COMPANY LAW IN EAST ASIA

COMPANY LAW IN EAST ASIA

Edited by

ROMAN TOMASIC

Ashgate

DARTMOUTH

Aldershot • Brookfield USA • Singapore • Sydney

Published by
Dartmouth Publishing Company Limited
Ashgate Publishing Limited
Gower House
Croft Road
Aldershot
Hants GU11 3HR
England

Ashgate Publishing Company
Old Post Road
Brookfield
Vermont 05036
USA

British Library Cataloguing in Publication Data
Company law in East Asia
  1.Corporation law – East Asia
  I.Tomasic, Roman
  346.5'066

Library of Congress Cataloging-in-Publication Data
Company law in East Asia.
    p. cm.
  Includes bibliographical references (p.).
  ISBN 1–85521–965–4
  1. Corporation law—East Asia. I. Tomasic, Roman.
KNC309.C66 1998
346.5'066—dc21
                                    98-8634
                                       CIP

ISBN 1 85521 965 4

Typeset by Manton Typesetters, 5–7 Eastfield Road, Louth, Lincs, LN11 7AJ, UK.

Printed and bound in Great Britain by MPG Books Ltd, Bodmin, Cornwall

Contents

List of Abbreviations

ASC	Australian Securities Commission
ASEAN	Association of South East Asian Nations
ASIC	Australian Securities and Investment Commission
BAPEPAM	The Capital Market Supervisory Agency (Indonesia)
BHP	Balai Harta Peninggalan (Indonesia)
BKPM	The Capital Investment Coordinating Board (Badan Koordinasi Penaman Modal) (Indonesia)
CA	Companies Act 1965 (Malaysia), Companies Act (Singapore) and the Companies Act 1956 (Brunei Darussalam)
CC	Commercial Code (Japan)
CCC	Civil and Commercial Code 1928 (Thailand)
COMECON	Council for Mutual Economic Assistance
CPV	Communist Party of Vietnam
CRA	Company Registration Authority (China)
CSRC	China Securities Regulatory Commission
CSTL	The Chattel Secured Transactions Law (Taiwan)
FIC	Foreign Investment Committee (Malaysia)
GDP	gross domestic product
GNP	gross national product
HKSAR	Hong Kong Special Administration Region
IOSCO	International Organization of Securities Commissions
KLSE	Kuala Lumpur Stock Exchange (Malaysia)
KMT	Kuomintang (Nationalist Party) (Taiwan)
LLCA	Limited Liability Act 1938 (Japan)
MIB	Melayu Islam Beraja (Malay Islamic Monarchy) (Brunei Darussalam)
MOEA	Ministry of Economic Affairs (Taiwan)
MOF	Ministry of Finance (Taiwan)
MOFTEC	Ministry of Foreign Trade and Economic Cooperation (China)
MPI	Ministry of Planning and Industry
NPC	National People's Congress (China)
NZSC	New Zealand Securities Commission
OECD	Organization for Economic Cooperation and Development

OTC	'over the counter'
PNG	Papua New Guinea
PLCA	Public Limited Companies Act 1992 (Thailand)
RGELS	Rules Governing Examination of the Listing of Securities (Taiwan)
ROC	Republic of China
SCRES	State Commission for Restructuring the Economic System (China)
SCSPC	State Council's Securities Policy Committee (China)
SEA	Securities and Exchange Act 1992 (Thailand)
SEHK	Stock Exchange of Hong Kong
SEC	Securities and Exchange Commission (Thailand) (Philippines)
SEL	Securities Exchange Law (Taiwan)
SET	Securities Exchange of Thailand
SFC	Securities and Futures Commission (Hong Kong) (Taiwan)
SIA	Securities Industry Act (Malaysia)
SMES	small and medium-sized enterprises
TNCs	transnational companies
TSE	Taiwan Stock Exchange

1 An Introduction

ROMAN TOMASIC*

Company law in many parts of Asia is currently undergoing considerable change. These changes have many causes. Some of these causes can be found in the need to reform outdated laws which are no longer considered to be appropriate to contemporary economic and political circumstances. Other explanations for the rush to reform the company laws in many Asian countries may be found in pressures coming from international sources, such as multinational corporations, international financial institutions and professional groups. To some degree, the pressure to achieve some kind of harmonization in international or crossborder corporate law practice in the region has also been a factor in stimulating reform efforts.[1] Yet another factor which has influenced company law reform in the region has been the pressure to lower business costs and to use more streamlined bodies of company law for this purpose.

In each country or legal system discussed in this book, the precise mix of factors which have influenced law reform has differed, but what is very clear is that company law has begun to be seen to play a much more important role in regard to matters such as corporate governance and corporate social control. The financial crisis which beset Asian economies in mid 1997 has also focused attention on other corporate law ideas, such as corporate insolvency, conflicts of interest on the part of corporate controllers and corporate borrowing and capital raising.

The chapters in this book seek to provide an in-depth overview of the background and the operation of company law ideas in a number of legal systems in Asia. The countries or legal systems covered here are primarily to be found in East and South East Asia, namely China, Japan, South Korea, Taiwan, Hong Kong, Vietnam, Thailand, Malaysia, Singapore, Indonesia, Brunei and the Philippines. The book also discusses the company laws of Australia, New

Zealand and Papua New Guinea. Due to a paucity of legal materials, it has not been possible to cover the company laws of Cambodia, Laos and Myanmar. We also have not sought to cover the company laws of the legal systems of South Asia. Perhaps the latter countries can be left to another volume although English language materials on these South Asian jurisdictions are relatively easily accessible.[2] The book also includes a chapter by Professor David Campbell on the meaning of the rule of law in the context of Asian company law reform.

Chapters 1–7 deal with company laws in Japan, Korea, the Peoples' Republic of China, Hong Kong and Taiwan. Chapters 8–17 contain discussions of company laws in Vietnam, Thailand, Malaysia, Singapore, Indonesia, the Philippines, Brunei, Papua New Guinea, New Zealand and Australia.

The discussion of each body of company law in the chapters which follow Chapter 2 adopts a largely standard format so as to ensure some degree of comparability between jurisdictions and to ensure that broadly similar questions are addressed by each author. Each chapter has been prepared by a company law authority who has sought to bring together the principal sources of company law in each jurisdiction. Wherever possible, each chapter also draws upon local legal expertise, either in the form of a local co-author (where the author is not based in that jurisdiction) or through resort to informal advice from local experts in the company law of the particular jurisdiction.

The authors of each country or legal system chapter were asked to discuss a set number of topics or issues which became the section or sub-section headings of each chapter. Sometimes a number of these topics are more conveniently discussed together, such as where there is limited legal material on a particular topic or where it is considered more appropriate in a particular context to discuss a topic in a different order. In some jurisdictions some areas of company law, such as takeovers and securities laws, are relatively underdeveloped or even non-existent and so less attention is devoted to these areas.

Each chapter begins with an introduction to the legal system of each jurisdiction and is followed by an overview of the relevant corporate law statute in that jurisdiction. This is followed by a discussion of the nature and powers of corporate regulatory bodies in the jurisdiction; a discussion of the types of companies which may be formed in that jurisdiction and the powers and capacities of these companies. Each chapter then goes on to discuss the company formation process, and the internal and external administration of companies. Finally, each chapter also discusses takeover and securities laws in each jurisdiction as well as such other areas as may be appropriate.

Generally, therefore, each author discusses his or her jurisdiction's body of company law by reference to the following issues or headings:[3]

1 An introduction to the nature of the legal system in each country, its history and judicial and regulatory structure
2 A description of the corporation law statute (and case-law) in the jurisdiction

  - The constitutional basis of the company law
  - How the company law came into being
  - Who is responsible for changing the law?
  - The principles, if any, underlying the company law
  - How the legislation is interpreted (rules of interpretation)

3 The nature and powers of corporate regulatory bodies in the jurisdiction

  - A description of the powers of company regulatory bodies
  - The role of regulatory bodies in policy formation, practice and so on
  - The mechanisms for the review of regulatory action

4 A description of the types of companies, their powers and so on

  - A description of the types of local companies
  - The recognition of foreign companies in the jurisdiction
  - The legal capacities and powers of companies

5 Company formation

  - The registration of companies, promoters and so on
  - The corporate constitution (for example memorandum and articles)
  - The restrictions on the use of certain names
  - Membership and share capital requirements
  - The amendment of corporate constitution
  - Company registers

6 The internal administration of companies

  - The registered office and name
  - The duties, powers and responsibilities of officers
  - Meeting procedures
  - The audit and accounting rules

- The annual return and other registers
- Shareholder protection rules (for example minorities)
- The relationship between management and shareholders
- Corporate financial transactions (for example, charges, share buy backs and receivers)

7   The external administration of companies

- The rules regarding arrangements and reconstructions
- Voluntary administration and corporate rescue provisions
- Company winding up rules, tests for insolvency, grounds for winding up and mechanisms for initiating insolvency proceedings
- The protection of creditors and the ranking of claims
- Control of insolvency practitioners

8   Takeover rules

- An introduction to company takeover rules (statutory or voluntary)
- Takeover thresholds
- Disclosure requirements and shareholder protection
- The role of lawyers, experts and the regulator in takeovers
- Mechanisms for the review of takeover activity

9   An introduction to securities regulation in the country/jurisdiction

- The relationship between stock exchange(s) and corporate regulation
- The types of securities regulated
- The legal effect of listing rules and business rules of the stock exchange(s)
- Market conduct rules and sanctions for securities misconduct

10 Miscellaneous

- The powers of the courts
- Civil remedies
- Offences
- Who may initiate proceedings?
- The registration and control of persons under the legislation (for example auditors, liquidators and experts)

It should be noted that the majority of Asian legal systems are based on civil law ideas drawn from countries such as Germany, the Netherlands and France, although these ideas have often been affected by common law systems (principally, by ideas from the US and UK common law systems).[4] These civil law systems operate around broad codes which seek to set out the principles applying to a particular area and, generally, are not modified or developed through the courts by resort to the doctrine of precedent. Judges in the civil law tradition have less authority than common law judges, with civil law judges usually being career administrative officials whereas common law judges would usually come directly from a career at the private Bar.[5]

This is to be contrasted with common law systems which rely heavily upon both case-law developed by the courts and statutory enactments.[6] Only Hong Kong, Malaysia and Singapore have common law systems of the kind that are also found in Australia, New Zealand and Papua New Guinea. Common law systems, therefore, depend upon the existence of a body of case-law which forms the precedents which company lawyers in that jurisdiction would use when a matter is interpreted or litigated. However, as there has been relatively little company law litigation in East Asia, legal precedents from other jurisdictions have often been drawn upon in resolving disputes. Such precedents have been drawn from countries such as Britain, Australia and the United States.

For example, the common law jurisdictions in Hong Kong, Singapore and Malaysia would frequently draw upon authorities and statements of legal principle from the United Kingdom and from Australia. In the more recent reforms of the company laws of jurisdictions influenced by civil law, such as Indonesia, the Philippines, Vietnam and China, US ideas have been drawn upon to some degree, although none of these jurisdictions has slavishly merely adopted foreign bodies of company law; however, this may have been done in earlier times.[7] US company law ideas have also been influential in Indonesian, New Zealand and Hong Kong reform efforts.

US influences have also been apparent in Japan, Korea and Taiwan through the impact of US postgraduate legal education upon legal practitioners working in the corporate law field. However, even this important influence has not meant that local factors have not had an impact on the form and content of company law ideas adopted in each jurisdiction. This is especially so in jurisdictions based on civil law ideas which have been affected by socialist ideas, such as China and Vietnam, where the categorization of the system becomes considerably more complex. Earlier German legal ideas have had an influence on Japan, Taiwan, Korea and China, whereas earlier Dutch legal ideas have had an influence in Indonesia. What is apparent, however, is that a hybridization of legal systems is emerging in some legal systems and that company law is increasingly being influenced by common law ideas where it operates within what is still basically a civil law system. The addition of local cultural variables adds yet another layer to the complexity of company law and practice in Asia.

Each chapter, therefore, looks closely at the history and constitutional structure of each legal system and the legal mechanisms or procedures which are in place to mobilize their respective bodies of company law. However, local cultural, historical and political factors will continue to play an important role in affecting the mobilization of corporate law in Asian legal systems.

Although it is not the aim of this introduction to summarize each of the chapters in this book, a number of inter-related themes emerge from these chapters. Some of these issues are discussed by Professor Campbell in Chapter 2.

Various other themes would be familiar to company lawyers and some of these may be mentioned here briefly. First, there is a tension in company law between the extent to which such laws are primarily facilitative or coercive and whether these laws are optional or mandatory in character. There has long been an argument in company law debates regarding the primary function of company law. Thus, it has been asked whether company law should aim to ensure compliance with strictures regarding business conduct or, alternatively, merely lay down the broad parameters or boundaries for acceptable business conduct and be primarily concerned with facilitating business activity.

As authors on company law such as Stone[8] in the United States and Tomasic and Bottomley[9] in Australia, have shown, there are major limits to corporate law as a regulatory or coercive device. The limits of corporate law are attributed in part to the importance of cultural factors in the structure of corporate action. Thus, far more important than corporate law are the cultural variables which are at work within the corporation. To be effective, corporate sanctions need to be linked to the sub-cultural and organizational dimensions of the corporation.[10] The use of serious corporate sanctions against corporate misconduct or the misconduct of corporate officers has been notoriously difficult and costly, so that criminal sanctions have been less effective in changing conduct by and within the corporation than well-targeted civil remedies and internal corporate compliance programmes.[11]

Company law has increasingly been seen as a set of rules which it is more efficient for a business to adopt rather than to have to negotiate these rules anew in the marketplace each time that it wishes to undertake commercial transactions. Law and economics scholars have supported this line of thinking about company law, tending also to see the corporation itself (or more correctly the firm) as a nexus of contracts.[12] Corporation law has increasingly come to be seen as a set of mandatory and optional rules which are provided to facilitate business activity. These kinds of debates are beginning to be echoed in different parts of Asia, such as in the work of the recent company law inquiry in Hong Kong and in the company law reform efforts in New Zealand. The debates in the latter jurisdiction have also had an effect on company law reform elsewhere in the region, such as in Vietnam and in Papua New Guinea.

A second key theme in company law debates has been that of corporate governance. Increasingly, we are seeing international corporate governance debates being extended into the Asian and the Pacific region. This has seen the emergence of debates regarding the roles of boards of directors, independent and executive directors, the company chairman, supervisory boards, audit committees and stakeholder groups, such as large shareholders, pension funds and employees.[13] The dominance of so many Asian companies by strong family groups[14] or by the state has tended to limit the impact of this debate, although it is likely that this will change following the financial crisis which has beset most Asian economies since mid 1997. However, the state still continues to play an important role in many Asian economies, having the effect of severely limiting the free play of market forces. This has led to what might be described as the rule by law rather than the rule of law in some Asian countries.[15] This issue is taken up further by Professor Campbell in Chapter 2. Heavy state ownership of companies in many Asian countries has also served to limit the extent to which corporate law principles have been able to be applied freely in these countries. However, the Asian economic crisis of late 1997 and 1998 may begin to loosen the reliance which has been placed upon state control of markets and economic activity in these jurisdictions.

A third key concern is the manner in which company law serves as a means of dealing with corporate debt problems, such as the problem of insolvent trading by companies. One of the traditional areas of concern in company law has been with the winding up of companies, corporate restructuring and the appointment of receivers over corporate assets. This concern has become increasingly significant, of course, since the currency collapses of 1997 and is likely to lead to a new interest in corporate insolvency laws. However, insolvency laws will always have to operate in a cultural context, especially in Asia.[16] At the same time, Asian insolvency laws are slowly being amended to introduce more effective means of rescuing companies which are in financial difficulties. Illustrations of this kind of reform effort are to be found in Hong Kong, Singapore and now China, with its heavily indebted state-owned enterprises.

A final general issue which might be considered here is that of capital raising by Asian companies. The emergence of stock exchanges in many Asian countries has seen increasing trading in the securities of Asian-based companies. This has meant that corporate regulatory bodies and stock exchanges have had to take an increasing interest in the application of company laws. In some Asian jurisdictions, such as Singapore and Hong Kong, companies and securities laws work reasonably effectively.[17] Singapore's handling of the collapse of Barings is testimony to the high standards of security regulation in that jurisdiction.[18] However, this is not the case in some very well-developed Asian legal systems, such as Japan and Korea, if the number of recent securities market abuses and irregularities is a guide.

Other countries in the region, such as China[19] and Vietnam, are still developing their securities market rules and institutions, so that it will be some time yet before they match the kinds of securities market practices found, for example, in the United States. However, as not all corporate capital raising takes place on stock exchanges, company law rules will continue to be important in this area.

Company law in an advanced economy is unlikely to be static, so that, as practitioners are well aware, any understanding of this area will need to accommodate this process of change and include an understanding of regulatory practice, court cases and law reform and business debates. Given the pivotal role of company law in providing a mechanism for the containment of risk and for the raising of capital, it is inevitable that corporate law and practice in each jurisdiction will tell us a lot about the organization of economic activity in these places. However, we are still only beginning to fully understand the nature of corporate law in Asian countries and hopefully this book will serve both to bridge the gap and to facilitate further inquiries and research in this area.

Notes

*   University of Canberra.
1   See generally, Taylor, V. (1995), 'Harmonising Competition Law within APEC: US-Japan Disputes on Vertical Restraints', *Australian Journal of Corporate Law*, **5**, 379.
2   See for example, Wickremasinghe, K. (1992), *Wickremasinghe's Company Law of Sri Lanka (Revised 2nd edition)*, Colombo: Kimarli Wickremasinghe; Fernando, H.M. (1995) *Sri Lanka – Its Company Law Stock Exchange Company Commercial Practice*, Colombo: H.M. Fernando.
3   Sometimes use of these headings has been departed from where the author has considered it appropriate depending on the local circumstances.
4   See for example, Smith, M. (1997), 'Private Law and Public Control of Commercial Activity in Japan – the Role of the Codes', in J. Gillespie (ed.), *Commercial Legal Development in Vietnam: Vietnamese and Foreign Commentaries*, Singapore:

Butterworths Asia, 261–276. See also, Ruru, B. (1995), 'Development of Equity and Bond Markets: History and Regulatory Framework Indonesia', *Australian Journal of Corporate Law*, **5**, 326.

5   See generally, Weeramantry, C.G., (1982), *An Invitation to the Law*, Sydney: Butterworths, 50–52; and Von Mehren, A.T. (1963), *Law in Japan: The Legal Order in a Changing Society*, Cambridge: Harvard University Press.

6   Llewellyn, K.N. (1960), *The Common Law Tradition: Deciding Appeals*, Boston: Little, Brown and Company; Stone, J. (1985), *Precedent and Law: Dynamics of Common Law Growth*, Sydney: Butterworths; Holmes, O.W. (1963), *The Common Law*, Boston: Little, Brown and Co; Twining, W. (ed.) (1986), *Legal Theory and Common Law*, Oxford: Basil Blackwell.

7   See for example, Le Dang Doanh (1996), 'Economic Reform in Vietnam: Legal and Social Aspects and Impacts', *Australian Journal of Corporate Law*, **6**, 289.

8   Stone, C. (1975), *Where the Law Ends, The Social Control of Corporate Behavior*, New York: Harper & Row.

9   Tomasic, R. and Bottomley, S. (1993), *Directing the Top 500: Corporate Governance and Accountability in Australian Companies*, Sydney: Allen & Unwin.

10 See further, Jackall, R. (1988), *Moral Mazes: The World of Corporate Managers*, New York: Oxford University Press.

11 See further, Tomasic, R. and Bottomley, S., note 9, above; Tomasic, R. (1993), 'Corporations Law Enforcement Strategies in Australia: The Influence of Professional, Corporate and Bureaucratic Cultures', *Australian Journal of Corporate Law*, **3**, 192; and Fisse, B. and Braithwaite, J. (1993), *Corporations, Crime and Accountability*, Melbourne: Cambridge University Press.

12 See further, Easterbrook, F.H. and Fischel, D.R. (1991), *The Economic Structure of Corporate Law*, Cambridge: Harvard University Press; Romano, R. (ed.) (1993), *Foundations of Corporate Law*, New York: Oxford University Press; Tomasic, R. (1995), 'A note on law and economics thinking about corporate law', *Canberra Law Review*, **2**, 155.

13 See for example, Low Siew Cheang (1996), *Corporate Powers: Controls, Remedies and Decision-making*, Kuala Lumpur,: Malayan Law Journal Sdn Bhd.

14 See generally, Redding, N.S. (1990), *The Spirit of Chinese Capitalism*, New York: Walter de Gruyter. See also, Steward, S. and Donleavy, G. (eds) (1995), *Whose Business Values? Some Asian and Cross-Cultural Perspectives*, Hong Kong: Hong Kong University Press.

15 See generally, Tomasic, R. (1995), 'Company Law and the Limits of the Rule of Law in China', *Australian Journal of Corporate Law*, **4**, 470.

16 See further, Tomasic, R. and Little, P. (1997), *Insolvency Law and Practice in Asia*, Hong Kong: FT Law & Tax.

17 O'Hare, J. (1996), 'Regulation of the Securities Industry in Hong Kong: The Securities and Futures Commission', *Australian Journal of Corporate Law*, **6**, 178; Neoh, A. (1995), 'The Capital Markets of Hong Kong: Opportunities and Challenges of the Future', *Australian Journal of Corporate Law*, **5**, 334.

18 Lim, M. and Tan, N. (Inspectors) (1995), *Baring Futures (Singapore) Pte Ltd: The Report of the Inspectors appointed by the Minister for Finance*, Singapore: Ministry of Finance. Also see generally, Gapper, J. and Denton, N. (1996), *All that Glitters: The Fall of Barings*, London: Hamish Hamilton; Leeson, N. and Whitley, E. (1996), *Rogue Trader*, London: Little, Brown & Company (UK).

19 Gao, Xi-Qing (1996), 'Developments in Securities and Investment Law in China,' *Australian Journal of Corporate Law*, **6**, 228.

2 What is Meant by 'the Rule of Law' in Asian Company Law Reform?

DAVID CAMPBELL*

1 Introduction

The recent resumption by the People's Republic of China (PRC) of sovereignty over the former British territory of Hong Kong has posed perhaps the most acute example of the major problem facing business law throughout Asia. General commitment to capitalist economic development in Asia, from which arguably only North Korea now remains a clear dissentient, requires the development of the legal framework necessary for capitalist enterprise, particularly company law, in countries within which the development of such a law has either remained vestigial or indeed has been actively opposed.

It is manifest that such a development poses a quite enormous legislative problem, one that can be met only by commitment of concomitantly enormous resources to company law inception or reform. What is in one sense even worse is that it is now beginning to be recognized within company law – although it was through the more theoretical perspectives of comparative law[1] and the sociology of law[2] that the problem was perceived initially – that the reception of legislation cannot be governed by (although obviously it is influenced by) the quality of the drafting of the legislation. Any accurate estimate of the reception of a law must pay regard to what here will be called the institutions relating to (the relevant) law prevailing in the country in which the law is to be implemented. The existence of, as it were, the requisite *material* institutions – in essence the sufficient resources (including a competent and committed legal personnel) – to not merely promulgate but enforce the law is an obvious issue. As these resources, although apparently (potentially) sufficiently available in, say, Hong Kong or Singapore, are restricted in other countries

11

or even apparently absent in, say, Cambodia or Laos, this problem is serious. However, there is a need to focus on a less immediately tangible but, it would seem, even more important issue, which is the existence of the requisite *cultural* institutions.[3] By this is meant, in essence, the existence of a 'culture' in the affected population sufficiently sympathetic to the law to make its reception in anything like the way intended by its promulgators sufficiently likely to make the whole effort worthwhile.

The predominant way this problem has been addressed in relation to company law has been that the development of the requisite culture for the reception of that law has been regarded as a matter of the inculcation of 'the rule of law'. It is claimed that as capitalism is based on rational economic calculability, capitalist development requires a legal framework of sufficient predictability to allow such calculability to be a predominant feature of economic action. The presence of the rule of law is to guarantee sufficient fairness and predictability. However, the rule of law has not been, and continues not to be, a dominant feature of the majority of the Asian polities, which are characterized by poor levels of rationality in decision-making and outright corruption, and its inculcation therefore is a prerequisite of economic development.

Establishing the conditions within which the technical resources of neoclassical economics can be brought to bear on the problems of Asian development is certainly essential, but it will be argued here, with particular reference to the law intended to facilitate capitalist enterprise, that understanding this establishment to be essentially a matter of the inculcation of the rule of law as a condition of technical, economic calculability is mistaken. As has been argued elsewhere, analysis of the business law of the advanced capitalist countries shows that there is a crucial ethical dimension to economic action.[4] Increasingly it is being recognized that an effective law of contract[5] and an effective company law[6] require an ethically endorsed framework for cooperation between involved parties which cannot be reduced to technical predictability. Indeed, the very technicality of the understanding of the relationship of law and economic development as a matter of support of self-interested economic calculation actually cuts against the ethicality which is central to the creation of those institutions necessary to promote economic activity which enhances welfare. However, in the neoclassical economics dominating the discussion, the cultural institutions in which this ethicality is based typically are not recognized, so that, to the extent that they exist, they remain merely 'intuitive', 'hidden structures'.[7]

With the policy focus being so restrictedly technical, the necessity of the development of ethical institutions in countries without a developed capitalist economy typically has not been recognized. In the best structuralist fashion, however, their absence has been terribly marked by the thwarting of the economic and legal policies devised in ignorance of them. For this reason, the pursuit of the establishment of the rule of law in Asian company law reform presently seems to threaten a markedly sub-optimal welfare outcome.

2 Corruption in Asian Countries

At the recent celebration of India's and Pakistan's 50 years of independence, a principal theme of the Indian President's speech, broadcast throughout the nation and reported throughout the world, was that the future prosperity of his country principally depends on its ability to reduce the volume of corruption in its economic and political spheres.[8] Although one can but applaud the honesty and courage which allowed President Narayanan to mark such an occasion in this way, that he felt it necessary to do so is but one particularly striking piece of evidence that it is unarguable that corruption seriously hinders the economic development of Asian countries. Of its nature, corruption does not allow of any sort of definite assessment of its extent or impact, but the accumulated evidence of the seriousness of the problem is on any reasonable standard overwhelming.

The most comprehensive attempt to collate that evidence of which the author is aware is the 'Corruption Index' produced by Transparency International, a private organization founded in 1993 by a former official of the International Bank for Reconstruction and Development (World Bank) which aims to perform a function in respect of the monitoring of economic corruption rather like that of Amnesty International in respect of political oppression. Indonesia, the PRC and Pakistan are the three most corrupt countries according to this index, and the Asian countries are all clustered at the top of the index by comparison to the west European countries and the United States of America (USA).[9] Similar judgments are made by the Country Assessment Service of Business International, another private firm of investment risk analysts.[10] The picture which emerges from the World Bank's own international table of 'Obstacles to Doing Business' is to the same effect,[11] and that picture is drawn, although as it were in the opposite way, from the clustering of these countries towards the bottom of the 'Rule of Law Index' produced by the International Country Risk Guide, in which a positive correlation is claimed between adherence to the rule of law and rates of *per capita* growth.[12]

Rather than discussing the detail of this evidence (much of which the author would readily acknowledge is very poor), let us accept here the broad picture of the Asian countries as subject to such a degree of economic corruption that that corruption is a significant variable in determining (by lowering) the rate of economic development of those countries.

3   The Neoclassical Development Strategy for Asia and the Rule of Law

The solution to this problem, one of the core elements of the 'neoclassical development strategy'[13] for Asia advocated by international economic organizations and avowedly pursued by the governments of almost all poor Asian countries, is taken to be the extension of the rule of law to, or within, the corrupt countries. As expressed by the World Bank, the development of Asian countries is handicapped by the uncongeniality of the 'climate'[14] they provide for capitalist enterprise. This uncongeniality has many features, including the existence of 'infrastructural bottlenecks' (for example lack of communications and transport) which state action may be taken to eradicate.[15] However, fundamentally, such state action is to be confined as far as possible and, certainly, to extend as little as possible into the direction of investment decisions. As the World Bank has it:

> Enterprise reform is – and will remain for the rest of this decade – an important priority for East Asian countries. This is true for socialist economies in transition from a centralised command system to a decentralised market system and for other countries with large public sectors and difficult public finance situations … . These efforts [should] encompass measures to foster private sector development as well as competition between enterprises (public and private), privatise state enterprises and activities that were previously public monopolies, and strengthen the financial sector's ability to finance increased private sector capital requirements and to lend to public or private enterprises on the basis of commercial criteria.[16]

With fundamental economic decisions taken by private enterprises under the 'market-friendly' approach[17] recommended by the World Bank in its 1991 *World Development Report*,[18] the state's role is one of direction only to the minimum extent possible. Its principal role is to be the provision of the legal environment of predictability in which such decisions can be taken in an economically rational fashion. In the language of information economics, the extension of the rule of law gives a 'time consistent' horizon within which individuals and firms may plan. It limits the 'rent-seeking' actions of those aiming to exploit the 'moral hazard' constituted by the illegitimate asymmetries of information and bargaining (including outright coercive) power which are endemic in corrupt conditions:

Time consistency plays an important role in designing effective policies and contracts, particularly in the presence of asymmetric information. A policy is time consistent if, when it is put in place, no changes in it are anticipated by affected policies over the period specified for the policy ... one implication of time consistent policies is that fewer resources may be devoted to rent seeking ... in a political environment which is monocentric, and in which transparency and accountability for public actions are very low, there are likely to be few checks and balances [on] rent seeking activities. This strongly suggests the need for developing an independent and impartial judiciary and the attendant legal infrastructure.[19]

Translated from economic theory into concrete legal policies, this view of the relationship between law and development leads to the strong advocacy of the extension of the rule of law. In a typical statement, Susan Esserman, Acting General Council of the US Department of Commerce, said the following of the development of economic relations between the PRC and the USA:

> Central to comprehensive engagement and the continued growth and stability of our economic relations is the development of and adherence to the Rule of Law ... . The 'Rule of Law' involves the development, implementation and enforcement of a public body of law – not necessarily a system of laws and regulations that mirrors [that of] the United States, but one that shares the fundamental characteristics of openness, fairness, transparency, accessibility and predictability ... . The Rule of Law is ... critical, on a day-to-day basis, to businesses, both US and Chinese, attempting to hammer out the business deals that give life and substance to [those relations]. Clear rules and effective mechanisms for resolving commercial disputes are vitally important to businesses for several reasons. First, business depends absolutely on predictability. Investment and marketing decisions, the forms in which business will be conducted, pricing and distribution arrangements – each of these decisions, and of course many others, depends vitally on the ability to plan ahead. Second, business depends on the prompt, efficient and, hopefully, amicable resolution of problems when they arise. The legal framework within which business operates must provide mechanisms that work fairly and in a cost-effective manner to permit resolution of disagreements.[20]

Against the background of the previous and almost universal failure of the entire range of development strategies adopted by poor countries since the Second World War, the 'East Asian miracle'[21] provided very welcome members for a set of 'newly industrializing countries',[22] a set which, it had come to be feared, might never have *any* members. However, to ascribe the 'miracle' to the neoclassical strategy is very problematic, as extensive state intervention is a marked feature of the Asian economies.[23] The intention here is not to refer only to the communist or former communist countries, but to all the other countries,[24] including by far and away the major non-communist economy, that of Japan.[25] For this reason, what typically are taken to be exemplars of the neoclassical strategy are not so much all Asian economies[26] but the four 'dragon' economies[27] of Hong Kong, Singapore, South Korea and Taiwan.[28] However, even this is very problematic, as (ignoring the strong state in Singapore), South Korean and Taiwanese development have been brought about by markedly interventionist policies,[29] to the extent that, rather comically in the context, Hong Kong's Financial Secretaries have always somewhat resented the bracketing of their own relatively market-based economic policies with those of the other 'dragons'.[30]

As, in the author's opinion, even to describe the economy of Hong Kong as *laissez faire* is highly misleading,[31] the accuracy of attributing the rates of growth of the Asian economies to neoclassical development strategy, as it is generally understood, is uncertain. However, so poor has been the performance not only of the former command economies but of the corrupt states of the former third world countries that it is possible to accept the plausibility of arguments that the extent of state direction of economic activity should be reduced. Decisions over this are, or should be, a matter of careful assessment, based on detailed empirical study, of the appropriate governance structures for particular circumstances. What needs to be argued, however, is the way that the reduction of the scope of the state is to lead to capitalist development is extremely poorly understood in the neoclassical development strategy.

This poor understanding has led to two policy mistakes, the second of which emerges from what was intended to be a change of policy in response to the first. That first mistake was to ignore the necessity of the development of the market as an institution at all. The neoclassical development strategy turns on the shortcoming which the social sciences other than neoclassical economics, and latterly institutional economics, have shown to be central to neoclassical economics, which is to ignore the social constitution of markets. Even if one accepts the first or basic theorem of welfare economics,[32] that the fully contingent market of general equilibrium theory[33] is 'Pareto optimal'[34] in that it is a perfectly efficient mechanism for the allocation of goods according to revealed preferences, this is by no means to say that the pursuit of a market-friendly strategy is correct in all circumstances. The fully contingent market is a market with zero transactions costs, that is to say with information gathering and communication costless. However, information gathering and communications costs will *always* be positive, so the existence of such markets is 'a very unrealistic assumption':

In order to carry out a market transaction, it is necessary to discover who it is that one wishes to deal with, to inform people that one wishes to deal and on what terms, to conduct negotiations leading up to a bargain, to draw up a contract, to undertake the inspection needed to make sure that the terms of the contract are being observed, and so on.[35]

Once this is appreciated, then the establishment of the institutions which allow necessary information gathering and communication is essential. Seen not from the point of view of theoretical economics but from concrete economic and legal policy, the market is one such institution, the institution which allows exchange to take place. Markets in this sense paradoxically have little or no role in the neoclassical strategy, as markets there are the products of rational economic action and not, as they should be seen, as the prerequisites of such action:

> Markets are institutions that exist to facilitate exchange, that is, they exist in order to reduce the cost of carrying out exchange transactions. In an economic theory which assumes that transaction costs are non-existent, markets have no function to perform ... the influence of the social institutions which facilitate exchange being completely ignored.[36]

An example may serve to illustrate the point, and what better example than that modern talisman the stock exchange, in which the workings of the empirical market are so little understood that 'the market' is widely thought[37] to operate automatically:

> commodity exchanges and stock exchanges ... are normally organised by a group of traders (the members of the exchange) which owns (or rents) the physical facility within which transactions take place. All exchanges regulate in great detail the activities of those who trade in these markets (the times at which transactions can be made, what can be traded, the responsibilities of the parties, the terms of settlement, etc.), and they all provide machinery for the settlement of disputes and impose sanctions against those who infringe the rules of the exchange. It is not without significance that these exchanges, often used by economists as examples of a perfect market and perfect competition, are markets in which transactions are highly regulated (and this quite apart from any government regulation that there may be). It suggests, I think correctly, that for anything approaching perfect competition to exist, an intricate system of rules and regulations would normally be needed.[38]

Although, as we have seen, the international development agencies are perfectly well aware of the problems discussed in information economics, they tend to portray the market as a solution to problems identified with moral hazard based on corrupt state activities. The market may have such a role to play, but it is not itself a solution. It requires institutions which limit the moral hazard it itself creates. Of course, in a fully contingent market, these problems are eliminated, but there is no possibility of such a market and to base policy on the belief that there is is profoundly mistaken:

> Contemplation of an optimal system may suggest ways of improving the system, it may provide techniques of analysis that would otherwise have been missed, and, in certain special cases, it may go far to providing a solution. But in general its influence has been pernicious. It has directed economists' attention away from the main question, which is how alternative arrangements will actually work in practice. It has led economists to derive conclusions for economic policy from a study of an abstract model of a market situation ... Until we realise that we are choosing between social arrangements which are all more or less failures, we are not likely to make much headway.[39]

Really quite dreadful consequences have followed from institutionally ignorant attempts to restructure formerly non-capitalist economies along capitalist lines in the period since the end of the Cold War. It is instructive to draw attention to an example which should guide Asian policy formulation, that provided by the poorly thought out encouragement of markets in the former Council for Mutual Economic Assistance (COMECON) countries. Following the collapse of communism in these countries, a period of accelerated capitalist development has taken place in them. On the usual economic indicators, absolute rates of economic growth have been substantial. However, the welfare costs of this growth have been extreme. To take the most important example, the economy of Russia, the leading Republic of the former Union of Soviet Socialist Republics, now is characterized by a form of highly exploitative private enterprise under which mass deprivation and the use of coercion in economic affairs is so common that that economy would, by civilized bourgeois standards, be regarded as gangsterism rather than capitalism.[40] The Russian example merely takes to an extreme what is endemic to these former communist countries now pursuing capitalist development.[41]

Of the Asian countries, only the PRC, North Korea and perhaps (although not in the author's opinion) Vietnam would seem, because of their formerly highly centralized command economies, to be threatened with a possible degree of collapse akin to what has happened to COMECON. (Things could hardly get worse in Cambodia.) However the lesson of the COMECON countries should be learned by all, for it is not at all clear that the poor Asian countries have anything like the established commercial and ethical institutions for necessary capitalist development. That lesson is clear:

It makes little sense for economists to discuss the process of exchange without specifying the institutional setting within which the trading takes place since this affects the incentives to produce and the costs of transacting. I think this is now beginning to be recognised and has been made crystal clear by what is going on in Eastern Europe today ... . The value of including ... institutional factors in the corpus of mainstream economics is made clear by recent events in Eastern Europe. These ex-communist countries are advised to move to a market economy, and their leaders wish to do so, but without the appropriate institutions no market economy of any significance is possible.[42]

Far more cautious counsels than international economic organizations such as the Asian Development Bank, the Asia-Pacific Economic Congress and the World Bank have proven to be have urged the recognition of the necessity of the development of the requisite institutions which will (so far as possible) ensure that only such markets as are nationally held to be legitimate will be created.[43] Unfortunately, it is obvious that these more cautious counsels have played only a small part in the formulation of the neoclassical development strategy for Asia. However, the case they make is perfectly clear. Without attention being paid to the creation of cultural institutions which will allow the development of markets in ways which will enhance welfare in the manner claimed, that development can have unintended welfare-reducing consequences which may well outweigh the positive effects of capitalist development.

Surely it is manifest that this institutional criticism of neoclassical development theory has very considerable force.[44] In the light of the growing acceptance of institutional economics in economic theory and the bearing out of its implications for development theory by the experience of the former COMECON countries, the international development agencies seem to have accepted the strength of the institutional criticisms of the neoclassical development strategy and have begun to develop institutionally sensitive policies. This has been an emerging theme of, for example, World Bank publications since the 1991 *World Development Report* and now dominates the 1997 *Report*, which is subtitled *The State in a Changing World*. Although still maintained in regard of the divestiture of state-owned enterprises,[45] the former overriding – indeed almost exclusive – concern to reduce the volume of state activity now is more balanced by recognition of the state's role not merely in physical infrastructural provision but also in 'Securing the Economic and Social Fundamentals'.[46] The abiding concern to reduce corruption[47] is tempered now by positive efforts aimed at 'Reinvigorating Institutional Capability'[48] in which markets will be fostered.[49]

Although expressed in terms still remarkable for their degree of complacency, this recognition of past fault is very welcome. It is, however, itself seriously limited and constitutes the second major policy mistake in the neoclassical development strategy. It is at this point that that the rule of law figures so strongly, because overwhelmingly the emergence of markets is treated largely as a matter of economic calculation which will take place once the rule of law is sufficiently established. The necessity of institutions is recognized now, but that recognition is confined to the framwork of technical predictability provided by the rule of law:

> Markets rest on a foundation of institutions. Like the air we breathe, some of the public goods these institutions provide are so basic to daily economic life as to go unnoticed. Only when these goods are absent, as in many developing countries today, do we see their importance for development. Without the rudiments for social order, underpinned by institutions, markets cannot function ... . The absence of these critical supports for property rights gives rise to ... the lawlessness syndrome. Firms ... are subject to [a] triple curse on markets: corruption, crime and an unpredictable judiciary that offers little prospect of recourse ... . Containing lawlessness is necessary ... but it may not be sufficient. Information and coordination problems can also impede development by undermining markets ... a problem often found in low-income countries. Information problems occur because people and firms inevitably have limited information and understanding or because the rules of the game are unclear ... . Coordination of economic activity is difficult because self-interested people and firms behave strategically ... . The presence of moral hazard ... hinders firms from taking opportunities for mutual gain ... . Firms need an environment that induces them to allocate resources efficiently, to improve productivity, and to innovate. And unless firms are confident that policies will remain reasonably stable over time, they will fail to invest, and growth will lag.[50]

In statements purporting to encourage economic development, such as Ms Esserman's discussed above, the key function of the rule of law is to provide predictability within which economic calculation can take place. However, on more detailed examination this widely accepted policy can be seen to be much more complicated than it appears.[51] Although the role for the rule of law in the refined neoclassical development strategy for Asia is, on the face of it, the purely technical one of supporting calculation, it is argued here that it is impossible to sustain this exclusively 'technical' quality when the jurisprudential plausibility of the rule of law as only predictability is examined in depth. Indeed, the notion of the application of the rule of law to Asia is particularly problematic when one recognizes that the meaning of that rule is unclear within the advanced capitalist countries.[52]

4 Objections to the Refined Neoclassical Economic Development Strategy for Asia

The stress on the rule of law as a predictable system turns on taking a legal system to be a system of validity in the way most thoroughly analysed by Kelsen. A legal system specifies the primary norms for the creation of secondary norms which purport to apply sanctions to particular acts, and jurisprudence is the identification of the system of norms which are valid in that they are created in the way the legal system specifies. Therefore, the legal system is composed of a chain of norms identified not at all by content but by the form of their creation:

> norms of the law ... are not valid by virtue of their content ... The validity of a legal norm cannot be called into question on the ground that its content fails to correspond to some presupposed substantive value, say a moral value. A norm is valid *qua* legal norm only because it was arrived at in a certain way – created according to a certain rule, issued or set according to a specific method. The law is valid only as positive law, that is, only as law that is issued or set. In this necessary requirement of being issued or set, and in what it assures, namely, that the validity of the law will be independent of morality and comparable systems of norms – therein lies the positivity of the law.[53]

What emerges particularly clearly from Kelsen's picture of the nature of the chain of validity is the pure *legalism* of the concept of justice which follows from the view of a legal system he articulates:

> 'Justice' in [the] sense [of a legal system viewed in terms of pure validity] means legality; it is 'just' for a general rule to be actually applied in all cases where, according to its content, this rule should be applied. It is 'unjust' for it to be applied in one case and not in another similar case ... . Justice, in the sense of legality, is a quality which relates not to the content of a positive order, but to its application.[54]

It will be obvious to those familiar with Kelsen's work that these quotations, taken from works originally published between 1934 and 1945, articulate Kelsen's then strong commitment to a neo-Kantian moral philosophy, in which commitment to ultimate values is not open to rational discussion but is merely a question, in politics ultimately determined by might, of the effective maintenance of one's interests:

> The norms which are actually used as standards of justice vary from individual to individual and are often mutually irreconcilable ... . A social order that is just from the liberal's point of view is unjust from

the socialist's point of view ... . Liberalism and socialism are by no means the only ideals of justice. The norm of justice has a different meaning for a pacifist and an imperialist, for a nationalist and an internationalist, for a religious believer and an atheist. Primitive man has another conception of justice than the civilised man. It is impossible to determine the norm of justice in a unique way. It is ultimately an expression of the interest of the individual who pronounces a social institution to be just or unjust ... . There is, however, only one positive law. Or – if we wish to account for the existence of the various national legal orders – there is for each territory only one positive law ... the question as to whether in a concrete case a definite behaviour is legal or illegal, is ... decided by the competent legal authority.[55]

It is this that affords the peculiar purity to Kelsen's jurisprudence of this period, which concentrates on justice as validity by emphatically severing this concept of justice from other concepts of justice based in, for example, ethics or sociology:

The Pure Theory of Law is a theory of positive law ... . It characterises itself as a 'pure' theory of law because it aims at cognition focused on the law alone, and because it aims to eliminate from this cognition everything not belonging to the object of cognition, precisely specified as the law. That is, the Pure Theory aims to free legal science of all foreign elements. This is its basic methodological principle. The principle may appear obvious, but a glance at traditional legal science ... shows just how far tradition is from meeting the requirement of purity. In an utterly uncritical way, jurisprudence has been entangled in psychology and biology, in ethics and theology ... . The Pure Theory of Law seeks to delimit clearly the object of its cognition [in opposition to] the prevailing methodological syncretism.[56]

Given such an, as it were, purely technical jurisprudence, justice as legality (which must itself be 'an irrational ideal'[57]), cannot be confined to merely democratic and/or liberal regimes:

From the standpoint of [legal] science, free from any moral or political judgements of value, democracy and liberalism are only two possible principles of social organisation, just as autocracy and socialism are. There is no scientific reason why the concept of law should be defined so as to exclude the latter.[58]

Accordingly, justice based on the rule of law as predictability, can embrace a wide range of political regimes:

Justice in this sense is compatible with and required by any positive legal order, be it capitalistic or communistic, democratic or autocratic. 'Justice' means the maintenance of a positive order by a conscious application of it. It is justice 'under the law'.[59]

It is this formalism of justice as legality that, as we have seen, allows the development banks to ask the Asian countries, and Ms Esserman to ask the PRC in particular, to adopt what seems *prima facie* a very demanding policy, the adoption of a hitherto undeveloped or imperfectly developed system of legality as at least a very important part of its governance structure for business. The formality of the rule of law is to allow the bracketing of fundamental questions about ultimate interests – whether, say, law issued under forms of one-party, monarchical, aristocratic or even settled despotic rule is legitimate – so long as such commercial agreements as are made are adhered to along the predictable lines of the rule of law.

5 The Significance of the Rule of Law in the Relationship of the Orient and the Occident

It is not necessary for us to take a position on Kelsen's particular moral philosophy to recognize the significance of the identifying theme of positive jurisprudence which it expresses with such clarity. The rule of law as a system of predictability can embrace a wide range of political regimes. Obviously, some tyrannies are of their nature unpredictable, and so cannot construct a legal system which is just even in Kelsen's terms. Asia has had its examples of such tyrannies until very recently, and even today has tyrannies of such arbitrariness that they markedly impair the legality of their legal systems even if they do not (at present) call their basic efficacy into question. These tyrannies are amongst the most egregious causes of misery in the world, and it is important to say that their criticism, in which the extension of legality can serve a valuable if hardly undisputed part, is a principal task for international political and legal action. I will say no more about this here.

On reflection, it becomes clear that the argument for the extension of the rule of law based on the facilitation of economic development typically does *not* follow the technical argument for the rule of law as predictability through to its politically agnostic, amoral conclusion. It typically is *not* envisaged that the rule of law will operate neutrally in respect of the political regime in which it is established. It typically is argued that it will change that regime, ultimately bringing it more into conformity with the bourgeois social structure of the advanced capitalist economies.

The reduction of economic action to a question of *calculability*, of the rational maximization of individual utilities, is, of course, at the heart of neoclassical economics. As Gossen had it in the first comprehensive statement of what we now know as those economics:

Man wants to enjoy life and makes it his goal to increase pleasures enjoyed throughout life to the highest possible level ... there are a large numbers of pleasures in life that man can obtain immediately; yet these pleasures have the consequence of imposing later, disproportionate deprivations. On the other hand, the most elevated, the purest pleasures, become comprehensible, become real pleasures, only after man has educated himself for their appreciation. Therefore ... in order to measure the true magnitude of a specific pleasure, not only must account be taken of its magnitude, but also all the sacrifices imposed by its enjoyment must be subtracted from it ... . In other words: *Enjoyment must be so arranged that the total life pleasure should become a maximum* ... this maximisation [is] viewed by all men without exception as life's ultimate purpose.[60]

Although Gossen's location of utility maximization within an explicitly theocratic scheme for the interpretation of God's purposes (which lawyers perhaps will most easily recognize as an economic parallel to Austin's utilitarian guide to legislation[61]) is, of course, not an intrinsic part of modern neoclassical economics; those economics typically do attribute the economic orientation of action to given qualities of human nature. The author does not accept this philosophic anthropology, which identifies individual utility maximization through rational quantitative calculation as a general human characterisitic such as 'choice'. This has been stated repeatedly elsewhere[62] and will not be taken up here. Instead, we will turn immediately to work which locates the rational economic orientation of action within a specific social context.

By far and away the most sociologically and historiographically sustained account of the development of this orientation of action is that of Weber. The obvious relevance of that account to our concerns here has been pointed out repeatedly.[63] Weber draws a particularly strong parallel between the formalism of the rule of law and the formalism of neoclassical economic theory. For Weber, the ideal types of legal rational domination and of capitalist economic calculation are built up on the basis of the, as it were, purely technical orientation to action which he describes as 'instrumentally rational action':

Social action ... may be ... *instrumentally rational*, that is, determined by expectations as to the behaviour of objects in the environment and of other human beings; these expectations are used as 'conditions' or 'means' for the attainment of the actor's own rationally pursued and calculated ends ... . Action is instrumentally rational when the end, the means and the secondary results are all rationally taken into account and weighed. This involves rational consideration of alternative means to the end, of the relations of the end to the secondary consequences, and finally of the relative importance of different possible ends ... . Action will be said to be 'economically oriented' so far as ...

it is concerned with the satisfaction of a desire for 'utilities'. 'Economic action' is any peaceful exercise of an actor's control over resources which is in its main impulse oriented towards economic ends. 'Rational economic action' requires instrumental rationality in this orientation ... . The universal predominance of the market consociation requires ... a legal system the functioning of which is *calculable* in accordance with rational rules.[64]

Weber's account of the dominance of rational economic action in the West is based on the most thoroughly worked out sociology of orientations to action and extensive historical study of the development of those orientations, at the heart of which is his monumental account of the consequences of the world religions for the development of economic action:

A product of modern European civilisation, studying any problem of universal history, is bound to ask himself to what combination of circumstances that fact should be attributed that in Western civilisation, and in Western civilisation only, cultural phenomena have appeared which (as we like to think) lie in a line of development having *universal* significance and value ... the Occident has developed capitalism both to a quantitative extent, and (carrying this quantitative development) in types, forms and directions which have never existed elsewhere ... . But in modern times, the Occident has developed, in addition to this, a very different form of capitalism which has appeared nowhere else: the rational capitalistic organisation of (formally) free labour ... the peculiar modern Western form of capitalism has been, at first sight, strongly influenced by the development of technical possibilities. Its rationality is today essentially dependent on the calculability of the most important technical factors ... the *technical* utilisation of scientific knowledge ... was certainly encouraged by economic considerations, which were extremely favourable to it in the Occident. But this encouragement was derived from the peculiarities of the social structure of the Occident ... Among those of undoubted importance are the rational structures of law and administration. For modern rational capitalism has need, not only of the technical means of production, but of a calculable legal system and of administration in terms of formal rules ... . Such a legal system and such administration have been available for economic activity in a comparative state of legal and formalistic perfection only in the Occident. We must hence inquire where that law came from ... . Every such attempt ... must, recognising the fundamental importance of the economic factor, above all take account of economic conditions. But at the same time, though the development of economic rationalism is partly dependent on rational technique and law, it is at the same time determined by the ability and disposition of men to adopt certain types of practical rational conduct.[65]

The neoclassical development strategy for Asia now turns on the geographical 'universalization', or 'globalization' as it commonly is put, of private enterprise, and specifically the development within the Orient of the rationalization of the Occident.[66] Leaving entirely aside the question of how useful is the vexed notion of globalization to describe the changes in the world economy to which it refers, what one must say is, of course, that there is nothing that Weber would have regarded with more horror.[67] Weber's moral despair at the disenchantment of the world concomitant upon universal rationalization[68] falls out of the exclusive focus which neoclassical development strategy places on the technical superiority Weber conceded to rational economic action. The most extravagant claims are, in fact, being made for the Westernizing impact of the rule of law on Asian countries,[69] to the point where the subsumption of Hong Kong to the PRC which was mentioned at the beginning of this chapter is, to some, the beginning of the former's 'takeover' of the latter![70]

6   The Role of Ethics in Economic Calculation and in the Rule of Law

That this projected subsumption of Asian countries to bourgeois political culture in line with the extension of the rule of law may not be culturally sensitive or appropriate, in the sense that it will necessarily involve challenging claimed 'East Asian values' of, say, deference to established authority, is a point that has been made repeatedly. This point is most often made in the political sphere by those satisfied with their own dominance of that sphere,[71] but it certainly can be made in relation to business values.[72] A point which is emerging, and which is of relevance to us here, is not so much whether this subsumption is appropriate but whether it will work. This question is not just one of whether the Asian economies will grow. Many of them have grown quickly and most of them have grown significantly. However the welfare consequences of growth are not entirely entailed in the absolute rates of that growth. Forms of growth that involve vast environmental despoliation, the exploitation of labour, the degradation of living conditions for labour, the accentuation of illegitimate social inequalities and the growth of repressive apparatuses to suppress opposition to forms of growth which involve these consequences, all of which are common to Asia,[73] do not necessarily improve the welfare function. The international development agencies centrally recognize this in their stress on the 'sharing' of the wealth produced by capitalist growth.[74] The author does not agree with their typical claim that the 'Essence' of the 'East Asian Miracle' actually has been 'Rapid Growth with Equity',[75] but it is not necessary to take this up here in the course of what are meant to be comments intended to achieve these agreed goals of equity and legitimacy.

7   The Social Constitution of the Rule of Law

The contradiction within the rule of law, and economic development based on it, to be identified lies in the purported non-ethical, technical quality of legalism on which economic calculation is claimed to be based. The Pareto optimality of general competitive equilibrium is reached by the exploration of all mutually beneficial opportunities for exchange motivated by individual utility maximization. Pareto optimality specifically is reached by the eschewing of ethical concern, leaving welfare optimization to the spontaneous order[76] of the invisible hand.[77] At the point of Pareto optimality, the market is in equilibrium because there are no further mutually beneficial exchange opportunities and, vitally importantly, it has been brought there by the uncoordinated working out of voluntary exchanges which automatically identify the point of Pareto optimality by reaching an equilibrium. The beautiful symmetry of the model lies in its being driven by voluntary exchange and working only because it is so driven. This is the source of the power of the rejection of 'patterned principles'[78] of distribution in favour of the 'pure procedure'[79] of the market in liberal political philosophy, for any state imposition of a 'fair' distribution of goods *must* prevent the perfectly efficient distribution which would be voluntarily reached at general competitive equilibrium.[80]

In this way, the concept of spontaneous order very valuably stresses the individual freedom inherent in competitive equilibrium, but this stress appears to work against the appreciation that such order can emerge only when an antecedent problem of order, the Hobbesian problem of order,[81] is solved. *Exactly the same* orientation of action towards individual utility maximization which, under the right institutional constraints can be shown to produce optimal economic outcomes will, in the absence of those constraints, produce seriously deleterious outcomes. The argument that unconstrained selfishness leads to the disorder of life being 'solitary, poor, nasty, brutish and short'[82] historically[83] and theoretically precedes the argument for the order of the invisible hand, but the wide reception of the latter argument seems to have largely extinguished the understanding that it not only is consistent with but requires the former argument. Rapacious capitalism and welfare-enhancing capitalism are merely the two sides of the coin of individual utility maximization.

In the above quotation from Weber's discussion of the concept of economic action, it will be recalled that economic action is defined as 'any peaceful exercise of an actor's control over resources which is in its main impulse oriented towards economic ends'. The use of the qualifier 'peaceful' is to deal with the obvious point that force and fraud may very well be useful means to pursue 'the satisfaction of a desire for "utilities"'.[84] If the neoclassical concept of economic action is to yield spontaneous economic order, it is clear that the claim that economic action is solely motivated by individual utility maximization should actually be understood to be such maximization constrained within the bounds of 'peacefulness':

> Economic action demands stable conditions. The extensive and lengthy process of production is the more successful the greater the periods of time to which it is adapted. It demands continuity, and this continuity cannot be disturbed without the most serious disadvantages. This means that economic action requires peace, the exclusion of violence.[85]

This conception of the relationship of economic life and political obligation in terms of the former taking place within the bounds set by the latter is, of course, the foundation of liberalism, and its success as a political philosophy cannot be overestimated. However, for the purpose of dealing with the Asian countries' problems we are addressing here, it has the most serious defects. Morality and obligation are kept to liberal bounds. Within those bounds is a system of economics in which freedom is identified with license, because the moral obligation which sets the bound is abandoned within those bounds, where individual utility maximization takes place. Liberalism, therefore, describes a tension which Kant captured perfectly as 'unsocial sociability'.[86] However, seeking to create a capitalist economy by merely focusing on the generation of the technical conditions for individual utility maximisation is contradictory. The creation of a market is equally, and more fundamentally, a moral issue, as a welfare-maximizing market *creates* the possibility of individual utility maximization only by *limiting* the scope of such maximization.[87]

The concentration on the amoral, technical dimension of the rule of law in economic and legal policies based on neoclassical development theory places far too much emphasis on the development of the possibility of individual utility maximization at the expense of recognition of the necessity of constraining that possibility within ethical limits that make realization of that possibility welfare enhancing rather than potentially extremely harmful.[88] In lifting the virtual anathema which they had placed on the state in poor countries, the international development agencies have begun to recognize this. Their consequent stress on the rule of law is most welcome. There is no alternative to furnishing a proper publicly determined ethical institutional environment for the market if the market is to be welfare optimizing. The point to be made is that no amount of development of the technical aspect of the rule of law will furnish the necessary institutions to actually develop that rule.

8 The Cultural Institutions that Make Possible the Rule of Law and the Existence of Markets

Sensible economic and legal policies advocating markets must attempt to secure the transparency and reliability of those markets and, fundamentally, this is an ethical matter.[89] We can, should we wish to do so, encourage action economically oriented towards individual utility maximization, but only if that action is confined within certain non-individualistic limits.[90] Exchange is possible only within the limits of an agreed and relatively fixed normative framework. The transparency and reliability of communication of preferences through exchange depends on common understandings which it would be impossibly costly to have to renegotiate for each exchange, or, what is more, continually to monitor whether others have not unilaterally departed from them were such departures legitimate. This requires an agreed, non-individualistic, ethical structure:

> The basic question is how best to emit those signals which will lead to accepted and understood ethical authority relations and the conditions for their stability. The latter depends on some combination of perceptions and of the reality of mutual self-interest.[91]

It is crucial to appreciate the economic significance of 'norms of social behaviour' as 'There is a whole set of customs and norms which might be ... interpreted as agreements to improve the efficiency of the economic system ... by providing commodities to which the price system is inapplicable.' These 'commodities' are those of trust and cooperation, which cannot really be bought in any direct way, but are of great utility because 'in the absence of trust, it would become very costly to arrange for alternative sanctions and guarantees, and many opportunities for mutually beneficial co-operation would have to be foregone'.[92] There is 'an element of trust in every transaction'[93] because 'Non-market controls, whether internalised as moral principles or externally imposed, are to some extent essential for efficiency.'[94]

Neoclassical economics typically denies this ethical dimension to economic action for it holds, in a most formalistic fashion, that such action can unfailingly be accounted for as the sophisticated outcome of calculation. The rule of law is adhered to through prudential calculation in what tellingly is called the social contract,[95] and 'trust' thus becomes understood as merely sophisticated self-interest,[96] and, as such, can be abandoned when it is prudential to do so. It can hardly be denied that this purely instrumental attitude to the law does widely obtain. However, this is the fundamental problem, and is so because it does not describe the properly ethical attitude to the rule of law when justice, rather than legality, obtains. In the author's opinion, fundamental economic trust cannot be established simply through adherence to the pure technique of legalism, because legal systems are not systems of pure validity and, therefore, *the rule of law is, fundamentally, not a legal matter*. In the pursuit of the purity of jurisprudence, Kelsen, as we have seen, sought to distinguish pure jurisprudence from the methodological syncretism of including, say, ethics and sociology in jurisprudence. He was at pains not to deny the usefulness of such approaches in their proper place, but that place emphatically was not in following the chain of validity to describe the legal system:

> Legal sociology ... asks, say, what prompts a legislator to decide on exactly these norms and to issue no others, and it asks what effect his regulations have had. It asks how religious imagination, say, or economic data influence the activity of the courts, and what motivates people to behave or to fail to behave in conformity with the legal system. The law comes into question in enquiries of this sort only as a material datum, as a fact in the consciousness of those human beings issuing legal norms or complying with or violating them. The object of such cognition, then, is not actually the law itself, but certain parallel phenomena in nature ... . The Pure Theory of Law, as a specifically legal science, directs its attention not to legal norms as the data of consciousness ... but rather to legal norms ... . And ... encompasses material facts only where these facts are the content of legal norms.[97]

At its heart, this strong distinction between the ability to describe the legal system in terms of validity and the simultaneously possible but separate statement of sociological reasons why the legal system is as it is is wrong. The commitment to the value of predictability as an essential component of fairness[98] is at the heart of what is of supreme political value in legalism and the rule of law. However, the predictability that is of such value is not the solely technical matter that is described in Kelsen's pure notion of validity. Not just legislation but adjudication, enforcement and statutory interpretation are not and cannot be purely technical matters, but are conducted by legal personnel (and others involved) within a framework of understanding of the valuable social goals towards which adjudication, enforcement and statutory interpretation are directed. Rather than argue this at length here, reference will only be made to Llewellyn's description of the sense of predictability or certainty as 'reckonability' which follows from recognizing this social context in which the law jobs are carried out:

> [We should] include in 'the Law', along with the rules of law, all the rest of the doctrinal environment ... . It is enough to mention here the general conceptual frame, the vibrant though almost unspoken ideals, the force-fields in doctrine and attitude which strain toward or against movement in any contemplated direction, the going techniques and going organisation of the work of Law-Government ... . And the consequent certainty of outcome is the truest certainty legal work can have, a certainty not reached by deduction but by dynamics, moving in step with human need yet along and out of the lines laid out by [the] history of the Law and of the culture; the certainty, then, not of logical conclusion from static *universal*, but of that *reasonable regularity* which is the law's proper interplay with life.[99]

If *this* sense of the predictability of the rule of law, as not fundamentally technique but as ethical commitment, is accepted, then of course it becomes essential to attempt to create 'the rest of the doctrinal environment', which I am calling the cultural institutions, as part of the attempt to extend the rule of law. This is not a question of pure calculation based on pure legalism but of ethical commitment to the creation of spheres of social life within which (bounded) economic calculation and (reasonable) legalism nationally are deemed appropriate.[100] A moment's reflection on what we have seen of the treatment of the rule of law in neoclassical development theory shows this emphatically has not been the way this issue has been understood.

9 Conclusion: One Obvious Observation and One Less Obvious Observation about Corruption in the Advanced Capitalist Countries

It is quite right to point out that corruption is hardly restricted to what once were regarded as third, or indeed second, world countries, but is common enough in the advanced capitalist economies.[101] In the majority of accounts, corruption is, as has recently been stated, 'always elsewhere'.[102] That this is not so is an obvious point but one it is necessary, certainly at the moment for a citizen of the United Kingdom, to recognize. Although this will not be argued here, the author does not take this recognition to involve denying what is implicit in the indices of corruption mentioned above, that the problem is far worse in former second and third world countries.

The crucial and rather less obvious point is that denying the prevalence of corruption in Asian countries is not in the best interests of the mass of the population of those countries. The point is not relativistically to appreciate Asian economic 'values'.[103] Instead, appreciating the crucial importance of the development of the rule of law and development based on it,[104] the issue is properly to understand what that development means, indeed what 'the rule of law' means. When subject to a very simplistic idea of improving the rationality of economic action by imposition of the rule of law which cannot begin to come to terms with the extent of the institutional changes necessary for the creation of welfare-enhancing markets, those countries' economic policies are riven by the very contradiction that besets the rule of law in former first world countries. The ideology of capitalist economic calculation represented in neoclassical economic technique represents economic action as a technical matter following from the nature of economic action as if that action were in some way an ineluctable given rather than a social construct. This utterly distracts attention from the major work of ethical and legal institutional change which is necessary to create welfare-enhancing markets. In the space left, those who are in a position to exploit the asymmetries of power which are central to capitalist economies, typically endogenous capitalist and political elites and transnational companies (TNCs) can pursue their narrow self-interest at the expense of their fellow citizens under the cover of the market.

Of its nature, this problem will be far worse in former second and third world countries because they do not have the history of the socialization of the market which is common to the advanced capitalist countries. That this socialization is hardly complete even in the advanced capitalist countries, and that the major capitalist corporations are not sufficiently subject to public scrutiny and control, is clear enough from the current crisis of company and securities law and the desperate search for more adequate regimes of corporate governance based on such notions as the stakeholding company. For TNCs and international public and private bodies to seek to implement in Asia merely 'technical' company law reforms under the rubric of the rule of law creates the space for domestic and international capitalists to adopt substantive policies in Asian countries which would be unacceptable in first world countries. No or far too little attention is paid to the creation of a nationally legitimate ethical environment for business. When interpreted formalistically by domestic and international capitalists in the legalistic framework, the rule of law provides a manifestly inadequate check on the scope of the profit-making activities these capitalists will pursue.

Particularly after the experience of the former COMECON countries, that capitalist development should continue to take this path in Asia would be a gross demonstration of the inability of the TNCs, the international development agencies and the domestic economic and political elites to enhance the welfare of the majority of the people of Asia in economic, efficient and effective ways. The current rehabilitation of the state in the policies of the international development agencies *must* be carried through to a recognition that it is not primarily the development of the technical aspect of the rule of law but the public determination of an ethical institutional framework for business that is a necessary condition of welfare-optimizing capitalist development. This is true in Asia and, indeed, everywhere.

Acknowledgement

Earlier versions of this chapter were read to the Conference on 'The Hidden Structures of Law', International Institute for the Sociology of Law, Oñati, Spain, May 1997 and to the Company Law Section of the Annual Conference of the Society of Public Teachers of Law, University of Manchester, September 1998.

Notes

* Professor of Law, Department of Law, University of Leeds, Leeds LS2 9JT. The author is grateful to Les Moran and Sol Picciotto for their comments on this chapter.

1 Zweigert, K. and Kötz, H. (1987), *Introduction to Comparative Law* (2nd edition), Oxford: Clarendon Press, 15–17.

2 Seidman, A. and Seidman, R.B. (1994), *State and Law in the Development Process*, New York (USA): St Martin's Press, 44–51.

3 North, D. (1990), *Institutions, Institutional Change and Economic Performance*, Cambridge: Cambridge University Press, Chapter 1.

4 Campbell, D. (1997), 'The Relational Constitution of Contract and the Limits of "Economics": Kenneth Arrow on the Social Background of Markets', in S. Deakin and J. Michie (eds), *Contracts, Co-operation and Competition: Studies in Economics, Management and Law*, Oxford: Oxford University Press, Chapter 12.

5 Campbell, D. (1980), 'The Social Theory of Relational Contract: Macneil as the Modern Proudhon', *International Journal of the Sociology of Law*, 18, 75; Campbell, D. and Harris, D. (1993), 'Flexibility in Long-term Contractual Relationships: The Role of Co-operation', *Journal of Law and Society*, 20, 166; and Campbell, D. (1996), 'The Relational Constitution of the Discrete Contract,' in D. Campbell and P. Vincent-Jones (eds), *Contract and Economic Organisation: Socio-legal Initiatives*, Aldershot: Dartmouth Publishing, Chapter 4.

6 Campbell, D. (1990), 'Adam Smith, Farrar on Company Law and the Economics of the Corporation', *Anglo-American Law Review*, 19, 185; Campbell, D. (1996), 'Why Insider Dealing Is Wrong', *Legal Studies*, 16, 185 and Campbell, D. (1997), 'The Role of Monitoring and Morality in Company Law: A Criticism of the Direction of Present Regulation', *Australian Journal of Corporate Law*, 7, 343.

7 Podgorecki, A. (1977), 'The Hidden Structures of the Law', paper presented to a conference on '*The Hidden Structures of the Law*', International Institute for

the Sociology of Law, Onāti, Spain (available from A. Podgorecki, Department of Sociology, Carleton University, Ottawa, Ontario, K1S 5B6, Canada).

8   Thomas, C. (15 August 1997), *The Times*, 11.

9   http://www.gwdg.de:80/~uwvw/icr.htm

10   Wheeler, D. and Mody, A. (1992), 'International Investment Location Decisions', *Journal of International Economics*, **33**, 57.

11   The World Bank (1997), *World Development Report 1997: The State in a Changing World*, Oxford: Oxford University Press, Box 3.1.

12   Knack, S. and Keefer, P. (1995), 'Institutions and Economic Performance: Cross-Country Tests Using Alternative Institutional Measures', *Economics and Politics*, **7**, 207.

13   The World Bank (1993), *The East Asian Miracle*, Oxford: Oxford University Press, 82–83.

14   The World Bank (1991), *World Development Report 1991: The Challenge of Development*, Washington DC (USA): The World Bank, Chapter 4.

15   The World Bank (1994), *Sustaining Rapid Development in East Asia and the Pacific*, Washington DC (USA): The World Bank, 26–30.

16   As note 15, above, 30–31.

17   We will ignore the various 'approaches' to development set out in documents of the international development agencies during the last decade, such as 'functional approach to growth' set out in World Bank (1992), *World Development Report 1992: Development and Environment*, Oxford: Oxford University Press, 87–90, and specifically applied to East Asia in World Bank, as note 13, above, Figure 2.1. Although purportedly different, it is fair to say that these approaches add nothing but pleonasm to the neoclassical development strategy.

18   As note 14, above, 6–7. See World Bank (1987), *World Development Report 1987: Industrialisation and Foreign Trade*, Oxford: Oxford University Press, Chapter 4.

19   Asian Development Bank (1994), *Asian Development Outlook 1994*, Oxford: Oxford University Press, Boxes 1.5, 1.6.

20   Esserman, S.G. (1996), 'The Rule of Law in China: A US Perspective', address to a conference on *'China Today: Justice and Business in the People's Republic'*, San Francisco (USA) (available from The China Business Forum, The US-China Business Council, Suite 200, 1818 N St, Washington DC 20036, USA).

21   Wonoroff, M. (1986), *Asia's Miracle Economies*, New York (USA): ME Sharpe.

22   Belassa, B. (1980), *The Newly Industrialising Countries in the World Economy*, New York (USA): Pergamon Press.

23   Pack, H. and Westphal, L.E. (1986), 'Industrial Strategy and Technological Change: Theory *vs* Reality', *Journal of Development Economics*, **22**, 87; and Wade, R. (1990), *Governing the Market: Economic Theory and the Role of Government in East Asian Industrialisation*, Princeton (USA): Princeton University Press.

24   Fishlow, A. *et al.* (eds) (1994), *Miracle or Design: Lessons from the East Asian Experience*, Washington DC (USA): Overseas Development Council.

25   Itoh, M. *et al.* (1988), 'Industrial Policy as a Corrective to Market Failures', in R. Komiya *et al.* (eds), *Industrial Policy of Japan*, New York (USA), Academic Press, Chapter 9; and Wade, R. (1996), 'Japan, the World Bank and the Art of Paradigm Maintenance: The East Asian Miracle in Political Perspective', *New Left Review*, **217**, 3.

26   Naya, S. (1990), *Private Sector Development and Enterprise Reforms in Growing Asian Economies*, San Francisco (USA): International Centre for Economic Growth, Chapter 8 heroically attempts to push the data on most Asian countries into this mould.

27   Vogel, E.F. (1991), *The Four Little Dragons*, Cambridge (USA): Harvard University Press.

28   P-w Liu, (1992), *Economic Development of the Four Little Dragons*, Hong Kong: Hong Kong Institute of Asia Pacific Studies, 25–26; and Senese, D.J. (1981), *Asianomics*, Washington DC (USA). The Council on American Affairs, Chapter 3.

29   Amsden, A. (1989), *Asia's Next Giant: South Korea and Late Industrialisation*, Oxford: Oxford University Press; Leuddeu-Neurath, R. (1988), 'State Intervention and Export Oriented Development in South Korea', in G. White (ed.), *Developmental States in East Asia*, New York (USA): St Martin's Press, Chapter 3; and Wade, R. (1988), 'State Intervention and "Outward Looking" Development: Neoclassical Theory and Taiwanese Practice', in G. White (ed.), *Developmental States in East Asia*, New York (USA): St Martin's Press, Chapter 2.

30   Jacobs, P. (17 October 1986), *South China Morning Post (Business Post)*, 1.

31   Campbell, D. (1993), 'Economic Ideology and Hong Kong's Governance Structure After 1997', in R. Wacks (ed.), *Hong Kong, China and 1997*, Hong Kong: Hong Kong University Press, Chapter 4.

32   Arrow, K.J. (1983), 'Pareto Optimality with Costly Transfers', in K.J. Arrow, *Collected Papers* (volume 2), Cambridge (USA): Belknap Press, 290.

33   Arrow, K.J. and Debreu, G. (1983), 'Existence of an Equilibrium for a Competitive Economy', in K.J. Arrow, *Collected Papers* (volume 2), Cambridge (USA): Belknap Press, Chapter 4.

34   Pareto, V. (1971), *Manual of Political Economy*, New York (USA): Augustus M. Kelley, Chapter 6, section 33.

35   Coase, R.H. (1986), 'The Problem of Social Cost', in R.H. Coase, *The Firm, the Market and the Law*, Chicago: University of Chicago Press, 114.

36   Coase, R.H. (1986), 'The Firm, the Market and the Law', in R.H. Coase, *The Firm, the Market and the Law*, Chicago: University of Chicago Press, 7–8.

37   In fairness, the World Bank's own evaluation of the developmental role of private financial institutions in the 1989 *Development Report* is much more sensibly nuanced than the general market-friendly approach advocated in the 1991 *Report*. World Bank (1989), *Development Report 1989: Financial Systems and Development*, Oxford: Oxford University Press.

38   As note 36, above, 9–10. See Coase, R.H. (1994), 'The Institutional Structure of Production', in R.H. Coase (ed.), *Essays on Economics and Economists*, Chicago (USA): University of Chicago Press, 12.

39   Coase, R.H. (1964), 'The Regulated Industries: Discussion', *American Economic Review (Papers and Proceedings)*, **54**, 195.

40   Menshikov, S. (1990), *Catastrophe or Catharsis*, London: Inter-Verso.

41   Los, M. (1997), 'Ahead of the Law: The "Virtual" Nature of Postcommunist Ownership Patterns', paper presented to a conference on *'The Hidden Structures of the Law'*, International Institute for the Sociology of Law: Oñāti, Spain (available from M. Los, Department of Sociology, Carleton University, Ottawa, Ontario K1S 5B6, Canada).

42   As note 38, above, 12, 6. See North, D.C. (1994), 'Economic Performance Through Time', *American Economic Review*, **84**, 366.

43   Chen, J. (1996), 'Market Economy and the Internationalisation of Civil and Commercial Law in the People's Republic of China', paper presented to a workshop on *'Legal Institutions and the Rule of Law in East Asia'*, Asia Research Centre, Murdoch University, Australia (available from J. Chen, School of Law and Legal Studies, Level 3, Martin Building, La Trobe University, Bundoora, Victoria 3083, Australia); Gillespie, J. (1996), 'Law and Development in the "Market Place": An East Asian Perspective', paper presented to a workshop on *'Legal Institutions and the Rule of Law in East Asia'*, Asia Research Centre, Murdoch University, Australia (available from J. Gillespie, Centre for Asian Business, Deakin University, Geelong, Victoria 3217, Australia); and Jayasuriya,

K. (1996), 'Corporatism and Judicial Independence Within Statist Legal Institutions in East Asia', paper presented to a workshop on *'Legal Institutions and the Rule of Law in East Asia'*, Asia Research Centre, Murdoch University, Australia (available from K. Jayasuriya, Asia Research Centre, Murdoch University, Murdoch, WA 6150, Australia).

44   Williamson, O.E. (1996), *The Mechanisms of Governance*, Oxford: Oxford University Press, 337–340.

45   World Bank, (1995), *Bureaucrats in Business*, Oxford: Oxford University Press.

46   As note 11, above, 41.

47   As note 11, above, Chapter 6.

48   As note 11, above, Part 3.

49   As note 11, above, Chapter 4.

50   As note 11, above, 41–45.

51   Upham, F. (1994), 'Relational Practices and the Marginalisation of Law', *Law and Society Review*, **28**, 67.

52   Jayasuriya, K. (1996), 'Rule of Law and Capitalism in East Asia', *Pacific Review*, **9**, 357; Jones, C.A.G. (1994), 'Capitalism, Globalisation and the Rule of Law', *Social and Legal Studies*, **3**, 195; and Tomasic, R. (1995), 'Company Law and the Limits of the Rule of Law in China', *Australian Journal of Corporate Law*, **4**, 470.

53   Kelsen, H. (1992), *Introduction to the Problems of Legal Theory*, Oxford: Clarendon Press, 56.

54   Kelsen, H. (1949), *General Theory of Law and State*, Cambridge (USA): Harvard University Press, 14.

55   Kelsen, H. (1957), 'Value Judgments in the Science of Law', in H. Kelsen, *What is Justice*, Berkeley (USA): University of California Press, 228–289.

56   As note 53, above, 7–8.

57   As note 54, above, 13.

58   As note 54, above, 5.

59   As note 54, above, 14.

60   Gossen, H.H. (1983), *The Laws of Human Relations*, Cambridge (USA): MIT Press, 3–4.

61   Austin, J. (1955), *The Province of Jurisprudence Determined*, London: Weidenfeld, Lecture 2.

62   Campbell, D. (1994), 'Ayres *versus* Coase: An Attempt to Recover the Issue of Equality in Law and Economics', *British Journal of Law and Society*, **21**, 434; Campbell, D. (1996), 'On What is Valuable in Law and Economics', *Otago Law Review*, **8**, 489; Campbell, D. as note 4, above; and Campbell D. and Picciotto, S., 'Exploring the Relationship Between Law and Economics: The Limits of Formalism', *Legal Studies*, **18**, 249.

63   Trubeck, D. (1972), 'Max Weber on Law and the Rise of Capitalism', *Wisconsin Law Review*, 721; and Trubeck, D. (1972), 'Towards a Social Theory of Law: An Essay on the Study of Law and Its Development', *Yale Law Journal*, **82**, 1.

64   Weber, M. (1978), *Economy and Society*, Berkeley (USA): University of California Press, 24, 26, 63, 337.

65   Weber, M. (1976), *The Protestant Ethic and the Spirit of Capitalism*, London: Allen and Unwin, 13, 20, 21, 24–25, 26.

66   Silbey, S. (1997), '"Let Them Eat Cake:" Globalisation, Postmodern Colonialism and the Possibilities of Justice', *Law and Society Review*, **31**, 207.

67   Ewing, S. (1987), 'Formal Justice and the Spirit of Capitalism: Max Weber's Sociology of Law', *Law and Society Review*, **21**, 487.

68   As note 65, above, 180–183.

69   Ohmae, K. (1990), *The Borderless World*, New York (USA): Harper Business.

70   Cheung, S. (1986), *Will China Go 'Capitalist'?* (2nd edition), London: Institute of Economic Affairs.
71   Robinson, R. (1996), 'The Politics of "Asian Values"', *Pacific Review*, **9**, 309.
72   Enderle, G. (1995), 'An Outsider's View of the East Asian Miracle', in S. Stewart and G. Donleavy (eds), *Whose Business Values?*, Hong Kong: Hong Kong University Press, Chapter 7.
73   Islam, I. and Chodury, A. (1997), *Asia-Pacific Economies*, London: Routledge.
74   As note 13, above, 158–166.
75   As note 13, above, 8.
76   Hayek, F.A. (1976), *Law, Legislation and Liberty*, Chicago (USA): University of Chicago Press, Volume 1.
77   Mandeville, B. (1970), *The Fable of the Bees*, Harmondsworth: Penguin; and Smith, A. (1976), *The Wealth of Nations*, Oxford: Oxford University Press, 412.
78   Nozick, R. (1974), *Anarchy, State and Utopia*, New York (USA): Basic Books, 155–160.
79   Rawls, J. (1971), *A Theory of Justice*, Cambridge (USA): Belknap Press, 83–90.
80   As note 76, above, Chapter 9.
81   Parsons, T. (1968), *The Structure of Social Action* (2nd edition), New York (USA): Free Press, 89–94.
82   Hobbes, T. (1968), *Leviathan*, Harmondsworth: Penguin Books, 186.
83   Keynes, J.M. (1973), *The General Theory of Employment, Interest and Money*, London: Macmillan, 359–362.
84   As note 64, above, 63.
85   von Mises, L. (1981), *Socialism*, Indianapolis (USA): Liberty Classics, 36.
86   Kant, I. (1983), 'Idea for a Universal History with Cosmopolitan Intent', in I. Kant, *Perpetual Peace and other Essays*, Indianapolis (USA): Hackett, 31–32.
87   Casson, M. (1991), *The Economics of Business Culture*, Oxford: Clarendon Press, Chapter 2.
88   McKinnon, R.I. (1992), 'Spontaneous Order on the Road Back From Socialism: An Asian Perspective', *American Economic Review (Papers and Proceedings)*, **82**, 31.
89   Sitkin, S. and Roth, N. (1993), 'Explaining the Ineffectiveness of Legal "Remedies" for Trust/Distrust', *Organisation Science*, **4**, 367–392.
90   Campbell, D., as note 4, above. The rest of this paragraph is based on a section of this chapter.
91   Arrow, K.J. (1983), 'The Organisation of Economic Activity: Issues Pertinent to the Choice of Market *Versus* Non-market Allocation', in K.J. Arrow, *Collected Papers*, Vol. 2, Cambridge (USA): Belknap Press, 151.
92   As note 91, above, 151–152.
93   Arrow, K.J. (1984), 'Information and Economic Behaviour', in K.J. Arrow, *Collected Papers* (Volume 4), Cambridge (USA): Belknap Press, 150.
94   Arrow, K.J. (1984), 'The Economics of Moral Hazard: Further Comment', in K.J. Arrow (ed.), *Collected Papers* Vol. 4, Cambridge (USA): Belknap Press, 104–105.
95   Gauthier, D. (1990), 'The Social Contract as Ideology', in D. Gauthier (ed.), *Moral Dealing*, Ithaca (USA): Cornell University Press, Chapter 14.
96   Coleman, J. (1990), *Foundations of Social Theory*, Cambridge (USA): Belknap Press, Chapter 8.
97   As note 53, above, 14.
98   As note 79, above, Chapter 1.
99   Llewellyn, K.N. (1960), *The Common Law Tradition*, Boston (USA): Little Brown, 185–186.
100 Walzer, M. (1983), *Spheres of Justice*, Oxford: Basil Blackwell, Chapter 4.

101   Huntingdon, S.P. (1996), 'The West Unique, Not Universal', *Foreign Affairs*, **75**, 28.
102   Thomas, P.A., 'Corruption and the Law', unpublished paper (available from P.A. Thomas, Cardiff Law School, University of Wales College of Cardiff, PO Box 427, Cardiff, CF1 1XD, UK).
103   As in Appelbaum, R.P. (1997), 'The Future of Law in a Global Economy', paper presented to a workshop on *'Changing Legal Cultures'*, International Institute for the Sociology of Law, Oñati, Spain (available from R.P. Appelbaum, Department of Sociology and the Centre for Global Studies, University of California at Santa Barbara, Santa Barbara, CA 93106, USA).
104   Dworkin, R. (1978), 'Liberalism', in S. Hampshire (ed.), *Public and Private Morality*: Cambridge, Cambridge University Press, Chapter 6.

3 Company Law in Japan

STEPHEN BOTTOMLEY*

1   A Brief Introduction to the Japanese Legal System

A proper examination of the nature and history of the Japanese legal system would take us back to the second century. This is not the place for such an extensive survey.[1] For present purposes it is sufficient to note the changes that have taken place since the mid-nineteenth century – the period of modernization of Japanese law. Taking this as the starting point, it is possible to describe two significant periods of legal and political change.

The first period, known as the Meiji restoration, lasted from the 1860s through to the early twentieth century. This period saw a shift from the essentially feudal system of the Tokugawa shogunate to a political system based on Western-style government and a legal system based on a European (principally German) civil law model. As one commentator puts it, during this period, '[u]nlike countries which introduced foreign law within their system of indigenous law, Japan almost entirely abandoned traditional law and turned to foreign law'.[2] It was in this period that the first major legal codes were enacted, in particular the Civil Code and the Commercial Code.

The second period of reform occurred in the post-Second World War period, under the supervision of the Supreme Command of the Allied Powers. This period witnessed the beginning of a strong US influence on the development of the Japanese legal system. The present Japanese Constitution was enacted in 1946 (replacing the Constitution of 1890) and although the pre-War codes remained in place, all were revised in order to bring them into line with the new Constitution.

Japanese law is, therefore, primarily a codified system, supplemented by case-law. There are five major codes: the Civil Code 1896, the Commercial Code 1899, the Criminal Code 1907, the Code of Civil Procedure 1890 and the Code of Criminal Procedure 1948 (all as amended). Of these, the Civil Code has the widest application, covering matters such as agency, the legal capacity of juridical persons, property, the law of obligations (contract and tort), family law and the law of succession. The Commercial Code covers general matters, such as trade names and commercial registration, as well as company law, commercial transactions (sale of goods and insurance) and maritime commerce. Alongside the Codes there are many other statutes (such as the Securities and Exchange Law), ordinances and regulations which deal with more specific issues which are relevant to the conduct of business.

The Japanese judicial system is established by the Constitution. At the base of the court hierarchy are the Summary Courts and, above them, the District Courts. According to Oda, the latter are the primary court of first instance, having original jurisdiction in most civil cases.[3] Appeals from these courts are heard by the High Courts, which also have a limited original jurisdiction in certain civil cases, such as *habeas corpus* and *mandamus* hearings. The Supreme Court is at the apex of the court hierarchy, exercising a narrowly defined appellate jurisdiction.

The role of the courts is to apply the provisions of the various codes to particular fact situations. Necessarily this involves interpretation of the statutes. Although there is no formal doctrine of precedent in Japanese law, it is the case that courts are generally careful to follow their own precedents and also give due consideration to the decisions of higher courts.[4]

2   Japanese Company Law: A General Description

2.1   *The Origins of Japanese Company Law*

Japanese company law is found primarily in the Commercial Code 1899 (as amended).[5] That Code is divided into four parts, or books, dealing respectively with general provisions, companies, commercial transactions and maritime commerce. Book II of the Code deals with company law and covers the incorporation, governance, accountability, financing and dissolution of three types of corporate entity (described below in section 4.1). Book II is supplemented by the Law on Limited Liability Companies[6] as well as the Law on Commercial Registration. In addition, the Securities and Exchange Law[7] deals with the regulation of the securities market.

The first Japanese Commercial Code was introduced in 1890 and represented a combination of French and German laws. However, the present system of company law is based on the Commercial Code of 1899, which was modelled more on the German Commercial

Code of 1897. The company law part of the Commercial Code has undergone a number of major amendments, many of which have been responses to developments in US corporate law and practice. This is especially true of the post-Second World War amendments which, for example, introduced a US-style board of directors into the management structure of the Japanese publicly held company.[8] More recently, negotiations between Japan and the United States concerning the improvement of trade imbalance between the two countries (the Structural Impediment Initiative) led to the 1993 amendments to the Commercial Code which introduced greater protection of shareholders' interests.[9]

Thus, Japanese company law is a distinct hybrid of German (with some French) civil law and US corporate law concepts, influenced by Japanese societal and cultural forces.[10]

2.2 *Who is Responsible for Changing the Law?*

The Constitution grants supreme and exclusive legislative authority to the bicameral Diet. The process of legislative reform usually features bureaucratic involvement, with the original bill being drafted by the relevant ministry, perhaps with the advice of specialist advisory committees attached to the ministry.

In the case of the Commercial Code, the relevant ministry is the Ministry of Justice. There is a standing committee under the auspices of the Ministry of Justice which reviews the Commercial Code. The Committee is comprised of lawyers, bureaucrats and academics.[11] Once presented to the Diet, the bill will be discussed in both houses, although the lower chamber (the House of Representatives) may pass a bill even though the upper house has rejected it.

2.3 *How the Legislation is Interpreted*

There is a hierarchy amongst the various Codes which follows the rule that a more specific provision will prevail over a more general provision. For example, with respect to business matters, the Civil Code – being the most general of the statutes – will yield to a more specific provision in the Commercial Code. In this connection, note that Article 1 of the Commercial Code (cited hereafter as CC) provides that 'As to a commercial matter, the commercial customary law shall apply if there are no provisions in this Code; and the Civil Code shall apply, if there is no such law.' Thus, it has been observed that 'Japanese legal scholars and practitioners must become adept at manoeuvring through the Codes [and] ... more often than not, manoeuvring among the Codes is a matter of making and arguing for conceptual linkages rather than of following explicit references which are incorporated as a matter of law ... .'[12] The following description of the company law provisions in the Commercial Code must be read with this in mind.

3   The Nature and Powers of Corporate Regulatory Bodies in the Jurisdiction

Regulation of corporate law in Japan is the responsibility of the Ministry of Justice, acting through its Local Legal Affairs Bureaus. The Ministry of Finance, via the Securities and Exchange Law, has jurisdiction over takeovers, stock exchange listings, supervision of securities businesses, securities market surveillance and, together with the Bank of Japan, foreign corporations.[13]

In carrying out their regulatory functions, Japanese administrative agencies rely to a considerable degree on unofficial administrative guidance (*gyōsei shidō*) in addition to legislation and subordinate regulations. The practice of administrative guidance has been described as a regulatory technique that, although generally non-binding, seeks to conform the behaviour of regulated parties to broad administrative goals.[14] For example, the Ministry of Finance might impose restrictions on certain securities trading activity by administrative guidance rather than by relying on statute.

4   Descriptions of Types of Companies

4.1   *A Description of Types of Local Companies*

There are four types of company created by Japanese law. The Commercial Code creates three types of company: the general partnership or *gōmei-kaisha*, the limited partnership or *gōshi-kaisha*, and the joint stock company or *kabushiki-kaisha* (CC, Article 53). The fourth type of company is the limited liability company or *yūgen-kaisha*, created by the Limited Liability Company Act 1938 (hereafter LLCA). Both statutes define a company as an association incorporated for the purpose of engaging in commercial transactions as a business (CC, Article 52; LLCA, Article 1).

The *gōmei-kaisha* is an incorporated unlimited liability partnership. It is similar to the general partnership found in the Australian, English and US legal systems, but with the additional attributes of corporate status and perpetual succession. These partnerships are governed by Book II, Chapter II, of the Commercial Code. Only natural persons may be partners (CC, Article 55). The partners have unlimited joint and several liability for the company's debts (CC,

Article 80). Each partner has the right to represent the company and to administer its affairs, although it is possible for one particular partner to be designated to represent the firm, either by unanimous agreement or by the articles of incorporation (CC, Articles 70 and 76). The Commercial Code requires unanimous agreement of partners prior to: any change to the articles of incorporation (CC, Article 72); the transfer by one partner of his or her share to another person (CC, Article 73); or one partner engaging in conduct which competes with the company's business (CC, Article 74). A partner may retire from the company, but will remain liable for a period of time for company debts which were incurred while he or she was still a partner (CC, Article 93). A partner may be expelled by a majority vote of other partners on the grounds of failing to contribute, unauthorized competition with the company or dishonesty (CC, Article 86). As a result of these various limitations, this form of company is not widely used, representing approximately only 0.3 per cent of incorporations in 1991.[15]

The second type of company, also a form of incorporated partnership, is the *gōshi-kaisha* or limited partnership. This is similar to the limited partnership found in some Australian states and in the United States. This type of company is generally governed by the same provisions as for the unlimited liability partnership (CC, Article 147), but with the following differences. In a limited partnership there are two classes of members: those with unlimited liability for the debts of the company, and those whose liability is limited to the amount of money or property they have contributed (CC, Articles 146 and 150). An unlimited liability member can only transfer his or her equity with the approval of all other members, whereas a limited liability member needs only the approval of the unlimited liability members (CC, Articles 147 and 154). Only unlimited liability partners can represent the company and carry out its business (CC, Articles 151 and 156). Although this is the more popular partnership form in Japan, this type of company is nevertheless not used widely, accounting for approximately 1.3 per cent of incorporations in 1991.[16]

Third, there is the stock company, or *kabushiki-kaisha*. As its description suggests, this is a form of incorporation based on the joint stock idea. This form is used by most large enterprises and accounted for nearly 50 per cent of incorporations in 1991.[17] The liability of shareholders is limited to the value at which they have subscribed for their shares (CC, Article 200). Subject to any restriction in the company's articles of incorporation, shareholders have the right to transfer their shares (CC, Article 204). The only type of restriction envisaged by the Commercial Code is the requirement for the approval of the directors before the transfer of shares (CC, Article 204). There is a minimum capital requirement of 10 million yen (CC, Article

168-4). There must be a minimum of three directors, who are appointed by the general meeting of shareholders (CC, Articles 254 and 255). The Commercial Code stipulates that the board of directors is 'to decide the administration of the affairs of the company' (CC, Article 260), and at least one director must be nominated as a representative director, having authority to represent the company individually (CC, Article 261).

The fourth type of company is the limited liability company, or *yūgen-kaisha*, governed by the Limited Liability Company Act 1938. This form of incorporation is used mainly for small enterprises and family businesses – it equates roughly with the US close corporation. It is the second most popular type of company, accounting for approximately 48 per cent of all incorporations in 1991.[18] Such a company must have at least one director (LLCA, Article 25) and each director has the power to represent the company (LLCA, Article 27). The number of members is limited to 50 (LLCA, Article 8) and the liability of members is limited in the same way as for the joint stock company. There are close controls on share transfers such that a transfer to non-members requires the approval of a general meeting (LLCA, Article 19). There is a minimum capital requirement of 3 million yen (LLCA, Article 9).

As the types of company which are based on incorporated partnerships are not widely used, the remainder of this chapter will concentrate on joint stock companies, with some comparative references to limited liability companies.[19]

4.2   Recognition of Foreign Companies

Foreign companies may carry on business in Japan, but only by either registering as a foreign company or by incorporating a Japanese subsidiary. The first option involves appointing a representative in Japan, and establishing and registering a branch office. The Foreign Exchange and Foreign Trade Control Law 1949 imposes reporting requirements on branch offices. Until registration has been effected, a foreign company cannot engage in commercial transactions as a continuing business in Japan (CC, Article 479). In general, a foreign company is deemed to be subject to the same general laws as are applied to a Japanese company of corresponding type (CC, Article 485-2). More particularly, where a foreign company establishes its principal office in Japan, or conducts its principal business in Japan, then it must comply with Japanese company law provisions (CC, Article 482). As a second option, a foreign business can incorporate a domestic company under Japanese law. This would usually take the form of a *kabushiki-kaisha* (see section 4.1 above).

4.3 *The Legal Capacities and Powers of Companies*

Under the Commercial Code, a company is a juridical person (CC, Article 54), and thus its legal capacity must be considered by reference to the general provisions in the Civil Code dealing with juridical persons.[20] A joint stock company is required to state its objects in its constitution (CC, Article 166(1)). The Civil Code provides that a juridical person has those rights and liabilities which fall within the scope of those objects (Civil Code, Article 43). Any transaction beyond the scope of the objects is void. Thus, a company's capacity to enter into legally effective agreements is limited by the scope of its objects. This is, in effect, the doctrine of *ultra vires*, which has been statutorily abolished in Australian company law. However it appears that Japanese courts take a broad interpretation of objects clauses, thereby reducing the disadvantage which this restriction can have on persons who deal with a company in an otherwise *ultra vires* transaction.[21] Oda notes, as an example, a 1970 Supreme Court decision in which it was held that political donations of a reasonable amount are not *ultra vires* in that they are part of the social role of the company.[22]

Japanese courts have decided cases in which they have lifted the veil of incorporation and disregarded the formal legal status of the company.[23] Nevertheless, there has been no definitive judicial enunciation of the rule.[24] Neither does the Commercial Code contain an express statement of this rule, although there are some provisions in the Commercial Code which make directors personally liable (for example Article 266-3, which makes directors liable to third parties, see section 6.2, below).

5 Company Formation

5.1 *The Registration of Joint Stock Companies*

A company comes into existence when the registration of incorporation has been effected (CC, Article 57). The registering authority will be one of the Local Legal Affairs Bureaus of the Ministry of Justice.

The Commercial Code establishes two alternative methods by which a joint stock company can be registered: either private incorporation[25] or incorporation by subscription. The first step in either method requires the promoters of the company to prepare articles of incorporation (CC, Article 165). The contents of the articles are dealt with more fully in section 5.2, below, but it is relevant to note here that they must state the total number of shares which will be issued at the time of incorporation. The total amount of shares to be issued at the time of incorporation must be at least one-quarter of the company's total authorized share capital (CC, Article 166(3)).

The process of private incorporation involves the promoters taking all of the shares which are to be issued at the time of incorporation. The promoters must make prompt payment of the full issue price for the shares, either in cash or in the form of property. The promoters also have a duty to appoint directors (a minimum of three) and auditors for the company (CC, Articles 170 and 255).

One of the first duties of the directors is to apply to the court for the appointment of an inspector to investigate whether the incorporation procedures have been complied with. In particular, the inspector must investigate the propriety of any payment for shares which has been made by the promoters in the form of property, together with any special benefits or remuneration which the promoters have received, and similar matters (CC, Article 173). The inspector reports the findings of the investigation to the court. An investigation is not required where:

- the payments in the form of property are less than 20 per cent of the company's capital or less than (5 million yen); or
- the property takes the form of marketable securities, the market value of which is higher than the value stipulated in the articles; or
- the property is real estate, the value of which has been appraised by a real estate appraiser (CC, Article 173(2) and (3)).

Registration of the company is effected within two weeks of completion of the investigation procedure (CC, Article 188).

In the process of incorporation by subscription the promoters take up only part of the shares issued on incorporation. They then invite subscriptions for the remaining shares. When all of the shares have been subscribed for and payment of the issue price has been made in full the promoters then convene a general meeting of members (CC, Articles 177 and 180). The primary functions of this meeting are to appoint the directors and auditors, and to hear a report from the promoters about the process of incorporating the company (CC, Articles 182 and 183). The general meeting has the power to alter any improper arrangements or benefits which have been made or received by the promoters. The company is registered within two weeks after the meeting has been held (CC, Article 188).

An important difference between the two methods of incorporation is that the former involves court intervention, whereas in the latter it is the general meeting which reviews the incorporation process. For this reason, it has been suggested, incorporation by subscription is the more popular method.[26]

The basic duties of a company promoter, therefore, are to prepare proper articles of incorporation, to appoint directors and auditors, and to ensure that shares issued on incorporation are fully paid for. Failure to discharge these duties gives rise to civil and criminal liability under the Commercial Code. The promoters and directors are personally liable to pay for any shares which are issued on incorporation but are not paid for (CC, Article 192). If the promoters fail to perform any of their duties in relation to incorporation, they are jointly and severally liable to the company. If that failure is caused by gross negligence or wrongful intent, the liability extends to third persons (CC, Article 193). If the company incurs damages in a situation where a promoter seeks to gain a benefit for himself or herself or for a third person, or to cause damage to the company, then the promoter is criminally liable (Article 486). Related offences arise where the promoter conceals facts from the general meeting, wrongfully acquires shares in the company, distributes profits in contravention of the articles or any law, or disposes of company property outside of the scope of the company's business (CC, Articles 489, 490, 491 and 493). These provisions apply also to directors and auditors.

Registration of a company is recorded in the Commercial Register, a public document which is maintained by local registry offices. Any matter which the Commercial Code requires to be registered must be entered in the Commercial Register. This includes alterations to matters which have been previously registered. On incorporation, the matters which must be registered include:

- the company's objects, trade name, authorized share capital and manner of giving public notices;
- the address of the company's main office and branch offices;
- the details of each class of shares to be issued;
- the details of any convertible shares to be issued;
- the names of all directors and auditors; and
- the names and addresses of each representative director.

The doctrine of constructive notice applies to matters entered into the Commercial Register: a third party who has dealings with a company is presumed to know about all of the company's publicly registered matters unless there is reasonable cause for not knowing (CC, Article 12). The courts have reportedly given the words 'reasonable cause' a very narrow interpretation.[27]

5.2 *The Corporate Constitution*

The corporate constitution of a joint stock company is embodied in its articles of incorporation. This document combines the effect of the memorandum and articles of association in Anglo-Australian corporate law.

Under Article 166(1) of the Commercial Code the articles of incorporation of a joint stock company must contain:

- the objects of the company (see section 4.3, above);
- the trade name of the company;
- the total number of shares authorized to be issued;
- the amount of each par value share, if any are to be issued;
- the total number of shares to be issued at the time of incorporation (including whether they are shares with or without par value);
- the address of the company's principal office;
- the manner in which the company is to give its public notices; and
- the full name and permanent residence of each promoter.

In addition to these mandatory inclusions, the Commercial Code states that certain matters will not be effective unless they have been stated in the articles (CC, Article 168). This includes the identity, ownership and value of any property which the company will take over after incorporation, and the amount of any remuneration which the promoters of the company are to receive. In addition to all of these matters, the following items will usually be included in the articles of incorporation: the number of directors the company is to have, the timing of general meetings of shareholders, and any restriction on the right of shareholders to transfer shares. As noted in section 4.1, above, the only type of restriction referred to in the Commercial Code is a requirement for the approval of the directors before the transfer of shares (CC, Article 204). Ishiyama points out that this type of restriction categorizes a company as privately held, and he goes on to note that this describes most companies in Japan.[28] It should also be noted that the articles may also stipulate the period for which the company is to exist, or some other circumstances the occurrence of which will lead to the company's dissolution (see section 7.2, below).

Each promoter must sign the articles of incorporation, but the articles do not take effect until they have been attested by a notary public (CC, Article 167).[29]

5.3   Trade Names

Trade names are regulated by the Commercial Code. A company's name must include the words '*gōmei-kaisha*', '*gōshi-kaisha*', or '*kabushiki-kaisha*' as appropriate, to indicate the type of company (CC, Article

17). Other provisions deal with the dishonest use of trade names and the effect of a transfer of trade name (see generally, CC, Articles 16–33). There are limitations on the registration of trade names. Thus, a trade name which has already been registered in a city, town or village cannot be registered in the same area in respect of the same kind of business (CC, Article 19). A corollary of this, however, is that registration of a trade name is only effective in the jurisdiction in which it is registered.

5.4   Membership and Share Capital Requirements

Membership in a joint stock company is evidenced by the holding of a share certificate. A share certificate contains details of the shares (type and amount), the shareholder and the company. A transfer of shares requires the delivery of share certificates (CC, Article 205).

The Commercial Code imposes certain share capital requirements as prerequisites to incorporation of a joint stock company. First, it is necessary for at least one-quarter of the company's authorized share capital to be issued and paid up before the company can be incorporated (CC, Article 166(3)). Second, there is a minimum capital requirement of 10 million yen (CC, Article 168-4). This is intended to restrict the use of this company form to large businesses. By comparison, the minimum capital requirement for a limited liability company is 3 million yen (LLCA, Article 9).

A joint stock company may issue shares with or without a par value (CC, Article 199), although the board of directors can resolve to convert shares of one type into the other (CC, Article 213). Par value shares must be of an equal amount, and they cannot be issued at a discount (CC, Article 202(2)). Each par value share issued by a joint stock company at the time of incorporation must have a value of at least 50 000 yen; the same figure applies to the issue price of shares without par value issued at the time of incorporation (Articles 166(2) and 168-3). Par value shares are reportedly the more common type issued by Japanese companies.[30]

A joint stock company can issue different classes of shares which vary on matters such as their dividend rights and rights to surplus assets. In general, however, shares cannot vary in their voting rights: the Commercial Code provides that each share has one vote (CC, Article 241). The exception to this is preference shares, which may be issued without voting rights so long as the total number of non-voting preference shares does not exceed one-third of the total issued shares (CC, Article 242(1) and (3)).[31] A company may issue convertible shares whereby a shareholder of one class can demand the conversion of those shares into shares of another class (CC, Article 222-2).

5.5   *The Amendment of Corporate Constitution*

The articles of incorporation may only be altered by a special resolution of a general meeting of shareholders (CC, Article 342). Where the alteration will affect the rights of a class of shareholders, a special resolution of a meeting of shareholders in that class is also required (CC, Article 345). In either case, a special resolution requires a majority of at least two-thirds of shareholders who hold more than one-half of the issued share capital (or of the shares in the affected class) (CC, Articles 343 and 345(2)).

Certain types of article alterations are regulated specifically. The company's authorized share capital cannot be increased beyond four times the total number of issued shares (CC, Article 347). An alteration to insert a requirement for the directors to approve any transfer of shares requires a majority vote of one-half of shareholders who hold more than two-thirds of the issued share capital (thus altering the normal special resolution requirement; CC, Article 348).

5.6   *Company Registers*

A joint stock company is required to maintain a register of shareholders (CC, Article 223). This register must contain the name and address of each shareholder, details of the type of shares held and the date of acquisition. The significance of this register lies in the fact that a notice is validly sent to a shareholder if it is sent to the address in the register. Moreover, a transfer of shares is not effective against the company until the matter has been entered in the register of shareholders (CC, Articles 206(1) and 224).

6   Internal Administration of Companies

6.1   *Registered Office and Name*

A joint stock company must register its trade name and the addresses of its principal office and each branch office as a prerequisite to registration (CC, Article 188(2)). Subsequently, details of any changes to the principal or branch offices must be registered.

6.2   *The Duties, Powers and Responsibilities of Directors and Auditors*

6.2.1   Directors   Other than those directors who are appointed by the promoters on incorporation, the directors of the company are appointed by the general meeting of shareholders. The Commercial Code specifies a minimum of three directors, but it is usual for boards of joint stock companies to be much larger, often with 30 or more directors. The term of a director's appointment under the Commercial Code is two years (CC, Articles 254, 255 and 256), but it is common for this to be renewed. In practice, directors are typically appointed from within the company, drawing on individuals who have risen through the ranks of management. Thus, there are few outside (or non-executive) directors appointed, and many of these are representatives of the company's main bank or major shareholders in the same *keiretsu* (see further, section 6.6, below).

Typically, boards in large companies are structured hierarchically. The highest positions are those of chairman (an honorary position) and president. Beneath the president are several vice-presidents, followed by the senior managing directors. Below these levels are the managing directors and, finally, the ordinary directors, both of which are involved in more specific aspects of the daily management of the company. For further discussion about Japanese boards, see section 6.6, below.

A person is disqualified from appointment as a director if he or she is mentally incompetent, bankrupt, or has had a criminal conviction. A director can be removed from office at any time by a special resolution of a general meeting of shareholders (CC, Articles 254-2 and 257; for special resolutions, see section 6.3, below).

The board must appoint one or more representative directors (CC, Article 261).[32] It is common practice for the board chairman and the president to be appointed to this position. A representative director has powers similar to those of a senior manager in an Australian, English or US corporation. That is, although the board of directors has the general power to supervise the management of the company's business, it is the representative directors who carry out the business of the company, manage its day-to-day affairs and who have the power to represent the company. Nevertheless, certain matters cannot be delegated to the representative directors and must be decided by the board. These are major acquisitions of property; large loans; the appointment and dismissal of senior employees; and the establishment of, alterations to or discontinuance of branches or parts of the company (CC, Article 260(2)). This provision was inserted in 1981 in response to concerns about the lack of supervision by boards over representative directors.

The relationship between the directors and the company is governed by the Civil Code provisions on mandates. Thus, a director has an obligation to use 'the care of a good manager', and to report to the company about management matters when requested (Civil Code, Articles 644 and 645). Under the Commercial Code, each director is under a broad obligation to obey any applicable laws or ordinances, the articles of incorporation and any resolution adopted at a general meeting. Directors are also under a general duty of good faith: they must 'perform their duties faithfully on behalf of the company' (CC, Article 254-3). The Commercial Code imposes more specific duties relating to conflicts of interest. First, a director who intends to enter into a transaction which falls within the type of business carried on by the company must make full disclosure to the board and obtain the board's approval beforehand. If this approval is not obtained, then the board may nevertheless deem the transaction to have been done on the company's behalf and seek an account of profits from the director. Second, a director who intends to acquire property from the company, sell property to the company, take a loan from the company, or enter into any transaction with the company must obtain the approval of the board (CC, Articles 264 and 265).[33]

The Commercial Code states that the board has a duty to decide on the administration of the company's affairs and to supervise the individual directors in the execution of their duties (CC, Article 260). The Supreme Court has held that this duty of supervision is not limited to matters raised before the board but extends to active supervision of representative directors.[34]

This idea of collective board responsibility flows through into the idea of collective liability for breaches of duty. Directors are jointly and severally liable to the company for any loss arising out of a wrongful distribution of profits, loans to another director, a director's transactions with the company, or any act which breaches the law or the articles of incorporation. Each director who has assented to the board's resolution is deemed to have done the act, and any director who has failed to express dissent is deemed to have assented to the board's resolution. Directors can be released from liability only with the unanimous consent of all the shareholders, except in the case of a director's transaction with the company, in which case a special resolution (defined in section 6.3, below) is sufficient (CC, Article 266).

As a general rule, it is the company which is liable for damages to third parties caused by the actions of the directors (Civil Code, Article 44(1), applied by CC, Articles 78 and 261). However, this only applies where the directors have acted in the performance of their duties. Directors are directly liable, jointly and severally, to third parties where they are guilty of wrongful intent or gross negligence in the discharge of their duties to the company, or where they make a false entry about important matters in an application for shares or debentures, a prospectus, the company accounts, or other similar document (CC, Article 266-3).[35] The third party must be able to show that there is a causal relationship between the harm and the director's breach. This has been an important provision in the hands of company creditors.

6.2.2 Auditors In the Japanese company law system auditors are given a significant role in corporate governance which goes beyond checking the company's financial statements. According to the Commercial Code, auditors are one of the three organs of the company (the other two being the general meeting of shareholders and the board of directors). The corporate governance role of auditors is considered here, whereas their role regarding the financial statements is dealt with in section 6.4, below.

The auditor requirements for joint stock companies vary according to whether the company is classified as large, medium-sized or small.[36] A large joint stock company is one which has capital exceeding 500 million yen or liabilities exceeding 20 billion yen. A small joint stock company is one with capital of 100 million yen or less. A joint stock company which falls in between these two extremes can be regarded as medium-sized. Special audit provisions apply to large and small joint stock companies. These provisions are drafted as specific exceptions and modifications to the audit provisions in the Commercial Code.[37] For medium-sized companies, the standard Commercial Code provisions apply.

All companies must appoint one or more statutory (or inside) auditors. The auditors are appointed by the general meeting, and their relationship to the company is covered by the same provisions of the Civil Code that apply to directors. Similar disqualifications about appointment apply to auditors as for directors, with the addition that an auditor cannot simultaneously be a director, manager or employee of the company or of an affiliated company. It is common practice for retiring directors or ex-employees to be appointed as auditors. As with directors, an auditor can be removed from office by a special resolution of the general meeting (CC, Article 276; Article 280 referring to Articles 254, 254-2 and 257). A large company must appoint a minimum of three auditors at least one of which must be an outside appointment – that is, a person who has not been a director, manager or employee of the company or any of its subsidiaries for the previous five years.[38] These auditors constitute a board of auditors, sometimes called a supervisory board (Special Exceptions Law, Articles 18 and 18-2). The general meeting of a large company must, with the approval of the board of auditors, also appoint an accounting auditor. The accounting auditor must be either a certified public accountant or an auditing corporation, and is concerned with auditing the company's financial statements. (Unless stated otherwise, the reference to auditors here does not include the accounting auditor.)

The primary duty of an auditor in large and medium-sized companies is to 'audit the execution by the directors of their functions'. Thus, an auditor has the power to investigate the affairs of the company and the state of its property, and may require a director or employee at any time to give a report of the business. Auditors in large and medium-sized companies are entitled to attend and participate in board meetings, but they cannot vote. The auditors are also required to report to the general meeting about any proposal or document which the directors intend to put to the meeting. The report should indicate the auditor's opinion about whether the proposal or document complies with the law or the articles of association, or is otherwise 'seriously unreasonable'. If a director is acting outside the scope of the company's objects or in contravention of a law, ordinance or the articles, and serious damage to the company may result, then an auditor may seek an injunction. Where there is litigation between a director and the company, it is the auditor's duty to represent the company in that action (CC, Articles 260-3, 274, 275, 275-2 and 275-4). In addition to these powers, the board of auditors in a large company can determine the company's auditing principles and the methods for investigating the company's financial situation (Special Exceptions Law, Article 18-2). Note that none of the provisions referred to in this paragraph apply to small joint stock companies; the powers and duties of the auditor in a small company are much more limited, being confined to investigating the accounts (Special Exceptions Law, Articles 22 and 24).

With regard to a joint stock company of any size, the auditors are jointly and severally liable to the company for breach of any of their duties. This liability may be joined to that of the directors in appropriate cases. Auditors are also liable to third parties in the same way as directors and, like directors, may be released from liability by a unanimous vote of all shareholders (CC, Articles 277, 278 and 280).

6.3   General Meetings

The powers of the general meeting of shareholders to decide issues by resolution are limited to the matters set out in the Commercial Code and in the company's articles of incorporation (CC, Article 230-10).

An ordinary general meeting must be convened at least once a year and, if the company pays dividends more than twice a year, the meeting must be convened at least once in each financial period. Notice of the meeting must state the matters to be resolved at the meeting. A shareholder who has for the previous six months held at least either 1 per cent of the company's issued share capital or 300 shares can request that certain matters be included on the agenda of the meeting (CC, Articles 232, 232-2 and 234), although this is apparently an exceptional occurrence.[39]

The power to convene general meetings lies with the board of directors, except where the Commercial Code provides otherwise.

One such exception is the right of minority shareholders to demand that directors convene an extraordinary general meeting. This right may only be exercised where the members' shareholding for the previous six months has been at least 3 per cent of the company's issued share capital. If there is a delay in convening the meeting, the shareholder(s) may convene the meeting with the permission of the court (Articles 231 and 237).

General meetings are chaired by a person who is either to be elected at the meeting or is prescribed in the articles of incorporation. The directors and auditors are required to give explanations about any matters which are raised by the shareholders, unless there is reasonable cause not to do so (for example the matter does not relate to the agenda or some investigation is needed into the matter) (CC, Articles 237-3 and 237-4).

Voting takes place on the basis of one vote per share (CC, Article 241) and proxy voting is permitted. In most cases decisions at a general meeting must be made by an ordinary resolution. This includes the appointment and remuneration of directors and auditors, approving the annual accounts and the appointment of a liquidator. An ordinary resolution requires a 'majority of votes of the shareholders present who hold shares representing more than one-half of the total number of issued shares' (CC, Article 239).

However, some matters require either a special resolution or an extraordinary resolution. A special resolution requires 'two-thirds or more of the votes of the shareholders present who hold shares representing more than one-half of the total number of issued shares' (CC, Article 343). The following list is indicative of the type of matter for which a special resolution is required:

- the transfer of the whole or a major part of the company's business (CC, Article 245);
- the making, altering or rescinding of a contract for leasing the whole of the business, the giving of a mandate to manage the business, or the sharing with another person of the profits and losses of the business (CC, Article 245);
- the take over of the entire business of another company (CC, Article 245);
- the removal of a director (CC, Article 257);
- any alteration to the company's articles of incorporation (CC, Articles 342 and 343);
- a reduction of share capital (CC, Article 375);
- the dissolution of the company (CC, Articles 404 and 405);
- the amalgamation of the company with another (CC, Article 408).

An extraordinary resolution requires the majority of more than one-half of all the shareholders who hold shares representing two-thirds or more of the total number of issued shares (CC, Article 348). Such a resolution is required, for example, to release a director from liability for a transaction involving self-dealing or conflict of interest (CC, Article 266(6)). In some instances – for example, releasing auditors from liability – the Commercial Code requires the unanimous consent of all shareholders.

A resolution of the general meeting may be rescinded by the court on the application of the shareholders, directors or the auditors.[40] The application must be made within three months of the resolution being passed. The grounds upon which the application may be made are that there has been a procedural impropriety, that the resolution breaches the articles or that the resolution is unreasonable due to the special interests of the majority shareholder. The court has a discretion not to rescind where the procedural impropriety was not serious (CC, Articles 247, 248 and 251).

Despite the provisions of the Commercial Code regarding general meetings, it has been observed that general meetings of joint stock companies are largely ineffective, and that 'the general meeting of shareholders has become almost a ceremonial or rubber-stamping body'.[41] General meetings may last for only 30 minutes and will usually involve little by way of questions from the shareholders. This issue is dealt with further in section 6.6, below.

6.4   Accounting and Audit Requirements

The accounting and audit requirements for joint stock companies vary in detail depending on whether the company is large, medium-sized or small (see section 6.2, above, for an explanation of these terms). The basic requirement is that every financial period the directors must prepare the following documents: a balance sheet, a profit and loss account, a business report, proposals for the distribution of profits or losses (CC, Article 281). These documents must be presented to the auditors for audit prior to the annual general meeting of the company. In the case of a large company, the documents must be presented to the board of auditors and the accounting auditor (see section 6.2, above).

The auditors must present an audit report on the accounts to the directors which deals with matters such as the auditing method used, any omissions or false statements in the accounts, whether the accounts and reports properly record the state of the company's property and comply with relevant laws and the articles of incorporation, and details of any unjust act or serious violation of law or the articles by the directors (CC, Article 281-3). These detailed requirements do not apply to an audit report in a small joint stock company.

Copies of the accounts and the audit report must be kept at the company's main office and branch offices for specified periods, and are available for inspection by any shareholder or creditor. In addition (and with the exception of small joint stock companies), copies must be attached to the notice of the general meeting.

With regard to large companies, the powers of the accounting auditor are defined more extensively. The accounting auditor may investigate the accounting books of the company at any time and request a director or manager to report on the accounts. The auditor may also investigate the condition of the company's business and property. Any unfair practice or breach of the articles or law must be reported to the board of auditors (Special Exception Law, Articles 7 and 8).

6.5 Shareholder Protection Provisions

The Commercial Code contains a number of provisions which are aimed at protecting the interests of shareholders in publicly held companies. Whether they have this effect in practice is a question that is dealt with in section 6.6, below.

The following list is indicative of these shareholder protection provisions, some of which have been referred to elsewhere in this chapter:

- A shareholder who holds at least either 1 per cent of the company's issued capital or 300 shares, and has done so for six months, can request that certain matters be included on the agenda of the meeting (CC, Article 232-2).
- One or more shareholders who hold at least 3 per cent of the company's issued capital and have done so for six months can demand that directors convene an extraordinary general meeting (CC, Article 237).
- Directors and auditors are required to give explanations about any matters requested by the shareholders at a general meeting, unless there is reasonable cause not to do so (CC, Article 237-3).
- Any shareholder who holds at least 3 per cent of the issued capital may demand to inspect the company's books, records and account documents, and can make extracts. The directors can refuse the demand if they reasonably believe either that it is made to harass managers of the company, the shareholder is associated with a business competitor, the shareholder intends to offer the information for profit to others, or an unreasonable time for inspection has been set by the shareholder (CC, Articles 293-6 and 293-7).

- Any shareholder who holds at least 10 per cent of the issued capital may apply to the court for the appointment of an inspector to investigate the company's affairs if there is cause to suspect that there has been an act of dishonesty or a serious contravention of any law, ordinance or the articles of incorporation in connection with the administration of the company (CC Article 294).

Another significant protection is that shareholders have the right under Articles 267 and 268 of the Commercial Code to bring a representative action on behalf of the company to enforce the duties of the directors.[42] The first step in such an action is for a shareholder to request the company to commence an action against the directors. It is the role of the statutory auditor to represent the company in considering this request (CC, Article 275-4). To have standing, the shareholder must have held a share in the company continuously for at least six months prior to making the request. If the company fails to act on the request within 30 days, the shareholder may then initiate proceedings on the company's behalf. The shareholder need not wait for the 30-day period if the company would thereby suffer irreparable damage. Other shareholders and the company itself may intervene in the action.

If the company (via the auditor) believes that the shareholder in a derivative action is acting with wrongful intent, then the company may request a court order that the shareholder provide security for costs (CC, Article 267(5) and (6)). In deciding whether there is wrongful intent, the courts have tended to focus on the possible detrimental effect on the directors of the company, rather than on the company itself.[43]

Where the derivative action is successful, any shareholders involved in the action may recover any reasonable expenses they have incurred from the company. If the action is unsuccessful, the shareholders are not liable to the company for damages unless they are guilty of 'wrongful intent' (CC, Article 268-2 (1) and (2)).

A related right is found in Article 272 of the Commercial Code. The provision applies where a director engages in activity on behalf of the company, and that activity falls outside the objects of the company, is against the articles of incorporation or contravenes a law or ordinance, and may therefore cause irreparable damage to the company. In such a case any shareholder who has held a share continuously for at least six months may demand that the director cease the activity.

6.6 Corporate Governance and the Relationship between Management and Shareholders

Perhaps the most widely noted feature of Japanese corporate organization is the *keiretsu*. Although its meaning is imprecise, this term usually refers to a large and complex network of interdependent companies held together by cross-shareholdings, shared directorships and mutual trading relationships. Companies in the group often have diversified businesses. Approximately 50 per cent of all listed Japanese companies are members of a *keiretsu*, and the 'Big Six' *keiretsu* (Daiichi-Kangyo, Fuji, Mitsubishi, Mitsui, Sanwa and Sumitomo) together are said to own 25 per cent of all issued share capital in Japan.[44]

A *keiretsu* ordinarily includes at least one bank ('the main bank') which is usually the major lender to the group, but it has more than a simple financing role. The bank is also likely to be a substantial shareholder in the group. More significantly, the main bank acts as a monitor and supervisor of company performance, often on behalf of other creditor banks.[45] It also plays a crucial role in decisions about whether to rescue or liquidate insolvent companies in the *keiretsu*. Therefore, the main bank performs functions which in other Western corporate law systems are performed by a variety of agents in the market.[46] For this reason, the main bank has been described as 'the dominant intermediary' in the group.[47] Approximately 50 per cent of the shares in large Japanese companies are held by banks and insurance companies.[48] Moreover, the dominant shareholdings in a *keiretsu* are usually held on a long-term basis – the purpose of these shareholdings is to establish stable business relationships rather than to make short-term gain. According to one estimate, nearly two-thirds of Japanese equity capital is held on this long-term basis.[49] This is a significant factor in the low level of takeover activity in Japan.

Another organizational feature of the large *keiretsu* is the presidential association, made up of the presidents of each of the core companies in the *keiretsu*. Given the existence of cross-shareholdings between the companies, each president also represents a significant shareholder in the other companies. A presidential association may meet once a month to plan the group's strategies and policies.[50] These associations are not a formal requirement of the Commercial Code, nor of the articles of incorporation of the various companies, and thus fall outside any of the formal accountability mechanisms.

As noted earlier, within each company, the board of directors typically consists almost entirely of executive directors who have earned their position by progression up through company's management hierarchy. The small number of outside directors on the board is likely to consist of representatives of the company's main bank and other major shareholding companies in the same *keiretsu*. Thus, in practice, boards typically direct their loyalty towards managers and company employees rather than towards the shareholders. Similarly, the statutorily appointed auditors, although legally accountable to the general meeting of shareholders, are usually drawn from the ranks of former corporate employees and so are likely to defer to the company president.[51] Thus, the capacity of the board of auditors to supervise the conduct of directors can be compromised.

In practice, the large size of the boards in most publicly held companies means that board meetings are not an appropriate forum in which to manage the company. Instead, this task is commonly performed by an informal committee comprised of the president and the representative directors.

There is little shareholder involvement in the general meetings of publicly held companies. One reason for this is the presence of so-called 'professional shareholders' (*sōkai-ya*). As one commentator describes it:

> '*sōkai-ya* are hired by management to attend meetings to ensure that no debate takes place, that no embarrassing questions are asked, and that the meeting runs smoothly and ends quickly. These men each own a few shares to gain entrance to the meeting, and are paid handsomely from corporate funds ... .'[52]

In 1981 the Commercial Code was amended in an attempt to limit the activities of the *sōkai-ya*: Article 294-2 prohibits a company from offering any proprietary benefit to a person in relation to the exercise of shareholders' rights. Any director, auditor, manager or other employee who offers such a benefit is liable to a fine or imprisonment (CC, Article 497). Further penalties apply to making or receiving unlawful solicitations (CC, Article 494). There is evidence to suggest that these laws have not been entirely effective in eliminating the practices associated with the *sōkai-ya*.[53]

6.7   Corporate Financial Transactions

6.7.1   Buy backs   A joint stock company is prohibited from acquiring its own shares or from taking more than 5 per cent of its shares as security, except in a limited number of situations. These are set out in Article 210 of the Commercial Code, being situations where:

- the shares are to be cancelled;
- the company is merging with, or acquiring, the whole of the business of another company, and that other company owns shares in the first company;

- the acquisition is a necessary part of exercising the company's rights (for example exercising rights as a creditor against a debtor who holds shares in the company);
- the shares are part of a broken lot (CC, Article 230-8-2);
- one or more shareholders who oppose a particular resolution of the general meeting (such as a merger or transfer of business) demand the repurchase of their shares at fair value (CC, Article 245-2, 349(1) and 408-3);
- the articles contain a restriction on the transfer of shares and the company requests the transferor to sell the shares to the company (CC, Articles 204-3, 204-3-2 and 204-5).

A further exception to the buy-back prohibition permits a company to acquire up to 3 per cent of its own shares for the purpose of transferring them to its employees. There are procedural restrictions on this type of acquisition, including the need for an ordinary resolution at a general meeting of shareholders (CC, Article 210-2).

Any promoter, director, auditor, manager or other employee who is involved in a breach of the prohibition in Article 210 is criminally liable (CC, Article 489).

6.7.2 Dividends Dividends must be paid out of profits and, unless there are classes of shares with different dividend rights, they must be paid in proportion to the number of shares held by each shareholder. For this purpose, the calculation of profits must take into account the need to maintain the company's stated capital. Dividends can be paid in cash or, if the general meeting decides, in the form of shares. If the articles permit, directors of a company may resolve to distribute an interim dividend. Before paying an interim dividend, the directors must be confident that there will be profits at the end of the financial year (CC, Articles 222, 290, 293, 293-2 and 293-5).

6.7.3 Reductions of capital A company may, by special resolution of its general meeting, reduce its stated share capital. The manner of reduction is to be decided by the same resolution. Creditors of the company must be notified within two weeks after the resolution has been passed, and be given an opportunity to object to the reduction. Furthermore, an action to have the reduction nullified can be brought within six months after the resolution. The action can be brought by a shareholder, a director, a liquidator, an administrator in bankruptcy, a creditor or (except in the case of a small joint stock company) an auditor (CC, Articles 375–380).

6.7.4 Debentures A company may invite subscriptions for debentures if the board of directors passes a resolution to this effect. The company must then appoint a debenture management company to manage the debentures and to look after the interests of the debenture holders.[54] The debenture management company must be either a bank, a trust company or a company licensed under the Secured Bonds Trust Law. The duties of the debenture management company are to 'impartially and faithfully manage debentures on behalf of debenture holders', and to exercise 'the care of a good manager' (CC, Articles 296-297-3).

The debenture management company has authority to act on behalf of the debenture holders in such matters as protecting their claims and receiving payments from the company. To discharge this function, the management company may seek the court's permission to investigate the company's financial affairs (CC, Articles 309 and 309-3).

A company may also issue convertible debentures and debentures with a pre-emptive right to new shares.

6.8   Capital Raising

A company may raise finance by a fresh issue of shares. Unless the articles of incorporation require a decision by the general meeting, this is a matter to be decided by the board of directors. Amongst other things, the directors must decide whether or not the shares will have a par value, the issue price of the shares, and whether pre-emptive rights to the new issue will be given to existing shareholders. All shares in a single issue must have the same price and be issued on the same terms and conditions. If the price at which the shares are to be issued is especially favourable to people who are not already shareholders, then the general meeting must pass a special resolution approving of the share issue (CC, Articles 280-2 and 280-3).

The directors must also prepare an application form for subscribers to the new issue, which includes the following information: the amount of the company's authorized share capital, the total number of shares to be issued, whether they have par value, the particulars of each class of shares (if more than one class is being issued), the amount to be paid on subscription and whether there are any restrictions on the right to transfer shares (CC, Article 280-6).

The Securities and Exchange Law 1948 requires a company which is making a public offer of securities, the aggregate value or selling price of which is at least 500 million yen, to file a securities registration statement with the Ministry of Finance. This statement contains detailed information regarding the company's business operations and its financial situation. In addition, the company must prepare a prospectus which provides investors with the information contained in the registration statement.[55] For the purposes of this requirement, the Securities and Exchange Law 1948 defines a public offer of securities as a solicitation or offer which is made to 'many and unspecified persons'. This phrase, in turn, is defined by the Ministry of Finance to mean an offer that is made to 50 or more persons. In other words, the prospectus requirements do not apply to offers to less than 50 persons.[56]

7 The External Administration of Companies

7.1 *Company Re-organizations*

The Commercial Code provides a process for re-organizing a company which is close to insolvency (see generally, CC, Articles 381–403). An application for a court-ordered re-organization can be made if there is a danger of the company becoming insolvent or of its liabilities exceeding its assets. The application may be made by a director, auditor, shareholders who hold at least 3 per cent of the issued share capital, or creditors whose claims equal at least 10 per cent of the company's capital.

If the court makes an order for the institution of a process of re-organization, this fact shall be registered with the company's local registry. Once an order has been made, no proceedings for insolvency, composition, or related matters may be commenced, and any proceedings already effected shall be discontinued.

In making its order, the court has the discretion to do any of the following (CC, Article 386):

- to impose restrictions on the affairs of the company, together with measures to preserve company property;
- to prohibit any alterations to the register of shareholders;
- to order the inspection of the affairs of the company and its property. The court must then appoint an inspector who will have the power to investigate the circumstances in which the company's business has been unsatisfactory and whether or not any promoter, director or auditor has been dishonest or negligent. After the investigation is completed, the inspector must report to the court on whether there is a reasonable prospect for the company's re-organization; whether any promoter, director or auditor should be held liable; whether it is necessary to supervise or manage the company's affairs or property; whether it is necessary to take measures to preserve the company's property, or the property of any promoter, director or auditor;
- order the preparation of a plan of re-organization or composition and its execution;
- order for the removal of a director or auditor. The court may

also then: appoint a re-organizing committee, which has the responsibility of preparing a plan for re-organization;

- prohibit any release of a director or auditor from their responsibilities, including rescission of any releases already made;[57]
- make an assessment of the amount of any claim for damages arising from the responsibility of a promoter, director or auditor, including ordering the preservation of property with respect to such a claim;
- order the supervision or the management of the affairs of the company and its property. An order for supervision shall be carried out by a court-appointed supervisor. An order for management shall be carried out by a court-appointed receiver, who will have exclusive power to represent the company, administer its affairs, and manage and dispose of its property.

An inspector, re-organizing committee, supervisor or receiver will have the power to demand a report on the company's affairs from a promoter, director, auditor or manager, and may inspect the company's books, documents and finances.

If there is no reasonable prospect for the re-organization of the company, the court must make an adjudication of insolvency in accordance with the Law on Bankruptcy 1922.

7.2   *Dissolution and Liquidation of a Company*

The Commercial Code provides that a company may be dissolved on any of the following grounds (Articles 404 and 405):

- the articles of incorporation specify a period of duration for the company which has expired, or some other reason or circumstance is specified in the articles;
- the company is merging with another company;
- the company is bankrupt;
- the court has ordered the dissolution of the company; or
- the general meeting of shareholders has passed a special resolution in favour of dissolution.

In addition, the court may order dissolution of a company on the application of one or more shareholders who hold (or have held) at least 10 per cent of the company's issued share capital. The court must be satisfied that there are unavoidable reasons for dissolution, either because the company's management is deadlocked, causing irreparable injury to the company, or the managing or disposing of the company's property is grossly improper and the company's existence is thereby in danger (CC, Article 406-2).

On dissolution, the directors become the liquidators of the company, except in the case of a dissolution by merger or where the company is bankrupt. It is possible for the articles of incorporation of the general meeting to appoint someone else as a liquidator. Failing any of these mechanisms, the court shall make an appointment. The general meeting of shareholders can resolve to remove a liquidator from office, except one which has been appointed by the court (CC, Articles 417 and 426).

The first task of the liquidator is to investigate the company's property, prepare an inventory and a balance sheet, and to present this material to a general meeting of shareholders for approval prior to filing it with the court (CC, Article 419). The specific duties of the liquidator are to wind up the company's affairs; to obtain performance of, and to perform, any obligations; and to distribute the surplus assets (CC, Articles 124 and 430). In the case of a special liquidation (see section 7.3, below), the liquidator has a duty to impartially and faithfully discharge the business of the liquidation for the benefit of the company, shareholders and creditors (CC, Article 434). In addition to these specific duties, a liquidator has the same powers as the directors and auditors of the company, and is subject to the same general duties of good faith and care as apply to the directors of the company (CC, Article 430).

7.3 Protection of Creditors

Within two months of having been appointed, the liquidator must publish at least three notices to creditors, requiring them to present their claims within a stipulated period (which cannot be less than two months). Each notice must state that any creditor who fails to present a claim will be excluded from the liquidation. In addition to these general notices, the liquidator must give a similar notice to each creditor who is known to the company (CC, Articles 421 and 422).

During the period stated in the notice, the liquidator cannot deal with the claim of any creditor unless the court gives permission. That permission is restricted to small claims, secured claims and claims which are not likely to prejudice other creditors (CC, Article 423).

The liquidator cannot distribute any company assets to shareholders until all of the company's obligations have been discharged. Any surplus assets at the end of the liquidation shall be distributed amongst shareholders, either according to the rights attaching to their shares or otherwise in proportion to the number of shares which they hold (CC, Articles 131, 425 and 430).

If there are grounds to suspect that the company's liabilities exceed its assets, the liquidator must file an application for a special liquidation. An application for this process can also be made by the liquidator, a creditor, shareholder or auditor if there are circumstances which would seriously impede the carrying out of the liquidation (CC, Article 431). During the course of special liquidation the court may order an inspection of the company's affairs and, on receiving a report from the liquidator, may make orders of a similar type as for a re-organization (see section 7.1, above).

The key feature of a special liquidation is the holding of a creditors' meeting. A creditors' meeting can be convened by the liquidator or by creditors who represent at least 10 per cent of the total amounts due to creditors. The liquidator must submit a report of the investigation into the company's affairs, together with a balance sheet and an inventory, to the meeting. In addition, the liquidator must give an opinion on the prospects of carrying out the liquidation. The meeting may decide to appoint an inspecting committee, which will have the power to demand reports from the directors, auditors, managers and other employees of the company (Articles 439, 443 and 444).

The liquidator must obtain the consent of the inspecting committee or, if there is none, the meeting of creditors, before disposing of any company property, borrowing money, bringing a legal action, making a compromise and agreement for arbitration, or relinquishing a right. Similarly, the liquidator must seek the opinion of an inspecting committee before making a proposal for an agreement of settlement to a meeting of creditors (CC, Articles 445 and 447).

8   An Introduction to Takeovers

8.1   Introduction

Japan has a low level of takeover activity compared with other Western countries. The common explanation for this is the practice of cross-shareholdings, whereby large parcels of shares in a company are held by affiliated companies and financial institutions within the company's corporate group (or *keiretsu*). As a consequence, there is relatively low trading of shares: one estimate is that approximately only 30 per cent of shares in Japanese corporations are traded on the market. This does not make a company immune to takeovers, but it does tend to raise the potential cost of an unwanted takeover bid.[58]

8.2   Takeover Rules

Takeover bids are regulated by the Securities and Exchange Law and by ministerial ordinances. The takeover rules apply to all acquisitions of shares of a reporting company, other than purchases made on a stock exchange or in the over-the-counter market. There are a number of exceptions to this requirement, including:

- acquisitions which will result in a holding of less than 5 per cent of the outstanding shares in the company;
- acquisitions for the purpose of redemption of securities;
- acquisitions from less than ten persons during a 60-day period (that is, private acquisitions).

The bidder is first required to publish a notice of the intended bid in at least two national daily newspapers. On the same day the bidder must file a registration statement with the Minister of Finance. The registration statement must give details of:

- the purpose of the offer;
- the duration of the offer – the offer must be open for at least 20 days and not more than 60 days;
- the number of shares to be acquired – the bidder may set minimum and maximum acceptance levels;
- the offer price;
- the source and amount of funds to be used;
- the current level of shareholding by the bidder and affiliates;
- the identity of the bidder and its affiliates.

A copy of the registration statement is sent to the target company and either to its stock exchange (if the company is listed) or to the Japan Securities Dealers Association.

During the period of the offer, the bidder is prohibited from acquiring shares in the target company other than in accordance with the terms of the offer. The terms and conditions of the offer may be varied during this period, but only if this does not prejudice the target company shareholders (such as by reducing the offer price or reducing the period of the offer). The bidder may withdraw the offer only if it has been made on the express condition that withdrawal may occur if there is any material change in the financial position of the target company which defeats the purpose of the takeover bid, and if such a change has occurred. The offer may also be withdrawn if there are material changes (such as insolvency) in the circumstances of the bidder. In contrast, a shareholder who has accepted the offer may withdraw that acceptance at any time during the offer period.[59]

8.3   Other Disclosure Requirements

The Securities and Exchange Law requires any shareholder who acquires a beneficial interest in more than 5 per cent of the issued shares in a company whose shares are listed or are registered on the over-the-counter market to notify the Ministry of Finance within five days of the acquisition. The notification takes the form of a report, which includes the name and address of the acquirer, details of the shares held in the company, the source of funds used to finance the acquisition and the purpose of the acquisition. A copy of the report is sent to the company and to the stock exchange (or to the Japan Securities Dealers Association if the shares are not listed). Subsequent to the initial report, any material change which affects the contents of the report must also be reported. This includes any increase in shareholding of 1 per cent or more.[60]

9   An Introduction to Securities Regulation in Japan[61]

The main body of regulation of the securities market in Japan is found in the Securities and Exchange Law 1948, which was modelled on the US Securities Act of 1933 and the Securities Exchange Act of 1934.[62] The Act regulates public offers of securities, secondary trading and the conduct of securities firms and dealers associations.

9.1   *Stock Exchanges and Other Regulatory Bodies*

Stock exchanges in Japan are regulated by the Securities and Exchange Law 1948. There are eight stock exchanges operating in Japan of which the largest is the Tokyo Stock Exchange followed by the Osaka then the Nagoya Exchanges.[63] The other exchanges operate at Kyoto, Hiroshima, Fukuoka, Niigata and Sapporo. Securities which are listed on the Tokyo, Osaka or Nagoya exchanges are divided into different divisions; the first division is reserved for large scale listings by large, established companies, whereas the second (or third) division is for smaller, newer companies. Membership of the exchanges is restricted to licensed securities companies. The listing of securities on an exchange requires the approval of the exchange itself (and, therefore, compliance with its listing rules) and of the Ministry of Finance.

The Securities and Exchange Law also establishes the Securities and Exchange Council as an associated body of the Ministry of Finance. This council administers the regulatory powers of the Ministry of Finance with regard to securities trading. It also has a role in amendments to the Law. In addition there is the Securities Bureau of the Ministry of Finance, the various divisions of which exercise powers under the Securities and Exchange Law and other laws, such as the Securities Investment Trust Law and the Investment Advisory Act.

The Securities and Exchange Surveillance Committee (established in 1992, under the Ministry of Finance) has a market-surveillance function and investigates improper securities transactions, such as insider trading.

Finally, there are a number of other self-regulatory bodies, most notably the Japan Securities Dealers Association, which is primarily concerned with regulating over-the-counter trading of unlisted securities. This association operates under the supervision of the Ministry of Finance.

9.2 Types of Securities Regulated

The Securities and Exchange Law applies to a wide range of securities, including those issued by joint stock companies (*kabushiki-kaisha*) and certain types of co-operative financial institutions. The Law does not apply to interests in limited liability companies (*yūgen-kaisha*). In relation to joint stock companies, the securities regulated are listed shares, bonds (including convertible bonds), warrants, call options and foreign securities which are listed on a Japanese stock exchange.[64]

9.3 Market Conduct Rules and Sanctions for Securities Misconduct

The Securities and Exchange Law prohibits a number of unfair, manipulative or fraudulent securities trading practices, only some of which are canvassed here.

Insider trading in securities of a listed company is prohibited by Articles 166 and 167 of the Law. Under Article 166, it is an offence for a corporate insider who has knowledge of a material fact to deal in securities until the information has been made public. Under Article 167 it is an offence for a person (known as a 'tender offer insider') who has knowledge of non-public information about a tender offer to trade in securities of that company. The Law provides extensive definitions of each of the terms 'insider', 'material fact' and being 'made public'; these definitions, which are supplemented by cabinet orders, are presented here in summary form only.[65]

9.3.1 Insider There are two types of insider. A 'corporate insider' is defined to include any company officer, representative or employee who obtains knowledge of material facts in connection with his or her office, and any shareholder who obtains knowledge by exercising the right to inspect the company's books under Article 293-6 of the Commercial Code (see section 6.5, above). Any person to whom a corporate insider communicates material facts is subject to the same prohibition. A 'tender offer insider' is any person who has a similar relationship with a tender offeror as a corporate insider has to the company.

9.3.2   Material fact   A 'material fact' is defined as:

- a company decision to implement (or reverse the implementation of) any one of a number of specified matters, including a share issue (public or private), a reduction of capital, a dividend declaration, the acquisition of a business, the development of a new product, a merger or takeover offer or the dissolution of the company;
- the occurrence of any one of a number of defined events, such as losses arising from the company's business operations, a change in the principal shareholder or a change which might cause the company to be delisted;
- information on the company's business results or projections; or
- any material fact about the company's management, business or property which may have a significant influence on an investor's investment decisions.

9.3.3   Made public   A material fact is deemed to have been made public if it is published in a document such as an annual report or other document filed with the Ministry of Finance and is available for public inspection, or if 12 hours have elapsed after a director or other authorized company representative has publicized it to two members of the media.

A breach of the insider trading prohibition is a criminal offence. The maximum penalty is a fine of 50 000 yen and/or imprisonment for six months.

The Securities Exchange Law also prohibits fraud and financial misconduct in relation to securities transactions, short selling and various forms of market manipulation, such as the fictitious purchase and sale of shares, the spreading of rumours, price fixing or stabilization and the generation of an artificial appearance of frequent trading in securities.

In addition to criminal penalties, the Law allows a company to recover profits which are obtained by its officers or principal shareholders through the purchase and sale of the company's shares during a period of six months or less (so-called 'short swing' profits).

10   Penalties

Chapter VII of Book II of the Commercial Code specifies a number of penalties in relation to the incorporation and management of companies. Space precludes a thorough review of these provisions, but the following examples give some idea of the extent of these sanctions.

Promoters, directors, auditors, managers and employees who are commissioned to carry out specific matters relating to the company's business are liable if:

- they breach their duties to the company with a view to benefiting themselves or a third party, or of causing damage to the company, and the company suffers damage – the penalty is imprisonment for up to seven years and/or a fine of up to 3 million yen (CC, Articles 486 and 492);
- they make a false statement to a court or a general meeting about the taking up of shares or payment for shares which are issued on or after incorporation; wrongfully acquire shares on the company's account; distribute profits or interest in contravention of the law or the articles of incorporation; or dispose of the company's property in speculative transactions that fall outside the scope of the company's business (this offence also extends to inspectors) – the penalty is imprisonment for up to five years and/or a fine of up to 2 million yen (CC, Articles 489 and 492).

Promoters or directors who have issued shares in excess of the total number of shares to be issued by the company are liable to imprisonment for up to five years or a fine of up to 2 million yen (CC, Article 492-2).

There are various offences associated with demanding or receiving bribes in connection with voting at a company meeting or with bringing legal action (such as a representative action) (CC, Articles 494–495).

The Commercial Code also prescribes non-penal fines for a wide range of conduct which is in breach of provisions in the Code, such as:

- neglecting to register something or to give a public notice, as required by the Code;
- failing to permit or obstructing the inspection of documents as provided for by the Code;
- making a false statement to government authorities or a meeting of the company;
- failing to enter a change of shareholders in the register of shareholders;
- failing to convene a general meeting of shareholders as ordered by the court.

The non-penal fine for any of these breaches is up to 1 million yen, (CC, Article 498).

Bibliography

Beyer, V. (1993), 'Judicial Development of a Business Judgment Rule in Japan', *Bond Law Review*, **5**, 209.

CCH Australia, *Doing Business in Asia*, Volume 1, Japan.

de Vere Stevens, K.B. (1996), 'Should We Toss Foss?: Toward an Australian Derivative Action', *Australian Business Law Review*, **25**, 127.

Gilson, R. and Roe, M. (1993), 'Understanding the Japanese Keiretsu: Overlaps Between Corporate Governance and Industrial Organization', *Yale Law Journal*, **102**, 871.

Hirose, A. (1991), 'Changes in Japanese Securities Laws', *Harvard International Law Journal*, **32**, 508.

Ishiguro, T. (1991), 'Japan Amends its Securities Laws', *International Financial Law Review*, 25.

Ishiyama, T. (1996), 'The Company Law in Japan (1)', *Waseda Bulletin of Comparative Law*, **15**, 56–65.

Kobayashi, T., Mihara, H. and Sugimoto, F. (1996), 'Japan', in M. Stamp and C. Welsh (eds), *International Insider Dealing*, London: FT Law & Tax.

Kojima, H. (1992), 'Japan', in E. Gaillard (ed.), *Insider Trading: The Laws of Europe, the United States and Japan*, Boston: Kluwer.

Kuniya, S. and Veda, H. (1992), 'Japan', in J. Buhart (ed.), *Joint Ventures in East Asia: Legal Issues*, London: Graham & Trotman/International Bar Association.

Matsui, I. (1991), 'The Regulation of Insider Trading in Japan – Comparing with American Law', *Comparative Law*, **8**, 83.

Milhaupt, C.J. (1994), 'Managing the Market: The Ministry of Finance and Securities Regulation in Japan', *Stanford Journal of International Law*, **30**, 423.

Oda, H. (1992), *Japanese Law*, London: Butterworths.

Sheard, P. (1989), 'The Main Bank System and Corporate Monitoring and Control in Japan', *Journal of Economic Behaviour and Organisation*, **11**, 399.

Szymkowiak, K. (1994), 'Sokaiya: An Examination of the Social and Legal Development of Japan's Corporate Extortionists', *International Journal of the Sociology of Law*, **22**, 123.

Tateishi, N. and Clemente, J. (1996), 'Securities Law and Regulation of Financial Markets', in G. McAlinn (ed.), *The Business Guide to Japan*, Reed International.

Viner, A. (1993), 'The Coming Revolution in Japan's Board Rooms', *Corporate Governance*, **1**, 112.

Watanabe, S. and Yamamoto, I. (1993), 'Corporate Governance in Japan: Ways to Improve Low Profitability', *Corporate Governance*, **1**, 208.

Yanagida, Y., Foote, D., Stokes, E., Johnson, J., Ramseyer, M. and Scogin, H. (eds) (1994), *Law and Investment in Japan: Cases and Materials*, Cambridge: Mass. Harvard University Press.

Yoshimoto, K. (1993), 'Company Law Amendment on the Supervisory System and Corporate Governance in Japan', *Osaka University Law Review*, **41**, 23–31.

Notes

* Professor of Commercial Law, Faculty of Law, Australian National University. The author thanks Professor Hisaei Itoh, Faculty of Law, Chuo University, Tokyo, whose assistance and advice was important in the preparation of this chapter. Of course, the responsibility for any errors that remain is the author's. Thanks also go to Veronica Taylor, Law School, University of Melbourne, for

assistance in locating information about securities regulation in Japan. This chapter describes the law as at January 1997, unless stated otherwise.

1   A useful review of this history can be found in Oda (1992), Chapter 2.
2   Ibid., 26.
3   Ibid., 68.
4   See Beyer (1993), 209, 211; see also Yanagida *et al.* (1994), 49.
5   This chapter refers to the Commercial Code as amended at June 1994.
6   Law No. 74, 1938.
7   Law No. 25, 1948.
8   Significant amendments to the company law provisions of the Commercial Code were made by Law No. 72, 1938; Law No. 167, 1950; Law No. 21, 1974; Law No. 74, 1981; Law No. 64, 1990; Law No. 62, 1993; and Law No. 66, 1994.
9   See Yoshimoto (1993), 23, 27.
10 See Yanagida *et al.* (1994), 23.
11 It is common for the Ministry of Justice to circulate draft amendments to institutions with expertise in the area (including universities) for comment.
12 Yanagida *et al.*, note 4, above, 33.
13 See further, Milhaupt (1994), 423.
14 Young, M., *Judicial Review of Administrative Guidance: Governmentally Encouraged Consensual Dispute Resolution in Japan*, extracted in Yanagida *et al.* (1994), 125.
15 Calculated from figures in Ishiyama (1996), 56 at 58.
16 Ibid.
17 Ibid, 59.
18 Ibid.
19 Many of the LLCA provisions are similar in effect to the company law provisions in the Commercial Code.
20 The Limited Liability Company Act 1938 contains a similar provision (Section 1(2)).
21 ODA (1992), 266.
22 Ibid., 144.
23 See cases extracted in Yanagida *et al.* (1994), 305–310.
24 See Beyer (1993), 212.
25 This term is used by Oda (1992), 267.
26 Ibid., 268.
27 See Hamada, M. (1982), 'The Relationship Between the Commercial Registration System and Provisions that Protect Reliance on External Appearances in Japan', *Journal of Comparative Corporate Law and Securities Regulation*, 4, 143, extracted in Yanagida *et al.* (1994), 294–296.
28 Ishiyama, (1996), 64.
29 This provision also applies to limited liability companies – LLCA, Section 5.
30 ODA (1992), 272.
31 Non-voting preference shares have a statutory right to vote in certain instances, mainly concerning failure to pay preferential dividends – Article 242(1).
32 By comparison, the members of a limited liability company have a discretion about appointing a representative director. If this is not done, then each director represents the company: LLCA, Article 27.
33 LLCA, Articles 29 and 30, impose similar duties on directors of a limited liability company.
34 *Kobayashi v Hashimoto*, 27 Minshu 655 (1973) cited in Yanagida *et al.* (1994), 302.
35 See also LLCA, Article 30-3.
36 These are descriptive terms and are not found in the legislation itself.
37 Law for Special Exceptions to Commercial Code Concerning Audit, etc., of

Kabushiki-Kaisha 1974 [hereinafter referred to as Special Exceptions Law]. This Law was amended in 1981, 1990 and 1993.

38   Despite this restriction, a director or employee of an affiliated company can be appointed as an auditor: Hiraide, Y., 'The Structure of Company Management and Shareholder Control', unpublished paper, Faculty of Law, Chuo University, April 1997. The author is grateful to Prof. Hiraide for providing a copy of this paper.

39   Yoshimoto (1993), 26

40   Auditors cannot seek rescission in the case of a joint stock company with a capital of Y 100 million or less: Law for Special Exceptions to Commercial Code Concerning Audit of Kabushiki-Kaisha 1974, Article 25.

41   ODA (1992), 278.

42   These sections also apply to limited liability companies: LLCA, Article 31.

43   de Vere Stevens, 127, 137.

44   Gilson and Roe, (1993), 871, 882 at note 47 (citing Kester); Viner (1993), 112, 114.

45   The monitoring role of the main bank has been interpreted by some US commentators as a substitute for the absence of an active takeovers market. See Sheard (1989), 399; and Gilson and Roe (1993), 871, 882.

46   Gilson and Roe (1993), 879.

47   Watanabe and Yamamoto (1993), 208, 214.

48   Gilson and Roe (1993), 883.

49   Prevezer, M. and Rickets, M. 'Corporate Governance: The UK compared with Germany and Japan', in N. Dimsdale and M. Prevezer (eds) (1994), *Capital Markets and Corporate Governance*, Oxford: Oxford University Press, 123.

50   Viner (1993), note 44, above, 114.

51   Yanagida *et al.* (1994), 276, Viner (1993), 113.

52   Survey (1983), 'Corporate Governance in Japan: The Position of Shareholders in Publicly Held Corporations', *University of Hawaii Law Review*, 5, 135, extracted in Yanagida *et al.*, (1994), 495.

53   See Szymkowiak, K. (1994), 123.

54   A debenture management company is not required if the amount of each debenture is more than 100 million yen (CC, Article 297).

55   Tateishi and Clemente (1996), 179; ODA (1992), 309.

56   Tateishi and Clemente (1996), 179–180.

57   If the release was effected more than one year prior to the court order, rescission can only be made if the release was for a dishonest purpose (CC, Article 386(1)).

58   See articles and discussion extracted in Yanagida *et al.* (1994), 513–519.

59   For more detail, see Ishiguro (1991), 25; and Hirose (1991), 508.

60   Hirose (1991) notes that this requirement, introduced in 1990, is based on Section 13(d) of the US Securities Exchange Act 1934.

61   This section of the chapter relies on secondary sources.

62   Note also the Foreign Securities Firms Law 1971, and the Foreign Exchange Law 1949.

63   Information about the Tokyo Stock Exchange can be found at http://www.tse.or.jp/ea.

64   See further, Kobayashi, Mihara and Sugimoto (1996), 322, 323.

65   For further details, see Kobayashi, Mihara and Sugimoto (1996), 322, 323; Matsui (1991), 83; and Kojima (1992).

4 Company Law in Korea

MICHAEL DIRKIS[1]

1 Introduction

1.1 Demographics

The Republic of Korea (South Korea) is on the southern half of the Korean peninsula, which lies between Japan and China. It is 98,190 square kilometres in land area[2] with a population estimated in mid-1997 of 46 million people.[3]

1.2 Brief History

Korea has existed as an identifiable autonomous, cultural and political region[4] since the establishment of the first Korean kingdom, Chosun, by Tangun in 2333 BC.[5] The Kingdom of Chosun (the 'land of morning calm'), which encompassed parts of Manchuria, the eastern littoral of China, areas north of the Yangtze River and the Korean peninsula, was ruled by Tangun's descendants for more than a millennium.[6] The expansion of the Chinese Yen Dynasty in the third century BC, resulted in the loss of Chosun's territory west of the Liao River. Chinese influence steadily increased, culminating in 109 BC with the Chinese Han Dynasty invasion and the subsequent division of Chosun into four Han-controlled provinces.

The decline of the Kingdom of Chosun and the Chinese occupation paved the way for the gradual emergence from tribal groupings of three states in southern Korea: the Kingdoms of Paekche and Shilla in the south, and the Kingdom of Koguryo (37 BC to 668 AD) in the north. All three kingdoms adopted Buddhist hierarchical structures[7] and promulgated state codes and a legal system to rule their people.[8] These early codes appear to have been influenced by the Chinese T'ang administrative statutes.[9]

As the kingdoms developed, they engaged in competition with each other and with the occupying Chinese to the north. As Koguryo (being the most northern of the kingdoms) was engaged in constant battle with the Sui and T'ang Chinese,[10] Shilla was building a closer relationship with the T'ang. Ultimately, it was through this alliance with the T'ang that Shilla first defeated Paekche in 660 and then Koguryo in 668. However, rather than allowing Shilla to rule Paekche and Koguryo the T'ang installed their own military governments. This led to conflict between the former allies, with Shilla defeating the T'ang in 671. With the repulsion of a subsequent T'ang invasion in 674, Shilla controlled the majority of the peoples of the three kingdoms.[11] Despite these defeats, the T'ang territorial claims to Paekche and Koguryo were not abandoned until 735.

The new Kingdom of Shilla, which existed between 668 and 935, was a Buddhist aristocratic state.[12] Despite 200 years of relative peace and prosperity, by the ninth century Shilla was being torn apart by inter-clan conflict. Rebel leaders created the state of Latter Paekche in 900 and the state of Latter Koguryo in 901.[13] In 918, Wang Kon gained control of Latter Koguryo and overthrew the government of Shilla. The new state's population was boosted by immigrants from Parhae with its fall to the Chinese in 926. Finally in 935, Latter Paekche surrendered and the King of Shilla abdicated, enthroning Wang Kon as King of a unified Korea (the Koryo Dynasty).

The Koryo Dynasty, which ruled from 918 to 1392, provided the transition from the Buddhist aristocratic state of Shilla to the Confucian Yi dynasty.[14] The Koryo dynasty survived despite Mongol invasions[15] and ultimate Mongol subjugation. As a result, the Koryo laws were Chinese influenced[16] and Confucianism emerged as the new political ideology.[17] From the 1340s, due to rebellion in China, Mongol influence declined. However, attempts by King Kongmin to reform the government and remove Mongol influences in fact led to the decline of the Koryo Dynasty. He created dissatisfied officials, military officers and land owners due to the removal of pro-Mongol officials and his attempts to reverse the Mongol legacy of centralizing land with favoured officials. A further factor was a conflict between Buddhist and Confucian scholars.[18]

In 1389 General Yi Song-gye seized power. In 1392 he was installed on the throne, the kingdom was renamed Chosun and he was re-named T'aejo.[19] The Yi Dynasty T'aejo created ruled Chosun from 1392 until 1910. T'aejo initially sought to consolidate all existing laws in the Six Codes of Governance (*Kyongje Yukchon*). This process led to the adoption in 1395 of the Chinese Great Ming Legal Code (*Tae Myongnyul Chikhae*).[20] As government had been divided into six departments,[21] the Code reflected this structure by being divided into six sub-codes. The official language was Chinese.

As with all prior Korean kingdoms, Chosun also suffered invasion. In 1592 the Japanese invaded (the Hideyoshi invasion). A bloody seven-year war ensued, ending with the assistance of China's Ming Dynasty. In 1627 and 1636 the Manchu invaded, forcing Korea to repudiate their loyalty to the Ming. However, to limit Chinese influence in its domestic affairs the Yi kings established a practice of seeking '... *pro forma* "enfeoffments" from the Chinese Emperor, partly to flatter the Chinese ego and partly to reinforce legitimacy at home'.[22] This relationship with China resulted in Chinese law continuing to be the major influence on Korean law during the Yi Dynasty.

There were many major achievements during the Yi Dynasty. During the early 1400s King Sejong oversaw the creation of the Korean alphabet.[23] In the 1450s King Sejo introduced the Grand Code for State Administration (*Kyongguk Taejon*), which provided the constitutional basis for dynastic administration.[24] The Uniform Land Tax Law was seen as the Dynasty's ultimate achievement in the late seventeenth century as it resulted in increased commercialization of the economy and led to the abandonment of commercial monopolies.[25] This process of codification of laws continued throughout the Yi Dynasty, with the laws becoming more elaborate. It culminated in the enactment of the the Comprehensive Code of Administration (*Taejon Hoet'ong*) in 1866.

Ultimately the Yi Dynasty was destabilized in the late nineteenth century by the competing interests of neighbouring powers. In 1876 the Kanghwa Treaty was signed with Japan (after constant military threats since 1868), forcing Korea to recognize the Meiji Government and forcing it into external commercial undertakings. After 1882, Korea signed treaties with the major Western powers after much urging from China. Civil unrest following a military mutiny in 1882 and a Japanese-sponsored coup d'etat in 1884 were both suppressed by the Chinese troops. The Tonghak Rebellion of 1894 provided the opportunity for both China and Japan to send in troops, with the Chinese ambitions in Korea ending in the Sino-Japanese war of 1894–99. Subsequently, with the demise of China, Russia competed with Japan for control, with the Russian interest also ceasing following defeat by the Japanese (in the Russo-Japanese War of 1904). With that victory, Japan claimed Korea as a protectorate. As a result, Japanese laws became the sole influence. This process commenced with the enactment in 1905 of the Complete Criminal Code (*Hyongpop Taejon*), which was based upon the Japanese Penal Code of 1882.[26] Korea was annexed as a Japanese colony in 1910. As a result, the Japanese civil law system was introduced.

With the defeat of Japan in 1945, Korea was jointly occupied by the United States and the Soviet Union, divided at the thirty-eighth parallel. A *de facto* North Korean government under Il-Sung Kim emerged under Soviet sponsorship in 1946. A failure between the then two super powers to agree on unification of Korea led to the United States using United Nations sponsored elections in the south to create the Republic of Korea (South Korea) in 1948 (the First Republic), under dominance of Syngman Rhee. Competing claims to legitimacy between the two governments ensued. In 1950 the impending repression of the 'communist' guerrillas by the southern government, the return of troops from the Chinese civil war and Soviet military aid led Il-Sung Kim to invade South Korea. A bitter and bloody war ensued. By 1953 the war had reached a stalemate along the thirty-eighth parallel, leading to an armistice. This armistice represents the peace agreement between north and south as a formal peace agreement was never negotiated.

From 1953 weak and corrupt civilian governments ruled South Korea until 16 May 1961 when a coup installed a military junta (the Second Republic). The junta ruled by fiat until 1963 when a new constitution was promulgated and coup leader Chung Hee Park became President (the Third Republic). In 1972 martial law was restored and modified the Constitution extensively (the Fourth Republic or *Yusin* system). Following the assassination of Chung Hee Park in 1979, a civilian government preceded another military coup in 1980, which installed Doo Hwan Chun (the Fifth Republic). The Sixth Republic came into being in February 1988 with the ninth amendment to the Constitution, following large scale civil unrest. A process of liberalization and political reform began, resulting in local elections in 1991 and free presidential elections in December 1992.[27]

1.3   Economic Information

The South Korean economy is a command capitalist system, where enterprises are privately owned but government agencies provide administrative guidance.[28] Although state-owned enterprises dominate steel, oil refining, chemicals and utilities, the major economic players are large, Japanese style, trading companies (*chaebol*). These companies account for one-third of all industrial production.

South Korea has one of the fastest growing economies, being the twelfth largest economy in the world.[29] South Korea's gross domestic product (GDP) in 1996 was US$ 490.5 billion,[30] whereas its gross national product (GNP) in mid 1997 was US$ 491.1 billion.[31] In recognition of this economic strength, South Korea became the twenty-ninth member of the Organization for Economic Cooperation and Development (OECD) in October 1996. However, in late 1997 and early 1998 the rate of economic growth has slowed dramatically due to the fall in value of the Won as a result of the 'Asian economic crises'.

1.4 The Legal System

South Korea has a civil law system. Under the Constitution, there are three branches of government. The Constitution vests legislative power in the National Assembly,[32] executive powers in the Executive Branch (headed by the president)[33] and judicial authority in 'courts composed of judges' (the Supreme Court being the highest court).[34] As a result, the primary source of law is in the statutes passed by the National Assembly.[35] Other sources of law include decrees issued by the president, cabinet and the ministries and decrees made by the National Assembly.[36] In respect of the administration of the courts, the Supreme Court is authorized under the Constitution to make rules governing administration.[37] Ratified treaties and recognized rules of international laws are also recognized as having the same operation as domestic statutes.[38]

The Republic's laws are derived from a number of influences. The penal and administrative laws (which were developed between 1392 and 1910 under the Yi Dynasty) are Chinese in origin. In fact the six-code structure (the *yukpop*), which is the core of the South Korean legal system, is Chinese influenced.[39] The other influences are the German civil law statutes and jurisprudence (introduced by the Japanese between 1910 and 1945) and Anglo-US influences on the commercial laws.[40] The more contemporary influences on Korean legislation are German and Japanese codes.[41]

1.5 The Judicial System

The Court Organization Act provides for six courts:[42] the Supreme Court, High Courts, Patent Courts, District Courts, Family Courts and Administrative Courts.[43]

The court of first instance in most civil and criminal cases is the District Court.[44] Each District Court's jurisdiction is subdivided into Civil District Courts and Criminal District Courts, which are in turn divided into single judge and collegiate trial divisions (Branch Courts).[45] The jurisdiction also includes further divisions into Juvenile Branch Courts[46] and Circuit Courts (*shi* or *kun* courts).[47] Most matters are heard at first instance by a single judge, but criminal cases involving long periods of imprisonment are tried in the collegiate division.[48] An appellant division in the District Court may also hear appeals from cases decided by single judges.

There are also three specialist courts that hear matters at first instance. The Family Court, which is organized in a similar way to the District Court (that is subdivided into single judge, collegiate trial and appellant divisions), is the court of first instance for family issues.[49] The Patent Court hears cases at first instance in patent, design and trademark disputes,[50] whereas the Administrative Court hears specific administrative disputes at first instance.[51]

The High Courts (also known as Appellant Courts) have appellate jurisdiction in respect of appeals from the collegiate divisions of the District Courts, and have primary jurisdiction in hearing appeals from the Administrative Courts and the Patents Courts.[52]

The highest court under the South Korean judicial system is the Supreme Court, which hears criminal and civil appeals from the District Courts, and appeals from the High Courts.[53] It will also hear appeals from the courts of first instance in exceptional cases.

As well as the courts provided for under the Court Organization Act, the Constitution provides for a Constitution Court,[54] to deal with a range of constitutional issues. Its jurisdiction involves the consideration of constitutional issues referred by other courts, constitutional issues referred by petition, issues of impeachment, the dissolution of political parties, disputes between state agencies and disputes between state agencies and local government.[55]

Finally, there are also Courts-Martial[56] and special procedures for small claims.[57] The legal profession is regulated under the Lawyer Act.[58]

2   The Corporation Law Statute

2.1   *The Constitutional Basis of the Company Law*

The constitutional basis for all South Korean laws (including corporate law) is Article 40 of the Constitution, which enables the statutes to be passed by the National Assembly.

2.2   *How the Company Law Came into Being*

The first company law in Korea was the Japanese Commercial Code which 'forcedly applied' in Korea in 1910 after colonization.[59] Although originally the Japanese Commercial Code of 1890 was a mixture of French and German concepts, the Code at the time of introduction into Korea reflected mainly German concepts (following its revision in 1899). Subsequent amendments in 1911 and 1938 generally adopted German reforms. However, some concepts adopted, such as convertible debentures and non-voting shares, had an Anglo-US origin.[60]

Following the creation of the Republic of South Korea in 1948, a committee was established to reform the company law to make it more responsive to Korean society. Progress was slow. Finally, the legislative arm of the military government, the Supreme Council for

National Reconstruction (*kukka chaegon ch'oegohoeui*), passed the Commercial Code[61] on 19 January 1962. The old Japanese law was abolished. The Code has been amended six times since promulgation,[62] the last amendments being enacted on 29 December 1995.[63]

2.3 Who is Responsible for Changing the Law?

The Ministry of Finance has a supervisory role over corporations law and is responsible for corporate law reform.[64] The Ministry for Justice is responsible for drafting the law.

2.4 What Principles Underlie the Company Law?

The corporate law contained in the Commercial Code is still derived from German continental law, but does incorporate many US influences, such as the adoption of the authorized capital system (*sukwonchaponjedo*) and management powers being vested in the board of directors (*isahoe*) rather than with the shareholders (*chuju ch'onghoe*).

2.5 How the Legislation is Interpreted (Rules of Interpretation)

Guidance for interpretation is provided for in the codes. Where the provisions of the Commercial Code do not cover a commercial situation, Article 1 states that customary law shall apply. In the absence of customary law, the Civil Code applies. Article 1 of the Civil Code states,[65] by implication, that where there is no provision of civil law that applies, then sound reasoning shall apply.

As the legal system is civil, there is implicitly no doctrine of precedent. However, it is argued that as Article 8 of the Court Organization Act states that the interpretation of law by an Appellant Court (a ruling) shall have binding force over the inferior courts, that '... the precedent of a higher court, especially of the Supreme Court, has binding force'.[66] In reality, however, higher court decisions are not universally legally binding, as Article 8 only states that judgments are only binding upon a lower court in the same legal proceeding (that is after the case is remanded).[67] Thus, outside the proceedings in which the specific judgment was delivered, a higher court judgment will at best only have *de facto* influence on subsequent decisions of the lower courts.[68]

Outside the laws and regulations, administrative guidelines, policies and directives can play an important role in the operation of the law in many areas.[69] Haywood argues that these administrative rules can play an even larger part than laws and decrees.[70] This arises as many of the laws have wide discretions, giving ministries latitude in their determining the application of the laws. In addition, many authors state that scholarly writings are also influential in judicial interpretation.[71]

3   The Nature of Corporate Regulatory Bodies

3.1   Corporate Regulatory Bodies

Although the Ministry of Finance has the dominant regulatory role in respect of companies, other bodies regulate specific aspects of corporate activity. Thus, although the Ministry of Finance has a supervisory role over corporations law and securities law[72] and is responsible for corporate law reform, the market regulation of the trading of securities is undertaken by the Korean Stock Exchange, the Securities and Exchange Commission, the Securities Supervisory Board and the Securities Finance Corporation.[73] In a similar way, the regulatory powers are split between the general corporate regulatory provisions under the Commercial Code and the securities regulatory provisions under the Securities and Exchange Act.

Whereas direct investment by foreign corporations is governed by Ministry of Finance, in the case of large scale investment the Foreign Capital Project Deliberative Committee has a role.[74] A similar situation exists in respect of foreign exchange controls (imposed upon domestic juristic persons and foreign corporations operating in South Korea).[75] The Ministry of Finance has responsibility for exchange control, but its regulatory control is subject to cabinet supervision,[76] and the Bank of Korea has a partial role.[77] The Ministry for Justice is responsible for drafting all laws, including the corporate law.

3.2   Mechanisms for the Review of Regulatory Action

The Administrative Court's jurisdiction includes the power to hear cases arising under the Administrative Litigation Act.[78] Under this Act, the court has the power to hear revocation applications against any administrative actions, including those undertaken in the regulation of corporations.[79] The High Court has primary jurisdiction in hearing appeals from the Administrative Court,[80] whereas the Supreme Court hears appeals from the decisions of the High Court in administrative cases.[81]

4 Types of Companies and their Powers

4.1 A Description of Types of Local Companies

The Civil Code[82] provides for two kinds of legal (juristic) persons (*popin*): profit and not-for-profit associations (*sadan*) or foundations. An association will be a 'company' (*hoesa*) under the Commercial Code if the association is incorporated for the purpose of engaging in commercial transactions and the acquisition of gains.[83] Four types of companies are provided for under the Commercial Code.[84] They are a partnership company (*hapmyong-hoesa*), a limited partnership (*hapcha-hoesa*), a stock company (*chusik-hoesa*) and a limited company (*yuhan-hoesa*). The Japanese Commercial Code also recognizes these four corporate forms.[85]

The most common corporate structure is the joint stock or share company (*chusik-hoesa*), which account for over 90 per cent of companies in South Korea.[86] Shareholders are only liable for their contributions to the company.[87] The law specifically regulating joint stock companies is found in Chapter IV of the Commercial Code (Articles 288–542).

The limited liability company (*yuhan-hoesa*) is a corporation whose members' liability is limited to the capital contributed.[88] Share holding is limited to a minimum of two shareholders or a maximum of 50 shareholders.[89] The transfer of shares to a third party is restricted.[90] It is the favoured vehicle for small enterprises. Although it is based upon the Japanese *Yugen Gaisha* and the German *Gesellschaft*, it is similar also to the US closed corporation.[91] The law regulating limited liability companies is found in Chapter V of the Commercial Code (Articles 543–637).

The unlimited partnership company (*hapmyong-hoesa*) is similar to a common law partnership except it is a legal entity. The unlimited partnership company requires two or more partners,[92] who bear both joint and severable, unlimited liability.[93] The transfer of shares in unlimited partnership companies is restricted.[94] The law regulating unlimited partnership companies is found in Chapter II of the Commercial Code (Articles 178–267).

The final corporate form is the limited partnership company (*hapcha-hoesa*). It is similar to the US limited partnership, with partners with unlimited liability and other partners whose liability is limited to their capital contribution.[95] Limited liability partners cannot be involved in the management and operation of the company nor can they represent it.[96] Generally, the rules governing unlimited liability partnership companies apply in respect of limited partnership companies.[97] Chapter III of the Commercial Code (Articles 268–287) contains the special rules for limited partnership companies that are needed due to the existence of two classes of members (that is partners with limited liability and those without). Given the small number of different regulatory sections, in the following text limited partnership companies and unlimited partnership companies will be discussed as one, with any differences highlighted.

4.2   Recognition of Foreign Companies in the Jurisdiction

The law regulating the recognition of foreign companies in South Korea is found in Chapter VI of the Commercial Code (Articles 614–621). If a foreign company intends to engage in commerce in South Korea, that company is required to appoint a representative, establish an office and register it as if it were a branch of a South Korean incorporated company.[98] Such a company will be subject to the same laws as apply to similar South Korean corporate forms and will be deemed to have been incorporated in South Korea.[99] A company's business office may be closed by a court if its objects are illegal, if it fails to commence business within 12 months of registration, if its representative has acted illegally or on the same grounds that a domestic corporation can be dissolved.[100]

4.3   The Legal Capacities and Powers of Companies

Under the Commercial Code, all corporate forms are juristic persons which have the power in their own right (as distinct from their owners) to contract, own property, carry on business and to sue or be sued.[101]

5   Company Formation

Although, in theory, foreigners may establish any one of the four corporate forms,[102] it appears that the unlimited partnership company and the limited partnership company are not open to be formed by foreigners, nor are foreigners allowed to participate in them.[103] This embargo occurs despite the absence of specific legislative provisions.[104]

5.1   The Registration of Companies

5.1.1   A joint stock company (Chusik-hoesa)[105]   The first step in incorporation of a joint stock company is the preparation of the articles of incorporation, which are signed and sealed by the promoters (*palkiin*).[106] There are no restrictions on who can be a promoter.[107] Where the articles do not contain details of the class and number of shares, the issue price of the shares (where not issued at par value) and the amount and number of shares to be issued, the details are determined by the promoters.[108] The articles need to be attested to by a notary public (*kongjungin*) to be effective.[109] At least three promoters are required for incorporation,[110] and each promoter must subscribe to at least one share.[111] The total number of shares issued upon incorporation must amount to more than 25 per cent of the total number of authorized shares.[112]

The next steps in the incorporation process vary according to whether incorporation involves promotive subscription (*palkisolip*) or general subscription (*mojippsolip*). Promotive subscription occurs when the promoters subscribe to the total number of shares to be issued upon incorporation,[113] whereas under general subscription the promoters subscribe to some of the shares, the balance of the shares authorized to be issued upon incorporation being subscribed upon invitation.[114]

Where there is promotive subscription, the directors are required to apply to the local District Court for the appointment of an inspector to supervise the incorporation.[115] The inspector will inquire into arrangements under which the promoters are entitled to receive benefits or remuneration, or arrangements under which property has been given in exchange for shares.[116] The inspectors will also look at the incorporation costs borne by the company and whether the incorporation was carried out in accordance with the articles.[117] The inspector must prepare a report for the court certifying whether the transactions with the promoters are fair.[118] A copy of the report is also sent to the promoters, who have the opportunity to produce an explanation to the court if necessary.[119] The court upon examining the report and any explanations provided by promoters may approve of the arrangements or take remedial action.[120] This investigation and court approval process can be time consuming and costly. However, it can be simply avoided by the subscription being taken up by only one non-promoter subscriber. Thus, to avoid cost it is widely recommended that such a non-promoter subscriber should be used.[121]

Once the all the shares authorized to be issued upon subscription have been subscribed and paid for by the promoters, they are required to appoint the directors and auditors.[122] This is done by majority vote of the promoters, the number of votes of each promoter being determined by the number of shares to which they subscribed.[123]

Where incorporation is by subscription, once all the shares authorized to be issued have been subscribed[124] and paid for, promoters are required to organize the first general meeting of the company.[125] The purpose of the inaugural general meeting (*ch'anglip ch'onghoe*) is to elect directors and auditors,[126] and to consider reports on the incorporation prepared by the promoters or inspectors.[127] These reports arise in two ways. First, the promoters are required to seek the appointment of an inspector by the local District Court to report on the fairness of these costs of arrangements whereby the promoters are entitled to receive benefits or remuneration, and the fairness of arrangements under which property has been given in exchange for shares.[128] Second, the promoters are required to submit a report to the inaugural general meeting outlining the acceptances of shares, payment details, any details of arrangements whereby the promoters are entitled to receive benefits or remuneration, arrangements under which property has been given in exchange for shares or where the expenses of incorporation have been met by the company.[129]

In order to elect the directors at the initial general meeting, a resolution needs to be passed by a two-third majority of those present, where those present represent more than half of the total shares subscribed.[130] The directors are also entitled to investigate the incorporation issues in light of the promoters' and investigators' report.[131] Where improper actions have occurred, the directors can seek shareholder approval for abandonment of incorporation[132] or claim damages against the promoters.[133] The promoters are jointly and severally liable in negligence.[134]

The incorporation will be registered (*soliptunggi*) within two weeks following either the court approval (in the case of promotive subscription), or the acceptance of the incorporation reports by the initial general meeting of members (for general subscription).[135] The application for registration must be made on a joint application of the directors and must contain particulars such as the company's object, the trade name, the total number of shares authorized to be issued, the amount of each share, the manner in which the company will give public notices, the total capital, the total number and class of issued shares, the location of each branch, the period of duration of the company, the triggers for dissolution, the full name and domicile of each director and auditor, and the powers of the representative director.[136] Other documents, including financial records, are also required.[137]

As well as having the effect of conferring corporate existence, incorporation also denies a subscriber recession on the grounds of mistake, fraud, duress or defects in application requirements.[138] However, the incorporation is still subject to nullification for two years following incorporation by lawsuit commenced by a shareholder, director or auditor.[139]

5.1.2 A limited company (Yuhan-hoesa)   The first step in incorporation of a limited company is the preparation of the articles, which are signed and sealed by two or more members of the company.[140] The articles need to be attested to by a public notary (*kongjungin*) to be effective.[141] Once a limited company comes into existence, a meeting must be called to elect directors.[142]

Upon subscription of shares incorporation will be registered within two weeks.[143] The application for registration must be made by two or more members and must contain particulars such as the company's object, the trade name, the location of the principal office and of each branch, the total capital, the capital contribution of each member, the particulars of each director, the powers of the representative director, the period of duration of the company, the triggers for dissolution and the particulars of the auditors.[144]

As with joint stock companies, the incorporation of a limited company is subject to nullification for two years after incorporation.[145]

5.1.3 *Partnership companies* (Hapmyong-hoesa and Hapcha-hoesa)

Partnership companies (both unlimited and limited) are incorporated by the articles of incorporation being executed jointly by two members of the company.[146] Registration of the articles of incorporation and branch offices is required.[147] The application for registration of an unlimited partnership company must be made on behalf of all members and must contain particulars such as the company's object, the trade name, the full name and domicile of each member, the subject-matter and value of the capital contribution of each member, the period of duration of the company, the triggers for dissolution, the identity of corporate representatives and the powers of those representatives.[148] For limited partnership companies the information contained in the application for registration includes all the information required to be in the articles and details of whether the liability of each member is limited or unlimited.[149] The incorporation of partnership companies is subject to nullification for two years after incorporation by an action initiated in the local District Court by a member[150] or by a creditor (where incorporation is prejudicial to the creditor).[151]

5.2 *The Corporate Constitution (Memorandum, Articles and so on)*

5.2.1 *A joint stock company* (Chusik-hoesa)

The articles of a stock company must include details such as the company's object, the trade name, the total number of shares authorized to be issued and the number to be issued upon incorporation, the amount of each share, the location of the company's principal offices, the manner in which the company will give public notices and the full name and domicile of each promoter.[152] The absence of these required details can lead to the articles being declared void and, thereby, threaten incorporation.[153]

The articles should also include other details, which do not affect validity but the absence of which can affect the operation of the company.[154] They include:

- the so-called 'abnormal incorporation' requirements[155] (that is details of arrangements whereby the promoters are entitled to receive benefits or remuneration, arrangements under which property has been given in exchange for shares or where the expenses of incorporation have been met by the company[156]);
- the period of duration or the causes of dissolution;[157]
- the particulars of the classes of shares, the numbers in each class and where shares are not issued at par, the number and issue price of such shares;[158]
- the powers to redeem shares;[159] and
- the rules relating to reduction of capital.[160]

Any other powers may be included in the articles, provided they are not contrary to the law.[161]

5.2.2   *A limited company* (Yuhan-hoesa)   The articles of a limited company must include details such as the object, the trade name, the total number of shares authorized to be issued, the total amount of capital, the amount of one unit of contribution, the number of contribution units to be acquired by each member, the location of the company's principal office and the attestation of the public notary.[162] As with joint stock companies, the articles of limited companies should also include details such as:

- the 'abnormal incorporation' requirements (that is details of arrangements under which property has been given in exchange for shares or where the expenses of incorporation have been met by the company[163]);
- the procedures for determining directors and the identity of representative directors;[164]
- the period of duration or the causes of dissolution;[165]
- the restrictions on transfer of shares;[166]
- the procedures for the appointment of an auditor;[167]
- the rules for the distribution of profits;[168] and
- the rules relating to voting.[169]

5.2.3   *Partnership companies* (Hapmyong-hoesa and Hapcha-hoesa)
The articles of incorporation of a partnership company must include details such as the company's object, the trade name, the full name and domicile of each member, the capital contribution, the location of the company's principal and branch offices and the date of execu-

tion.[170] For limited partnerships the articles must specify whether a member's liability is limited or unlimited.[171] The articles of partnership companies should also include other details such as whether all unlimited liability members are able to manage the business, the respective powers of managing members,[172] the period of duration or the causes of dissolution,[173] and the grounds for expulsion of members.[174]

5.3 Restrictions on the Use of Certain Names

The Commercial Code permits registration of any trade name by a corporation[175] and that trade name is recorded in the articles.[176] Provision registration of a trade name may be sought prior or during the incorporation process for a joint stock company.[177] The name must include the words that indicate it is a company.[178] A name will be registered even if a name has been previously registered, provided the applicant does not carry on the same business in the same city.[179] The misuse of a trade name[180] can give rise to penalties and liability to damages.[181]

5.4 Membership and Share Capital Requirements

5.4.1 A joint stock company (Chusik-hoesa) A joint stock company can exist with only one member.[182] The minimum capital requirement for a joint stock company is at least 50 million Won.[183] The minimum amount of any share is 5 000 Won and the coupon price of each share must be equal.[184] At least 25 per cent of the total number of authorized shares must be issued and paid for upon incorporation.[185]

To ensure creditor protection joint stock companies are required to establish a reserve fund to the value of half of the stated capital.[186] In order to achieve this, companies are required to set aside 10 per cent of dividends annually.[187] Companies are also required to contribute to the reserve any surpluses on any capital transactions, including:

- share premiums;
- any amount in excess of the new reduced capital amount, where a capital reduction has been undertaken; and
- any amount in excess stated capital of a newly merged entity, where a merger has been undertaken.[188]

This reserve fund can only be used to make good a capital loss.[189] In order to use the reserve fund a favourable resolution of members at a general meeting is required.[190]

Although prior to 1996 issued shares were generally able to be transferred without restriction, the 1995 amendments subject all share transfers to the directors' approval (subject to the Articles granting directors such powers).[191] Restrictions also apply when a share in a newly incorporated company is transferred before the issuance of a share certificate. In this instance, the share transfer will not be effective against the company until six months has elapsed from the date of incorporation.[192]

5.4.2   A limited company (Yuhan-hoesa)   The membership of a limited company is restricted to a minimum of two and a maximum of 50 persons.[193] This number may be exceeded where the shares are transferred by a testamentary gift.[194] The minimum capital requirement for a joint stock company is 10 million Won.[195] The minimum amount of any share is 5 000 Won and the amount of each share equal.[196] The liability of a member is limited to the amount of the member's contribution to the company.[197]

The transfer of shares is generally restricted. Where the transfer is to a third party, it can only proceed if a special resolution is passed at a general meeting (by half of the members holding three-quarters of the votes of all members) agreeing to the transfer.[198] These restrictions can be further enhanced under the articles.[199] Where the transfer is between members, the restrictions are set by the articles.[200]

5.4.3   Partnership companies (Hapmyong-hoesa *and* Hapcha-hoesa)
A partnership company is required to have at least two members.[201] There are no minimum capital requirements for a partnership company. The transfer of shares in unlimited and limited partnership companies is restricted. For a member with unlimited liability a share transfer requires the consent of all other members,[202] whereas for members with limited liability a share transfer requires the consent of all members with unlimited liability.[203] A share may also be transferred to a successor upon the death of the member, where permitted by the articles.[204]

The membership of an unlimited partnership may be terminated voluntarily by the member giving six months' notice, provided the articles have not fixed a duration date or the company's existence is not determined by a member's life expectation.[205] A retiring member remains liable for obligation incurred while a member for two years after retirement.[206] Membership may also terminate upon the occurrence of an event specified in the article, consent of all members, death, incompetency, bankruptcy or expulsion.[207] A member joining the company becomes liable for all obligations, even those incurred before joining.[208]

The situation in respect of limited liability members of limited partnerships is somewhat different. Where a limited liability member dies, the member's successor automatically becomes a member of the company.[209] Similarly, where a limited liability member becomes incompetent, the member remains a member.[210]

5.5 Amendment of the Articles of Incorporation

5.5.1 A joint stock company (Chusik-hoesa) In order to alter the articles of incorporation of a joint stock company, a special resolution is required to be passed at a general meeting.[211] The resolution requires a favourable vote by two-thirds of the members present who represent more than a third of the total number of shares issued.[212] Where more than one class of share has been issued and the resolution may prejudice one class, a general meeting of that class of members is required and a resolution must be passed by two-thirds of the members of that class present who represent more than half of the total number of shares of that class issued.[213]

5.5.2 A limited company (Yuhan-hoesa) In order to amend the articles of incorporation a special resolution is required at a general meeting.[214] The resolution requires a favourable vote by half of the members holding three-quarters of all votes.[215]

5.5.3 Partnership companies (Hapmyong-hoesa *and* Hapcha-hoesa)
In order for the articles of a partnership company to be altered all members must agree.[216]

5.6 Company Registers

Company registers only are required under the Commercial Code in respect of joint stock and limited companies. The transfer of a share between a third person and a limited company is not effective until registered in the register of members.[217] Similarly, the transfer of non-bearer share in a joint stock company is only effective when registered in the register of members or where a transfer agent has registered the transfer.[218]

Where the share is a bearer instrument, the register plays no role, as the transfer of a share is effective when there is delivery of a share certificate and there is a presumption that the possessor of the certificate is the owner.[219]

6   The Internal Administration of Companies

6.1   *Registered Office*

The location of a company's principal office is crucial under the Commercial Code. The locality of its principal office determines the domicile of a company[220] and a company's existence depends upon its incorporation being effected at the locality of its principal office.[221] Further, a general meeting of a joint stock company can only be held at its principal office or in an adjacent location.[222]

Given the importance of the principal office, the Commercial Code imposes requirements upon all corporate entities to include the location of their principal and branch offices in their articles of incorporation[223] and their registration of incorporation documentation,[224] and to register any changes in the location of these offices.[225] The registration procedures are the same for all corporate forms.[226] Essentially, any changes to the location of branch or principal offices or the establishment of new branch offices requires registration within two weeks at the new location of the principal or branch office,[227] or registration within three weeks at any new established office.[228]

6.2   *Duties, Powers and Responsibilities of Officers*

6.2.1   A joint stock company (Chusik-hoesa)   The minimum number of directors is three, but the articles can permit more. A director's term of appointment cannot exceed three years,[229] but the director can be re-elected after serving that three-year term. Directors are appointed at the general meeting.[230]

A director can be removed by special resolution passed by the general meeting.[231] Where the meeting refuses to remove a director who has been dishonest or has contravened the articles, then a minority of shareholders (representing not less than 5 per cent of the issued shares) may demand that the court remove the director.[232] Where a vacancy occurs causing the number of directors to fall below the number prescribed by statute or the articles, the retiring director remains a director until a replacement is appointed or the court appoints a replacement.[233]

Remuneration for directors is determined by the articles or by a general resolution of shareholders.[234] Meetings of the board of directors can be convened by any member unless a convenor has been appointed.[235] The notification period is usually one week, but this period may be shortened by the articles or by the consent of all the directors and the auditor.[236] A majority of directors constitutes a quorum, with a resolution being effectively passed if there is a favourable vote by the majority of directors present.[237] Minutes must be prepared and are signed and sealed by the directors and auditors.[238]

The major task for the board of directors is the administration and management of the company[239] and the supervision of the representative director.[240] Thus, the resolutions the board is empowered to pass include resolutions in respect of:

- the management of the company;
- the appointment and dismissal of a manager;
- the establishment or abolition of a branch;[241]
- the convening of a general meeting;[242]
- the approval of financial statements;[243] and
- the approval of a director transacting with the company of the director's own account or on account of a third party.[244]

The board may appoint a particular director to represent the company (the representative director).[245] The representative director has the authority to represent the company and is authorized to do all judicial and non-judicial acts related to the company's business.[246]

Many large corporations have established a non-statutory standing committee (*sangmuhoe*) consisting of full-time directors, who form a group management conference or an informal directors' discussion group.[247] Choi argues that although it allows for flexible and rapid decision-making for large stock corporations, it has the effect of reducing the board of directors as an endorsing entity for the committee's decisions.[248]

A director is not permitted to vote upon a resolution in which the director has an interest, nor can the presence of that director be used to establish a quorum on that issue.[249] If a director acts in contravention of the articles or the law, or is negligent, he or she is jointly and severally liable for damages to the company[250] and to a third person.[251] Shareholders can institute a representative action to seek remedial action, including injunctions against actions by the directors.[252]

Unlike Australia, the United States and the United Kingdom, the vast majority of directors of joint stock companies in South Korea are employees of the corporation.[253] Thus, despite the above-mentioned statutory safeguards, the board's lack of independence from its dominant shareholder and its representative directors means that the representative director or dominant shareholder will normally dictate proceedings. Therefore, questions or alternative opinions are not usually raised at board of directors' meetings.[254] Choi's research further indicates that in most unlisted companies the management has characteristics such as:

family-oriented patrimonial management is considered to be the best
method of management, favouritism prevails in personnel management, as secret funds, tax evasion, and so on are made because of close
ties between politics and business with lack of sense, modern book-
keeping system and social liability of corporations are usually
disregarded.[255]

Choi argues that this lack of separation between ownership and
management, combined with poor management practices, can, at the
basic level, lead to the failure of companies to adopt advances in
management and technology and, ultimately, lead to insolvency.[256]

6.2.2   A limited company (Yuhan-hoesa)   As limited companies have
fewer members than joint stock companies and limited companies
are in theory more closely held than joint stock companies, the Commercial Code is less prescriptive in setting out the obligations and
duties of limited company directors. As the membership of limited
companies is restricted to 50 members, a limited company is only
required to have one director (although more can be appointed).[257]
Where there is only one director, that director is deemed to represent
the company.[258] Where there are two or more directors, the general
meeting (or the articles) can either nominate one director to represent
the company or permit the directors to act jointly.[259]

Where several directors represent the company, a resolution is
effectively passed if there is a favourable vote by the majority of
directors.[260] The actions the directors are empowered to carry out
include:

- the management of the company;
- the appointment and dismissal of a manager;
- the establishment or abolition of a branch;[261]
- the convening of a general meeting;[262] and
- the preparation of financial statements.[263]

Unlike joint stock companies where the board of directors can
approve a director transacting with the company of the director's
own account or on account of a third party, in a limited company the
consent of the auditor or the consent of all members is required.[264]

6.2.3   Partnership companies (Hapmyong-hoesa *and* Hapcha-hoesa)
As partnership companies are the most closely held form of corporations and the least regulated, it follows that there is little regulation
of the obligations and duties of partnership company directors under the Commercial Code. Every member has the right to administer
the business of an unlimited liability partnership company alone[265]

or jointly.[266] Similarly, every unlimited member has the right to administer the business of a limited liability partnership company.[267] However, limited members are prohibited from administering the limited partnership's business.[268] In both partnership forms a representative member can be appointed,[269] as can a manager.[270] A person who represents a partnership company is authorized to undertake all judicial and extra-judicial acts relating to the company,[271] and render the company liable for any wrongs caused.[272]

6.3   Meeting Procedures and the Powers of Shareholders

6.3.1   A joint stock company (Chusik-hoesa)   The convening of general meetings is determined by the directors.[273] An ordinary general meeting is usually held annually[274] at the end of the period for settlement of accounts.[275] For most Korean companies the meetings are held in late February.[276] Choi argues that the reason for the common date is due to an attempt by the large companies to restrict the influence of professional agitators (*chonhoekoon*) at general meetings. *Chonhoekoon* are thugs, owning small share holdings, who are employed by companies to keep order at general meetings. However, *chonhoekoon* can also act against the company and obstruct the meeting if they consider the remuneration to be inadequate[277] or if they are employed by other parties to do so. The result of all company meetings being scheduled in late February is that shareholders with diverse share holdings are unable to attend meetings and exercise their rights.[278]

Notice in writing is required to be sent to each shareholder at least two weeks before the meeting,[279] or, where bearer shares have been issued, a public notice of the meeting must be issued three weeks before the meeting.[280] The meeting should be held at the principal office or in an adjacent location.[281] As the validity of most resolutions requires the attendance by shareholders representing a quarter of the issued capital, this is the quorum required at a general meeting.[282] In practice, the quorum is difficult to secure for most companies as most speculative shareholders do not attend and the meeting dates coincide.[283]

Each share entitles a shareholder to a vote,[284] except in the case of preference shares, which may be non-voting or have limited voting rights.[285] Non-voting shares are not taken into account when ascertaining issued shares for the purpose of a quorum.[286] Members holding bearer stock must lodge a certificate with the company one week before the meeting to be entitled to vote.[287] Persons can also vote by proxy.[288] Solicitation of proxy voting rights in respect of listed shares is forbidden unless approved by Presidential Decree.[289] Breach of this rule will render the person liable to a maximum penalty of two years' imprisonment or a fine of 10 million Won.[290] A member is not permitted to vote on a resolution in which the member has an interest.[291]

The types of general resolutions (the adoption of a resolution by a majority of the members present who represent more than a quarter of the total number of shares issued[292]) passed at general meetings include those to:

- elect directors and auditors;[293]
- appoint inspectors[294] and liquidators;[295]
- adjourn or postpone a general meeting;[296]
- approve financial statements;[297]
- approve the distribution of profit with new shares;[298]
- remunerate directors, auditors and liquidators;[299] and
- approve the liquidation of the company.[300]

The types of special resolutions (the adoption of a resolution by a two-third majority of those present, where those present represent more than one-third the total shares subscribed) passed at general meetings include those to:

- remove a director or auditor;[301]
- pass resolutions at the first general meeting, including the election of the directors;[302]
- alter the articles of incorporation;[303]
- approve major variations to the company's business (transferring it, acquiring a new business or altering significant commercial aspects of the business which affect control and profit share);[304]
- approve a merger or dissolution;[305]
- appoint persons to a committee to oversee a merger;[306]
- approve the continuance of a company whose duration has expired or an event specified in the articles for termination has occurred;[307]
- approve the acquisition of property used continually in the business, where it is to be acquired within two years of incorporation and its value exceeds 5 per cent of the capital;[308]
- approve the issue of convertible debentures or debentures with preemptive rights to non-shareholders;[309] and
- approve the issue of shares at a price below par value.[310]

The high quorum required to pass a special resolution, particularly those resolutions related to the business operation, can create potential difficulties for the financial management of the company. Although the quorum required for a special resolution in most cases was reduced by the 1995 amendments to a third of all issued shares, Kim's argument (that the high quorum potentially allows persons with only a third of issued shares – or even less in practice – to exercise a veto on such crucial business decisions of the board) is still valid.[311]

Unanimous consent is required for resolutions in four situations. The first three situations where unanimous consent is required are where resolutions are proposed to release promoters,[312] directors[313] and auditors[314] from liability to the company where they have acted in contravention of the articles or law, or where they have been negligent. The final situation requiring unanimous resolution is where the company seeks conversion from a joint stock corporation into a limited corporation.[315]

If a resolution is contrary to the articles or the procedure for calling a general meeting, or the passing of a resolution is faulty, then the directors, shareholders or auditors may bring an action to revoke the resolution.[316]

As the Commercial Code does prescribe the procedures to be adopted in general meetings and most companies have not enacted by-laws meeting, the procedures adopted are determined by custom.[317] Choi argues that, in practice, the annual general meetings conducted by most stock corporations are short in duration, held only to satisfy the statutory requirements.[318] In many cases there are five agenda items and only five or fewer shareholders are permitted to speak to each item.[319] Most speeches are less than five minutes long,[320] there is usually no voting and only rarely dissent on issues regarding management of the company or its financial statements.[321] Minutes of the meeting must be recorded.[322]

An extraordinary general meeting can be called whenever necessary.[323] Minority shareholders, representing not less than 5 per cent of the issued shares may demand that the directors convene a meeting to discuss issues of concern.[324] With court approval, they are entitled to convene the meeting themselves.[325] The court can also allow directors to convene a general meeting if a report of an inspector indicates dishonesty or grave contravention of law.[326] An auditor may also call a statutory meeting.[327]

6.3.2 *A limited company* (Yuhan-hoesa) The convening of general meetings is determined by the directors,[328] or it may be convened with the consent of all members.[329] Also, minority shareholders, representing not less than 5 per cent of the issued shares may also demand that the directors convene a meeting to discuss issues of concern.[330] A temporary general meeting can be convened by an auditor.[331] The general meeting is usually held annually.[332] Notice in writing is required to be sent to each shareholder at least one week before the meeting, or a shorter period specified in the articles.[333]

Except where otherwise provided in the articles or the Commercial Code, a general resolution is passed if adopted by a majority of the members present, provided they represent at least half of the voting power of members.[334] Each member shall have one vote for each unit of contribution. However, this entitlement may be altered by the articles.[335] Persons can also vote by proxy.[336] A member is not permitted to vote on a resolution in which the member has an interest.[337] The types of general resolutions passed at general meetings include those to:

- appoint directors, representative directors and auditors;[338]
- appoint or remove a manager;[339]
- appoint an inspector[340] or a liquidator;[341]
- increase capital;[342]
- adjourn or postpone a general meeting;[343] and
- approve the liquidation of the company.[344]

The types of special resolutions (the adoption of a resolution by half of the members holding three-quarters of the votes of all members[345]) passed at general meetings include those:

- where a member seeks to transfer part or the whole of his or her interest to a third party;[346]
- to amend the articles of incorporation;[347]
- to approve major variations to the company's business (transferring it, acquiring a new business or altering significant commercial aspects of the business which affect control and profit share);[348]
- to approve a merger or dissolution;[349]
- to appoint persons to a committee to oversee a merger;[350] and
- to approve the continuance of a company whose duration has expired or an event specified in the articles for termination has occurred.[351]

Unanimous consent is needed where the company seeks conversion from a limited corporation into a joint stock corporation.[352]

If a resolution is contrary to the articles or the procedure for calling a general meeting, or the passing of a resolution is faulty, then the directors, shareholders or auditors may bring an action to revoke the resolution.[353] Minutes of the meeting must be recorded.[354]

6.3.3 *Partnership companies* (Hapmyong-hoesa *and* Hapcha-hoesa)

As partnership companies are small, closely held entities, the Commercial Code does not prescribe any requirements to be followed in the conduct of a general meeting. The Code does, however, prescribe the quorum required to pass specific resolutions. Where a resolution relates to the day-to-day operation of the company, then a resolution is passed by a majority of members. Examples of these resolutions include those to appoint a member to administer the business,[355] the appointment of a liquidator[356] and the appointment or removal of a manager.[357]

Where a resolution affects the existence of the business or affects members' rights, the unanimous consent of members is required. Examples of these resolutions are those to alter the articles,[358] dissolve the company[359] or to voluntarily liquidate the company.[360] For a member with unlimited liability a share transfer requires the consent of all other members,[361] whereas for members with limited liability a share transfer requires the consent of all members with unlimited liability.[362] If a company's duration has expired or an event specified in the articles for termination has occurred, the continuance of the company can be approved by a resolution of all the members.[363] If there are dissenting members, the company may still continue with the dissenting members being deemed to have retired.[364]

No member is permitted to compete with the company, become an unlimited member or become a director of a competing company without the consent of all the members.[365] A member who does this without consent may be required to transfer profits arising from the conflict to the company and may be liable for damages.[366] Similarly, business may be transacted between the company and a member only with the consent of all the members.[367]

6.4 Audit Rules

6.4.1 A joint stock company (Chusik-hoesa) The Commercial Code provides for the position of a statutory auditor. The system is based on the German model, but has been modified by the Anglo-US audit concept.[368] The auditor's role is to monitor the directors' performance of their duties by receiving reports from the directors and investigating the affairs of the company.[369] The wide investigative powers available to auditors were further expanded in 1995 to allow auditors to investigate subsidiary companies.[370] The auditor may attend board meetings, participate in those meetings and report any wrongdoing by directors.[371] An auditor examines the accuracy and honesty of documents prepared by the directors for the general meetings.[372] Directors are also required to immediately report to an auditor any facts which indicate a probable loss by the company.[373]

An auditor is appointed at the general meeting.[374] Any shareholder who is holding 3 per cent of the total number of shares issued (or a lower amount prescribed by the articles) is restricted to exercising only the votes attributable to the 3 per cent (or lesser amount) in the election of the auditor.[375] The auditor's term is three years.[376] Remuneration for the auditor is determined by the articles or by a general resolution of shareholders.[377]

An auditor director can be removed by special resolution passed by the general meeting.[378] Where the meeting refuses to remove an auditor who has been dishonest or who has contravened the articles, then shareholders, representing not less than 5 per cent of the issued shares, may demand that the court remove the director[379] or institute a representative action to seek remedial action against actions by the auditor.[380] Auditors who are negligent are liable for damages to the company and third parties.[381]

Despite these sanctions and the auditor's wide powers, Choi argues that the auditor system does not work properly.[382] This arises as the auditor is usually appointed from within the company, at the recommendation of the representative director.[383] As the auditor is appointed by the executive, it is impossible for him or her to be independent.[384]

As well as the statutory auditor, a joint stock company with assets in excess of 4 000 million Won must be audited by an external auditor.[385] External auditors are also required for listed companies, companies intending to list and securities corporations.[386]

6.4.2   A limited company (Yuhan-hoesa)   Where the articles so provide, limited companies may have one or more statutory auditors.[387] Where specific auditors are not appointed in the articles, the auditors are appointed at a general meeting.[388] As with joint stock companies, the auditor's role is to monitor the directors' performance of their duties by receiving reports from the directors and investigating the affairs of the company.[389] Remuneration for auditors is determined by the articles or by a general resolution of shareholders.[390]

An auditor can be removed by special resolution passed by the general meeting.[391] Auditors who are negligent are liable for damages to the company and third parties.[392] Shareholders representing not less than 5 per cent of the issued shares may demand that the company enforce the liability of the auditor.[393]

6.5   Annual Return and Other Registers

Generally, all traders are required to keep books of accounts which accord with fair and proper accounting practices.[394] The trader is specifically required to prepare a balance sheet every 12 months.[395] The books must be retained for 10 years, while slips or similar documents are only required to be kept for five years. Records can be kept in the form of microfilm, microfiche or electronically stored data.[396]

Outside of these requirements special requirements for the various corporate forms are set out in the following paragraphs.

6.5.1 A joint stock company (Chusik-hoesa) The directors of joint stock companies are required to prepare at each settlement term (a period not exceeding 12 months, usually ending on 31 December[397]) for approval of the board a balance sheet, profit and loss statement, a profit distribution or deficit statement and a business report.[398] These reports must be submitted to the auditor six weeks prior to the annual general meeting and the auditor is required to prepare a report certifying the validity of the accounts.[399] The documents are submitted to the general meeting and any shareholders or creditors may inspect these records or obtain a copy of them.[400] Access to more detailed information is limited to shareholders owning not less than 5 per cent of the issued shares.[401] The company can only refuse access to these shareholders if it can prove that the access is improper.[402] The company's records are to be retained for five years.[403]

6.5.2 A limited company (Yuhan-hoesa) The directors of limited companies are required to prepare at each settlement term a balance sheet, profit and loss statement, a profit distribution or deficit statement and a business report.[404] These reports must be submitted to the auditor, if one is appointed, four weeks prior to the annual general meeting and the auditor is required to prepare a report certifying the validity of the accounts.[405] The documents are submitted to the general meeting.[406] The records are to be retained for five years.[407]

6.5.3 Limited partnership companies (Hapcha-hoesa) As all members of partnership companies and all unlimited members of limited partnerships have the right to administer the partnership's business, there are no specific financial record inspection powers for these members.[408] However, as limited members of limited partnerships have no right to administer the partnership's business, the members are given the right at the end of each business year, to inspect the company's books and investigate the status of its business and its property.[409] Court approval can be obtained to investigate the company's affairs where grave reasons exist.[410]

6.6 Shareholder Protection Rules

6.6.1 A joint stock company (Chusik-hoesa) Minority shareholders (that is shareholders representing not less than 5 per cent of the issued shares) in joint stock companies are provided limited protective rights under the Commercial Code. These rights permit minority shareholders to take action against the company and includes the right to:

- demand that the directors convene a meeting to discuss issues of concern[411] (with court approval they are entitled to convene the meeting themselves);[412]
- demand in writing to inspect the company's accounts;[413]
- request the holding of action by a director or liquidator who proposes to act or is acting in contravention of the articles and laws, causing irreparable damage to the company;[414]
- demand the company take action to enforce liability against a promoter, director, auditor or liquidator;[415]
- seek from the court the removal of a director, auditor or liquidator;[416] and
- seek court appointment of an inspector where there is cause to suspect dishonesty or grave contravention of law.[417]

In February 1998 enhanced powers for minority shareholders were announced, including the dismissal of executives through collective law suits.[418] To stop an unfair dilution of all shareholders' voting rights or the shareholders' interest in dividends and company assets, the Commercial Code provides for preemptive rights for existing shareholders in respect of new share issues, except where the articles provide otherwise.[419] A further safeguard exists in respect of indirect methods of diluting shareholders rights, such as the issue of convertible debentures or debentures with preemptive rights to non-shareholders. Protection is provided by requiring that a special resolution of members be passed at a general meeting to approve the issue of these debentures.[420]

6.6.2   *A limited company* (Yuhan-hoesa)   Limited company minority shareholders (that is shareholders representing not less than 5 per cent of the issued shares) are also given limited protective rights under the Commercial Code. Minority shareholders may:

- demand that the directors convene a meeting to discuss issues of concern;[421]
- demand that the company take action to enforce liability against a promoter, director, auditor or liquidator;[422]
- request the holding of action by a director or liquidator who proposes to act or is acting in contravention of the articles and laws causing irreparable damage to the company;[423] and
- seek from the court the removal of a director or liquidator.[424]

In addition, in limited companies, to stop an unfair dilution of shareholders' voting rights or the shareholders' interest in dividends and company assets, the Commercial Code provides for preemptive rights for existing shareholders in respect of new share issues.[425]

Where shares are to be issued other than in accordance with existing preemptive rights, a special resolution must be passed by the members.[426]

6.6.3 Punishments In order to deter wrongful actions by promoters, directors and auditors, the Commercial Code provides for penalties where such persons have committed certain offences. These offences include misappropriation by promoters, directors and other members,[427] endangerment of company property,[428] false reporting by a director or auditor,[429] using false statements to induce investment,[430] bribery[431] and negligence.[432] The punishments include monetary penalties, imprisonment and confiscation of gains.[433]

6.7 Capital Raising, Retention and Reduction

6.7.1 Capital raising by a joint stock company (Chusik-hoesa) As joint stock companies are the only corporate form in which share holding is freely transferable and which has the capacity to have numerous members, they are given wide capital-raising capacity under the Commercial Code. Joint stock companies can raise capital after incorporation by issuing shares[434] and debentures.[435]

The decision to issue shares is determined by the board of directors unless the articles specify shareholder approval.[436] Where shares are not to be issued to the public, a prospectus is not required. However, the application form supplied to prospective shareholders is required to include some basic financial information.[437] Existing members are given preemptive rights in respect of new share issues, except where the articles provide otherwise.[438] Where shares are issued at a price less than par, a special resolution must be passed by the members.[439]

The decision to issue debentures is determined by the board of directors.[440] The total amount of debentures shall not exceed twice the amount of the reserve fund and stated capital.[441] Each debenture must have a coupon price of not less than 10 000 Won and the coupon price of each debenture in each class shall have an equal value.[442]

Subscription for new debentures cannot be invited until the previous debenture subscription has been repaid.[443] A special resolution must be passed by a general meeting to approve the issue of convertible debentures or debentures with preemptive rights to non-shareholders.[444]

Where shares or debentures (securities[445]) are offered to the public or a company is seeking to list securities, the company is required to be registered under the Securities and Exchange Act.[446]

6.7.2   Capital raising by a limited company (Yuhan-hoesa)   The capital of limited companies can be increased if a special resolution of shareholders is passed.[447] Existing members are given preemptive rights in respect of new share issues.[448] Where shares are to be issued other than in accordance with existing preemptive rights, a special resolution must be passed by the members.[449]

6.7.3   Capital retention in a joint stock company (Chusik-hoesa)   To prevent dissolution of its capital, a joint stock company is:

- prohibited from acquiring its own shares except where the shares are to be amortized, or where the companies are merged;[450]
- limited in pledging its shares (the number of shares pledged cannot exceed more than 20 per cent of the issued shares);[451]
- prohibited from acquiring more than 40 per cent of the issued shares of its holding company (unless it is to facilitate a merger, takeover of parent or the transfer of the business);[452] or
- prohibited from reducing capital by share amortization, where the source of funds is retained profits.[453]

However, companies can issue redeemable shares[454] and convertible shares.[455]

6.7.4   Capital reduction in a joint stock company (Chusik-hoesa)   The stated capital of a joint stock company can be reduced by the passing of a special resolution of members.[456] This decision is subject to objections by creditors and debenture holders.[457]

7   The External Administration of Companies

7.1   Rules Regarding Arrangements and Reconstructions (Including Voluntary Administration)

In South Korea only insolvent joint stock companies (*chusik-hoesa*) are allowed to restructure or reorganize under the Corporate Reorganization Act.[458] Whilst undertaking restructuring or reorganizing under this Act, the stock company is able to continue trading. The process can be instigated by the insolvent company, a creditor (whose claim against the company amounts to more than 10 per cent of its capital, or by a shareholder who holds more than 10 per cent of the company's shares.[459]

Upon the filing of a reorganization petition with the District Court, the court, in order to determine whether the reorganization should commence, appoints an inspecting commissioner to investigate the circumstances leading up to the petition and to report on whether the grounds for reorganization have been met.[460] If the court determines that a reorganization is required, it will appoint a trustee to manage the company's assets and business.[461] The effect of this order is to prevent any actions by creditors to take any recovery action.[462]

At the preliminary stages the trustee is required to:

- file a draft reorganization plan;[463]
- prepare a draft timetable for meeting all claims by creditors (secured and unsecured) and shareholders; and
- report to all creditors at a meeting to inform them about the reorganization plan.[464]

Creditors must consider the draft plan at a subsequent meeting and may prepare an alternative plan which is filed with the court.

Upon completion of these preliminary steps, the court must convene a meeting of all creditors to seek approval for the plan.[465] The court will make the necessary orders, if it sees fit, upon approval of the plan by the creditors. The trustee will normally implement the plan.

7.2   Company Winding Up Rules

Generally, the rules for the liquidation of corporations are dealt with under the Commercial Code, whereas the bankruptcy rules are dealt with under the Bankruptcy Act.[466]

7.2.1   Winding up joint stock companies (Chusik-hoesa)   Under the Commercial Code,[467] a joint stock company can be dissolved:

- under its articles of incorporation, if a specified period of duration expires or a specified event occurs;
- by a resolution of a general meeting of shareholders (voluntarily);
- if a merger takes place;
- upon bankruptcy; or
- due to a court order.

For a joint stock company to be dissolved voluntarily, a meeting of shareholders must be called,[468] at which two-thirds of the shareholders[469] representing more than half of the issued shares pass a resolution calling for the dissolution of the company.[470] Upon passing the resolution the directors are required to give notice of the decision[471] and the dissolution must be lodged with the commercial recording office.[472] The reason for dissolution must be recorded and the shareholders' minutes submitted.[473]

7.2.2   *Winding up limited liability companies* (Yuhan-hoesa)   The same triggers for dissolution apply to limited liability companies as apply to joint stock companies.[474] In addition, the Commercial Code provides for the dissolution of a limited liability company if the membership is reduced to one member.[475] For a limited liability company to be dissolved voluntarily, a meeting of shareholders must be called, at which two-thirds of shareholders representing more than half of the issued shares pass a resolution calling for the dissolution of the company.[476]

7.2.3   *Winding up partnership companies* (Hapmyong-hoesa *and* Hapcha-hoesa)   Under the Commercial Code,[477] a partnership company (limited or unlimited) can be dissolved for similar reasons as limited liability companies (expiration of term, consent of all members, one member, merger, bankruptcy or court order). In addition, a limited partnership company is dissolved if all the unlimited members leave or if all the limited members leave.[478]

In order for a partnership company to be dissolved voluntarily, all the members must agree.[479] Where a member's share in a partnership company is subject to attachment, the consent of that creditor is also required.[480]

7.3   Liquidation

7.3.1   *Liquidating joint stock* (Chusik-hoesa) *or limited liability companies* (Yuhan-hoesa)   As the rules governing the liquidation of joint stock companies apply generally in respect of limited liability companies,[481] and given the small number of different regulatory sections, the following text discusses the liquidation rules applying to the two corporate forms as one, with any differences highlighted.

Upon dissolution of a joint stock company or a limited liability company, the directors cease to act for the company and responsibility shifts to the liquidators.[482] Unless the articles or the Commercial Code directs otherwise, the directors automatically become a liquidator,[483] except in bankruptcy.[484] The court can also appoint a liquidator[485] as can the shareholders by a majority vote.[486] Although in theory a liquidator may act alone, in practice at least two liquidators are appointed.[487] Liquidators, other than court appointed liquidators, can be removed by a resolution of shareholders.[488] Where a liquidator is unfit or has acted in contravention of his or her duties, any shareholder, holding not less than 1/500 of the issued share or any other person interested can apply to the court for the liquidator's removal.[489]

Within two weeks of the appointment the liquidator of a joint stock company must report to the court the reason for corporate dissolution, the date and the liquidator's particulars.[490] Two public notices are also required,[491] as well as a personal notice to all known creditors.[492] The liquidator is required to prepare a inventory of the assets and liabilities of the company and a balance sheet and submit them to shareholders, the court and company auditors.[493] The liquidator may also finalize any pending business, realize assets and distribute any surpluses.[494] If a liquidator discovers a deficiency, the liquidator should apply for a declaration of bankruptcy.[495] Failure to do so may subject the liquidator to ten years' imprisonment or a fine of ten million Won.[496]

Creditors of a joint stock company must be invited to present their claims within two months of the second public notice or their claims will be disregarded.[497] Generally, creditors cannot be paid during this period. However, if the amounts are small and the payments will not prejudice other creditors, the court may approve early payment.[498]

After paying all debts, the surplus assets may be distributed to shareholders according to their entitlement to surpluses.[499] Upon completion of the liquidation, the liquidator must prepare a final statement of accounts for shareholders' approval.[500] After approval, the statement must be lodged with the commercial recording office.[501]

Liquidators are assigned the same obligations to the company and third parties as are imposed upon directors.[502] Thus, a liquidator who is negligent or who contravenes the articles or law is liable for damages to the company, or, if the negligence is gross or wrongful, liable to third parties.[503]

7.3.2 Liquidating partnership companies (Hapmyong-hoesa *and* Hapcha-hoesa)   Where a partnership company is dissolved due to a merger, bankruptcy or a court order, the court can also appoint a liquidator.[504] In all other cases members can appoint a liquidator by a majority vote.[505] For limited partnerships that majority of members consists only of the members with unlimited liability.[506] If a liquidator is not appointed, the member administering the business becomes the liquidator.[507] In practice at least two liquidators are appointed, although in theory a single liquidator may act.[508]

Within two weeks of the appointment or the assumption of duties the liquidator must register the liquidator's particulars.[509] Public notice must be given to creditors, as well as a personal notice to all known creditors.[510] The liquidator is required to investigate the affairs of the partnership company, to prepare a statement of the company's property, an inventory and a balance sheet, and to submit them to members.[511] The liquidator may also finalize any pending business, realize assets and distribute any surpluses.[512] If a liquidator discovers a deficiency, the liquidator should apply for a declaration of bankruptcy.[513]

Creditors must be invited to present their claims or their claims will be disregarded.[514] Generally, creditors cannot be paid until the time period for registering all claims has elapsed.[515] After paying all debts, the surplus assets may be distributed to shareholders according to their entitlement to surpluses.[516] Where assets are insufficient, the liquidator may call upon members (that is all members in an unlimited liability partnership and unlimited liability members in a limited liability partnership) to make a contribution[517] and call upon limited liability members (in a limited liability partnership) to meet any amounts not yet contributed.[518] Upon completion of the liquidation, the liquidator must prepare a final statement of accounts for shareholders' approval.[519] After approval, the statement must be lodged with the commercial recording office.[520]

Liquidators of a partnership company are assigned the same obligations to the company and third parties as are imposed upon directors.[521] Thus, a liquidator who is negligent or who contravenes the articles or law is liable for damages to the company, or if the negligence is gross or wrongful, liable to third parties.[522]

7.4   Bankruptcy

Corporate bankruptcy is quite rare in Korea as companies in financial difficulties are usually liquidated after an accommodation being reached with creditors following a reorganization.[523] Proceedings for corporate insolvency are undertaken under the Bankruptcy Act, principally where a company is unable to pay its debts when they become due.[524] Bankruptcy may also arise if liabilities exceed assets.[525] As property used as security for debts is not considered part of the company's assets, secured creditors will enforce their claims independently of the Bankruptcy Law. However, if the secured assets prove to be insufficient to meet an outstanding claim, this procedure is available to secured creditors to make up any short-fall.[526]

Proceedings are initiated by the filing of a petition with the District Court.[527] As bankruptcies are rare, there are few appellate decisions to clarify these procedures.[528] The petition can be made by a debtor or creditor,[529] or a director or liquidator.[530] The court will then decide whether grounds for bankruptcy exist. Debtors seek to halt proceedings by submitting a plan involving continuation of the business.[531]

If judgment for bankruptcy is given, then the size of the estate determines the process adopted. Where the estate is small (less than five million Won), the court in consultation with creditors will make the administrative decisions.[532] In all other cases the court will appoint a receiver and may set a date:

- by which all claims against the company must be filed;

- for the first creditors' meeting; and
- by which the validity of all claims will be established by an investigation.[533]

Upon the appointment of the receiver, the bankrupt loses control of its property.[534] The receiver is responsible for the assets and management of the company,[535] and is the representative for the estate in any litigation.[536] The receiver is required to report to the creditors at the first meeting on the financial position of the company and the circumstances that contributed to its insolvent position. The creditors' consent is required at various stages of the bankruptcy and for the making of any concessions.[537] They are also entitled to appoint advisers and to decide upon the continuation of the business.[538] If creditors holding more than three-quarters of the debt agree to accept a partial payment in satisfaction of their debt, then all creditors are bound.[539]

Upon adjudication of bankruptcy, the debtors' obligations become due and payable.[540] The receiver can declare certain payments prejudicial to creditors where they were made during specified periods prior to insolvency or the petition for bankruptcy.[541] The receiver may also institute legal action to overturn or set aside any acts of the debtor company which were intentionally prejudicial to the creditors and seek the restoration of these payments to the estate.[542] Where contracts are partially performed by a third party, the receiver may demand completion or cancel the contract, or the third party may require the receiver to elect whether to rescind or request performance.[543]

Bankruptcy ceases upon the assets being distributed to creditors, on the unanimous agreement of all creditors,[544] or when the costs of proceedings exceed the value of the bankruptcy estate.[545]

7.5 *Protection of Creditors and the Ranking of Claims*

In a company insolvency the debts of the company are ranked as follows:

- fund claims (items such as the cost of the bankruptcy);
- preference claims (includes claims given preference by other statutes, such as amounts owed to employees and taxes,[546] and lien holders on general property[547]);
- ordinary claims; and
- less preferred claims (debts arising after the determination of insolvency).[548]

For secured interests[549] priority of claim is generally determined by the date of the security, with the earlier security generally having priority.[550] This applies particularly to immovable property, where the first or earlier registration of the interest has priority.[551] However, in respect of movable property, priority is given to the creditor in possession unless the statute specifies otherwise.[552]

8   Takeover and Merger Rules

8.1   *An Introduction to Merger and Takeover Rules*

Takeovers in Korea of unlisted companies are conducted by a merger mechanism and the takeover of listed companies is by share acquisition. The mechanisms under the Commercial Code that allow all companies to merge[553] operates either by merging the target company with the predator company or by dissolving both companies and bringing a new, combined entity into existence.

8.1.1   Joint stock companies (Chusik-hoesa)   A joint stock company is dissolved by merger.[554] A merger agreement requires approval by a special resolution of members (the adoption of a resolution by a two-third majority of those present, where those present represent more than a third of the total shares subscribed).[555] The company is required within two weeks of the merger decision to give public notice to creditors and individual notice where creditors are known to the company.[556] A creditor is deemed to consent to the merger in the absence of any objection and is required to be paid out if the creditor does object.[557]

Where a merger proceeds, the merged entity's registration must be altered.[558] The resulting entity of a merger involving a joint stock must be a joint stock or a limited company.[559] The merged company is the successor to the rights and duties of preceding companies.[560]

8.1.2   A limited company (Yuhan-hoesa)   The rules for merging a limited company are similar to those applying to a joint stock company. A limited company is dissolved by merger.[561] The merger agreement must be approved by a special resolution of members (the adoption of a resolution by half of the members holding three-quarters of the votes of all members).[562] The company is required within two weeks of the merger decision to give public notice to creditors and individual notice where creditors are known to the company.[563] A creditor is deemed to consent to the merger in the absence of any objection, and is required to be paid out if the creditor does object.[564]

Where a merger proceeds, the merged entity's registration must be altered.[565] The resulting entity of a merger involving a limited company must be a joint stock or a limited company.[566] The merged company is the successor to the rights and duties of preceding companies.[567]

8.1.3 *Partnership companies* (Hapmyong-hoesa *and* Hapcha-hoesa)

The merger requirements for partnership companies are similar to those discussed above. A limited partnership can also reorganize and become an unlimited partnership, provided the members agree.[568] Two partnership companies can also merge to form a joint stock company with the consent of all the former members.[569] A partnership company is dissolved by merger.[570] The consent of all the members is required for a merger.[571] The company is required within two weeks of the merger decision to give public notice to creditors and individual notice where creditors are known to the company.[572] A creditor is deemed to consent to the merger in the absence of any objection and is required to be paid out if the creditor does object.[573]

Where a merger proceeds, the merged entity's registration must be altered.[574] The merged company is the successor to the rights and duties of preceding companies.[575]

8.2 *Merger Thresholds*

The Monopoly Regulation and Fair Trading Act prohibits any action which substantially restricts competition in a particular field of trade.[576] The Act seeks to regulate two types of mergers, the so-called 'anti-competitive combinations' and the 'unfair combinations'.

The anti-competitive combinations rules apply to 'entrepreneurs', that is persons (both individuals and judicial)[577] who have a specified level of paid-in capital (five billion Won) or a specified asset base (total assets exceeding 20 billion Won).[578] A company satisfying these thresholds is prohibited from entering into uncompetitive combinations without approval of the Commissions.[579] Uncompetitive combinations can arise from the acquisition of shares (including equity), the creation of interlocking directorships, mergers, the lease of a substantial part of a company's business or by the formation of a new corporation.

The second form of prohibited merger is the merger that is achieved through compulsion or unfair practices (unfair combinations). The prohibition against this activity applies to all firms, regardless of whether a restriction of trade occurs.[580]

8.3 *Disclosure Requirements*

8.3.1 *Mergers* The following discussion focuses on the market domination provisions, which impact upon merger activity. The Fair Trade Commission requires notification that merger or acquisition activity is required where:

- a company acquires or owns 20 per cent of the issued shares (excluding Article 370: non-voting shares) or equity of another company;
- a non-judicial person owns 20 per cent or more of two or more competing companies;
- an officer or employee of a company is an officer in a competing company;
- a company intends to merge or take over a company, or establish a new company; or
- a company intends to subscribe 20 per cent or more of the shares in a new company.[581]

In respect of mergers or takeovers, entrepreneurs are required to notify the Commission 30 days prior to the commencement of acquisition activity.[582] For acquisitions or interlocking of directorships, notification is required within ten days of the event.[583]

8.3.2   Listed Companies   On top of the merger controls a person who controls more than 5 per cent of a listed company must report his or her ownership to the Korean Stock Exchange and the Securities and Exchange Commission.[584] These reports are available to the public.[585] Where that holding varies by 1 per cent or more, the shareholder is required to give further notification.[586] In addition, listed companies that operate in industries important to the economy (the so-called 'public corporations') have share ownership limitations.[587]

8.4   The Role of the Fair Trade Commission

As the Korean covernment sees mergers as a important means of encouraging economic growth,[588] the administration and structure of its anti-monopoly legislation reflect this view. The principle anti-trust legislation is the Monopoly Regulation and Fair Trading Act.[589] The Act is enforced by the Minister of Economic Planning through the Fair Trade Commission.[590] Actions can be taken privately through the judicial system or through the Commission's administrative procedures. The law has two focuses: first, to stop anti-competitive business practices (for example price maintenance), and, second, to stop market domination by the formation of anti-competitive or unfair combinations. It covers both domestic arrangements and international agreements.[591]

8.5   Mechanisms for the Review of Merger Activity

To determine whether the transaction is legal, the Commission uses the Combination of Enterprises Examination Guidelines. The Commission has 30 days to review a merger, but the time limit may be extended to 60 days in exceptional circumstances.

If an activity contravenes the Act, the Commission has the power to stop the merger, force the resignation of the officers, force the divesting of all or part of the shares and any other steps deemed necessary.[592] As unlawful combinations are only voidable on a court decision, the Commission can also bring an action to nullify any unlawful merger or incorporation.[593] Penalties range from ten million Won for a false merger report[594] to imprisonment for up to two years and fines of 50 million Won for violating the merger provisions.[595]

However, the Commission will allow such activities if it deems the merger necessary in order to rationalize the industry ('the rationalization of industry exception') or to reinforce its international competitiveness ('the international competitiveness exception').[596] The entrepreneur bears the burden of proof.[597]

In order to establish the rationalization of industry exception, the entrepreneur must establish that:

- the combination is the only way that the industry can be restructured to deliver efficiency gains;
- it is difficult to assemble the scale of investment in terms of equipment and organization required for that activity through normal means; or
- the merger is necessary to satisfy the national interest.[598]

In order to establish the international competitiveness exception, the entrepreneur must establish either that the merger will increase international competitiveness in price and quality or that it will lead to an increase in exports.[599]

Other exceptions exist for mergers executed in accordance with industry promotion laws such as the Basic Small and Medium Enterprise Act.[600]

9 An Introduction to Securities Regulation

9.1 *The Relationship between Stock Exchange(s) and Corporate Regulation*

The regulatory regime established under the Securities and Exchange Act (which regulates securities[601]) consists of the Ministry of Finance, the Korean Stock Exchange, the Securities and Exchange Commission, the Securities Supervisory Board and the Securities Finance Corporation. The most important is the Ministry of Finance, which determines security market policies[602] and plays a supervisory role, including:

- reporting on public offer prices;[603]
- licensing securities businesses and branches of foreign securities companies;[604]
- licensing investment advisory businesses;[605]
- approving the appointment of the chief director, non-permanent directors, auditors and full-time employees of the Korean Stock Exchange and monitoring its activities;[606]
- approving membership of the Securities and Exchange Commission and appointing the deputy and assistant directors of the Securities Supervisory Board;[607] and
- licensing the Securities Finance Corporation.[608]

The Securities and Exchange Commission is an independent entity that has the role of reviewing and supervising the issue of securities, ensuring fairness in the markets, regulating mergers and supervising security institutions.[609] The day-to-day work of the Commission is carried out by the Securities Supervisory Board.[610] The institutions under the supervision of the Commission include:

- the Securities Finance Corporation,[611] which has the role of financing many market transactions including lending money for market promotion and for underwriting;[612]
- the Securities Dealers Association, which has the role of ensuring that dealers have high standards of practice, that trading is fair and that investors are protected;[613] and
- the Securities Depositing Board, which is responsible for transferring securities.[614]

The Korean Stock Exchange was established for the purpose of providing a fair and stable market for securities.[615] It is a non-profit, government-run corporation set up under the Securities and Exchange Act to establish securities markets and to regulate the listing of securities.[616]

9.2   Types of Securities Regulated

Companies of a specific size are required to be registered with the Securities and Exchange Commission if:

- they intend to list securities;
- they intend to offer non-listed securities to the public;
- they seek to invite subscription for securities; or

- a merger is being undertaken by a non-listed corporation and a listed corporation.[617]

A 'security' for the purposes of the Securities and Exchange Act is defined to include a government, municipal or government enterprise bond, a corporate bond, a certificate of contribution, a stock certificate and a right.[618] Registration is not required in respect of government, municipal or government enterprise bonds. The requirements specified for a company include that:

- the shareholders' equity exceeds one billion Won;
- the yearly sales volume exceeds five billion Won;
- the loans exceed one billion Won; or
- there are more than 1 000 persons employed.[619]

Registration is also required for tenders.[620] Until registration has been effected, no trading in securities is permitted.[621]

For public offering a prospectus is usually required.[622] The information required in the prospectus is prescribed by the Commission. Where a person relies on a prospectus which contains a false statement or omits a material fact, that person is entitled to compensation for any loss.[623] The persons liable include the directors, the accountants and the appraiser who certified certain matters to be true and correct, the underwriters and even the persons delivering the prospectus.[624] Liability will not lie with these persons if the investor knew the facts were false or if despite due diligence by the person, the false fact or omission was not discoverable.

9.3 *Market Conduct Rules and Sanctions for Securities Misconduct*

There are a number of sanctions for misconduct set out in the Securities and Exchange Act. A securities business can have its licences cancelled or business suspended where it has acted contrary to the Act[625] as can an investment adviser.[626] Penal sanctions also apply.[627]

Where a listed company fails to advise the Commission and Korean Stock Exchange of an event that affects viability (such as the fact that it has financial difficulties, for example a bank has refused credit, it has reorganized, capital has been reduced, a dissolution event has occurred, it has suffered a major loss or changed its article) the Commission can delist the company and recommend that its shareholders discharge its officers.[628] Penal sanctions also apply.[629]

There are also two major insider trading prohibition provisions. First, where any officer, employee or major shareholder of a company makes a gain from selling shares within six months of purchase, they may be required to pay that gain to the company.[630] Second, the

Act provides that a person who possesses sensitive information not available to the public is not permitted to use that information (or engage another party to do so on his or her behalf) in connection with transactions in respect of the company's securities.[631] A person is widely defined to include an officer, employee, agent, major shareholder of the company, a member of an agency that regulates the company or a person who contracts with the company.[632] If such a person does so, he or she is liable for damages.[633] Penal sanctions also apply.[634]

10   Miscellaneous

10.1   Limitations on Foreign Investment Portfolio Investment

Foreign individuals and foreign-controlled companies resident in Korea are able to invest in securities on the Korean Stock Exchange subject to a number of restrictions. Under the Regulations on Trading of Securities by Foreigners, individual foreign investment is limited to 1 per cent of the issued shares of a company, whereas the aggregate foreign investment is limited to 20 per cent of the issued shares of a company. Further limitations apply to holdings in Pohang Iron and Steel Co. and Korea Electric Power Corp. Foreigner's aggregate holdings are limited to 1 per cent and 15 per cent of issued shares, respectively. However, in September 1996, the Ministry of Finance and Economy announced that these aggregate investment limits will be abolished in the year 2000.[635] From 1997 the aggregate investment limit will increase by 3 per cent annually and the general individual investment limit will be increased to 10 per cent in the year 2000.[636] This 10 per cent limitation was further extended in February 1998, when the Ministry of Finance and Economy announced (in response to the International Monetary Fund rescue package) a further relaxation of these foreign investment requirements. Legislation was introduced to permit foreign investors to buy up to a third of a company's shares without the approval of the board of directors.[637] However, it is argued that these new rules will have little impact as it will be impossible to conduct a hostile takeover of prime properties owned by chaebols due to the removal of cross-ownership limitations on chaebols and the continuation of the limitations on foreign investment in strategic industries (such as electricity).[638]

Until 1996 foreign investors resident outside Korea were limited to investments in domestic and international investment trusts. From September 1996, the Ministry of Finance and Economy announced new avenues for non-residents to invest in Korea. They are investment in listed stocks, investment in non-guaranteed convertible bonds issued by small and medium-sized companies, investment in low-rate public/government bonds designated by the Securities Exchange Commission and stock index futures.

10.2 Incentives for Direct Foreign Investment

The Foreign Capital Inducement Act applies to any foreign direct investment, loans and technology transfers.[639] Direct investment can be by way of the formation of a subsidiary in South Korea, the establishment of an office or a joint venture arrangement (contractual). For any foreign direct investment, loans and technology transfers to proceed, approval is required from the Ministry of Finance[640] and, in the case of large scale investment, approval from the Foreign Capital Project Deliberative Committee is needed too.[641]

Incentives available to such foreign investment under the Foreign Capital Inducement Act include:

- the right to remit dividends and profits;[642]
- reduction and exemption from tax and customs duties,[643] including exemptions for registered foreign-investment enterprises from income tax, corporate tax and acquisitions tax, exempting capital goods from customs duties and consumption taxes as well as providing exemption from tax for specific personnel;[644] and
- substantial protection for foreign-owned property.[645]

The Foreign Capital Project Deliberative Committee will only offer these inducements where it is deemed necessary.[646]

Notes

1 BEc (ANU), LLB (Adelaide), GDLP (SAIT), LLM (Commercial) (Adelaide), Senior Lecturer in Law, University of Canberra.
2 Tradeport, (1997) *South Korea World Factbook*, US Department of Commerce – National Trade Data Bank, at http://www.tradeport.org/cgi-bin/banner.pl/ts/countries/skorea/wofact.html
3 Republic of Korea, National Statistics Office (1997) at http://nsohp.nso.go.kr/graph/ef-major9703.htm
4 Cha, J.S. (1997) 'South Korea' in A.S. Gutterman and R. Brown (eds), *Commercial Laws of East Asia*, Hong Kong: Sweet and Maxwell Asia, 457.
5 Genzberger, C.A. *et al.*, *Korea Business*, San Rafael: World Trade Press, 3.
6 Republic of Korea, Overseas Information Service (1997) at http://www.kois.go.kr/history/koreahis/ancient/tangun.htm
7 The Kingdom of Koguryo adopted Buddhism as royal creed in 372, whereas the Kingdom of Shilla adopted Buddhism in 528; as note 6, above, at http://www.kois.go.kr/history/koreahis/ancient/three.htm

8   The Kingdom of Koguryo enacted its first legal code (*yul*) in 373, whereas Shilla promulgated its first code and sub-statutes (*yullyong*) in 520; Kim, C. (1987), *Korean Law Study Guide*, San Diego: Cross-Cultural Associates, 3.

9   Although the existence of these laws is recorded, the actual laws are not in existence. A civil government document dated 755 AD suggests T'ang influence; see Kim, as note 8, above, 4 and 5.

10   It was Koguryo that finally captured the last of the Chinese provinces, Nangnang (Lolang in Chinese), in 313.

11   A smaller state, Chin (later named Parhae), was established following the fall of Koguryo by a former Koguryo general (Tae Cho-yong) in Manchuria and soon gained control of most of the former Koguryo territory; as note 5, above, http://www.kois.go.kr/history/ koreahis/ancient/Parhae.htm

12   As note 6, above, http://www.kois.go.kr/history/koreahis/ancient/shilla.htm

13   As note 6, above, http://www.kois.go.kr/history/koryo.htm

14   *Encyclopedia of Asian History* (1988), New York: Charles Scribner's Sons, 336.

15   There were seven invasions from 1231 to 1257; Pyong-Choon, H. (1967), *The Korean Political Tradition and Law*, Seoul: Hollym Corporation, 7.

16   The organization of codes and the penalties operative between 960 and 1279 were influenced by the Chinese T'ang and Sung Dynasties, and the administrative codes promulgated between 1276 and 1368 exhibit the characteristics of the Chinese Yuan Dynasty; see Kim, as note 8, above, 5.

17   As note 14, above, 336.

18   As note 6, above, http://www.kois.go.kr/history/koryo.htm

19   As note 6, above, http://www.kois.go.kr/history/korwahis/e-chosun/state.htm

20   See Kim, as note 8, above, 5.

21   As note 20, above, 6. The departments were personnel (*i*), revenue (*ho*), rites (*ye*), war (*pyong*), punishment (*hyong*) and works (*kong*).

22   See Pyong-Choon, as note 15, above, 102.

23   As note 6, above, http://www.kois.go.kr/history/korwahis/e-chosun/sejong.htm

24   As note 6, above, http://www.kois.go.kr/history/korwahis/e-chosun/sejo.htm

25   As note 14, above, 336.

26   As note 20, above, 6.

27   For a short history, see West, J.M. and Yoon, D.-K. (1992), 'The Constitutional Court of the Republic of Korea: Transforming the jurisprudence of the vortex?', *The American Journal of Comparative Law*, **49**, 73.

28   Choi, J.-S. (1994), 'The organizational structure of stock corporation in Korea – The disparity between law and practice', *Korean Journal of Comparative Law*, **22**, 1, 3.

29   Korean International Trade Association (1997) at http://www.geocities.com/Tokyo/4041

30   '1996 Country Reports On Economic Policy and Trade Practices', in *Korea: Economic Policy and Trade Practices Report* (1996) US Department of State report submitted to the Senate Committees on Foreign Relations and on Finance and to the House Committees on Foreign Affairs and on Ways and Means, January 1997 at http://www.tradeport.org/cgi-bin/banner.pl/ts/countries/skorea/ecopol.html

31   As note 3, above, http://nsohp.nso.go.kr/intro/e-intro4.htm

32   The Constitution, Law No. 1, 17 July 1948 (as amended), Article 40.

33   As note 32, above, Article 66.

34   As note 32, above, Article 101.

35   As note 32, above, Article 40.

36   As note 32, above, Articles 64 and 75.

37   As note 32, above, Article 108.
38   As note 32, above, Article 6.
39   The six codes are the Constitution, Civil Code, Criminal Code, Commercial Code, Code of Civil Procedure and the Code of Criminal Procedure; as note 20, above.
40   International Legal Services Advisory Council (1995), *Legal Services Country Profile: Republic of Korea* (2nd edition), , Canberra: Attorney-General's Department, 7.
41   *Doing Business in Asia* (1991 looseleaf), Singapore: CCH Asia Limited, para. KOR 20–002.
42   The Court Organization Act, Article 3(1), wholly amended by Law No. 3992, 4 December 1987 (formerly Law No. 51, 26 September 1949).
43   The Court Organization Act, Articles 11–25-2 regulate the Supreme Court, Articles 26–28 the High Courts, Articles 28-2–28-4 the Patent Courts, Articles 29–36 the District Courts, Articles 37–40 the Family Courts and Articles 40-2–40-4 the Administrative Courts.
44   As note 43, above, Article 3(1).
45   As note 43, above, Articles 3(1) and (2).
46   As note 43, above, Article 3(2).
47   As note 43, above, Articles 3(2), 33 and 34.
48   As note 43, above, Article 32. The jurisdiction of the collegiate division of the District Court includes the power to hears cases that:

   ● the collegiate division has decided to hear; or appeals against single judge decisions;
   ● civil cases as specified in the Supreme Court Regulations;
   ● criminal cases where penalty is death or imprisonment exceeding one year, but not offences under Articles 2(1), 3(1) and 3(2) of the Military Services Act (Law No. 2259, 31 December 1970), Article 3 of the Act Concerning Punishment of Violent Crime (Law No. 625, 20 June 1961) and Articles 331 and 332 of the Criminal Code (Law No. 239, 18 September 1953).

49   As note 43, above, Article 40.
50   As note 43, above, Article 28-4: The jurisdiction includes the power to hear cases that arise under Article 186(1) of the Patent Act (wholly amended by Law No. 4207, 13 January 1990), Article 35 of the Utility Model Act (wholly amended by Law No. 4209, 13 January 1990), Article 75 of the Design Act (wholly amended by Law No. 4208, 13 January 1990), and Article 86 of the Trademark Act (wholly amended by Law No. 4210, 13 January 1990).
51   As note 43, above, Article 40-4. The Administrative Court's jurisdiction includes the power to hear cases arising under the Administrative Litigation Act (wholly amended by Law No. 3754, 15 December 1984).
52   As note 43, above, Article 28.
53   As note 43, above, Article 14.
54   As note 32, above, Articles 111 to 113.
55   Article 2 Constitution Court Act, Law No. 4017, 5 August 1988 (as amended). The court is based upon the model adopted in the Austrian Federal Constitution 1920. See West, J.M. and Yoon, D.K. (1992), 'The Constitutional Court of the Republic of Korea: Transforming the jurisprudence of the vortex?', *The American Journal of Comparative Law,* **49,** 73, 77.
56   The Courts Martial Act, Law No. 3993, 4 December 1987 (as amended).
57   The Small Claims Trial Act, Law No. 2547, 24 February 1972 (as amended).
58   The Lawyer Act, wholly amended by Law No. 3594, 31 December 1982.
59   For a concise history of the development of South Korean company law, see

Yoo, H. (1973), 'To form a stock corporation in Korea – A comparative study with American law', *Korean Journal of Comparative Law*, **1**, 101, 106.

60   Blakemore, T.L. and Yazawa, M. (1953), 'Japanese Commercial Code Revisions', *American Journal of Comparative Law*, **2**, 12, 13.

61   The Commercial Code, Law No. 1000, 20 January 1962 (as amended).

62   It was first amended in 1962, 1984, twice in 1991, and once in 1994 and 1995.

63   For a discussion of the 1995 amendments which have had effect from 1 October 1996, see Sohn, K.-H. (1996), 'News – South Korea – Legislation – Commercial Code', *Asian Commercial Law Review B-23*.

64   Sonn, J.-C. (1975), 'A comparison of the major proposals for amendment of stock company law in the revision of the Korean Commercial Code', *Korean Journal of Comparative Law*, **3**, 156.

65   Article 1 states: 'If there is no provision in law applicable to certain civil affairs, the customary law shall apply to them, and if there is no customary law applicable to them, sound reasoning shall apply to them.'

66   Kwack, Y.C. *et al.* (1973), *Credit and Security in Korea*, St Lucia: University of Queensland Press, 12. They were considering an equivalent provision, Article 18 of the former Court Organization Law, Law No. 51, 26 September 1964.

67   As note 59, above, 105. Yoo was also considering the former Article 18.

68   As note 59, above. This view is also adopted by the CCH editors of *Doing Business in Asia*, as note 41, above, para. KOR 20-003.

69   Kim, D.H. (1992), 'Legal aspects of foreign investment in Korea', *Hastings International and Comparative Law Review*, 227, 231.

70   Haywood, S.F. (1989), 'Foreign investment and licensing in Korea', *University of British Columbia Law Review*, **23**, 405, 406.

71   For example, as note 41, above, para. KOR 20-005.

72   Articles 7, 28 and 70-2 of the Securities and Exchange Act (Law No. 2920, 22 December 1976 (as amended)).

73   As note 72, above, Articles 71, 118, 130 and 145.

74   Foreign investment is discussed in detail in section 10.2, below.

75   Article 2 of the Foreign Exchange Control Act, (wholly amended by Law No. 4447, 27 December 1991).

76   As note 75, above, Article 7(1).

77   As note 69, above, 236.

78   As note 43, above, Article 40-4.

79   Article 9 of the Administrative Litigation Act. The administrative actions available under the Act are actions for revocation of an administrative decision, actions to declare an administrative decision null and void and actions to force an administrative officer to perform his or her duty.

80   As note 43, above, Article 28.

81   As note 43, above, Article 14.

82   Chapter III of the Civil Code, Law No. 471, 22 February 1958 (as amended).

83   As note 61, above, Article 169.

84   As note 61, above, Article 170.

85   As note 69, above, 239.

86   As note 28, above, 3 and 4. In 1991 of the 90 553 corporations registered, 73 614 were joint stock companies, 2 938 limited partnership companies, 407 unlimited partnership companies, 3 094 limited companies, 9 716 noncommercial companies and 784 foreign companies. Of the 73 614 joint stock companies, only 694 companies were registered on the Korean Stock Exchange.

87   As note 61, above, Article 331.

88   As note 61, above, Article 553.

89   As note 61, above, Articles 543 and 545.

90   As note 61, above, Article 556.
91   As note 69, above, 240.
92   As note 61, above, Article 178.
93   As note 61, above, Article 212.
94   As note 61, above, Article 197.
95   As note 61, above, Article 268.
96   As note 61, above, Article 278.
97   As note 61, above, Article 269.
98   As note 61, above, Article 614.
99   As note 61, above, Articles 617 and 621.
100 As note 61, above, Articles 619 and 176(2)–(4).
101 As note 61, above, Article 171.
102 As note 69, above, 238.
103 As note 5, above, 168.
104 Cha (as note 4, above, 471) argues that the restrictions arise for legal reasons (such as Article 173 of the Commercial Code that limits a company from being a limited member) and practical reasons.
105 An overview of this process and sample documentation in English are available at Hwang Mok Park and Jin Law Firm's home page at http://www.korealaw.com/korealaw/library/incorp-mem.html
106 As note 61, above, Article 289.
107 It is advisable if they are natural persons that the promoters be Korean nationals, over 20 years old. See note 59, above, 111.
108 As note 61, above, Article 291.
109 As note 61, above, Article 292.
110 As note 61, above, Article 288. The number of promotors was reduced from seven to three under the 1995 amendments to the Commercial Code. Sohn claims that this change, which brought Korean law into line with the requirements of most other jurisdictions, will reduce paperwork and related incorporation expenses (see note 63 above at para. B-24).
111 As note 61, above, Article 293.
112 As note 61, above, Article 289(2).
113 As note 61, above, Article 295.
114 As note 61, above, Article 301.
115 As note 61, above, Article 289.
116 As note 61, above, Articles 290, 295 and 299.
117 As note 61, above, Article 299.
118 As note 118, above.
119 As note 118, above.
120 As note 117, above.
121 As note 59, above, 106 and as note 4, above, 167.
122 Article 296(1) Commercial Code.
123 As note 61, above, Article 296.
124 As note 61, above, Articles 301–307 which set out the process of subscription.
125 As note 61, above, Article 308.
126 As note 61, above, Article 312.
127 As note 61, above, Article 313.
128 As note 61, above, Articles 290 and 310.
129 As note 61, above, Articles 290 and 311.
130 As note 61, above, Article 309.
131 As note 61, above, Article 313.
132 As note 61, above, Article 315.
133 As note 61, above, Article 314.
134 As note 61, above, Article 323.

135   As note 61, above, Article 317(1).
136   As note 61, above, Article 317(2).
137   Article 249 of the Non-Contentious Case Procedure Law, cited in Yoo, as note 59, above, 152–3.
138   As note 61, above, Article 320(1).
139   As note 61, above, Article 328. The powers of the court and associated matters (such liability and effect of nullification) are set out in Articles 186–193.
140   As note 61, above, Article 543.
141   As note 61, above, Articles 292 and 543(3).
142   As note 61, above, Article 547.
143   As note 61, above, Article 549(1).
144   As note 61, above, Article 549(2).
145   As note 61, above, Article 552.
146   As note 61, above, Articles 178 and 269
147   As note 61, above, Articles 180, 181 and 269.
148   As note 61, above, Article 180.
149   As note 61, above, Article 270.
150   As note 61, above, Articles 184 and 269.
151   As note 61, above, Articles 185 and 269. The powers of the court and associated matters (such liability and effect of nullification) are set out in Articles 186–194.
152   As note 61, above, Article 289(1).
153   As note 59, above, 126.
154   As note 59, above, 127.
155   As note 61, above, Article 311.
156   As note 61, above, Article 290.
157   As note 61, above, Article 302(2).
158   As note 61, above, Articles 291 and 344(2).
159   As note 61, above, Article 345(2).
160   As note 61, above, Articles 302(2) and 343(2).
161   As note 59, above, 127.
162   As note 61, above, Article 543(2).
163   As note 61, above, Article 544.
164   As note 61, above, Articles 546(1) and 562(2), (3).
165   As note 61, above, Article 549(2).
166   As note 61, above, Article 556(1).
167   As note 61, above, Article 568(2).
168   As note 61, above, Article 580.
169   As note 61, above, Articles 572(2) and 575.
170   As note 61, above, Article 179.
171   As note 61, above, Article 270.
172   As note 61, above, Articles 200 and 273.
173   As note 61, above, Articles 227 and 269.
174   As note 61, above, Articles 217 and 269.
175   As note 61, above, Article 22.
176   As note 61, above, Articles 178 and 269 (for partnership companies), 289 (joint stock) and 543 (limited liability).
177   As note 61, above, Article 22-2.
178   As note 61, above, Article 19: The words to be included are 'hapmyong-hoesa', 'hapcha-hoesa', 'chusik-hoesa' or 'yuhan-hoesa'.
179   As note 61, above, Article 22.
180   As note 61, above, Articles 20, 23 and 24.
181   As note 61, above, Article 28.
182   As note 69, above, 242.

183 As note 61, above, Article 329(1).
184 As note 61, above, Article 329(4) and (2).
185 As note 61, above, Article 289(2).
186 As note 61, above, Article 458.
187 As note 136, above.
188 As note 61, above, Article 459.
189 As note 61, above, Article 460.
190 As note 61, above, Article 461(1).
191 As note 61, above, Article 335(1). Sohn claims that these new restrictions will not generally apply to companies listed on the Korean Stock Exchange (note 63, B-24). The change may not be totally dramatic as Articles 335-2–335-7 also provide for an appraisal remedy if the board refuses permission to transfer the shares. It is claimed that this will have great advantages for joint ventures, ensuring continuity of partners, but has the disadvantage of entrenching the current board's control: see Sohn, note 63 above at para B-24 and B-25.
192 As note 61, above, Article 335(2).
193 As note 61, above, Articles 543 and 545(1).
194 As note 61, above, Article 556(2).
195 As note 61, above, Article 546(1).
196 As note 61, above, Article 546(2).
197 As note 61, above, Article 553.
198 As note 61, above, Article 556(1).
199 As note 198, above.
200 As note 61, above, Article 556(3).
201 As note 61, above, Articles 178 and 269
202 As note 61, above, Articles 197 and 269.
203 As note 61, above, Article 276.
204 As note 61, above, Article 219.
205 As note 61, above, Article 217.
206 As note 61, above, Article 225.
207 As note 61, above, Article 218. The grounds for expulsion are set out in Article 220.
208 As note 61, above, Articles 213 and 269.
209 As note 61, above, Article 283.
210 As note 61, above, Article 284.
211 As note 61, above, Article 433.
212 As note 61, above, Article 434.
213 As note 61, above, Article 435.
214 As note 61, above, Article 584.
215 As note 61, above, Article 585.
216 As note 61, above, Articles 204 and 269.
217 As note 61, above, Article 557.
218 As note 61, above, Article 337. The details to be entered on the register are set out in Article 352. Also see generally Articles 353 and 354 and, in respect of share certificate requirements, Articles 355–360.
219 As note 61, above, Article 336.
220 As note 61, above, Article 171(2).
221 As note 61, above, Article 172.
222 As note 61, above, Article 364.
223 As note 61, above, Articles 289 (for joint stock companies), 543 (for limited companies) and 179 and 270 (for partnership companies).
224 As note 61, above, Articles 317 (for joint stock companies), 549 (for limited companies) and 180 and 271 (for partnership companies).

225   As note 61, above, Articles 319(2) (for joint stock companies), 549(3) (for limited companies) and 181–183 and 269 (for partnership companies).
226   As note 61, above, Articles 319(2) (for joint stock companies), 549(3) (for limited companies) and 269 (for limited partnership companies) adopt rules applying for unlimited partnership companies contained in Articles 181–183.
227   As note 61, above, Articles 181(1), 182(1) and 183.
228   As note 61, above, Articles 181(2), 182(2) and 183.
229   As note 61, above, Article 383(1) and (2).
230   As note 61, above, Article 382(1).
231   As note 61, above, Article 385(1).
232   As note 61, above, Article 385(2).
233   As note 61, above, Article 386.
234   As note 61, above, Article 388.
235   As note 61, above, Article 390(1).
236   As note 61, above, Article 390(2) and (3).
237   As note 61, above, Article 391. The quorum required can be increased by the articles.
238   As note 61, above, Article 391–3.
239   As note 69, above, 244.
240   As note 61, above, Article 393(2).
241   As note 61, above, Article 393(1).
242   As note 61, above, Article 362.
243   As note 61, above, Articles 447 and 447-2.
244   As note 61, above, Article 398.
245   As note 61, above, Article 389(1).
246   As note 61, above, Article 389(3) (incorporating Articles 208(2) and 209).
247   As note 28, above, 25.
248   As note 249, above.
249   As note 61, above, Article 391(2).
250   As note 61, above, Article 399.
251   As note 61, above, Article 401.
252   As note 61, above, Articles 402 and 403.
253   As note 28, above, 2.
254   As note 254, above.
255   As note 28, above, 7.
256   As note 28, above, 30.
257   As note 61, above, Article 561.
258   As note 61, above, Article 562(1).
259   As note 61, above, Article 562(2) and (3).
260   As note 61, above, Article 564(1).
261   As note 260, above.
262   As note 61, above, Article 571.
263   As note 61, above, Articles 579 and 579-2.
264   As note 61, above, Article 398.
265   As note 61, above, Article 200(1).
266   As note 61, above, Articles 201, 202 and 208.
267   As note 61, above, Article 273.
268   As note 61, above, Article 278.
269   As note 61, above, Articles 207 and 269.
270   As note 61, above, Articles 203 and 274.
271   As note 61, above, Articles 209 and 269.
272   As note 61, above, Articles 210 and 269.
273   As note 61, above, Article 362.
274   As note 61, above, Article 365(1).

275   As note 28, above, 8.
276   As note 28, above, 9.
277   As note 28, above, 9–10.
278   As note 28, above, 10.
279   As note 61, above, Article 362.
280   As note 61, above, Article 363(3).
281   As note 61, above, Article 364.
282   Article 368(1) of the Commercial Code.
283   As note 28, above, 1 and 9 (for details of all the reasons given by companies for low shareholder attendance, see 18–23).
284   As note 61, above, Article 369.
285   As note 61, above, Article 370. Preference shareholders are only usually entitled to vote on resolutions affecting their priorities. The issue of preference shares by companies is limited to 25 per cent of issued shares.
286   As note 61, above, Article 371.
287   As note 61, above, Article 368(2).
288   As note 61, above, Article 368(3).
289   The Securities and Exchange Act, Article 199.
290   As note 289, above, Article 209.
291   As note 61, above, Article 368(4).
292   As note 61, above, Article 368(1).
293   As note 61, above, Articles 384 and 409.
294   As note 61, above, Articles 366(3) and 367.
295   As note 61, above, Article 531. It is also required for the removal of liquidators: Article 539.
296   As note 61, above, Article 372.
297   As note 61, above, Article 449.
298   As note 61, above, Article 462-2.
299   As note 61, above, Articles 388, 388 via 415, and 388 via 542(2) respectively.
300   As note 61, above, Article 540(1).
301   As note 61, above, Articles 385(1) and 415.
302   As note 61, above, Article 309. This special resolution still requires the resolution to be adopted by a majority of the members present, who represent more than half of the total number of shares issued.
303   As note 61, above, Articles 433–435.
304   As note 61, above, Article 374.
305   As note 61, above, Articles 518 and 522(3).
306   As note 61, above, Article 175(2).
307   As note 61, above, Article 519.
308   As note 61, above, Article 375.
309   As note 61, above, Article 516-2(4).
310   As note 61, above, Articles 518 and 522(1).
311   As note 69, above, 244.
312   As note 61, above, Article 324.
313   As note 61, above, Article 400.
314   As note 61, above, Article 415.
315   As note 61, above, Article 604.
316   As note 61, above, Articles 376–381.
317   As note 28, above, 10.
318   As note 28, above, 1.
319   For details of Choi's research, see note 28, above, 10–13.
320   As note 28, above, 11.
321   As note 318, above, 1.
322   As note 61, above, Article 373.

323   As note 61, above, Article 365.
324   As note 61, above, Article 366(1).
325   As note 61, above, Article 366(2).
326   As note 61, above, Article 467(3).
327   As note 61, above, Article 412-3.
328   As note 61, above, Article 571(1).
329   As note 61, above, Article 573.
330   As note 61, above, Article 572.
331   As note 61, above, Article 571(1).
332   As note 61, above, Article 578.
333   As note 61, above, Article 571(2).
334   As note 61, above, Article 574.
335   As note 61, above, Article 575.
336   As note 61, above, Article 578.
337   As note 61, above, Article 578.
338   As note 61, above, Articles 547, 562(2) and 586.
339   As note 61, above, Article 564(2).
340   As note 61, above, Article 578.
341   As note 61, above, Article 613(1).
342   As note 61, above, Article 588.
343   As note 61, above, Article 578.
344   As note 61, above, Article 613(1).
345   As note 61, above, Article 585(1).
346   As note 61, above, Article 556(1).
347   As note 61, above, Article 585.
348   As note 61, above, Article 576.
349   As note 61, above, Articles 598 and 609(2).
350   As note 61, above, Article 599.
351   As note 61, above, Article 610.
352   As note 61, above, Article 607.
353   As note 61, above, Article 578.
354   As note 61, above, Article 578.
355   As note 61, above, Articles 201 and 269.
356   As note 61, above, Articles 269 and 287.
357   As note 61, above, Articles 203 and 274.
358   As note 61, above, Articles 204 and 269.
359   As note 61, above, Articles 227 and 269.
360   As note 61, above, Articles 247 and 269.
361   As note 61, above, Articles 197 and 269.
362   As note 61, above, Article 276.
363   As note 61, above, Articles 229 and 269.
364   As note 363, above.
365   As note 61, above, Article 198(1).
366   As note 61, above, Article 199.
367   As note 61, above, Article 198(1).
368   As note 28, above, 43.
369   As note 61, above, Article 412. Under Article 412-3 the auditor has the right to call an extraordinary general meeting to address any allegations of wrongdoing by directors.
370   As note 61, above, Article 412-4.
371   As note 61, above, Article 391-2.
372   As note 61, above, Article 413.
373   As note 61, above, Article 412-2.
374   As note 61, above, Article 409(1).

375   As note 61, above, Article 409(2) and (3).
376   As note 61, above, Article 410.
377   As note 61, above, Article 388 (via 415).
378   As note 61, above, Article 385(1) (via 415).
379   As note 61, above, Article 385(2) (via 415).
380   As note 61, above, Article 403(1) (via 415).
381   As note 61, above, Articles 401 (via 415) and 414.
382   As note 28, above, 33 and 34.
383   As note 28, above, 35.
384   As note 28, above, 2.
385   Article 2 of the External Audit of Joint Stock Corporation Act, Law No. 3297, 31 December 1980.
386   Article 182 of the Securities and Exchange Act. The documents that need to be externally audited are prescribed in Articles 46(2) and 81 of the Enforcement Decree of the Securities and Exchange Act, Presidential Decree No. 8436, 9 February 1977.
387   As note 61, above, Article 568(1).
388   As note 61, above, Article 568(2).
389   As note 61, above, Article 569.
390   As note 61, above, Article 388 (via 570).
391   As note 61, above, Article 385(1) (via 570).
392   As note 61, above, Article 414 (via 570).
393   As note 61, above, Article 565 (via 570).
394   As note 61, above, Article 29.
395   As note 61, above, Article 30(2). The methodology for valuing fixed and floating assets is set out in Article 32.
396   As note 61, above, Article 33(1).
397   As note 61, above, Article 30(2); see note 69, above, 249.
398   As note 61, above, Articles 447 and 447-2. Accounting methodology to be adopted in respect of asset valuation, share issue costs, par value shortfall, debenture balance and amortization of capitalized interest are set out in Articles 452–457.
399   As note 61, above, Articles 447-3 and 447-4.
400   As note 61, above, Articles 449 and 448(2) respectively.
401   As note 61, above, Article 466(1).
402   As note 61, above, Article 466(2).
403   As note 61, above, Article 448(1).
404   As note 61, above, Articles 579(1) and 579-2. Accounting methodology to be adopted in respect of asset valuation and share issue costs are set out in Articles 452 and 453 (via Article 583(1)).
405   As note 61, above, Article 579(2) and (3).
406   As note 61, above, Article 583(1).
407   As note 61, above, Article 579-3.
408   As note 61, above, Articles 200 and 273 respectively.
409   As note 61, above, Articles 273 and 277(1).
410   As note 61, above, Article 277(2).
411   As note 61, above, Article 366(1).
412   As note 61, above, Article 366(2).
413   As note 61, above, Article 466.
414   As note 61, above, Articles 402 and 542(2).
415   As note 61, above, Articles 324, 403, 415 and 542(2).
416   As note 61, above, Articles 385(2), 415 and 542(2).
417   As note 61, above, Article 467(1).

418   Burton, J. (1998), 'Korea to allow foreign takeover bids', *Financial Times* (UK) 2 February, 8.
419   As note 61, above, Articles 418(1) and 420(5).
420   As note 61, above, Articles 513(2) and 516-2(4).
421   As note 61, above, Article 572.
422   As note 61, above, Articles 565, 570 and 613(2).
423   As note 61, above, Articles 567 and 613(2).
424   As note 61, above, Articles 565 and 613(2).
425   As note 61, above, Article 588.
426   As note 61, above, Article 587.
427   As note 61, above, Article 622.
428   As note 61, above, Article 625.
429   As note 61, above, Article 626.
430   As note 61, above, Article 627.
431   As note 61, above, Articles 630 and 631.
432   As note 61, above, Article 635.
433   As note 61, above, Article 633.
434   As note 61, above, Articles 416–432.
435   As note 61, above, Articles 469–516-10.
436   As note 61, above, Article 416.
437   As note 61, above, Article 420.
438   As note 61, above, Articles 418(1) and 420(5).
439   As note 61, above, Article 417.
440   As note 61, above, Article 469.
441   As note 61, above, Article 470.
442   As note 61, above, Article 470.
443   As note 61, above, Article 471.
444   As note 61, above, Articles 513(2) and 516-2(4).
445   Defined in Article 2(1) of the Securities and Exchange Act.
446   As note 445, above, Article 3.
447   As note 61, above, Article 586.
448   As note 61, above, Article 588.
449   As note 61, above, Article 587.
450   As note 61, above, Article 341.
451   As note 61, above, Article 341-2.
452   As note 61, above, Article 342-2.
453   As note 61, above, Article 343.
454   As note 61, above, Article 345.
455   As note 61, above, Articles 346–351.
456   As note 61, above, Article 438.
457   As note 61, above, Article 439(2) and (3).
458   Corporate Reorganization Act, Law No. 1214, 12 December 1962 (as amended). This law is modelled on the Japanese Corporate Reorganization Law, Law No. 172, 7 June 1952 (as amended). As eligibility for reorganization under the Corporate Reorganization Act is limited to stock companies, partnerships (*hapmyong-hoesa*), limited partnerships (*hapcha-hoesa*), limited company (*yuhan-hoesa*) and unincorporated organizations are unable to use the Act. Hong, I. (1980), 'A comparative study of American and Korean Corporate Reorganization Laws', *Korean Journal of Comparative Law*, 8, 1, 28; Hong, I. (1988), 'A comparative study of American and Korean Corporate Reorganization Laws', in C.-J. Kim (ed.), *Business Laws in Korea* (2nd edition), Seoul: Panmum Book Company Ltd, 377, 401.
459   Article 3 of the Corporate Reorganisation Law.
460   As note 459, above, Article 26.

461 As note 460, above.
462 As note 459, above, Article 67(1). Creditors are estopped from lodging a petition for adjudication in bankruptcy, or an application for composition or foreclosure of assets by a secured creditor.
463 See Hong (1988), as note 458, above, 387.
464 As note 459, above, Article 187-9.
465 Each category of creditor is required to give approval. Approval of the plan is required:

- by unsecured creditors holding two-thirds of the debt;
- where postponement of secured debts is proposed, secured creditors holding three-quarters of the secured debts;
- where reduction or extinguishment of secured debts is proposed, all secured creditors and a majority of shareholders.

See generally note 458, above, 388.
466 Bankruptcy Act, Law No. 998, 20 January 1962 (as amended).
467 As note 466, above, Articles 227 and 517.
468 As note 466, above, Articles 362, 363 and 390.
469 Consisting of those present and those holding proxies.
470 The resolution required is specified in Article 518 of the Commercial Code and the rules governing the adoption of the resolution are specified in Article 434.
471 As note 61, above, Article 521.
472 As note 61, above, Article 228 (via Article 530).
473 Kim, Y.-M. and Woo, C.-R. (1988), 'A brief survey of Korean Corporate Liquidation and Bankruptcy Law', in C.-J. Kim (ed.), *Business Laws in Korea* (2nd edition), Seoul: Panmum Book Company Ltd, 418, 420.
474 As note 61, above, Articles 609 and 227.
475 As note 474, above.
476 As note 61, above, Articles 585 and 609(2).
477 As note 61, above, Articles 227 and 269.
478 As note 61, above, Article 285(1).
479 As note 61, above, Article 247(1).
480 As note 61, above, Article 247(4).
481 As note 61, above, Article 613.
482 Kim and Woo (1988) as note 470 above, 420; Kim, Y.-M. and Woo, C.-R. (1980), 'A brief survey of Korean corporate liquidation and bankruptcy law', *Korean Journal of Comparative Law*, 8, 45, 47.
483 As note 61, above, Articles 531(1) and 613(1).
484 As note 61, above, Article 1; and Article 82 of the Civil Code.
485 As note 61, above, Articles 531(2) and 613(1).
486 As note 61, above, Articles 531(1) and 613(1).
487 Kim and Woo (1988) as note 473, above, 420; as note 482, above, 47.
488 As note 61, above, Articles 539(2) and 613(2).
489 As note 485, above.
490 As note 61, above, Articles 532 and 613(1).
491 As note 61, above, Articles 535(1) and 613(1).
492 As note 61, above, Articles 535(2) and 613(1).
493 As note 61, above, Articles 533, 534 and 613(1).
494 As note 61, above, Articles 542 and 612.
495 As note 61, above, Article 542; and Article 93 of the Civil Code.
496 As note 61, above, Articles 635 and 622.
497 As note 61, above, Articles 535(1) and 613(1).

498   As note 61, above, Articles 536 and 613(1).
499   As note 61, above, Articles 344(1), 538 and 612.
500   As note 61, above, Articles 540(1) and 613(1).
501   As note 61, above, Article 264 (via 542 and 613).
502   As note 61, above, Articles 542 and 613.
503   As note 61, above, Articles 399 and 401 (via 542 and 613).
504   As note 61, above, Articles 252 and 269.
505   As note 61, above, Article 251(1).
506   As note 61, above, Article 287.
507   As note 61, above, Articles 251(2) and 287.
508   Kim and Woo (1988) as note 473, above, 420; Kim and Woo (1980), as above, 47.
509   As note 61, above, Articles 253 and 269.
510   As note 61, above, Articles 247 (via 232) and 269.
511   As note 61, above, Articles 256 and 269.
512   As note 61, above, Articles 254 and 269.
513   As note 61, above, Articles 254(4) and 269; and Article 93 of the Civil Code.
514   Article 88(2) of the Civil Code.
515   As note 514, above, Article 90.
516   As note 61, above, Articles 260 and 269.
517   As note 61, above, Articles 258 and 269.
518   As note 517, above.
519   As note 61, above, Articles 263 and 269.
520   As note 61, above, Articles 264 and 269.
521   As note 61, above, Articles 265 and 269.
522   As note 61, above, Articles 399 and 401 (via 265 and 269).
523   Kim and Woo (1988), as note 473, above, 423; Kim and Woo (1980), as note 482, above, 50.
524   Article 116 of the Bankruptcy Act.
525   As note 524, above, Article 117.
526   As note 524, above, Articles 84–88.
527   As note 524, above, Article 122.
528   Kim and Woo (1988), as note 473, above, 423; Kim and Woo (1980), as note 482, above, 50.
529   As note 524, above, Article 122.
530   As note 524, above, Article 123.
531   As note 524, above, Article 262.
532   As note 524, above, Article 332; and generally Articles 330–338.
533   As note 524, above, Article 132.
534   As note 524, above, Article 132.
535   As note 524, above, Article 7.
536   As note 524, above, Article 152.
537   As note 524, above, Articles 188 and 184.
538   As note 524, above, Articles 170 and 187.
539   As note 524, above, Articles 278 and 304: compulsory composition.
540   As note 524, above, Article 16.
541   As note 524, above, Article 64.
542   As note 538, above.
543   As note 524, above, Article 50.
544   As note 524, above, Article 319.
545   As note 524, above, Articles 135 and 325.
546   As note 524, above, Articles 38 and 40.
547   As note 524, above, Article 32.
548   As note 524, above, Articles 37–43.

549 Security of commercial credit is by hypothec (mortgage) (*chodanggwon*), pledge (*chilgwon*), assignment as security (*yangdo tambo*), retention of title (*shoyuken ryuho*) and the use of a trust (*shint'ak*). The laws governing the security of debt are principally the Civil Code, the Code of Civil Procedure (Law No. 547, 4 April 1960 (as amended)) and the Trust Act (Law No. 900, 30 December 1961 (as amended)). There are other laws that require specific registration depending on the nature of the property secured; for example the Heavy Machinery Mortgage Act (Law No. 1855, 23 December 1966). For a detailed discussion of secured charges, see Coleman, R. (1979), 'The Japanese and Korean Law of secured transactions', *Hastings International and Comparative Law Review*, **2**, 21; and Reid, K. and Tomasic, R. (1997), 'Japan, South Korea and India', in R. Tomasic and P. Little (eds), *Insolvency Law and Practice in Asia*, Hong Kong: FT Law and Tax Asia Pacific.

550 For example where a number of pledges are created in respect of the same assets then the earlier pledge has preference: Article 33 of the Commercial Code.

551 As note 41, above, para. KOR 75-504.

552 As note 41, above, para. KOR 75-504.

553 As note 61, above, Article 174(1).

554 As note 61, above, Article 517.

555 As note 61, above, Article 522. Under Article 522-3 an appraisal-of-share remedy is available to shareholders who oppose a merger.

556 As note 61, above, Article 530(2).

557 As note 556, above.

558 As note 61, above, Article 528.

559 As note 61, above, Article 174(2).

560 As note 61, above, Article 530(2).

561 As note 61, above, Article 609.

562 As note 61, above, Article 598.

563 As note 61, above, Article 603.

564 As note 564, above.

565 As note 61, above, Article 602.

566 As note 61, above, Article 174(2).

567 As note 61, above, Article 603.

568 As note 61, above, Article 286.

569 As note 61, above, Article 525.

570 As note 61, above, Articles 227 and 269.

571 As note 61, above, Articles 230 and 269.

572 As note 61, above, Articles 232(1) and 269.

573 As note 61, above, Articles 232(2), (3) and 269.

574 As note 61, above, Articles 175, 233, 238 and 269.

575 As note 61, above, Articles 175, 235 and 269.

576 As note 61, above, Article 2 Monopoly Regulation and Fair Trading Act, wholly amended by Law No. 4198, 13 January 1990. What constitutes a particular field of trade is determined by reference to the product market (the nature of goods or services, including substitute goods and services being dealt in) and the geographic market (that is the number and nature of competitors, consumer behaviour and transportation inefficiencies).

577 As note 576, above, Article 2.

578 These levels are prescribed in Article 11 of the Enforcement Decree of the Monopoly Regulation and Fair Trading Act, wholly amended by Presidential Decree No. 12979, 14 April 1990.

579 As note 576, above, Article 7(1).

580 As note 576, above, Article 7(3).

581   As note 576, above, Article 12(1).
582   As note 576, above, Article 12(4).
583   As note 576, above, Article 12(3).
584   Article 200-2(1) of the Securities and Exchange Act.
585   As note 584, above, Article 200-2(2).
586   As note 584, above, Article 200-2(1).
587   As note 584, above, Articles 199(2) and 200.
588   Abir, D. (1996), 'Monopoly and merger regulation in South Korea and Japan: A comparative analysis', *International Tax and Business Lawyer*, **13**, 143, 157 and 173.
589   The other legislation aimed at curtailing anti-competitive behaviour (price restraint and cartels) is the Price Stabilization Act, Law No. 2798, 31 December 1975. This law represented a reversal of South Korean government policy, which had been aimed at encouraging economies of scale; see note 588, above, 154.
590   The Fair Trade Commission is part of the Economic Planning Board.
591   As note 576, above, Articles 32–34-2 impose restrictions on international agreements.
592   As note 576, above, Article 16.
593   As note 576, above, Article 16; Article 17 (for penalties).
594   As note 576, above, Article 29.
595   As note 576, above, Article 25.
596   As note 576, above, Article 7(1) and Chapter III (generally). Abir argues that the breadth of these exemptions, combined with bureaucratic indifference means that the stated free trade objectives of the legislation cannot be met. In fact, the government's reluctance to use these laws in an attempt to encourage the growth of industries is short-sighted as it has the opposite effect of creating barriers to entry and thereby limiting growth; see note 581, above, 160-1, 170-3 and 175.
597   As note 576, above, Article 7(2).
598   As note 576, above. The last ground is broad, allowing latitude for the exercise of ministerial discretion.
599   As note 576, above. The entrepreneur must demonstrate how these goals will be achieved by the merger. He or she will need to point to facts such as that the merger will promote technology, optimize management, optimize marketing offshore and so on. An example of a failed attempt is *Don Yang Chemical Industrial Co Ltd* (Corrective Order No. 82.1, 13 January 1982 Medium and Small Enterprise Basic Law, 1982 Monopoly Regulation and Fair Trading Law Decision 153) cited in note 588, above, 158 and 159. Dong Yang acquired 50 per cent of a competitor. Dong Yang argued that the merger would reduce production costs by 13 per cent by reducing transport and packaging costs, technology exchange and reduction in overlapping research and development. The Commission found that these claims were not supportable and, given that the merger would result in a monopoly in the hydrogen peroxide market, Dong Yang, was required to divest its holdings.
600   The Basic Small and Medium Enterprise Act, wholly amended by Law No. 4897, 5 January 1995.
601   Article 1 of the Securities and Exchange Act.
602   Park, J. (1988), 'Securities Market in Korea', in *Securities Markets in Asia and Oceania* (2nd edition), 'Japan: The Asian Securities' Analysts Council Securities, 349.
603   Article 7 of the Securities and Exchange Act.
604   As note 603, above, Articles 28 and 28-2.
605   As note 603, above, Article 70-2.

606 As note 603, above, Articles 78 and 112.
607 As note 603, above, Articles 119 and 133.
608 As note 603, above, Article 145.
609 As note 603, above, Article 118.
610 As note 603, above, Article 130.
611 As note 603, above, Article 145.
612 As note 603, above, Article 147.
613 As note 603, above, Article 162.
614 As note 603, above, Article 147.
615 As note 603, above, Article 71.
616 As note 615, above.
617 As note 603, above, Articles 3 and 4.
618 As note 603, above, Article 2(1).
619 As note 603, above, Article 3; and Article 3(1) of the Enforcement Decree of the Securities and Exchange Act.
620 As note 603, above, Articles 21–27.
621 As note 603, above, Article 10.
622 As note 603, above, Articles 8, 12 and 13.
623 As note 603, above, Article 14.
624 As note 623, above.
625 As note 603, above, Articles 55 and 57.
626 As note 603, above, Article 70-2.
627 As note 603, above, Articles 208, 209, 214 and 215.
628 As note 603, above, Articles 186 and 193.
629 As note 603, above, Article 211.
630 As note 603, above, Article 188.
631 As note 603, above, Article 188-2.
632 As note 631, above.
633 As note 603, above, Article 188-3.
634 As note 603, above, Article 208.
635 'Custody – Korea' (1996/7), VII(10), *AsiaMoney*, 92.
636 As note 635, above.
637 As note 418, above.
638 Kirk, D., 'Seoul shields chaebol from hostile bidder', *International Herald Tribune* (UK), 5 February 1998, 15.
639 Articles 2 and 3 of the Foreign Capital Inducement Act.
640 As note 639, above, Articles 7(1), 19(1), 23(1), 25(1) and 29(1).
641 As note 639, above, Article 7-3(3) states that the minister can only approve insignificant investment. Article 8(4) of the Enforcement Decree of the Foreign Capital Inducement Act, wholly amended by Presidential Decree No. 11,469, 30 June 1989 (as amended) states that insignificant investment is amounts less than one billion Won for manufacturers and less than 3 billion won for other industries. Investment referred to the committee is that greater than 100 million US dollars; as note 69, above, 235.
642 Article 4 of the Foreign Capital Inducement Act.
643 As note 642, above, Articles 5, 14–17. The criteria for the reduction of taxes and customs duty are set out in Articles 13–19-4 of the Enforcement Decree of the Foreign Capital Inducement Act.
644 As note 642, above, Article 14.
645 As note 642, above, Article 6.
646 Article 13 of the Enforcement Decree of the Foreign Capital Inducement Act.

5 Company Law in China

ROMAN TOMASIC* AND JIAN FU**

1 Introduction

1.1 A Brief Introduction to the History of China's Company Law

Company laws have been enacted in China in 1904 (Qing Dynasty), in 1914 (Republican), in 1929 (Nationalist), in 1946 (Nationalist) and in 1993 (People's Republic of China – PRC). All of these laws have reflected a considerable degree of central government control and have had limited impact on the organization of business activity in China. Historically, Chinese governments have not encouraged commerce, perhaps due to the long-standing policy of national isolation and what some have described as a Confucian disdain for the world of business. This meant that the state provided minimal protection for private business, so that, by default, the family and relationships of trust became a more secure basis for business activity than formal bodies of law, such as company law.[1]

Company law ideas have been circulating in China since the early years of this century, with China's first Company Law (*Gongsilü*) being issued by the Qing Dynasty's Ministry of Commerce in 1904. The Ministry of Commerce had itself only been established in 1903. However, this 1904 law and subsequent company law reforms had little impact on the structure of Chinese business organization. This may be attributable in part to a fear of incorporation on the part of business, especially smaller businesses. There was a fear of government intervention through the company registration process, but an even more fundamental problem, as described by Li Chun, was that:

> [t]he idea that members of the public would be invited to join one's business and share in its control and profits was indeed repugnant. On the other hand, the notion that one's money be put into the pocket of some strangers for them to run a business was just as unthinkable.[2]

135

Prior to 1904 there was very little Chinese business law. Qing China did not have a commercial code and other laws, such as the Great Qing Code, were primarily penal in character.[3] As Kirby notes, until this time 'commercial law, as a field, simply did not exist'.[4] This failure of Chinese law to develop along lines which were familiar in the West was related to the failure of capitalism and the failure of an independent business class to develop in old China. This was emphasized by the leading China scholar, J.K. Fairbank, when he observed that:

> [t]here was no idea of the corporation as a legal individual. Big firms were family affairs. Business relations were not cold impersonal matters governed by the general principles of the law and of contract in a world apart from home and family. Business was a segment of the whole web of friendship, kinship obligations, and personal relations that supported Chinese life.[5]

However, forms of business partnership did exist, although none of these were legal entities; guarantors also played an important role in Chinese business at this time. Kirby notes that the introduction of the 1904 Company Law was in part aimed at overcoming the constraints of these forms of partnership and guarantorship as well as seeking to achieve a greater degree of national sovereignty.[6]

The 1904 Company Law was the product of the Imperial Law Codification Commission whose work reflected a reformist period which saw the adoption of Western legal ideas as important to the economic development of China and the abolition of the hated system of the extraterritorial application of Western laws in China. This system had been in existence since the 1840s.[7] The 1904 Company Law, which drew broadly upon both English and Japanese company law models, established a number of different types of companies, created them as juristic persons and introduced the idea of the limited liability company limited by shares.[8] After the collapse of the Qing Dynasty in 1911, and the emergence of early Chinese Republican governments, the 1904 Company Law was replaced (in 1914) with the much more detailed Ordinance Concerning Commercial Associations, which was based on German commercial law ideas.

However, after the defeat of the warlords and the establishment of the government of the Republic of China in Nanjing in 1928, a new company law was subsequently enacted by the Nationalists in 1929. The Nationalists saw commercial law in narrowly instrumentalist terms, namely as a means of promoting greater state control over the private sector.[9] This law revised the 1914 Company Law and imposed severe restrictions on companies and greater penalties for breaches of the law. Article 1 of the 1929 Company Law also introduced a new purpose for the establishment of companies, stating that they were a legal person which was 'formed with a view to profit'.[10] Except for the adoption of the corporate form by state enterprises, by 1942 only 28 per cent of China's private industrial firms had adopted any of the corporate forms which were created by these laws and older forms of business organization (such as partnerships and the family-based firm) continued to predominate. Somewhat reminiscent of contemporary patterns of organization in China, Kirby notes that by 1943 state-controlled enterprises accounted for 70 per cent of the paid up capital of public and private companies operating in Nationalist-controlled areas.[11]

With the end of the Second World War a New Company Law (*Xin Gongsifa*) was enacted in 1946. This new law reflected the end of a century of foreign extraterritorial privilege in China with the result that China's company law now applied to British and US citizens and introduced a stricter regime for the recognition of foreign companies which could be registered under the new Chinese company law.[12] The new law also reflected the rise of increasingly socialized state-dominated public enterprises with the creation of a new type of limited company having no more than ten limited liability shareholders. As Kirby observes, this was described by some commentators at the time as 'bureaucratic capitalism'. He added that the state became the primary user of the corporate forms permitted by the Company Law.[13] By this time, some 70 per cent of all industry in China was controlled by the government and over half of the government enterprises were reorganized as limited companies or, less frequently, into limited share companies.

After the successful overthrow of the Nationalist government, all pre-communist laws were repealed in 1949 with the inauguration of the People's Republic of China. The 1946 Company Law was repealed and in 1950 new regulations were introduced for the nationalization or collectivization of all organizations. Between 1950 and 1994 there was no comprehensive national body of law providing for the incorporation of business enterprises, although 1979 saw the introduction of a Law on Joint Ventures and in 1988 the Law on State Enterprises was introduced. In addition, the Enterprise Bankruptcy Law (For Trial Implementation) was passed in 1986 and, in the same year, the General Provisions of the Civil Law of the People's Republic of China (Article 41) introduced the concept of legal personality as applied to organizations such as collective and state-owned enterprises. There have, however, been regional or local experiments in company law reform in places such as Shenzhen and Shanghai.

The enactment of a more comprehensive body of company law had to wait until 1993; this law was described by its chief drafter as 'the first law on companies since inauguration of the People's

Republic of China'.[14] China's present Company Law was adopted and promulgated in December 1993 and came into force on 1 July 1994. Although this is still a somewhat sparse enactment, in part reflecting a civil law drafting style, it has re-introduced a broad range of fundamental company law ideas into the Chinese system and made these available for use by a broad range of enterprises. However, despite its parallels with various foreign bodies of law, drawing especially upon Japanese and German models, it is a Company Law with distinctly Chinese characteristics. It is also a Law that will inevitably be subject to further reform, something which seems to be characteristic of company laws in many jurisdictions.

Before going on to describe the key provisions of this new PRC Company Law, it is useful to provide a brief overview of the nature of the legal system in which the new Company Law operates.

1.2   A Brief Overview of the Chinese Legal System

During the two decades since the end of the Cultural Revolution, China has developed a legal system with a strongly stated commitment to rule by law,[15] the enhancement of a sense of legality amongst the community and the reduction of arbitrariness in official decision-making. In 1978, at the third plenary session of the Eleventh Central Committee of the Communist Party of China, Deng Xiaoping called for a strengthening of the legal system by the removal of personalized features. As Deng noted at that time, '[d]emocracy needs to be institutionalised and legalised so that such a system and such laws would not change merely because of a change of leadership or a change in the leaders' views and attention'.[16] This was followed by a prolonged period of law reform aimed at filling the many gaps which existed in the legal system at that time. After the turmoil of the Cultural Revolution, law was also seen as an important means of maintaining order and stability, something which was seen to be needed urgently in China. In its 1981 Resolution on the Interpretation of the Law, the Standing Committee of the National People's Congress noted that:

> Some people have a weak sense of legality due to the serious sabotage of the socialist legal system caused by ... [various] ... counter-revolutionary cliques and the baneful influence they spread in this regard. On the other hand, little has been done to publicize the legal system, and many people are far from familiar with it. The Standing Committee of the National People's Congress holds that state institutions at all levels and all people's organizations should do more to publicize and educate people in the socialist legal system ... .

The NPC Standing Committee added that:

The vast numbers of cadres and masses, particularly the leading cadres at all levels and the law-enforcement personnel in public security organs, procuratorates and courts should be educated in such a way that they will consciously observe and correctly apply the laws, handle the various disputes among the people according to law, and know how to use the law as a weapon against all criminal acts that undermine the socialist legal system.[17]

Lubman has noted that:

[l]aw was inextricably entwined with politics from the birth of Maoist China and politicized into irrelevance during the Cultural Revolution; only in recent years has it begun to evolve, unevenly and slowly, into a distinct body of rules and institutions.[18]

The close relationship between the state apparatus and the role of the Communist Party of China is an illustration of this link between politics and the legal or constitutional structure of the state. The Constitution of the People's Republic of China deals with the structure of the Chinese State under seven main categories: (1) the National People's Congress; (2) the President of the People's Republic of China; (3) the State Council; (4) the Central Military Commission; (5) the Local People's Congresses and Local People's Governments at Various Levels; (6) the Organs of Self-Government of National Autonomous Areas; (7) the People's Courts and the People's Procuratorates.

Lubman suggests that the Chinese judicial system is merely another bureaucratic hierarchy among the many which make up the Chinese state.[19] It is true that the judicial system is a bureaucratic hierarchy, but there are nevertheless signs of increasing change in judicial institutions which in time are likely to more closely resemble Western civil law models.[20] However, judges appointed to People's Courts in China do not enjoy the security of tenure of some common law judges. Article 36 of the Organic Law of the People's Courts provides that 'People's Congresses at all levels have the power to remove from office the presidents of the People's Courts whom they have elected'. No limits on this power of removal, or criteria for its exercise, are laid down. Similarly, Article 63(4) of the Constitution of the PRC (as amended in 1993) empowers the National People's Congress to remove from office the President of the Supreme People's Court.

The Preamble to the PRC Constitution proclaims that China 'is a unitary multi-national state ...'. It should also be noted that the Chinese legal system is fundamentally a unitary one and is not based on the Western idea of the separation of powers.[21] Similarly, although the Chinese state is a hierarchical one, and contains 23 provinces, five autonomous regions and four large cities which are directly under central government control, it is not regarded as a federal system but as a unitary one.[22] Despite the unitary theory which underlies the Chinese system of state and law, the reality of the Chinse legal system and Chinese law has however been described as one of 'excessive fragmentation'.[23] The maintenance of central control in a system as large and diverse as that of China must inevitably face serious problems of fragmentation or what might be called 'centre-periphery' problems. This is especially evident through the challenges to national authority provided by the forces of localism in China's provinces and special economic zones.

Also, the civil law assumptions upon which the legal system rests are such that the role and structure of the judiciary differ from those found in most common law systems.[24] Other factors which limit the influence and power of Chinese judges are their generally poor levels of legal training, their links to local political and administrative structures, their relatively low status and their low incomes.[25] Of course, if the training of Chinese judges falls short of Western standards, the legal profession in China has even further to go in terms of achieving increased levels of professionalism, standards of legal education and law firm culture.[26] This reflects in part the historically insignificant role played by lawyers in relation to the application of Chinese laws.[27]

Nevertheless, the judiciary in China is an integral part of the system of government. Courts exist at the national, provincial and local levels and, as Du and Zhang point out, 'judicial institutions in China function under the unified leadership of state institutions of power. Therefore, judicial independence exists only in regard to other institutions of state power.'[28] At the top of the judicial system is the Supreme People's Court, with other courts being the High People's Courts found at the provincial level, the Intermediate People's Courts found in cities and prefectures, Local People's Courts found at the county and district level, and divisions of the Local People's Courts found in some towns and villages. Chinese courts tend to contain a number of divisions. Although the distinction between civil law and economic law is somewhat fuzzy, the People's Courts contain an economic division which deals with economic law cases, such as those relating to company law. Civil cases usually involve individuals and individual property, whereas economic cases mainly involve enterprises or other economic entities. The economic division is one of the divisions found in each court; the other divisions may include the criminal, the civil and the administrative divisions.[29]

The Supreme People's Court is increasingly adopting a law-making and interpretative role, although the formal constitutional position in China has been that only the legislature has the power to interpret its laws, although this power may be delegated.[30] Thus, since 1955, the Supreme People's Court has been delegated power to interpret laws.[31] Also, in 1981, the NPC Standing Committee was given interpretative powers as well as the power to make decrees on the meaning of laws where there was some uncertainty.

Furthermore, the 1981 Resolution on Improved Interpretation of the Law stated that '[i]nterpretation of questions involving the specific application of laws and decrees in court trials shall be provided by the Supreme People's Court'. The Supreme People's Procuratorate is also given power to interpret questions involving the application of laws and decrees in the procuratorates' procuratorial work. In the event of there being a conflict of opinions between the Supreme People's Court and the Supreme People's Procuratorates, this is to be resolved by the NPC Standing Committee. The State Council, which is the central executive body of the Chinese state, is also given powers of interpretation of laws and decrees which do not relate to judicial or procuratorial work.[32] The PRC Constitution, which was amended in 1993, also deals with the question of the interpretation of laws and in Article 67 gives interpretative powers to the NPC Standing Committee.

Chinese courts are also beginning to issue case reports of their decisions,[33] although this practice falls short of the development of a doctrine of precedent.[34] The changing law-making role of the courts may be seen in the opinions which are issued from time to time on the implementation of new legislation, such as the Supreme People's Court's 1991 Opinion regarding the implementation of the 1986 PRC Bankruptcy Law[35] and its 1988 Opinion regarding the implementation of the PRC General Principles of Civil Law.[36] Such Opinions as these have been seen to amount to law-making by the Supreme People's Court.[37] As well as the Opinions issued by the Supreme People's Court, courts at all levels may decide not to deal with a matter, regarding it as being beyond their competence, and instead decide to refer the matter to another branch of government. This has been seen as an illustration of the judicial restraint which is commonplace in the Chinese legal system.[38]

However, the implementation or enforcement of civil and economic law judgments made by Chinese courts is still relatively limited, with the effect of undermining confidence in these courts. In part, this failure is due to the reluctance of the courts to use coercive measures, especially where there is some blame on both sides of a matter. Furthermore, the enforcement of economic law judgments against state enterprises presents problems, especially where the court and state enterprise are responsible to the same local authority or, alternatively, where the judgment may lead to the closure of the enterprise and the unemployment of workers.[39]

The principal law-making institution of the Chinese state is the National People's Congress (NPC). People's Congresses in the provinces, autonomous regions and municipalities directly under the control of the central government are also empowered to make laws in areas in which the NPC has not enacted laws or in areas not reserved for the NPC. Under Article 100 of the Constitution, such local laws must not conflict with the PRC Constitution or with laws and regulations which have been passed at the national level. In addition to the NPC, the Standing Committee of the NPC has substantial law-making powers and may enact or amend all laws other than those which are reserved for the NPC. As there will usually be a substantial interval between the meetings of the NPC, the NPC Standing Committee plays an important law-making role when the NPC is not sitting. The State Council also has rule-making powers and may make administrative regulations.[40] Finally, it should be noted that the Communist Party of China also has some, if declining, influence over the law-making process.[41]

Under the Constitution of the People's Republic of China, new legislation may only be proposed by certain designated state organs, although there are clearly informal influences or pressures for change (such as from senior policy advisers) which may also lead to reform.[42] Some activists may be responsible for initiating important law reforms by persuading an approved agency to promote a reform proposal; an example of this is to be found in the efforts of Cao Siyuan, who is widely regarded as the 'father' of China's 1986 Enterprise Bankruptcy Law.[43] However, the State Council and various ministries are responsible for most legislative initiatives put before the NPC and the NPC Standing Committee. Inter-agency bargaining is much relied upon to build a consensus for legal reform initiatives, which tends to be incremental in nature.[44] Sometimes this process can take many years, as has occurred in relation to legislative reforms in regard to securities laws and bankruptcy laws, although it can be accelerated by obtaining strong support for a change from a key patron. Progress in the law reform process may be accelerated by evidence from the trial implementation of laws in particular provinces, cities or special economic zones, as happened with the 1986 enterprise bankruptcy law.

Finally, turning briefly to the executive arm of Chinese government, the State Council is described in Article 85 of the PRC Constitution (as amended in 1993) as 'the executive body of the highest organ of state power; it is the highest organ of state administration'. Under the direction of the Premier, the State Council comprises Vice-Premiers, State Councillors, Ministers in charge of ministries and commissions, the Auditor-General and the Secretary-General. Ministers in charge of ministries and commissions are responsible for the work of their respective agencies. Such agencies include the Ministry of Justice, the Ministry of Finance, the State Economic and Trade Commission and the State Council's Office for Restructuring the Econnomic System (formerly the State Commission for Restructuring the Economic System (SCRES)).[45]

A number of organs are also directly under the control of the State Council and these include the Legal Affairs Office of the State Council (formerly the Legal Affairs Bureau of the State Council) and the Securities Committee of the State Council. The China Securities Regulatory Commission (CSRC) is directly responsible to the State Council even though it was the executive arm of the State Council's Security Policy Committee (SCSPC) which was dismissed in March 1998.[46] Overlapping jurisdiction in areas of economic and financial law leads to some degree of administrative restraint on the part of ministries and commissions, so consultation between agencies is often undertaken or, alternatively, decision-making by agencies may even be avoided in order to minimize potential conflict.[47]

2   Corporation Law Statute and Case-law in China

2.1   Introduction to the Company Law of China

The Company Law of the People's Republic of China was enacted in December 1993 and came into force in mid 1994.[48] The Law contains 11 chapters and 230 Articles or Sections. The Company Law was passed by the 5th Plenary Session of the Standing Committee of the Eighth National People's Congress and was promulgated by order of the President, coming into force on 1 July 1994.[49] Where companies have been incorporated under earlier procedures, such as the Opinions on Standardization of Joint Stock Limited Companies and the Opinions on Standardization of Limited Liability Companies, or other rules or local regulations, Article 229 of the Law requires that these companies should comply with the new procedures under the Company Law within a time to be prescribed. In the meantime, such companies will continue to exist alongside companies which have been incorporated and registered under the Company Law.

Prior to and following the passage of the Company Law, various other administrative rules applying to companies have been passed, such as the 1994 Provisions of the State Council on the Listing of Joint Stock Companies Outside Mainland China and the 1991 Provisions on Administration of Enterprise Name Regulation.[50] Reference should also be made to the PRC Administration of Company Registration Regulations and the Opinion on these regulations issued by the State Administration for Industry and Commerce in 1995.[51] In March 1996

Tentative Provisions, issued by the State Administration for Industry and Commerce on the Administration of Registration of Company Registered Capital, became effective.[52] Finally, reference should also be made here to the Articles of Association for PRC Companies, established in accordance with the 1993 Companies Law, which must be adopted where a company is seeking listing outside the PRC.[53]

2.2   How China's Company Law was Made

The process of enacting China's Company Law may be divided into a number of distinct stages.[54] The process of reform involved eight markedly different drafts of the Law each introduced by a proponent seeking to have its draft enacted by the NPC. Frustrated by the plethora of proposals, the NPC eventually drafted its own version of the Law.[55] The following overview illustrates the lengthy and difficult process of law-making, spanning more than a decade, which was involved in the formulation and enactment of the new Company Law.

The relevant ministries and commissions of the State Council first proposed company law rules and drafted the Limited Liability Company Regulation and the Joint Stock Company Regulation. The proposal for a company law was first submitted in February 1982 by the Economic Law Research Centre of the State Council in its 1982–1986 Five Year Legislative Plan. In 1983 the draft Company Organizational Law was prepared by the then State Economic Commission and the Ministry of Foreign Economics and Trade (now the Ministry of Foreign Economic and Trade Co-operation). In August 1985 a drafting group, headed by the then State Economic Commission, was established to draft company regulations. In January 1986 the drafting group drafted the Limited Liability Company Regulation and Joint Stock Company Regulation (draft for inquiry).

Thereafter, in October 1986, the Limited Liability Regulation (draft for investigation) was passed by the State Economic Commission. However, in April 1988 the State Economic Commission was dissolved, but the SCRES continued the task of drafting. It prepared the Limited Liability Company Regulation (draft) and the Joint Stock Company Regulation (draft). The Legislative Affairs Bureau of the State Council and the SCRES investigated and studied these Company Law drafts. In November 1988 the State Council then convened a seminar on these two regulations. After that time, the Legislative Affairs Bureau decided to enact a company law which was to take the place of the regulations. In August 1990 the Legislative Affairs Bureau and the SCRES jointly drafted the Limited Liability Company Law (draft for investigation) and submitted it to the State Council. After that a number of seminars were convened to discuss the revision of this draft.

The State Council subsequently discussed and approved the draft Limited Liability Company Law. On 2 August 1991 the draft Limited Liability Company Law was discussed at the 88th Session of the State Council. Many legal issues, especially those relevant to state-owned companies were found still not to be very clear at this session. As a result of the urgent need to provide interim regulations in this area, the SCRES issued two opinions to provide guidance. These were the Standardization Opinion on Limited Liability Companies and the Standardization Opinion on Joint Stock Companies. These decrees were produced due to delays which had occurred in preparing the new Company Law. On 15 July 1992 Premier Minister Li Peng convened the 109th Session of the State Council which investigated and approved the draft Limited Liability Company Law. On 15 August 1992 the State Council put this draft before the 27th Session of the Standing Committee of the Seventh National People's Congress.

In November 1991, the Limited Liability Company Law, among other laws, was inserted into the legislative plan of the Standing Committee of the NPC. On 28 August 1992 the 27th Plenary Session of the Standing Committee of the Seventh NPC was convened at which the Limited Liability Company Law was discussed and investigated. Most of the members of the Standing Committee thought that this Law was too narrow to meet the needs of practice. A meeting of the chairmen of the Standing Committee decided to ask the Legislative Affairs Commission to draft a broader Company Law based on the draft of the State Council's Limited Liability Company Law.

On 6 November 1992 the Legislative Affairs Commission completed the first draft of the Company Law in which there were eight Chapters containing 224 Articles. In the process of drafting, the Legislative Affairs Commission drew upon the experience of both foreign countries and domestic areas in the development of companies laws. China's Company Law was mainly influenced by the company laws of Japan, Germany, Great Britain, the United States, Hong Kong and other countries. However, the influence of German and Japanese law was probably the greatest. Insights were also gained from the opinions of the SCRES of the State Council, the Interim Regulation on Joint Stock Company of the Shanghai Municipal Government and the Company Regulation Draft of the Shenzhen Special Economic Zone drafted by Guangdong Provincial Government, and the State Council's 1991 draft Limited Liability Company Law and its 1992 draft Limited Liability Company Law. From November 1992 to January 1993 about 20 seminars were held to discuss and revise the draft Company Law. On 22 June 1993 the Second Session of the Standing Committee of the Eighth NPC for the second time investigated the revised draft Company Law.

The Legislative Affairs Commission again held more than 30 seminars on the Company Law draft from April to May of 1993. From 26 July to 31 July of 1993 the Law Committee of the NPC, the Financial and Economic Committee of the NPC and the Legislative Affairs Commission jointly convened a seminar on the revised draft Company Law. Legal experts, economic experts, and representatives from joint stock enterprises, the State Council's relevant ministries and commissions, and state organs of some provinces gave their opinions on the draft Company Law.

From 2 December to 7 December 1993 the Law Commission of the NPC again investigated the Company Law draft in accordance with the spirit of the 3rd Plenary Session of the Fourteenth Central Committee of the Communist Party of China and suggested that the revised draft Company Law be investigated by the 5th Plenary Session of the Standing Committee of the Eighth NPC. From 20 December to 29 December 1993 the 5th Plenary Session of the Standing Committee of the Eighth NPC investigated the revised Company Law draft. The Law Commission and the Legislative Affairs Commission then revised the draft according to the opinions received from the members of the Standing Committee of the NPC On 29 December 1993 China's Company Law was eventually passed by the 5th Plenary Session of the Standing Committee of the Eighth NPC. In the Law it was provided that the Law will come into effect on 1 July 1994, as it did.

2.3   Who is Responsible for Changing China's Company Law?

The lengthy process of debate which led to the enactment of the Company Law in December 1993 illustrates the range of organizations which continue to have an interest in the application of this Law. Under the PRC Constitution, a law (*falü*), such as the Company Law, may be formally amended by either the NPC (Article 62(3)) or by its Standing Committee (Article 67(2)). It has even been the case that legal rules and regulations have been approved by the State Council without first having been approved by the NPC. Although this practice may be questionable constitutionally, so far it has not been questioned by the NPC or by the courts.[56] The State Council is empowered by Article 89(2) of the Constitution to submit proposals for the reform or amendment of a law to the NPC or to the NPC Standing Committee. The State Council is also empowered by Article 89(13) of the Constitution 'to alter or annul inappropriate orders, directives and regulations issued by the ministries or commissions'.

Proposals for reform may come to the State Council through a Ministry or a Commission. For example, the CSRC, the State Economic and Trade Commission and the Ministry of Foreign Trade and

Economic Cooperation (MOFTEC) may make suggestions for reform. However, as the Company Law is very sparse and needs to be applied to a wide range of circumstances, it is also necessary to supplement this law by the making of regulations (*fagui*) and rules (*guizhang*). Such regulations and rules will be approved by the State Council and drafted by bodies such as the State Economic and Trade Commission, the CSRC and the SCSPC. For example, in 1995 MOFTEC promulgated guidelines and regulations relating to foreign companies which wished to go public or which sought to form investment vehicles in the form of holding companies.[57] The stock exchanges in Shanghai and Shenzhen and the local People's Congresses in these cities may also play an important role in formulating securities regulatory rules.

Before a proposed reform will be considered by the State Council, a relevant commission or ministry must obtain approval for the inclusion of a proposed regulation in the State Council's legislative plan for that year. This plan is formulated by the Bureau of Legislative Affairs of the State Council and is approved by the Standing Committee of the State Council. Obtaining a slot in this legislative plan is not always easy and much lobbying is involved in securing a place in the programme. However, if a proposed regulation does secure a place in the programme, a joint drafting committee may be formed, comprising representatives from the Bureau of Legislative Affairs and the proposing agency (such as the CSRC). A key question to be considered at this stage is whether the proposed regulation is within the competence of the proposing agency. Other agencies will be consulted and asked to make inputs, where this is appropriate (these may include the Ministry of Finance, the Ministry of Justice and the People's Bank of China). Also, an effort will be made to determine whether the proposed regulation is in harmony with existing Chinese laws and regulations. A revised draft of the regulation will then be presented to the State Council's Standing Committee for approval.[58]

Customary practices (*guanli*) and institutionalized state practices regarding corporatization may also be important supplements to the law as enacted by the legislature.[59] As we have seen, Opinions released by the Supreme People's Court could also have a bearing upon the interpretation and implementation of a law such as the Company Law, as has occurred with the Opinion on the 1986 Enterprise Bankruptcy Law. Under the Constitution, interpretations of the Company Law may also be made by the NPC and the NPC Standing Committee.

It seems inevitable that China's Company Law will be subject to further reform as China gains more experience with the application of the existing legislation. These further reforms will occur either through the enactment of a more thoroughgoing statute or through the drafting of supplementary rules and regulations. Professor Fang suggests that the Company Law is inevitably a transitional body of law as its drafters were grappling with a serious dilemma, namely how to reconcile the existing system of administrative permits which arose as part of the planned economy (such as the quota system which exists for issuing and listing shares) with the new more market-oriented approach.[60] The legislation reflects a particular stage of economic and legal development in China, so that its reform will no doubt remain on the law reform agenda. However, in view of the lengthy process of law-making which led to the enactment of this legislation, further reforms may well be postponed for some time.

2.4   Principles which Underlie China's Company Law

The decision to enact a new Company Law reflects debates regarding the movement towards the development of a market economy which have been underway in China since the early 1980s following Mr Deng Xiaoping's now famous tour of southern China. At that time, Deng called for greater economic reform and a movement away from a state planning approach to markets. This new approach was described by Deng as the building of socialism with Chinese characteristics based on the need to 'proceed from Chinese realities'.[61] The enactment of the Company Law is one of a large number of pieces of new legislation aimed at providing a legal structure for 'socialist market' enterprises.[62] It was enacted after the commencement of corporatization experiments in both state and collective sectors of the Chinese economy. The beginning of enterprise reform was marked by the *Decision by the Central Committee of the Communist Party of China on the Reform of the Economic System* passed on the 20th October 1984. This Decision sought to create enterprises that were relatively independent as economic entities, which had an independent business manager and which were responsible for their own losses and profits.[63]

Earlier corporatization efforts saw the introduction of laws such as the 1988 Law on Industrial Enterprise and the State Council's Rural Collective Enterprise Regulations (issued in 1990).[64] Thus, Article 2 of the Law on Industrial Enterprises provides that the enterprise shall have the status of a legal person. Then, in October 1992, the 14th Congress of the Chinese Communist Party declared that the Party would seek to put in place a socialist market economy in China. In July 1992 the State Council approved the Regulation on Transforming the Managerial System of State-owned Industrial Enterprises. This was followed by the November 1993 Decision of the 14th Congress of the Chinese Communist Party which considered further issues regarding the establishment of a socialist market economy and required that state enterprises be transformed into modern corporate entities with redefined ownership rights, a capital structure with the state as a shareholder and the use of new management principles.[65] When the PRC Constitution was amended in 1993, Article 16 was amended to refer to 'state-owned enterprises' instead of 'state [run] enterprises'. Under the 1982 Constitution, state enterprises were required to fulfil their obligations under the 'state plan'. The reference to a 'state plan' was dropped in the 1993 version of Article 16 as part of the move to achieve greater economic decentralization. The passage of the Company Law continued this line of development and may also be seen as a means of seeking to deal with the serious problems arising from the ailing state sector.

The General Provisions set out in Chapter 1 of the Company Law contain a number of guiding principles. The goals of establishing a 'modern enterprise system' and the promotion of 'the socialist market economy' are stated in Article 1 of the Law. Moreover, in conducting its operations, a company is required to 'strengthen the construction of socialist culture' (Article 14). Chapter 1 of the Company Law contains a limited number of key definitions which reflect basic principles which are to be established by this Law. Thus, the Law states that the company will have a separate legal identity in that it will be 'an enterprise legal person' (Article 3). The company is required to operate independently and be responsible for its own profits and losses (Article 5). Two basic types of 'company' are provided for in Article 2: the 'limited liability company' and the 'joint stock limited company'. One of those responsible for the drafting of this legislation has observed that, as the economy develops and as the enterprise system is reformed, the limited liability company will in time become the predominant form of corporate structure in China.[66]

Thus, in contrast to the system of state planning of production, the company is required to organize its own production activities in accordance with market demand and to do this independently. However, although stating this broad principle of independence, this principle is limited to some degree, as it has been in other countries. Thus, Article 5 states that the company should act independently 'under the macro-adjustment and control of the State'. This qualification to the independence principle suggests that elements of state control persist, which is hardly surprising where state-owned assets are involved. This qualification is emphasized by Article 14, which provides that companies must be prepared to 'accept supervision of the government and the public'. At the very minimum, this means that companies will be subject to external regulation, although the full parameters of such state regulation or control are uncertain.

Ambiguity of this kind is to be found in other parts of the legislation and will no doubt be clarified as the Law is tested or applied.[67]

Article 3 also provides for the limitation of the liability of shareholders to the amount of capital that each has subscribed as a member. Although the company is regarded as being separate from its members and it is entitled to the entire property of the legal person, where state-owned assets are held by the company, Article 4 provides that the ownership of these assets rests within the state. This is a somewhat awkward approach as there will inevitably be the possibility of different opinions on whether an asset belongs to the company or to the state. However, it does reflect the view that privatization of state assets should be avoided for a variety of reasons, such as the difficulty of adequately valuing assets, the lack of a developed system of taxation collection and the undesirable consequences of concentrating capital in private hands.[68] It is unclear how the state's rights as a shareholder are to be exercised in such circumstances. Nevertheless, the question of the ownership of state assets has been one of the key debates in the PRC and is, of course, also central to Western legal debates about the separation of ownership and control in companies. However, it is clear, as Bian suggests, that one effect of the Company Law is that 'the state's right to own company property will be circumscribed to a considerable extent'.[69]

Article 4 also lays the foundations for corporate governance by stating that the shareholders are empowered to make major decisions and select management personnel in proportion to the amount of capital that they have invested in the company. This approach is developed in subsequent Chapters of the Law, such as in Article 38 which empowers the shareholders' meeting of a limited liability company 'to decide on the business policy and investment plan of the company'. Surprisingly, the same power is also given to the board of directors of such a company under Article 46 of the Law. However, it is the role of the company's manager 'to organize the implementation of the annual business plans and investment plans of the company' (Article 50).

Furthermore, the Company Law provides for the addition of another governance layer by providing for the establishment of a supervisory board in a limited liability company and in a joint stock limited company (Articles 54 and 124). If the experience with similar provisions found in the 1988 Law on Industrial Enterprises is to be a guide, it is likely that employees and shareholders will have less authority in managerial decision-making than the words of the new Company Law might suggest.[70] Another distinctive feature of corporate governance which is stated in the General Provisions is the commitment to the strengthening of labour protection, the education of employees and the organization and support of trade union activity (Articles 15 and 16). In this regard, it may also be noted that the Company Law provides for the presence of a Communist Party cell in each company by allowing the 'grass-root organizations of the Communist Party of China' to carry on their activities in companies (Article 17). This provision parallels Article 8 of the 1988 Law on Industrial Enterprises.

Finally, as Fang has noted, the Company Law is an important development in PRC law and procedure because of its departure from the long-standing principle of administrative authorization or the exercise of administrative permit power. Article 8 of the Company Law now provides that a company which meets the registration criteria laid down by the Company Law must be registered, subject to complying with any examination and approval procedures specifically laid down in law. Professor Fang notes that earlier pre-registration examination and approval procedures placed considerable power in the hands of various administrative bodies and suggests that this 'permit power may be curtailed by the implicit *ultra vires* (*yuequan wuxiao*) principle contained in Article 8 of the Company Law.[71]

Similarly, Bian Yaowu, one of those responsible for the drafting of the legislation, has noted that the independent legal status of companies will mean that they will no longer be subordinated to the administrative organs of the Chinese state, provided that they carry on their business in accordance with the law.[72] Bian notes the significance of the movement away from the pre-registration examination and approval system to a system in which the registration of a company will normally be automatic, provided that the legal conditions for the establishment of a company are satisfied.[73] However, examination and approval procedures will continue to apply where a wholly state-owned company seeks to transfer its assets: Article 71.

2.5 How the Company Law is to be Interpreted

Apart from the General Provisions set out in Chapter 1 of the Company Law, the Law contains no specific rules of interpretation. Some reference to the interpretation of China's laws was made in the earlier discussion of China's legal system. As we have seen, the interpretation of the Company Law may be undertaken by a number of bodies, such as the NPC, the NPC Standing Committee and the Supreme Peoples' Court. Although, in theory, the interpretation of the Company Law is partly a matter for the courts, especially the Supreme People's Court, doubts have been expressed about the capacity of Chinese judges to handle disputes arising in this area.

For example, one American observer has noted that:

because a large proportion of Chinese judges lack sufficient education, it is doubtful that the Chinese judiciary, as an institution, has the ability to understand and address disputes that centre around highly technical issues, such as those often involved in securities litigation.[74] Because of such difficulties, economic disputes have often been referred to alternative dispute handling bodies, such as the China International Economic and Trade Arbitration Commission, rather than being dealt with by the courts. The interpretation made by such bodies may be useful in developing practical solutions to legal uncertainty in the absence of judicial interpretations.

3   The Nature and Powers of Corporate Regulatory Bodies in China

No single regulatory body is primarily responsible for overseeing China's Company Law. This in part reflects the manner in which the Company Law was drafted. Instead of being influenced by the State Council or one of its departments, the Law was drafted by the Legislative Affairs Commission of the NPC and, after only minor changes, it was submitted directly to the NPC Standing Committee for approval. As a result, no implementation measures were formulated to ensure that the Company Law conformed to the existing law and no single agency was designated as the 'department in charge' of implementing this Law.[75] Instead, a variety of agencies have responsibility for different aspects of the administration of the Company Law. These include the Company Registration Authority (CRA); the State Council's department of security administration (the CSRC), the State Administration for State-owned Assets Management, a people's government at the provincial level and the State Council. These agencies may seek to issue regulations and rules regarding the implementation of the provisions of the Company Law which are within the agencies' area of responsibility. They may also seek to promote reform of the Law.

Examples of the agencies which have responsibility for various areas of the Company Law are set out below. For example, Article 77 of the Law provides that before a joint stock limited company can be incorporated, approval must be obtained from a department which has been authorized to do so by the State Council or by a people's government at the provincial level. Furthermore, the CRA must register the capital of a joint stock limited company (Article 78). In the case of a limited liability company, Article 27 provides that the CRA will be required to receive a capital verification certificate before it grants registration to a company or issues the company's business licence. However, the CRA is not an entirely independent agency. In its liability provisions, the Company Law contemplates the possibility of a department which is at a higher level than the CRA forcing the CRA to approve the registration of a company (Article 223).

If shares in a joint stock limited company are to be offered to the general public, the sponsors of the company are required by Article 84 to submit an application for the share offering to 'the department of security administration' under the State Council. This department is the CSRC. The approval of this department must be obtained before shares can be offered to the general public. This is a system which serves a function broadly akin to the pre-vetting of prospectuses which has existed in some other countries. Furthermore, where shares are to be offered to the general public outside the PRC, pursuant to Article 85, the State Council's department of security administration must also approve such an offering by a joint stock limited company.

Similar approval procedures are set out in Article 139 where new shares are issued by a company and the shares are to be issued to the general public. The Company Law gives the State Council other responsibilities, such as the responsibility to devise rules for the issue of shares at a premium or above their par value (Article 131); to draft separate regulations for the issue of classes of shares which are not provided for under the Company Law (Article 135); to lay down conditions for the listing of a company's shares and for the transfer of such shares (Articles 152 and 153); and to lay down procedures for the issue of company bonds by a joint stock limited company (Article 161).

In the case of the formation of wholly state-owned companies, Article 64 provides that these are to be established by a state-owned investment institution or by a department which has been so authorized by the state. The State Council needs to give its consent before a wholly state-owned company can exercise the rights of an asset owner (Article 72). Similarly, to facilitate the restructuring of state-owned enterprises as limited liability companies, the State Council is required by Article 21 to formulate 'implementation procedures and specific measures' for this purpose.[76]

A people's government at the provincial level may also have a role to play in the administration of provisions of the Company Law. For example, the merger or division of a joint stock limited company will have to be approved by either a department authorized by the State Council or by a people's government at the provincial level (Article 183). Similarly, Article 77 provides that the people's government at the provincial level may also approve the incorporation of a joint stock limited liability company.

No provision is made in the Company Law for the enforcement of the provisions imposing sanctions, although Chapter 10 of the Law does provide a variety of sanctions which might be applied.

Regulatory responsibilities under the law are allocated to a variety of agencies, further accentuating the problems of enforcement.[77]

3.1   *Mechanisms for the Review of Regulatory Action*

The legal procedures for the review of the decisions of corporate regulatory commissions and departments are in an early stage of development and have generated a lively debate. The 1989 Administrative Procedure Law lays down rules for the review of administrative decisions by the people's courts.[78] In 1990, this was followed by the adoption by the State Council of the Regulations on Administrative Review and the Regulations on Administrative Supervision. Also, for example, Article 227 of the Company Law provides for administrative review of a decision by the Company Registration Authority to refuse registration as a company where the prerequisites for registration have been satisfied. The 'underdevelopment of administrative law' in China and the existence of 'gaps' in this emerging body of administrative law and practice have been pointed to by scholars. Thus, much new legislation only confers powers upon agencies without providing sanctions for the abuse of these powers.[79]

The speed with which legislative reforms in the area of economic law have been introduced has led some to criticize bodies such as the CSRC as acting arbitrarily or even *ultra vires* when securities regulations are issued. Thus, Professor Fang argues that 'the abuse of administrative powers that is impeding China's smooth and stable transition from a planned to a market economy constitutes the most serious problem [needing solution]'.[80] He adds that under the Administrative Procedure Law it is not possible for the victim of arbitrary administrative action to challenge the rationality or constitutionality of an administrative enactment which is generally applied and that 'the court can review only whether an administrative decision against a plaintiff is inconsistent with the relevant administrative statute, which, in all probability, was drafted by the defendant itself'.[81] Therefore, Fang calls for the introduction of judicial review of the legality of administrative rules and procedures.

In contrast, Professor Gao Xiqing, the former Chief Counsel for the CSRC, takes issue with Fang's criticisms. Gao acknowledges that the:

> CSRC was established as the administrative, supervisory, and enforcement arm of the SCSPC. The CSRC does not have administrative status in name due to the urgent need for a regulatory body at the time of its formulation...The current labelling of the CSRC is only that, a label. In fact, the CSRC is in every other respect an administrative body.[82]

However, Professor Gao argues that the Chinese courts do have the authority to overturn any decisions made by the CSRC and have done so from time to time.[83] However, bodies such as the CSRC are clearly still evolving.

In addition to administrative review, the Company Law provides for the imposition of administrative sanctions. Thus, administrative penalties are provided for under Article 223 where the Company Registration Authority is forced by a higher authority to register a company which fails to meet the legal requirements for registration. Administrative sanctions are also provided for by Article 213 where state-owned assets are converted into shares at a depressed value.

4 Types of Companies and their Powers under the Company Law

4.1 The Limited Liability Company and the Joint Stock Company

China's Company Law provides for the establishment of two main company forms: the limited liability company and the joint stock limited company. The principal differences between these two forms is to be found:

- in the number of members that each may have (the limited liability company is limited to 50 members, whereas the membership of the joint stock limited company does not have an upper limit: see Article 20);
- the limits imposed on the transfer of shares in limited liability companies (by Article 35); and
- the prohibition on raising funds from the general public which is imposed on limited liability companies.

The minimum capital requirements and the management structures of these two types of company are also different. However, both company forms enjoy limited liability whereby the liability of shareholders is limited to the amount which has been subscribed by each shareholder.[84]

Each of these two basic company forms is divided into two types of company, according to whether they are wholly state-owned or listed. The four types of company which are therefore provided for in the Company Law are as follows:

- limited liability companies (which have smaller capital requirements, simpler governance structures and less readily transferable shares);

- wholly state-owned companies (which are limited liability companies with a single shareholder and simpler governance structures);[85]
- joint stock limited companies (which are larger enterprises whose shares are more readily transferable); and
- listed companies (which are joint stock limited companies which are authorized to list and trade their shares on a stock exchange).[86]

It is also possible to convert a company from one type of company to another; for example, Articles 98–100 provide for the conversion of a limited liability company into a joint stock limited company.

4.1.1 Scope of business   Companies formed under the Company Law must specify the scope of their business in their articles of association (Article 22(2) and Article 79(2)). Presumably, this is to be interpreted as introducing an *ultra vires* doctrine into Chinese Company Law. However, Article 11 states that the articles of association are binding upon a company, its shareholders, directors, supervisors and managers. Although Article 11 requires companies to 'engage in business activities within their registered scope of business', this scope of business clause in a company's articles may be changed by resort to the usual procedures for the amendment of the articles. Such a change must be registered with the CRA. Additional laws and regulations may impose further restrictions where the company's business is in an area which requires special approval. Although no specific sanctions are imposed upon companies for failing to strictly comply with their scope of business clause, action may be brought by a relevant authority as Article 14 provides that the 'legitimate rights and interests of companies shall be protected by the law and shall be inviolate'.

4.1.2 Powers   Turning to some of the rights of a company as provided for in the 1993 Company Law, it may be noted that the company as a legal person has the right to the control of the entire property which is based upon the capital contributions made by its shareholders (Article 4). In the case of larger wholly state-owned companies, these may be authorized to exercise the rights of asset owners (Article 72). The powers and functions of the company can be examined by reference to the powers of the various organs of the company, such as the general meeting of shareholders, the board of directors, the company's manager and the supervisory board.

4.1.3 The shareholders' meeting   If we begin with the powers of the shareholders' meeting, these are set out in Articles 38 and 103. These powers include the election and removal of directors and the setting of the remuneration of directors; the power to decide upon the business policy and investment plan of the company; the right to approve the annual budget plan of the company; the power to examine and approve plans for a profit distribution or a distribution of dividends or an increase or decrease of the company's registered capital; the shareholders' meeting also has the power to amend the company's articles provided that the amendment has the support of two-thirds of those with voting rights (Articles 40 and 107).[87] However, the shareholders' general meeting of a joint stock limited company must not remove a director without reason (Article 115). In the case of a limited liability company, Article 47 provides that the shareholders' meeting 'may not unwarrantedly dismiss a director prior to the expiration of his term of office'.

The limited liability company shareholders' meeting also has the power to approve the assignment of a shareholder's capital contribution to another person (Article 38(10)). In contrast, in a joint stock limited company, the shareholders' meeting does not have this power as shares are freely transferable. However, a wholly state-owned company is not required to have a shareholders' meeting, although its board of directors is authorized to exercise some of the powers and functions of the shareholders' meeting (Article 66).

4.1.4 The board of directors The powers of the board of directors are set out in Article 46, in the case of a limited liability company, and in Article 112, in the case of a joint stock limited company. The powers of the boards of each type of company are in similar terms and include: the convening of shareholders' meetings; the implementation of resolutions of shareholders' meetings; deciding on the company's business and investment plan; the formulation of the company's annual budget and final accounts, plans for the distribution of profits or for dealing with losses, plans for the increase or reduction of capital, and plans for the merger, reconstruction or dissolution of the company; the establishment of the company's internal management organs; the appointment and dismissal of the company's manager and the remuneration of the manager and deputy managers; and, finally, the formulation of the company's basic management system.

However, it should be noted that in small scale limited liability companies with a small number of shareholders, these need not have a board of directors and may instead merely have an executive director who may also be the company's manager; that person will also be the company's legal representative (Article 51). In the case of a joint stock limited liability company, the chairman of the board will be the company's legal representative (Article 113). The board of directors of a joint stock limited company must have between five and 19 members; whereas a larger limited liability company must have a board of between three and 13 members (Articles 112 and 45 respectively). The term of office of a director must be stipulated by the articles and may not exceed three years (Articles 47 and 115).

4.1.5   The manager   The functions and powers of the manager of each type of company are set out in Articles 50 and 119 of the Company Law. These are similar and are as follows: responsibility for the company's production, operation and management; the implementation of the resolutions of the board; the organization and implementation of the company's annual business and investment plans; the drafting of plans for the establishment of the internal management structures of the company and the company's basic management system; the formulation of specific internal rules and regulations for the company; the appointment and dismissal of deputy managers and other management personnel and the appointment and dismissal of the company's chief financial officer; and, finally, the exercise of other functions and powers which are set out in the company's articles or which are granted by the board.

4.1.6   The supervisory board   An additional layer of corporate governance is the supervisory board, whose members may also attend meetings of directors as non-voting members. The members of the supervisory board are drawn from representatives of shareholders and employees of the company and the proportion drawn from each of these categories is to be set out in the company's articles of association (Articles 52 and 124). Only larger scale limited liability companies need to have a supervisory board, although no guidance is given in the Law as to what constitutes a larger company; this will presumably be determined by regulations. In the case of smaller companies, they may have one or two supervisors instead of a supervisory board; although a larger company of this type must have at least three supervisors (Article 52). The supervisory board of a joint stock limited company must have at least three members (Article 124).

The functions and powers of the supervisory board of each type of company are set out in Articles 54 and 126. These are as follows: the examination of the company's financial affairs; the supervision of the conduct of the directors and the company's manager; the power to demand that the directors and the manager correct any damage which has occurred to the company through their conduct; proposing that an interim meeting of shareholders be called; as well as such other functions as are stipulated in the articles. Various restrictions are placed upon those who can serve as supervisors or as members of the supervisory board: Articles 57–59 and 128. For example, directors and managers are excluded from being supervisors or members of the supervisory board.

4.2 Recognition of Foreign Companies in China

Prior to the enactment of the Company Law, joint ventures with foreign companies were common.[88] Existing joint ventures which are governed by earlier laws will not be affected by the Company Law (Article 19). However, Chapter 9 of the Company Law provides a system of the establishment of branches of foreign companies in China. There is a significant amount of state control over foreign investment activity in China.[89] Article 199 permits a company which has been registered in another jurisdiction to establish a branch within China. Before a foreign company's branch can be issued with a business licence by the CRA, the foreign company wishing to set up a branch must first apply to the relevant authority and submit relevant documentation, such as its articles of association and certificate of registration. In the past, the MOFTEC has exercised such preliminary approval powers in regard to foreign investment in China.[90]

Once a foreign company has set up a branch in China, it is required to appoint a representative or agent who will take charge of the operations of the branch within China. The State Council may prescribe the minimum amount of operating funds which such a branch office must have to support its operations (Article 201). However, the branch office does not have the status of a legal person in China and the foreign company will be liable for the operations of the company in China (Article 203), and the business activities of the foreign company branch must comply with the laws of China and must 'not harm the social and public interest of China' (Article 204). The Company Law also provides that the 'lawful rights and interests of such branches shall be protected by the laws of China' (Article 204). However, where a foreign company establishes a branch in China without authorization, it will be liable to rectify this or be closed down and it may also be liable to the imposition of a fine of not less than 10 000 yuan or more than 100 000 yuan.

A foreign company may also apply to have its name registered in China. This may be done under Article 29 of the 1991 Provisions on Administration of Enterprise Name Regulation, approved by the State Council and promulgated by the State Administration for Industry and Commerce as the competent authority.[91] If successful, the foreign company will be issued with a Certificate of Enterprise Name Registration.

5   Company Formation

The pre-conditions for the formation of limited liability companies and joint stock limited liability companies have some similarities (see Articles 19 and 73), although the Company Law lays down more detailed provisions for joint stock companies in view of their capacity to issue shares to the general public. Thus, the company must have a minimum number of shareholders (in the case of a limited liability company) or sponsors (in the case of a joint stock company), its share capital must comply with the minimum requirements for that type of company, its articles of association must be formulated by its shareholders or sponsors, the company must have a name and an organizational structure which complies with the requirements for that type of company and the company must have fixed premises.

As we have seen, a limited liability company must have at least two and no more than 50 shareholders, whereas a joint stock company must have at least five sponsors (Articles 20 and 75). The minimum registered capital of a limited liability company will vary between 100 000 yuan and 500 000 yuan, depending on the type of business that it proposes to conduct: Article 23. In contrast, the minimum registered capital of a joint stock company is ten million yuan, although in the case of a listed company, this minimum amount will be 50 million yuan (Articles 78 and 152). The contents of the articles of association of each type of company are set out in the Law (Articles 22 and 79). The articles of a limited company must contain conditions for the transfer of the capital contributions made by shareholders.

A joint stock company may be incorporated in one of two ways: by sponsorship or by share offer. Incorporation by way of sponsorship requires the sponsors to subscribe for all shares which are to be issued in the company, whereas with incorporation by way of share offer, sponsors would only subscribe for a proportion of the shares with the remaining shares being offered to the general public (Article 74). Otherwise, the articles must specify additional matters, such as the name and domicile of the company, its scope of business, the names and titles of its shareholders and/or sponsors, the rights and obligations of shareholders, the name of the company's legal representative and its registered capital. The articles of a joint stock company must also set out the methods of incorporation, the total number of shares to be issued, the methods for the distribution of the company's profits and the methods by which notices and announcements are to be issued to members.

Where shares are to be issued by a limited liability company, the Company Law lays down procedures for the issue to the shareholders of capital contribution certificates and for capital verification.

Capital contribution certificates must contain certain prescribed information, such as the name of the company, its date of registration, its registered capital and the name of the shareholder (Article 30). Joint stock companies will issue shares instead of capital contribution certificates. Verification is especially important where a capital contribution is not made in cash, but is made in kind (see Articles 24 and 80). The valuation of such non-cash contributions must be made in accordance with the relevant valuation rules and regulations.

Where shares are to be issued to the general public, the sponsor of a joint stock company must subscribe for at least 35 per cent of the total shares to be issued (Article 83). Before shares can be offered to the public, the sponsors are required to prepare a prospectus and an application to make a share offer and submit these and other documents for approval to the department of security administration in the State Council (Article 84). The documents which must be submitted include: approved documents for the incorporation of the company, the company's articles of association, the company's business forecast, the names and titles of the sponsors and the number of shares to be subscribed by them, the forms of capital verification and a capital verification certificate, the name and address of the bank which is to accept the subscription monies on behalf of the company and the name of the selling agencies, related agreements and the prospectus.

The prospectus must comply with the requirements of Article 87 and specify the number of shares which have been subscribed for by the sponsors, it must also state the face value of the shares and the issue price of each share, the total number of shares to be issued, the rights and obligations of subscribers and the term of the share offer. The prospectus must also include a statement to the effect that the subscribers may withdraw their share subscriptions if the share offer is not fully subscribed within the time limit which has been set. The information required by Article 87 is also to be set out in the subscription forms (Article 88). Shares being issued by a company are to be distributed by a securities agency which has been established under the law and subscription monies will be collected by a bank which has agreed to collect subscription monies on behalf of the company (Articles 89 and 90). Funds received by way of a share subscription must then be verified by a statutory capital verification institution which will then produce a verification certificate.

After the issue of the capital verification certificate, the sponsors of a joint stock limited company have 30 days in which to convene the inaugural meeting of the subscribers (Article 91). The requirements for the inaugural meeting are set out in Article 92: the meeting must examine the sponsor's report, adopt the company's articles of association, elect members of the board of directors and the supervisory board, examine and verify the expenses which have been incurred during the incorporation process, and verify the valuation of the property used by the sponsors to pay for their subscription. The inaugural meeting may also resolve not to incorporate the company in the event of a change in the business operation conditions or due to *force majeure* (Article 92). Thereafter, the board of directors have 30 days in which to submit relevant documents to the CRA. These documents include the minutes of the inaugural meeting, the capital verification certificate, the articles of association, the financial audit report, the names and addresses of the directors and members of the supervisory board and the name and address of the company's legal representative (Article 94). The CRA then has 30 days in which to make a decision regarding the registration of the company (Article 95).

5.1   The Corporate Constitution

Reference has been made above to the content requirements for the articles of association which are laid down in Article 22 and 79, respectively, of the Company Law. Companies seeking listing outside the PRC must adopt articles of association which have been prescribed by the Securities Office of the State Council.[92] The shareholders' meeting is empowered to amend the company's articles of association (Articles 38(12) and 103(11)). The articles may normally be amended by the shareholders' general meeting provided that the amendment has the support of the holders of at least two-thirds of the shares (in the case of a limited liability company: Article 40) or two-thirds of those present with the power to vote (in the case of a joint stock company: Article 107).

5.2   Restrictions on the Use of Certain Names

The Company Law as such does not place any restrictions upon the use of particular company names, apart from requiring the inclusion of the words 'limited liability company' or 'joint stock limited company' in the name of the company, as appropriate (Article 9). This is a matter provided for by regulations. In 1991 the Provisions on Administration of Enterprise Name Regulation were approved by the State Council and promulgated by the State Administration for Industry and Commerce as the competent authority.[93] These provisions apply to all enterprise persons. Also, Article 224 provides penalties for the unlawful use by an unregistered company of the phrases 'limited liability company' or 'joint stock limited company' and provides for rectification orders or banning as well as the imposition of fines of not less that 10 000 yuan or more than 100 000 yuan.

Article 9 of the 1991 Provisions states that enterprise names must not contain contents which are detrimental to the state and to the public interest, they must not be names which cause fraud or misunderstanding on the part of the public; also prohibited are the use of names of foreign countries and international organizations, the names of political parties, government or army departments, or names which are prohibited by laws or administrative regulations. Application must be made for the use in the enterprise name of the words '*Zhongguo*' or '*Zhonghua*' (both meaning China) or '*Guoji*' (meaning international). If it approves of the name, the State Administration for Industry and Commerce will issue a Certificate of Enterprise Name Registration within ten days of receiving the application and all relevant supporting material. Where the registered name of an enterprise is used without authority by another person, compensation may be payable for any loss incurred by the registered holder of the name and a fine of up to 50 000 yuan may be imposed (Article 27 of the Enterprise Name Provisions).

5.3 Membership and Share Capital Requirements of Companies

Different membership and capital requirements apply to limited liability companies and to joint stock limited companies. As we have seen, a limited liability company must have no less than two and not more than 50 members or shareholders (Article 20). However, a wholly state-owned limited liability company will only have a single owner, although it does not have shareholders as such (Article 66). No upper limit on membership is placed upon joint stock limited companies. Where the state is a shareholder, it is unclear how the state's rights as a shareholder will be exercised or which institution will hold these shares upon behalf of the state.[94] However, shares may be held in a company by another company registered under the Company Law, as provided for by Article 12.

Turning to the capital requirements for both types of companies, as we have seen, these matters are dealt with differently given the variations between each type of company. In the case of a limited liability company, the amount of its registered capital will vary depending upon the scope of its business (Article 23). Thus:

- where a company is primarily engaged in production, it must have a registered capital of at least RMB 500 000 yuan;
- where a company is primarily engaged in commodity wholesale activity, it must have a registered capital of at least RMB 500 000 yuan;
- where a company is primarily engaged in commercial retailing, it must have a registered capital of at least RMB 300 000 yuan;

and
- where a company is primarily engaged in science and technology development, consultancy or services, it must have a registered capital of at least RMB 100 000 yuan.

However, if it is considered that the minimum capital requirements for a particular trade or business need to be higher than the above limits, this higher figure may be stipulated by law or by administrative rules and regulations. In the case of an unlisted joint stock company, Article 78 provides that it must have a minimum registered capital of RMB ten million yuan, although a higher minimum amount may be stipulated by law or by administrative rules and regulations. At least half of the sponsors of a joint stock limited company must be domiciled in the PRC (Article 75).

A joint stock company may also offer its shares outside the PRC, provided that it obtains the approval of the State Council's department of security administration (Article 85).

In the case of a listed joint stock limited company, it must have a registered share capital of at least 50 million yuan and must have at least 1 000 shareholders each holding shares with a face value of at least 1 000 yuan; such a company must have issued at least 25 per cent of its shares to the general public.

5.4   Company Registers

The limited liability company is required to prepare a register of shareholders which contains the names and addresses of the shareholders, the amounts of capital contributed by each shareholder and the serial number of the capital contribution certificates given to shareholders (Article 31).

In the case of the joint stock limited company, Article 101 requires that it maintain various documents at its company office; these comprise the articles of association, a register of shareholders, the minutes of the shareholders' general meetings and the financial and accounting statements of the company. The minutes of meetings of shareholders are to be kept together with the roster of the signatures of the shareholders who have attended the meeting (Article 109). The shareholders have the right to examine the articles of association of the company, the minutes of the shareholders' general meetings and the financial and accounting statements (Article 110).

Where a company issues bonds, it is required by Article 169 of the Company Law to keep the counterfoils of the debentures which specify the name and address of the debenture holder, the date on which the holder acquired the debenture, the total amount of the debentures, their par value, the interest rate payable under the debenture and the method and time for repayment. The date of issue of the debentures must also be recorded.

The company must also keep statutory account books, as required by Article 175 of the Company Law. It must not keep any account books in addition to these books (Article 181).

5.5   Company Registered Office

A limited liability company must have a domicile. Like the company name, the company's domicile must be stated in its articles of association (Article 22). As we have seen, the articles must be lodged with the CRA (Article 27). Article 10 provides that the domicile of a company shall be the place where its main administrative organization is located. Similarly, the articles of a joint stock limited company must set out the domicile of the company (Article 79). The articles must be lodged with the department of security administration of the State Council where the company proposes to offer shares to the general public (Article 84). Where a joint stock company is incorporated by way of sponsorship, the articles of association must be lodged with the CRA (Article 82). In any event, the directors must submit a copy of the articles to the CRA within 30 days of the inaugural meeting of the company (Article 94).

6   The Internal Administration of Companies

In addition to the provisions of the Company Law, the articles of association will lay down some of the rules for the internal governance of companies. For example, Article 39 of the Company Law provides that the rules governing deliberations and voting procedures for shareholders' meetings are to be stipulated by the articles, except in so far as the Law has already done so. The articles will also lay down the procedures to be followed by the supervisory board (Article 127). The internal structure of companies has been discussed above when reference was made to the shareholders' meeting, the board of directors, the manager and the supervisory board. The directors and the company's manager are required to comply with the terms of the articles of association (Article 59).

Shareholders' meetings of a limited liability company are either regular meetings or interim meetings. The general meeting of shareholders of a joint stock company must be presided over by the chairman of the board of directors (Article 105). Similar provisions apply to limited liability companies which have set up a board of directors (Article 43). The shareholders' meetings of a limited liability company may appoint directors and members of the supervisory board as well as amend the articles (Articles 38 and 103). It is the task of directors to decide on the establishment of the company's internal management organs (Articles 46(8) and 112(8)).

Although the management of a company is usually the province of the board of directors and its manager or managers, the Company Law does give the general meeting certain management-like powers, such as the power to decide on the business policy and investment plan of the company (Articles 38 and 103). However, the frequency with which a joint stock limited company's members will meet can be as infrequent as once a year, as interim shareholders' meetings need not be convened except in certain specified unusual circumstances (Article 104; see also Article 43). However, the shareholders' meeting may be convened when a request to do so is made by one-third or more of the directors or supervisors or by one-quarter or more of the holders of voting rights in the company: Article 43. In the case of a joint stock limited company, shareholders holding 10 per cent or more of the company's shares may request the holding of a shareholders' general meeting; the board may also call such a meeting if it deems it necessary to do so (Article 104).

Finally, the supervisory board also plays a role in the internal administration of a company. The supervisors are empowered to attend meetings of the board of directors as non-voting members. In a limited liability company, Article 54 provides that the supervisory board shall exercise the following functions and powers:

- examining the financial affairs of the company;
- supervising the acts of the directors and of the manager;
- requiring that directors and the manager rectify any damage which their actions may have caused the company;
- proposing that an interim shareholders' meeting be called; and
- such other functions as may be stipulated by the company's articles.

Similar duties and powers are allocated to the supervisory board of a joint stock limited company by Article 126 of the Company Law. Certain persons are disqualified from serving as members of the supervisory board, including the company's directors, its manager and personnel who are responsible for the company's financial affairs (Articles 52 and 124).

6.1   *The Duties, Powers and Responsibilities of Officers*

The board of directors plays an important part in corporate governance. However, the Company Law only lays down limited rules regarding the duties and responsibilities of directors and other officers. This is a major omission given the importance of fiduciary duties of directors under Western company laws.[95] The monitoring of the actions of the board of directors and those of the manager is the task of the shareholders' meeting and of the supervisory board. Self-dealing and conflict of interest are fundamental problems in this area. The Company Law does seek to deal with some of these 'agency' problems through a variety of mechanisms, however, before looking at these, it may be useful to examine the powers and responsibilities of the directors and the manager. Articles 46 and 112 deal with these matters in similar terms. The statutory functions and powers of the board of directors are as follows:

- responsibility for the convening of shareholders' meetings and reporting to the meetings of shareholders;
- implementation of the resolutions passed at the shareholders' meeting;
- deciding on the company's business and investment plans (this needs to be done in collaboration with the shareholders' meeting);
- the formulation of the company's annual financial budget plan and the company's final accounts;
- the formulation of plans by the company for the distribution of profits and for the handling of losses;
- the formulation of plans for increasing or reducing the company's registered capital;
- the formulation of plans for the merger, reorganization or dissolution of the company;
- making decisions on the establishment of the internal organs of the company;
- responsibility for the appointment and dismissal of the company's manager; and
- responsibility for the formulation of the company's basic management system.

A manager who is responsible to the board of directors is required to be appointed by both a limited liability company (Article 50) and a joint stock limited company (Article 119), although a small limited liability company may have an executive director instead of a board of directors and that executive director may concurrently serve as the company's manager (Article 51). However, in the case of a joint stock limited company, the manager may be one of the directors of the company (Article 120). As with members of the supervisory board, the manager is required to attend the meetings of the board of directors, but does not have a vote at such meetings. The powers and functions of the company manager are as follows:

- responsibility for the production, operation and management of the company and the implementation of the resolutions of the board of directors;
- responsibility for organizing the implementation of the company's annual business and investment plans;
- responsibility for the drafting of plans for the establishment of the company's internal management organs;
- responsibility for formulating the company's basic management system;
- the formulation of specific rules and regulations for the company;
- the formulation of proposals (which are to be put to the board of directors) for the appointment and dismissal of deputy managers and persons who will be responsible for the company's financial affairs;
- responsibility for the appointment and dismissal of management personnel, other than those who are to be appointed or dismissed by the board of directors; and
- the performance of such other powers and functions as are provided for in the company's articles of association and as are authorized by the directors.

The control of the misappropriation of enterprise assets by managers and directors is also a central concern in company law. Simon has noted that enterprise reform in China has in the past 'occasioned the looting of state assets by ex-cadres'.[96] Professor Fang also points to the long-standing conflict of interest problems which have emerged where government officials have also been involved in business enterprises.[97]

The Company Law seeks to deal with some of the conflict of interest problems which face directors and corporate managers. For example, Article 58 provides that government officials may not concurrently serve as directors, supervisors or managers of companies; this provision applies to both limited liability companies and to joint stock limited companies (see Articles 123 and 128, respectively). However, this does not prevent a government official being nominated to a board; it only prevents simultaneous service as a government official and as a company board member or manager.[98]

The most general statement of the duties of officers found in the Company Law is set out in Article 59, although Articles 60–62 also impose further specific duties on directors, managers and supervisors. Thus, Article 59 requires that the directors and managers 'faithfully perform their duties' and that they 'maintain the interests of the company' and that they do not 'take advantage of their position, functions and powers in the company to seek personal gain'.

Similarly, Article 123 states that directors and managers of joint stock limited companies 'shall abide by the articles of association of the company, faithfully perform their duties and protect the interests of the company, and shall not use their positions, functions and powers in the company to seek personal gain'. More specifically, Article 59 also prohibits directors and managers from accepting bribes or other unlawful income or from misappropriating company property.

The prohibition in Article 59 on the misappropriation of company property is backed up by Article 60, which proscribes the misappropriation of company funds or the lending of company funds by directors. The latter section also proscribes the depositing of company funds into personal accounts of directors or into the personal accounts of other persons. Company assets are also not to be used as security for the personal debts of the company's shareholders or of other individuals.

A number of conflict of interest rules are set out in Article 61, which prohibits a director from directly or indirectly operating a business which is in the same area as that of the business of the company in which they are serving as a director or manager. Where a director breaches the Company Law in this way, Article 215 creates what is in effect a duty to account for profits by providing that the income derived from this competing business is to belong to the company.

Except as provided for in the company's articles or as approved by the shareholders' meeting, Article 61 also prohibits a director from entering into contracts or from conducting transactions with the company upon whose board the director sits. Finally, Article 62 imposes a duty of confidentiality upon directors, supervisors and managers. This duty of secrecy is subject to provisions of the law and approval by the shareholders' meeting.

A director may be removed from office by the shareholders' meeting, although this can only occur if the removal is warranted (Article 47) or if there is reason to do so (Article 115). Presumably, a breach of one of the above prohibitions will be sufficient cause for the removal of a director by the shareholders' meeting.

Various liability provisions also apply to misconduct or illegality upon the part of directors, supervisors or managers. For example, Article 63 provides that such officers will be liable to compensate the company if, in the performance of their duties, they cause damage to the company through violating the company's articles of association, laws, administrative rules or regulations. To some degree, codes of ethics or professional conduct apply to companies in relation to the way that they carry on their business (Article 14). However, these codes of ethics or professional ethics do not seem to apply specifically to directors and managers.

A number of further sanctions are imposed by Article 214 for breaches of the duties of a director, supervisor or manager. These provisions basically impose a duty to account to the company for the funds received or profits made. First, where a director, supervisor or manager accepts bribes, makes illegal gains or takes advantage of his or her position, the illegal gains will belong to the company. Where criminal behaviour has occurred, this is to be investigated in accordance with the law. Second, Article 214 provides that where a director or manager misappropriates company funds, he or she will be ordered to return these funds and any gains derived therefrom to the company. Once again, criminal sanctions may also be available. Third, Article 214 provides that where company assets are used as a guarantee for the personal debts of a shareholder of the company or some other person, a liability to pay compensation will arise and any gains derived from this misuse of company property will belong to the company.

6.2   Meeting Procedures

Procedures are laid down in the Company Law and in the articles of association for meetings of shareholders, for meetings of the board of directors and meetings of the supervisory board. The inaugural meeting of the company is also provided for (Articles 92–94). Thus, Article 39 provides that decisions of the shareholders' meeting of a limited liability company regarding an increase or decrease of the company's registered capital, the division, merger or transformation of the company, or its dissolution, must receive the support of two-thirds of the shareholders with voting rights. Similar requirements exist in relation to joint stock limited companies (Article 106). A two-thirds majority of shareholders present at a shareholders' meeting is required before an amendment can be made to the articles (Article 107).

Shareholders attending the shareholders' general meeting have one vote for each share that is held by them. This vote may be exercised by a proxy (Articles 106 and 108). Resolutions passed at a shareholders' general meeting must be minuted and authenticated by the directors (Article 109).

The shareholders' general meeting will usually be convened only once a year, although an interim meeting may be convened within two months of any of a number of circumstances occuring; such as the decline in the number of directors to less than the number required by law or to less than two-thirds of those required by the articles of the company; the shareholders' meeting must also be called if the directors or the supervisory board deem that it is necessary to hold an interim meeting or if 10 per cent or more of the company's shareholders request that such a meeting be held (Article 104). A general meeting of shareholders is to be presided over by the chairman of the board, or by the vice-chairman or another director if the chairman is unable to preside (Article 105).

In relation to meetings of the board of directors, Article 117 provides that the quorum for a meeting of the directors of a joint stock limited company is one-half of all the directors of the company; the board must comprise between five and 19 members (Article 112). The chairman of the board of directors of a joint stock limited company is given various functions by Article 114, including the function of presiding over the shareholders' general meeting and the examination of the implementation of resolutions of directors' meetings. The board of directors' meetings of a joint stock limited company must be held at least twice a year, with Article 116 requiring that directors be notified of these meetings at least ten days before the date of the meeting; the same period of notice is required for meetings of the board of a limited liability company (Article 49). In a limited liability company, meetings of the board are to be presided over by the chairman, or in his absence, by the vice-chairman or by a director designated by the chairman (Article 48).

Where a director is unable to attend a board meeting, that director may give written authority to another director to attend on his behalf. Minutes of the directors' meetings must be kept and these must be signed by the directors and clerks present at that meeting (Article 118). Where it is necessary to do so, the board of directors of a joint stock limited company may authorize its chairman to perform some of its functions or powers when the board is not meeting: Article 120. The procedures to be adopted by the board of directors may be set out in the articles of association of the company (Article 49).

Some rules are also laid down for the meetings of the supervisory board of a limited liability company (Articles 53 and 54) and a joint stock limited company (Articles 124–128). The articles of association will set out the procedures to be adopted at meetings of the supervisory board (Article 127).

6.3 Audit and Accounting Rules

Chapter 6 of the Company Law deals with the financial affairs and accounts of companies. Companies are required to establish their financial and accounting system in accordance with the law, administrative rules and regulations. Other laws have been passed which deal with the regulation of accountants[99] and with auditing practice.[100] At the end of each financial year, the financial accounts of companies registered under the Company Law must include a balance sheet, a profit and loss statement, a statement regarding any

changes in the company's financial position, a statement which explains the financial position of the company and a statement regarding
the distribution of profits (Article 175). A copy of the company's
financial and accounting report must be sent to each shareholder of a
limited liability company; in the case of a joint stock limited company, these financial records must be available for inspection 20 days
before the convening of the annual general meeting of shareholders.

A company is required to allocate 10 per cent of its after-tax profits
to a statutory common reserve fund and a further 5 per cent to a
statutory common welfare fund (Article 177). The statutory common
welfare fund is to be used for the collective welfare of the company's
staff and workers (Article 180), and the statutory common reserve
fund is to be used to make up for any losses of the company, to
expand production of the company or to increase the company's
capital by issuing new shares (Article 179). This emphasis on rein-
vestment is characteristic of enterprise laws in China, although it is
weaker in the Company Law than in other such laws.[101] Once any
losses have been made up and allocations have been made to the
common reserve fund and the common welfare fund, the company
may distribute the remaining profits to its shareholders (Article 177).

6.4   Shareholder Protection Rules

The Company Law does not have minority shareholder protection
rules as such, although shareholders are able to petition for the calling of an interim meeting of shareholders. Shareholders are also able
to bring matters to the attention of the supervisory board or the
supervisors. As the powers of the supervisory board are somewhat
limited (Articles 54 and 126), this is a poor mechanism for protecting
the interests of shareholders, especially minority shareholders. Also,
as Fang has observed, in China there are no provisions for the filing
of a derivative suit, either under the Civil Procedure Law or under
the new Company Law.[102] The common welfare fund which is provided for in Article 177 of the Law is available to provide for
employees of the company, but not in their capacity as shareholders.[103] The Company Law does pay particular regard to the conditions
of workers and staff (Article 15). However, shareholders are given a
wider range of powers, such as through the shareholders' meetings
(Articles 38 and 103) than is usual under other bodies of company
law.

6.5   Corporate Financial Transactions

As we have seen, joint stock limited companies may raise additional
capital through the issue of a prospectus. The issue of bonds by a

joint stock limited company or by a limited liability company must be authorized by a company's board of directors and must be part of a plan which has been approved by the meeting of shareholders (Article 163). The issue of bonds by a state-owned company must be authorized by the state-authorized investment institution or by a department which has been authorized by the state.

More detailed rules apply where such capital raising is to occur abroad through the listing of shares on a foreign exchange. Provision is also made in Chapter 5 of the Company Law for the issue of company bonds or debt securities, provided that various conditions (Article 161) are satisfied. These conditions relate to such matters as the rate of interest and the value of bonds which may be issued. Company bonds may be issued by a limited liability company or by a joint stock company and are transferable (Article 170). With the agreement of shareholders at a general meeting, convertible company bonds may be issued by the company (Article 172).

7   The External Administration of Companies

Chapter 8 of the Company Law deals with the bankruptcy, dissolution and liquidation of companies. Other bankruptcy-related rules may be found in the 1986 Enterprise Bankruptcy Law (which applies only to state-owned enterprises) and in Chapter 19 of the 1991 Civil Procedure Law.[104] Also of relevance in regard to the interpretation of the 1986 Enterprise Bankruptcy Law is the Opinion of the Supreme People's Court on the Law of the People's Republic of China On Enterprise Bankruptcy (For Trial Implementation) 1986, handed down by the court on 7 November 1991. A more comprehensive bankruptcy law is currently being drafted and is planned to be approved by 2000.

8   Takeover Rules

The Company Law also provides various rules for the merger and division of companies (Articles 182–188). Such a merger or division requires the approval of the shareholders' meeting. The merger or division of a joint stock limited company also requires the further approval of the department authorized by the State Council or by a people's provincial government (Article 193). The merger of a company must occur in one of two ways: by 'absorption' into another entity or by 'new establishment' of another entity into which the company is to be merged. Various disclosure and notice requirements need to be satisfied before a merger can proceed by way of either of these methods (Article 184).

9 An Introduction to Securities Regulation in China

Articles 151–158 of the Company Law deal with the operations of listed companies. These are highly regulated and the listing and trading of shares in a joint stock limited company needs the approval of the State Council or the department of securities administration (Article 151). The discussion of securities regulation in this section cannot do more than to briefly refer to this rapidly growing area of law and practice.[105]

China has yet to pass a comprehensive national securities markets law. In the meantime, temporary rules drafted by the CSRC have served as the basis for regulation in this area. The State Council's Provisional Ordinance on Managing the Issuing and Trading of Shares was issued in 1993. As Dowdle notes, this provisional ordinance:

> establishes the general structure of China's securities market, setting out fairly comprehensive provisions governing, among other things, the issuing and trading of shares, the acquisition of listed companies, the storage of share certificates, the clearing of accounts, transfer of ownership, public announcements by listed companies, and the punishment of illegal securities activities.[106]

The Provisional Ordinance has been supplemented by other regulations issued by the CSRC and other agencies, such as the Provisional Measures Prohibiting Securities Fraud, the Special Regulations on Listing and Issuing Shares Abroad by Companies Limited by Shares and the Mandatory Provisions for Companies Listed Abroad.

However, various securities rules were developed by the Shanghai and Shenzhen stock exchanges and their local municipal governments. As many of these rules were developed before the creation of the CSRC, these local rules have served as models for national rules subsequently developed by the CSRC.[107] The existence of different sources of authority in regard to securities matters created uncertainty in regard to jurisdictional authority, with the CSRC competing for authority against other national agencies as well as against regional governments and stock exchanges. One effect of this confusion was to further undermine the effectiveness of securities law enforcement in China. At the national level, for example, enforcement efforts by the CSRC must be undertaken in cooperation with the Ministry of Justice. Such joint responsibility also exists between the CSRC and the People's Bank of China.[108] Other agencies with responsibility for aspects of the securities area include the State Economy and Trade Commission and the Commission for the Restructuring of the Economic System. However, the CSRC is becoming increasingly powerful.[109]

Many commentators have pointed to the poor enforcement record of the CSRC in securities law matters. This problem is enhanced by the existence of vague legal concepts which lead to the lack of a clear view of what market manipulation will involve. There have been insider trading and market manipulation scandals on the Shanghai and Shenzhen stock exchanges, but the discussion of these is outside the scope of this chapter.

10 Offences

Chapter 10 (Articles 206–228) of the Company Law contains a number of liability provisions and sets out various penalties which will apply where a breach of the Law has been proved. Many of these have already been referred to above, especially in relation to issues of corporate governance. Other legislation will also be relevant in regard to criminal law breaches which may arise out of misconduct under the Company Law.

11 Conclusions

The 1993 Company Law of the PRC has significantly enhanced China's rules for the organization of business. These rules represent a major advance on earlier attempts at providing a suitable vehicle for business enterprise in China. The process of developing company law with 'Chinese characteristics' for such a diverse economy as that of China is likely to lead to further reform of China's company law rules and regulations over the next few years. It is clear that, although the 1993 Law is a major advance, it is a transitional statute in that it will pave the way for a more thorough-going piece of legislation in the future. This will obviously be based on the experience gained in the application or enforcement of this Law.

The lack of any real body of case-law in China on such matters as the duties of directors will need to be catered for by the enactment of more detailed regulations and legislation. Given the centrality of rules regarding the conduct of directors, this might require the enactment of new legislation or codes of conduct dealing with this area. Another major gap in the legislation is the lack of a single administrative body for the processing of administrative decisions and overseeing this area of law. There are far too many bodies which currently have to make decisions relating to company law matters. Hopefully this will be remedied in the not too distant future. Developing an improved system for the review of administrative or regulatory decisions affecting companies covered by the Company

Law will also be required. Company Law reform will remain an important activity in China as it has been in many Western countries, if only to cope with changing market circumstances.

However, the enactment of the 1993 Company Law reflects a real commitment to rule of law values by the government of the PRC and reflects an independent process of law-making which is much to be admired. Although the law is based on a variety of Western models, it is far removed from the styles of company law-making which have characterized many earlier periods of company law reform in developing countries; in the past, law-makers have often relied on what might be called 'legislation by xerox' or the simple expedient of copying foreign company laws, regardless of their appropriateness to local conditions. Although there is much in the Company Law which is familiar to Western lawyers and business persons, there are many 'Chinese characteristics' in this new legislation and its administration, and the challenge for the Chinese legal system and its companies will be to develop a Chinese company law jurisprudence which enjoys the confidence of the market both in China and abroad.

Notes

*   LLB (Syd), PhD (NSW), SJD (Wisconsin), Professor of Law and Director, National Centre for Corporate Law and Policy Research, University of Canberra, Australia.
**   LLB (Beijing), LLM (Canberra), PhD candidate (UNSW), Research Officer, National Centre for Corporate Law and Policy Research, University of Canberra, Australia; and formerly Section Chief of the Civil Law Department with the Commission for Legislative Affairs, National People's Congress, Beijing, PRC.
1   Redding, S.G. (1993), *The Spirit of Chinese Capitalism*, Berlin: de Gruyter, 121–122.
2   Quoted by Kirby, W.C. (1995), 'China Unincorporated: Company Law and Business Enterprise in Twentieth Century China', *Journal of Asian Studies*, **54**, 43, 50.
3   As note 2, above, 44.
4   As note 2, above, 45. Kirby notes (at 47) that although a Chinese joint stock company, the China Merchants' Steam Navigation Company, was chartered in 1872, it relied on guarantors for its contractual arrangements and did not enjoy limited liability; see further, Lai, C.K. (1993), 'The Qing State and Merchant Enterprises: The China Merchants' Company, 1872–1902,' in J.K. Leonard and J.R. Watts (eds), *To Achieve Security and Wealth: the Qing Imperial State and the Economy*, Ithaca: East Asia Program, Cornell University.
5   Fairbank, J.K. (1992), *China: A New History*, Cambridge, Mass.: Harvard University Press, 185–186; quoted by Kirby, As note 2, above, 46.
6   As note 2, above, 47.
7   As note 2, above, 43–44.
8   As note 7, above.
9   As note 2, above, 51.

10 See generally, Teesdale, J.H. (1932), 'A Short Analysis of the New Chinese Company and Partnership Law', *Journal of Comparative Legislation and International Law*, **14**, 247–254.

11 As note 2, above, 52–53. See generally, Kirby, W.C. (1990), 'Continuity and Change in Modern China: Chinese Economic Planning on the Mainland and in Taiwan, 1943–1958', *Australian Journal of Chinese Affairs*, **24**, 121–142.

12 As note 2, above, 55–56.

13 As note 2, above, 56.

14 Li, F. (1995), 'Legislative Consideration on Company Law, PRC', *China Law*, **1**, 76 at 76.

15 Keith, R.C. (1994), *China's Struggle for the Rule of Law*, New York: Macmillan-St Martins Press; See also, Jianfu, C. (1995), *From Administrative Authorisation to Private Law*, Dordrecht: Martinus Nijhoff.

16 Quoted by Chen, A.H.Y. (1993), *An Introduction to the Legal System of the People's Republic of China*, Singapore: Butterworths Asia, 33.

17 Resolution of the Standing Committee of the National People's Congress Providing an Improved Interpretation of the Law (adopted at the 19th Meeting of the Standing Committee of the Fifth National People's Congress, 10 June 1981).

18 Lubman, S. (1995), 'Introduction: The Future of Chinese Law', *The China Quarterly*, **141**, 1.

19 As note 18, above, 2.

20 See, for example, the agreement to the so-called Beijing declaration of judicial independence; see further, Malcolm, D. (1996), 'The Beijing Statement of Principles of the Independence of the Judiciary in the Lawasia Region', *The Australian Law Journal*, **70**, 299.

21 See generally Du, X. and L. Zhang (1990), *China's Legal System: A General Survey*, Beijing: New World Press, 79.

22 Chen, A.H.Y. (1993), *An Introduction to the Legal System of the People's Republic of China*, Singapore: Butterworths Asia, 49.

23 Dicks, A.R. (1995), 'Compartmentalized Law and Judicial Restraint: An Inductive View of Some Jurisdictional Barriers to Reform', *The China Quarterly*, **141**, 82 at 94.

24 As note 18, above. See further, Jones, W.C. (ed.) (1989), *Basic Principles of the Civil Law in China*, Armonk, NY: ME Sharpe; Jones points out (p. xvi) that the Chinese General Principles of Civil Law are based on the German Civil Code, which had itself influenced the Civil Code which now operates in Taiwan.

25 As note 18, above, 6–7.

26 See, for example, Alford, W.P. (1995), 'Tasselled Loafers for Barefoot Lawyers: Transformation and Tension in the World of Chinese Legal Workers', *The China Quarterly*, **141**, 22; Gelatt, T. (1991), 'Lawyers in China: the past decade and beyond', *New York University Journal of International Law and Politics*, **23**, 751; Zheng, H. (1988), 'The evolving role of lawyers and legal practice in China', *American Journal of Comparative Law*, **36**, 473.

27 See generally, Li, V. (1978), *Law without Lawyers*, Stanford: Stanford Alumni Association; and Bodde, D. and Morris, C. (1967), *Law in Imperial China*, Cambridge, MA: Harvard University Press.

28 Du, X. and L. Zhang (1990), *China's Legal System: A General Survey*, Beijing: New World Press, 81.

29 As note 22, above, 107–108.

30 See generally, Keller, P. (1989), 'Legislation in the People's Republic of China', *University of British Columbia Law Review*, **23**, 653.

31 Resolution Regarding the Question of the Interpretation of Laws, adopted by the 17th Session of the Standing Committee of the First National People's

Congress, 23 June 1955; The Interpretation Resolution 1955 was replaced by the Interpretation Resolution 1981; See further: Dicks, A.R. (1995), 'Compartmentalized Law and Judicial Restraint: An Inductive View of Some Jurisdictional Barriers to Reform', *The China Quarterly*, **141**, 82, 87–90.

32   Resolution of the Standing Committee of the National People's Congress Providing an Improved Interpretation of the Law, adopted at the 19th Meeting of the Standing Committee of the Fifth National People's Congress, 10 June 1981.

33   See generally, Leung, P. (ed.) (1995), *China Law Reports (1991)*, Singapore: Butterworths Asia; and *Zhongguo Shenpan Anli Yaolan* (An Anthology of Adjudicated Cases in China) (1992), edited by the China Senior Judges Training Centre and the People's University of China Law Faculty, Beijing, China People's Public Security University Press.

34   See generally, Liu, N. (1991), '"Legal Precedents" with Chinese Characteristics: Published Cases in the Gazette of the Supreme People's Court', *Journal of Chinese Law*, **5**, 107.

35   Opinion of the 7 November 1991, Supreme People's Court, Law of the People's Republic of China On Enterprise Bankruptcy (For Trial Implementation) 1986.

36   See further, Jones, W.C. (1994), 'The Significance of the Opinion of the Supreme People's Court for Civil Law in China', in P.B. Potter (ed.), *Domestic Law Reforms in Post-Mao China*, Armonk, NY: ME Sharpe, 97–137.

37   As note 36, above, 98.

38   Dicks, A.R. (1995), 'Compartmentalized Law and Judicial Restraint: An Inductive View of Some Jurisdictional Barriers to Reform', *The China Quarterly*, **141**, 82, 100–102.

39   See further, Clarke, D.C. (1995), 'The Execution of Civil Judgments in China', *The China Quarterly*, **141**, 65, 69–79.

40   As note 39, above, 77–78. See also Tanner, M.S. (1995), 'How a Bill Becomes a Law in China: Stages and Processes in Lawmaking', *The China Quarterly*, **141**, 39; and Tanner, M.S. (1994), 'Organisations and politics in China's post-Mao law-making system', in P.B. Potter (ed.), *Domestic Law Reforms in Post-Mao China*, Armonk, NY: ME Sharpe, 56–96.

41   Tanner, M.S. (1994), 'The Erosion of Communist Party Control over Lawmaking in China', *The China Quarterly*, **138**, 381.

42   Tanner, note 40, above, 46.

43   Tanner, discusses this well-known example of the work of a 'policy entrepreneur', as note 41, above, 50–53.

44   As note 41, above, 53.

45   See generally, Fang, L. (1995), 'China's Corporatization Experiment', *Duke Journal of Comparative & International Law*, **5**, 149, 156ff.

46   China Securities Regulatory Commission, *China Securities and Futures Markets*, Beijing, China Securities Regulatory Commission, December 1995, 5.

47   As note 38, above, 102–103.

48   See generally, Art, R.C. and Gu, M. (1995), 'China Incorporated: The First Corporation Law of the People's Republic of China', *The Yale Journal of International Law*, **20**, 273.

49   The discussion of this legislation will be based on the English translation of the Company Law found in Volume 5 of *The Laws of the People's Republic of China*, Beijing: Science Press (1995), 269–318.

50   Both of these sets of provisions are reproduced in Wang, G.G. and Tomasic, R. (1994), *China's Company Law: An Annotation*, Singapore: Butterworths Asia, 177–216.

51   For a translation of this Opinion, see: 'Issues Concerning the Applicability of

the Administration of Company Registration Laws and Regulations to the Administration of Foreign Investment Enterprises Registration Implementation Opinion', April 1996, *China Law & Practice*, 30–36.

52   For an English translation of these provisions, see 'Administration of Registration of Company Registered Capital Tentative Provisions', June 1996, *China Law & Practice*, 30–36.

53   Securities Office of the State Council and the State Commission for Restructuring the Economic System, 'The Articles of Association of Companies Seeking a Listing Outside the PRC, Prerequisite Clauses', 8 May 1995, *China Law & Practice*, 19–64.

54   The discussion in this section draws upon the following work: Song, Y.N. and S. Liu (1994), *Textbook on China's Company Law*, Beijing, University Press of the Central Committee of the Communist Party of China. These authors divide the law making process into eight stages. The drafting of the new Company Law is also critically discussed by Fang, L. (1995), 'China's Corporatization Experiment', *Duke Journal of Comparative & International Law*, 5, 149, 252–259.

55   Unpublished paper by Professor M.W. Dowdle, entitled 'Regulatory Enforcement in China: Lessons from the China Securities Regulatory Commission', 6 February 1996, 11. See also Yaowu, B. (1995) 'Issues related to the legislative structure of the new company law', in B. Bachner and H.L. Fu (eds), *Commercial Laws in the People's Republic of China*, Singapore: Butterworths Asia, 21–29.

56   Gao, X. (1995), 'The Perceived Unreasonable Man – A Response to Fang Liufang', *Duke Journal of Comparative & International Law*, 5, 271, 281.

57   Gao, X. (1996), 'Developments in Securities and Investment Law in China', *Australian Journal of Corporate Law*, 6, 228. Professor Gao notes (at 232) that other regulations which have filled in gaps left by the Company Law include regulations regarding H shares and the mandatory articles of association for H share companies, the B Share Rules and the implementation rules for these, the State Share Management Rules and the amendments which have been made to the Criminal Code to deal with corporate offences.

58   As note 55, above.

59   Fang, L. (1995), 'China's Corporatization Experiment', *Duke Journal of Comparative & International Law*, 5, 149.

60   As note 59, above, 253.

61   Evans, R. (1993), *Deng Xiaoping and the Making of Modern China*, London: Penguin Books, 252–253.

62   See further, Simon, W.H. (1996), 'The Legal Structure of the Chinese "Socialist Market" Enterprise', *The Journal of Corporation Law*, 276. See also generally, Connor, A.W. (1991), 'To Get Rich is Precarious: Regulation of Private Enterprise in the People's Republic of China', *Journal of Chinese Law*, 1, 9.

63   Jiang, Q. (1995), 'Like Wading Across a Stream: Law, Reform and the State Enterprise', in B. Bachner and H.L. Fu (eds), *Commercial Laws in the People's Republic of China*, Singapore: Butterworths Asia, 3.

64   The Law on Industrial Enterprise Owned by the Whole People 1988, in *The Laws of the People's Republic of China*, Volume 3, 141, Beijing: Science Press; Rural Collective Enterprise Regulations (Xiangzhen Jiti Suoyouzhi Qiye Tiaoli), issued by the State Council 1990; See also generally, Chen, J. (1993), 'Securitization of State-owned Enterprises and the Ownership Controversy in the PRC', *Sydney Law Review*, 15, 59; Tang, J. and Ma, J.C. (1985) 'Evolution of Urban Collective Enterprises in China', *China Quarterly*, 104, 614; and references to other writing on corporatization in China cited by Simon, as note 62, above, 287, note 78.

65   As note 63, above, 9.

66   Bian, Y. (1995), 'Issues Related to the Legislative Structure of the New

Company Law', in B. Bachner and H.L. Fu (eds), *Commercial Laws in the People's Republic of China*, Singapore: Butterworths Asia, 22–23.

67   For a discussion of the effects of litigation on the development of Chinese corporate law, see note 59, above, 238–251.

68   See the discussion of these and other considerations by Simon, as note 62, above, 270.

69   As note 66, above, 23.

70   See further, note 62, above, 274.

71   As note 59, above, 254. Fang's lengthy discussion in this article also contains a list of major problems of arbitrariness which he sees as arising as a result of the incompatibility of the corporatization experiment and the existing legal framework, 261–262.

72   As note 69, above, 23.

73   As note 66, above, 24.

74   Dowdle, as note 55, above, 14–15.

75   As note 59, above, 253–254.

76   See further, Regulation on the Supervisory Management of State-owned Enterprise Assets, approved by the State Council on 24 July 1994.

77   Dowdle, as note 55, above, 11.

78   See further, Administrative Procedure Law of the People's Republic of China, adopted at the 2nd Session of the Seventh National People's Congress on 4 April 1989, in *The Laws of the People's Republic of China*, Volume 3, 285, Beijing: Science Press.

79   As note 16, above, 203 and the references given there. Also see the 1989 Law on Administrative Litigation and the useful discussion of the operation of this law by Professor Chen, 181–184.

80   As note 59, above, 266–267.

81   As note 59, above, 266.

82   Gao, X. (1995), 'The Perceived Unreasonable Man – A Response to Fang Liufang', *Duke Journal of Comparative & International Law*, 5, 271, 281.

83   As note 82, above, 281.

84   See further, Wei, Y. (1995), 'The Regulatory Framework of China's Company Law', in B. Bachner and H.L. Fu (eds), *Commercial Laws in the People's Republic of China*, Singapore: Butterworths Asia, 30–46.

85   However, it should be noted that Article 74 of the Company Law does allow for the restructuring of a state-owed enterprise as a joint stock limited company. Article 21 also provides for the restructuring of state-owned enterprises as companies. Separate implementation rules and procedures are provided for this purpose.

86   See further, Gensler, H. (1995), 'Company Formation and Securities Listing in the People's Republic of China', *Houston Journal of International Law*, **17**, 399, 401; See Simon, as note 62, above, 291.

87   In the case of a joint stock limited company, the resolution must be supported by two-thirds of those shareholders voting at a general meeting of shareholders.

88   See generally, Decision of the National People's Congress Regarding the Revision of the Law of the People's Republic of China on Chinese-Foreign Equity Joint Ventures, adopted by the NPC on 4 April 1990; the Sino-Foreign Joint Venture Implementation Rules, promulgated on 4 September 1995; and the Law of the People's Republic of China on Foreign-Capital Enterprises, effective as of 12 April 1996; See also, Wu, Y. (1994), 'Joint ventures of the People's Republic of China', *Corporate and Business Law Journal*, **7**, 15; Gelatt, T.A. (1988), 'China's New Cooperative Joint Venture Law', *Syracuse Journal of International Law*, **15**, 187; Lee, O. (1983), 'Formation of Contract and Contract

Through Multinational Joint Ventures: Indonesia, China and the Third World', *International Lawyer*, **17**, 257; and McLauchlin, B. and Lau, C. (1996), 'Are cooperative joint ventures losing their appeal?', *China Law & Practice*, (June) 22.

89   For a more detailed discussion of China's foreign investment rules, see Potter, P.B. (1995), 'Foreign Investment Law in the People's Republic of China: Dilemmas of State Control', *The China Quarterly*, **141**, 155, 166–173; See also generally, *China's Foreign Economic Legislation*, Beijing: Foreign Language Press; and *China's Laws for Foreign Business*, Sydney: CCH Australia Ltd.

90   See Potter, as note 89, above, 171.

91   Reproduced in Wang and Tomasic, as note 50, above, 195–216.

92   Securities Office of the State Council and the State Commission for Reform of the Economic System, 'The Articles of Association of Companies Seeking a Listing Outside the PRC, Prerequisite Clauses', 8 May 1995, *China Law & Practice*, 19–64.

93   As note 91, above.

94   See Simon, as note 62, above, 289.

95   See generally, Nikkel, M.I. (1995), '"Chinese Characteristics" in Corporate Clothing: Questions of Fiduciary Duty in China's Company Law', *Minnesota Law Review*, **80**, 503, 530ff.

96   See Simon, as note 62, above, 299.

97   As note 59, above, 255.

98   As note 59, above, 259.

99   The Accounting Law of the People's Republic of China was adopted in December 1993 and amended in January 1995; this is concerned with the regulation and standardization of accounting practice in China.

100   Audit Law of the People's Republic of China, adopted on 31 August 1994 and effective as of 1 January 1995.

101   Simon, as note 62, above, 294.

102   As note 59, above, 251.

103   See further Simon, as note 62, above, 293.

104   See further, Tomasic, R. and Little, P. (1997), *Insolvency Law and Practice in Asia*, Hong Kong: FT Law & Tax, 24–25, for a list of the various PRC laws dealing with corporate insolvency.

105   See further, Chen, D. (1995), The Regulation of Secured Transactions in Emerging Chinese Stock Markets', in B. Bachner and H.L. Fu (eds), *Commercial Laws in the People's Republic of China*, Singapore: Butterworths Asia; Nie, Q. (1995), 'Legal Structure of the Securities Market in China', in B. Bachner and H.L. Fu (eds) *Commercial Laws in the People's Republic of China*, Singapore: Butterworths Asia, 81–92; Gao, S. and Chi, F. (eds) (1996), *The Chinese Securities Market*, Beijing: Foreign Language Press; Gao, X. (1996), 'Developments in Securities and Investment Law in China', *Australian Journal of Corporate Law*, **6**, 228; and note 59, above, 149.

106   As note 55, above, 6.

107   As note 55, above, 5.

108   As note 55, above, 10.

109   See further, Tomasic, R. (1998), 'An Overview and Assessment of the Draft Securities Law of the People's Republic of China', *Australian Journal of Corporate Law*, **9**.

6 Hong Kong Company Law

CHEE KEONG LOW*

1 Introduction

Hong Kong is administered by the government of the Special Administrative Region of the People's Republic of China pursuant to the terms of the Sino-British Joint Declaration on the Question of Hong Kong,[1] a legally binding international agreement which was registered at the United Nations by both the British and Chinese governments on 12 June 1985. The constitutional basis of the Hong Kong government and legal system is set out in the Basic Law of the Hong Kong Special Administrative Region (HKSAR) of the People's Republic of China[2] as promulgated by the National People's Congress (NPC). The Joint Declaration and the Basic Law are the two constituent documents which enshrine the underlying principle of 'one country, two systems', providing the HKSAR with a high degree of autonomy and the maintenance of its capitalist economic framework together with its common law system for at least 50 years after the changeover of sovereignty from 1 July 1997.

The hierarchy of the judiciary, in descending order, is the Court of Final Appeal, the Court of Appeal, the Court of First Instance, the District Court and the Magistrate's Court. The central court system is supported by a number of tribunals, namely the Lands Tribunal, the Labour Tribunal and the Small Claims Tribunal, as well as by the Coroner's Court and the Juvenile Court. The principle of judicial independence is guaranteed under Article 85 of the Basic Law, which states that the courts shall exercise their powers independently, free from any interference. Nonetheless, its jurisdiction is limited by Article 19 which expressly provides that the courts may not preside over the laws relating to Hong Kong which have been passed by the NPC or its Standing Committee, and over issues which involve acts of state such as defence and foreign affairs.

A distinction between barristers and solicitors is maintained by the legal profession. The former are supervised by the Bar Association, whereas the latter fall within the purview of the Law Society, both of which are regulated under the Legal Practitioners Ordinance.[3] Solicitors currently have no right of audience in the higher courts, although those with at least ten years' advocacy experience in the lower courts and the tribunals may be appointed as judges of the Court of First Instance. The tradition of having barristers instructed by solicitors continues to date, with the Bar Association steadfastly opposed to moves which would establish a fused profession. Original jurisdiction for matters connected with the Companies Ordinance vest with the Court of First Instance. However, the prosecution of offences under the Companies Ordinance will initially be brought to the Magistrate's Court. Where an accused is arrested and charged, a decision will be made as to whether the matter is to proceed in the District Court or by indictment to the Court of First Instance.

2   Companies Legislation

2.1   Background to Company Law in Hong Kong

The Companies Ordinance[4] (hereafter the Ordinance), forms the core of the regulation of companies in Hong Kong, and is supplemented by various subsidiary legislation, namely the Companies (Disqualification Orders) Regulation, the Companies (Forms) Regulations, the Companies (Reports on Conduct of Directors) Regulation, the Companies (Requirements for Documents) Regulation, the Companies (Winding-up) Rules and the Companies (Disqualification of Directors) Proceeding Rules. The Ordinance does not purport to be a comprehensive statute covering all aspects of company law. As companies are artificial creations of legislation, the law has been developed through the interaction, and interdependence, of case and statute law. Section 2 of the Ordinance provides for its definitions and interpretations, and is supplemented by the Interpretation and General Clauses Ordinance[5] which appears to favour the Mischief Rule of statutory interpretation[6].

The evolutionary development of the Ordinance mirrored that of the English Companies Act, reflecting the unique historical status of Hong Kong as a colony of the United Kingdom for some 156 years prior to 1 July 1997. Section 3(1) of the Application of English Law Ordinance[7] provided for the incorporation of the English common law and equity into the Hong Kong legal system, a framework which will be preserved under Article 8 of the Basic Law so long as these are not inconsistent with the provisions of the latter. As a result,

English company law often bears a high degree of significance to the general principles supporting the regulatory framework in Hong Kong and remains of persuasive authority in the interpretation of equivalent statutory provisions. Nonetheless, the influence of English law is expected to wane given the recent trend of increasing divergence between the jurisdictions as a consequence of the different pace of company law reform and the unique demands which are imposed upon the United Kingdom as a member of the European Union.

2.2   Law Reform

The Standing Committee on Company Law Reform was established in 1984 to advise on amendments required to the Ordinance as and when experience has shown them to be necessary. The Standing Committee is chaired by a judge of the Court of First Instance with its 20 or so members comprising representatives from a cross-section of the community. It has been instrumental in ensuring that the Ordinance remain responsive to the day-to-day needs of the business sector and the community at large. In 1993 it proposed that the government undertake a comprehensive review of the Ordinance to address one of its principal deficiencies, namely its increasing lack of coherence as a result of it becoming unwieldy. The two-year review culminated with the publication of the consultancy report in March 1997, which proposed the adoption of a traditional 'core company law' approach to the reform of the Ordinance, the latter being a term of reference coined recently by the New Zealand Law Reform Commission.

3   The Nature and Powers of Corporate Regulatory Bodies

3.1   The Registrar of Companies

The provisions of the Ordinance affect approximately 480 000 companies, including almost 700 which are listed on the Stock Exchange of Hong Kong (SEHK), inundating the Companies Registry with voluminous paperwork generated by ever increasing compliance requirements. The latter also acts as the secretariat to the Standing Committee on Company Law Reform and has assumed a trading fund status since 1993 which requires it to be held accountable for its self-sufficiency and commercial viability.

The Companies Registry is supervised by the Registrar of Companies, who is appointed the Chief Executive of the HKSAR and entrusted with the responsibility for the administration of the

Ordinance.[8] However, despite the relative importance of the office, the Ordinance makes no specific provisions with respect to the powers and duties of the Registrar.[9] Although the Twelfth Schedule to the Ordinance sets out a table of punishments for offences, the levels of penalties are prescribed under the Criminal Procedure Ordinance[10] and may only be enforced by a court order.[11] The foregoing may have been a contributory factor to the reason why the Companies Registry has not been particularly active in its mandate to ensure compliance with, and enforcement of, the Ordinance.

3.2   *The Regulation of Listed Companies*

Companies which issue publicly listed securities are governed by other legislation, including the Securities and Futures Commission Ordinance,[12] the Securities Ordinance,[13] the Protection of Investors Ordinance,[14] the Securities (Insider Dealing) Ordinance,[15] and the Securities (Disclosure of Interests) Ordinance.[16] The two principal regulatory bodies entrusted with securities regulation are the Securities and Futures Commission (SFC) and the SEHK.

The SFC was established as a body corporate in May 1989 in accordance with the recommendations of the Securities Review Committee, the latter having been set up to review the inadequacies of the securities and futures markets in Hong Kong following the unprecedented closure of the SEHK in the wake of the global stock market crash of October 1987. The SFC is an independent regulatory body which administers the Securities Ordinance and is empowered to, *inter alia*, supervise the stock and futures exchanges, regulate its intermediaries and products, and promote self-regulation within these industries. It also regulates takeovers and mergers, enforces securities laws to protect investors and market integrity, and reports occurrences of insider trading to the Financial Secretary. In addition, the SFC may make recommendations for the reform and development of laws pertaining to the securities and futures industries.

The SEHK is a company owned by its member brokers and has had the exclusive right to operate a stock exchange since April 1986 pursuant to the Stock Exchanges Unification Ordinance.[17] Its principal obligation is to ensure that its facilities provide for an orderly and fair market in the trading of securities.[18] In performing this duty, the SEHK is required to act in the interests of the investing public. The SEHK is empowered to make rules and regulations which cover two broad aspects, namely regulations governing its members and rules which must be complied with by listed companies. The latter is set out in the Rules Governing the Listing of Securities on the SEHK (Listing Rules),[19] which lays out both the initial listing requirements and the strict continuing obligations which must be adhered to. Clearing, share depository and settlement facilities are managed by the Hong Kong Securities Clearing Company Limited, a non-profit distributing company limited by a guarantee which is 50 per cent provided for by the SEHK. Although the SEHK is a self-regulatory organization, it remains subject to the control of the SFC.

4   The Types of Companies

4.1   Local Companies

The Ordinance recognizes three types of local companies which are classified according to the liability of their members, namely companies limited by shares, companies limited by guarantee and companies without limited liability.[20] However, only the first type is widely used in Hong Kong. Companies limited by guarantee are common only for charitable and non-profit-making organizations. Unlimited liability companies are rare in Hong Kong, as they offer their members few advantages over a partnership and enjoy no significant disclosure requirements. A company limited by guarantee without a share capital may only be incorporated as a public company, but the restriction does not apply for such companies having a share capital.

The Ordinance makes a distinction between private and public companies.[21] The former has the meaning assigned to it, whereas the latter is defined by exclusion, namely a company which is not a private company. Private companies must limit the number of members to 50 and impose restrictions on the right to transfer shares. In addition, such companies are prohibited from inviting the public to subscribe for its shares or debentures. The principal advantages of a private company are its ability to keep its financial information private,[22] and the ability to appoint a body corporate as a director[23] to facilitate privacy of control.

Listed companies are defined by the Ordinance as those for which shares are listed, whether in whole or in part, on the SEHK.[24] This special category of public company is subject to a number of additional controls, including those imposed under the Listing Rules, the Securities Ordinance,[25] the Securities (Disclosure of Interests) Ordinance[26] and the Securities (Insider Dealing) Ordinance.[27] The principal quantitative requirements to facilitate the consideration of an application by the Listing Division of the SEHK are highlighted by Table 6.1 below.

Table 6.1   Listing Requirements of the SEHK

Track record	Three years (profits of HK$ 20 million in most recent year; HK$ 30 million in total for two preceding years)
Latest audited accounts	Not more than six months prior to listing document
Public interest in issuer	Must be sufficient
Market value of issuer	HK$ 100 million
Value of shares held by public	HK$ 50 million
Percentage of shares held by public	25% (10% if issuer's capitalization is over HK$ 4 billion)
Number of shareholders	Three for each HK$ 1 million of issue, minimum 100
Market value of class of securities listed	HK$ 50 million
Shareholder conflict of interest	Prohibited
Voting rights of shares	Must be equal
Management presence in Hong Kong	Required

Source: Stock Exchange of Hong Kong

4.2   *Foreign Companies*

A corporation and body corporate are construed to include both a corporation sole and a company incorporated outside Hong Kong.[28] The Ordinance recognizes overseas companies which are essentially foreign companies with a place of business in Hong Kong.[29] The Ordinance does not define a 'place of business' in an exhaustive manner. The term includes a share transfer or share registration office, or any place used for the manufacture or warehousing of any goods, but excludes a place not used by the company to transact any business which creates legal relations.[30] All overseas companies must register themselves with the Registrar of Companies within one month of their establishing a place of business in Hong Kong.[31]

4.3   *Legal Capacities and Powers*

As artificial legal entities, the capacity of companies to engage in activities is limited by their objects clauses in their memorandum of association. However, companies are not required to state their objects, the absence of which will confer upon the company the powers of a natural person.[32] Companies which were incorporated with objects clauses and which have not amended these will continue to be restricted by the same.[33] Accordingly, a company may not exercise any power which has been excluded by its memorandum or articles of association, although any act which was carried out in contravention of those restrictions is not invalid.[34] To avoid the uncertainties which had been brought about by the doctrine of *ultra vires*,[35] the new Section 5C abolishes the doctrine of constructive notice in relation to both the memorandum and articles of association, and for any returns or resolutions lodged with the Registrar of Companies.[36]

5   Company Formation

5.1   *Registration Procedures*

The association of persons is prohibited under certain circumstances unless the formal process of incorporating a company is undertaken.[37] This requires the promoter[38] to lodge with the Registrar of Companies the memorandum and articles of association of the company[39] together with a statutory declaration that the provisions of the Ordinance have been complied with.[40] The company will be registered upon the payment of the requisite fees[41] and the Registrar issuing the certificate of registration.[42] The company hereafter possesses all the attributes of a separate legal entity.[43]

5.2   *Promoters*

As fiduciaries of the company, the promoter has a common law obligation to act *bona fide* in the interest of the company which is being promoted. Promoters must avoid any actual or potential conflicts of interests with the company and ensure full and frank disclosure of all material information.[44] In addition, he or she must refrain from disclosing any confidential information gained from his or her role as a promoter. The principal remedies for breach of promoters' duties are rescission of the contract on the grounds of misrepresentation and damages.[45]

5.3   *Corporate Constitution*

The corporate constitution of the company comprises of its memorandum and articles of association. The former is a prerequisite for registration of the company[46] and must contain the name of the company together with its share capital, liability and subscriber clauses.[47] The objects clause is no longer mandatory, although companies will continue to be so bound should they be incorporated with these. Companies need not lodge their articles of association, namely provisions which regulate its internal management and operations, in order to be incorporated.[48] Where companies choose to register their articles, these must be in the English language and signed by each of the subscribers to the memorandum in the presence of a witness.[49] The memorandum and articles create a contract under seal between the company and each member, and between the members themselves.[50] As the memorandum governs the relationship of outsiders dealing with the company, its provisions shall prevail above those of the articles should there be any inconsistencies between the two.

The memorandum may only be altered in the manner provided for by the Ordinance.[51] A company may amend its articles by special resolution but these shall be subject to the provisions of the Ordinance[52] and its memorandum.[53] In addition, such alterations should be *bona fide* for the benefit of the company as a whole in order to ensure that the majority do not exercise such powers to the detriment of the minority.[54] To ensure that members are not adversely affected by any alteration to the memorandum or articles, they are not bound by any such amendments which require them to take, or subscribe for, more shares than the number which they held, or which would in any way increase their liability at the date of the alteration unless they expressly consent in writing to the same.[55]

As the memorandum must be printed in the English language, every company must have an English name.[56] A company limited by shares or guarantee must have the word 'Limited' or its abbreviation 'Ltd' at the end of its name.[57] No company may be registered by a name which is the same as a name in the Registrar's Index of Company Names or that of a body corporate established under an Ordinance.[58] In addition, the Chief Executive of the HKSAR may refuse the registration of a company whose name might constitute a criminal offence, is offensive or otherwise contrary to public interest.[59] The consent of the Chief Executive is also required where the proposed name gives the impression that the company is connected to the government of the HKSAR or the government of Mainland China or any department of either government.[60]

5.4   Membership and Share Capital Requirements

A company may issue shares up to the limit of its authorized capital.[61] Where shares are issued, they are allotted to the holders who become members after their names are entered into the register of members. Companies must have a minimum share capital of $ 2 divided into two shares of $ 1 each, although this need not be denominated in

Hong Kong dollars.[62] Accordingly all companies must have at least two members,[63] which may be attained by subscribing to the memorandum, applying for and receiving an allotment of shares, accepting the transfer of shares from another member or receiving shares by transmission on the death or bankruptcy of a member.[64]

5.5 Company Registers

All companies are obliged to state in their memorandum that they shall maintain a registered office in Hong Kong, the address of which must be given to the Registrar within 14 days of incorporation.[65] The principal purpose of this is to enable legal documents, notices and other communications to be served on the company. Upon its incorporation, a company must establish registers to record particulars with respect to its:

- directors and secretaries;[66]
- debenture-holders;[67]
- charges;[68]
- members;[69]
- substantial shareholders;[70] and
- the interests in shares and debentures held by its chief executive and directors.[71]

6 The Internal Administration of Companies

6.1 The Powers of the Officers

The two principal organs of the company are its board of directors and its members in a general meeting, each of which may be regarded as agents of their company, with their respective powers set out in the articles. In practice, the general management of the company usually rests with its directors[72] who are given the right to exercise all of the company's powers unless specifically excluded under the Ordinance or by its articles.[73] The members in a general meeting may not override the directors where the issue pertains to the management of the company.[74]

The powers of the board of directors are often drafted in a wide manner to include the power to pay the promotion and formation costs of the company; to borrow money; to charge its assets, property, business or unpaid capital; to issue debentures; or to give security for a debt, liability or obligation of the company. They also have the power to recommend dividends, convene general meetings of members and to authorize the common seal of the company to be affixed to certain documents such as deeds, share certificates and transfers of land. The power of management is usually vested in the board of directors collectively at a properly convened board meeting,[75] although this may be delegated.[76]

6.2   Duties of Officers

As fiduciaries of the company, directors owe certain duties to the company on whose board they serve and these may be categorized as follows:

- to act *bona fide* in the interests of the company which is gauged subjectively;[77]
- to exercise powers for their proper purpose;[78]
- to retain their discretionary powers;[79]
- to avoid conflicts of interests;[80] and
- to exercise care, diligence and skill.[81]

6.3   The Procedure for Meetings

Board meetings are usually convened by a director or by the secretary on the instructions of a director of the company. Notice of meetings may be dispensed with if these are held on a regular basis but otherwise it may be despatched together with the agenda. The quorum is usually two, although this may be increased by the articles.[82] Decisions of the board are arrived at by a simple majority of those directors who are present and entitled to vote.[83]

The will of members is expressed at their meetings, the calling and conduct of which is governed primarily by the articles of the company. The three common types of meetings are the annual general meeting, the extraordinary meeting and the class meeting. A company must hold an annual general meeting at least once in each calendar year[84] to provide its members with the opportunity to obtain information and question the directors regarding the affairs of the company. If the company fails to hold the meeting, the court may call a meeting or direct the calling of a meeting and give any ancillary or consequential directions as it deems fit.[85] Matters which are usually considered at these meetings include the tabling of the various accounts and reports,[86] the election of directors, the declaration of dividends and the appointment of auditors.[87] A general meeting other than the annual general meeting is called an extraordinary general meeting.[88] A class meeting refers to those meetings held by members of a particular class of shares.[89]

Meetings of members must be convened by written notice.[90] Where a special resolution is to be proposed at a meeting, the requisite timeframe is at least 21 days.[91] A special notice[92] is required under certain circumstances, namely for the removal of an auditor,[93] the appointment as auditor[94] of a person other than the retiring auditor, the filling of a casual vacancy in the office of the auditor[95] and the reappointment of a retiring auditor who was appointed to a casual vacancy by the directors.[96] All notices must specify the time, date and venue of the meeting together with the general nature of the business to be conducted. Failure to provide the requisite notice as specified by the articles will render the proceedings void unless so rectified by unanimous agreement of members.[97] Unless otherwise provided by the articles, a quorum is two members personally present,[98] although the court may order that a meeting be held with only the presence of one member.[99] Voting is usually conducted by a show of hands with each member present having one vote,[100] but a poll may be demanded by the members.[101]

6.4 Accounting and Audit Rules

The disclosure of financial information enables the members to assess the performance of the management of the company, thereby enhancing the quality of corporate governance. The Ordinance stipulates the preparation of a balance sheet and profit and loss statement which reflects a true and fair view of the financial position of the company.[102] These accounts must be made up to a date not more than six months from the date of the annual general meeting,[103] and must be sent to its members no less than 21 days prior to the meeting.[104] Certain private companies are exempt[105] from most of the accounts provisions if this is agreed to unanimously by its members in writing.[106] Although exempt, these companies must comply with the provisions of the Eleventh Schedule.[107] Overseas companies are required to submit their accounts to the Registrar at least once every calendar year within 15 months of the preceding submission.[108]

Every company must appoint an auditor prior to its inaugural annual general meeting.[109] The auditor owes both contractual and statutory duties to the company. The former requires the auditor to exercise a reasonable degree of care and skill in the carrying out of the audit in an independent manner so as to present an opinion as to whether the accounts represent a true and fair view of the financial position of the company. An auditor is statutorily bound to present his or her report which is laid before the annual general meeting.[110] In addition, an auditor is under a duty to report any deficiencies, failures or shortcomings in the course of his or her audit.[111]

6.5 Annual Returns

The directors must make out a report, which is signed by the chairman of the meeting or the company secretary,[112] with respect to the financial position of the company and its activities. This report has the effect of verifying the accounts and contains the matters as prescribed by Section 129D(3). The directors' reports of an exempt company must be attached to its balance sheet showing the state of the company's affairs, the amount of dividends recommended by the directors and the amount proposed to be transferred to reserves.[113]

6.6 The Relationship between Management and Shareholders

With the division of power between the company in a general meeting and its board of directors, there needs to be a delicate balancing of these competing interests. Although the rule of the majority usually prevails,[114] the equitable principles of fairness and justice serve to protect the interests of the minority from any abuse of power by the directors or the majority shareholders of the company. This protection is effected at two levels, namely by the common law and through statutory provisions.

6.7 Shareholder Protection

The rule in *Foss v Harbottle*[115] has two aspects, namely the internal management rule and the proper plaintiff rule. The former recognizes that in the affairs of companies the will of the majority prevails; the latter is a recognition of the separate legal identity of the company.[116] This rule is subject to the four common law exceptions[117] as set out below. If the minority can bring themselves within any of these, they will be permitted to bring an action against the company, its majority shareholders and/or its directors. They are:

- where the act of the company is *ultra vires*;[118]
- where the act of the company requires a special resolution;[119]
- where a member's personal rights are infringed;[120] or
- where the majority commits a fraud on the minority.[121]

Although a fifth exception, namely where the interests of justice require,[122] was suggested in other common law jurisdictions, this is unlikely to gain acceptance in Hong Kong.[123]

The principal statutory remedies for the protection of minority shareholders are Sections 168A[124] and 177(1)(f).[125] The former provides for a range of remedies where the act complained of is unfairly prejudicial to the interests[126] of some part of the members of the company. The extensive terminology enables the court to order a remedy where it is of the opinion that:

> affairs of the company are being conducted, or the powers of the directors are being exercised, in a manner that is unfairly prejudicial[127] to one or more of the members including himself or herself, or in disregard for his or her interests as members or shareholders;[128] or

> some act of the company has been done or is threatened, or that some resolution of the members or any class of them has been passed or is proposed, which unfairly discriminates against or is otherwise prejudicial to, one or more members or debenture holders of the company.[129]

Where the applicant successfully establishes his or her case, the courts have a very wide discretion in determining the appropriate order with a view to bringing to an end or remedying the matters complained of.[130] These include an order, whether singularly or in combination:

- restricting the commission or continuation of any act;
- regulating the future conduct of the affairs of the company;
- authorizing such proceedings in the name of the company against such persons as the court sees fit;
- for the purchase of the shares of the company by other members or by the company itself (the latter is tantamount to a court-approved reduction of capital); and
- altering the memorandum and/or articles of association of the company which takes immediate effect without the need for calling a general meeting.

6.8 Corporate Financial Transactions

6.8.1 Charges Companies incorporated on or after 31 August 1984 are conferred a number of powers[131] including the general power to borrow on either a secured or unsecured basis.[132] A charge[133] is a common security granted under a debenture to secure a loan. A system of registration[134] is provided for charges, the principal purpose of which is to enable those dealing with the company to determine whether a particular asset of the company has been so encumbered. However, unlike other jurisdiction, the Ordinance does not set out a scheme of priorities for holders of competing registrable charges and this remains governed by the principles developed under general law.

6.8.2 Receivership The charge is usually granted pursuant to the terms of a debenture which invariably contains a clause for the appointment of a receiver and/or manager in the event of a default of its obligations by the company.[135] The appointment may also be made by the High Court where it appears just and convenient to do so.[136] Although Part VI of the Ordinance deals specifically with receiverships, these relate primarily to administrative matters and the importance of the general law should not be ignored given the non-exclusivity of the statutory provisions.

6.8.3   Share buy backs   Subsidiaries are not allowed to be members of their holding companies.[137] To prevent any abuse of the concept of the separate legal entity, a company is also prohibited from purchasing or subscribing for its own shares.[138] However, the Ordinance provides for a detailed code to enable companies to purchase their own shares under certain circumstances.[139] If so authorized,[140] listed companies may purchase their own shares through a general offer on the SEHK or other recognized stock exchanges or by other means.[141] These buy-backs must be financed either by distributable profits or out of the proceeds of a fresh issue of shares.[142] Unlisted companies require special resolutions to undertake share buy backs.[143]

6.8.4   Financial assistance   Companies are generally prohibited from providing financial assistance for the purchase of their own shares.[144] In essence, the provisions allow unlisted companies to provide such financial assistance where it will be financed out of distributable profits and has been approved by a special resolution. In addition, directors must sign a statutory declaration attesting to the solvency of the company, namely that it will be able to repay its debts as they fall due over the next 12 months.[145] Additional requirements are imposed on listed companies.[146] Breach of the provision renders the company liable to a fine and its defaulting officers to imprisonment and/or pecuniary penalty.[147] At common law, a transaction which breaches Section 47A is illegal and, hence, void.[148]

7   The External Administration of Companies

7.1   Schemes of Arrangement

Apart from being placed in receivership where the terms of a debenture so provides, the options available to a company in financial difficulties include the implementation of an appropriate scheme of arrangement or liquidation.[149]

Although a member is not bound by any alteration to the memorandum or articles which effectively increases his or her liability,[150] this is subject to the provisions with respect to arrangements and reconstruction.[151] The company may undertake a scheme of arrangement involving a compromise or moratorium with its creditors. The former allows the company to defer the payment of debts to its creditors until some point of time in the future, whereas the latter refers to the acceptance by the creditors of a lesser sum than that which is owed as full settlement of their claims. An arrangement may also involve only the rights and liabilities of the members themselves as would be the case in a reorganization of the company.[152] Such schemes are also applicable to takeovers.[153] Once approved by the court, the scheme is binding on the company, its members and creditors alike.[154]

7.2 Liquidation

The other alternative available to companies in financial difficulties is outright liquidation.[155] This may proceed in one of three ways, namely by a creditors' voluntary winding up,[156] through the special Section 228A procedure[157] or by the court,[158] with the last option being the most common of the three. An applicant for the compulsory winding up of a company must be accompanied by affidavits in support. The date of commencement of the winding up is the date of the filing of the petition, although the actual date of the court hearing and order may be some months thereafter.[159]

7.3 Grounds for Winding Up

The test of solvency of a company is not restricted to an analysis of its balance sheet, namely that it has more liabilities than it has assets. The applicant must establish that the company is unable to pay its debts as they fall due, taking into account its actual, contingent and prospective liabilities. The Ordinance provides for a simple method of determining insolvency, namely the failure to adequately meet a statutory notice of demand.[160]

The court may also order the winding up of a company where it is just and equitable to do so.[161] This provision has been liberally interpreted so as to allow the court to exercise its discretion to make such an order where the minority shareholders have been harshly done by.[162] The existence of a deadlock[163] and the failure of substratum[164] are also common grounds for the granting of a winding up order under this heading. In addition, the court may consider applications by a member alleging unfair prejudice based on the surrounding circumstances.[165] As with all equitable remedies, the person who seeks such an order from the court must do so with clean hands.[166]

7.4   The Role of the Liquidator

The appointment of a liquidator is a common feature of winding ups. Neither an undischarged bankrupt nor a body corporate may be appointed to this office.[167]

The liquidator assumes the power of the board of directors upon his or her appointment. The liquidator is given powers under the Ordinance[168] and his or her actions are binding on the company given the agency relationship which exists. As a fiduciary, the liquidator owes a number of duties to the company[169] the most important of which include the proper administration of the liquidation, the preservation of assets, its realization and its distribution as dividends to creditors.

7.5   Proof of Debt and Ranking of Claims

Creditors must prove their debts in order to have any entitlements.[170] The policy of the Ordinance is that, unless otherwise provided for, all provable debts rank equally and if there are insufficient funds to meet these in full they are to be paid proportionately. The scheme of priority of payment accords privilege to secured creditors whose claims are paid out of the assets subject to the charge.[171] Unsecured creditors are paid out of assets which are not subject to such encumbrances and from any other asset which may be recovered by the liquidator.[172] In the unlikely scenario that there are surplus assets after the distribution to creditors, special leave of court must be obtained by the liquidator before the members may participate in the same.[173]

8   Takeover Rules

8.1   The Framework

The Hong Kong Code on Takeovers and Mergers (hereafter the Takeovers Code) is based on the broad principle approach as adopted by the United Kingdom in its City Code on Takeovers and Mergers. The Takeovers Code is not legally enforceable, but emphasizes the spirit of its rules which are grounded on the principles that:

- The identity of the offeror be made known to the directors and members, who must in turn be afforded reasonable time to consider the proposal;
- The offeror provides such information as is necessary to facilitate an informed judgment as to the merits of the offer by the members of the target company; and

- All members of the target company be given an equal opportunity to participate in the offer.

The Takeovers Code was integrated with the Code on Share Repurchases (hereafter the Share Repurchase Code) on 1 April 1992 in view of the substantial degree of overlap between the two codes. The day-to-day oversight of the Codes is conducted by the Takeovers and Mergers Executive, which comprises executive staff of the SFC.[174] Matters pertaining to disciplinary actions, review of decisions of the Takeovers and Mergers Executive and the determination of policy are considered by the Takeovers Panel.[175] The ultimate appellate body is the Takeovers Appeal Committee,[176] whose function is limited to the review of the sanctions imposed by the Takeovers Panel in the exercise of its disciplinary powers. As all of the above are statutory bodies, their decisions are subject to judicial review.[177]

8.2 The Takeover Threshold

The Takeovers Code aims to regulate acquisition of shares in a target company which effect a change in its control, the latter of which is set at 35 per cent or more of the voting shares. A mandatory general offer to all shareholders of the target company is mandated[178] unless an exemption or waiver has been granted by the Takeovers and Mergers Executive.[179] All offers must be in writing, with the same terms and conditions, and sent to every shareholder of the target company. The offer document must contain the information as prescribed under Schedule I of the Takeovers Code.

8.3 Duties of the Board of Target Companies

The Takeovers Code imposes a number of duties on the board of the target company to ensure that they have regard to the interests of the shareholders.[180] At the minimum, the directors must act honestly and not mislead their shareholders. They must appoint independent advisers and make the substance of the objective advice available to shareholders.[181] Where documents are prepared, they must conform to the same standard of care as if they were prospectuses.[182]

8.4 Sanctions

The breach of any provision of the Takeovers Code attracts sanctions which may be imposed by the Takeovers Panel.[183] Where there has been a breach of either the Takeovers Code or of a ruling by the Takeovers and Mergers Executive, the Takeovers Panel may:

- issue a private reprimand, public statement which involves criticism or a public censure;
- report the matter to the SFC and such other regulatory authority, whether domestic or overseas (as is necessary);
- ban the persons from acting or continuing to act in a particular capacity or from appearing before the Takeovers and Mergers Executive or Takeovers Panel for a specified period; and/or
- impose such other action as it thinks fit in the circumstances.

9   Securities Regulation

9.1   *The Regulators*

The principal regulators of the securities industry in Hong Kong are the SFC and the SEHK. The current scheme of regulation is applied at two levels, namely the regulation of the markets and the licensing of persons engaged in the securities industry. Diagram 6.1 below provides for an overview of the existing regulatory framework.

The SFC is an independent non-governmental statutory body[184] whose primary functions[185] include the administration of securities laws,[186] pursuit of the continuing development of the markets and constant improvement of the regulatory framework. The administration of the Securities Ordinance[187] comes within the purview of the SFC and is perhaps its most important function. The SFC is accountable to the government of the HKSAR for the discharge of its responsibilities and reports to the Financial Secretary.[188] The chairman and directors of the SFC are appointed by the Chief Executive of the HKSAR[189] who must also approve its annual budget which is tabled before the legislature.[190]

The SEHK is a limited liability company owned by its member brokers and has been given the exclusive right to operate a stock exchange under the Stock Exchange Unification Ordinance.[191] It is a self-regulatory body responsible for the supervision of its members and for the approval of listing documents and corporate announcements. Membership on the SEHK is secured through the purchase of a seat on the exchange company. These persons must be registered under the Securities Ordinance and have to meet the Financial Resources Rules as imposed by the SFC, subject to such additional requirements as may be determined by the SEHK. The SEHK is empowered to make rules which cover regulations governing its members and rules to be complied with by listed companies. It assumed the front line responsibility for the authorization of prospectuses in 1993 and administers the Listing Rules of the Stock

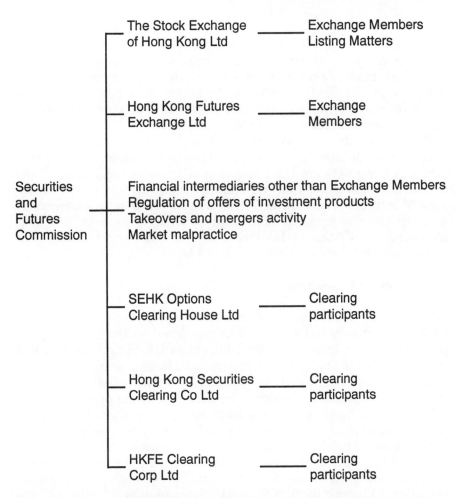

Diagram 6.1   Regulatory Structure of the Securities and Futures Industry

Exchange, which are both additional and complementary to listed companies' common law and statutory obligations.

9.2   *Regulatory Framework*

The influence of securities regulation as applied across the British Commonwealth is evident in Hong Kong given its status as a colony of the United Kingdom for some 156 years until 1 July 1997.[192] Primary markets are essentially governed by the prospectus provisions of the Companies Ordinance, which set out the requirements regarding the format and contents.[193] The SEHK vets and approves all prospectuses of listing applicants and the role of the Registrar of Companies is merely to register the prospectuses which have been authorized by the SEHK.[194] A minimum subscription must be attained before shares can be allotted[195] and the company must actually get listed on the SEHK, otherwise the allotment is void.[196] The remedies for misstatements and non-disclosures in prospectuses are derived from both the common law[197] and statutes.[198]

Apart from the Companies Ordinance, the Securities Ordinance and the SFC Ordinances, the principal pieces of legislation governing secondary markets are the Protection of Investor Ordinance,[199] the Securities (Insider Dealing) Ordinance[200] and the Securities (Disclosure of Interests) Ordinance.[201] This framework is supplemented by an increasing number of non-statutory codes issued by the SFC, including the Codes on Takeovers and Mergers and Share Repurchases and the Code on Unit Trusts and Mutual Funds.

9.3   Licensing Requirements

Part VI of the Securities Ordinance requires persons engaged in the securities industry to be licensed or registered by the Licensing Department of the Intermediaries Division of the SFC.[202] As this is a major way to ensure that such persons and their activities are supervised, the principal objective of the SFC is to ensure that only fit and proper persons are so licensed. The character of the person is taken into account, together with the interests of the public. The SFC retains the discretion of rejecting applications from persons whom they have reason to believe will not perform their duties effectively, honestly and fairly. All registered persons must comply with the Code of Conduct which embraces the seven principles developed by the International Organization of Securities Commission. Members of the SEHK are exempt from this provision as they are subject to fundamentally similar requirements as imposed by the Code of Conduct of the SEHK.

9.4   Prohibited Market Activities

Insider dealing, short-selling and the creation of false markets are the principal forms of securities misconduct. Short-selling[203] is the practice of selling securities not owned by the seller at the time of the sale and for which no exchange recognized stock borrowing arrangement has been previously entered into. The creation of a false or misleading appearance with respect to the market or price of securities, regardless of whether there is an intention to induce another person to enter the market, is prohibited.[204]

10   Miscellaneous

10.1   *Powers of the Court*

The Ordinance provides the court with certain powers so that it may effectively enforce the same. For example, the court may grant relief to an officer or auditor of the company where it appears that he or she has acted honestly and reasonably and ought fairly to be excused.[205] This applies where the action against the officer or auditor is founded upon negligence, default, breach of trust or breach of duty. The court may also, on the application of the defendant, require that the company provide security for costs where it brings an action as a plaintiff.[206]

10.2   *Offences*

The Ordinance sets out a series of offences in Sections 271–277 and Sections 349–355. The former relates to offences antecedent to or in the course of winding up of the company, including falsification of books,[207] fraudulent trading[208] and misfeasance or breach of duty.[209] Liquidators of companies are obliged to report actual or suspected offences by its officers or members to the Attorney-General, whose duty it is to determine whether proceedings are to be instituted against these parties.[210]

Miscellaneous offences are dealt with by Sections 349–350A which impose penalties for the provision of false statements, destruction of books, improper use of the term 'Limited' or 'Incorporated', and the failure to give notice of paid up capital. The principal provisions with respect to punishment of offences are set out in Section 351 and the Twelfth Schedule to the Ordinance. Apart from setting out the details of sanctions which are to be imposed, the latter also shows whether the offence is one which is punishable on conviction, on indictment or on summary conviction. It prescribes the maximum fines and term of imprisonment together with the applicable default penalties. All fines paid under the Ordinance become part of the general revenue of the HKSAR.[211]

10.3   *Reforms*

The increasing complexity of company law and the apparently uncoordinated piecemeal amendments to the Ordinance since its enactment in 1865 prompted the government to commission a review of the Ordinance.[212] The two-year review culminated with the production of the report by the consultants in March 1997,[213] which proposed a return to core company law. In a nutshell, this proposal seeks to separate the regulation of matters pertaining to companies[214] from those which govern the issue of securities and administration of insolvent companies. Simplification and coherence appear to be the principal guiding forces of the proposal which should hopefully result in the enactment of an Ordinance which is less unwieldy when compared with its existing 17 Part, 365 Sections and 15 Schedules counterpart.

A rationalization of the existing scheme of securities regulation has also been proposed by the SFC which released a consultation paper and draft Composite Securities and Futures Bill on 15 April 1996.[215] No timeframe has yet been set for the submission of the draft Bill to the legislature, as the SFC is considering the comments from the recently concluded period of public consultation.[216]

The Law Reform Commission has also advocated the enactment of a corporate rescue procedure in its Report on Corporate Rescue and Insolvent Trading which was released on 31 October 1996. This will provide for an effective half-way house for financially distressed companies as it will allow for their restructuring under a protected regime.[217] This proposal has received the support of the business and professional communities, although its progress through the legislative process is somewhat clouded by the proposed return to core company law.

Bibliography

Arjunan, K. and Low, C.K. (1996), *Lipton & Herzberg's Understanding Company Law in Hong Kong*, Sydney: LBC Information Services.

CCH Asia Limited (1993), *Hong Kong Company Law & Practice*, Singapore: CCH Asia.

Low, C.K. (1998), 'Securities Regulation' in F. Kan (ed.), *The Business Guide to Hong Kong*, Sydney: Butterworths-Heinemann Asia, Chapter 9.

Smart, P., Lynch, K. and Tam, A. (1997), *Hong Kong Company Law: Cases, Materials and Comments*, Singapore: Butterworths Asia.

Notes

* Associate Professor in Corporate Law, School of Accountancy, The Chinese University of Hong Kong
1 Commonly referred to as the Joint Declaration.
2 Commonly referred to as the Basic Law.
3 Cap. 159 of the Laws of Hong Kong.
4 Cap. 32 of the Laws of Hong Kong.
5 Cap. 1 of the Laws of Hong Kong.
6 Section 19 of the Interpretation and General Clauses Ordinance (Cap. 1).
7 Cap. 88 of the Laws of Hong Kong.
8 Section 303(2) of the Companies Ordinance provides for the appointment of

the Registrar by the Governor, whose office has ceased with the changeover of sovereignty. This provision is likely to be amended with the reference to the Governor being substituted with the Chief Executive, given his status prior to and after 1 July 1997. This chapter is written on the assumption that this and all other similar provisions in the Ordinance which refer to Governor shall be amended in the aforesaid manner and accordingly all references will be to the Chief Executive of the HKSAR although the amendment has not been effected at the time of writing.

9   Although the Registrar exercises some powers, these are not set out in a distinct part of the Companies Ordinance but are instead dispersed throughout. For example, Section 22A empowers the Registrar to demand that a company abandon a misleading name, Sections 290A and 291 allow for the striking off of companies, and Section 348D permits the Registrar to keep records in a non-documentary form.

10   Cap. 221 of the Laws of Hong Kong.

11   Section 306 of the Companies Ordinance.

12   Cap. 24 of the Laws of Hong Kong.

13   Cap. 333 of the Laws of Hong Kong.

14   Cap. 335 of the Laws of Hong Kong.

15   Cap. 395 of the Laws of Hong Kong.

16   Cap. 396 of the Laws of Hong Kong.

17   Cap. 361 of the Laws of Hong Kong.

18   Section 27A of the Stock Exchanges Unification Ordinance.

19   Commonly referred to as the Listing Rules.

20   Section 4(2) of the Companies Ordinance.

21   Section 29 of the Companies Ordinance.

22   Section 109(3) of the Companies Ordinance. See also Section 141D for additional exemptions.

23   Section 154A(3) of the Companies Ordinance. However this only applies to an exempt private company namely one which is not a member of a group of companies of which a listed company is a member.

24   Section 2 of the Companies Ordinance. There are only about 700 companies of this type, representing only a minute fraction of the approximately 480 000 registered limited liability companies in Hong Kong.

25   Cap. 333 of the Laws of Hong Kong.

26   Cap. 396 of the Laws of Hong Kong.

27   Cap. 395 of the Laws of Hong Kong.

28   Section 2(3) of the Companies Ordinance.

29   Section 332 of the Companies Ordinance. These companies are regulated by Part XI of the Ordinance. See *South India Shipping Corp Ltd v Export-Import Bank of Korea* [1985] 1 WLR 585.

30   Section 341 of the Companies Ordinance.

31   The requisite documentation is set out in Section 333(1) of the Companies Ordinance.

32   Section 5A of the Companies Ordinance which was introduced with the enactment of the Companies (Amendment) Ordinance in February 1997.

33   Section 5B of the Companies Ordinance.

34   Section 5B(1b) of the Companies Ordinance. However, Section 5B(2) permits a member to bring an action to restrain the company from acting in breach of its memorandum or articles of association.

35   See *Pearl Island Hotel Ltd v Li Ka-yu* [1988] 2 HKLR 87 and *European Asian Bank v Reicar Investments Ltd* [1988] 1 HKLR 45 for examples of the application of the doctrine in Hong Kong.

36   However, the absence of any reference to the word 'register' means that the

doctrine of constructive notice continues to apply to charges created by the company, as the Registrar of Companies is statutorily obliged to maintain a Register of Company Charges pursuant to Section 83 of the Companies Ordinance.

37   The Companies Ordinance does not directly specify who must incorporate. Unless otherwise exempted, Section 345(1) prohibits the formation of an association or partnership consisting of more than 20 persons that has as its objective the acquisition of gain by the association, partnership or its individual members.

38   A promoter is a person who is involved with the formation of a company, whether actively or passively, as can be seen in *Twycross v Grant* (1877) 2 CPD 469 and *Tracy v Mandalay Pty Ltd* (1953) 88 CLR 215. The definition of a promoter in Section 40 of the Ordinance is only applicable where the person is involved in the preparation of a prospectus.

39   Only the lodgement of the memorandum of association is mandatory under Section 9 of the Companies Ordinance. The lodgement of the articles of association is not compulsory as the company will be assumed to have adopted the model articles as contained in Table A of the First Schedule to the Companies Ordinance. However, companies limited by guarantee and unlimited liability companies must lodge their articles of association.

40   This may be made by a solicitor of the High Court engaged in the formation of the company or a person named in its articles of association as a director or secretary. It must be produced for the Registrar, who may accept the declaration as sufficient evidence of compliance under Section 18(2) of the Companies Ordinance.

41   Section 304. The structure of fees payable is set out in the Eighth Schedule to the Companies Ordinance.

42   Sections 16(2) and 18(2) of the Companies Ordinance.

43   Sections 16(2) and 17(1) of the Companies Ordinance.

44   See for example, *Erlanger v New Sombrero Phosphate Co.* (1878) 3 App Cas 1218 and *Gluckstein v Barnes* [1900] AC 240.

45   For instances involving fraudulent misrepresentation. See *Re Leeds and Handley Theatres of Varieties Ltd* [1092] 2 Ch 809. Damages may also be awarded in lieu of rescission at the discretion of the courts pursuant to Sections 2 and 3(1) of the Misrepresentation Ordinance (Cap. 284).

46   Section 15 of the Companies Ordinance must be printed in English pursuant to Section 4(1). A model memoranda is set out in the First Schedule to the Ordinance and should be followed as closely as circumstances permit.

47   Section 5 of the Companies Ordinance. The subscriber clause applies only to companies with a share capital, as it indicates the number of shares which subscribers agree to take. The memorandum must also specify the amount of capital of the company and its division into shares of a fixed amount for companies with a share capital.

48   Section 9 of the Companies Ordinance. Where such companies do not lodge articles, the regulations contained in Table A of the First Schedule to the Ordinance will apply to the extent that they are not excluded or modified. This provision, however, does not apply to companies limited by guarantee or unlimited liability companies, both of which must lodge their articles of association to facilitate their registration.

49   Section 12 of the Companies Ordinance.

50   Section 23(1) of the Companies Ordinance.

51   Section 7 of the Companies Ordinance. Alterations to the objects clause must conform to the procedure as set out in Section 8. The name of the company may only be altered in the manner as provided under Section 22. The altera-

tion of the capital clause may be effected by Section 58 which sets out the procedure to facilitate a reduction of capital. Cognisance should also be taken of Section 64 where the proposed reduction of capital varies the class rights of members as stated in the articles of association.

52 For example, Section 58 of the Companies Ordinance prohibits the reduction of issued capital without confirmation by the court. Part IIA states that a company may not alter its articles so as to authorize a declaration of dividends out of capital.

53 Section 13 of the Companies Ordinance.

54 See, for example, *Allen v Gold Reefs of West Africa Ltd* [1900] 1 Ch 656, *Greenhalgh v Arderne Cinemas Ltd* [1951] Ch 286 and *Dafen Tinplate Co. Ltd v Llanelly Steel Co.* [1920] 2 Ch 124.

55 Section 25 of the Companies Ordinance.

56 Most companies also have a Chinese name which is printed on its certificate of incorporation.

57 Sections 5(1)(a) and 94 of the Companies Ordinance, the principal purpose of which is to place a person on notice that he or she is dealing with a company whose members have limited liability. The use of such terms without proper incorporation is an offence under Section 350. The Registrar is empowered by Section 21 to exempt a company from including the word 'Limited' in its name where it is formed for the purpose of promoting commerce, art, science, religion or any other useful object and where it will apply its profit and income to the furtherance of these objects. Such companies will also be prohibited from distributing any dividends.

58 Section 20 of the Companies Ordinance. The index is a register for both locally incorporated and overseas companies.

59 Section 20(1)(c) and (d) of the Companies Ordinance.

60 Section 20(2) of the Companies Ordinance, which also requires the Chief Executive to give consent where the name includes any word or expression as specified by an order made pursuant to Section 22B such as 'Royal', 'Building Society', 'Chartered', 'Kaifong', 'Savings' and 'Trust'. Caution should also be exercised in the choice of names to ensure that no action will arise from the common law tort of passing off. See, for example, *Land Power International Holdings Ltd v Inter-Land Properties* (HK) Ltd [1995] 2 HKC 146 and *Computer Land Ltd v Registrar of Companies* [1986] HKC 49.

61 This amount may subsequently be increased by an ordinary resolution pursuant to Section 53(1)(a) of the Companies Ordinance if so authorized by the articles of the company. Although the allotment of shares in excess of the authorized capital is void, an application may be made to the court under Section 57C for its validation.

62 See *Re Scandinavian Bank Group plc* [1988] Ch 87.

63 Section 4(1) of the Companies Ordinance. A limit of 50 members is imposed upon private companies under Section 29(1).

64 Section 8(2) of the Companies Ordinance mandates that membership be effected by entry into the register of members.

65 Section 92(2) of the Companies Ordinance.

66 Section 58(1) of the Companies Ordinance. Pursuant to Section 158(2) and (3) the register must contain the personal details of its directors and secretaries including their names, residential addresses, nationalities and identity or passport numbers. If the office is held by a body corporate, its corporate name and registered or principal office address should be stated. Directors of publicly listed companies must have the particulars of their directorships in all other Hong Kong incorporated or overseas companies reflected in the register under Section 158(2A).

67   Section 74A of the Companies Ordinance.
68   Section 89 of the Companies Ordinance, together with copies of the instruments creating these charges as required under Section 88.
69   Section 95 of the Companies Ordinance.
70   Section 16 of the Companies Ordinance Securities (Disclosure of Interests) Ordinance, (Cap. 396).
71   Section 29 of the Companies Ordinance Securities (Disclosure of Interests) Ordinance (Cap. 396).
72   The word 'director' is defined in Section 2(1) of the Companies Ordinance to include any person occupying the position of director even though he or she may be described by another name. Thus the focus is on the substantive function served by the individual in determining whether he or she is a director of the company.
73   Article 82 of Table A of the First Schedule of the Companies Ordinance is a common example of such a provision which creates a statutory contract between the company and its members pursuant to Section 23(1) of the Companies Ordinance.
74   See, for example, *Automatic Self-Cleansing Filter Syndicate Co. v Cunninghame* [1906] 2 Ch 34 and *National Roads & Motorists Association v Parker* (1986) 4 ACLC 609.
75   *Guinness plc v Saunders* [1990] 2 AC 663. However, this strict requirement was relaxed in *Runciman v Walter Runciman plc* [1992] BCLC 1084, where the court held that a formal meeting may be dispensed with if the decision is made unanimously by the members of the board.
76   Article 109 of Table A allows the board to delegate some of its powers to a managing director. The rules governing the proceedings of the board are set out in the articles or determined by the board itself. For example, Article 100 of Table A enables the directors to meet together as a board and to regulate their meetings as they think fit.
77   *Re Smith and Fawcett Ltd* [1942] 1 All ER 542. There is no breach of duty where a director acts in a manner which he or she honestly believes is in the best interests of the company. The courts are generally reluctant to override the business judgments of directors and it is for the person alleging the breach of duty to bear the onus of proving his or her case.
78   This wider duty requires the director to exercise the powers for the purpose it was granted. The onus is on those alleging the improper exercise of power to prove his or her case and the courts are generally reluctant to interfere unless this is clearly demonstrated by the facts of the case. See, for example, the decisions of the Privy Council in *Howard Smith Ltd v Ampol Petroleum Ltd* [1974] AC 821 and *Lee Tak Samuel v Chou Wen Hsien* [1984] HKC 409. Such actions have been upheld by courts where the power to issue shares has been abused and where directors unreasonably refuse to register a transfer of shares.
79   The position of a director is akin to that of a trustee in that he or she cannot limit the exercise of his or her future discretion, an example of which is an agreement entered into by directors providing that they will vote in a certain way at future board meetings. However, the position of a nominee director remains unclear as the issue of divided loyalty may arise, that is whether the nominee owes the duty to the company or the shareholder who appointed him or her. See, for example, *Scottish Co-operative Wholesale Soc. Ltd v Meyer* [1958] 3 All ER 66, *Berlei-Hestia (NZ) Ltd v Fernyhough* [1980] 2 NZLR 150 and *Whitehouse v Carlton Hotel Pty Ltd* (1987) 5 ACLC 421.
80   This obligation prevents directors from putting themselves in a position which creates the appearance that they are acting in their own interests. Directors are deemed to be constructive trustees for the company of any property or

profit which they acquire from such a breach of duty: *Carrian Investments Ltd v Wong Chong-po* [1986] HKLR 945. As such, unless expressly allowed and/or disclosed, directors may not make personal profits out of their office. This duty also prohibits a director from accepting a bribe or other undisclosed benefit, misusing company funds, taking up corporate opportunities, using confidential information or competing with the company. See, for example, *Cook v Deeks* [1916] 1 AC 554, *Regal (Hastings) Ltd v Gulliver* [1942] 1 All ER 378, *Attorney General for Hong Kong v Reid* [1994] 1 AC 324 and *Kishimoto Sangyo Co. Ltd v Akihiro Oba* [1996] 2 HKC 260.

81 Although the minimal standard of care as enunciated by Romer J. in *Re City Equitable Fire Insurance Co. Ltd* [1925] Ch 407 continues to be applied in Hong Kong, this standard may gradually increase with the enactment of Part IVA (Sections 168C–168T) of the Companies Ordinance which seeks to disqualify certain persons from assuming the office of director. This group includes those who are deemed incompetent or irresponsible, those who persistently breach provisions of the Ordinance or have been convicted of an indictable offence and those who are liable for fraudulent trading in the course of the winding up of a company. It remains to be seen as to whether the Hong Kong courts will adopt recent judicial pronouncements promoting higher standards of care namely *Norman v Theodore Goddard* [1991] BCLC 1028, *Re D'Jan of London Ltd* [1993] BCC 646 and *Daniels v Anderson* (1995) 16 ACSR 607.

82 Article 101 of Table A.

83 Directors, although present, may be ineligible to vote due to *inter alia* potential or actual conflicts of interest as outlined by Article 86(2) of Table A. Where an equality of votes arises the chairman of the meeting is given a second or casting vote under Article 100. Resolutions by the board may also be effected in writing if this is signed by all the directors as provided for in Article 108.

84 Section 111 of the Companies Ordinance. The company need only hold such a meeting once in its first two years provided that its inaugural meeting is held within 18 months of its incorporation. Thereafter, these annual meetings must be held no later than 15 months from the last preceding annual general meeting unless an extension of time has been granted in writing by the Registrar.

85 Section 111(2) of the Companies Ordinance. The application must be initiated by a member of the company and failure on the part of the company or its officers to comply will attract a penalty of not exceeding $ 50 000 together with a daily default fine where applicable.

86 Section 122 of the Companies Ordinance. These comprise the profit and loss account or income and expenditure statements, the balance sheet, and the directors' and auditor's reports.

87 Section 131(8) of the Companies Ordinance, which includes the fixing of the remuneration of the auditor.

88 These are usually convened by the directors pursuant to Article 51 of Table A. However, members may request the convening of such a meeting under Section 113 of the Companies Ordinance where they hold at least 10 per cent of the paid up capital carrying voting rights if the company has a share capital. Otherwise the 10 per cent threshold is determined with reference to the total voting rights.

89 Section 5(4)(a) of the Companies Ordinance requires that a company having a share capital state its amount of share capital and its division into fixed amounts in its memorandum. However, the directors of the company are conferred wide powers under Article 2 of Table A to issue shares of different classes, each carrying various rights and restrictions. Class meetings are usually held separately from general meetings of all members to discuss and vote on matters which affect the legal rights of the particular class.

90   Section 114 of the Companies Ordinance specifies a 21-day minimum require-
      ment for an annual general meeting and 14 days for other meetings, but this
      may be increased by express provisions in the articles. Such a notice applies
      equally to class meetings.
91   Section 116 of the Companies Ordinance. This may be waived or reduced
      with the consent of members who collectively hold at least 95 per cent of the
      voting shares. Kaplan J. held in *SFC v Stock Exchange of Hong Kong* [1992] 1
      HKLR 135 that the day of posting, the day of deemed receipt and the day of
      the meeting were to be excluded from the calculation of the requisite notice.
      See also Article 132 of Table A.
92   Section 116C of the Companies Ordinance specifies the timeframe for such
      notices as 28 days if served on the company, or 21 days if given by the
      company or made by way of advertisement in a newspaper.
93   Section 132(1)(d) of the Companies Ordinance.
94   Section 132(1)(a) of the Companies Ordinance.
95   Section 132(1)(b) of the Companies Ordinance.
96   Section 132(1)(c) of the Companies Ordinance.
97   *Re Express Engineering Works Ltd* [1920] 1 Ch 466. Article 53 of Table A pro-
      vides that an accidental omission to provide notice to a member or its
      non-receipt is not an irregularity which would invalidate proceedings and the
      resolutions which were purportedly passed.
98   Section 114A(1) of the Companies Ordinance. This definition includes proxies
      and representatives of member corporations: Article 55 of Table A. The latter
      must be authorized by its board of directors to assume the powers pursuant
      to Section 115(1).
99   Section 114B of the Companies Ordinance. See also *Re Totex-Adon Pty Ltd and
      the Companies Act* [1980] 1 NSWLR and *Cheng Yuk Lin v Chan Choi Wah* [1993] 1
      HKC 52.
100   Article 64 of Table A. Proxy votes are not usually counted in such a manner of
      voting.
101   Article 60 of Table A. The calculation of votes is determined by the voting
      rights held by the person present and includes proxies *per* Article 69.
102   Section 122 of the Companies Ordinance and the Tenth Schedule to the Ordi-
      nance. Given its fluidity, the precise meaning of 'true and fair' is left largely to
      the accounting profession and is generally accepted as including the applica-
      tion of accounting policies appropriate to the company in question, compliance
      with all relevant statutory disclosure requirements and the usefulness of the
      financial information in the hands of its recipients. Section 126 mandates the
      preparation of consolidated accounts where related companies operate within
      a group.
103   Section 122(1A) of the Companies Ordinance. The timeframe for exempt pri-
      vate companies and companies limited by guarantee is nine months preceding
      its annual general meeting. In all cases, the balance sheet should be prepared
      as at the date to which the profit and loss account is made out, that is they
      must have the same balance date.
104   Section 129G of the Companies Ordinance. Non-compliance is an offence
      against the Ordinance which attracts a penalty for both the company and the
      officers in default.
105   Referred to hereafter as 'exempt companies' for convenience.
106   Section 141D of the Companies Ordinance. The consent of the members must
      be obtained every financial year for the exemption to continue. Companies
      carrying on a banking, insurance or securities business cannot claim this
      exemption. It also does not apply to a private company which has, or is, a
      subsidiary of another company registered under the Ordinance, or which

operates a trade or business of accepting loans and money, or owns and operates ships and aircraft engaged in the carriage of cargo between Hong Kong and places outside of Hong Kong.

107 Section 141D(1)(b) of the Companies Ordinance which requires the company to keep proper books of accounts and have a balance sheet. Every company must keep such accounting records as is necessary to facilitate the preparation of true and fair accounts which may be conveniently and properly audited.

108 Section 336 of the Companies Ordinance. The submission comprises its balance sheet and profit and loss account, together with its group accounts, and the directors' and auditor's reports where applicable.

109 Section 131(3) of the Companies Ordinance. This duty rests with the directors of the company. The company in a general meeting assumes this duty from the first annual general meeting. An auditor may not be a body corporate and must be an independent person who is qualified under the Professional Accountants Ordinance (Cap. 50).

110 Section 141 of the Companies Ordinance. This report states the opinion of the auditor as to whether the accounts have been properly drawn up in accordance with the provisions of the Ordinance and whether they give a true and fair view of the matters which have to be dealt with pursuant to Section 123. To do so the auditor must investigate whether proper books of accounts have been kept by the company and whether the balance sheet and profit and loss account are in agreement with the former.

111 Section 141(4) and (6) of the Companies Ordinance. Auditors are obliged to devise their audit procedures in a manner which would assist in the detection of errors or fraud, failure of which could constitute a breach of duty. See generally, *Pacific Acceptance Corp. Ltd v Forsyth* (1970) 92 WN (NSW) 29, *WA Chip & Pulp Co. Pty Ltd v Arthur Young & Co.* (1987) 5 ACLC 1002 and *Daniels v Anderson* (1995) 13 ACLC 614. However, it is noteworthy that the Law Amendment and Reform (Consolidation) Ordinance (Cap. 23) allows the apportionment of damages in actions for the tort of negligence where there has been contributory negligence by either the injured party or some other person.

112 Section 129D of the Companies Ordinance.

113 Section 141(1) of the Companies Ordinance.

114 See, in particular, the internal management rule from *Foss v Harbottle* (1843) 2 Hare 461; 67 ER 189, which is based on the reluctance of the courts to interfere with internal irregularities which are capable of being ratified by an ordinary resolution.

115 (1843) 2 Hare 461; 67 ER 189. This has been applied in *Tan Poh Lean v Hong Kong Communications Equipment Co. Ltd* [1983] 2 HKC 488.

116 See *Saloman v Saloman & Co. Ltd* [1897] AC 22 and Section 16(2).

117 *Per* Jenkins LJ. in *Edwards v Halliwell* [1950] 2 All ER 1064.

118 This exception refers to illegal and criminal acts of the company as well as to acts which were beyond the objects and powers as set out in the memorandum of association. See *Simpson v Westminister Palace Hotel Co.* (1860) 8 HL Cas 712 and *So Kwan Nane v Kowloon Stock Exchange Ltd* [1973–1976] HKC 315.

119 See *Cotter v National Union of Seamen* [1929] 2 Ch 58 and *Edwards v Halliwell* [1950] 2 All ER 1064.

120 See *Pender v Lushington* (1877) 6 ChD 70, *Ram Krssendas Dhanuka v Satya Charan Law* (1949) LR 77 IA 128 and *Residues Treatment & Trading Co. Ltd v Southern Resources Ltd* (1988) 6 ACLC 1160.

121 In *Allen v Gold Reefs of West Africa* [1900] 1 Ch 656 it was held that, in the context of company law, the majority must use their voting power to act *bona fide* for the benefit of the company as a whole. Failure to meet this duty

would constitute fraud on the minority. The word 'fraud' means an abuse of power whereby the majority secures an unfair gain at the expense of the minority. The injured party may either be the minority or the company, and the onus is upon the person who alleges to establish the purported abuse of power: *Peters American Delicacy Co. Ltd v Heath* (1939) 61 CLR 457. See generally, *Menier v Hooper's Telegraph Works* (1874) 9 Ch App 350, *North-West Transportation Co. v Beatty* (1887) 12 App Cas 589, *Anglo-Eastern (1985) Ltd v Karl Knutz* [1988] 1 HKLR 322 and *Tan Eng Guan & Chan Wing Chong v Southland Co. Ltd* [1996] 2 HKC 100.

122   Per Street J. in *Hawkesbury Development Co. Ltd v Landmark Finance Pty Ltd* [1969] 2 NSWR 782 and Vinelott J. in *Prudential Assurance Co. Ltd v Newman Industries Ltd (No. 2)* [1982] 2 All ER 841. However, the English Court of Appeal expressed doubts over the position taken by Vinelott in handing down its decision in *Prudential Assurance Co. Ltd v Newman Industries Ltd (No. 2)* [1982] 1 All ER 354.

123   Per Megarry V.-C. in *Estmanco (Kilner House) Ltd v Greater London Council* [1982] 1 All ER 437; [1982] 1 WLR 2, Silke V.-P. in *Anglo-Eastern (1985) Ltd v Knutz* [1988] 1 HKLR 322 and Knox J. in *Smith v Croft* (No. 2) [1988] Ch 114.

124   Based on Section 210 of the English Companies Act 1948, now Section 459 of the 1985 Act.

125   Identical to Section 222(f) of the English Companies Act 1948, now contained in Part XVII of the 1985 Act. This is discussed below under 'External Administration of Companies'.

126   The word 'interests' has been widely defined to include a legitimate expectation such as the payment of dividends by the company to its members upon its winding up: *Yun Jip Auto Services v Yuen Sau Fai* [1990] 1 HKC 20.

127   The test for unfairly prejudicial is an objective one. The applicant must establish that both unfairness and prejudice co-existed with respect to the conduct complained of. See *Re Taiwa Land Investment Co. Ltd* [1981] HKLR 297 and *Re Saul D. Harrison & Sons plc* [1995] 1 BCLC 14.

128   Although an applicant need not be a member at the time of the petition, he or she should have been a member at the time of the alleged conduct: *Lou Thiam Siong v Hwa Aun Co. (Hong Kong) Ltd* [1989] 1 HKC 443.

129   This would include actions whose facts are similar to those in *Ebrahimi v Westbourne Galleries Ltd* [1972] 2 All ER 492. See *Re Lai Kan Co. Ltd* and *Re Safe Steel Furniture Factory Ltd* [1988] 1 HKLR 257. Other examples include actions which prevent the company from trading or acting in accordance with the fundamental shareholders' agreement: Re *Mediavision Ltd* [1993] 2 HKC 629, and the making of a rights issue designed to dilute the equity of certain shareholders: *Tseng Yueh Lee, Irene v Metrobilt Enterprises Ltd* [1994] 2 HKC 684.

130   Section 168A(2) of the Companies Ordinance.

131   Section 5(5) of the Companies Ordinance and the Seventh Schedule to the Ordinance. These powers are usually granted to the board of directors under Article 81 of Table A. However, these may be amended by the members in general meeting, and in any event the consent of the general meeting is required where the amount borrowed exceeds the nominal capital of the company.

132   Paragraph 12 of the Seventh Schedule to the Companies Ordinance.

133   Though not defined by the Companies Ordinance, the term applies to both legal and equitable charges and includes any security for repayment of a debt thereby incorporating mortgages and charges in the strict legal sense.

134   Part III of the Companies Ordinance, namely Sections 80–91.

135   This is referred to by Section 298A of the Companies Ordinance as an appointment under an instrument which is also commonly known as a private

appointment or an appointment out of court. The terms of the debenture govern the appointment and set the parameters of the powers of the receiver and/or manager: *Re B. Johnson & Co. (Builders) Ltd* [1955] 2 All ER 775.

136 Section 21L of the Supreme Court Ordinance. See *Mandarin Resources Corporation Ltd v Cheng Heng Soon Civ,* App No. 146 of 1987, 20 April 1988 (unreported). The status of such an appointee has been clarified by Lord Haldane in *Parsons v Sovereign Bank of Canada* [1913] AC 160.

137 Section 28A of the Companies Ordinance. However, Section 28(4) allows two companies to purchase shares in each other so long as the holding subsidiary relationship does not arise.

138 Section 58(1A) of the Companies Ordinance. To allow the same would be tantamount to an open invitation for the company to return its capital to its members. See *Trevor v Whitworth* (1887) 12 App Cas 409.

139 Sections 49B–49S of the Companies Ordinance. These were derived from, and are broadly similar to, the current Chapter VII of Part V of the English Companies Act 1985, albeit with some differences. However, Section 49B(6) prohibits a company from buying back its own shares where the result of such a transaction would be to leave its capital comprising of only redeemable shares.

140 Section 49B(1) of the Companies Ordinance states that the source of this authority is the articles of the company.

141 Section 49BA of the Companies Ordinance. General offers must be authorized by an ordinary resolution of the general meeting as are stock market purchases, although the mandate for the latter may be on a renewal one-year basis. All other purchases may only proceed by way of special resolution by independent members.

142 Sections 49B(3) and 49A(1) of the Companies Ordinance respectively. The company must cancel the shares which it purchases. Buy-backs out of capital are permissible under the circumstances as outlined under Section 49B(4).

143 These may only proceed by way of a purchase contract pursuant to Section 49D or a contingent purchase contract under Section 49E of the Companies Ordinance.

144 This prohibition extends that as expounded by the House of Lords in *Trevor v Whitworth* (1887) 12 App Cas 409 and is now reflected by Sections 47A-47G of the Companies Ordinance. Exemptions are provided in certain circumstances as outlined in Section 47C, including assistance given in good faith in the interest of the company or where it is merely incidental to a larger purpose: *Brady v Brady* [1989] AC 755. English decisions on the matter are likely to be adopted in Hong Kong given the fact that the current provisions were effectively taken from Chapter VI of Part V of the Companies Act 1985. The principal distinction is that the Hong Kong version divides companies into listed and unlisted entities rather than the public and private company approach used in the United Kingdom.

145 These provisions are detailed in Sections 47E–47G of the Companies Ordinance.

146 Section 47D of the Companies Ordinance.

147 Section 47A(3) of the Companies Ordinance.

148 See *Dressy Frocks Pty Ltd v Bock* (1951) 51 SR (NSW) 390 and *Heald v O'Connor* [1971] 2 All ER 1105. However, the courts have been prepared to uphold that part of the transaction which may be severed from the others which have been tainted by this illegality: *Carney v Herbert* [1985] AC 301.

149 Although the ensuing discussion relates primarily to companies in financial distress, these options are available to financially sound companies. For example, a corporate restructuring may be implemented as a prelude to a listing on the stock exchange, whereas a member's voluntary winding up might be

appropriate where the purpose of the entity has been realized. The procedure for such liquidations is set out in Sections 228–239A of the Companies Ordinance.

150   Section 25 of the Companies Ordinance.

151   Sections 166–168 of the Companies Ordinance.

152   Section 166(5) of the Companies Ordinance. See *Re Hongkong and Shanghai Banking Corporation Ltd* [1991] 2 HKLR 111.

153   Section 168 of the Companies Ordinance allows the successful bidder to compulsorily acquire the remaining shares of a target company where the 90 per cent threshold has been attained. Likewise, it allows the minority to compel the bidder to purchase their shares at this juncture.

154   Section 166 of the Companies Ordinance sets out the procedure involved. A scheme will only be binding if it is approved by the required three-quarters in value of creditors or members and is subsequently sanctioned by the court. However, the scheme will only be effective when a copy of the court order is lodged with the Registrar for registration.

155   It is possible for companies to resort to informal corporate rescues or workouts. However, these are governed by normal contractual principles as there are no express provisions for the same under the Companies Ordinance. Although judicial management has been advanced as an option by the Law Reform Commission as published in its Report on Corporate Rescue and Insolvent Trading in October 1996, this remains a recommendation and has yet to be legislated upon.

156   Sections 241–248 of the Companies Ordinance.

157   This allows directors of a company to resolve that it be wound up on the grounds that its liabilities prevent the company from carrying on its business. A statutory declaration must be lodged with the Registrar and a meeting of the company and its creditors must be convened within 28 days from the date of this filing. This procedure is aimed at preserving the assets of the company where its directors are of the opinion that it would be futile to carry on trading and which would otherwise invariably lead to a grab race between creditors.

158   Such applications for the compulsory winding up of a company may only be made by a person listed in Section 179(1) of the Companies Ordinance, which includes the company, its creditors and contributories. The applicant must establish one of the grounds as envisaged under Section 177(1), although in practice the most common are the inability to pay debts and the just and equitable ground.

159   Section 184(2) of the Companies Ordinance.

160   Section 178(1)(a) of the Companies Ordinance allows any creditor to whom the company owes a debt in excess of HK$ 5 000 to serve such a demand on the company. If the company fails to pay the said sum or to secure or compound it to the reasonable satisfaction of the company within three weeks, it is deemed to be unable to pay its debts for the purposes of Section 177(1)(d).

161   Section 177(1)(f) of the Companies Ordinance.

162   See generally, *Re Quality International Ltd* [1964] HKLR 669 and *Ebrahimi v Westbourne Galleries Ltd* [1973] AC 360. A winding up order was granted where the courts opined that the directors of the company lacked probity and lost the confidence of its members: *Loch v John Blackwood Ltd* [1924] AC 783 and *San Imperial Corp. Ltd (No. 2)* [1980] HKLR 649.

163   See *Re Yenidje Tobacco Co. Ltd* [1916] 2 Ch 426 and *Re Cirtex Co. Ltd* [1987] 3 HKC 21.

164   See *Re Eastern Telegraph Co. Ltd* [1947] All ER 104, *Re Tivoli Freeholds Ltd* [1972] VR 445 and *Re Mediavision* [1993] 2 HKC 629. However, no order will be

granted by the court if it can be shown that the principal objects of the company can still be performed by the company: *Re Chinese Estates Ltd* [1976] HKLR 369. The onus of establishing the failure of substratum rests with the applicant. The respondent may allege that the applicant is acting unreasonably in not pursuing alternative remedies, but bears the onus of proving this pursuant to Section 180(1A) of the Companies Ordinance.

165 *Per* Godfrey J. in *Tseng Yueh Lee Irene v Metrobilt Enterprise Ltd* [1994] 2 HKC 684, 690.

166 Re *Cirtex Co. Ltd* [1987] 3 HKC 21 and *Re Shiu Fook Co. Ltd* [1989] 2 HKC 3; see *Re London School of Electronics Ltd* [1986] Ch 211.

167 Section 278 of the Companies Ordinance, the contravention of which renders the appointment void.

168 Sections 199 and 226 of the Companies Ordinance. See also the Companies (Winding Up) Rules.

169 Section 204 of the Companies Ordinance allows the official receiver to supervise the performance of these duties by the liquidator. If a breach of duty is established, the court may take such action as it thinks fit including an order that the liquidator make good the loss incurred as a result of his or her breach: *Commissioner for Corporate Affairs v Harvey* [1980] VR 669.

170 Section 263 of the Companies Ordinance. The amount of a debt is generally computed as at the date of commencement of winding up. This includes damages, although this is confined to instances of breaches of contract, promise or trust under Section 264. However, where the company is solvent, the creditor may prove as yet unascertained damages arising from claims in tort. Section 264 provides for the application of the rules of bankruptcy in the winding up of insolvent companies.

171 The claims of holders of floating charges may be postponed to those of preferential creditors as outlined in Section 265 of the Companies Ordinance to include claims by employees and other statutory debts.

172 These may include, for example, recovery of invalid floating charges under Section 267 of the Companies Ordinance and the recovery from the officers of the company under Sections 275 or 276.

173 This is not required in the case of a voluntary winding up.

174 Section 9 of the Securities and Futures Commission Ordinance (Cap. 24).

175 This committee is established under the terms of Section 6(1) of the Securities and Futures Commission Ordinance (Cap. 24).

176 Section 6(1) of the Securities and Futures Commission Ordinance (Cap. 24).

177 *R v The Panel on Takeovers and Mergers; Ex parte Datafin and Prudential Bache Securities Inc.* [1987] 2 WLR 699.

178 Rule 26 of the Takeovers Code. This applies when a person acts in concert with associates to acquire 35 per cent or more of the voting shares in the target company or where a creeping takeover is being implemented. The latter requires an acquisition of 5 per cent or more of the voting shares over a period of 12 months where the person and his or her associates already hold between 35 to 50 per cent of the same in the target company.

179 These are set out in the Notes to Rule 26 and include shareholders coming together to act in concert, the application of the chain principle through which a person indirectly controls one company by the purchase of another, foreclosure on security for a loan and urgent rescue operations.

180 Rule 4 and paragraph 6 of the General Principles. These reflect the principles enunciated by the Privy Council in *Howard Smith Ltd v Ampol Petroleum Ltd* [1974] AC 821. This rule also prohibits certain unilateral conduct by the board of the target company without shareholder approval, namely those which are designed to frustrate the offer.

181   Rule 2 of the Takeovers Code.
182   Rule 9 of the Takeovers Code.
183   Paragraph 12 of the Introduction. This may be imposed by the Takeovers and Mergers Executive with the consent of the party to be disciplined.
184   It was established on 1 May 1989 under the Securities and Futures Commission Ordinance (Cap. 24).
185   Its functions are set out in Section 4 of the Securities and Futures Commission Ordinance (Cap. 24).
186   The word 'securities' is defined extensively under Section 2(1) of the Securities Ordinance (Cap. 333) to include shares, stocks, debentures, funds, bonds and options in respect of the same.
187   Cap. 333 of the Laws of Hong Kong. This Ordinance regulates the formation and conduct of stock exchanges, relations between stock exchanges and the issuers of securities, the licensing and conduct of dealers in securities and investment advisers, and improper market practices.
188   Section 12 of the Securities and Futures Commission Ordinance (Cap. 24).
189   Although the Securities and Futures Commission Ordinance (Cap. 24) currently uses the word 'Governor', this will be amended to read 'Chief Executive'.
190   Section 14 of the Securities and Futures Commission Ordinance (Cap. 24).
191   Cap. 361 of the Laws of Hong Kong. The SEHK opened in April 1986 following the amalgamation of the then four operating exchanges, namely the Hong Kong Stock Exchange, the Far East Stock Exchange, the Kam Ngan Stock Exchange and the Kowloon Stock Exchange.
192   The Securities Ordinance (Cap. 333) is derived from its early Australian counterpart, the Securities Industry Code of New South Wales. However, unlike other jurisdictions, the regulatory framework in Hong Kong has not kept pace with recent developments within the industry, the result being an increasingly unwieldy regime spread across 11 different Ordinances.
193   Sections 37–41A and the Third Schedule to the Companies Ordinance. This checklist approach has, unfortunately, resulted in the prospectus being a highly technical and legalistic document, comprehensible only by those with considerable financial expertise.
194   Section 38D of the Companies Ordinance. The SFC retains the responsibility for the authorisation for registration of prospectuses issued by non-listing applicants.
195   Section 42 of the Companies Ordinance.
196   Section 44B of the Companies Ordinance.
197   These include actions for misrepresentation, breach of contract and negligent misstatements.
198   This is spread across three Ordinances, namely Sections 40, 40A, 45 and 46 of the Companies Ordinance, Sections 3, 7 and 8 of the Protection of Investors Ordinance (Cap. 335) and Section 139 of the Securities Ordinance (Cap. 333).
199   Cap. 335 of the Laws of Hong Kong. This Ordinance makes it an offence for any person to induce another to deal in securities through fraudulent means or by reckless misrepresentation. It also imposes restrictions on the issue and distribution of material inviting the public to subscribe for securities.
200   Cap. 395 of the Laws of Hong Kong. Insider dealing is not a criminal offence in Hong Kong. The specific circumstances of insider dealing are set out in Section 9 of the Ordinance with the available defences stated in Section 10. There are no provisions for civil remedies by investors as the sanction is a penalty of up to 300 per cent of the profits made or loses avoided.
201   Cap. 396 of the Laws of Hong Kong. Directors and substantial shareholders (the latter defined as holders of more than 10 per cent of the share capital of the company) are required to disclose their interests in the company and its

associates. The disclosure by substantial shareholders is mandated when they attain 10 per cent and whenever their shareholding changes by 1 per cent, whereas directors must disclose all of their transactions regardless of amount. This notification must be made to both the company and the SEHK within five days of the transaction.

202 These certificates of registration are granted on a permanent basis, although it may be suspended or revoked at any time (subject to the rules of natural justice) when the holder is deemed not to be a fit and proper person. See Sections 55 and 57 of the Securities Ordinance (Cap. 333).

203 Section 80 of the Securities Ordinance (Cap. 333).

204 Section 135 of the Securities Ordinance (Cap. 333). Such activities include churning, namely transactions which involve no change in the beneficial ownership of those securities, and such other activities which inhibit the free market forces.

205 Section 358 of the Companies Ordinance. Such an application may also be brought pursuant to Section 358(2) in anticipation of a breach. If so granted, the costs of the legal proceedings may be paid for by the company: Section 165(c).

206 Section 357 of the Companies Ordinance. In exercising this jurisdiction, the court should attempt to do justice to each of the litigants having due regard to the facts and issues of the case, the solvency of the company and the relative burden of such an order.

207 Section 272 of the Companies Ordinance.

208 Section 275 of the Companies Ordinance.

209 Section 276 of the Companies Ordinance.

210 Section 277 of the Companies Ordinance.

211 Section 352 of the Companies Ordinance.

212 This followed a recommendation for the same by the Standing Committee on Company Law Reform. See pp. 52–53 of the Committee's Tenth Annual Report 1993/94.

213 The report has been widely circulated for public comments with the consultation period closing on 31 December 1997. However, its enactment is not expected for a number of years and the eventual framework may be somewhat different from the proposal given the initial reactions to it.

214 This includes the incorporation, powers and functions of the separate organs of the company, the provisions with respect to accounts and audit, and the control of foreign companies. The term 'core company law' was coined by the New Zealand Law Reform Commission, whose reforms of the early 1990s are being adopted as a model for the simplification of the Companies Ordinance.

215 The draft Bill consists of 15 Parts and eight Schedules, with the aim of consolidating the regulation of the securities and futures industries which is currently spread across 11 separate Ordinances.

216 Some amendment is envisaged in view of the comments received. The Hong Kong Association of Banks expressed some reservations over provisions which might impact upon their business, and the submission by the SEHK included an indication that it would have tremendous difficulties in giving support to the passing of the draft Bill in its present published form.

217 The proposed provisional supervisor may effect an immediate 30-day moratorium which could thereafter be extended for a further six months on application to the court. This will allow him or her to formulate plans for the rescue of the company without being unduly hampered by the competing claims and interests of creditors. It also provides for the protection of the rights of employees who may be affected by the reorganization of the company.

7 Company Law in Taiwan

NEIL ANDREWS* AND ANGUS FRANCIS**

1 Introduction

The law governing the activities of companies in Taiwan, like the Taiwanese legal system and regulatory structure, reflects a complex heritage. Taiwanese company law and regulation remains heavily influenced by its origin in the imperial Chinese system of government and law, the Japanese and German civil law traditions imported in the late imperial and republican periods, and more recently, by the common law tradition embodied in the commercial law and practice of the United States. Only by taking into account the intricate interplay of these disparate legal traditions with Taiwan's elaborate political and regulatory structures and the economic forces which transformed Taiwan after 1945 can contemporary Taiwanese company law and its practice be understood.

1.1 The Constitution and the Separation of Powers

Taiwan, which was ceded in 1895 by China to Japan, was restored to China in 1945. Within four years it was the only remaining part of Chinese territory under the control of the Nationalist Party, the Kuomintang (KMT), following its withdrawal from the mainland in 1949.

The Constitution, which was promulgated on the mainland in 1947 by the National Constituent Assembly of the Republic of China, remains the fundamental law. It follows the formal fivefold separation of powers instituted by Sun Yat-Sen.[1] The executive power is vested in the President and power is further divided between the National Assembly and the five Yuans: Executive, Legislative, Judicial, Control and Examination.[2]

The Executive Yuan resembles the cabinet in other constitutions. It is presided over by the Premier. It consists of the Vice-premier, five to seven ministers of state and a number of chairs of commissions having cabinet rank. These include the Minister for Finance and the chairs of the Securities and Futures Commission (SFC) and the Fair Trading Commission.[3]

Legislative power is divided between the National Assembly and the Legislative Yuan. The National Assembly's powers essentially relate to amendments to the Constitution, and the recall of the President. The Legislative Yuan has law-making powers and some powers to control the Executive Yuan.[4]

Judicial power is vested in the Judicial Yuan[5] which is constituted by the Council of Grand Justices. It has responsibility for the judicial system, including the Supreme Court, the Administrative Court and the Committee on the Discipline of Public Functionaries. The Council of Grand Justices includes in its membership non-legally qualified former senior politicians.[6] It has the power to 'unify' the interpretation of other laws and, as the Constitutional Court, the power to interpret the Constitution.[7] All judicial power is required to be exercised by independent and impartial judges in accordance with law and free from any interference.[8]

The Control and Examination Yuans continue a separation of power formulated by the imperial government. The Control Yuan perpetuates the imperial Censorate. Now a quasi-judicial body, it monitors the actions of government and the implementation of government policies and corrects officials.[9] It may impeach, censure and audit. Its powers are greater than those of the ombudsman or parliamentary commissioners in Western states. The Examination Yuan is responsible for the examination, employment and management of all civil service personnel. It continues the imperial tradition of competitive public examinations for the civil service.[10]

Changes to the Constitution in 1994, claimed to be a revision of a cabinet system of government, freed the President from having instruments countersigned by ministers. It has further tilted constitutional ambiguity towards a presidential system, which was the reality under the rule of the Chiang family from 1928 to 1988.[11]

The Constitution also establishes a federal division of powers between the central and provincial governments. Below the provincial level there is a system of county government. In 1994 some of the powers of the Executive Yuan were transferred to the Province of Taiwan and its elected governor.[12] In January 1997 the central government announced an intention to abolish the provincial government.[13]

1.2   *Taiwanese Law*

1.2.1   Chinese law   The legal system in Taiwan continues that of the Republic of China (ROC) before 1949.[14] It is a codified civil law system overlaid on imperial Chinese law. Under the last two emperors of the Qing Dynasty (1644–1911) from 1902 the imperial government commenced a programme of law reform to develop a system of European-style codes and courts. Over two decades later the KMT completed this programme.[15] The basic codes, promulgated in the late 1920s and early 1930s, followed Japanese models, which were heavily influenced by German codes. Since 1945, particularly in areas of commercial law, there has been increasing borrowing from Anglo-US common law.

Despite the introduction of Western codes and courts, the 3 000-year-old Chinese legal system has remained significant. The first European observers of imperial Chinese law and some writers of the late imperial period were impressed by its codification, rationality, leniency and systematic administration through a large empire.[16] Subsequently it has been frequently to the political and economic advantage of Western states to criticize it. Those advantages have extended from continuing the privileges of extraterritoriality to reaping the monopoly profits of intellectual property. Repeated representations are of a legal system gradually emerging from a state of legal impoverishment. Often these are based on a narrow Western positivist conception of law: that obligations between individuals, companies and the state are governed by rules made by state institutions.[17] If not obeyed, punishment or payment of damages follows. Legal obligations are only those that are enforceable under this law. A 'strong' legal system adheres to the obligations imposed by state law-making institutions. The contemporary Taiwan codes and courts, which emerged during the 1920s and 1930s in China, are criticized as a 'weak' form of law or as opposed to 'the rule of law'.

This model of law ignores the possibility of binding obligations without recourse to state law.[18] In traditional Chinese society the obligation arose from the relationship between the parties involved. The character of that relationship, and the social expectations which governed it, determined the proper conduct. Social expectations emerged from the community's major political and social philosophies of Confucianism and Legalism. These were concerned with social rules establishing the greatest order and stability in a large administrative state.[19] As their primary aim was to preserve public order, private commercial transactions between individuals and commercial groups were regarded as insignificant. The result was that 'there was no conception of civil law, of the claims and suits of citizens as between themselves'.[20] Law's ranking below social morality in significance is shown in the penal and administrative character of the imperial legal codes. The Qing Code penalized those who encouraged litigation or managed it for profit.[21] This source of people's obligations to each other and to the state in social and cultural norms distinguished China from many Western states. Yet all systems have their contradictions and even in the imperial period commercial disputes did come before magistrates where the parties had failed to be reconciled by other processes.[22]

1.2.2   The civil codes   Taiwan's legal system has been heavily influenced by European civil law. The loss of Taiwan to Japan at the end of the Sino-Japanese War made change, including law reform, a critical issue in China after 1895.[23] The period of relative peace between 1928 and 1937 enabled law reforms, started in the late empire, to be completed. The KMT government promulgated the Code of Civil Procedure (1928, revised 1935), the Civil Code (1929), the Company Law (1929), the Bankruptcy Law (1935) and a number of other codes. These codes still form the basis of Taiwanese law. They are largely based on Japanese codes. The Chinese law reformers saw similarities between the two countries, including extraterritoriality, which the Japanese codes successfully ended. They perceived, like the Japanese, that the civil law tradition was more compatible with Chinese law and values than the common law. The civil law was also conveniently codified with the German codes both recent and comprehensive.[24]

In spite of the Japanese colonization of Taiwan, the codified law has, as on the mainland, not had a great effect on commerce. It was alien and frequently ignored in favour of commercial social norms and custom:

> The Nationalist government from about 1928 built up in China an impressive array of modern courts administering modern codes of rules in the adjudicative mode, Western style ... But the whole structure was an elaborate facade without any real substance behind it. The Western system never won acceptance by the Chinese people, the great bulk of whom simply ignored it and continued in their traditional ways and practices unaffected.[25]

In Taiwan these 'bodies of rules have been, to a certain extent, internally inconsistent and incomplete and not uniformly implemented'.[26]

1.2.3   Anglo-US common law   American commercial dominance, the economic relationships between Taiwan and the United States and the US education of many Taiwanese lawyers have since 1945 increasingly influenced Taiwan's legal system. A number of US civil and commercial laws have been directly borrowed. These include amendments to the Law of Negotiable Instruments, the Maritime Law, the Insurance Law, the Civil Code (in the form of the Chattel Secured Transactions Law) and the Company Law. Yet, it is open to question too whether this Anglo-US common law influence has had much effect on local commercial practice.

1.3 The Court Structure

The Judicial Yuan exercises the judicial power with some quasi-judicial and administrative powers being exercised by the Control Yuan. The Judicial Yuan is constituted by a President and 15–17 Grand Justices. As the Council of Grand Justices, they have the power to interpret the Constitution and to unify the interpretation of other laws. As the Constitutional Court, they may dissolve political parties. They also supervise the other courts: the Supreme Court, the High Courts, the District Courts, the Administrative Court and the Committee on the Discipline of Public Functionaries.

At the lowest level of the general court system are the District Courts. These are courts of first instance with jurisdiction over almost all criminal prosecutions and all civil claims not exceeding NT$ 300 000. The court sits in divisions, including financial divisions, constituted generally by a single judge. Decisions of a single judge may be reviewed by a panel of three judges. An appeal lies to the High Court. Appeals are heard by panels of three judges. From the High Court appeal lies on matters of law to the Supreme Court, the final court of appeal. It sits in seven civil divisions and ten criminal divisions with panels of five judges. As in other civil law jurisdictions, there are few limits on appeal and the court hears a large volume of cases.

The separate Administrative Court is based on the French distinction between civil and administrative law. It is more judicial than its French equivalent. It hears appeals from individuals claiming violation of rights by administrative actions of government agencies. Panels of five judges determine these cases. Their decisions are final with the exception of some limited grounds for retrials. They may not make a decision less favourable to an individual than that appealed against. The Committee on the Discipline of Public Functionaries is another special tribunal. It determines accusations of malfeasance or dereliction or neglect of duty against public office holders made by the Control Yuan or requests for disciplinary action by heads of government agencies and departments.

Company and securities law matters, subject to any statutory requirement to use arbitration or mediation, can be litigated in the courts. Traditional attitudes lead to most disputes being resolved without litigation. The presence of international law firms and the adoption of US-style laws may lead to a greater involvement by lawyers in dispute resolution and litigation.[27] The increasing professionalization of Taiwanese lawyers may add to this.[28]

1.4   The Regulatory Structure

In addition to the legal system, including its administrative courts, Taiwan has a developed regulatory structure, reflecting the fact that the government retains considerable power over the economy. In the areas of company and securities law and regulation the principal agencies are the Ministry of Economic Affairs (MOEA), which administers the Company Law and the SFC, a commission in the Ministry of Finance (MOF) which administers the Securities Exchange Law (SEL).

Any decision or action which exceeds the legal authority of the agency, or which is based on an abuse of power is unlawful. The Law of Administrative Appeal, following the French model, permits a person whose rights have been violated by a government agency to petition its immediate supervising authority. If that is unsatisfactory, the petitioner can appeal to the next highest authority. Where the decision is confirmed or the appeal is not determined within three months an appeal lies to the Administrative Court.

The Control Law provides another means of redress. Individuals may initiate proceedings against public officers for malfeasance or neglect of duty by filing a written complaint with the Control Yuan. The Control Yuan may also investigate the operations of the Executive Yuan and its agencies for violation of the law or dereliction of duty. It may propose corrective measures to the ministry or commission concerned, which must take the appropriate action and report to the Control Yuan in writing. The Legislative Yuan's committees also have investigatory powers.

The Ministry of Justice, which advises the Executive Yuan on matters of law and acts for them in legal proceedings, may also investigate crimes. Its criminal function is overshadowed by the Procurate. Each court with criminal jurisdiction has associated with it procurators who investigate and prosecute criminal offences. They have the same status as a judge. As part of their investigation, they may summon and examine witnesses.

2   A Description of the Corporation Law

2.1   The Constitutional Basis of the Company Law

Promulgated in 1929, the Company Law was made under a previous constitution of the ROC.[29] The present Constitution has a number of provisions enabling all three levels of government to legislate for companies.

Article 111 of the Constitution allocates power on a federal basis. It provides that matters not specifically mentioned in the other Articles:

> shall fall within the jurisdiction of the Central Government if it is national in nature, within that of the Province if it is provincial in nature, and within that of the County if it is county in nature. In case of dispute, the matter shall be settled by the Legislative Yuan.

Under Article 107(2), the central government has power to make criminal, civil and commercial laws. Under Article 108(1), it has the specific and delegatable power to legislate and take executive action over industry, commerce and stock exchanges.

Other Articles give considerable power to the central government, reflecting the socialist philosophy of the KMT when the Constitution was promulgated in 1947. Article 145 specifies that:

> With respect to private wealth and privately operated enterprises, the State shall restrict them by law if they are deemed detrimental to the balanced development of national wealth and people's livelihood.

Article 149 complements this by providing that: 'Financial institutions shall, in accordance with law, be subject to State control.'

Additional Article 9, adopted in 1994, declares that:

> The State shall encourage development of and investment in science and technology, facilitate the upgrade of industry, promote the modernization of agriculture and fishery, emphasize the exploitation and utilization of water resources, and intensify international economic cooperation.

2.2   How the Company Law Came into Being

2.2.1   'Merchant practices under official supervision'   Chinese commerce and law had developed a number of institutions analogous to those which have contributed concepts to Western company law. Merchant guilds, families or lineages had developed some corporate features. Joint stock business partnerships, for example, had sometimes developed structures similar to holding companies.[30] No arrangement of rules analogous to the company had been produced before contact with the chartered companies, granted monopolies by European states, to trade with Asia. As Braudel has argued, these companies originated in the relationship between princes and rich merchants and are a 'sophisticated and domineering' form of capitalism compared with the 'down-to-earth' form found in domestic markets which can be made 'almost transparent' by 'competition'.[31] China had the latter,

but not the former. In the imperial period great wealth could only be achieved within the 'state apparatus', so that this form could only exist within the limits laid down by the state, which was hostile to any individual who became '"abnormally" rich'.[32] Yet this model of the company has lingered and created expectations, subsequently entrenched, in Taiwanese company administration. The first is an acceptance that the state will have considerable control over enterprises conducted in a company form. The second is shareholders enjoying good dividends with little interest in the management of the enterprise.[33]

The model was used by imperial officials to divert Chinese investment from the joint stock companies operating illegally in the treaty ports.[34] Features of the eighteenth-century state control of the Dutch and British East India companies and the Bank of England were adopted.[35] These entities have been described as *'kuan-te shang-pan'*, that is 'merchant practices under official supervision'.[36] In 1867 Yung Wing first suggested a joint stock company to Governor-General Li Hung-Shang of Chihli, the province which surrounded Beijing. Yung proposed a shipping company, restricted to Chinese shareholders, to recover shipping in Chinese waters from European states. This was implemented in 1873 when Li ordered that regulations and by-laws be drawn up for the China Merchants Steam Navigation Co. It established an office in Shanghai to encourage Chinese investors in foreign companies to invest in it.[37] It was followed by a number of other firms incorporated by imperial edict resulting from memorials laid before the throne.[38] These entities had schizoid legal personalities. The China Merchants Steam Navigation Co. was a joint stock company with shareholders, but it was also part of the government administration in the Commissioner for Northern Ports and, ultimately, the Ministry of Posts and Telegraphs. They were directed by imperial officers exercising the powers of the board. The shareholders' interests were protected where this was consistent with state interest. They united Chinese and Western practices. Following Western practice, they enjoyed state monopolies and patronage in business and tax concessions. The state was also a shareholder with state funds, including military funds, invested in them.[39] The Chinese tradition of commercial activity as a public service and a responsibility of government was continued by them.[40] The threat of state intervention, in the ethical duty of the emperor to do economic justice, is argued to have deterred overseas Chinese in particular from investment in them.[41]

The model was rejuvenated by the KMT which, historically, opposed *laissez-faire* capitalism.[42] After 1945 it planned economic development with significant state ownership of capital in an increasingly socialized economy.[43] A new form of limited company was created. It permitted state-owned industry to become companies with the central, provincial and county governments as shareholders together with minority private investors. When the KMT was defeated on the mainland governments owned 70 per cent of industry, half of which had been reorganized in this form.[44] On Taiwan the pattern was continued where possible as its agricultural economy, created to feed Japan, was increasingly industrialized.[45]

2.2.2 *Earlier company laws*   Uncertainty about legal personality and limited liability were significant in inhibiting the use of joint stock partnership outside those organized by the state. Under Chinese law, the managing partners were liable for debts irrespective of shares. Silent partners (those who have only contributed capital) could only be made liable for the remaining debts with difficulty, although, by negotiation, they frequently made some contribution.[46] In Taiwan in the late Qing period there were numerous joint stock partnerships and some *de facto* recognition of them as legal persons. Fear of liability, however, limited their size.[47]

In 1903 an imperial edict required the Imperial Law Codification Commission to codify commercial law. Commercial law was chosen as the large number of foreign companies operating in China had exposed the inadequacies of the existing law. In late 1904 the emperor approved the draft Commercial Code, largely modelled on English commercial law with some Japanese influence.[48] It was promulgated by the newly created Ministry of Commerce in early 1904. It continued the policy of Governor-General Li of encouraging Chinese entrepreneurs by permitting them to operate through a corporate form. It was also the first step to remove the justifications for extraterritoriality enjoyed by foreign citizens. It included 131 Articles under the title 'Company Law'.[49] Additional regulations provided for the registration of limited partnerships and joint stock companies. Article 32 on its face imposed joint and several liability on partners, making such liability desirable.[50]

Lack of reform of the court system led to the Ministry of Commerce dealing with disputes referred to it by the courts.[51]

In 1914 the company provisions of the Commercial Law of 1904, in a substantially amended form reflecting Japanese law, were promulgated as 251 Articles under the title 'Ordinance Concerning Commercial Associations'. It became the substantial basis for subsequent company laws.[52]

2.2.3 *The present law*   The present Company Law was promulgated on 26 December 1929 and came into force on 21 February 1931. It then contained 231 Articles.[53] Largely based on the law of 1914, 90 articles had been revised. The other major codes drafted in this period provided for corporate legal personality.[54] It was part of a conscious state building by the KMT in which the end of extraterritoriality and the promotion of industry were important planks. The Company Law reflected this in increased state control of companies and increased penalties. These were criticized for preventing 'law-abiding people from developing their businesses'.[55]

The Company Law was substantially revised in 1946 to assist in the accumulation of capital for the expansion of industry, to take over Japanese-owned industry and to attract foreign investment following the relinquishment of extraterritoriality by China's wartime allies. This had required companies controlled by foreigners and foreign-registered companies to register under the Company Law of 1929 and its restrictive provisions. Most refused to do so and their governments, particularly the government of the United States, pressured for less state control over companies.[56] Further revisions of the law in Taiwan in 1966, 1968, 1970 and 1980 introduced features of Anglo-US company law. The 1966 and 1968 revisions adopted schemes of authorized capital and protected shareholders, particularly minority shareholders, recognizing the separation of ownership from control. The 1970 amendments simplified the process for reorganization.[57]

2.3   Who is Responsible for Changing the Law

The MOEA in the Executive Yuan has primary responsibility for the Company Law.[58] Any amendments to the Company Law need to be approved by the Executive Yuan Council and passed by the Legislative Yuan. Legislation may be referred to a committee of the Legislative Yuan before the second of three readings. At the second reading it can again be referred to a committee. The second reading provides considerable opportunity for debate. If passed at the third reading stage, it may be subject to consideration by the Executive Yuan Council which can request the legislature to reconsider it. The final stage is approval by the President.[59]

Changes to regulations made under the law are made by decree of the MOEA. In respect of corporate securities and companies with publicly issued shares, the responsibility also rests on the SFC and the MOF.[60] Regulations are required to be submitted to the Legislative Yuan. If it finds that the regulations oppose, change or contradict the enabling or other statutes or deals with a matter which should be the subject of a statute, it may require them to be amended or disallow them.[61]

Before the 1990s the Legislative Yuan was a rubber stamp and the Executive Yuan agencies, which represented the views of the KMT, were able to make laws in spite of the opinions of the business community. The process of democratization and the legislators' need for commercial patronage of one form or another has given the business community some power over changes to legislation. Some economic legislation in particular has only been passed after protracted negotiated compromises, coordinated by a new *ad hoc* committee composed of office holders and KMT officials who are, also, no longer shielded from business pressure. The KMT and the Executive Yuan officers are still able, generally, to get their own way. They are the patrons of the economic think-tanks, and are able to make ambit policy claims, exploit tensions between business communities and threaten 'tax audits' or other strict application of uncertain laws.[62]

2.4 What Principles, If Any, Underlie the Company Law?

The Company Law, when promulgated in 1929, was intended to promote the raising of capital for industrial and other development. The other aim of increasing state power to regulate business was strengthened in 1946. More recent amendments and the liberalization of the Taiwanese economy have led to greater emphasis now being given to the first rather than the second purpose.

The capital-raising aspects were confirmed in the 1980s by Article 156 requiring companies worth more than a fixed amount – NT$ 200 million was prescribed – to offer shares to the public. This has had an unintended effect. On the mainland, and also Taiwan, the public resisted investing in other people's businesses, and the families which ran these businesses have avoided strangers investing as shareholders. When a company reached this threshold, its controllers started another.[63]

State control is still, however, a significant purpose. The combined effect of Articles 6, 15 and 129 restrict a company from engaging in activities not specified in its articles of association at the time of registration and approved by the relevant government authority regulating the area of business activity. The relevant authorities have been willing to approve only a limited number of activities. Consequently, permission is generally sought for one of those limited purposes and the company then engages in any which are profitable.[64] The effect of Article 10 makes the company a hostage to the relevant authority and the MOEA. On complaint by such an authority, the MOEA may order the company to cease the unauthorized activities. If it fails to do, whether or not there is a further complaint, its directors may be fined. If it then fails to do so, it may be dissolved. This has also led to a proliferation of companies. It has been easier to start a new company and get such approval.[65] Foreign applicants have found that local competitors are favoured.[66]

Only a small percentage of firms are registered as companies. Registration with the government had been a deterrent on the mainland. This persists in Taiwan. Fear of government interference may be greater in Taiwan and may explain other phenomenon. Up to 40 per cent of Taiwan's economy has been underground.[67] Between 1945 and 1949 two million people from the mainland fled to Taiwan, joining the six million Taiwanese. This was a traumatic event and the division still marks Taiwanese society and commerce. The KMT felt constrained to permit considerable commercial freedom to the Taiwanese, but in corporate commerce it often exchanged entry rights to a lucrative oligopoly for cooperation and loyalty.[68] Both Chinese and Taiwanese populations, however, have been slow to incorporate.[69]

2.5   How the Legislation is Interpreted

Taiwan has, unusually for a civil law system, a formalized use of precedent. This is recognized by the Constitution. The Council of Grand Justices may give a unifying interpretation of the law. The discrete neglect of some shows that these decisions may have limited force.[70] The Organic Courts Law provides for certain Supreme Court decisions to have a similar function, if a lower status.[71] The Supreme Court may designate a decision as having binding force, but only the essential minimum, rather than the full text, is published.[72] This follows the practice established in the first two decades of the Republic. Faced with considerable uncertainty, the judges followed Qing practice and referred questions, once reserved for higher tribunals or the Emperor, to the Supreme Court in Beijing, even when its jurisdiction was limited to only parts of China.[73] Other decisions are not binding, but judges follow their own decisions, and those of the higher courts both out of habit and to increase their chances of promotion.[74]

Legislation, including the Company Law, has not been subject to the same detailed gloss as in other civil law jurisdictions and many conflicting interpretations have not been the subject of judicial interpretation.[75]

General principles of statutory interpretation derive from the Constitution and from legislation dealing with conflicts between laws within Taiwan and between domestic and international law. Continuing stress on the spirit, rather than the letter of the law, and, to a lesser extent, the absence of agreement amongst lawyers on how to interpret can still generate uncertainty.[76]

A hierarchical rule of construction, reflecting constitutional priorities, determines the validity of legislation:

Laws must not violate the Constitution. Regulations must not violate
the Constitution or laws. Regulations made by a subordinate branch
of government must not violate those by the superior branch.[77]

This has now developed, through interpretation, into judicial review
for inconsistency.[78]

Where there is conflict between laws at the same level, the more
specific law prevails over the more general law.[79] This is significant
in the application of the Company Law to foreigners, including overseas Chinese. Company Law, Article 98 does not permit foreigners to
control companies limited by shares as one half the shareholders are
required to have a Taiwan domicile. Article 18 of both the Investment
by Foreign Nationals Law and the Investment by Overseas Chinese
Law are interpreted as specific legislation derogating from this requirement. Consequently, foreign-owned and -controlled companies
are incorporated as companies under the Company Law, Article 2.[80]

The constitutional provision that treaties have the status of law is
of increasing significance as the Taiwanese economy international-
izes, although this has not been subject to any clear determination by
the Council of Grand Justices.[81] It appears that treaties made after a
law has been promulgated override the law. Laws promulgated after
a treaty has been made are considered on a case-by-case basis.[82]

There is still an expectation that people will act reasonably according to good customs and propriety in respect of each others' rights
and entitlements rather than by strict conformity with formal rules.
Custom, for example, specifically continues as a source of law. Contrary forces generate tension in interpretation.[83] The Chinese language,
which 'places a value on ambiguities which leave several possibilities open', facilitates a continuing reliance on the spirit of the law.
Codes such as the Company Law, with their greater specificity, point
to the letter of the law. The SEL, which is drafted in a similar way,
has been construed in a narrow and technical way, deterring investors from taking any action except in the clearest cases.[84] Other, more
recent, commercial legislation avoids black-letter law in a level of
generality which surprises Westerners forgetful of aspects of their
own legal systems.[85] The precise language of the Company Law, its
conflicting provisions and its poor fit with social expectations suggests 'that much of it seems not designed to encourage compliance
but to represent official sanctions open to manipulation for economic
or political advantage'.[86] Adding to these problems are difficulties in
accessing documents with legal effect issued by both the Judicial and
Executive Yuans.[87]

3   The Nature and Powers of Corporate Regulatory Bodies in the Jurisdiction

3.1   *The Description of Powers of Company Regulatory Bodies*

The MOEA is the principal corporate regulatory body. It is a department of the Executive Yuan directed by a minister who is a member of the Executive Yuan Council. It has the power to delegate its functions to cognate agencies – 'local authorities' – of the provincial government and municipal governments under the direct jurisdiction of the Executive Yuan. These have their own constitutional powers relating to companies.[88] As part of the Executive Yuan, the MOEA is still powerful, able to dispense favours both to politicians and the business community seeking special arrangements or even classified information for insider trading.[89]

The MOEA's sole power to incorporate companies and to recognize foreign companies is dealt with in Sections 4 and 5 below. Under the Company Law, Article 10, the MOEA, of its own volition, or on complaint of shareholders or a government agency, may order companies to commence their proposed business operations or, where the business operation undertaken is inconsistent with that proposed, to cease a particular business operation. If disobeyed, the MOEA may dissolve the company. Where shareholders take action to dissolve a company, the court is required to request the opinion of the MOEA and the central government agency responsible for the area of enterprise of the business operation.[90] The court is also required to ask the opinion of the MOEA, the central government agency responsible for the area of enterprise and the MOF, where a company which has publicly issued shares seeks a reorganization because of financial difficulties.[91] It has the power, on its own motion, to revoke the registration of companies which have been dissolved.[92]

Article 21 gives the MOEA powers of inspection. It, and the central government agency responsible for the area of enterprise, may send inspectors, including accountants and lawyers retained for that purpose, to inspect the operational and financial conditions of a company. Under Article 22 it may order the company to present all relevant documents and information, but must keep them confidential and return them in 15 days. Article 384 authorizes the MOEA to inspect registered foreign companies.

The MOEA is responsible, but acting through the Ministry of Justice and the relevant Procurate, for the prosecution of offences relating to misrepresentations in respect of any incorporation.[93]

The MOEA also has other miscellaneous powers to give directions to companies and to rectify failures to observe requirements of the

Company Law. For example, when a company fails to organize an election of supervisors, it may order that such an election be held.[94]

The SFC has primary responsibility for regulating corporate securities and trading in securities on the Taiwan Stock Exchange (TSE) and in over-the-counter transactions.[95] It consists of nine commissioners including a chair and a deputy-chair. Its members are appointed by the MOF, the MOEA, the Central Bank of China, the Council for Economic Planning and Development and the Ministry of Justice. Its basic objectives are:

- to promote sound development of the capital market and encourage the raising of capital through securities; and
- to improve the mechanism of the stock market and promote fair, just and open trading.

It also aims to develop securities businesses and strengthen the supervision of accountants and raising their professional standards and skills.[96]

Its six divisions exercise the following supervisory functions: First Division: primary market administration, including the raising of capital;[97] Second Division: supervision of securities firms and licence holders and the Securities Dealers' Association;[98] Third Division: secondary market supervision, including the administration and supervision of information services for shareholders in publicly held companies including soliciting proxies, the education of securities industry personnel and the investigation of illegal trading;[99] Fourth Division: regulation of securities-related services, including mutual funds ('securities investment trust enterprises'), securities finance enterprises permitting short sales or purchases on margins, securities investment consultants, script depositaries, and supervising overseas Chinese and foreigners investing in the securities markets;[100] Fifth Division: supervision of the futures industry and its personnel;[101] Sixth Division: the regulation and supervision of certified public accountants under rules administered by the MOF;[102] the Auditor's Office: audits the SFC and plays a similar role to the Sixth Division in respect of auditing generally;[103] and, the Office of Legal Affairs: legal issues, including the revision of laws regulating publicly owned companies and securities markets, and international dealings.[104]

The SFC has the power to investigate companies with publicly issued shares, to order compliance with the legal requirements for companies and to impose sanctions for failure to observe the requirements. It has similar powers of investigation in respect of applications for the approval of public offerings. It may also investigate and seize material from securities firms.[105]

3.2   *The Role of Regulatory Bodies in Policy Formation and Practice*

The MOEA has principal responsibility for the formulation of policy and its implementation, whether by legislation or regulatory practice.[106] The relevant divisions are the Commerce Department, which formulates commercial policies and measures, and a Committee of Laws and Regulations, which is responsible for the formulation, revision, compilation and explanation of laws and regulations.[107] The MOEA is developing broad plans for the modernization of Taiwanese business[108] and for the improvement of the Taiwanese investment environment.[109] It is considering amendments to the Company Law which will remove from it 'paternalistic' provisions. These are essentially the remnants of the policy of controlled economic development developed by the KMT in the 1930s and 1940s for protection of shareholders' interests in reorganizations.[110] Its recent focus has not been on company law but on wider issues of deregulation and internationalization of the economy in which other agencies are also involved.[111] The Council for Economic Planning and Development, constituted by a large number of government departments and agencies, for example, has encouraged the development of the financial markets, taxation and other concessions, in the hope of converting Taiwan into a regional and international centre.[112]

The focus on markets has made the SFC, and the MOF in which it is located, more significant in the formulation and implementation of new policy. The SFC has the main responsibility for formulating policy changes to laws relating to publicly owned companies and securities trading. The major policy changes have been part of global change; deregulation of these areas and foreign investment. The MOF has had a significant role in these developments.[113] Within the SFC, the Office of Legal Affairs is principally involved in policy formulation and reform of law and regulations. The First Division of the SFC has had major responsibility for the process of internationalization, the introduction of new financial instruments. The Second Division has formulated the rules and policies which are implemented by the TSE and the Securities Dealers' Association.[114] The Fifth Division worked on changes to the SEL to permit the establishment of local derivative markets. It had primary responsibility for the Futures Trading Law.[115] The Sixth Division has been most active in pushing for changes in accurate financial information disclosure. It is closely involved with the Accounting Research and Development Foundation in developing and revising Statements of Financial Accounting Standards and Statements of Audit Standards and promoting a change to unified accounting accounts and codes.[116]

3.3 Mechanisms for the Review of Regulatory Action

As noted in Section 1.4, above, Taiwan has processes for the review of government decisions similar to French administrative law. A person injured by an unlawful or improper administrative measure may file an administrative appeal with the next highest administrative level. The MOEA has a Committee of Administrative Appeal to deal with such applications.[117] Decisions of commercial regulators are frequently reviewed by the Administrative Court.[118]

Also as noted in section 1.4, above, officers who abuse their power or neglect their duty, or government agencies not implementing government policy, can be the subject of a complaint to the Control Yuan. It may impeach the officers before the Committee on the Discipline of Public Functionaries of the Judicial Yuan. The Control Yuan also has powers of censure and audit.

4 A Description of Types of Companies, Their Powers and So On

4.1 A Description of Types of Local Companies

The Company Law enables the creation of the following business entities:

- limited company (private or proprietary limited company):
  - more than five but no more than 21 shareholders,
  - shareholder's liability extends only to capital they contribute,
  - may not raise funds from the public,
  - limitations on the capacity of members to transfer their shares,
  - comparable to the private or proprietary limited company in other jurisdictions;
- company limited by shares (public limited company):
  - more than seven shareholders,
  - shareholder's liability is restricted by the shares they own,
  - may raise funds by allowing the public to purchase or subscribe for shares,
  - comparable to public limited companies in other jurisdictions;
- unlimited company:
  - two or more shareholders,
  - shareholders have unlimited joint liability for a company's obligations;
- unlimited company with restricted liability shareholders:

- some shareholders have limited liability and others unlimited.

4.2   *The Recognition of Foreign Companies in the Jurisdiction*

Chapter VII of the Company Law governs the recognition of foreign companies. In addition, foreign investment is subject to the Investment by Foreign Nationals Law and the Investment by Overseas Chinese Law, and the policy and guidelines promulgated by the Investment Commission and by the Industrial Development and Investment Centre – both within the MOEA.

In order to establish a branch in Taiwan, foreign companies must go through two procedures: recognition and registration.

For recognition the Company Law in Article 435 requires that a foreign company supply the MOEA with details in relation to the parent company. These details include:

- the name, type and nationality of the company;
- the business of the company and its intended business in Taiwan;
- the total amount of capital, shares, kinds of shares, par value of each share and the paid up amount;
- the amount of funds set aside for its intended business in Taiwan;
- the address of its head office and branch office in Taiwan;
- the date of incorporation and the date it began business;
- the names, nationalities and addresses of company directors;
- the names, nationalities and addresses of its representatives in Taiwan and their powers of attorney;
- if an unlimited company or an unlimited company with limited liability shareholders, then the number of shares subscribed to and the amount paid on such shares by each of them;
- copies of its articles of incorporation;
- if it is a franchise business, a copy of the franchise agreement;
- if it is a franchise business according to the laws of Taiwan, a copy of the franchise;
- the company's intended business plan for its operations in Taiwan; and
- the minutes of the meeting of the shareholders or board of directors approving the application for recognition.[119]

Documents accompanying the application for recognition must have a Chinese translation attached.

Before the MOEA will recognize a foreign company, it must be satisfied that the company is incorporated under foreign law.[120] Furthermore, it must designate a local representative.[121] Applications, including applications to establish a branch, should be lodged by the local representative.[122] An application for recognition by a foreign company's representative must be accompanied by documents to prove the nationality and authority or power of attorney of the representative.[123]

Once the MOEA gives a foreign company a 'certificate of recognition' it has the same rights and obligations, and will be subject to the same powers of the MOEA, as a Taiwanese company.[124] The MOEA's jurisdiction extends to the examination of its books of accounts, records and any other documents relating to its business.[125] Its rights include the right to purchase and own land, subject to MOEA approval[126] which is gained through an application to the relevant local authority.[127] Obligations imposed upon it include the keeping of a copy of its articles of incorporation in its representative's or its branch office.[128] The insolvency provisions of the Company Law also apply to it.[129] Finally, a certificate of recognition may be revoked by the MOEA.[130] If a certificate of recognition is surrendered or revoked then its business operations in Taiwan will be subject to liquidation.[131]

4.3 The Legal Capacities and Powers of Companies

No provision in the Company Law equates a company with a natural person. Article 1 defines a company as a 'corporate juristic person organized and incorporated in accordance with this law for the purpose of profit making'. As a result, companies incorporated under the Company Law must operate in accordance with the powers and restrictions granted and imposed by the Company Law.

Important restrictions imposed on all companies include that:

- a company cannot be a shareholder of unlimited liability in another company or a partner of a partnership business;
- when a company is a limited liability shareholder in another company, the total amount of its investment in such other companies cannot exceed 40 per cent of the amount of its own paid-up capital unless
  - it is a professional investment company;
  - its Articles of Incorporation allow;
  - it has obtained the consent of its shareholders; or
  - a unanimous resolution is passed at the shareholders' meeting of an unlimited or limited company, or a majority resolution is passed at a shareholders' meeting for a company limited by shares.[132]

- a company must not engage in any business outside the scope of its registered business;[133] and
- a company must not act as a guarantor unless permitted by law or its Articles of Incorporation.[134]

5   Company Formation

5.1   *The Registration of Companies*

Companies must be incorporated and certified by the MOEA.[135] The incorporation of a company, establishment of a branch office, recognition of a foreign company and establishment of its branch office are confirmed when the MOEA issues the appropriate certificate.[136]

5.1.1   Limited companies (private or proprietary company)   An application to register the incorporation of a limited company must be made by all the directors of the company.[137] It must be made within 15 days of the adoption of the articles of incorporation of the company.[138] These must be attached to the application.[139] The application must set out the following particulars:

- all those particulars required to be set out in its articles of incorporation by virtue of Article 101 of the Company Law (see Section 5.2, below);
- testimonials to prove full payment for shares; and
- for non-cash purchases of shares, a description or valuation of the property.

Officers of the MOEA then consider the application and notify the company of any matters needing clarification. There are tough penalties for directors who fail to answer the MOEA's enquiries within the time it sets.

5.1.2   Company limited by shares (public limited company)   Where the application to register is made by a company limited by shares, it must be by more than 50 per cent of the directors and at least one supervisor.[140] Where a company limited by shares is organized by promotion, an application for registration of incorporation must include:

- the articles of incorporation;
- the shareholders' roster;
- the total number of issued shares;
- where property is transferred for shares, the name of the

transferor, a valuation of the property, and the number of shares
given in consideration of the transfer;

- the expenses of incorporation to be paid by the company and
the amount of remuneration or special benefit payable to promoters;
- in a case where special shares are issued, the total number of
such shares and the par value of each share;
- documents that evidence the full payment of shares; and
- the names and addresses of directors and supervisors.[141]

The following additional information must be included in an application for registration of incorporation of a company limited by
shares where the company is to be established by soliciting shares:[142]

- matters approved at the inaugural meeting of shareholders;
- approval for the share issue from the SFC;
- the report presented by the directors, supervisors or inspectors
to the inaugural meeting of shareholders;
- the minutes of the inaugural meeting;
- if relevant, evidence of compliance with the Company Law
requirements for consolidations and mergers, such as notice to
creditors or public announcements.

*5.1.3 Unlimited company and unlimited company with limited liability
shareholders*[143]   An unlimited company and an unlimited company
with limited liability shareholders must within 15 days of drawing
up their articles of incorporation register for incorporation.[144] An
application must be made by all shareholders.[145] It must include a
number of particulars, including the name of the company, the business to be undertaken, the name and address of its shareholders and
the location of its head office.[146] It must be accompanied by the
articles of incorporation.[147]

5.2   The Corporate Constitution

The articles of incorporation form the constitution of a company incorporated under the Company Law. They perform the functions of the
memorandum of association and articles of association of the corporate constitution of other jurisdictions. In particular, they are the primary
incorporation instrument and also the principal means of regulating
the internal affairs of the company. The Company Law lays down
specific requirements for them for the different corporate forms.

5.2.1   Limited company (private or proprietary limited company)   The
shareholders of a limited company must, by unanimous agreement,

execute, sign and seal the Articles of Incorporation. A copy of them is to be kept at the head office of the company and with each shareholder.[148] Those of a limited company must set out:

- the name of the company;
- the business of the company;
- the name and address of each shareholder;
- the amount contributed by each shareholder;
- the distribution of profit and loss;
- the address of the head office, and of any branch offices;
- the directors and chairman;
- the conditions for dissolution;
- the manner of making public announcements by the company; and
- the date of execution of the articles of incorporation.

5.2.2   Company limited by shares (public limited company)   A company limited by shares must have seven or more persons as promoters.[149] The promoters must by unanimous agreement execute, sign and seal the articles of incorporation, which must include the following:

- the company name;
- the business undertaken;
- the total shares and par value of each share;
- the address of the head office;
- the manner for making public announcements;
- the number and tenure of directors and supervisors; and
- the date of execution of the articles of incorporation.[150]

Article 130 of the Company Law highlights six matters that will be of no effect unless provided for in the articles of incorporation. They are:

- the establishment of a branch office;
- the first instalment of issued shares (if shares are issued by instalment);
- the causes for dissolution of the company;
- the preference shares;
- any special benefits for promoters and the name of all beneficiaries; and
- the amount of corporate bonds convertible to shares.

5.2.3   Unlimited companies   Article 41 of the Company Law sets out the requirements for the articles of incorporation of an unlimited company. They include:

- the name of the company;
- the business of the company;
- the name and address of each shareholder;
- the total amount of capital and contribution of each shareholder;
- the valuation of property contributed by shareholders to the capital of company;
- the ratio of distribution of profit and loss;
- the address of the head office and branch offices;
- the name of the shareholder designated to represent the company (if any);
- the name of shareholder designated to run the business of the company (if any);
- the causes for dissolution (if any); and
- the date of execution of the articles.

The articles of incorporation of an unlimited company may also set out the rules for its internal regulation and administration.[151] Those of an unlimited company with limited liability shareholders must state the above particulars and also stipulate whether the liability of a shareholder is limited or unlimited.[152]

5.3 Restrictions on the Use of Certain Names

The name of a company must indicate to what class of company it belongs.[153] A company must apply to the MOEA for approval and reservation (for a specified time) of its company name before registration of incorporation.[154] Conversely, business may not be conducted in the name of a company whose incorporation has not been registered.[155] There are restrictions imposed upon the use of similar company names where companies are in the same line of business. This restriction applies despite the fact that the companies may belong to different classes or operate in different localities. Where the companies operate in different lines of business, the company registered last must include in its name words that clearly distinguish it from the other. A company may also not use a name that misleadingly associates it with a government agency, public-spirited organization, or that may offend against public order or custom.[156]

5.4 Membership and Share Capital Requirements

5.4.1 Capital The minimum amount of capital of a limited company (private or proprietary limited company) or a company limited by shares (public limited company) is set down in the Rules Governing the Minimum Amount of Capital of A Limited Company or a Company Limited by Shares (Rules Governing the Minimum Amount of Capital) promulgated by the MOEA, Executive Yuan on 29 June 1988. These rules are issued in accordance with Articles 100 and 156 of the Company Law.

Article 2 of the Rules Governing the Minimum Amount of Capital lays down the following capital requirements for companies operating in different business areas:

- public housing construction: NT$ 25 million;
- business building construction: NT$ 35 million;
- off-shore fishery: NT$ four million;
- car production: NT$ 100 million;
- international tourist hotel: NT$ 65 million;
- general tourist hotel: NT$ 26 million;
- mining: NT$ five million;
- professional investment: NT$ 50 million;
- management of construction business: NT$ 50 million; and
- waste pollution water disposing: NT$ five million.

In all other cases, the minimum amount of a limited company's paid-in capital must be NT$ 500 000 and for a company limited by shares NT$ one million. Where a limited company or company limited by shares operates two or more enterprises, the minimum amount of its paid in capital is the minimum of paid-in capital of the two or more enterprises.[157] The Company Law also has additional capital requirements for companies limited by shares and limited companies.

5.4.2   Companies limited by shares (public limited companies)   At least 25 per cent of the capital of a company limited by shares must be paid in at registration. Companies with capital of NT$ 200 million or more will be caught by Article 156 of the Company Law. It provides that when the capital of a company has reached or exceeded an amount fixed by the MOEA (NT$ 200 million), its shares must be issued in public. The public issuance requirement brings with it a number of other regulatory measures. As a result of this, many companies in Taiwan limit their paid-in capital to one dollar less.[158] However, approved foreign investment companies are exempt from the public issuance and offering requirements when the foreign investment is greater than 45 per cent of the total capital.[159]

Foreign Investment Approved projects under the Investment by Foreign Nationals Law are exempt from the Company Law requirement that all companies with paid up capital of more than NT$ 200 million publicly issue their shares provided that 45 per cent or more of the enterprise is owned by foreigners.[160]

5.4.3 Limited companies (private or proprietary limited companies) The MOEA has the power to decree the minimum capital requirement for a limited company taking into account the nature of its operations and the 'existing situation'.[161] A limited company cannot reduce its minimum capital.[162] The whole of this amount must be paid upon registration. It must be paid in full by the shareholders and must not be paid in instalments or solicited from non-shareholders.[163] There is also a mandatory contribution to a reserve of 10 per cent of after-tax profits. This requirement does not apply where the reserve amounts to the authorized capital. A company may also, by the provisions of its Articles of Incorporation or with the unanimous agreement of all shareholders, appropriate another sum as a special reserve.[164]

A majority of shareholders may agree to increase the capital.[165] When filing such an application for registration, a limited company must submit, together with the particulars already lodged at registration of the company, the following documents:

- the amended articles and a comparative table of the amended clauses;
- the shareholders' consent to the increase in writing;
- a list of directors elected after the increase of capital.[166]

5.4.4 Membership A limited company (private or proprietary limited company) must have more than five and less than 21 shareholders.[167] The liability of the shareholders is limited to the extent of their capital contribution.[168] At least one-half of the shareholders must be resident citizens holding 51 per cent or more of the combined capital.[169] Furthermore, there must be more than one but no more than three directors. The directors are elected from among the shareholders. Where there are several directors, the articles of incorporation may specifically provide for a chairman of directors to represent the company externally. The chairman must be a resident citizen.[170]

Each shareholder has one vote regardless of capital contribution. However, the articles of incorporation may provide that votes are to be allocated according to the shareholder's contributions to capital.[171] The company must keep a shareholders' roster, which includes:

- the contribution of each shareholder;
- the name and address of each shareholder; and
- the date of payment of contribution to the capital.[172]

Following incorporation, a company must issue share certificates.[173] The share certificates, which are to be signed and sealed by the body of directors, are required to state:

- the company name;
- the date of incorporation;
- the name of the shareholder and the amount of contribution; and
- the date the certificate was issued.

If the name of the transferee is not inscribed in the share certificate and the name and address of the transferee are not entered in the shareholders' roster, the transfer of the share certificate will not be valid as against the company.[174] In addition, shareholders cannot transfer their capital contribution to another person without the consent of a majority of other shareholders. Directors are required to have the unanimous consent of all other shareholders before they may transfer their capital contribution.[175]

Shareholders who are not involved in the business of the company may conduct an audit of the affairs of the company.[176] For the purposes of conducting the audit, they have the power to require those who do conduct the business to furnish information on the business condition of the company and to examine the company's books, assets and other relevant documents.[177]

In the case of companies limited by shares (public limited companies) a minimum of seven promoters, at least one-half of whom are residents of Taiwan, is required.[178] There is no minimum number of shares per shareholder. This means that non-residents may hold all but four shares. There must be a minimum of three shareholders. However, unlike limited companies, there is no maximum. Another difference is that companies limited by shares must also have at least one supervisor. The supervisors and the directors must all be elected from among the shareholders. The chairman and at least one supervisor must be resident citizens.

Foreign investment approval under the Investment by Foreign Nationals Law and the Investment by Overseas Chinese Law exempts foreign investment companies from the Company Law restrictions regarding nationality of shareholders, directors and supervisors (in addition to the requirements covering minimum amounts of investment by citizens, employees' pre-emptive subscription rights on newly issued shares, and sites for holding shareholders' and board of directors' meetings). There has also been further relaxation of residency requirements for foreign white-collar workers. Following the introduction of the revised Employment Service Law in June 1997, they can now obtain permanent employment in Taiwan.[179]

5.5 The Amendment of Corporate Constitution

5.5.1 Limited company (private or proprietary limited company) The modification of the articles of incorporation of a limited company are governed by the same rules as govern the modification of the articles of incorporation of an unlimited company. Article 47 of the Company Law simply provides in relation to unlimited companies that 'any modification or alteration in the Articles of Incorporation of a company shall be agreed upon by all of the shareholders'. Article 417 specifies that a limited company, when filing such an application, must lodge its amended articles of incorporation and a comparative table of the amended clauses.

5.5.2 Company limited by shares (public limited company) Subject to the articles of incorporation, a company limited by shares may only amend them by a majority resolution adopted at a meeting of shareholders attended by shareholders representing over two-thirds of the total number of issued shares. The attendance requirement is reduced to a majority of the total number of issued shares for companies that have publicly issued shares.[180] If a company limited by shares has issued special shares, any alteration of the articles of incorporation which is prejudicial to the interests of the special shareholders must be adopted by a meeting of them and by a majority resolution at a shareholders' meeting attended by shareholders representing two-thirds of total issued shares.[181]

6 The Internal Administration of Companies

6.1 Registered Office

The company's head office serves as its registered office. The address of the head office must be stated in the articles of incorporation submitted to the MOEA on incorporation. The MOEA will refer all notices to the head office and it will be the place of any investigation into the company's accounts. This is the same for unlimited companies, unlimited companies with limited liability shareholders, limited companies, and companies limited by shares.

6.2 The Duties, Powers and Responsibilities of Officers

6.2.1 Company limited by shares (public limited company) The Company Law contains basic provisions on the duties, powers and responsibilities of directors and officers of a company. In particular, it has a number of sections governing the role of directors and the board of directors of a company limited by shares. Before considering those sections, it is necessary to outline its provisions dealing with the appointment of directors of a company limited by shares.

A company limited by shares is required to have at least three directors. They are elected at a meeting of shareholders from among the shareholders.[182] A director may only hold office for a period of three years, subject to re-election. If a new director cannot be elected immediately after the expiration of the term of office of an outgoing director, the outgoing director must continue to perform his or her duties until a new director is re-elected. The MOEA has the power to set a time limit for a new election. Failure to hold an election in the stipulated time will make the directors liable to a penalty. The MOEA can set successive time limits and a penalty will be imposed for each failure.[183]

Once elected, directors or boards of directors of a company limited by shares have various statutory duties under the Company Law. Most importantly, they must act in accordance with the articles of incorporation, the resolutions adopted at shareholders' meetings, and the general laws and regulations of Taiwan. Directors will be liable to compensate the company for any damage or loss caused by a resolution that was adopted in contravention of these. However, directors who disagree with the resolution, on the record or in writing, will not be liable.[184]

Shareholders have various remedies against directors for wrongful acts. Article 199 allows a director to be removed from office by a resolution of shareholders. Individual shareholders, if they have continuously held shares for one year or more, may lodge a request to the board to stop the act.[185] An individual shareholder, who has continuously held 3 per cent or more of the total number of issued shares for a year or more, may, in the absence of a shareholders' resolution, apply within 30 days to a court for an order that a director be removed from office for causing loss or damage to the company.[186]

A meeting of shareholders may also resolve to institute court proceedings against a director. The company must proceed with the court action within a month of the resolution.[187] In the proceedings, the supervisors will act for the company and the meeting of shareholders may also appoint another representative.[188] A shareholder who has continuously held 5 per cent or more of the total number of issued shares for a year or longer may request in writing for a supervisor to institute proceedings against a director.[189] Shareholders who bring actions against directors may be liable to compensate directors and the company for any loss or damage resulting from an unfounded action.[190]

The board of directors is given the role of determining the business transactions of the company. Unless the articles of incorporation require a matter to be decided upon by resolution at a shareholders' meeting, all matters may be decided by the board.[191] Directors are required to attend meetings of the board in person unless the Articles permit a director to be represented by another director by proxy.[192] The absent director must issue a power of attorney before each meeting setting out the authority of the proxy at that meeting. A director cannot be proxy for more than one other director. A director residing overseas may register the appointment of a shareholder as his permanent proxy with the MOEA.[193]

Managing directors may be elected by the board. The minimum number of managing directors is three and the maximum is one-third of the total number of directors. A chairman or vice-chairman must be elected by the managing directors from among themselves. Managing directors exercise the power and authority of the board whilst the board is in recess. The managing directors must exercise the board's power and authority 'in accordance with law or ordinance, Articles of Incorporation, resolutions of the meeting of shareholders and resolutions of the Board'.[194]

There are domicile and nationality requirements for the chairman, vice-chairman, and the managing directors. The chairman and vice-chairman must be domiciled citizens, and at least one-half of the managing directors must be domiciled.[195]

Supervisors of a company limited by shares (public limited company) originate in the Japanese and German laws that form the basis of the Company Law. They have been described as a kind of internal auditor. They are elected at a meeting of shareholders from among themselves.[196] They are subject to the same election rules and terms as directors.[197]

Their powers include:

- investigating the financial and business condition of the company;
- examining the books, records and other documents of the company;[198]
- requesting the board of directors to make reports on the business and financial condition of the company;
- instructing the board of directors to cease an act that contravenes the law or the company's articles of incorporation;[199]
- checking all statements and records submitted by the board to the shareholders;
- reporting findings of the condition of the company to the shareholders;[200]
- convening a meeting of the shareholders;[201]
- representing the company in negotiations with directors acting in their individual capacity;[202] and

- appointing a public accountant to conduct an investigation of the company's books.[203]

A supervisor cannot be, at the same time, a director, manager, or employee of the company. A supervisor is also liable to compensate the company for any negligent act that causes the company loss or damage.[204]

6.2.2 Limited company (private limited company) The Company Law does not contain many provisions regulating the conduct of directors and officers of a limited company. Aside from nationality and domicile requirements for directors, the directors of a limited company must:

- not, without the unanimous consent of all other shareholders, transfer all or part of their contribution to the capital of the company to another person or persons;[205] and
- set aside an after-tax reserve of 10 per cent of profits.[206]

There is no provision for supervisors. Instead, the internal audit function of the limited company is largely in the hands of shareholders who do not conduct its business.[207]

6.2.3 Unlimited company Shareholders of the unlimited company are the 'responsible persons' when it comes to the conducting of its business.[208] One shareholder may be designated to represent the company, otherwise individual shareholders have the right to conduct the business.[209] The internal relations of an unlimited company are governed by the articles of incorporation.[210] Shareholders who are not involved in the running of the business may require the shareholders who are to supply information on its business position.[211]

Shareholders must conduct the business in accordance with laws and ordinances, decisions of the shareholders, and the articles of incorporation.[212] A shareholder may be expelled from the company, by unanimous agreement of all other shareholders, for:

- inability to contribute the required capital;
- engaging in the same business as the company or being a shareholder of another unlimited liability company;
- improper conduct detrimental to the interest of the company; or
- failure to attend to important duties of the company.

6.2.4 Unlimited company with limited liability shareholders The shareholders are also considered to be the officers of the unlimited company with limited liability shareholders. The Company Law imposes different duties, powers and restrictions on unlimited and limited liability shareholders. Limited liability shareholders may not dispose of their capital contribution without the majority consent of the unlimited liability shareholders.[213] A shareholder of limited liability may at the end of the business year examine the accounts and the business and financial condition of the company.[214] Limited liability shareholders cannot conduct the business of the company.[215]

6.3 Meeting Procedures

As in other jurisdictions, meetings of the shareholders and directors of a company form the basis of decision-making for companies operating in Taiwan. The discussion of meetings in this context looks at the use of meetings as the usual form for regulating the company. Other meetings, with their own special rules, may be held by other groups, for example creditors.

6.3.1 Company limited by shares (public limited company) Shareholders' meetings may be convened by the board.[216] Notice must be issued to individual shareholders and the public.[217] Regular meetings of shareholders are also held at least once a year.[218] Shareholders who have continuously held more than 3 per cent of shares for more than a year may propose in writing to the directors that a shareholders' meeting be convened.[219] Article 174 of the Company Law requires resolutions at shareholders' meetings to be adopted by a majority. The quorum required for a valid resolution is one-half of the total number of voting shares.[220] Tentative resolutions may be passed where one-third of the total number of voting shares are present. The tentative resolution may become a resolution if passed at a shareholders' meeting held one month later if a quorum is present or one-third of total voting shares voted for the resolution.[221]

Shareholders may grant proxies through powers of attorney forms stating the scope of authority granted. A person may not hold proxies for more than 3 per cent of the total voting shares.[222] Shareholders may be disqualified from voting if they have a personal interest in the matter.[223]

Resolutions adopted at a shareholders' meeting must be recorded in the minutes of the meeting. The minutes of the meeting must be kept with the list of shareholders present at the meeting and the powers of attorney granting proxies.[224] The shareholders' meeting may also:

- examine the statements and records of accounts prepared by the board;

- examine the reports of the supervisor; and
- make resolutions on the distribution of profit, dividends and bonuses.[225]

A two-thirds resolution is required if the company intends to:

- enter, amend or terminate a lease of the company's business or joint operations;
- transfer any essential part of its business or assets; or
- be transferee of another's whole business or assets, which may have significant impact on the business operation of the company.[226]

6.3.2   Limited company (private or proprietary limited company)   The meeting requirements for a limited company are not regulated by the Company Law but by its articles of incorporation. Directors are required, annually, to prepare and send books of accounts to the shareholders for approval. If no objection is raised by shareholders within one month of delivery of the accounts, they are deemed to have been approved.[227] Only after the accounts have been approved are the directors discharged from their liabilities, except for any unlawful conduct.[228]

Other matters, such as notice and quorums, must also be determined by the articles of incorporation. This same approach is taken with unlimited companies and unlimited companies with limited liability shareholders.

6.3.3   SEL requirements   In respect of companies which have issued shares to the public Article 26(1) of the SEL requires that on convening a shareholders' meeting material particulars with an explanation must be given of any transactions under Article 209(1), Article 240(1) and Article 241(1). These involve self-dealing by directors, the payment of dividends by new shares or the issue of new shares on a pro-rata basis, respectively.

6.4   Audit and Accounting Rules

Upon registration, all companies must start books of accounts. The fiscal year is 1 January to 31 December subject to a different fiscal year being approved by the national tax office. At the end of the fiscal or financial year, every company operating in Taiwan is required to submit to shareholders for their approval, or to the shareholders' meeting for ratification, the accounts of the company, consisting of:

- the business report;
- the balance sheets;
- an inventory of principal properties;
- a profit and loss statement;
- a statement of shareholders' equity changes;
- a cash flow statement; and
- the proposal for distribution of profit or loss.[229]

The MOEA has the power to require the company to submit the accounts to it or it may examine the accounts at the company's premises.[230] It may appoint a certified public accountant, a lawyer or other professional to assist in the inspection.[231] It also has the power to order the company to present information concerning the accounts.[232]

Books of account must be signed by the manager or general manager of the company.[233] Shareholders also have the right under the Company Law – including Articles 48, 109 and 118 – to inspect the accounts or cause them to be inspected. Article 110 requires that the directors of a limited company send the accounts to shareholders at the end of each financial year for their approval.

In the case of a company limited by shares, accounts prepared by the board must be available for inspection by shareholders at the head office at least ten days prior to the regular shareholders' meeting. Shareholders may bring their lawyers or certified public accountants when inspecting the accounts.[234] After ratification of the accounts at the shareholders' meeting, copies of the accounts must be provided to each shareholder, and to any creditor upon request.[235] Supervisors may request that the board deliver the accounts to them in advance of the regular shareholders' meeting.[236]

Where the capital of a company, other than a public enterprise, exceeds NT$ 30 million, its balance sheet, profit and loss statement, statement of shareholder's equity changes, and cash flow statement must be audited and certified by a certified public accountant.[237] Listed companies must publish their financial statements at least four months after the close of the financial year. A listed company's reports must be approved by the board and the shareholders' meeting, audited, and certified by two certified public accountants.[238]

Listed companies and securities companies must also file financial statements with the SFC. Article 36 of the SEL requires a company with publicly issued shares, within four months of the end of the fiscal year, to announce to the public and file with the SEC, the audited financial reports approved by the directors and recognized by the supervisor. This is also required, unless the SFC has given a dispensation, within two months of the close of the half year. In respect of the other two quarters, reports certified by a public accountant must be announced and filed with the SEC within one month. Operating accounts must also be announced and filed within ten days of the end of each calendar month. The audit and certification should be carried out in accordance with the standards laid down by the Financial Accounting Foundation of Taiwan.[239]

6.5   *Shareholder Protection Rules*

The Company Law is premised on majority rule in company affairs. However, in the 1960s amendments were made to incorporate developing Anglo-US principles for the protection of minority shareholders.[240] Most of these provisions relate to a company limited by shares (public limited company).

The first remedy that such shareholders have is to request the company to buy back all of their shares at the prevailing and fair price.[241] Article 186 provides that shareholders who have served a notice in writing on the company, expressing their intention to object to an act prior to a resolution at the shareholders' meeting, and who also object at the meeting, may make such a request. If there is no agreement on the price, the court may determine it.[242] Once a company ceases the offending act, the right of the shareholders to have their shares bought back lapses.[243]

Shareholders in such companies who believe that the procedure for convening a meeting of shareholders or the method of resolution is in violation of the general law or of the company's articles of incorporation may apply to the court within one month of the resolution for an order that the resolution be annulled.[244] They may also apply to the court for an order that a resolution is null and void if it is contrary to the general law or the articles of incorporation.[245]

6.6   *Relationship between Management and Shareholders*

The relationship between managers and shareholders in the various types of companies are subject to similar rules. The duties of managers may be stipulated in the articles of incorporation and also in the contracts between the manager and the company.[246] The essential role of the manager is to implement the resolutions and decisions of the directors and shareholders. Managers are not allowed to modify or alter the decisions of shareholders conducting the business of the company, or resolutions of the shareholders' meeting or the board.[247] Managers are also confined to the scope of the authority conferred to them in the articles of incorporation or the contracts with the company.[248]

To avoid potential conflicts of interest, the Company Law does not permit managers to be managing officers of other companies or to engage in the same kind of business as the company, unless this is agreed to by a majority of the shareholders or directors conducting the business of the company.[249] These restrictions on the power of a manager do not invalidate transactions involving *bona fide* third parties.[250]

Managers are liable to compensate the company for any loss or damage as a result of:

- violating any law or ordinance;
- contravening the articles of incorporation;
- modifying or altering the decisions of the shareholders conducting the business of the company, or the resolutions adopted at the shareholders' meeting or at the meetings of the board; or
- exceeding the scope of their authority.[251]

The appointment, remuneration and discharge of managers are to be decided by:

- a majority of shareholders in the case of a limited company, an unlimited company and an unlimited company with limited liability shareholders; or
- a majority of directors in the case of a company limited by shares.[252]

6.7 Corporate Financial Transactions

6.7.1 Charges   Taiwan's domestic finance market is predominantly asset-based. As a result, financial transactions tend to be dependent to a large extent on the taking and enforcing of some form of security.[253] The Civil Code, the Chattel Secured Transactions Law (CSTL) and the Negotiable Instruments Law are the major laws governing the creation of charges.

A mortgage over real property is defined in the Civil Code as a right to receive performance of an obligation from the proceeds of sale of an immovable asset which has been given as security for the obligation of a debtor or by a third person without any transfer of possession.[254] No title to property passes under a real mortgage. Instead, the mortgagee holds a security interest over the property.[255] A mortgage must be in writing and will gain priority over general creditors, and subsequently registered mortgages, only when registered.[256]

Chattel mortgages are covered by the CSTL. The CSTL also deals with trust receipts. All chattel security interests must be in writing to be effective between the parties and must be registered to be effective as against a *bona fide* third party.[257] In contrast to a real mortgage under the Civil Code, chattel mortgagees under the CSTL may enforce their security without judicial assistance if debtors fail to perform the contract or the mortgaged property is removed, sold, pledged, transferred or otherwise disposed of.[258]

Likewise, in the case of trust receipts granted by trust agreement if the trustee does not fulfil the contractual obligations, removes the collateral without consent, pledges or grants a mortgage over the collateral, or disposes of the collateral other than as provided for in the contract, the grantor of the trust is entitled to retake possession of the collateral without judicial intervention.[259] A major problem with trust receipts is that they cannot act as floating charges. As they must be created over specific items, once those items are manufactured into something else, the trustor's ownership of the goods is lost and the security becomes worthless.[260]

Pledges are also provided for under the Civil Code. A pledge may be made in respect of both moveable property or other rights. A pledge made in relation to moveables gives the right to take possession of the property of a debtor, or of a third party, as security for an obligation. A pledge made in respect to rights only covers transferable claims or other rights and to non-transferable claims.[261] In addition to mortgages, trust receipts and pledges, the other means financiers use to secure loans to companies includes guarantees and promissory notes. Promissory notes are particularly effective because once default has occurred it is a criminal offence under the Negotiable Instruments Law for a debtor to touch the assets. Corporate guarantees are also important for financiers because companies tend to operate in groups, often with a strong family focus, and financiers look beyond the credit risk of the named borrower.[262]

6.7.2 Share buy-backs There is a general prohibition in Article 167 of the Company Law against companies limited by shares buying back their own shares. It provides that 'a company shall not redeem or buy back any of its own shares, nor accept any of them as security'. There are a number of exceptions to this general prohibition. The first exception is found in Article 167 itself: a company may buy-back shares from a shareholder who is in liquidation or adjudged bankrupt.

The next exception has already been discussed in the context of shareholders' rights. Article 186 entitles shareholders to request that the company buy back their shares where the shareholders have objected to a company doing a particular act. Shareholders are also entitled to have their shares bought back where they object to a proposed consolidation or merger.

6.8   Capital Raising

Taiwan has the fourth largest equity market in the region after Japan, Korea and Australia.[263] This is in spite of five factors which have slowed and limited its official growth so that in 1991 new public offerings raised only US$ 1.5 billion.[264] The first is a continuation of the Japanese practice of banks as significant suppliers of capital. This relationship banking network is limited as the banks are also risk adverse and have restricted themselves to a few companies.[265] Second, businesses frequently borrow through their relationships with customers or suppliers.[266] Third, underwriting is not developed and the process is frequently a farce with the underwriters conducting a lottery among family members of the issuing group who buy and sell to one another in order to get the price of the shares above the permitted SFC flotation price.[267] Fourth, perhaps reflecting a continuing distrust of government, there has been an informal and underground financial sector of colossal dimensions. Its scale is now reduced as a result of government pressure to suppress it forcing 'kerb-side' lenders to move to shop fronts.[268] Fifth, much industrial activity is still in state-owned enterprises or in small to medium-sized companies neither of which use or need listing, although privatization of state corporations is reducing the significance of this.[269]

As mentioned, the Company Law continues to seek to promote capital investment through the corporate form and employee share ownership. All companies with a paid up capital of more than NT$ 200 million are required to publicly issue their shares unless the government agency responsible for the enterprise consents.[270] If 45 per cent or more of the enterprise is owned by foreigners in a foreign investment approved under the Investment by Foreign Nationals Law, this is not required.[271] The Company Law also requires, unless the government agency responsible for the enterprise agrees, 10–15 per cent of new shares to be reserved for employees.[272] There are a number of restrictions, based on lack of profitability and authorized capital, on a company issuing shares.[273] Under Article 22 of the SEL, a maximum of 10 per cent of the shares in companies not listed on the TSE or 'over the counter' (OTC) are to be offered for sale unless a shareholder's meeting has approved a higher allotment. These provisions specifically derogate from provisions of the Company Law which would permit existing shareholders to exercise pre-emptive rights.[274]

The 1988 reforms to the SEL provided for a two-tier review system for public offerings. They continued a merit review system.[275] They established a registration system for all public offerings under which applications for particular public offerings become effective 30 days after lodgement with the SFC.[276]

There are no specific exceptions to registration on the basis of private placements to individuals. It is possible, if there is no fraud and no general solicitation, that such placements may not fall within the definition of securities which defines them as offered to 'the public'. Specific offers to a few wealthy, informed individuals would therefore fall within Article 22.[277]

Companies listing their shares on the TSE must comply with the TSE rules made under Article 140 of the SEL, the Rules Governing Examination of the Listing of Securities (RGELS).[278] They require an application to the TSE and, depending on the enterprise sector in which the company is engaged, the consent of the government agency in charge of that sector. Dispersed shareholding is encouraged by requiring a proportion of the common and preferred stock to be available for a public offering prior to listing.[279] Companies already in existence which are seeking listing in the first two classes are required to have the dispersal required for their relevant class as indicated in Table 7.1.[280]

There are two further categories of listed companies. The third category consists of technology-based enterprises which are approved by the ministry responsible for the enterprise area. They must hold an 'unequivocal opinion' from it that they have developed a product with market potential, have a paid up capital of at least NT$ 200 000 000, be recommended by underwriters who agree to sell the stock on a firm commitment basis, and have a current net worth of not less than 66 per cent of the paid up capital. In addition, certain shareholders and officers who hold more than 5 per cent of issued shares are required to deposit specified proportions of them with a specified organization on undertaking not to sell them for two years.[281] The fourth category is for hotel businesses and government incorporated enterprises in which the government holds shares, which have been designated as national economic reconstruction 'important enterprises'.[282]

There have been a number of changes to these requirements considered in recent years. At the end of 1996 the SFC and the TSE were considering amalgamating the first three categories using the criteria for the second category, with the criteria for the third category as an alternative.[283] Increasing popular resistance to high pollution in the early 1990s saw more stringent environmental legislation. When this led to decreasing investment in certain industries, the TSE added pollution control performance to the guidelines for stock listing review.[284]

Table 7.1

Category	1[285]	2[286]
Number of years in existence	At least five years	At least five years
Amount of paid up capital	NT$ 600 000 000 in the two most recent fiscal years	NT$ 300 000 000 in two most recent fiscal years
Profitability	Profit recorded for the three most recent fiscal years with: (i) operating profit in the two most recent years of 10 per cent or more of paid up capital; (ii) operating profit in the two most recent years of NT$ 120 000 000 being not less than 6 per cent of paid up capital; (iii) either of the first two criteria are met in the two most recent years; or, (iv) the operating profit for the five most recent years represents 5 per cent or more of the paid up capital.	Profit recorded for the most recent fiscal year with: (i) operating profit in the most recent year of 10 per cent or more of the paid up capital; (ii) both the operating and pre-tax profit in the two most recent years must be not less than 6 per cent of paid up capital, or the average is not less than 6 per cent with the last year better than the previous year; or, (iii) both the operating and pre-tax profit in the five most recent years represent 3 per cent or more of the paid up capital.
Capital structure	Before profit distribution for the most recent year represents 33 per cent or more of the total assets.	None
Dispersion of shareholdings	At least 2 000 stock holders with at least 1 000 holding 1 000– 50 000 shares which represent 20 per cent or more of issued shares, or at least 10 000 000 shares.	At least 1 000 stock holders with at least 500 holding 1 000–50 000 shares which represent 20 per cent or more of issued shares, or at least 10 000 000 shares.

7   The External Administration of Companies

Corporate insolvency is dealt with in both the Company Law and the Bankruptcy Law (1935).[287] The Company Law contains provisions which deal with the liquidation of companies and the reorganization of companies limited by shares. On the other hand, the Bankruptcy Law, which applies to individuals, partnerships, corporations and associations, makes provision for the composition and bankruptcy of companies.

Like the Company Law, the Bankruptcy Law was part of the law reform movement undertaken during the last years of the Qing dynasty and completed by the KMT. Several attempts at drafting a bankruptcy code were made. One was finally being promulgated by Imperial Edict in 1906 only to be revoked in 1907.[288] However, when the KMT government appointed the Civil Codification Commission in 1928 to draft a new bankruptcy law it was able to draw on the Imperial Edict, a draft of the Beijing Codification Commission of 1915, a draft of the Ministry of Justice and the Provisional Rules for the Liquidation of Indebtedness of Merchants.

The present regulation of insolvency reflects principles the Commission adopted. It sought to preserve the traditional practice of parties informally reconciling their differences. A member of the drafting committee wrote in 1935:

> The Chinese people have long been accustomed to settling their differences and difficulties in an amicable manner; great leniency is generally shown to a *bona fide* insolvent debtor. Bankruptcy is not regarded, as is done in Europe, as a semi-criminal offence. A debtor, be he a merchant or not, is usually permitted to settle his debts by all manner of means. When he has failed in his own effort, he may request some third party to mediate.[289]

Furthermore, the Commission incorporated the traditional practice of a merchant seeking assistance from the local chamber of commerce where negotiation and mediation led to no agreement. This was also enshrined in a scheme of non-judicial composition. According to the drafting committee:

> A debtor is permitted, before any application for bankruptcy has been presented, to apply to the court or the chamber of commerce for an amicable settlement. In fact, even after the proceedings for bankruptcy have been commenced, the debtor may still propose a scheme for composition to his creditors.[290]

7.1 Rules Regarding Arrangements and Reconstructions

7.1.1 Compositions A composition under the Bankruptcy Law seeks to allow a company's debt to be dealt with by agreement between the creditors and the company, without bankrupting the company. Both the debtor and creditor may apply for a composition. A company may apply if it is unable to pay its debts.[291] It can apply to the courts or the local chamber of commerce for a supervised composition.[292] There are no significant differences between the two forms.[293] Importantly, Article 4 of the Bankruptcy Law stipulates that a composition entered into in another jurisdiction will not be effective against the property of the debtor company in Taiwan.

The company's application must include a statement of assets, a list of creditors and debtors, and the proposed composition plan.[294] No appeal is allowed from the decision of the court, which must be made within seven days of receipt of the application.[295] A judge acts as supervisor, and an accountant, or other person chosen by the local chamber of commerce, is appointed as assistant supervisor.[296] The court must publish the general reasons for granting the application, the name of the supervisor, the place where the composition is to be conducted, the period within which claims by creditors are to be reported, and the date of the creditors' meeting.[297]

Within one month of the end of the notified period for reporting claims by creditors, a creditors' meeting, presided over by the supervisor, must be held.[298] Representatives of the debtor company must attend. If the debtor fails to attend, the supervisor must declare the meeting closed and make a report to the court, which will then adjudicate on the bankruptcy.[299]

The role of the supervisor is to report on the results of investigations conducted into the state of the debtor company's assets and business and to provide an opinion to creditors concerning the proposed composition plan. Next, the supervisor must attempt to bring about agreement between the respective parties.[300] If objections are raised by the debtor or other creditors against a claim of a creditor then the supervisor must make an immediate ruling on the dispute.[301] The creditor may appeal to the court against this decision.[302]

The composition plan may be accepted by a majority vote of the creditors present at the meeting if they amount to more than two-thirds of the total amount of unsecured claims.[303] If the composition plan is rejected, the supervisor must declare the composition procedure closed and make a report to the court which will then adjudicate on the bankruptcy.[304] According to Articles 29 and 37, the composition plan is subject to court approval and does not bind a secured creditor. If the court disapproves of the plan, the settlement agreement reached is unconscionable or fraudulent, or the debtor does not comply with the plan, the court must adjudge the debtor bankrupt.[305] In the case of a plan undertaken under the supervision of the local chamber of commerce, court approval is not required.[306] This is consistent with the general principles enunciated by the drafting committee in 1935.

7.1.2   Consolidation and mergers   The Company Law makes specific provision for the consolidation and merger (and the necessary dissolution and re-incorporation) of companies. In the case of a company limited by shares, Article 316 requires that a dissolution, consolidation or merger must be passed by a majority of the shareholders present at a shareholders' meeting attended by more than 75 per cent of the total number of issued shares. In relation to other companies, a company may be merged or consolidated with the unanimous consent of all shareholders.[307]

7.2   Voluntary Administration and Corporate Rescue Provisions

7.2.1   Reorganization   Before 1966, there was no form of corporate rescue available in Taiwan. That year the Company Law was amended to incorporate court-ordered company reorganizations, similar to the then US and Japanese provisions for company reorganisation.[308] The scheme is limited to a company which publicly issues shares or corporate bonds.[309] As has already been discussed, this means that if a company falls within the scope of Article 156 of the Company Law it will be able to have recourse to a court-supervised restructuring designed for potentially viable but insolvent companies.

Professionals have been critical of the process.[310] The main criticism is that companies seek to avoid bankruptcy. Once a petition for reorganization is approved by the court, bankruptcy and composition proceedings are halted for the duration of the reorganisation.[311] As the courts are under no time limit to grant a petition, approval of a petition and plan for reorganization usually takes up to two years.[312] This creates considerable opportunities for the dissipation of the company's assets.

Furthermore, there is no clear standard for granting such a petition. Article 288 of the Company Law states that an application must not be granted where the company has been declared bankrupt; is subject to a composition already approved by the court; has been dissolved; or is not 'worthy of operation according to the standard of reasonable financial bearing of expense'.

Other problems with the reorganization process include the creditors' lack of opportunity to contest the reorganization petition. The court is not required to advertise the receipt of a petition or to issue notices to known creditors.[313] This also applies to applications made by the debtor company or 'interested parties' to the court for a stay on proceedings against the company prior to the reorganization petition being granted, including proceedings for bankruptcy, composition and compulsory execution.[314] Finally, once a petition is granted the company is effectively in the control of the reorganizers who can be, and often are, the directors of the company.[315]

7.3 *Company Winding Up Rules, Tests for Insolvency, Grounds for Winding Up, Mechanisms for Initiating Insolvency Proceedings*

7.3.1 Bankruptcy A bankruptcy petition may be lodged by either the debtor or creditor. A court will declare bankruptcy where a debtor company is unable to pay off its debts. However, if a bankruptcy petition is lodged during a composition, the court will dismiss the application if there is a possibility that the composition procedures will be successful.[316] A trustee in bankruptcy will be appointed and the trustee will make an application to the court for the holding of a creditors' meeting. The creditors' meeting may pass resolutions concerning:

- the election of supervisors to represent the creditors during the bankruptcy process;
- how the bankrupt's estate is to be administered; and
- whether the business of the bankrupt should continue.[317]

Bankrupt companies which have discharged their debts may ask the court to restore their rights. If they fail to discharge their debts entirely, they may petition the court for restoration of their rights after three years from the close of bankruptcy proceedings or execution of a reconciliation agreement.[318]

7.3.2 Liquidation Liquidation of companies is dealt with by the Company Law. In relation to companies limited by shares, there is an ordinary and special liquidation procedure. An ordinary liquidation is basically a voluntary liquidation in which the directors are the liquidators. Creditors may apply for the appointment of a court-appointed liquidator in a special liquidation. A special liquidation involves greater court scrutiny and creditor input. Creditors may appoint an inspector to overview the activities of the liquidator and to report to the court.[319] There is also provision for the liquidation of limited companies, unlimited companies and unlimited companies with limited liability shareholders. The shareholders liquidate unless a liquidator is appointed by the court on the application of a concerned person, or a majority of shareholders agree to appoint a liquidator.

7.4   *Protection of Creditors and the Ranking of Claims*

7.4.1   Bankruptcy   The method for the distribution of assets found in the Bankruptcy Law includes the distribution to creditors *pro rata*, with secured creditors having exclusive rights in respect of the secured property.[320] Article 112 of the Bankruptcy Law provides that 'obligatory claims' enjoy priority in the distribution of the bankrupt's estate. These priority claims are found in other laws, such as the Business Tax Law, the Labour Standards Law and the Law Governing Workers Financial Welfare.

7.4.2   Compositions   Following the approval of a composition application, no civil proceedings may commence or continue against the debtor company. However, this restriction does not apply to secured creditors.[321] Article 108 of the Bankruptcy Law exempts them from any composition proceedings and gives them the right to enforce their securities at any time. On the other hand, unsecured creditors are only protected from any 'gratuitous act' of the debtor company. Article 15 of the Bankruptcy Law defines this as any transaction entered into between spouses, lineal relatives or relatives of dependants living together, and transactions where the debtor company disposes of property at prices 50 per cent below the market price, conducted by the debtor after the application for composition. Such an act will be of no effect.

7.4.3   Reorganizations   If a reorganization petition or an application for a stay on proceedings is granted, all litigation, bankruptcy proceedings or composition proceedings are suspended against the debtor company. The secured creditor is not exempt from this rule.[322] Both secured and unsecured creditors must pursue their claims through the reorganization process. This entitles them to attend meetings of concerned persons of the company and to vote on the reorganization plan proposed by the reorganizers.[323] The number of votes allocated to creditors will depend on the amount of their claim.

7.4.4   Liquidation   In the case of companies limited by shares, there is protection for creditors in the form of mandatory notice requirements and also in the priority payment requirements provided for in the Company Law.[324] There is also the added requirements of creditors' meetings, the appointment of a liquidation inspector to act on behalf of creditors, and the inspector's approval of a number of the liquidator's acts, including the disposal of company property.[325] The inspector has a number of other powers that can be utilized on behalf of the creditors. Where a limited company, unlimited company or an unlimited company with limited liability shareholders is being liquidated, creditors are protected only to the extent that if the assets of the company are not sufficient to meet its liabilities, the liquidator must file an application for bankruptcy.[326] The creditors must then pursue their claims in accordance with the provisions of the Bankruptcy Law.

7.5   Control of Insolvency Practitioners

There is no registration or regulation of insolvency practitioners in the Bankruptcy Law or the Company Law. Apart from the respective professional qualifications for lawyers and accountants, there are no specific requirements. The Company Law and Bankruptcy Law simply require that certain positions be filled by public accountants or legal representatives. However, there is a widespread reluctance on the part of both lawyers and accountants to become involved in insolvencies. This stems from social perceptions of the process.[327] This reluctance extends to the role of supervisor in a reorganization procedure.

Article 285 of the Company Law requires that supervisors in a reorganization report on the financial condition of the company, including the assets and the potential viability of the company, and any negligence or impropriety on the part of the management. This necessitates the appointment of supervisors with the accounting and business skills to conduct an adequate investigation. However, the choice of supervisors is at the discretion of the court. Article 289 of the Company Law provides that the court must select a supervisor with 'specialised knowledge and experience in the operation of the business or of such a company or banking institution'. In the past, courts have tended to appoint supervisors that are favourable to the management of the company. This has also undermined the independence and credibility of the position of supervisor, so much so that, again, professionals are reluctant to accept appointment to the position by the courts.

8   Takeover Rules

8.1   An Introduction to Company Takeover Rules

Chinese companies are generally described as family owned and controlled. This, it is said, results from the strong trust within the family which is absent in relations with strangers or the state.[328] The large government-owned companies previously dominating the economy, which originated in the socialist phase of the KMT, do not fit easily with these social or corporate stereotypes. Many companies do. Neither form is prone to takeovers, particularly the Anglo-US hostile acquisition. At the end of 1992 ten large family-owned conglomerates represented 31 per cent of the market value of the TSE. There are signs that this structure is breaking down partly as a result of the need to obtain growth capital. Some families still maintain 30–35 per cent holdings to defeat changes requiring super-majorities. Others have sold below this limit.[329] Other problems result from families entering their third generation of ownership.[330] Some, the exceptions, are separating ownership from control.[331] Others are repeating the previous pattern, but at a higher level. Strategic alliances between families, including non-Taiwanese families, impose partnership-like concepts over the corporate conglomerate controlled by the families in the alliance.[332]

In spite of the dispersal rules of the TSE, listed companies are often narrowly held by individuals and the government.[333] Institutional investors, including local pension funds, are not active, although foreign institutions are increasingly so.[334] Takeovers have been friendly and driven by demand for increased market share,[335] and the need to diversify[336] and harvest research and development.[337] Some have been driven by the diversification of organized crime with gangsters muscling in on 13 listed companies using voting rights purchased from shareholders. In 1996 when 100 gangsters, in black dinner jackets and silver ties, from the Highest Alliance black society intimidated shareholders to take control of a listed company, Kao Hsing Chang Iron and Steel, the government responded.[338]

Crossborder takeovers overseas are driven by government encouragement for international markets.[339] Acquisitions have been made by both Taiwanese companies overseas and by foreign companies in Taiwan.[340] When pressure by the US government appreciated the currency by 45 per cent between 1986 and 1988, foreign targets became cheap.[341] Acquisitions in Taiwan by foreign companies of limited companies with publicly issued shares have had to be friendly.[342] Strict government control has immunized them from hostile takeovers.[343] Where foreign firms face no direct barriers others exist. When government policy permitted new foreign securities firms to set up, no regulations implementing it were made.[344] Subsequently a 12 month waiting period was imposed.[345] The finance industry has also been described as one of 'special permission'.[346] Taiwanese companies also have not been immune from this regulatory pressure. The SFC has been reluctant to permit them to guarantee the loans of overseas subsidiaries.[347]

Crossborder takeovers have also been used to avoid this regulation.[348] Taiwanese companies have acquired foreign companies to avoid bans on investment with the mainland, including dealings in securities.[349] Foreign companies have acquired Taiwanese companies to avoid restrictions on foreign ownership of certain enterprises, such as cable television.[350] Some Taiwanese companies, unable to obtain permission for other reasons, have followed their example.[351]

Increased activity in takeovers was indirectly promoted by changes made to the Company Law in 1990 to encourage further investment by companies. Previously they could not invest more than 40 per cent of their capital in other companies. They may now do so if they are holding companies and are specifically empowered by their articles or have the approval of the general meeting on a case-by-case basis.[352]

Takeovers of companies which have not publicly issued shares are regulated by the Company Law. Takeovers of companies with publicly issued shares are subject to the SEL and regulated by the SFC. Article 25 of the SEL prohibits a person from making a 'public tender offer to purchase the securities' of such companies outside the TSE or the OTC market without the permission of the SFC. Where these companies are listed on the TSE, they are also subject to those listing rules relating to takeovers.

The Fair Trading Law, promulgated on 4 February 1992, imposes anti-trust and unfair competition restrictions on mergers. These include transactions where more than one-third of the voting shares or capital of another enterprise is being acquired.[353] It requires pre-merger notification and approval, where:

- the merged enterprise will have one-third or more of the market share;
- one of the enterprises being merged has one-quarter or more of the market share; or
- one of the enterprises being merged had sales for the previous year which exceeded the FTC's publicly announced sales criteria. In April 1992 the FTC fixed sales revenues in excess of NT$ 2 billion. In 1993 this was increased to NT$ 10 billion.[354]

The law is administered by a Fair Trading Commission within the Executive Yuan. There is doubt about its commitment to enforcing the law. Few actions have been taken against large companies.[355] When it has taken action, unfair competition has not been its principal motivation.[356]

8.2 Takeover Thresholds

Takeovers are regulated along a scheme similar to the US Williams Act of 1988.[357] Takeovers of companies with publicly issued shares are subject to provisions in the SEL and regulated by the SFC in rules made pursuant to Article 25 of the SEL. The SEL and the rules set out the thresholds and the particular action required when the threshold is reached. First, the SEL seeks to regulate the sale of significant parcels of shares amounting to more than 10 per cent of the total shares on issue for all companies with publicly issued shares. Second, it requires all takeovers of such companies to be approved by it or, where the company is listed on the TSE, to comply with its listing rules relating to shares beneath a certain value in public offers or large block transactions.

Under Article 22(2) of the SEL, if a director, a member of the supervisory board, a manager or a person holding more than 10 per cent of the total shares on issue wishes to transfer shares he or she can only do so by an offer to the public after filing for the approval of, and obtaining registration by, the SEC. A transfer than can take place in one of two ways. First, where the shares have been held for a particular period, it may be by sale on the TSE or in an OTC market three days after the registration. The price must be within the daily transfer allowance ratio permitted by the TSE. This is not required if there are less than 10 000 shares involved. Second, within the same time limits, the shares may be sold by private placement. Purchasers who buy these shares are subject to the same provisions if they wish to transfer the shares. This provision is ignored with many takeovers being treated as private transactions.[358] Breach of the law relating to the transfer of shares can be a ground for the TSE suspending trading in those shares.[359]

Until 1995, the SFC had made no rules for takeovers outside the TSE and OTC markets. The rules made after 1995 require any investor or enterprise holding one-third of a targeted firm's shares to purchase over 50 per cent if they continue to buy shares. This must be done on the open market outside the TSE and the OTC. The target company is to be served with a notice which it must make public within ten days. It must notify major shareholders who control over 1 000 shares within 15 days. The acquisitions should be completed within 20–60 days. The acquirers cannot take action against the same targeted firm within one year from a previous attempt failing. Penalties for non-compliance include imprisonment from one to seven years.[360]

The TSE has made rules, approved by the SFC, under Art 138 of the SEL regulating sales of shares which may carry control. Buyers may acquire, in a public offer by a securities firm, up to 20 per cent if the outstanding shares are below a particular threshold. The TSE also allows block transfers of more than 500 000 shares through a broker where the shares and the purchase price have been deposited in advance.[361]

8.3 Disclosure Requirements and Shareholder Protection

Takeovers are regulated partly by disclosure of significant shareholdings. When a takeover proposal is made, more complex requirements must be observed.

If the takeover is by way of merger, the Company Law requires the approval of a merger resolution by the majority at a meeting at which 75 per cent of issued shares are represented. It is possible for the articles to provide for higher majorities and quorums. If the company has publicly offered shares and there is no quorum, a vote of 75 per cent or more for the merger will suffice.[362] As noted earlier, shareholders who dissent have the right not to vote and to have their shares purchased at a fair price.[363]

This provision does not apply to foreign nationals or overseas Chinese as the Company Law does not contemplate non-citizens acquiring a company. Such transactions are possible, but they are required to comply with the Investment by Foreign Nationals Law or the Investment by Overseas Chinese Law.[364]

Where the company has publicly issued shares Article 43-1 of the SEL requires a person who possesses (individually or jointly with another) 10 per cent of the shares to file a report with the SFC within ten days. It should detail any financial arrangements relating to the shares. Article 25 requires a company, on becoming eligible to issue shares to the public, to notify the SFC of the par value of shares held by directors, supervisors, managers or persons holding more than 10 per cent of the total shares on issue. If there are any changes in these holdings, the holder must notify the company by the fifth day of the month and it must inform the SFC by the fifteenth day of the month. If the holder pledges the shares, the company must be notified of this within five days. It must report this to the SFC and make a public announcement within another five days.

Where, under the rules made in 1995, an investor or company which holds one-third of a targeted firm's shares is required to purchase over 50 per cent, that investor or company must give notice to the targeted company. The targeted company must make the potential takeover public within ten days and notify major shareholders who control over 1 000 shares within 15 days. The acquisition should be completed within 20–60 days. The acquirers cannot take action against the same targeted firm within one year after a previous attempt has failed.[365]

Both the Company Law and the SEL give protection to minority shareholders against the use of proxies. The SFC has made rules under Article 22 of the SEL. Article 177 of the Company Law also offers protection against the misuse of proxies. The common practice of shareholders selling voting rights, often earning more than dividends, produced a difficult regulatory issue. A number of listed companies were stealthily taken over by black societies which had purchased these voting rights. These societies developed a more brazen form of takeover through intimidating shareholders' meetings. The government, at the beginning of 1997, promised to introduce legislation to prevent this from happening and to ban the sale of voting rights.[366]

8.4   Role of Lawyers, Experts and the Regulator in Takeovers

Until 1989, admission to the legal practice affected lawyers' abilities to professionally perform skilled complex corporate or securities transactions or litigation. Admission was tightly controlled, privileging judges, procurators or retired military officers over the pre-1945 Taiwanese. Judges, including the Council of Grand Justices, and procurators are still not required to have professional legal training.[367] Lawyers have a number of roles in takeovers. They are lobbyists, advisers on the legal implications of takeovers and the financial arrangements relating to them, and promoters and drafters of new laws.[368] The regulatory environment of 'public restrictions, private disregard'[369] and the connection of a number of lawyers with government and the KMT makes lawyers significant intermediaries between companies and the state in obtaining approvals and indications that regulatory agencies will not take action.

Corporate advising is now a competitive area with increasingly widespread professional knowledge of law relating to companies and securities. As companies have become more internationally oriented, there has been an increase in crossborder mergers and acquisitions advising. There has been also a change in attitude towards paying for such advice.[370] The size of law firms has not permitted specialization, although competition from foreign firms has led to some mergers of local firms.[371] Foreign law firms, with localized branches, may have an advantage in advising on complex corporate financial transactions because of their expertise and size. Their advent resulted partly from a demand for services in intricate transactions.[372] They may be competing against, or working with, foreign financial experts on whom Taiwan's large listed companies have relied heavily to objectively evaluate possible acquisitions. Some unlisted companies have employed financial services companies for similar reasons. This financial advising sector has had negligible local competition.[373] Foreign law firms without localized branches are restricted to advising on transactions which have a connection with the domestic or international law of their home jurisdiction.[374]

The ability of shareholders to protest and to offer their shares for purchase requires a determination of a 'fair' price, but this has not led to a lucrative business for independent experts in made-to-order fairness opinions.

8.5 Mechanisms for the Review of Takeover Activity

Any decisions made by the SFC or another government agency are reviewable in accordance with the law outlined in Section 3.3, above. Decisions made by the TSE are made in a contractual relationship between the listed company and the exchange with the SEL giving the SFC a number of powers to terminate the contract at the request of the TSE or the listed company.[375]

9 An Introduction to Securities Regulation in Taiwan

Trading in securities, after 1945, was subject to the Exchange Law promulgated in 1935. This was the law, supplemented by the Securities House Regulations, made under the National General Mobilization Law, which applied to the TSE when it was established in February 1962. The drafting of a new law commenced, as it was already clear that the Exchange Law permitted too many improper practices. A market crash in 1965 led to the TSE being closed for ten days and gave new urgency to the drafting. Yet it was not until 30 April 1968 that the SEL was promulgated. It remains the law regulating trading in corporate securities.[376] It is based on provisions from the 1948 Japanese Securities Exchange Law and the US Securities Act of 1933 and Securities Exchange Act of 1934.

It has had four significant amendments. In July 1981 the SFC was transferred from the MOEA to the Ministry of Finance. A number of amendments in May 1983 provided for the establishment of securities investment trust companies,[377] the regulation of proxies at shareholders' meetings and of certified public accountants certifying financial statements to shareholders and investors and to more effectively recover insider trading profits. In January 1988 the most extensive amendments increased the regulation of securities firms and the TSE. It permitted foreign broking firms to establish offices in Taiwan or to enter into joint ventures with Taiwanese firms. It also made insider trading illegal and clarified the limits of civil liability for breaches of the law. Following a review by a SFC task force in June 1990, it was again amended to give the SFC the power of judicial investigation and to bring civil actions, to increase penalties, to recognize the reorganization of the functions of the Securities Dealers Association and the TSE and the internationalization of securities trading.[378]

The regulation of securities trading is the responsibility of the SFC. The TSE is responsible for the regulation of trading on the TSE, subject to the supervision and direction of the SFC. A Securities Dealers Association is intended to apply some self-regulation to securities intermediaries. In 1962 18 companies were listed on the TSE. Further listings were slow. Corporate managers preferred to obtain long-term loans from banks to listed share issues. They also preferred close control and little disclosure. Government encouragement followed through tax cuts both to the company and to shareholders on their dividends. In the late 1970s these were increased and, by 1980, 102 companies were listed.[379] At the end of 1996 382 companies were listed on the TSE. In that year, 23 out of 36 applicants for listing were listed for the first time.[380]

In addition, there is a developing OTC market, where the securities are traded by investors through price negotiation at the securities dealers' places of business. At the end of 1994 a computerized OTC securities exchange was opened, again with capped foreign ownership limits.[381] The OTC market has also undergone rapid growth. By February 1997 there were over one million individual accounts, 20 times the number in February 1996 with few of the new accounts overlapping with other accounts.[382]

The secondary securities markets have been described as 'casinos' and 'not yet for widows and orphans'.[383] They are extremely volatile despite limits on price movements.[384] Some argue that there will be little change until there is deregulation of currency exchange and profit repatriation[385] and other existing regulatory controls which make access to the market cumbersome for foreign investors[386] and impose a cap on it.[387] Some of the most capricious and arbitrary, such as permitting applications to be made in a short period each year, are disappearing. The SFC believes that increased investment by institutional investors will 'introdu[ce] more mature investment behaviour'.[388] Some large Asian investment funds have purchased on the TSE. There has also been a significant increase in the level of foreign investment in shares traded on it. In 1996 foreign institutions held stock worth US$ 27.08 billion, a threefold increase from 1995.[389] Foreign institutions by the end of that year held more stock than local mutual funds.[390]

In 1982 an OTC market was established for trading in government and corporate bonds. In 1988 corporate equities were included. In 1991 some venture capital firms were included. The decision to list corporate equities was to enable companies too small to list on the TSE to make public offers. The SFC made guidelines with which they must comply.[391]

The Fair Trading Law will not impinge generally on corporate or securities transactions, although it includes unfair trade practices within its purpose of removing impediments to competition.[392] It does not extend, under Article 5, to an act performed by an enterprise under another law which would include acts under the Company Law and the SEL.[393]

9.1   The Relationship between the TSE and Corporate Regulation

The TSE was established in 1962 by 43 private and government institutions. It remains the only stock exchange, although the government has given some indications that a second exchange may be established.[394] It is a company-type stock exchange under Article 124 of the SEL specifically prohibited from listing its shares on itself.[395] Its board is composed of 15 directors. The board of supervisors has three members. The SEL requires that at least one-third of the board members be relevant non-shareholders' professionals, and designated by the competent authority; the remaining positions are elected among shareholders at the shareholders' meeting.[396] The board, which is argued to be too narrowly constituted, is appointed by the SFC which has strong formal and informal control over it. The KMT continues to influence the TSE. The chair of the TSE board is chosen by it.[397] In early 1996, when prices fell dramatically due to tension between Taiwan and China, institutions associated with the KMT entered the market to push prices up.[398] It became a member of the International Organization of Securities Commissions (IOSCO) in 1992.[399]

Under Article 139 of the SEL, the TSE may list the shares of a company. Article 142 prevents securities from being traded unless the SFC has consented. The SFC may impose restrictions on that trading. Under Article 156, it may suspend or restrict trading if there are questions about the viability of the company, if it has engaged in deceptive or dishonest practices, or if the securities are subject to abrupt rises and falls and it is likely to affect market orders or 'impair public interest'. In other circumstances, where continued trading would affect the market or 'impair the public interest', the SFC may take similar action with the approval of the Ministry of Finance.

The rules of the TSE give it the power to suspend trading for a considerable number of reasons.[400] Under Article 148, the TSE must inform the SFC if it suspends or reinstates the trading in listed securities.

Articles 141 and 143 require that the contract between the listing company and the exchange must be approved by the SFC. Pursuant to Article 144 the TSE can terminate that contract if this is approved by the SFC. The listed company may apply to the TSE to terminate the contract and may do so if the SFC gives its approval under Article 145.

Additional disclosure is required by the SEL from listed companies.[401] In addition to the periodic disclosures required by Article 38 it requires disclosure, within two days of 'any matter, the occurrence of which has had a significant impact on shareholders equity on the price securities'.

The TSE requires that a listed company file these reports and the resolutions, operating reports and financial statements with the TSE following its general meeting.[402]

The TSE's efforts to lift the standards of corporate governance through market discipline are subject to significant limitations. The TSE itself is not free of scandal.[403] There is an absence of reliable information. Disclosure provisions are inefficient and inadequately enforced, which is why banks remain a primary source of capital.[404] When companies have fallen into difficulties, they have not been delisted but assigned to a limbo called 'full delivery'. This is similar to the Tokyo practice of shifting stocks which fail to meet the big board requirements to the OTC market. These stocks have often been traded by pools to cheat the investors who join in.[405] The emergence of management funds led to further, rather than fewer, problems. Local investors sought to influence these funds to buy the shares of companies associated with these investors.[406] There are indications that the TSE market is not 'efficient'[407] and subject to seasonal taxation variations in particular.[408] A clearer restriction on market discipline can be seen in the limits on the permitted deviation of the price of stock from the previous day's close. This follows the practice of the Seoul and Tokyo exchanges. These limits are intended to provide small cooling-off periods, particularly in the event of a crash. In other exchanges similar action may be taken by officers exercising discretionary powers to stop trading if it is necessary or desirable. The result, however, is that the listed price may vary from a 'true' market price.[409]

9.2   Types of Securities Regulated

Securities are defined in Article 6 of the SEL in a limited way. The definition includes: government bonds, shares, stock or bonds issued as a result of a public offer by a corporation, certificates which are issued in respect of the securities already mentioned, subscription warrants for new stocks and new stock warrants. In addition, the Ministry of Finance, under its power to do so in the same Article, has designated as securities beneficiary certificates of securities investment trust companies and foreign stock and shares, government bonds, corporate bonds and beneficiary certificates which have been offered to the public or traded.[410]

9.3   The Legal Effect of Listing Rules and Business rules of the TSE

The SEL requires the TSE to provide in its by-laws or operational rules for the listing of securities and the use of its market, and a range of other matters relating to the conduct of the exchange.[411] The SFC may, by Article 161, 'in order to protect the public interest or the interest of investors', order the TSE to amend its articles, business rules, by-laws or any other rules or to suspend them.[412] Article 165 requires that brokers and others using the TSE must comply with orders made by the supervisory personnel of the SFC.

The relationship between the TSE and the brokers and dealers who operate through it is based on contract[413] and those contracts are terminated if the SFC revokes the broker's licence or the broker suspends its business.[414]

Articles 141 and 143 also specify that the relationship between the TSE and the listing company is based on a contract. Article 143 requires that contract to be approved, together with the charges and fees imposed, by the SFC. Government bonds are excepted by Article 149. They must be listed if the SFC so orders and the listing requirements do not apply to them.

9.4 Market Conduct Rules and Sanctions for Securities Misconduct

The SEL imposes liability for fraudulent trading, deceptive trading, market manipulation and insider trading. It also regulates margin trading and short selling.[415] The TSE has a surveillance programme, administered by a special task force, which operates while the market is open and also reviews trading after the close to detect abnormalities. It further investigates abnormalities detected.[416] The Third Division of the SFC receives reports from the TSE on matters which warrant further investigation as part of its role in supervising the secondary markets.[417]

9.4.1 Deceptive and fraudulent trading Deceptive and fraudulent trading is subject to civil liability under Article 20 of the SEL. Such conduct in markets was a feature of imperial law.[418] This Article is based on § 17 of the US Securities Act 1933, § 10b of the US Securities Exchange Act of 1934 and Rule 10b-5 made under that later Act. It prohibits the offering of securities to the public. It also prohibits issuing or trading in securities either fraudulently or in a manner which misrepresents or misleads a third person. The inclusion of false or misleading information in financial reports or statements made or filed by the issuer of securities is prohibited. These are criminal offences under Article 171 which imposes a maximum penalty of seven years' imprisonment and a maximum fine of NT$ 750 000. This provision is little known to the legal profession. The SEL generally has been narrowly construed by the courts deterring investors from taking any action except in the clearest cases.[419]

9.4.2   Market manipulation   Article 155 groups various unrelated activities together as the offence of market manipulation. Manipulating public markets was also an offence under the Qing Code.[420] The Article applies to the TSE and, with appropriate changes, to securities traded in the OTC market. It is based on § 9 of the US Securities Exchange Act 1934. It imposes civil liability on persons engaging in that conduct in favour of any buyer or seller with whom they dealt. Breach of the provision is a criminal offence under Article 171. Actions which breach the provision are:

- failing to deliver securities, or tender the purchase price, in a transaction on the exchange in a manner which may disrupt the market;
- creating the appearance of a transaction in which rights in securities are transferred without transferring those rights;
- colluding with purchasers and sellers in transactions for the purpose of raising or depressing the price of securities;
- conducting transactions in the name of an individual or his or her nominee for the purpose of raising or depressing the price of securities by purchasing at a high price or selling at a low price;
- spreading a false rumour or misrepresenting information for the purpose of affecting the price of a security on the exchange; or
- directly or indirectly performing any manipulative act which affects the price of a security listed on the exchange.

Most actions have been under the fourth ground. Those charged have escaped liability under a whimsical interpretation of 'purchasing at a high price and selling at a low price'. The courts have relied on the evidence of those charged whether they believed the price was 'high' or 'low'. The provision, consequently, has not been effective in preventing market manipulation.[421] Serious investigations do take place although they have exposed activities which have led to a further loss of confidence in the market.[422] On the other hand, well publicized cases have gone uninvestigated because of the political connections of the investors who benefited with the KMT and the major opposition parties.[423]

9.4.3   Insider trading   The Swiss management institute, IDM, in July 1996 ranked the TSE 38 out of 45, on a descending scale, of stock exchanges subject to insider trading. The SFC reacted by taking action to attract and reassure foreign investors.[424] By late 1996 it was investigating more than 80 listed firms following probes into share transactions by board members, supervisors and managers of the companies.[425] The impression remains amongst Taiwanese business executives that insider trading is prevalent.[426]

Insider trading is dealt with in two provisions in Articles 157 and 157-1. Article 157 enforces disgorgement of profits. A director, supervisor, officer or shareholder who holds more than 10 per cent of the company's shares can be required to surrender to the company any profit earned, within six months, from the sale or purchase of listed shares. The action must be brought within two years. A shareholder can request the directors and supervisors to bring the claim. If they fail to do so and the company suffers a loss or damages, the directors and supervisors are jointly or severally liable. The provision is based on § 16b of the US Securities Exchange Act 1934. Since the late 1980s regular actions have been brought under this Article[427] and the TSE carries out regular screenings of trading by insiders to check whether profits required to be disgorged have been.[428]

Article 157-1 prohibits inside trading and is limited in similar ways to US law. It applies only to corporate insiders and their tippees. This suggests that it is based on policies of abuse of a relationship or misappropriation of corporate property. It applies to directors, supervisors and officers of the company, an owner of more than 10 per cent of the issued shares, a person who is engaged in professional or regulatory work involving the company or anyone to whom these people have passed the information. The information is required to materially affect the price of the shares and not to have been disclosed to the general public. Insiders have a defence that they had good reason to believe that the information had been disclosed. Insider trading could fall within Article 20, the general fraud provision. The relationship between the two Articles is not clear.

Article 157-1 provides that any person who deals with insiders is entitled to recover from them the difference between the price at which they bought or sold and the average closing price of the shares for the ten days following the disclosure of the information to the public. The court may triple the difference 'where the seriousness of the violation warrants'. Until 1993 there had been only three criminal prosecutions and no civil cases brought under this provision. Only one of the prosecutions had resulted in a conviction. The courts have construed the provision more narrowly than the SFC has.[429]

10 Miscellaneous

10.1 *The Powers of the Courts*

Courts have significant power to adjudicate on company disputes. As indicated, the division between civil and administrative law separates the courts dealing with disputes within the company from those between the company and state regulators.

The main limitations on the courts' powers arise from the tradition of non-recourse to state law in resolving disputes and to the judicial system giving priority to alternative ways of resolving disputes. As seen in Sections 6.6–6.8, above, courts offer a number of remedies to shareholders aggrieved about the management of a company. Similarly, they play a role in the external administration of a company, if at times in competition with chambers of commerce. In civil matters involving property worth only a small amount, mediation may be required before any legal action can be instituted.[430]

The state endorsement of private arbitration is most clearly seen in Articles 166–170 of the SEL, which prescribe rules for arbitration in disputes about securities transactions. Parties may agree to resolve any disputes by arbitration.[431] Arbitration is compulsory in disputes arising from securities transactions between the TSE and securities firms or between securities firms whether or not the parties have agreed to arbitration.[432] If a securities firm does not comply with an arbitration award, the SFC may suspend it from operating.[433] Claims for damages under the SEL must be made within two years of claimants learning that they have a claim or within five years of the transaction giving rise to the claim.[434]

Courts retain the power to repeal any arbitrator's award if it is void.[435] Parties, after an action is commenced, may, by agreement, reach a settlement which avoids a final judgment being given.[436] Parties may compromise their differences and reach new agreements at any time.[437]

10.2 Civil Remedies

As indicated, parties seeking a resolution of a commercial conflict have a choice between the judicial system or private commercial arbitration. Litigation is regarded as expensive and slow with judgments not necessarily reflecting the merits or the law.[438]

10.3 Offences

The Company Law contains a number of offences for failure to comply with the law which appear in particular Articles. For example, under Article 103 a person required to keep a shareholders' roster who fails to do so is liable to be fined. Similarly, Article 210 imposes a punishment for failure to keep books or failure to make them available for inspection. More serious offences relating to false statements and dishonesty are contained in the Criminal Code or the Special Criminal Code.

Security market offences are dealt with in Section 9.4, above. Chapter VII of the SEL contains a number of penal provisions.[439] Individuals responsible for breaches of the SEL by a company are liable to punishment for the offence.[440]

10.4 Who May Initiate Proceedings?

The Company Law, as indicated in Section 3.1, above, contains a number of provisions permitting the MOEA to bring applications for breaches. In respect of actions by directors (as indicated in Sections 6 and 7, above) directors, supervisors, shareholders and creditors have access to the courts to protect their interests. The SFC has the power to bring civil actions for breaches of the SEL, generally where securities have been issued to the public.[441] The TSE has a contractual relationship with listed companies entitling it to seek remedies for breach of contract.

As indicated above, the Ministry of Justice advises the Executive Yuan and its agencies, such as the MOEA and the Ministry of Finance on matters of law and acts for them in any legal proceedings. It has a limited role in respect of the investigation of crimes,[442] which is the primary responsibility of the procurate of the appropriate court.[443] The SFC has similar powers for the investigation of criminal offences.[444]

10.5 Registration and Control of Persons under the Legislation

The MOEA has few functions in this regard. The SFC, through the Sixth Division, regulates and supervises certified public accountants under the regulations made by the Ministry of Finance.[445] The SEL requires a number of securities-related activities to be approved and licensed by the SFC under rules made by the Ministry of Finance. These include the operation of the following enterprises: securities investment trusts, securities financing, securities investment consulting, security depository and 'any other enterprise which operates securities-related services'.[446] The approval may be revoked for breaches of the law.[447] Employees of such firms must meet the standards imposed by the SEL and the SFC.[448] They may be subject to SFC sanctions for breaches of any law.[449]

Notes

*   University of Canberra.
** Mallesons Stephens Jacques, Brisbane
1   The Provisional Constitution of the Political Tutelage Period promulgated in 1931 by the Nationalist Government, which it replaced, contained this separa-

tion of powers. The separation has its origin in the imperial constitution in which the emperor held the legislative, executive and judicial powers with independent powers of examination and censorship (control). Sheng, R.C.W. (1937), 'The Legislative Yuan of China Today', *China Law Review*, 9, 297, 297–298; Chiu, H. (1993), *Constitutional Development and Reform in the Republic of China on Taiwan*, Baltimore: School of Law, University of Maryland, 5–9; Wu, J.C.H. (1932), 'The Struggle Between Government of Laws and Government of Men in the History of China', *China Law Review*, 5, 53, 64.

2   The President and Vice-President are now directly elected. Constitution, Additional Article 2(1). Under Article 43 in financial or economic crises, the President, if the Legislative Yuan is in recess, may, by a resolution of the Executive Yuan Council and in accordance with the Emergency Orders Law, issue emergency orders.

3   Constitution, Article 55. The premier is nominated by the President and confirmed by the Legislative Yuan. Kwang, M.C.H. (1995), 'Taiwan – The Republic of China: A Profile of Recent Constitutional Changes and Legal Developments', in A.E.-S. Tay and C.S.C. Leung (ed.), *Greater China: Law Society Trade*, Sydney: Sydney Law Book Co., 59, 67–68.

4   Constitution, Chapter VI.

5   Constitution, Chapter VII and Article 77.

6   The Organic Law of the Judicial Yuan, Article 4, requires that no more than one-third be from the following groups: legislators of more than nine years' standing, politicians with legal qualifications or judges of the Supreme Court of more than ten years' standing. In practice, the members are generally senior politicians, senior judges and professors of law. Chiu, H. and Fa, H.J. (1994), 'Taiwan's Legal System and Legal Profession', in M.A. Silk (ed.), *Taiwan Trade and Investment Law*, New York: Oxford University Press, 21, 28 and note 54.

7   Constitution, Article 79. Additional Article 4.

8   Constitution, Article 80.

9   Constitution, Chapter IX and Article 90. The Control Yuan's powers are set out in Articles 95–98. Article 104 requires it to appoint an Auditor-General who has extensive powers to investigate government expenditure. Biddulph, S. (1993), 'Continuity in the Relationship Between Law and Administration', in M. Lee and A.D. Syrokomla-Stefanowska (eds), *The Modernization of the Chinese Past*, Sydney: Wild Peony, 42, 45. Theoretically, the Censorate under the imperial system could inspect and condemn the acts of the sovereign himself, although Staunton notes 'this must be little more than a fiction of state'. Staunton, G.T. (trans) (1810), *Ta Tsing Leu Lee: Being the Fundamental Laws and A Selection from the Supplementary Statutes of the Penal Code of China*, London: T. Cadell and W. Davies, 182.

10   The Examination Yuan is established by Chapter VIII and Additional Article 5 of the Constitution. Under Article 86 all public servants, members of professions and technicians must be examined by it. Article 88 states that it is independent of other branches of government.

11   Kwang, as note 3, above, 66–67; Cooper, J.F. (1996), *Taiwan's 1995 Legislative Yuan Election*, Baltimore: School of Law, University of Maryland, 34. Lien, appointed Premier in 1996, is also the Vice-President. His name was not submitted to the Legislative Yuan for approval. 'Taiwan Review 1997', *Quest Economics Data Base*, 1 May 1997, Reuters. The Legislative Yuan in May 1996 resolved that the President appoint a new Premier. The President did not do so. 'DPP Chairman Calls for Lien to Resign', *China News*, 13 May 1997, Reuters.

12   Kwang, as note 3, above, 67–68.

13   'Taiwan Review 1997', as note 11, above.

14   Following the Chinese Communist Party coming to power in 1949, the administration of the ROC relocated to Taiwan. The ROC continues to claim that it is the legitimate government of all China. Consequently, it does not view itself as an independent country, but as a province of China under the administration of the ROC.

15   Chen, J. (1995), *From Administrative Authorisation to Private Law*, London: Martinus Nijhoff, 9–16.

16   Tay, A.E.-S. (1986), *Law in China: Imperial, Republican and Communist*, Sydney: Centre for Asian Studies, University of Sydney, 6; Staunton, as note 9, above, 'Preface' i-xxxv; Alabaster, E. and Alabaster, C. (1968), *Notes and Commentaries on Chinese Criminal Law and Cognate Topics*, Taipei: Ch'eng-Wen (original edition published, London, 1899).

17   Blakeney, M. (1996), 'Intellectual Property Reform in the Asia Pacific Region', *Australian Journal of Corporate Law*, **6**, 23; Drahos, P. (1996), 'Global Law Reform and Rent-Seeking: The Case of Intellectual Property', *Australian Journal of Corporate Law*, **6**, 45; Jones, C. (1994), 'Capitalism, Globalization and the Rule of Law: An Alternative Trajectory of Legal Change in China', *Social and Legal Studies*, **3**, 195–221; Scogin, H.T. (1994), 'Civil "Law" In Traditional China: History and Theory', in K. Bernhardt and P.C.C. Huang (eds), *Civil Law in Qing and Republican China*, Stanford: Stanford University Press, 13, 19–23. Twentieth century positivists have found it more difficult to answer the question of 'What is law?' Hart, H.L.A. (1994), *The Concept of Law*, Oxford: Clarendon Press, 2nd edition, 13.

18   Cohen, J.A., Edwards, R.R. and Chen, F.C. (1980), *Essays on China's Legal Traditions*, Princeton: Princeton University Press, 226, 236; Trubeck, D.M., Dezaley, Y. and Buchanan, R. (1994), 'Studies of the Internationalization of Legal Fields and the Creation of Transnational Arenas', *Case Western Reserve Law Review*, **44**, 407, 479–80. Jones describes the complex commercial relationships in the banking system of Ningpo which represented institutions analogous to partnerships, franchises, agencies and guilds. Mann Jones, S. (1972), 'Finance in Ningpo: The "Chi'en Chuang", 1750–1880', in W.E. Willmott (ed.), *Economic Organization in Chinese Society*, Stanford: Stanford University Press, 47, 60–67, 77.

19   Chiu, H. and Fa, J. (1994), 'Taiwan's Legal System and Legal Profession', *Occasional Papers/Reprints: Series in Contemporary Asian Studies*, Baltimore: School of Law, University of Maryland, 1.

20   Chen, as note 15 above, 7.

21   It was an offence to incite others to bring litigation or to manage litigation for profit. Staunton, as note 9, above, Section CCCXL, 376. Taiwanese are becoming more willing to sue. Lawsuits are no longer regarded as declarations of war. *Taiwan Business: The Portable Encyclopedia For Doing Business With Taiwan* (1994), San Rafaele: World Trade Press, 180.

22   In the nineteenth century Taiwan civil cases consumed the magistrates' time. Cohen, Edwards and Chen, as note 18, above, 26, 55. In northern Taiwan the 'corporate lineage' was frequently involved in litigation. Allee, M.A. (1994), *Law and Local Society in Late Imperial China: Northern Taiwan in the Nineteenth Century*, Stanford: Stanford University Press, 251–252, 255–256.

23   Cameron, M.E. (1931), *The Reform Movement in China 1898–1912*, Stanford: Stanford University Press, 26, 44.

24   Chen, as note 15, above, 13.

25   Stephens, T.R. (1987), 'The Shanghai Mixed Court and the Ming Sung Umbrella Case 1926', *Australian Journal of Politics and History*, **33**, 77, 85.

26   Biddulph, as note 9, above, 59. This is said of the imperial period and of the People's Republic of China (PRC). It is equally true of Taiwan.

27   Large accountancy firms, with government contacts, may be as equally well placed. Trubeck, Dezaley and Buchanan, as note 19, above, 479–480.

28   Chiu, H. (1991), 'Contract Management and Dispute Resolution', in J.T. McDermott (ed.), *Legal Aspects of Investment and Trade with the Republic of China*, Baltimore: School of Law, University of Maryland, 44, 53; Kaufman-Winn, J. (1991), 'Banking and Finance in Taiwan: The Prospects for Internationalisation in the 1990s', *International Lawyer*, 907, 948.

29   Chiu, as note 1, above, 7.

30   Kirby, W.C. (1995), 'China Unincorporated; Company Law and Enterprise in Twentieth-Century China', *Journal of Asian Studies*, **54**, 43, 45–46. The older form of partnerships can be seen as the unlimited liability company and the joint liability company. Hung, W.S.H. (undated), *Outlines of Modern Chinese Law*, Shanghai, 213, 223.

31   Braudel, F. and Ranum, P.M. (trans) (1977), *Afterthoughts on Material Civilization and Capitalism*, Baltimore: Johns Hopkins University Press, 62–63.

32   Braudel, F. and Reynolds, S. (trans) (1982), *Civilization and Capitalism 15–18th Century, Vol II, The Wheels of Commerce*, Cambridge: Harper & Row, 588–589; Godley, M.R. (1981), *The Mandarin Capitalists From Nanyang: Overseas Chinese Enterprise in the Modernisation of China, 1893–1911*, Cambridge: Cambridge University Press, 178; Le Fervour, E. (1988), *Western Enterprise In Late Ch'ing China: A Selective Survey of Jardine, Matheson & Company's Operations, 1842–1895*, Cambridge: Harvard University Press, 82.

33   Cheng, Y. (1956), *The Foreign Trade and Industrial Development of China: An Historical and Integrated Analysis through 1948*, Washington: University Press of Washington, 38–39.

34   A number of states permitted companies, in breach of their treaties, to engage in industrial activities. This was regularized when the Treaty of Shimonoseki conceded the right to establish industries to Japan. Other states then acquired this right through most favoured nation clauses. Feuerwerker, A. (1995), 'China's Nineteenth Century Industrialization: The Case of the Hanyeping Coal & Iron Company Ltd', in A. Feuerwerker (ed.), *Studies in the Economic History of Late Imperial China: Handicraft, Modern Industry and the State*, Michigan: Ann Arbor, Center for Chinese Studies, University of Michigan, 165–166.

35   Neal, L. (1990), *The Rise of Financial Capitalism: International Capital Markets in the Age of Reason*, Cambridge: Cambridge University Press, 9; Bowen, H.V. (1995), 'The Bank of England During the Long Eighteenth Century, 1694–1820', in R. Roberts and D. Kynaston (eds), *The Bank of England: Money, Power and Influence 1694–1994*, Oxford: Clarendon Press, 5, 5–7.

36   Feuerwerker, as note 34, above, 181–182. This is indicated by the name of the China Merchants Steam Navigation Co. which can be literally translated as 'a public – or government bureau to invite merchant [investment] in steamships'. Feuerwerker, A. (1958), *China's Early Industrialization: Sheng Hsuan – Huai (1844–1916) and Mandarin Enterprise*, Cambridge: Harvard University Press, 110.

37   As note 36, above, 96–99.

38   They include the Imperial Telegraph Administration, the Hua-Sheng Textile Mill, the Imperial Bank of China and the Hanyeping Coal and Iron Company. Feuerwerker, A. (1995), 'Three Kuan-tu Shang-pan Enterprises' in A. Feuerwerker (ed.), *Studies in the Economic History of Late Imperial China: Handicraft, Modern Industry and the State*, Michigan: Ann Arbor, Center for Chinese Studies, University of Michigan, 201, 204, 222, 242–243; Grundy, R.S. (1895), *China Present and Past: Foreign Intercourse Progress Resources The Missionary Question Etc*, London: Chapman & Hall, 103, Appendix C, 394–398, Appendix D, 399–401; Le Fervour, as note 32, above, 81–82.

39 Feuerwerker, as note 36, above, 100, 124.
40 Articles 152 and 151 of the Qing Code provided for commercial agents, se-
    lected from amongst merchants, to supervise markets. Staunton, as note 9,
    above, 163–164; Feuerwerker, as note 34, above, 1, 34; Jacobs, N. (1958), *The
    Origins of Modern Capitalism in Eastern Asia*, Hong Kong: Hong Kong Univer-
    sity Press, 48.
41 As note 40, above, 44, 52, 55, 118.
42 On coming to power in 1928 it nationalized a number of enterprises, includ-
    ing banks. Kirby, as note 30, above, 53.
43 As note 42, above, 54. Chang, M.H. (1983), 'Sun Yat-sen's Program for the
    Economic Modernization of China', in A.J. Gregor and M.H. Chang (eds),
    Essays on Sun Yat-sen and the Economic Development of Taiwan, Baltimore: School
    of Law, University of Maryland, 4, 4–5.
44 Kirby, as note 30, above, 53–56.
45 Loh, J., Allen, D.E., Hiscock, M.E. and Roebuck, D. (1973), *Credit and Security
    in the Republic of China: The Legal Problems of Development Finance*, St Lucia,
    Queensland: University of Queensland Press, 10. Pang argues that the state
    and the KMT, have been central to the development of the country's economy
    and are also responsible for the increasing internationalization of the economy.
    Pang, C. (1992), *The State and Economic Transformation: The Taiwan Case*, New
    York: Garland Publishing; Huang, T. 'Chapter 11', in Lin, B.J. (ed.), *Asia and
    Europe: A Comparison of Development Experiences*, Taipei: Institute of Interna-
    tional Relations; Myers, N.L. (1994), *Statutory Encouragement of Investment and
    Economic Development in the Republic of China on Taiwan*, Baltimore: School of
    Law, University of Maryland, 4; Patrick, H.T. (1994), 'Comparisons, Contrasts
    and Implications', in H.T. Patrick and Y.C. Park, (eds), *The Financial Develop-
    ment of Japan, Korea, and Taiwan: Growth, Repression and Liberalization*, New
    York: Oxford University Press, 325, 333–335; Cheng, T.J. (1997), 'Taiwan in
    1996 – From Euphoria to Melodrama', *Asian Survey*, **37**, (No 1), 1 January,
    Reuters; 'IDB Plans to Nurture Internationally Competitive Software Compa-
    nies', *Taiwan Business News*, 18 March 1997, Reuters.
46 Jamieson, G. (1921), *Chinese Family and Commercial Law*, Shanghai: Kelly &
    Walsh, 121–122. Ordinance No. 53 of 1911, 'to provide for the registration of
    Chinese Partnerships and to enable partners therein to register and limit their
    liability', also reflects this principle. Jamieson, above, 129. See also the report
    from the *North China Herald*, 31 October 1890 of the *Bank of China v Chinese
    Shareholders*, in which Chinese holders of partly paid shares in an English
    incorporated company were found not liable to pay further calls on their
    shares on the basis of this principle. Jamieson, above, 178–179.
47 Kirby, as note 30, above, 46.
48 Fa, J.-P. (1980), *A Comparative Study of Judicial Review under Nationalist Chinese
    and American Constitutional Law*, Baltimore: School of Law, University of Mary-
    land, 22, note 19, 29; Cameron, as note 19, above, 171.
49 Kirby, as note 30 above, 43–44; Hung, as note 30, above, 212.
50 Jamieson, as note 46, above, 128. T.R. Jernigan noted that the directors of an
    unincorporated joint stock company would generally be regarded as the man-
    aging partners and the shareholders as silent partners. Family property could
    be required to be contributed depending on a common-sense view of a par-
    ticular case. If property had accrued to the family, such a decree might be
    made. It was enforced by the imprisonment of the individual for the offence
    of not paying a debt. This generally led to a compromise. *China In Law and
    Commerce*, New York: Macmillan, 1905, 94–96.
51 Kirby, as note 30, above, 43.
52 Hung, as note 30, above, 212.

53　Hung, as note 30, above 212.
54　The Civil Code, for example, in Title 4 deals with the concept of juristic person. Riasanovsky, V.A. (1938), *Chinese Civil Law*, Tientsin, 39–51.
55　Kirby, as note 30, above, 51–52 citing Zhaoyuan, Z. (1946), *Xin Gongsifa Jieshi* [New Company Law Annotated], Lixin: Shanghai.
56　Kirby, as note 30, above, 5–56.
57　Ma, H.H.P. (1973), 'General Features of the Law and Legal System of the Republic of China', in R. Cosway, H.H.P. Ma and W.L. Shattuck (ed.), *Trade and Investment in Taiwan: The Legal and Economic Environment in the Republic of China*, Taipei: China Council on Sino-American Cooperation in the Humanities and Social Sciences, 1, 12.
58　Company Law, Article 5.
59　Chiu and Fa, as note 6, above, 24.
60　In 1996, for example, the Finance Minister instructed the SFC to prepare revisions to the SEL to permit companies listed on the Taiwan Stock Exchange to buy back their own stocks on the open market. 'Legal Change to Allow Companies Buy Back Their Own Stock', *China Economic News Service*, 23 August 1996. LEXIS-NEXIS.
61　Law for Enacting National Statutes and Regulations, Article 7. Regulations on Deliberations of the Legislative Yuan, Article 8.
62　Chu, Y.-H. (1994), 'The Realignment of Business-Government Relations and Regime Transition in Taiwan', in A. McIntyre (ed.), *Business and Government in Industrialising Asia*, St Leonards: Allen & Unwin, 113, 128–131.
63　Kirby, as note 30, above, 50–51, 56.
64　Winn, as note 28, above, 948.
65　Kirby, as note 30, above, 56.
66　Cheeseman, B. (1997), 'Taiwan's Red Tape Trips Foreigners', *Australian Financial Review*, 5 June, 50.
67　Kirby, as note 30, above, 58.
68　Tsai, W.-H. (1994), *Towards Greater Democracy: An Analysis of the Republic of China on Taiwan's Major Elections in the 1990s*, Baltimore: School of Law, University of Maryland, 33 and note 31; Chu, as note 62, above, 116–117, 136.
69　In 1933 of the 2 243 Chinese-owned firms surveyed only 617 were organized as joint stock companies. The main reasons for this was the absence of a secondary market to trade shares and the expectation of shareholders that they would enjoy immediate returns. Feuerwerker, A. (1995), *The Chinese Economy 1870–1949*, Michigan: Ann Arbor, Center for Chinese Studies, University of Michigan, 102, 118. Only 1 per cent of firms were registered companies on the mainland in 1949; Kirby, as note 30, above, 56.
70　Loh, Allen, Hiscock and Roebuck, as note 45, above, 9.
71　Article 25 states: 'when a division of the Supreme Court in trying a case should entertain an opinion of law different from a precedent made by the same provision or some other division, the President of the Supreme Court should request the President of the Judicial Yuan to solve the question by calling a conference for the Alteration of Precedents.' A committee composed of the divisional heads of the Supreme Court selects representative cases which are condensed by the judges of the division that wrote the decision and are published, with the approval of the president of the court, as precedent. Ma, as note 57, above, 16.
72　Chiu, as note 28, above, 44, 53.
73　Chang, C.H., Liang, Y.L. and Wu, J.C.H. (1937), 'Sources of Chinese Civil Law', *China Law Review*, 9, 209. The approach then was that although precedents had no binding authority, a judge should 'draw inspiration and

instruction from them', where there was a unifying interpretation it should be followed. Chang, Liang and Wu, 211–212.

74 In the early 1980s the Appeal Courts had target rates for upholding lower court decisions: 45 per cent in civil cases and 55 per cent in criminal cases. Chiu, as note 28, above, 44, 53.

75 Cosway, R., Ma, H.H.P. and Shattuck, W.L. (1973), 'Introduction', in R. Cosway, H.H.P. Ma and W.L. Shattuck (ed.), *Trade and Investment in Taiwan: The Legal and Economic Environment in the Republic of China*, Taipei: China Council on Sino-American Cooperation in the Humanities and Social Sciences, vii.

76 Pound, R. (1981), 'Law Reform During 1937–1949', in J.C. Hsiung (ed.), *Contemporary Republic of China: The Taiwan Experience, 1950–1980*, New York: Praeger, 290–291.

77 Constitution, Article 171.

78 Chiu and Fa, as note 6, above, 25–26.

79 This follows the Qing Code, Article 35. Staunton, as note 9, above, 37.

80 Wallace-Semkow, B. (1994), *Taiwan's Capital Market Reform: The Financial and Legal Issues*, Oxford: Clarendon Press, 291 and note 41.

81 Constitution, Article 14. Chiu and Fa, as note 6, above, 26.

82 Decree of Judicial Yuan, 27 July 1931, No. 459, Appeal Case No. 1074, Sup Ct (1934) cited in *Taiwan Business*, as note 21, above, 177.

83 Goh, B.-C. (1993), 'Understanding Chinese Negotiation', *Australian Dispute Resolution Journal* 178, 184–185. Civil Code, Articles 1 and 2.

84 Lai, I.-J. (1994), 'Securities Regulation' in M.A. Silk (ed.), *Taiwan Trade and Investment Law*, New York: Oxford University Press, 337.

85 Tay, A.E.-S. and Leung, C.S.C. (1995) 'Introduction: The Relation Between Culture, Commerce and Ethics', in A.E.-S. Tay and C.S.C. Leung (eds), *Greater China: Law Society Trade*, Sydney: Sydney Law Book Co., 1, 6.

86 Winn compares this with the lack of integration of Japanese law into social practices. Excessive resources are required to enforce compliance. Consequently, it is ignored or officials bargain over its requirements Winn, as note 28, above, 948, drawing on Upham, F. (1987), *Law and Society in Postwar Japan*, 949. The Central Bank of China concedes that its rules are often confusing and ambiguous. Cheeseman, B. (1997), 'Taiwan Bank Branch Faces Delay', *Australian Financial Review*, 4 April, 58.

87 Cosway, Ma and Shattuck, as note 75, above, vii.

88 Company Law, Articles 5–7.

89 Chu, as note 62, above, 132.

90 Company Law, Article 11.

91 Company Law, Article 284.

92 Company Law, Article 397.

93 Company Law, Article 9.

94 Company Law, Article 217.

95 Lai, as note 84, above, 326, note 12, 349.

96 SFC, 'Introduction to the Securities and Futures and Exchange Commission' at <http://www.tse.com.tw/sec/introd/e_introd.html> and 'Organization of SEC' at <http://www.tse.com.tw/sec/org/e_org.html>

97 SFC, 'Primary market administration' at <http://www.tse.com.tw/sec/service/primary/e_primary.html>

98 SFC, 'Securities firms management' at <http://www.tse.com.tw/sec/service/manage/e_manage.html>

99 SFC, 'Administration of the secondary market' at <http://www.tse.com.tw/sec/service/supervise/e_superv.html>

100 SFC, 'Regulation of the securities related services' at <http://www.tse.com.tw/sec/service/related/e_related.html>

101   SFC, 'Supervision of the futures industry' at <http://www.tse.com.tw/sec/service/future/e_future.html>

102   SFC, 'Regulation of the certified public accountants' at <http://www.tse.com.tw/sec/service/account/e_account.html>

103   SFC, 'Audit control' at <http://www.tse.com.tw/sec/service/audit/e_audit.html>

104   SFC, 'Legal operations' at <http://www.tse.com.tw/sec/service/regulation/e_regula.html> and 'International affairs' at <http://www.tse.com.tw/sec/service/internat/e_intern.html>

105   SEL, Articles 38, 39 and 64.

106   MOEA, 'Economic Measures and Policies' at <http://www.moea.gov.tw/~meco/Intro_e/xmoe2.htm>

107   MOEA, 'Staff Units' at <http://www.moea.gov.tw/~meco/Intro_e/xmoe331.htm>

108   MOEA, 'Modernization of Business' at <http://www.moea.gov.tw/~meco/Intro_e/xmoe2211.htm #4>

109   MOEA, 'Improvement of Investment Environment' at <http://www.moea.gov.tw/~meco/Intro_e/xmoe2221.htm #1>

110   Klatt, G. (1997), 'Taiwan', in A.S. Gutterman and R. Brown (eds), *Commercial Laws of East Asia*, Hong Kong: Sweet & Maxwell Asia, 505, 521.

111   These include, within the Ministry, the Board of Foreign Trade, the Small and Medium Business Administration, the Investment Commission and the Commission of National Corporations. MOEA, as note 107, above. MOEA, Industrial Development Bureau, 'Development of Industries in Taiwan Republic of China' and 'Chapter 4. Promotional Measures and Strategies' at <http://www.moeaidb.gov.tw/etext/prom.htm#ch4–7>

112   Patrick, as note 45, above, 325, 346. The Council for Economic Planning and Development plans to attract Asia-Pacific regional headquarters of multinational enterprises. Republic of China, *Republic of China Year Book 1997*, 'Asia-Pacific Regional Operations Center' at <http://www.roc-taiwan.org/info/yearbook/ch10.htm>

113   The MOEA, the Ministry of Transportation and Communications, the Central Bank of China and the Government Information Office have also been involved. Republic of China, as note 112, above.

114   SFC, as notes 97 and 98, above.

115   Approved by the Executive Yuan, its passage was delayed in the Legislative Yuan. SFC, as note 101, above.

116   SFC, as note 102, above.

117   MOEA, as note 107, above. Its function is the 'examination, in accordance with the law, of petitions and appeals submitted by the people'.

118   Ma, as note 57, above, 22.

119   Company Law, Article 435.

120   Company Law, Article 371.

121   Company Law, Article 372.

122   Company Law, Article 437.

123   Company Law, Article 434.

124   Company Law, Article 375.

125   Company Law, Article 384.

126   Company Law, Article 376.

127   Company Law, Article 376.

128   Company Law, Article 374.

129   Company Law, Article 377.

130   Company Law, Article 378.

131   Company Law, Article 380.

132 Company Law, Article 13.
133 Company Law, Article 15.
134 Company Law, Article 16.
135 Company Law, Articles 6 and 387.
136 Company Law, Article 389.
137 Company Law, Article 411.
138 Company Law, Article 412.
139 Company Law, Article 413.
140 Company Law, Article 418.
141 Company Law, Article 419.
142 Company Law, Article 420.
143 Company Law, Articles 404–409 dealing with the incorporation of an unlimited company also apply to the incorporation of an unlimited company with limited liability shareholders.
144 Company Law, Article 405.
145 Company Law, Article 404.
146 Company Law, Articles 41 and 405.
147 Company Law, Article 406.
148 Company Law, Article 98.
149 Company Law, Article 128.
150 Company Law, Article 129.
151 Company Law, Article 42.
152 Company Law, Article 116.
153 Company Law, Article 2.
154 Company Law, Article 18.
155 Company Law, Article 19.
156 Company Law, Article 18.
157 Rules Governing the Minimum Amount of Capital, Article 3.
158 Kaufman-Winn, J. (1988), 'Creditor's rights in Taiwan: A Comparison of Corporate Reorganization Law in the United States and the Republic of China', **13**, *North Carolina Journal of International Law and Commercial Regulation*, 1994, 409, 441.
159 Ernst & Young, *Doing Business in Taiwan*, New York: Ernst & Young International, 30.
160 Investment by Foreign Nationals Law, Article 16.
161 Company Law, Article 100.
162 Company Law, Article 106.
163 Company Law, Article 100.
164 Company Law, Article 112.
165 Company Law, Article 106.
166 Company Law, Article 415.
167 Company Law, Article 98.
168 Company Law, Article 99.
169 Company Law, Article 98.
170 Company Law, Article 108.
171 Company Law, Article 102.
172 Company Law, Article 103.
173 Company Law, Article 104.
174 Company Law, Article 165.
175 Company Law, Article 111.
176 Company Law, Article 109.
177 Company Law, Article 48.
178 Company Law, Article 128.

179   Taiwan Industrial Development and Investment Centre (1997), *Taiwan Industrial Panorama*, **25**, (6), June.
180   Company Law, Article 277.
181   Company Law, Article 159.
182   Company Law, Article 192.
183   Company Law, Article 195.
184   Company Law, Article 193.
185   Company Law, Article 194.
186   Company Law, Article 200.
187   Company Law, Article 212.
188   Company Law, Article 213.
189   Company Law, Article 214.
190   Company Law, Articles 199, 214 and 215.
191   Company Law, Article 202.
192   Company Law, Article 205.
193   Company Law, Article 205.
194   Company Law, Article 208.
195   Company Law, Article 208.
196   Company Law, Article 216.
197   Company Law, Article 217.
198   Company Law, Article 218.
199   Company Law, Articles 218–222.
200   Company Law, Article 219.
201   Company Law, Article 220.
202   Company Law, Article 223.
203   Company Law, Article 219.
204   Company Law, Article 224.
205   Company Law, Article 111.
206   Company Law, Article 112.
207   Company Law, Article 119.
208   Company Law, Article 8.
209   Company Law, Articles 41, 45 and 46.
210   Company Law, Article 42.
211   Company Law, Article 48.
212   Company Law, Article 52.
213   Company Law, Article 119.
214   Company Law, Article 118.
215   Company Law, Article 112.
216   Company Law, Article 171.
217   Company Law, Article 172.
218   Company Law, Article 170.
219   Company Law, Article 173.
220   Company Law, Article 174.
221   Company Law, Article 175.
222   Company Law, Article 177.
223   Company Law, Article 178.
224   Company Law, Article 183.
225   Company Law, Article 184.
226   Company Law, Article 185.
227   Company Law, Article 110.
228   Company Law, Article 231.
229   Company Law, Article 20.
230   Company Law, Articles 20 and 21.
231   Company Law, Article 21.

232 Company Law, Article 22.
233 Company Law, Article 35.
234 Company Law, Article 229.
235 Company Law, Article 230.
236 Company Law, Article 228.
237 Company Law, Article 20.
238 SEL, Article 36. Ernst & Young, as note 159, above, 69.
239 As note 238, above, 63.
240 For a discussion of the emergence of minority rights in Anglo-US law, see Tomasic, R. and Bottomley, S. (1995), 'Chapter 15: Members and Rights and Remedies', in *Corporations Law in Australia*, Leichhardt: Federation Press, 419–453.
241 Company Law, Article 186.
242 Company Law, Article 187.
243 Company Law, Article 188.
244 Company Law, Article 189.
245 Company Law, Article 191.
246 Company Law, Article 30.
247 Company Law, Article 33.
248 Company Law, Article 33.
249 Company Law, Article 32.
250 Company Law, Article 36.
251 Company Law, Article 34.
252 Company Law, Article 29.
253 McGowan, T. (1994), 'Banking, Credit, and Finance: The Transactional Aspects', in M.A. Silk (ed.), *Taiwan Trade and Investment Law*, Hong Kong: Oxford University, 378.
254 Civil Code, Article 244.
255 Civil Code, Article 878.
256 Civil Code, Article 865.
257 CSTL, Article 5.
258 CSTL, Article 17.
259 CSTL, Article 34.
260 McGowan, as note 253, above, 380.
261 Civil Code, Article 109.
262 Hamilton, G. and Kao, G.-S. (1990), 'The Institutional Foundations of Chinese Business: The Family Firm in Taiwan', in C. Calhoun (ed.), *Comparative Social Research*, London: JAI Press, 135–153.
263 Park, K.K.H. and Schoenfeld, S.A. (1992), *The Pacific Rim Futures and Options Markets: A Comprehensive Country-by-Country Reference to the World's Fastest Growing Financial Markets*, Chicago: Probus, 252.
264 Semkow, B.W. (1992), *Taiwan's Financial Markets and Institutions: The Legal and Financial Issues of Deregulation and Internationalisation*, Westport: Quorum Books, 173.
265 Patrick, as note 45, above, 325, 329, 332–333.
266 Winn, as note 28, above, 919.
267 Rowley, A. (1987), *Asian Stockmarkets: The Inside Story*, Hong Kong: Far Eastern Economic Review, 123.
268 Winn, as note 28 above, 916, note 51, 917; Patrick, as note 45, above, 325, 329; Chiu describes 'underground investment firms which collected funds from small investors'. These reached huge sizes in the late 1980s, taking US$ 8 billion from over one million investors over five years and paying returns of 4 per cent a month. Action, after the December 1989, elections finally led to

their collapse. Chiu, H. (ed.) (1990), *Chinese Year Book of International Affairs,* 10, 144–153.

269   According to the MOEA, over 95 per cent of Taiwan's 930 000 registered companies are small and medium-sized enterprises (SMEs). They employ nearly 80 per cent of the total work force and account for half of the island's aggregate export value. Rowley, as note 267, above, 103.

270   Company Law, Article 156.

271   Investment by Foreign Nationals Law, Article 18.

272   Company Law, Article 267.

273   Company Law, Articles 269, 270 and 278.

274   SEL, Articles 22-1 and 28-1.

275   SEL, Article 22. Hsu, P. and Liu, L. (1988), 'The Transformation of the Securities Market in Taiwan, the Republic of China', *Columbia Journal of Transnational Law,* 27, 174.

276   SEL, Article 22.

277   Klatt, as note 110, above, 505, 528.

278   RGELS, Article 1.

279   RGELS, Article 2.

280   RGELS, Articles 2, 3, 4 and 6.

281   RGELS, Article 5.

282   RGELS, Article 6.

283   There were also indications that companies floated in association with the government's planned regional business headquarters project would be assessed under a new criteria of NT$ 1 billion of capital with net assets higher than 50 per cent of the paid up capital whether there were profits or losses in past years. 'Simpler Criteria – Stock Exchange', *China Economic News Service,* 8 October 1996. LEXIS-NEXIS.

284   Yeh, J.-R. (1996), 'Institutional Capacity Building Towards Sustainable Development: Taiwan's Environmental Protection in the Climate of Economic Development and Political Liberalization', *Duke Journal of Comparative and International Law,* 6, 229, 261 and note 111. TSE, RGELS, Article 9(5) (amended 1993).

285   RGELS, Article 4.

286   RGELS, Article 5.

287   Tomasic, R. and Francis, A. (1997), 'Taiwan', in R. Tomasic and P. Little (eds), *Insolvency Law & Practice in Asia,* Hong Kong: FT Law & Tax Asia Pacific, 67–100.

288   Allman, N. (1925), 'Bankruptcy Laws in China', *China Law Review,* 2, 218, 220.

289   Hsia, C.L. (1935), 'The Preliminary Draft of the Law on Bankruptcy', *China Law Review,* 1, 1, 3.

290   As note 289, above, 3.

291   Bankruptcy Law, Article 6.

292   Bankruptcy Law, Article 7.

293   Bankruptcy Law, Article 9.

294   Bankruptcy Law, Article 7.

295   Bankruptcy Law, Article 9.

296   Bankruptcy Law, Article 11.

297   Bankruptcy Law, Article 12.

298   Bankruptcy Law, Article 12.

299   Bankruptcy Law, Articles 31 and 32.

300   Bankruptcy Law, Article 25.

301   Bankruptcy Law, Article 26.

302   Bankruptcy Law, Article 30.

303   Bankruptcy Law, Article 27.

304 Bankruptcy Law, Article 28.

305 Bankruptcy Law, Section 3.

306 Bankruptcy Law, Article 47.

307 Company Law, Article 73.

308 For a discussion of this process, see Winn, as note 158, above, 424.

309 Company Law, Article 282.

310 Tomasic and Francis, as note 287, above, 75.

311 Company Law, Article 296 and Bankruptcy Law, Article 108.

312 Li, N. (1995), 'The Insolvency Regime in the Republic of China (Taiwan)', paper presented at the *INSOL Regional Conference*, Hong Kong, November 1995 (copy on file with authors).

313 Company Law, Article 284.

314 Company Law, Article 287.

315 Company Law, Articles 290 and 293.

316 Bankruptcy Law, Article 58.

317 Bankruptcy Law, Article 120.

318 Bankruptcy Law, Article 150.

319 Bankruptcy Law, Article 345.

320 Bankruptcy Law, Articles 108 and 95.

321 Bankruptcy Law, Article 17.

322 Company Law, Article 296 and Bankruptcy Law, Article 108.

323 Company Law, Articles 300–301.

324 Company Law, Articles 327–328.

325 Company Law, Article 346.

326 Company Law, Article 89.

327 Tomasic and Francis, as note 287, above, 87.

328 Fukuyama, F. (1996), *Trust: The Social Virtues and the Creation of Prosperity*, London: Penguin, 70.

329 Semkow, as note 80, above, 271.

330 In November 1995 shares in Taiwan's Formosa Plastics fell as investors worried about which of the 12 children of the founder would take over the business. 'The Overseas Chinese: Inheriting the Bamboo Network', *Economist*, 23 December 1995, Reuters.

331 Stan Shih's Acer computers is an example. As note 330, above.

332 Chavez, G. (1997), 'Bamboo Network Joins in the Funds', *Asia Times*, 19 May, Reuters.

333 Semkow, as note 80, above, 289, note 8.

334 *Taiwan Business*, as note 21, above, 213; Rowley, as note 267, above, 17.

335 'FTC Approves Cal's Plan to Buy Shares of Formosa Airlines', *China Economic News Service*, 30 August 1996, LEXIS-NEXIS; 'Eva buys shares of domestic airlines', *Business Taiwan*, 12 June 1995, LEXIS-NEXIS; Cheeseman, B. (1996), 'BTR Offloads Its Taiwan Ventures', *Australian Financial Review*, 10 September; Expansion through mergers to gain the advantages of size and scale are occurring in the finance industry. 'Leasing Companies – Deregulation is Spurring Development', *Business Taiwan*, 23 December 1996, LEXIS-NEXIS.

336 'FPG Buys PC Firm', *China Economic News Service*, 18 November 1983, LEXIS-NEXIS.

337 'Novartis Chief Urges More Incentives', *China News*, 3 May 1997, Reuters.

338 See note 366, below.

339 'MOF Encourages Taiwan Banks To Acquire Foreign Institutions', *China Economic News Service*, 27 July 1994, LEXIS-NEXIS; 'Insurance – Relaxed Investment Restrictions', *Business Taiwan*, 31 March 1997, LEXIS-NEXIS; 'Taiwan To Lower Income Tax Rate for Foreigners', *Reuters News Service*, 25 April 1997, Reuters.

340   Semkow, as note 80, above, 274–275, 280–281, 285, 287; American Institute –
       Taipei, 'The Financial Advisory Services Market in Taiwan', Financial Advi-
       sory Services, 1995 *National Trade Data Bank Market Reports*, 21 March 1995,
       LEXIS-NEXIS.
341   Wang-Ho, J. (1992), 'Taiwan and the Gatt', *Columbia Business Law Review*, 61,
       61.
342   'M-Systems to Acquire C-One Technology, Pretec Electronics', *EDP Weekly*, **38**,
       (18), 5 May 1997, Reuters.
343   Peng, J. (1995), 'Taiwan Raises Cap on Foreign Investments', *Reuters News
       Service*, 3 February, Reuters; Peng, J. (1995), 'Brokers Give Tepid Welcome to
       Taiwan Fund News', *Reuters News Service*, 3 February, Reuters.
344   American Institute – Taipei, as note 340, above.
345   SFC, 'News' at <http://www.tse.com.tw/sec/secnews/secnews.html>
346   R. Dawn, the director of finance division of the Taiwan Institute of Economic
       Research, quoted in Liu, J. (1994), 'Taiwan's Economic Boom Generates Finan-
       cial Scandal', *Reuters Asia-Pacific Business Report*, 13 October, LEXIS-NEXIS.
347   Engbarth, D. (1995), 'Taiwan: Taiwan Firms Prefer Caution', *Reuters News
       Service*, 13 July, Reuters; 'Yulon to Create Merger Between Auto Parts Compa-
       nies', *Taiwan Business News*, 26 March 1997, Reuters; 'Teco has Cool Ideas for
       Growth', *Reuters News Service*, 3 March 1997, Reuters; 'Toppan in Taiwan
       Merger, To Supply Terminal Products with Short Delivery Deadline', *Nihon
       Keizai Shimbun*, 28 February 1997, Reuters; 'Chinese Petroleum To Buy Shares
       in Middle-East Oil Company', *China Economic News Service*, 26 February 1997,
       LEXIS-NEXIS; 'RTRS-Govt Approves Kingstream Steel Plan', *Reuters News
       Service*, 6 March 1997, Reuters; 'Kingstream Says An Feng Merger Approved',
       Reuters News Service, 10 April 1997, Reuters; 'Semiconductors – Lite-On Ex-
       pands Global Base', *Business Taiwan*, 19 May 1997, Reuters.
348   'Taiwan SEC Leads Push for Euro CB Conversion', *Euroweek*, 31 July 1995, 28.
       'Relaxed Banking Rules leave Taipei 2% Higher', *Financial Times*, 4 April 1997,
       37.
349   Cheeseman, B. (1997), 'Taiwanese Sidestep Real Estate Ban', *Australian Finan-
       cial Review*, 30 June, 50; Cheeseman, B. (1997), 'Taiwanese Bank Beats China
       Ban', *Australian Financial Review*, 10 June, 45; Engbarth, D. (1995), 'Taiwan:
       Taiwan Firms Prefer Caution', *Reuters News Service*, 13 July, Reuters.
350   Tseng, O. (1995), 'Warner Uses Back Channels to Enter Local Cable TV Mar-
       ket', *Business Taiwan*, 20 March, Reuters.
351   'Cathay Life Stretches Tentacles Into Banking', *Business Taiwan*, 27 September
       1993, Reuters; 'FTC Fines Firms', *China Economic News Service*, 16 September
       1993, LEXIS-NEXIS; 'Fair Trade Ruling – Linyuan Group, Taiwan First Invest-
       ment And Trust', *China Economic News Service*, 8 July 1993, LEXIS-NEXIS.
352   Company Law, Article 13.
353   Fair Trading Law, Article 6.
354   The FTC revised the figure upwards on the basis that Taiwan's small and
       medium-sized enterprises are not able to monopolize or collude in the control
       of markets. Semkow, as note 80, above, 273.
355   Kwang, as note 3, above, 86.
356   'FTC Fines Firms', *China Economic News Service*, 16 September 1993. LEXIS-
       NEXIS; 'Fair Trade Ruling – Linyuan Group, Taiwan First Investment And
       Trust', *China Economic News Service*, 8 July 1993, LEXIS-NEXIS.
357   Klatt, as note 110, above, 528; Semkow, as note 80, above, 149.
358   As note 357, above, 273.
359   Item 16 of the Supplementary Provisions to the Concrete Criteria for Deter-
       mining the Inappropriateness for the Listing of Securities under each Item of
       Article 9 of the Rules Governing Examination of the Listing Rules of Securi-

ties of Taiwan Stock Exchange Corporation. Paragraph 18 of Article 9 of the Rules Governing Examination of the Listing Rules of Securities of Taiwan Stock Exchange Corporation refers to 'other events concerning the scope, nature or special circumstances of the enterprise that do not warrant an approval of stock listing by this Corporation'.

360 'Takeover Rules', *China Economic News Service*, 8 September 1995, LEXIS-NEXIS;
361 Semkow notes that this has not been used to takeover a listed company. Semkow, as note 80, above, 271.
362 Company Law, Article 316.
363 Company Law, Article 317.
364 Semkow, as note 80, above, 275, 290 and note 36.
365 Penalties ranging from one to seven years' imprisonment apply for breaching this provision. 'Takeover Rules', as note 360, above.
366 Proxy-buying had already caused problems in controlling listed firms. 'SEC To Close Loophole On Buying Proxies To Control Firms', *China Economic News Service*, 21 February 1995, LEXIS-NEXIS. 'Taiwan: Taiwan Politics – Soft-Pedalling China Issue; Crackdown On Gangs', Economist Intelligence Unit Country View, 10 January 1997, *Electronic Publishing*, Reuters; The sale of stock voting rights was prohibited from 19 December 1996. 'Taiwan: In Asia', *Toronto Globe and Mail*, 18 December 1996, Reuters; Cheesman, B. (1996), 'Taiwan cracks down on mob power at company meetings', *Business Times*, 11 November, 1. Trading in proxies had become a small industry. The new regulations have made it difficult for listed companies to obtain the required quorum of at least 50 per cent of shareholders for annual general meetings. The SFC claimed it would encourage more institutional investors to attend meetings. 'Editorial: Taiwan's Gangsta Rap', *Business Times*, 28 November 1996, 13; Cheung, T.M. (1996), 'Can PLA Inc Be Tamed?', *Institutional Investor*, 30 July, Reuters.
367 See note 28, above.
368 Hawk, B.E. (1995), 'Book Review: UK Merger Control: Law and Practice', *Fordham International Law Journal*, **18**, 1588, 1588.
369 Winn, as note 28, above, 952.
370 'Asia's Best Companies: The fight for the last frontier', *Euromoney*, December 1996, Issuers and Underwriters Supplement.
371 International Legal Services Advisory Committee (1993), *Legal Services Country Profile: Taiwan*, Canberra, Australia: Attorney-General's Department, 8–9.
372 Abel, R.L. (1994), 'Transnational Law Practice', *Case Western Reserve*, **44**, 737, 739–741.
373 American Institute – Taipei, as note 340, above.
374 Abel, as note 372, above, 737; 'Restrictions may be lifted on lawyers, language teachers', *China Post*, 11 August 1995, LEXIS-NEXIS.
375 SEL, Articles 141 and 143–145.
376 Lai, as note 84, above, 325–326.
377 Regulations for the Administration of Securities Investment Trust Fund Enterprises (Trust Regulations), effective 26 May 1983, and the Regulations for Governing the Management of Securities Investment Trust Fund Enterprises (Trust Fund Regulations), effective 10 August 1983.
378 Lai, as note 84, above, 326–327, 349.
379 Liang, C.H. and Skully, M.T. (1982), 'Financial Institutions and Markets in Taiwan', in M.T. Skully (ed.), *Financial Institutions and Markets in the Far East: A Study of China, Hong Kong, Japan, South Korea and Taiwan*, London: Macmillan, 170, 191–192.
380 TSE (1997), *Annual Report 1996*, Taipei, 2.
381 From February 1995 foreigners have been permitted to hold 12 per cent of market capitalization. 'Taiwan Review 1997', as note 11, above.

382   'Business Briefing: Taiwan', *Far Eastern Economic Review*, 27 February 1997, 55.
383   Semkow, as note 264, above, 173; Rowley, as note 267, above, 'Taiwan: Not Yet For Widows and Orphans', 99–126.
384   In the first five months of 1997 the TSE gained 26.5 per cent. 'Taipei Drops 3.5% and Ignores Profits Growth', *Financial Times*, 3 May 1997, 21.
385   Before the end of 1995, foreign exchange transactions required approval by the Central Bank of China and the SFC. The process took over three months and could only be done once a year. In March 1996, the previous requirement for clearance by the tax authorities was replaced by the requirement that all foreign investors appoint a tax filing agent. This agent has to be appointed before the first repatriation of earnings. The agent must perform an audit of the accounts and ensure all taxes have been paid. 'Clearing The Paper Trail', *Asia Money*, 7 (10) December 1996/January 1997, Asian Capital Markets Supplement.
386   Chen, J.H. and Huang, J.J.T. (1993), 'Taiwan's Evolving Stockmarket: Policy and Regulatory Trends', *Pacific Basin Law Journal*, 12, 34, 61. A foreign institution must nominate and apply through a local agent, and appoint a local custodian to hold all its Taiwanese assets to become a qualified foreign institutional investor. 'Clearing The Paper Trail' as note 385, above; 'KPMG, Taipei, Taiwan', *Accountancy*, 117, (1232), April 1996, 83–86.
387   Foreign capitalization has recently been lifted to 25 per cent of the whole market. The TSE also has been included in a Morgan Stanley index to emerging markets. 'Taiwan Review 1997', as note 11, above.
388   The Chair of the SFC cited in Chen and Huang, as note 386, above, 37 and note 14. Rowley, as note 267, above, 100.
389   'Business Briefing: Taiwan', *Far Eastern Economic Review*, 9 January 1997, 89 reporting figures released by the SFC.
390   'Business Briefing: Taiwan', *Far Eastern Economic Review*, 24 October 1996, 75.
391   Semkow, as note 363, above, 185–186.
392   Fair Trading Law, Article 1.
393   Consumer Protection Law, Article 12(1) may have implications for dealings with securities where there are standardized contracts, as such clauses are void if they contradict good faith or jeopardize the consumer's interests in other ways. Kwang, as note 3, above, 89.
394   The Minister of Finance, P. Chiu, announced to the Legislative Yuan that the SEL would be amended to permit a second stock exchange to be established as part of the government's effort to introduce competition into the market. 'MOF Wants Law Changed to Allow Second Taiwan Stock Exchange', *China Economic News Service*, 18 March 1997, Reuters.
395   SEL, Article 127
396   TSE, 'TSE Introduction: Organization And Functional Responsibilities' at <http://www.tse.com.tw/intro/intro1.html>
397   Rowley, as note 267, above, 101–102.
398   Newland, J. (1996), 'Hong Kong: Tokyo's Nikkei Leads the Way as Asian Bourses Rise', *Reuters News Service*, 1 February, Reuters. Republic of China, *Republic of China Yearbook 1997* at <http://www.roc-taiwan.org/info/yearbook/ch11.htm>
399   Wolff, S. (1995), 'Recent Developments in International Securities Regulation', *Denver Journal of International Law and Policy*, 23, 347, 401, note 367, citing *The Annual Conference of the International Organization of Securities Commissions*, 29 October 1992, 8.
400   Rules Governing Examination of the Listing of Securities, Article 9.
401   The first legislative provisions for companies under the Imperial Edict of 1904 provided for disclosure in the prospectus of whether the promoters of a joint

stock company had obtained 'any extra profit or have been promised such advantage by others [and] what sort of financial agreements with others have been entered into beforehand'. Jamieson, G. (1921), *Chinese Family and Commercial Law*, Shanghai: Kelly & Walsh, 127, citing Williams, E.T. (trans) (1904), *Recent Chinese Legislation*, Shanghai: Mercury.

402   Chang, S. (1993), 'Taiwan', in K.K.H. Park and A.W. Van Agtmael (eds), *The World's Emerging Stock Markets: Structure, Developments, Regulations and Opportunities*, Chicago: Probus Publishing, 101, 11; TSE (1988), 'Securities Market in Taiwan', in Asian Securities Analysts Council (ed.), *Securities Markets in Asia and Oceania* (2nd edition), Japan, 513, 552.

403   In October 1996 the SFC was questioning officers of the TSE about bribes of US$ 36 300 to US$ 254 500 alleged to have been paid to them by listed companies. 'Business Briefing: Taiwan', *Far Eastern Economic Review*, 31 October 1996, 63 quoting, *China Times Express*.

404   Patrick, as note 45, above, 325, 332–333; The TSE is seeking better disclosure. TSE, as note 380, above, 22.

405   Rowley, as note 267, above, 109. In the late 1980s there were about 20 of these stocks. The companies may be bankrupt in all but name with their assets disposed of, but they are still permitted to trade. SFC officers, seeking to clean this up, were assaulted by hit men engaged by the pool syndicates. As note 267, above, 113, 121.

406   As note 405, above, 116.

407   Pan, M.-S., Chiou, J.-R., Hocking, R. and Rim, H. (1990), 'An Examination of Mean Reverting Behaviour of Stock Prices in Pacific-Basin Stock Markets', in S.G. Rhee and R.P. Chang (eds), *Pacific-Basin Capital Markets Research*, Amsterdam: North-Holland, 333, 341–342.

408   Chou, S.-R. and Johnson, K.H. (1990), 'An Empirical Analysis of Stock Market Anomalies; Evidence from the Republic of China in Taiwan', in S.G. Rhee and R.P. Chang (eds), *Pacific-Basin Capital Markets Research*, Amsterdam: North-Holland, 283, 292–293.

409   Chiang, R. and Wei, K.C.J. (1990), 'Price Limits in Taiwan and Risk-Return Estimation', in S.G. Rhee and R.P. Chang (eds), *Pacific-Basin Capital Markets Research*, Amsterdam: North-Holland, 173, 173–174.

410   Lai, as note 84, above, 328 citing a Ministry of Finance letter dated 20 September 1988 ((77) T'ai Ts'ai Cheng Tzu (III) 8070) and a Ministry of Finance letter dated 18 September 1987 ((77)) T'ai Ts'ai Cheng Tzu (II) 6805).

411   SEL, Article 138.

412   Under Article 162, it may order the TSE to disclose information to it relating to its affairs which may lead to the use of this power.

413   SEL, Article 129.

414   SEL, Article 130.

415   TSE, as note 402, above, 530–531.

416   As note 415, above, 545. This was established in 1986 in the Stock Surveillance System Provisions. TSE, 'Market Surveillance' at <http://www.tse.com.tw/intro/intro4.html>

417   SFC, as note 99, above. In 1996 384 matters were investigated. Of these, 109 were referred to the SFC. TSE, as note 380, above, 24.

418   Article 39 of the T'ang Code punished the taking of goods or articles by fraud or cheating. Johnson, W. (trans) (1979), *The T'ang Code, Volume 1, General Principles*, Princeton: Princeton University Press, 214–215. It also punished 'forcing the market' in Article 32.2, defined in Article 142 as using fear or force to sell. Johnson, 181 and note 55.

419   Writing in 1993, Lai was aware of only one action under Article 20. Lai, as note 84, above, 337.

420   Article 154 made it an offence to 'monopoliz[e], or otherwise use undue influence in the market'. Staunton, as note 9, above, 164–165. In addition, it punished the use of false measures in Article 155 and obtaining property by false pretences in Article 274. As note 84, above, 165–166, 289–290.

421   Lai, as note 84, above, 343–344. In 1994 the SFC took action in 32 cases of stock manipulation. In January 1995 the manipulation in 1994 of the price of shares in a listed window-curtain maker, Nien Made, had serious consequences for the TSE. It led to a series of defaults by speculators estimated by the TSE to amount to NT$ 1 billion. 'Stock Exchange Reports Another Massive Stock Payment Default', *China Economic News Service*, 11 January 1995, LEXIS-NEXIS.

422   The SFC investigation into the manipulation of prices in Kao Hsing Chang Iron & Steel and Taiwan Fluorescent Lamp produced a crash on the money market and the TSE fell 4.9 per cent. 'Taiwan Braces for More Trouble in Financial Scandal; Asia: A Run On Short-Term Debt Is Feared. Fake-Debt Case May Be A Conspiracy Officials Say', *Los Angeles Times*, 7 August 1995, Part D, 4.

423   Liu, J. (1994), 'Taiwan's Economic Boom Generates Financial Scandal', *Reuters Asia-Pacific Business Report*, 13 October, LEXIS-NEXIS.

424   'SEC to Make Cracking Down on Insider Trading a Top Priority', *China Economic News Service*, 12 July 1996, LEXIS-NEXIS.

425   'Business Briefing: Taiwan', *Far Eastern Economic Review*, 31 October 1996, 63.

426   A poll by the Far Eastern Economic Review of executives indicated that 100 per cent were not satisfied with the existing law. Fifty per cent believed that insider trading occurs to a 'great extent' on the TSE and 50 per cent believed that it occurred 'to some extent'. The same percentage thought that the SFE was 'inefficient' in administering the law. 'Asian Executives Poll', *Far Eastern Economic Review*, 30 January 1997, 30.

427   Lai, as note 84, above, 348.

428   In 1996 it found NT$ 178 809 642 of profits which had not been disgorged. TSE, as note 380, above, 24.

429   Lai, as note 84, above, 339, 343.

430   Chiu, as note 28, above, 44, 51.

431   SEL, Article 166.

432   Kwang as note 3, above, 78.

433   Commercial Arbitration Law, Article 169.

434   SEL, Article 21.

435   Commercial Arbitration Law, Article 23.

436   Chiu, as note 28, above, 44, 51, citing Civil Procedure Code, Articles 403 and 427.

437   The Civil Code in Articles 736 and 737 provides for compromise contracts which terminate disputes or prevent the occurrence of future disputes and enforce the new agreement in place of the previous agreement.

438   *Taiwan Business*, as note 21, above, 180.

439   SEL, Articles 171–179.

440   SEL, Article 179.

441   Lai, as note 84, above, 349.

442   Republic of China, *Republic of China Year Book 1997*, 'Five Government Branches' at <http://www.roc-taiwan.org/info/yearbook/ch5.htm>

443   Chiu, as note 28, above, 44, 52.

444   Lai, as note 84, above, 349. 'SEC to Make Cracking Down on Insider Trading a Top Priority', as note 424, above.

445   Certified Public Accountants have 'a reputation for being what can politely be termed unprofessional'. Winn, as note 28, above, 947–948; Rowley, as note 267, above, 105. The SFC has been pushing for reform as it recognizes that the

absence of reliable information has had a negative impact on the market. Rowley, 106. SFC, as note 102, above.

446   SEL, Articles 18, 45,
447   SEL, Article 57.
448   SEL, Article 54.
449   SEL, Articles 56, 66.

8 Corporations in Vietnam

JOHN GILLESPIE*

1 Introduction

As a member of ASEAN, Vietnam is now emerging as a regional economic power. This is, however, a recent phenomenon. The 30-year struggle against France and the United States destroyed much of the country's infrastructure and geared its economy and legal institutions to war. By the early 1980s adherence to rigid Stalinist central economics had brought the economy of the recently unified country to the point of collapse. Admitting their policy failures, the Communist Party of Vietnam (CPV) commenced an economic reform programme called *doi moi* (renovation) in 1986.[1] Over a decade later, state and private production unleashed by these reforms had excited annual gross domestic product (GDP) growth to over 9 per cent.[2] The Asian economic crisis has now significantly reduced investment and growth.

Despite continuing drafting and procedural deficiencies, the basic regulatory framework is nearing completion. The recently enacted Civil Code 1995 and Commercial Law 1997, for example, now classify the relationships between public and private law in the area of property and contractual rights. As in China,[3] however, the implementation of law is suffused with party-state ideology and particularism, which erodes and at times subverts legal principles. The blurring between ideology and legal rights is nowhere more obvious than in the licensing of corporate entities. This symbiotic relationship between state ideology and legislative implementation, suggests that statutory prescription is never value free.

For this reason, a functional analysis of Vietnam's corporate laws, which ignores sources of validation, will reveal only a facsimile of actual processes. A first step in reconciling the gap between legal expectations and reality, is to outline the three major legal systems that have contributed to contemporary Vietnamese legal thought. They are East Asian, French and Soviet/Socialist models.

1.1   *The Legal Legacy*

Prior to French colonization, Vietnamese law was principally derived from localized versions of Chinese imperial codes and domestic village practices.[4] The codes criminalized some forms of private commercial practice, such as contractual fraud and duress. Unlike Western law, they only interacted vertically from the state to villages/clans and did not assist individuals to assert private rights horizontally against other individuals. Without universal, normative law, socio-legal relations rested on the *ad hoc* solutions gleaned from customary practices. A local equivalent to the Roman Law concept of corporation sole never developed.[5] As a consequence, private commercial relationships remained village-bound, escaping official attention unless they threatened tax collection or social order, the twin concerns of imperial rule. Without abstract legal principles, the notion that a 'legal personality' could exist outside personal authority failed to develop.

In contrast to village autonomy, the urban centres of Hanoi and, later, Hue were products of royal patronage. Trade was strictly controlled through a series of state monopolies and those practising authorized crafts joined together to form trade streets (*phuongs*).[6] Once again, lacking an abstract legal tradition, private commerce remained clan-based and did not develop into proto-corporate organizations capable of mobilizing trading capital and allocating profit and losses.[7] Encapsulated by the Confucian saying, 'Emphasize agriculture, commerce is peripheral' (*Trong nong mat thu ong*), state policy inhibited the emergence of large scale commercial organizations independent of Royal patronage and particularistic linkages.[8]

Under the transplanted trappings of a rights-based legal system, two parallel legal systems coexisted during the period of French colonization (1862–1954). The civil law system of France (including corporate entities)[9] applied to French citizens and other Europeans, whereas with the exception of a small bureaucratic and merchant elite the Imperial Code (*Gia Long*) (1813–1945) and customary practice continued to govern most Vietnamese. A judicial tradition of analysing and reinterpreting code-based rights continued until 1975 in the South. In the North, the legal system changed radically after the defeat of France in 1954.

Legal transformation in North Vietnam called for the methodical substitution of ancient customary and colonial rules with 'rational, progressive socialist legislation'.[10] French colonial law which discriminated between individuals on the basis of property, gave way to

Communist notions of class and nationalism. The few laws enacted were often not publicized, much less uniformly implemented.[11] Commercial regulation took the form of administrative directives, determining production targets, the price of raw materials, finished products, services, transport and most other tradable goods and services. As private commerce was officially discouraged, the only legally recognized corporate organizations were state-owned enterprises established by central and provincial authorities.[12] Until the *doi moi* economic reforms of 1986, law and CPV policy were largely interchangeable; implementing agencies did not distinguish between legislation and party resolutions.[13]

1.2 The Doi Moi *Reforms*

Socialist economic orthodoxy was openly challenged during the Fifth National Congress of the CPV (*Dan Cong San Vietnam*) in 1982.[14] A pilot scheme designed to excite more commercial autonomy within state-owned enterprises was introduced by Decree No. 25 C/P in 1982. What was needed, so the reformers argued, was a separation of the party from the day-to-day running of the economy. Little was done, however, until the Sixth National Congress of the CPV in 1986. By this time rampant inflation, falling production, a vibrant informal economy and the booming economies of Vietnam's capitalist neighbours could no longer be ignored. Admitting past errors, party policy abruptly changed and central command economic planning was abandoned in favour of a kind of state capitalism, euphemistically called the 'socialist orientated market economy'.[15] Overwhelmingly, reforms have focused on economic development, an objective nominated by the CPV as the country's most urgent national goal.[16]

Doi moi promotes three objectives:

- to transform Vietnam's highly centralized economy based on state ownership of the means of production, into a multi-sectored economy where the 'leading role' is reserved for state-owned enterprises regulated by 'socialist orientated market mechanisms';
- to instil greater regularity into social and economic transactions through legal, rather than ideological/moral apparatus; and
- to pursue an 'open door' policy that fosters cooperation and trading relationships between Vietnam and other countries.[17]

2   The Contemporary Political and Legal Systems: An Overview

2.1   *Communist Party*

According to Vietnam's Constitution of 1992 (the fourth since independence) the state is divided into five arms. They are the National Assembly, the president, the People's Procuracy, the People's Courts and the government (see Figure 8.1).

Before considering these bodies in detail, no discussion would be complete without examining the CPV. The antecedent party was formed by Ho Chi Minh primarily as a nationalistic, anti-colonial movement.[18] Although the party has an hierarchical organizational structure and adheres to the Leninist principles of democratic centralism, in reality it is a quite decentralized organization. As 'a leading force of the state and society', the party and its mass organizational arm (the Fatherland Front) has a constitutional duty[19] to guide and dominate virtually every facet of the public domain. However, constitutional theory limits this power, requiring the CPV to confine its activities to policy formulation without directly interfering in the workings of the state.[20] Some progress has been made in this regard; however, informal lines of control are maintained through a *nomenklatura* system, which ensures that party members occupy most senior state positions.[21]

2.2   *The National Assembly*

Within the state system the National Assembly is the primary legislature and it possesses powers to supervise the executive and the judiciary.[22] It is the only body authorized to enact and interpret constitutions, codes and laws, the highest legislative instruments. No longer a compliant 'rubber stamp' legislature, within the parameters of party policy, National Assembly delegates form issue-orientated factions, blocking or amending legislation that could adversely effect their constituencies.[23] Below the National Assembly, legislative branches operate at the provincial/city and village/district administrative levels (Peoples' Councils).

2.3   *The State President*

While the National Assembly is the paramount state organ, the president is the titular head of state. Apart from performing ceremonial duties, the president also recommends to the National Assembly the appointment and removal of various state officials (for example the deputy chief justice and deputy prime ministers).[24] After witnessing a powerful leader dismantle the Communist Party in the former

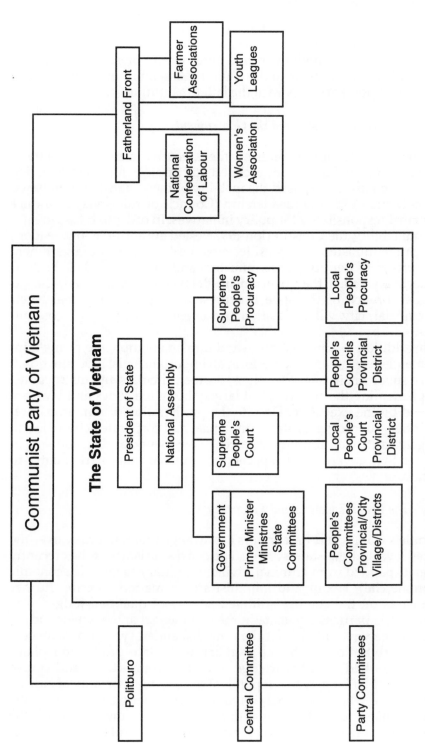

Figure 8.1   Political and Administrative Structure of Vietnam

Soviet Union, the CPV created the position of president to act as a counter-balance to the concentration of power in the hands of the prime minister. As both the prime minister and president are elected by and held accountable to the National Assembly, in theory the real balance of power resides with the latter institution.

2.4   The Prime Minister and the Government

Headed by the prime minister, the executive arm of the state is unquestionably the supreme architect and implementer of state policy. Economic reforms exposed the inability of the socialist system based on collective executive leadership (Council of Ministers) to induce personal responsibility for policy initiatives. In order to infuse greater accountability, the Constitution 1992 vested authority in 'one leader', the prime minister, who presides over a cabinet style of government comprised of deputy prime ministers and ministers.[25] This body is collectively called the government. Below the central level, the executive branch of the state is represented at three regional levels (provincial/city, village/district and *xa/phuong*) by people's committees.

In addition to administration and implementation, the prime minister and government also perform an important legislative function.[26] Most subordinate rules (decisions, decrees, circulars and instructions) implementing the superior, but largely hortative codes and laws are issued by the executive. Despite the proliferation of numerous prescriptive, subordinate rules, commercial and corporate activity is still largely controlled through an extensive network of discretionary licences that govern most aspects of commerce from market entry to bankruptcy.

2.5   The People's Courts and Procuracy

People's Courts and Procurators are arranged hierarchically over the three levels of the state system. The court's jurisdiction has recently been expanded from criminal, civil and military to include economic (commercial), labour and administrative[27] matters, placing further demands on the country's limited supply of qualified judges. The problem is particularly acute in the commercial arena, where judges were largely recruited from the now disbanded system of state economic arbitration. Although familiar with state production plans, arbitrators had little knowledge of market transactions and corporate law.[28] Market players[29] report that the day-to-day reality of judicial fora is one where personalities and power relationships dominate. When linked to dysfunctional debt enforcement mechanisms,[30] the courts offers few benefits to commercial litigants, and corporate structures and commercial transactions are framed with little regard for the possibility of litigation. During 1995 only four cases concerning company law were brought to court and these related to capacity to enter commercial transactions.[31]

3 Corporation Legislation

3.1 The Constitutional Basis of Company Law

Company laws based on the French models (*Droit de Société*) existed in the North before partition in 1954 and until reunification of the South in 1975. Thereafter the Stalinist command economy had no place for private commercial entities and only regulated the composition and activities of state-owned enterprises[32] (Decision 25–CP 21 January 1981). Immediately after 1954, private trade remained quite robust in the North, accounting for approximately 70 per cent of wholesale and 80 per cent of retail trade. According to official statistics, by 1960 most large scale private trading entities had converted to state or cooperative production, leaving a mere 12 per cent of retail trade[33] for small scale private traders. Other sources suggest a far greater role for private commerce. By the inception of *doi moi* over 40 per cent of state production passed through private distribution channels.[34]

Acknowledging the vibrancy of the private sector, the CPV reluctantly conferred political legitimacy upon private business activity in 1988.[35] Legal legitimacy had to wait until the enactment of the Law on Companies 1990 and Law on Private Enterprise 1990. These laws established the legal framework for individuals and legal entities to invest resources in commercial activities,[36] but display little attempt to formalize state policy promoting a 'socialist market economy'. As the following discussion reveals, bureaucratic discretion, rather than normative legalism, is still the preferred *modus operandi* of the party-state. Paradoxically, the development and eventual enactment of the Law on Companies took place under an orthodox socialist Constitution 1980; a document which discouraged, if not completely prohibited private commerce.[37] The legal institutionalization of the principles of *doi moi* and private rights over income-producing property eventually came with the enactment of the 1992 Constitution.[38]

The temporary constitutional invalidity of the Law on Companies and, by implication, entities incorporated before 1992, has never been formally acknowledged by the National Assembly. This is an omission which tends to confirm the relative imbalance between political and legal legitimacy. There are, however, more troublesome remnant, socialist constraints on private commerce. The most significant are the provisions in the Penal Code which criminalize speculative trading.[39] Until they are amended in line with the spirit of the *doi moi* reforms, commercial players rely on the forbearance of policing authorities. It is also important to realize that courts can not challenge the validity of legislative provisions by drawing general inferences from the Constitution,[40] only the National Assembly possesses the authority to interpret the Constitution.[41]

The re-emergence of private trade and light industries following *doi moi* reforms, prompted the enactment of a company law to extend state economic management and legalism to the vibrant, but unruly private sector. Company law was also used to standardize and modernize enterprise organization and practice. Corporate structures were needed to enable private capital to participate in joint ventures with foreign investors, in addition to raising capital from the domestic market. Initial drafts of the Law on Companies were prepared by a joint ministerial committee that drew upon the French company law model for inspiration.[42] The final bill was passed by the Eighth Sessions of the Eighth Legislature of the National Assembly on 21 December 1990. It commenced operation on 15 April 1991.

3.2   Changing the Company Law

The Ministry of Planning and Investment is in charge of corporate law reform (including the Law on Companies, the Law on Private Enterprise and the Law on State-Owned Enterprises 1995). Two different proposals for a new companies law are currently under consideration. One favours a uniform regulatory regime governing all corporate entities, whether foreign, state or privately owned. The other supports the existing system that distinguishes between corporations according to the nature of the managing authority.[43] Subdivisions based on management (that is state, cooperative, political organization and private) were derived from Soviet law[44] at a time when all companies were administrative apparatus 'owned' by the state.

Apart from inevitable concerns regarding national sovereignty, corporate reform focuses primarily on the cost of quarantining foreign investment companies from the domestic market. Existing legal rules based on the type of ownership, so reformers argue, unnecessarily complicate transactions and arbitrarily inhibit novel and adaptive ownership combinations.[45] This is a distinct disadvantage in a commercial setting where debt capital is expensive and difficult to raise. The real debate, however, surrounds the discretion of licensing authorities to control market entry. This is an issue at the very centre of law reform, as it concerns the ultimate destination of market reforms. Will private companies eventually operate in a law-based market economy, or remain within the parameters established by licensing authorities?

The Ministry of Justice is also closely involved in corporate law reform. In addition to its legislative coordinating role, it has line-ministry (*ho chu quan*) responsibility for regulating business license approvals at the provincial/city people's committee level (*uy ban phan dan*).[46] Before its abolition, the State Economic Arbitration Body also issued legislation governing company registration, this function has now been assumed by the Ministry of Planning and Industry (MPI). Finally, People's Committees issue sub-ordinate rules implementing superior legislation issued at the central level.[47]

4 Corporate Regulatory Bodies

4.1 People's Committees

Different regulatory authorities preside over the two procedural steps required to license[48] and register[49] companies. Licensing authority is devolved by the Law on Companies[50] and Law on Promotion of Domestic Investment 1994[51] to People's Committees at the provincial and city levels. Within the parameters set by central level guidelines, people's committees exercise delegated authority to enact procedural pathways and evaluative criteria.

Legislation delegates the ultimate licensing power to the chairmen of provincial/city Peoples' Committees.[52] In practice, however, industry-specific departments (assessment departments) within each People's Committee perform this function. The dominant business objective determines which department assumes responsibility for processing licence applications. Proposals to establish light industrial factories, for example, fall within the jurisdiction of industry departments, whereas construction departments generally assume responsibility for licensing building contractors.[53] Adding to the administrative confusion, most documents submitted in support of licence applications require certification from notaries[54] and other official bodies. Licensing invariably requires approval from many other departments, including land, housing and health. In fact, primary assessment departments may in practice play a relatively minor role in the evaluation process. The processing of companies with low capitalization levels is frequently devolved to district level People's Committees.[55]

4.2   *Planning Departments*

On completion of the assessment process, recommendations regarding the issue of business permits[56] are made to the People's Committee chairman. Where licenses are approved, promoters are required, as a second procedural step, to register their companies with provincial planning departments. Under the guidance of the MPI, these bodies ensure that national economic plans are researched and implemented at the local level.[57] Until recently, Economic Arbitrators registered companies.[58] After the abolition of this body on 1 July 1994, staff were transferred to the State Planning Committee (now the MPI), the others went to corresponding levels of the People's Court – the economic division.[59]

The substantive law[60] restricts planning departments to a purely mechanical function. Once satisfied that documentation is complete and regular, they register nascent companies, transforming them into judicial entities.[61] Practice suggests, however, that planning departments assume a broad discretion. For example, in Ho Chi Minh City the provincial planning department is the first point of reference for applicants.[62] It coordinates licence approvals between People's Committee assessment departments, and refers its own evaluation to the People's Committee chairman for a final decision. Once business licences are issued, all documentation is returned to planning departments for registration and certification by the local police department. This process is formalized by a stamp ('chop') on all official papers.[63] Even in provinces where the evaluative role of the planning department has not been formalized, applicants report that processes extend beyond document verification to include a re-evaluation of the merits of proposals. This occurs most often where capital is invested in low priority economic sectors. In short, the registration and policy functions of regional planning departments are frequently blurred.

The reasons for transferring responsibility for registration to the MPI, in preference to the Ministry of Justice, or some other authority remain obscure. The Ministry of Justice and the People's Courts,[64] for example, control a network of justice departments and courts in every province, whereas not every provincial government has a planning department. In addition to these structural advantages, as their portfolio responsibilities do not include economic planning, a certain degree of procedural neutrality may have been expected of the Ministry of Justice courts. Some commentators argue, however, that economic neutrality[65] was a political disadvantage since the central government sought to strengthen economic policy implementation at the local level.[66] This authority remains doubtful, where the ability of local planning committees to transcend loyalties to the

People's Committee that recruits, pays and promotes their officials is uncertain.

5   Companies and their Powers

5.1   *Commercial Entities*

Two basic kinds of private commercial organizations are regulated by law. The Law on Private Enterprises 1990 governs private enterprises (*doanh nghiep ta nhan*), which are similar in nature to sole proprietary, unincorporated associations. Without the protection of limited liability, proprietors are personally liable for all business activities.[67] Most private enterprises are small family-owned businesses with a low capital base; commercial entities with higher levels of capitalization must incorporate.[68] The Law on Companies 1990 establishes two types of companies (*cong ty*) for this purpose. They are loosely based on the French *Société anonyme*[69] (shareholding companies) and *Société à Responsabilité Limitée* (limited liability companies; *cong ty trach nhiem hua han*). However, the similarities are superficial: the French Law No. 66–537 on Commercial Companies 1966 contains 509 Articles, whereas its Vietnamese counterpart contains a scant 46 Articles.

Members of both types of companies, whether individuals or legal entities, proportionately share profits and losses to the extent of their capital contributions.[70] Only shareholding companies can issue shares and raise equity capital from the public.[71] Limited liability companies are geared for family-centred business.

By the end of 1996 over 2,000 private companies operated in Vietnam. Although most are small scale limited liability companies, an increasing number of shareholding companies have a substantial market capitalization.[72] Despite recent growth, overall this sector is minute compared with the capital controlled by state-owned enterprises; fewer than 500 private companies have equity capital exceeding five billion *dong* (US$ 500 000).[73]

5.2   *Company Definitions*

The Civil Code 1995 defines juridical entities in broader terms than the Law on Companies 1990. Juridical entities must:

- be established or recognized by a competent state authority;
- possess an organizational structure;
- separate ownership, control and legal responsibility for assets; and

- have the capacity to participate in legal relationships.[74]

The definition contains procedural and substantive functions described in language wide enough to accommodate both private and
state ownership. For example, the designation 'own or control' is
sufficiently expansive enough to include the management of state
assets by state-owned enterprises. Based on theory derived from
Soviet legislation,[75] these enterprises are vested with rights of management; ownership resides with the state.[76] Various types of
state-owned enterprises are considered by the Civil Code, these include commercial and non-commercial bodies established by state
apparatus (including the army, party and Fatherland Front Organizations).[77] They are established by specific enabling legislation,[78]
enacted either at the central or provincial governmental levels. Although they control approximately 85 per cent of all registered
enterprise assets, they generate less than 30 per cent of the GDP.[79]
Calls by reformers to discard Soviet legality that separately regulates
corporations according to their form of ownership, have so far been
rejected by the party. Finally, perpetual succession is not a prescribed
corporate attribute, as many private companies operate on fixed-
term business licences.

Numbering between 700 000 and one million entities, household
businesses, the most vibrant economic sector, remain largely unregulated.[80] This comparatively benign regulatory approach pragmatically
recognizes Vietnam's long history of 'fence breaking' (*vuot rao*). Even
under the command economy the public found ways to evade or
ignore rules promulgated by the party and state on almost every
subject imaginable.[81] At the height of state economic management,
private commerce flourished 'underground', infusing business practices with commercial norms and attitudes informed and moulded
by years of official suppression. As a consequence, both formal regulated and informal (largely, but certainly not entirely) unregulated
commercial entities follow personal clan and patron-client routes
and by-ways, in preference to state ideology and legal processes.
Calls by law-makers for a law-based state are often justified by the
need to enlist the lively informal sector to further state-mandated
development goals.[82]

5.3   *The Concept of Legal Personality*

Vietnamese legislation and academic commentary reveals little consideration of the Western debates surrounding the jurisprudential
meaning of legal personality.[83] Either oblivious to, or declining to
engage with, Western theories, on the few occasions where commentary exists, Vietnamese lawyers portray legal personality as an

institution recognized by law.[84] There is little attempt to blend traditional Vietnamese or socialist precepts with Western corporate forms. Indeed, the struggle in Western theory to justify the attribution of personal authority to an abstract legal body is a non-issue in Vietnamese jurisprudence. Without the Western underpinning of natural rights theory, it does not occur to Vietnamese lawyers that corporate rights require a source of legitimacy outside legislation and bureaucratic licences. Both natural and legal persons derive their legal capacity through state law. Thus, legal personality is a function of state authority, conferred through the licensing systems to selected natural persons. Vietnamese law-makers differentiate natural from legal persons along functional lines by reference to the independence of the latter from the former. Independence falls far short of Western notions of a legal 'mind', rather it is functionally explained as a separation of liability and property ownership.

5.4   Foreign Ownership

The Law on Companies 1990[85] expressly excludes the possibility of foreign ownership of domestic companies, a prohibition not found in the Civil Code 1995.[86] Legal persons are 'established on the initiative of individuals, economic organizations, political, socio-political or social organizations, socio-professional groups, social or charitable funds or by a decision of a competent State authority'.

The Law on Foreign Investment 1996 regulates the investment of foreign capital in domestic juridical entities. Four types of investment are permitted: business cooperation[87] (a contractual, non-equity joint venture), build-operate-transfer[88] (also contractual, non-equity joint ventures), only Vietnamese-foreign joint ventures[89] and wholly foreign-owned entities[90] are treated as Vietnamese juridical entities. Many aspects of corporate governance and the administration of foreign-owned juridical entities are governed by foreign investment legislation. Indeed, this *corpus* of rules is in most respects more detailed and prescriptive than the Law on Companies 1990. It remains unclear to what extent (if at all) the Law on Companies 1990 applies where the foreign investment regime is silent.

Making sense of a prescriptive legal framework which conveys little normative guidance, bureaucrats and judges routinely infer solutions from analogous provisions in legislation governing similar subject-matter. This technique is used to apply concepts selected from foreign investment regulations to domestic companies.[91] Provisions concerning financial regulation found in the Law on Foreign Investment 1996, for example, are applied to domestic companies.

Private international law provisions in the Civil Code 1995,[92] assess the legal capacity of foreign juridical entities according to the laws of their country of incorporation.[93] Where transactions are performed within the territory of Vietnam, capacity becomes a matter for Vietnamese law.[94] In other respects, foreign law only has currency within Vietnam where it does not contradict domestic rules and the basic principles of the Civil Code.[95] Transactions are subject to Vietnamese legal jurisdiction in the following circumstances:

- where the proper law is Vietnamese;
- where there is a proper law, but performance takes place in Vietnam;
- even where the proper law is that of another country, where the transaction is wholly made and performed in Vietnam; and
- where the transaction concerns immovable property located in Vietnam.[96]

5.5   *Legal Capacity and Powers of Domestic Companies*

The doctrine of *ultra vires*[97] appears to have a conditional applicability in Vietnam. Legal capacity is determined by, and is coextensive with, the 'rights and obligations' stipulated in company business licences.[98] These operational objectives are prescribed with considerable precision by licensing authorities (People's Committees). General powers to pursue authorized objectives are set out in the Law on Companies 1990[99] and include the ability to determine the place and scale of the business, raise capital, contract, hire labour, use foreign currency and make investments. Companies are also entitled to own land use rights,[100] buildings, movables and intellectual property. As it is unlawful to pursue economic objectives without a licence of some kind, pre-incorporation contracts are technically void, even if ratified post incorporation.

Companies are not permitted to expand their business capacity by including a 'shopping list' of associated or tangential objectives. It is possible, although not easy, to change or broaden business objectives.[101] The legal consequences of entering transactions which exceed corporate authority (legal capacity) has not been authoritatively established. It is clear that those who committed the company to the *ultra vires* contract, depending on the seriousness of the breach,[102] are liable for administrative[103] or criminal prosecution.[104] What is unclear, is whether the contracts remain enforceable. Although untested in the courts, doctrinal rules suggest that economic contracts (contracts for income-producing objectives) are invalid where any party is not licensed to perform specified contractual duties.[105] If this construction is correct, companies are not liable for commercial contracts which exceed their licensed objectives.[106]

6 Company Formation

As previously mentioned, different regulatory authorities preside over the two procedural steps governing incorporation. In the first instance, authority is devolved to provincial/city People's Committees to issue business licences as a precondition to incorporation. The second phase involves registration with planning departments attached to provincial/city People's Committees.

6.1 Business Licences

Applications to establish privately owned companies[107] (or private enterprises)[108] must first be lodged with the provincial/city People's Committee closest to the registered domicile(s) of the promoters. A *curriculum vitae* certified by the local district police verifying that the applicant is entitled to reside in that locality and is not subject to current criminal charges or an undischarged sentence, must accompany the application.[109] Contrary to the explicit terms of the governing legislation, some provincial governments selectively refuse to incorporate businesses belonging to promoters with criminal or political convictions.[110] Initially intended to regulate rural migration, residency rules now impede investment between the North and South and even from one province to another.

Once promoters have been vetted, the application and supporting documentation must be forwarded to the appropriate city/provincial level People's Committee. State[111] and private companies share the same registration system. Authorities are permitted 60–90 days to process licence applications or provide reasons for refusal.[112] Appeals against unfavourable decisions may be made in the first instance to the MPI.[113] Information required to support licence applications includes the following:[114]

- the names, ages and permanent address of the founding members (Article 14(1) of the Law on Companies 1990);
- the name and address of the proposed head office (Article 14(2) of the Law on Companies 1990);
- the objectives, branches and areas of business of the company (Article 14(3) of the Law on Companies 1990);
- the chartered capital and method of contributing capital (Article 14(4) of the Law on Companies 1990);
- an environmental impact statement (Article 14(5) of the Law on Companies 1990);
- a feasibility plan (Article 14(6) of the Law on Companies);
- a medical certificate (Article 5 of Circular No. 472, 29/9/93, Ministry of Justice); and

- educational qualifications (Article 6 of Circular No. 472, 29/9/ 93, Ministry of Justice).

The broad discretion exercised by assessment departments during the approval process is increasingly guided by prescriptive rules issued by line-ministries. This is particularly true where licensed goods and services fall within the 'restricted lists'.[115] In key sectors of the economy, such as tourism, central-level legislation prescriptively regulates corporate management and capitalization. The unifying intent of such rules is subverted at the local level, where assessment departments use their discretion over minimum levels of capitalization to discourage investment in activities that lie outside 'favoured' economic sectors.[116] Incorporation resembles the particularistic practices adopted in other East Asian jurisdictions, such as China and Indonesia. In contrast, since the mid-nineteenth century corporate status has been granted in the West, subject to nominal disclosure requirements.

The evaluation of promoters' medical histories provides further fertile ground for deferral or rejection. Similarly, with few standards controlling educational qualifications for professions or trades, assessment departments assume a broad subjective discretion to impute their own standards. Where raw material, labour and utility requirements for proposed businesses cannot be satisfied, or may strain local resources, an additional ground for rejection arises. Practice suggests that People's Committees often stray beyond these official criteria and base their decisions on the likely impact a proposed business may have upon its competitors, particularly those owned by the state.[117]

Despite numerous grounds for rejection, the preferred *modus operandi* employed by local officials is to apply indirect pressure to modify, delay or withdraw disfavoured proposals. Where applicants remain unresponsive, People's Committees may delay processing documents, charge excessively for relocation compensation and utility connection and impose highly restrictive environmental controls.[118] Some idea of the extent and depth of procedural barriers to market entry can be gauged from the incorporation of Song Thu Ltd, a company established in Ho Chi Minh City to operate a mini-hotel. Incorporation took eight months. During this time promoters submitted 40 documents, requiring 83 official seals and 107 signatures to 26 different official bodies. In contrast, those wishing to invest in priority areas of the economy are unlikely to encounter administrative hurdles and occasionally receive financial inducements from provincial planning departments.[119]

Applications are also rejected for reasons other than local development priorities. With the notable exception of politically powerful city people's committees, local officials are often reluctant to assume personal responsibility for approving or rejecting innovative business ventures, particularly those that lie outside officially authorized business areas. Administrative prudence is understandable in a system which reprimands bureaucratic adventurousness and rewards compliance.

6.2 Document Certification

Documents submitted to assessment departments require certification by designated authorities.[120] This process is particularly rigorous in the case of capital contributions. In addition to stipulating minimum capital requirements, assessment departments also determine the ratio of fixed to liquid assets. In contrast to the favourable conditions enjoyed by foreign investors, who may borrow an approved proportion of their invested capital,[121] domestic investors cannot contribute capital in the form of borrowings.[122] Only bank accounts or state bonds may be used to contribute the liquid asset component of working capital. A certificate verifying ownership of liquid assets must be issued by an appropriate bank or bond-issuing agency. While fixed capital requires certification by people's committees, notary publics must certify land valuations,[123] health, education, criminal and residency reports. Fees charged for these services vary significantly among provinces.

6.3 Registration

Once business licences are issued, promoters must register the nascent company with the local planning department. It is at this point that a juridical entity is created and the new company commences business.[124] Companies registered in one province are recognized and may trade throughout Vietnam as juridical entities. However, companies wishing to open branches or representative offices in other provinces must reapply for registration.[125] Each application requires a certified copy of the company registration and details of the proposed business, raw material, labour and utility requirements. Where people's committees decide that local infrastructure cannot support the proposed investment, applications may be deferred or refused. Documents verifying occupation rights are also necessary.

The jurisdictional fragmentation associated with pre-registration procedures suggests the emergence of a *de facto* federal legal system, which undermines the unitary constitutional framework. Despite an hierarchical constitutional structure, the Vietnamese state is in reality highly decentralized; local governments pursue their own development strategies.[126] As a consequence, companies registered in one province, may, for entirely parochial reasons, be precluded from establishing branch offices in neighbouring localities.[127] Localism hampers attempts at the central level to coordinate provincial economic development, often distorting the bureaucratic chain of command.

6.4   Corporate Constitutions

6.4.1   The elements of company charters   The Civil Code requires promoters to hold meetings to approve company charters prior to submitting applications for business licences and registration.[128] Charters are defined as written undertakings establishing the functions and activities of companies,[129] and must include the following eight items:

- the name of the entity;
- the purpose and scope of the operation;
- the head office;
- the legal capital, if any;
- the organizational structure, procedures for appointments and dismissals, and duties and powers of the management body and other bodies;
- the rights and obligations of the members;
- the procedures for amending and supplementing the charter; and
- the conditions for winding up.

The Law on Companies 1990 places a different emphasis on the subject-matter of corporate charters.[130] The point of departure arises from the broad range of juridical entities regulated by the Civil Code. The Law on Companies is narrowly focused on privately owned companies. The Civil Code employs broad language, for example, 'the charter capital (if any)',[131] contrasting with specific provisions found in the Law on Companies governing matters such as 'valuation of capital contribution',[132] registers of individual capital contributions and 'share issues'.[133]

The difference between the general and particular does not explain the stipulation in the Civil Code that charters should elucidate rights and obligation of members.[134] For the first time, charters are required to consider the sharing of power between boards of management and shareholders, canvassing complex issues such as the abuse of minority shareholders – matters that are currently unregulated by the the Law on Companies.[135] Of equal importance, the Civil Code[136] also requires corporate charters to elucidate the powers of company officials when legally representing the company. This is another area left virtually unregulated by the Law on Companies.

People's committees use their licensing discretion to closely scruti-nize charters, ensuring that company capacity does not exceed the ambit of business licences although collateral powers required to realize authorized business objectives are permitted. Authorities en-courage simple management structures that reflect the general regulatory issues covered in the Law on Companies.[137] More com-plex corporate structures reflecting the wider issues covered by the Civil Code are evidently routinely rejected.

6.4.2 Amending company charters All amendments to company char-ters require approval from company members[138] and provincial planning departments.[139] Particularly where changes seek to expand the range of business objectives, amendments may trigger a new licence application. It will be recalled that the legal capacity of com-panies is tied by the Civil Code to their licensed objectives.[140] For this reason, applications to expand business capacity are treated as fresh licence applications, which must follow all the procedural steps re-quired for business licensing.[141]

6.5 The Regulation of Company Names

During the registration process, company names are entered by pro-vincial level planning departments into business registration books. Certificates of registration bearing these names are issued to compa-nies.[142] Limited liability companies are required to choose names descriptive of their business activities or incorporating the name(s) of one or more of their founding members.[143] These restrictions do not apply to shareholding companies.[144] The Civil Code further stipu-lates that all company names must use Vietnamese letters or words that are distinguishable from names of other companies operating in the same field of endeavour.[145]

Although the regulation of names has the appearance of general-ity, enforcement is in practice disjointed and fractured. As previously discussed, there is no central register of companies, each provincial planning department maintains its own listing. Until the law is re-formed, the only practical means of protecting corporate names nationally is to establish company offices in all 57 provinces, a costly and time-consuming exercise.[146] Court action to compel companies using misleading or deceptive names to change their names, may theoretically be taken in the commercial division of provincial-level People's Courts. Again, in practice, there are no procedural rules supporting such actions and, for reasons already discussed, litigation is not a commercially viable option.[147]

6.6   *Membership and Capital Requirements*

Statutory rules governing membership and capital contribution differentiate limited liability and shareholding companies. The Law on Companies 1990 indicates that members are not liable for company debts beyond unpaid calls on shares.[148] Unfortunately, the drafters of the Civil Code did not precisely define the boundaries between juridical entities, corporate officials and members (the corporate veil).[149]

6.6.1   *Limited-liability companies*

Capital contributions stipulated in company charters must be fully subscribed by members before registration.[150] The state sets different minimum capital requirements for each economic sector, these range from US$ 5 000 for animal husbandry to US$ 50 000 for light industries and US$ 150 000 for mining and metallurgy.[151] Payment of capital into accounts opened in the company's name is a precondition for business licences' approval. Where contributions are not liquid in nature, members must meet prior to incorporation to determine valuations.[152] It is at this point that members formally adopt the company charter and select office bearers to control the internal affairs of the company, and a director to represent the company externally.[153] Charter capital can be increased by a resolution of members calling for further capital contributions or deductions from reserve funds.[154] Limited liability companies are forbidden from raising capital from the public.[155]

6.6.2   *Shareholding companies*

The authorized chartered capital of shareholding companies is divided into equal parts, each share has the same par value.[156] A minimum number of seven members[157] must subscribe for at least 20 per cent of the total capital authorized in the company charter. Where the entire authorized capital is not issued in shares to promoters, the remaining shares may be sold in a public issue.[158]

Promoters are required to convene a general meeting of shareholders to approve the corporate charter where:

- all issued shares have been sold;
- those who applied to take up a share have paid at least half the par value and are legally bound to pay the remainder;
- share capital has been contributed in the form of non-liquid assets and/or intellectual property.[159]

Although all shares must be of equal par value, there is no legal impediment to creating classes of shares with different rights of participation in profit distribution and capital on winding up (preference shares). Nevertheless, legal practitioners report that licensing authorities are reluctant to approve arrangements of this kind. Shares can, however, be divided into 'named' and 'bearer' categories.[160] The former are often issued by promoters to ensure a stable share registry. Named shares can only be transferred by majority vote of a board of management,[161] or on the expiration of two years after promoters have stood down as members of the board of management.[162] Bearer shares, in contrast, are freely transferable.[163]

6.6.3 Company registers   There is no legislation regulating share or member registers. By implication, however, some form of register is necessary for companies to record, issue and transfer share certificates.[164] Details of the same are usually found in company charters.

7 Internal Administation

7.1 Registered Offices and Names

Company registered offices (the head office) are located at the address specified in the company charter,[165] different addresses may be nominated for receipt of official communications. Branch offices established outside the province of incorporation[166] lack an independent legal status, and accordingly derive their legal authority through the juridical capacity of the companies' head office.[167]

Company names, together with words denoting limited liability or shareholding status, must be displayed on all company documents and signs.[168] Statutory sources do not specify the legal status of transactions which offend this requirement. It is clear though, that companies can only acquire 'civil rights and obligations' through transactions formed by legal representatives.[169] Legal authority is either acquired via a direct divestment of power from the company charter (such power is invested in official positions not individual people),[170] or delegation through powers of attorney.[171] No provision is made for ostensible authority. Thus, the representation implicit in the use of documents bearing the company name apparently has little bearing on the validity of contracts. Finally, although no legislation explicitly prohibits the use of blasphemous and offensive names or those appropriating state titles and institutional names, in practice, licensing authorities use their discretion to disallow names of this kind.

7.2 Corporate Governance

7.2.1 Company officials   In a society lacking a corporate culture and well-developed regulatory institutions, a detailed legislative framework prescribing behavioural norms that circumscribe the exercise of power by company officials is essential. As the following discussion reveals, Vietnam's regulatory system virtually ignores important issues of corporate governance, such as the standard of behaviour required of company officials and personal liability for contractual relationships with third parties.

7.2.2   General directors   Considerable scope exists for 'fine tuning' corporate governance in company charters,[172] as the Law on Companies 1990 leaves this area virtually unregulated. General directors are 'vested with full power to supervise the business activities of a company and are entitled to act on its behalf in all matters'.[173] Day-to-day powers of management are virtually unconstrained by the powers of members of limited liability companies to set broad policy objectives.[174]

General directors in both limited liability and shareholding companies legally represent their companies to third parties. Within 30 days of the grant of licence, companies are required to advertise in five consecutive issues of local and national newspapers details of the company, including the name of the general director.[175] This, however, is the only time companies are compelled to publicly disclose the identity of their personal legal representative(s). Regrettably, the Civil Code failed to clarify the applicability (if any) of the doctrine of constructive notice and, consequently, it is unclear whether public notification of any kind legally binds the public. When new general directors are appointed, no public notification is required. It is true that general directors' signatures are filed with the local police at the time of registering the company seal, but these records are not open for public inspection. In the absence of a public register, the only way third parties can verify the identity of general directors is to request notorized copies of appointment resolutions.[176] As general directors are designated as the highest legal representative,[177] bureaucrats commonly assume that only these office bearers are authorized to transact on behalf of companies. This narrow construction unnecessarily constrains business, as medium-sized to large companies routinely devolve authority to other officials through powers of attorney.[178]

Companies are held vicariously liable for, and can indemnify themselves against, damage[179] caused by 'officials thereof in the performance of an assigned duty'.[180] Although the Law on Companies is silent on this point, the previous discussion concerning *ultra vires* tentatively suggests that 'assigned duties' must coincide with the companies' business licence. In other circumstances, authorities demonstrate little reluctance to lift 'the corporate veil' and proceed directly against owner managers.

7.2.3 Board of management In addition to appointing general directors, limited liability companies with 12 or more members and shareholding companies are also required to elect a board of management and inspectors. Shareholding companies are managed by salaried[181] boards of management (board). Comprised of between three and 12 members, boards 'have full power to act on behalf of companies in making decisions on all matters relating to its objectives and interests, except those matters solely within the authority of the shareholders' meeting'.[182] In general, boards are not involved in daily business affairs, this is the preserve of general directors. Though relatively uncommon, some charters require board members to hold shares while they are in office.[183]

Boards elect chairmen from among their members[184] to convene board meetings according to the rules stipulated in the charter. Unless chairmen are also general directors, the board must appoint a director (from the board) to act as the personal representative of the company when supervising daily business activities.[185] This concept of 'legal representatives' acts as an encroachment on limited liability, according with Chinese, but diverging from Western practices. Perhaps more significantly, in a society where private commercial legal enforcement is virtually unknown, legal representatives are subject to administrative sanctions for the legal person's conduct.

7.2.4 Inspectors Shareholders elect and pay an allowance to two inspectors, one of whom requires 'familiarity' with accountancy, to perform a 'watch dog' role.[186] Among their duties, inspectors peruse books of accounts and annual reports, and oversee the financial management of the board, providing shareholders with an investigation report at the end of each financial year.

When necessary, emergency interim reports are presented to shareholders. Once again, if they exist, details concerning the procedures followed by inspectors are contained in company charters.

Apart from a few terse words prohibiting inspectors from joining the board, acting as the general director, or becoming spouses of these officials,[187] legislation is otherwise silent on the question of standards of behaviour expected of company officials. If regulated at all, these issues must be included in the company charter. The Law on Companies 1990 is now out of step with the Law on State Owned Enterprises 1995 in this regard.[188] A general duty to avoid conflicts of interest which might 'lessen their honesty and impartiality or provoke contradictions between the interests of the corporation and the interests of the individual is now required of boards of management in state-owned enterprises.[189] Prescriptive rules also forbid general directors and chairmen of the board of directors from establishing or participating directly or indirectly in private commercial entities. Practitioners report that regulatory authorities rely on administrative and criminal penalties to regulate corporate governance and few private companies have adopted codes of behaviour in their charters.

7.3   Meeting Procedures

Once again, there are few statutory rules governing members' meetings, leaving this important function to be regulated (if at all) by provisions in the company charter.[190] Shareholding companies are comparatively more highly regulated than limited liability companies in this regard. The quorum for inaugural meetings must, for example, comprise members representing at least three-quarters of the chartered (but not necessarily paid up) capital.[191] Resolutions are passed by a simple majority on all matters. Contrasting with the restrictive voting rules effecting foreign joint venture companies,[192] voting power in domestic companies is proportionally based on capital contributions.

Extraordinary shareholder meetings may be called by the board of management and inspectors to amend the charter and pass urgent resolutions, otherwise meetings are held annually at the end of each financial year.[193] Details concerning time limits governing the notice for calling meetings and methods of casting votes are once again left to the company charter.[194] This is an unfortunate practice in a legal setting where corporate legal advice is, with a few notable exceptions, of a uniformly low standard.[195] Practitioners report that voting is conducted by poll; the use of secret ballots and proxies is unknown.

7.4   Share Offers

The primary advantage of shareholding companies is their ability to raise capital by offering shares and bonds to the public. The public can participate in share offers at the time of formation or during the life of the company. Rules governing each form of offer differ slightly.

7.4.1   Pre-incorporation share offers   Where promoters elect not to take up their full share entitlement, the remaining share allotment may be offered to the public. Various provisions ensure that public subscribers clearly understand the market capitalization and development objectives of the company.[196] Information thought necessary to make rational investment decisions includes:

- the company name;
- the objectives;

- the head office location;
- the total prescribed and allotted capital;
- the total number of shares to be issued;
- the place of payment for shares; and
- the date and place where the company charter was registered.[197]

Money received from the public must be deposited in an account kept separate from other company finances. Public shareholder funds only become available once a business licence has been issued. If this has not happened within 12 months of the public offer, all funds must be returned to subscribers.[198]

7.4.2   Post-incorporation share offers   Approval from regional licensing authorities (provincial People's Committees) is required in order to raise capital from the public.[199] In addition to providing potential investors with appropriate information about prospective business objectives, companies must demonstrate that all prior capital issues were fully subscribed, business activities are under 'good and effective management', a bank will underwrite the offer and the timetable for the allotment is realistic and fair.[200] These prescriptive conditions are frequently undermined by the failure of licensing authorities to monitor compliance. This is another instance where the regulatory regime places too much emphasis upon pro-active control through discretionary gateways, while neglecting to monitor post-licence compliance.[201]

7.5   The Relationship between Members and Management

7.5.1   Limited liability companies   Like companies around the world an unequal division of power subsists between members and management in both limited liability and shareholder companies.[202] General directors of limited liability companies with less than 12 members exercise 'full power' over company activities.[203] Admittedly members have counter-balancing powers to set broad policy objectives, alter the company charter, and approve the distribution of profits, mergers, dissolutions and extensions of the company's operational life. However, without a regime of public disclosure or rights to inspect company records,[204] members lack sufficient information to effectively evaluate decisions taken by general directors. At the same time, general directors are closely acquainted with operational and financial details and can draw on company resources in contests with members. The ultimate threat of dismissal may force directors to account to members,[205] but this is a clumsy and time-consuming means of curbing aberrant behaviour. In reality, the overwhelming majority of limited liability companies are small,

family-centred organizations where dissent between management
and members is settled through informal personalistic relationships.[206]
Informants are unaware of any disputes of this kind finding their
way into the court system.

7.5.2   *Shareholding companies*   Like limited-liability companies, the
division of powers between shareholders and the board of management of shareholder companies is unequal. There are, however, several
differences. Although shareholders do not have a right to inspect
company accounts and records, inspectors are invested with these
powers[207] on behalf of shareholders. Both the board of management[208]
and inspectors[209] are responsible to shareholders for damages caused
by 'wrongdoings' carried out while discharging official duties.

Shareholders can remove members of the board of management
and inspectors at shareholder meetings,[210] but not general directors.[211]
Even these limited powers are substantially constrained, as only members of the board and inspectors are entitled to call extraordinary
shareholder meetings.[212] Without support from these officials, or similar powers embedded in the company charter, shareholders must
wait for the next annual general meeting to express their displeasure
and remove recalcitrant officials.

It is unclear whether, and on what basis, shareholders can take
legal action directly against board members and inspectors. The board
of management owes a duty to shareholders regarding 'any shortcomings in the management of the company including breaches of
the charter or of the law'.[213] However, it is the general director, not
the board who has responsibility for daily management of the company.[214] Although general directors are responsible to boards, it is
doubtful whether boards are correspondingly responsible to shareholders for the acts of the general director. If this construction is
correct, boards are only liable for damage resulting from miscon-
ceived policy objectives (a tenuous proposition) and breaches of the
charter and laws. Perhaps the drafters did not intend their words to
give rise to this inference, nevertheless their choice of words does not
seem to be inadvertent.

In describing legally enforceable 'civil obligations', the Civil Code
does not specify whether the duty owed by board members and
inspectors to shareholders subsists in contract or is a non-contractual
obligation. If contractual, it must be shown that on joining the company members agreed with each other, the company and company
officals to abide by the company charter.[215] Although possessing the
virtue of familiarity,[216] there are technical difficulties with transplant-
ing this theoretical construction into Vietnamese law. Share agreements
are not 'commercial contracts', as shareholders lack business registration within the meaning of the Commercial Law 1997.[217] Although

agreements of this kind fall broadly within the scope of civil contracts,[218] there are various conceptual objections to their legitimacy. For example, if the corporate charter forms the terms of the shareholders' contract, each time it is amended, board members and inspectors are bound by a process over which they have no control (except resigning). This form of unilateralism is forbidden by the Civil Code, which requires all parties to contracts to agree to contractual amendments before the same take effect.[219] According to the Law on Companies, boards of management and inspectors are collectively responsible to shareholders.[220] In a working environment where officials are constantly joining and leaving companies, collective contractual liability fails to accord with the principle of contractual privity.[221] Even if a theoretical exception is allowed, and shareholders' contracts are supported by the company charters, officials will escape contractual responsibility for breaches that do not offend charter provisions. Given the limited scope of most company charters, the basis of liability would be narrow indeed.

Perhaps the duty to shareholders is better construed in non-contractual terms (tort). Although the Civil Code does not specifically refer to this class of non-contractual duty, the general civil responsibility is sufficiently broad to cover damage to company and shareholder interests.[222]

There are currently no legislative provisions protecting the interests of minority shareholders. Unless protection is given in company charters (an unlikely prospect), legal action is only possible where officials or majority shareholders act unlawfully or breach the company charter.[223] Even though the Civil Code now requires charters to regulate the rights of members, abuses of voting power have not attracted the attention of regulatory authorities.

The preceding analysis assumes clear conceptual divisions between juristic persons, members and company officials that are rarely evident in Vietnamese practice. Since private corporations are comparatively recent market players, the infusion of local culture into the corporate forms is poorly understood. Anecdotal observations made by local legal practitioners portray a corporate culture not dissimilar to the Chinese experience,[224] where owners are managers and there is little genuine separation between family and company interests. Corporate and property structures follow familial lines of authority with little regard for legislative provisions.[225] In this particularistic environment, directors' and shareholders' interests are collapsed into a common family/group networks. Directors' duties are transmogrified into obligations to preserve family/group interests. This frequently involves co-opting influential state officials within family networks. Depending upon individual circumstances, the exercise of the 'director's duties' may involve hiring a relative of an official, outright bribery, or 'harmonizing' corporate and state interests by transferring part ownership to local authorities.[226]

7.6   Auditing

Auditing is a comparatively recent concept in Vietnam. Until 1990 all companies were state owned, paid tax, followed state-prescribed accounting procedures and in theory required no independent scrutiny.[227] Foreign-owned companies were the first required to audit their accounts,[228] independent verification now applies to state-owned enterprises[229] and will eventually extend to private companies.

The qualifications and responsibilities of auditors are regulated by the Ministry of Finance.[230] Until the new auditing statute is introduced, it is difficult to verify whether the auditing rules currently applied to foreign investment entities will, in part or whole, govern private companies. Under existing provisions, final audit reports must be certified, signed and sealed by an impartial auditing agency, on the basis of objectivity, truth and fairness. Auditors bear full personal responsibility for audit reports, which include the truthfulness and accuracy of accounting data, compliance with accounting standards, and recommendations and proposals to improve compliance (if any).[231] Four large transnational accountancy firms compete with two foreign joint ventures and eight domestic firms for the rapidly expanding auditing market.[232]

The shift to a national system of auditing is propelled by the belief that greater corporate accountability will induce higher levels of tax compliance. Without a uniform accounting system it is virtually impossible for the General Department for Taxation to accurately evaluate levels of corporate profitability.[233] Tax avoidance in this sector is accordingly rampant.[234]

7.7   Accounting

New accounting standards applicable to every type of business entity in all economic sectors came into affect on 1 January 1996.[235] They replaced a complex patchwork of regulations which had evolved on an *ad hoc* basis to enhance administrative scrutiny over state and private production.[236] Socialist economic accounting treated companies as arms of the state, accounting reports were not intended to, and consequently did not reflect complete and reliable company results.

In general, the new accounting system is designed to move away from socialist accounting principles, bringing financial analysis in line with international practice.[237] The draft provisions state, for example, that the accounting year now coincides with the calendar year and balance sheets are required to reflect the source and use of capital at the end of this period. Profit and loss accounts must contain sufficient information in relation to lawful revenues and expenditures to enable auditors to independently verify balance sheets. Accounting reports must also contain a description from the board of management, regarding company activities, trading results, appropriation of profits and losses together with proposals relating to future operations. Auditors are required to certify the objectiveness, authenticity and reasonableness of disclosed financial statements and data, and compliance with accounting regulations.[238]

7.8 Company Reporting

Company reporting is poorly regulated. Domestic, privately owned companies are required to advise provincial licensing authorities of changes to the registered place of business of the company, the company officials, the capital reductions and the share allotments. Alterations to company charters and public share offers[239] must be publicly disclosed, but only because they require approval from licensing authorities.[240] Statements revealing business plans must accompany financial records, which are confidentially filed with the General Department of Taxation.[241] This rather lax reporting regime contrasts with the rigorous disclosure required of companies with foreign invested capital.[242]

Disclosed information is in general not released to the public. Public policing of company compliance has yet to receive official acceptance and the state continues to assume virtually the entire enforcement burden.[243] Drafters of the forthcoming Law on Companies (tentatively scheduled for 1999), are currently considering whether in a mix-market economy it is appropriate to reduce the current reliance on pro-active licensing, in favour of a system of continuous public disclosure. Wedded to a culture of secrecy and economic management, bureaucrats have little to gain from reforms that will dismantle the licensing gateways which currently provide numerous opportunities for goal substitution.

8 Winding Up and Bankruptcy

8.1 Voluntary Winding Up

Just as market entry is tightly controlled by the government, dissolution is a creature of administrative discretion.[244] Voluntary winding up requires the vote of members representing at least three-quarters of the chartered capital. Companies may liquidate in any of the following circumstances:

- the duration of the company stipulated in the charter has expired;
- the objectives have been achieved;
- the objectives are no longer profitable;
- three-quarters of its charter capital has been lost or the company faces 'insurmountable difficulties'; or
- members representing at least two-thirds of the charter capital petition for dissolution.[245]

Once a dissolution resolution has been passed, a formal winding-up application must be lodged with the People's Committee which granted the initial business licence. A notice of the application disclosing the timetable and procedures governing liquidation of assets, settlement of debts and contractual obligations should be published in five consecutive issues of local and national newspapers.[246] Only where no claim has been made on the company after a period of 15 days from the expiration of the date set for discharging outstanding obligations, can the responsible People's Committee approve the application.[247] In short, members must guarantee full payment of liabilities. Dissolution may commence once approval is granted by licensing authorities and the liquidation of assets must follow the priority order stipulated in the Law on Business Bankruptcy 1993 (discussed below).

8.2   Involuntary Winding Up

In the command economy state-owned enterprises were treated as arms of the state, receiving funding whether financially viable or not. Bankruptcy and insolvency laws were unnecessary in an environment where financial success was not measured independently from state planning objectives.[248] The introduction of the mixed market necessitated a set of rules allowing non-viable enterprises, both state and privately owned, to exit after repaying creditor's claims according to an orderly set of rules. Proponents[249] of the Law on Business Bankruptcy 1993[250] asserted that far from being a social disaster, bankruptcy is an effective means of ensuring that efficient businesses flourish.

A combination of cultural, social and ideological factors[251] disrupted the adoption of a bankruptcy law based on Western market principles. For example, bankruptcy exposes state officials to an intolerable loss of status. There is no social security net to catch retrenched employees who, in any event, assert moral claims over the assets of state-owned enterprises. And, more importantly, the party has an ideological commitment to the retention of state economic management and actively opposes bankruptcies that transfer productive assets to the private sector. In this politicized environment, market forces alone could not be permitted to determine the fate of ailing companies. Instead, state-owned enterprises (in particular) survive or fail according to their respective political and economic importance.[252] Most cases are processed administratively by the Standing Central Steering Committee for Debt Solvency,[253] and to date courts have considered only 20 bankruptcy cases.[254] The peripheral importance of bankruptcy is shown in surveys indicating that bankruptcy laws and proceeding have a virtually negligible impact on business decision-making.[255]

8.2.1   Acts of bankruptcy   Exhibiting aspects of both French and Anglo-US bankruptcy law, the Law on Business Bankruptcy 1993 also contains principles derived from socialist property law (for example land is not treated as a fixed asset).[256] The definition of bankruptcy in the Law on Companies 1990 corresponds with the grounds for declaring companies bankrupt in the Law on Business Bankruptcy.[257] Both rather vaguely state that bankruptcy occurs when a company suffers losses in two consecutive years and is unable to repay its debts.[258] Unlike the Law on Companies 1990, the Law on Business Bankruptcy pays homage to the Vietnamese preference for non-adversarial processes, and enables companies to enter the equivalent of schemes of arrangement and reconstruction with their creditors. These provisions are loosely based on the French, *Relative à la Prévention et au Réglement Amiables des Difficultés des Enterprise* (Act No. 85–98 for the Prevention and Amicable Settlement of Difficulties in Companies, 25 January 1985).[259] Reconstruction is treated as a sequential step in the bankruptcy procedure.[260]

8.2.2   Bankruptcy petitions and property   Thirty days after repayment falls due,[261] three categories of creditors (secured, partially secured and unsecured) may petition for a debtor company's bankruptcy. In keeping with their central economic role, labour unions and employee associations may also petition for bankruptcy where companies fail to provide the payroll over three successive months.[262] Presumably to avoid wholesale bankruptcy of the estimated 50 per cent of unprofitable state-owned enterprises,[263] there is no 'automatic trigger' clause in the bankruptcy legislation.

For the purposes of bankruptcy, company assets include all fixed and current assets, outstanding debts and loans to third parties, cash, capital contributions and shares.[264] Rules defining state-owned enterprises' assets are still rather vague, but appear to include all property under the management of those enterprises, even where it is technically owned by the state.[265] The vulnerability of land allotments rights (the highest recognized form of land/licence) for distribution to creditors is highly controversial.[266] Improvements built on land are, in contrast, available in bankruptcy. What remains uncertain is whether it is possible to recover improvements without corresponding rights over the legal substratum.[267] No rights of receivership or mortgagee in possession are recognized in Vietnamese law.

8.2.3 Procedure   Three steps are involved in bankruptcy proceedings. First, after receiving a petition from creditor(s)[268] to initiate bankruptcy proceedings, provincial People's Courts[269] classify proven debts.[270] Second, a 'reconciliation conference' between the debtor company and creditors canvasses possible schemes of arrangement and reconstruction as an alternative to liquidation.[271] At least one-half of the total number of creditors representing at least two-thirds of the unsecured debts must vote to approve reconstructions before they become legally binding.[272] During the currency of the reconstruction, directors and boards of management remain responsible for trading results.[273] Companies under reconstruction are given a maximum period of two years to recover solvency. If they fail, the presiding judge may make a sequestration order and commence liquidation.[274]

Third, where creditors fail to endorse a reconstruction scheme within 60 days of its proposal, a sequestration order declares the company bankrupt and liquidation automatically commences.[275] Company assets are then placed under the control of an Asset Liquidation Committee formed by the local Office of Civil Judgments (under the control of Ministry of Justice).[276] This body administers bankruptcy proceedings for both voluntary and involuntary liquidation.

Asset Liquidation Committees recover, manage, value and realize all company assets.[277] Secured creditors take priority over other types of creditors, in the division of company assets. Unsecured creditors participate in remaining assets (if any) according to the following priority ranking:[278]

- fees and expenses connected with bankruptcy proceedings;
- unpaid wages and employee entitlements;[279]
- unpaid taxes;
- pro rata distribution to other proved creditors according to the respective value of outstanding indebtedness.

Surplus assets (if any), are paid to company members in proportion to their respective capital contribution (or share entitlement) or to the state bank where the bankrupt is a state-owned enterprise.

9 Amalgamations and Mergers

9.1 *Amalgamation*

The Civil Code distinguishes between amalgamation and mergers. Companies 'of the same kind' can agree to combine, forming new juridical entities.[280] The previously discussed business licensing and registration procedures apply to the creation of amalgamated entities. Where foreign capital is involved, approval from the MPI is also required.[281] Once approvals are given, the pre-existing legal entities are terminated[282] and all existing rights and obligations are transferred to the new entity. No detailed implementation rules have so far been enacted, and informants report that outside the state-owned enterprise sector this procedure is unknown.

9.2 *Mergers*

Non-hostile takeovers are also theoretically permitted by the Civil Code.[283] Unlike amalgamations, state approval is not required to create a merged entity, as one juridical entity continues and the other(s) transfers all existing rights and obligations before termination.[284] Hostile takeovers are unknown. Little research has been carried out in this area, however, there are several plausible explanations for the lack of takeover activity. Chief among these is the previously discussed cultural reluctance to organize business transactions along abstract legal lines. Surveys of business attitudes confirm that corporate structures are peripheral to business strategies and alliances.[285] At a functional level, pre-emptive rights[286] inhibit the free transfer of membership rights in limited liability companies, while the lack of equity markets has a similar effect on share transfers in shareholding companies.[287]

10 Securities Regulation

After years of debate, Vietnam established a securities market.[288] The government has also recently issued T-bills, bankers' acceptances and ten-year bonds, but the securities market will only trade company debentures, bonds and shares.

The market was established to finance company development and facilitate the eventual privatization (a process euphemistically called equalization (*co phan hoa*)) of selected state-owned enterprises.[289] Apart from appointing a central regulatory authority (National Securities Commission) and opting for a unified securities exchange incorporating both a capital and stock market, the detailed regulatory framework awaits enactment. Current debate favours a self-regulated, state owned, non-profit exchange, where membership is controlled by a licensing system operated by the National Securities Council.

Although drafting of implementing regulations is not complete, the researchers at the Central Institute for Economic Management (the primary research body in this area)[290] suggest that securities and exchange legislation must:

- define the powers and responsibilities of the National Securities Council;
- establish procedures and standards of conduct governing primary and secondary markets;
- protect investors through adequate disclosure, prohibiting market abuses; and
- curb insider trading and the use of fraudulent and deceptive practices.

The inability of well-funded stock exchanges to curb abuses in former socialist East European countries and China casts doubt on the short-term viability of the market. Commentators agree that if regulatory authorities are unable or unwilling to curb abuses compromising the issue of shares to the public, the legal system and bureaucracy are insufficiently developed to regulate a stock market.[291] It is also argued that the paucity of companies that meet listing requirements together with resistance among private companies to disclosing information conspire to produce 'thin', easily manipulated markets.

Notes

*   Senior Lecturer, Law School, Deakin University Melbourne. The author gratefully acknowledges the generous assistance and information provided by Do Duc Dam, Deputy Director of the Central Institute of Economic Management (the institution in charge of drafting the new company law), and lawyers at Leadco and I & L Associates, Hanoi.

1   See Hoi, K.D. (1994), 'Opening But Not Loosing Ourselves', *Nhan Dan* (The People), 25 February, 2; Spoor, M. (1988), 'State Finance in the Socialist Republic of Vietnam: The Difficult Transition from "State Bureaucratic Finance" to "Socialist Economic Accounting"', in D.G. Marr and C.P. White (eds), *Post War Vietnam, Dilemmas in Socialist Development*, Southeast Asian Project, Ithica: Cornell University, 111; Tri, V.N. (1990), *Vietnam's Economic Policy Since 1975*, Sydney: Allen and Unwin, 181–203.

2   Statistical Publishing House (1997), *So Lieu Thong Ke Chxhen 1991–1996* (Statistical Data, 1991–1996); Hanoi. See generally, Womeck, B. (1997), 'Vietnam in 1996', *Asian Survey*, 37, 1.

3 See generally, David, E. (1996),'Financial Reforms and Corporate Governance in China', *Colombia, Journal of Transnational Law*, **34**, 2, 469; Unger, J. (1996), 'Bridges: Private Business, and the Chinese Government and the Rise of New Associations', *The China Quarterly*, September, 147, 795; Fin, T. (1993), 'Legal Person in China': Essence and Limits', *American Journal of Comparative Law*, **41**, 261, 285–289.

4 See Hooker, M.B. (1986), *The Laws of Southeast Asia: The Pre-Modern Texts*, Singapore: Butterworths, 449–451; Tai, T.V. (1982), 'Vietnam's Code of the Lê Dynasty (1428–1788)', *American Journal of Comparative Law*, 30, 523, 523–525; Tai, T.V. and Hay, N.N. (1987), *The Lê Code: Law in Traditional Vietnam*, Athens: University of Ohio Press.

5 See Finer, S.E. (1990), 'Problems of the Liberal Democratic State: An Historical Overview', *Government and Opposition*, **25**, 3, 334, 325–340; Coser, L. (1984), 'Introduction', in E. Durkheim (ed.), *The Division of Labour in Society*, London: MacMillian, xxxvi–xlii.

6 See Reid, A. (1993), *Southeast Asia in the Age of Commerce 1450–1680*, volume 2, Chiang Mai: Silkworm Books, 91. Similar clan-based corporate behaviour is reported in China. See Chen, J. (1995), *From Administrative Authorisation to Private Law*, Dordrect: Martinus Nijhoff, 72–74; Lawton, P. (1996), 'Berle and Means Corporate Governance and the Chinese Family Firm', *Australian Journal of Corporate Law*, **6**, 3, 348, 351–353.

7 See Vien, N.K. (1987), *Vietnam: A Long History*, Hanoi: Foreign Languages Publishing House, 87; Whitmore, J.K. (1984), 'Social Organization and Confucian Thought in Vietnam'.

8 Reid, as note 6, above, 62–77.

9 The most popular forms of *les societélés commerciales* set out in the Code de Commerce were *société à responsabilité limitée* and *société anonyme*. The Law Codes of France, as they were in 1864 were promulgated in total in Cochin-China. The rules regulating corporations were applied throughout Vietnam, because there were no indigenous laws thought suitable for 'modern commercial organizations'. See Hooker, M.B. (1979), *A Concise Legal History of Southeast Asia*, Oxford: Clarendon Press, 157–159.

10 See Ginsbergs, G. (1979), 'The Genesis of the People's Procuracy in the Democratic Republic of Vietnam', *Review of Socialist Law*, **5**, 191; Lien, H.T. (1994), 'On the Legal System of Vietnam', *Vietnam Law and Legal Forum*, **1**, 33, 33–34.

11 See Vinh, P.H. (1965), 'The Obligatory Nature of Planning Targets', *Review of Contemporary Law*, **12**, 83, 83–84.

12 See Nguyen Ngoc Tuan, Ngo Tri Long and Ho Phuong (1996), 'Restructing of State-Owned Enterprises Towards Industrialization and Modernization in Vietnam', in Ng Chee Yuen, et al. (eds), *State Owned Enterprise Reform in Vietnam*, Singapore: Institute of South East Asian Studies, 19, 19–24.

13 See Duiker, W. (1977), 'Ideology and Nation-Building in the Democratic Republic of Vietnam', *Asian Survey*, **17**, 414–419.

14 See Circular No. 3831/TP Concerning Some Immediate work to be done by the Judiciary Sector to Implement the Fifth Party Congress Resolution, 11 June 1982, Minister of Justice.

15 See generally, Fforde, A. and de Vylder, S. (1996), *From Plan to Market: The Economic Transition in Vietnam*, Boulder: Westview Press, see World Bank (1993), 'Vietnam: Transition to the Market', Washington D.C.: World Bank.

16 See Central Committee of the CPV, 'Resolution on Industrialization from the Central Committee, Communist Party Seventh Session Seventh Party Congress', Voice of Vietnam, 11 August 1994, *BBC Monitoring Service*, Asia-Pacific, 19 August 1994. For a more detailed account, see Luoc, V.D. (1996), *Vietnam's*

Industrialization, Modernization and Resources, Hanoi: Social Sciences Publishing House, 30–46.

17   See Xuan, N.Q. (1995), 'Vietnam: Potential Market and New Opportunities', **19**, *Fordham Int'l Law Journal*, 32–33.

18   See Marr, D. (1981), *Vietnamese Tradition on Trial, 1920–1945*, Berkeley: University of California, 98–99.

19   Constitution 1992, Article 4.

20   See Muoi, D. (1994), 'Communist Party of Vietnam Seventh Central Committee's Political Report', *FBIS East Asian Daily Report 94-015*, 24 January, 65, 65–72.

21   The *nomenklatura* system established a list of appointments by the CPV, which ensures that key legislative, executive and judicial posts are occupied by party members. See Khng, R.H.H. (1992), 'The 1992 Revised Constitution of Vietnam', *Contemporary Southeast Asia*, **14**, 221–225; Thayer, C. (1992), 'Political Reform in Vietnam: Dô Mói and the Emergence of Civil Society', in R.F. Miller (ed.), *Civil Society in Communist Systems*, North Sydney: Allen & Unwin, 114–115.

22   Constitution 1992, Articles 83–84. See Mao, V. (1995), 'Renovation in Legislation', *Tap Chi Cong San (Communist Review)*, August, 3, 7.

23   See Manh, N.D. (1994), 'Some Thoughts on the Legislation by the National Assembly', *Nha Nuoc va Phap Luat* (State and Law), (4) 8.

24   Constitution 1992, Article l03.

25   Constitution 1992, Article 112. Law on the Organization of Government of the Socialist Republic of Vietnam 1992.

26   See Schot, A. (1996), *Legal Aspects of Foreign Investment in the Socialist Republic of Vietnam*, The Hague: Kluwer Law, 28–29.

27   Law on the Organization of the People's Court 1992; Oda, H. (1987), 'The Procuracy and the Regular Courts as Enforcers of the Constitutional Rule of Law: The Experience of East Asian States', *Tulane Law Review*, **61**, 1339.

28   Huyen, N.V. (1995), 'The Problems of Training Judges and People's Assessors', *Luat Hoc* (Jurisprudence), November, 33, 33–36.

29   See Schumacher, R. (1997), 'For Now, Vietnam Officials Leave Phan Thiet Golf Assets Untouched', *Asian Wall Street Journal*, 6 January, 3.

30   See Thuy, N.T. (unpublished) 'Dispute Resolution and Enforcement of Economic Judgments in Vietnam' (research report No. 8) Australian International Legal Cooperation Programme 1996, 21–33.

31   Interviews: H.H. Cuong, Director International Law and Cooperation Department Ministry of Justice, Hanoi, 1996–1997.

32   See Uc, D.T. (1994), 'Market and Law', *Vietnam Social Sciences*, **4**, 18, 19–21.

33   See 'The Non-State Trade Sector' (1994), *Vietnam Economic Review*, **3**, 35.

34   See Kiet, V.V. (1986), 'Report to the National Assembly on the 1987 Socio-Economic Development Plan', Hanoi Domestic Service, 26 December 1986, *FBIS Asia and Pacific Daily Report*, 30 December, K.9; see generally, Fforde and de Vylder, as note 15, above, 56–67.

35   Communist Party of Vietnam Resolution No. 16 of 1988.

36   See Binh, N.T. (1995), 'It's Time to Amend the Law on Companies', *Saigon Giai Phong* (Saigon Liberation) 3 July, 3.

37   Constitution 1980, Articles 24, 27.

38   Articles 15, 16, 21.

39   Penal Code 1986, Articles 165, 168 and 172 respectively.

40   See Gillespie, J. (1994), 'Private Commercial Rights in Vietnam: A Comparative Analysis', *Stanford Journal of International Law*, **30**, 21, 325, 333–336.

41   Constitution 1992, Article 84.

42   Law No. 66-537 on Commercial Companies 1966. See Senghor, V. (1994),

'France Lends a Hand for Legal Overhaul', *Vietnam Investment Review*, 10 October, 1.

43   For a wide-ranging discussion of corporate reform, see Dam, D.D. (unpublished), 'Administrative Reform: Changes to Meet the Requirements of the Market-Oriented Economy' (Research Paper No. 1) Australian International Legal Cooperation Programme 1996, 8–13.

44   See Ioffe, O.S. (1988), *Soviet Civil Law*, Dordrecht: Martinus Nijhoff, 34–46; Lucas, S. and Malter, Y. (1996), 'The Development of Corporate Law in the Former Soviet Republics', *Int'l Comp. L.Q.*, **45**, 365, 366–368.

45   See Binh, as note 36, above, 4; Bao, X. and Hong, N. (1995), 'Problems in Implementation of the Law on Companies', *Dien Dan Doanh Nghiep* (Entrepreneur Forum), 28 September, 11.

46   See Circular No. 472 PMDSKJ Providing Guidance for Procedures and Duration for Issuing Licences for the Establishment of Private Enterprises and Companies, 20 May 1993, Ministry of Justice.

47   For example, Official Dispatch No. 4556-4BNN Concerning the Resolution of Expired Business Licenses, 19 September 1992, Ho Chi Minh City People's Committee. See 'The People's Committee of Ho Chi Minh City Issues Regulations on Procedures for Issuance of Established Licenses and Business Registration, Certificates for Private Enterprises and Companies', *Sai Gon Giai Phong* (Saigon Liberation), 11 January 1995, 4.

48   Law on Companies 1990, Articles 14, 16.

49   Law on Companies, Articles 17, 18.

50   Law on Companies, Article 14.

51   See Decree No. 29 CP Stipulating Detailed Provisions for Implementation of the Law on Promotion of Domestic Investment, Article 26, 12 May 1995 (government).

52   Law on Companies 1990, Article 16.

53   Decision No. 19-BXD-CSXD Promulgating the Regulations on the Operation and Registration of Construction Consultancy Practices, 10 June 1995 (Ministry of Construction).

54   Decree No. 31-CP on the Organization and Operation of the State Notorization, 18 May 1996 (government).

55   Decree 222 HDBT Promulgating Regulations on a Number of Articles of the Law of Companies, 23 July 1991 (Council of Ministers).

56   Law on Companies 1990, Article 16; Circular No. 472 PMDSKJ, Article 3 (IV), 20 May 1993 (Ministry of Justice).

57   See 'Functions, Tasks and Organizational Structures of Planning Agencies under the Local People's Committee' (1995), *Vietnam Economic Review* (4), 38–40.

58   Law on Companies 1990, Article 17.

59   Circular No. 5 UB/TT-LB Providing Guidance on the Functions, Tasks and Organization of Planning Committees of Provinces and Cities, 10 July 1995 (State Planning Committee and Government Organization and Personal Committees).

60   As note 59, above.

61   The word 'juridical' is used in Vietnamese law to attribute legal personality according to the French concept of *personalité juridique*. See Nghi Din So 17-HDBT (Application Decree 17–HDBT), 16 January 1990.

62   Decree 46 CP, 7 January 1995 (Ho Chi Minh City People's Committee).

63   See World Bank 'Vietnam Economic Report on Industrial Policy', (Report No. 14645-VN) (1995), 17 October, 50–53.

64   It should be noted under the French Law on Commercial Companies, Articles 53–55 of Decree No. 67-237 Relating to the Commercial Register, 23 March

1967 (upon which the Vietnamese company law is loosely based), registration is processed by the courts.

65   See 'Continuation of Part Two of the Seventh Party Central Committee's Political Report Delivered to General Secretary Do Muoi', 20 January 1994, *FBIS East Asian Daily Report 94-016*, 25 January, 67–68.

66   This policy would bring Vietnam in line with the Chinese company registration system which is controlled by the State Administration for Industry and Commerce. See Epstein, E. (1995), 'Law and Legislation in Post-Mao China', in P. Potter (ed.), *Domestic Reforms in Post-Mao China*, New York: M.E. Sharp.

67   Law on Private Enterprise 1990, Article 2.

68   Decree No. 222, 23 July 1991 (Council of Ministers).

69   Law No. 66-537 on Commercial Companies 1966, Chapter IV.

70   Law on Companies 1990, Article 2.

71   Law on Companies, Article 20.

72   Source: Ministry of Planning and Investment 1996.

73   See Phan, N.D. (1996), 'The Development of Small and Medium Scale Enterprises', *Vietnam's Socio-Economic Development*, **8**, 3, 3–9.

74   Civil Code, Article 94. The Vietnamese definition differs from its counterpart in Article 37 General Principles of Civil Law (People's Republic of China) because it specifies the need for internal division of ownership and authority.

75   See Sadikov, O.N. (ed.) (1988), *Soviet Civil Law*, New York: M.E. Sharp, 50–67.

76   Law on State Enterprises 1995, Article 6 (state enterprises have the right to 'manage and use' capital, land and natural resources assigned by the state).

77   Civil Code 1995, Articles 110–115.

78   Law on State Owned Enterprises 1995.

79   Source: State Planning Committee Annual Report, January 1995.

80   Small scale business are not licensed and merely need to register with the local district or village People's Committee. Decree No. 66 HDBT, 2 March 1992 (Council of Ministers). See 'The Non-State Trade Sector' (1994) *Vietnam Economic Review*, **3**, 35, 35–37; Hue, D.D. (1994), 'Legal Regulation in Relation to Issuance of Permits to Establish Enterprises and Business Registration in Vietnam – The Present Situation and Some Recommendations', *Nha Nuoc va Phap Luat* (State and Law), **4**, 20, 21–23.

81   See Uc, as note 32, above, 18, 19–20; Marr, D. (unpublished), 'The Vietnam Communist Party and Civil Society', Vietnam Update Conference, Australian National University, Canberra, 11 November 1994, 3–4.

82   See Muoi, D. (1994), 'Continuation of Part Two 7th Party Central Committee Political Report', *FIBIS* East Asia Daily Report 94-016, 67; Trong, N.P. (1994), 'Market Economy and the Leadership Role of the Party', *Tap Chi Cong San* (Communist Review), January 1994, **29**, 29–33.

83   The literature in this area is vast. See Stoljar, S.J. (1973), *Groups and Entities – An Enquiry Into Corporate Theory*, Canberra: Australian National University Press; Tay, A.E.S. (1992), 'Introduction: The Juridical Person in Legal Theory, Law and Comparative Law', in A.E.S. Tay and C.S.C. Leuong (eds), 'Legal Persons and Legal Personality in Common Law, Civil Law and Socialist Law', *Indian Socio-Legal Journal*, 4; Blumberg, P. (1990), 'The Corporate Personality in American Law: A Summary Review', *American Journal of Comparative Law*, **38**, 49–69.

84   See Tuan, N.N. (1993), 'Renovating the Enterprise Model in Our Country', *Tap Chi Cong San* (Communist Review), December, 29–33; Phat, N.N. (1993), 'Conceptions on the Legal Status of Entrepreneurs in the Market Economy', *Nha Nuoc va Phap Luat* (State and Law), **2**, 24, 25–27. See Fu, at note 3, above, 269–277, 289–294. (Although still a fragile concept, the corporate veil in China is considerably more durable than its Vietnamese counterpart.)

85   Law on Companies 1990, Article 1.
86   Law on Companies, Article 95.
87   Law on Foreign Investment 1996, Article 5.
88   Law on Companies, Article 19.
89   Law on Companies, Articles 6–14.
90   Law on Companies, Article 15.
91   For a general discussion of this principle, see Minh, N.N. (1983), 'On the General Part of the Criminal Law of Vietnam', *Luat Hoc* (Jurisprudence), **3**, 3, 5.
92   Civil Code Article 832.
93   Civil Code Article 832(1)
94   Civil Code Article 832(2)
95   Civil Code Article 828.
96   Civil Code Article 834.
97   See generally, Ford, J.H. and Austin, R.P. (1995), *Ford and Austin's Principles of Corporations Law* (7th edition), Sydney: Butterworths, 482–485; Le Gall, J.P. and Morel, P. (1992), *French Company Law* (2nd edition), Longman, London: 68–73.
98   Civil Code 1995, Article 96(1); Law on Companies 1990, Article 13(1).
99   Article 12.
100 Land use rights are proprietary interests in land of variable tenure, only the state owns land outright, Land Law 1993, Article 1; Decree No. 65 CP Detailing the Implementation of the Ordinance on the Rights and Obligations of Domestic Organizations with State Allotted or Leased Land 1996 (government). See Veitbid Law Firm (1996), 'The Intricacies of Land-Use Rights', *Vietnam Investment Review*, 6 January, 16.
101 Law on Companies 1990, Article 21.
102 Law on Companies 1990, Article 44.
103 Decree No. 1 CP Sanctions Against Violation of Administrative Regulations in the Field of Trade, 3 January 1996, Article 4(3) (government).
104 Penal Code 1986, Article 168(1).
105 Commercial Law 1997, Articles 2, 5; Decree No. 11/TT-PL on Signing and Carrying Out Economic Contracts, 25 May 1992, Part Four (State Economic Arbitrators).
106 This position contrasts with the law in the People's Republic of China, where the doctrine of *ultra vires* does not apply in any circumstances. See Fu, note 3, above, 272–273.
107 Law on Companies 1990, Article 2.
108 Law on Private Enterprises 1990, Article 2.
109 Circular No. 472 PMDSKJ on Procedures for the Issue of Licenses for Branch or Representative Offices, 20 May 1993 (Ministry of Justice).
110 See Heng, L.H. (1992), 'The Law and Freedom to Carry Out Business', *Nha Nuoc va Phap Luat* (State and Law), **2**, 27–29.
111 Law on State Owned Enterprises 1994, Articles 17, 18.
112 Decree No. 29 CP Stipulating Detailed Provisions for Implementation of the Law on Promotion of Domestic Investment in May 1995, Article 27 (government).
113 Law on Companies 1990, Article 16.
114 See Linh, T. (1992), 'Companies Want Barriers to Growth Lifted', *Vietnam News*, 17 June, 2.
115 The provision of certain goods and services is either prohibited or closely regulated. Decree No. 2 CP Defining the Commodities and Services Banned from Commercial Business and the Commodities and Services Allowed for

Commercial Business Under Certain Conditions on the Domestic Market, 5 January 1995 (government).

116   See 'New Orientations of the Industrialization Policy of Vietnam', *Kinh Te Chau a Thai Binh Duong* (Asia-Pacific Economic Review), September 1994, 6; 43 per cent of all registered private businesses operate commercial services and 42 per cent operate industrial and handicraft factories: General Department of Statistics, Hanoi 1995.

117   Civil Code, Article 99.

118   See Phong, N. (1996), 'From Factories to Construction Sites', *Nhan Dan* (The People), 26 January, 2.

119   Funds are distributed from the National Fund for Investment Support. Decree No. 29 CP Stipulating Detailed Provisions for Implementation of the Law on Promotions of Domestic Investment, 12 May 1995, Articles 6–11, 27 (government).

120   Circular No. 472 PMDSKJ 20 May 1993 (Ministry of Justice).

121   Subject to the approval of the MPI; Law on Foreign Investment 1996.

122   Decree No. 222 HDBT Promulgating Regulations Making Detailed Provisions for a Number of Articles of the Law on Companies, 23 July 1991 (Council of Minsters).

123   Decree No. 31 CP on 16 Organization and Operation of the State Notorization, 18 May 1996, Articles 18, 26 (government).

124   Thong Tu So 06-TT/DRKD Cua Trong Tai Kinh Te Nha Nuoc (Circular No. 06-TT/DKKD of State Arbitration Authority), 29 July 1991.

125   Law on Companies 1990 Article 20; Circular No. 472 PMDSKJ on Procedures for the Issue of Licenses for Branch or Representative Offices, 20 May 1993 (Ministry of Justice).

126   See 'Basic Contents Mid-term Party National Conference Resolution', *Saigon Giai Phong* (Saigon Liberation), 19 March 1994, 2.

127   See Bao and Hong, as note 45, above, 11.

128   Civil Code, Article 99.

129   Law on Companies 1990, Article 10.

130   Article 10.

131   Civil Code, Article 99(2)(d).

132   Law on Companies, Article 10(3).

133   Law on Companies, Article 10(4).

134   Civil Code, Article 99(2)(f).

135   For example, Law on Companies 1990, Article 10(5). These matters are discussed in more detail below.

136   Civil Code, Article 102.

137   Law on Companies 1990, Article 27.

138   Law on Companies, Article 27 (limited liability companies), Article 37 (shareholding companies).

139   Civil Code, Article 99(3); Law on Companies 1990, Article 21.

140   Civil Code, Article 96 (1).

141   Law on Companies 1990, Article 21.

142   Law on Companies, Article 18.

143   Law on Companies, Article 26.

144   Law on Companies, Article 31.

145   Civil Code, Article 97.

146   Civil Code, Article 100; Law on Companies 1990, Article 20.

147   Without exception, all private Vietnamese lawyers interviewed by the author stated that courts would never be used for this purpose.

148   Law on Companies 1990, Article 2.

149 Civil Code, Article 103(3). (This provision simply repeats the Law on Companies 1990.)
150 Law on Companies 1990, Article 25(1).
151 See Thuyet, P.V. (1996), 'Legal Framework and Private Sector Development in Transitional Economies: The Case of Vietnam', *Law and Policy in International Business,* **27** (3), 541, 565.
152 Law on Companies 1990, at 27(1).
153 As note 152, above.
154 Law on Companies, Article 29.
155 Law on Companies, Article 25.
156 Law on Companies, Article 30(2).
157 Law on Companies, Article 30(1).
158 Law on Companies, Article 32. (This topic is discussed in more detail under 'External Administration of Companies'.)
159 Law on Companies, Article 32(6)(c).
160 Law on Companies, Article 30(3).
161 Law on Companies, Article 30(3).
162 Law on Companies, Article 39.
163 Law on Companies, Article 30(4).
164 Law on Companies, Article 36.
165 Civil Code, Articles 99(c), 90; Law on Companies 1990, Article 14(2).
166 Law on Companies 1990, Article 20.
167 Civil Code, Article 100(4).
168 Law on Companies 1990, Articles 26, 31.
169 Civil Code, Article 100(5).
170 Civil Code, Article 102(2); Decree No. 17 HDBT on Economic Contracts 1990, Article 5(2).
171 Civil Code, Article 102(3). Decree No. 17 HDBT on Economic Contracts 1990, Article 6(2).
172 Civil Code, Article 102.
173 Law on Companies 1990, Article 27(1). Similar provisions apply to shareholding companies, see article 40.
174 Law on Companies, Article 27(2). It should be noted that these powers are expressed in the permissive form 'may' and can, in theory, be excluded by the charter.
175 Law on Companies, Article 19(2).
176 Decree No. 17 HDBT on Economic Contracts, 16 January 1990, Article 6.
177 Law on Companies, Article 5(2).
178 Civil Code, Article 143(a).
179 Civil Code, Article 612 (includes personal and property damage).
180 Civil Code, Article 622.
181 Law on Companies 1990, Article 39.
182 Law on Companies, Article 38.
183 Law on Companies, Article 39.
184 Law on Companies, Article 38
185 Law on Companies, Article 40.
186 Law on Companies, Articles 41, 42.
187 Law on Companies, Article 43.
188 Law on State Enterprises 1995, Article 32. See Doanh, L.D. (1996), 'Legal Consequences of State-Owned Enterprise Reform', in N.C. Yuen, N.J. Freeman and F.H. Huyen (eds), *State-Owned Enterprise Reform in Vietnam,* Singapore: Institute of South East Asian Studies, 61, 70–72.
189 Decree No. 39 CP Promulgation the Model Statute on Organization and Operation of State Corporations 1995, Article 15 (government).

190   Law on Companies 1990, Article 27.
191   Law on Companies, Article 37(1).
192   Law on Foreign Investment 1996, Article 14. (Minority shareholders have a right of veto over important matters changing the company charter.)
193   Law on Companies, Article 37(2)(3).
194   Law on Companies, Article 37(3).
195   See Chi, B.K. (1996), 'Providing Legal Services in Vietnam: A Practitioner's Viewpoint', in S. Leung (ed.), *Vietnam Assessment: Creating a Sound Investment Climate*, Singapore: Institute of Southeast Asian Studies, 107, 108–111. Some domestic legal firms, such as Investconsult, provide a sophisticated level of commercial advice.
196   Law on Companies, Article 3.
197   Law on Companies, Article 32(4).
198   Law on Companies, Articles 32(5), 33.
199   Law on Companies, Article 34.
200   Law on Companies, Article 35.
201   See Bao and Hong, as note 45, above, 11.
202   To a lesser degree similar imbalances may be discerned in Law No. 66-537 on Commercial Companies 1966 (France), Chapter IV.
203   Law on Companies 1990, Article 27(3).
204   Such rights may in theory be included in the corporate charter.
205   Law on Companies 1990, Article 27(2)(b).
206   These comments are based on interviews with Vietnamese legal practitioners, little empirical research has been conducted. See generally, Tomasic, R. (1995), 'Company Law and Limits to the Rule of Law in China', *Australian Journal of Corporate Law*, 4, 470.
207   Law on Companies 1990, Article 41(1).
208   Law on Companies, Article 39.
209   Law on Companies, Article 42.
210   Law on Companies, Article 37(3)(c).
211   Law on Companies, Article 40.
212   Law on Companies, Article 37(3).
213   Law on Companies, Article 39.
214   Law on Companies, Article 40.
215   There is no statutory designation that the company charter operates like a contract. See Corporations Act 1989 (Australia), Section 180(1); 'Subject to this Law, the constitution of a company has the effect of a contract under seal:

(a)   between the company and each member;
(b)   between the company and each eligible officer [defined in Section 180 (5)) as "a director, the principal executive officer or a secretary of the company"];
(c)   between each member and each other member;
(d)   under which each of the above-mentioned persons agrees to observe and perform the provisions of the constitution as in force for the time being so far as those provisions are applicable to that person.'
216   This is company model favoured in Anglo-US jurisdictions. See Farrar, J.H., Furey, N.E. and Hannigan, B.M. (1991), *Farrar's Company Law*, London: Butterworths, 121–127.
217   The definition of economic contracts is broad enough to encompass agreements of this kind, however, contracts must be signed between legal entities or individuals holding business registration. Commercial Law 1997, Articles 1, 3; Decree No. 17 HDBT on Economic Contracts 1990, Article 5.

218   Civil Code, Article 395.
219   Civil Code, Article 417.
220   Law on Companies 1990, Articles 38, 42.
221   Civil Code, Article 404(3).
222   'A person who, by his/her fault intentionally or unintentionally ... adversely effects the honour, prestige or property of a legal person ... and thereby causes damages shall be liable for such damage.' Civil Code, Article 609.
223   Civil Code, Article 609.
224   Although there appears to be substantial similarities, as predicted by the similar neo-Confucian cultures, differences in the exercise of state power in Vietnam and China are likely to provoke different company-state relationships. See generally, Tricker, R.I. (1990), 'Corporate Governance: A Ripple on the Cultural Reflection', in S.R. Clegg and S.C. Redding (eds), *Capitalism in Contrasting Cultures*, New York: Walter de Gruyter; Tomasic as note 206, above, 470.
225   This proposition is confirmed by a survey of business attitudes, conducted in Hanoi and Ho Chi Minh City in 1995. See Vietnam State Planning Committee (unpublished), 'Firm Survey: Assessment of First Responses to New Economic Environment', Hanoi, March 1995, 4, 45–46.
226   *The Economist*, 27 May 1997. Huy Huang, Vietnam's largest private company is selling a part share to the Ho Chi Minh People's Committee, family wealth requires political patronage; Kiet, P.T. (1995), 'The Present Situation of the Non-State Owned Economic Sector in Cuong-Nam, Da Nang and Problems to be Solved', *Nghiem CUU Kinh Te* (Economic Problems), 8, 26, 29.
227   See Jenkins, G. and Terkper, S. (1993), 'Administrative Reform for Fiscal Systems in Transitional Economies: The Case of Vietnam', *Tax Rates International*, 29 March, 796.
228   Decree No. 12 Stipulating in Detail the Implementation of the Law on Foreign Investment, 18 February 1997, Article 66.
229   See Communist Party of Vietnam (1990), *Seventh National Congress Document*, Hanoi: Foreign Language Publishing House, 77; Circular No. 12 TC TCT Guidance on the Examination and Approval of Balance Sheets and Allocation of Income of State Enterprises, 22 February 1994 (Ministry of Finance).
230   Circular No. 22 TC-CDKT Guiding the Implementation of Decree No. 7 CP Regulating Independent Auditing (29 January 1994) April 1994.
231   Decree No. 7 CP On the Regulation of Independent Auditing in the National Economy, 29 January 1994.
232   See 'Auditing Companies in Full Swing in Vietnam', *Vietnam Law and Legal Forum* 3(30), 13; the first Vietnamese auditing firms were not registered until October 1995.
233   Law on Promotion of Domestic Investment 1994, Article 6; Law on Business Profit Tax 1990, Article 10.
234   See Heyde, R. and Kheng, C.T. (1996), 'Taxation in Vietnam – Taxation by Negotiation', *Vietnam Investment Review*, 25 March, 1.
235   Decision No. 1141/TC/QD/CDKT Promulgating the Business Accounting System, 1 November 1995 (Ministry of Finance); Circular No. 3256/TC/CDKT on the Implementation of the Business Accounting System, 24 November 1995 (Ministry of Finance).
236   See Spoor, as note 1, above, 122–131.
237   See Binh, T.N. (1995), 'Accounting Loopholes to Close Investors', *Vietnam Investment Review*, 3, April 1995, 11.
238   The new auditing rules are expected to closely follow the protocols developed in the foreign investment regime. Decree No. 12 CP 1997, Article 69.
239   Law on Companies 1990, Article 21.
240   Law on Companies, Article 74.

241   Circular No. 3256/TC/CDKT on the Implementation of the Business Accounting System, 24 November 1995 (Ministry of Finance).
242   Law on Foreign Investment 1996, Article 56(6). (Annual audited financial reports must be lodged with the MPI.)
243   Provincial Court Officials interviewed in January 1997 in Hanoi and Ho Chi Minh City were unaware of any private action taken against a company for non-compliance with the law or corporate charter.
244   Civil Code, Article 107.
245   Law on Companies 1990, Article 22.
246   Law on Companies, Article 23.
247   As note 246, above.
248   See Schot, as note 26, above, 339–340; Harmer, R. (1994), 'Commercial and Bankruptcy Laws in Vietnam', in G. Hassell and T. Truong (eds), *Infrastructural Development and Legal Change in Vietnam*, Melbourne: Centre for Comparative Constitutional Studies, 68–71.
249   See Hue, D.D. and Man, N.M. (1993), 'Some Issues on the Draft Bankruptcy Law', *Nha Nuoc va Phap Luat* (State and Law), **2**, 39.
250   The law applies to all company types and forms of ownership, private enterprises, cooperatives and businesses registered in accordance with Decree No. 66 HDBT, 2 March 1992 (Council of Ministers) Decree Providing Guidance on the Implementation of the Law on Business Bankruptcy, 23 December 1994, Article 1(2) (government).
251   See Harmer, as note 248, above, 68–70. For a broad comparative assessment of these issues, see Tomasic, R., Reid, K. and Francis, A. (1996), 'Insolvency Law Administration and Culture in Six Asian Legal Systems', *Australian Journal of Corporate Law*, **6**, 2, 249, 265–287.
252   See Hue and Man as note 249, above, 41–42.
253   Law on State Enterprises 1995 Article 23(1)(2). See 'Vo Van Kiet Attends Meeting on Debt Solvency', Hanoi, Voice of Vietnam in Vietnamese, 22 March 1994, translation, *FBIS Daily Report East Asia Service 94-056*, 23 March 1994, 58; Thuy as note 30, above, 33–42; Law on State Enterprises 1995, Article 24.
254   Unfortunately, published statistics do not break down aggregate numbers into types of companies and forms of ownership. See 'Settlement of Economic Lawsuits and Bankruptcy Declarations', *Vietnam Law and Legal Forum*, **2**, (2), 1996, 11.
255   See Vietnam Planning Committee, as note 225, above, 46.
256   Law on Business Bankruptcy 1993, Article 44(4).
257   Similar provisions apply to state-owned enterprises, Law on State Enterprises 1995, Article 22(2).
258   Law on Business Bankruptcy 1993, Article 2; Decree No. 189 CP Providing Guidance on the Implementation of the Law on Business Bankruptcy, 23 December 1994, Article 3 (government); Law on Companies 1990, Article 24.
259   See Ormesson, D., Crowley, C. and Marshall, T. (1991), 'France', in L. Nelson (ed.), *Digest of Commercial Laws of the World*, New York: Oceana Publications, 104.
260   Law on Business Bankruptcy 1993, Article 30.
261   Law on Business Bankruptcy, Articles 3, 9.
262   Law on Business Bankruptcy, Article 8.
263   See Lay, J. (1994), 'The New Bankruptcy Law in Vietnam', 11 *International Comparative and Commercial Law Review*, **11**, (4), 389, 389–390.
264   As note 262, Article 19.
265   Law on State Owned Enterprises 1995, Article 6; Civil Code, Articles 208–209.
266   The Civil Code suggests that only individuals and households may mortgage land use rights (Articles 727–732), however, the recently enacted Decree No.

65 CP 1996 (government) provides for this type of security.

267 Although Vietnamese law provides for outright ownership of houses and buildings, the Civil Code in Articles 181, 205–207 does not authoritatively determine how such rights differ for land use rights.

268 Law on Business Bankruptcy 1993, Article 9.

269 Law on Business Bankruptcy, Article 13.

270 Law on Business Bankruptcy, Articles 15–19, 21.

271 Law on Business Bankruptcy, Articles 27–34; Decree No. 189 CP Providing Guidance on the Implementation of the Law on Business Bankruptcy, 23 December 1994, Articles 13–14.

272 Law on Business Bankruptcy 1993, Article 29.

273 Law on Business Bankruptcy, Article 18.

274 Law on Business Bankruptcy, Article 20.

275 Law on Business Bankruptcy, Article 36.

276 Law on Business Bankruptcy, Article 15. See Schot, as note 26, above, 347. These bodies are headed by a judge of the local provincial People's Court and comprise of representatives drawn from courts, creditors, bankrupt companies, trade unions and local officials.

277 Law on Business Bankruptcy 1993, Article 17; Decree No. 189 CP Providing Guidance on the Implementation of the Law on Enterprise Bankruptcy, 23 December 1994, Articles 34–39.

278 Law on Business Bankruptcy 1993, Article 39.

279 Decree No. 92 CP 19, December 1995.

280 Civil Code, Article 104(2).

281 Law on Foreign Investment 1996.

282 Law on Foreign Investment, Article 104(2).

283 Law on Foreign Investment, Article 105.

284 Law on Foreign Investment, Article 105(2). It should be noted that state approval is indirectly required as the act of termination is subject to administrative discretion: Civil Code, Articles 107–108.

285 See Vietnam State Planning Committee, as note 225, above, 45–46; Gates C. (1995), 'Micro Economic Adjustments and Institutional Change in Vietnam: Issues, Observations and Remarks', *Vietnam's Socio-Economic Development*, 2, 21, 30–34.

286 Law on Companies 1990, Article 2, 5(2).

287 See Tai, N.D. (1996), 'Towards a Securities Market in Vietnam', *Vietnam's Socio-Economic Reform*, 5, 15, 23–24.

288 See Phung, T.V. (1998), 'Overview of the Decree on Securities and the Securities Market in Vietnam', *Vietnam Law and Legal Forum*, 4 (48), 19, 19–20; also Thanh, C.H. (1993), 'The State and the Formation of a Stock Exchange Market in Vietnam at the Moment', *Nha Nuoc va Phat Luat* (State and Law), 2, 16.

289 See Tai, N.D. (1996), 'The Equitisation of the State Enterprises', *Vietnam's Socio-Economic Development*, 8, 42; Huy, N.V. and Nghia, T.V. (1996), 'Government Policies and State-owned Enterprise Reform', in N.C. Yuen *et al.* (eds), *State Owned Enterprise Reform in Vietnam*, Singapore: Institute of South East Asian Studies, 56, 57–62.

290 See Tai, as note 287, above.

291 See Tuan, T.Q. (1997), 'Some Basic Measures to Speed up the Establishment of a Stock Market in Vietnam', *Economic Development Review*, January, 3–7. Tu, T. (1997), 'Challenges to Deal with on the Way to a Vietnamese Stock Market', *Tap Chi Kinh Te* (Economic Review), January, 3–7.

9 Thai Company Law

SAOWANEE ASAWAROJ* AND EUGENE CLARK**

1 Introduction

Thailand is a country of approximately 60 million people and is located in South East Asia. Until the Asian financial crisis, it had enjoyed a rapidly developing and increasingly diversified economy. This includes major exports of technical goods such as computers, air-conditioners, integrated circuits and appliances, to the United States and European Union. Other major exports include mining products, processed food, jewellery and rice. Although the major ethnic group are the Thai, the population also includes significant numbers of Chinese, Lao, Malay and Cambodians. The Chinese-Thai have been especially influential in business. Another major influence is religion with over 90 per cent of the population being Buddhist.[1]

Modern Thailand's legal system dates from the reign of King Rama V and involved the adoption of the Romano-Germanic legal system with further adaptations in the form of localized codes which have drawn from a variety of legal sources, including Japan, Germany and the United States.[2]

Thailand has a constitutional monarchy led by H.M. King Bhumibol Adulyadej (Rama IX) who is also commander-in-chief of the military. The king has a veto right over bills passed by the National Assembly, which veto may be overriden by a two-thirds majority vote of the National Assembly (Constitution, Chapter 5, article 94). The king is supported by a Privy Council appointed by the king to advise him on all matters related to his constitutional duties (Constitution, Chapter 2).[3]

A new constitution of the Kingdom of Thailand was approved in October of 1997. It is designed to bring about major changes in Thailand's government structure in order to create a better balance of power and greater checks on potential abuses of power and corruption. Thailand's legislature consists of a national assembly which in turn is divided into two houses – a House of Representatives (lower house) and a Senate (upper house). The House of Representatives consists of 500 members, 100 of whom are from the election on a party-list basis under Section 99 of the new constitution and 400 of whom are from the election on a constituency basis under Section 102. Members of the House of Representatives are determined on a proportional basis, with the population divided into constituencies called *Changwats*, each *Changwat* being entitled to one representative.

The Senate is primarily a house of review and is confined to scrutiny or veto of legislation proposed by the House of Representatives. It consists of 200 members (not belonging to a particular party) elected by the people on the basis of a certain number of senators from each *Changwat*.

The executive head of government is the prime minister who is appointed by the king from the members of the Lower House. The king appoints the prime minister and not more that 35 other ministers to constitute the Council of Ministers which is charged with carrying out the administration of state affairs. This appointment is made on the recommendation expressed by a resolution of the House of Representatives which must be passed by the votes of more than one-half of the total number of the existing members of the house. The prime minister and his cabinet members are not allowed to hold dual positions of MP and cabinet member. They must relinquish MP status before taking the post in the cabinet (Sections 118(7), 201 and 204). Ministers must not own, hold shares or work for companies. All their shares must be transferred to others before taking up ministerial office (Sections 208 and 209).

The new constitution also establishes the National Economic and Social Advisory council to provide consultation and advice to cabinet members on economic and social development and other related plans. Such plans must be approved by the Council before they can be formally announced. This will enhance the check-and-balance system and enable state projects to be carried out more effectively.

Government administration is part of one central system divided into approximately 80 departments, 76 provincial units and numerous local government units. Each province is divided into districts (*amphurs*) headed by a Chief District Officer (*Nai Amphur*). Districts in turn are comprised of sub-districts or communes (*tambols*) each representing about ten villages (*muban*). The leaders of *tambols* and *mubans* are elected under the supervision of a provincial governor.[4] Local government units or authorities either report to central government directly or have government officials as their chairpersons. Examples are the Bangkok Metropolitan Administration and the City of Pattaya.[5] Typically, each city will have a mayor and city council-lors who are elected.

The framework for local government is set forth in Chapter IX of the new constitution:

> Section 282. Subject to section 1, the State shall give autonomy to the locality in accordance with the principle of self-government according to the will of the people in the locality.
>
> Section 283. Any locality which meets the conditions of self-government shall have the right to be formed as a local administrative organization as provided by law.
>
> The supervision of a local administrative organization must be exercised in so far as it is necessary as provided by law but must be for protecting local interests or the interests of the country as a whole; provided, however, that it shall not substantially affect the principle of self-government according to the will of the people in the locality otherwise than as provided by law.
>
> Section 285. A local administrative organization shall have a local assembly and local administrative committee or local administrators.
>
> Members of a local assembly shall be elected.
>
> A local administrative committee or local administrators shall be directly elected by the people or shall be from the approval of a local assembly.
>
> An election of members of a local assembly and local administrative committee or local administrators who must be directly elected by the people shall be made by direct suffrage and secret ballot.
>
> Members of a local assembly, local administrative committee or local administrators shall hold office for the period of four years.
>
> A member of a local administrative committee or local administrator shall not be a Government official holding a permanent position or receiving a salary or an official or employee of a State agency, State enterprise or local administration.[6]

The court system and independent judiciary play an important role in Thai society.[7] At the top of Thailand's court hierarchy is the Supreme Court (*Sarn Dika*), which is the final court of appeal in all civil, bankruptcy, labour, juvenile and criminal matters. Then there is a middle level Court of Appeal (*Sarm Uthorn*) and various lower courts which hear matters in the first instance (*Sarn Chunton*) and which are divided into particular geographical areas (Provincial Courts) or according to subject-matter (for example civil cases, bankruptcy or juvenile).[8]

Thailand also has a Constitutional Court (see Section 2.1 of the text) and a system of Administrative Courts established under the new constitution (Chapter VIII, Part 4). Administrative Courts have the powers to try to adjudicate disputes between:

... a Government agency, State agency, State enterprise, local administration, or State official under the superintendence or supervision of the Government on one part and a private individual on the other part, or between a Government agency, State agency, State enterprise, local administration, or State official under the superintendence or supervision of the Government on one part and another such agency, enterprise, administration and official on the other part, which is the dispute as a consequence of the act or omission of the act that must be, according to the law, performed by such Government agency, State agency, State enterprise, local administration, or State official, or as a consequence of the act or omission of the act under the responsibility of such Government agency, State agency, State enterprise, local administration or State official in the performance of duties under the law, as provided by law. There shall be the Supreme Administrative Court and Administrative Tribunals, and there may also be the Appellate Administrative Court.

The new constitution (Chapter VI, Part 7) also creates a panel of not more than three ombudsmen who are appointed, by the king with the advice of the Senate, from the persons recognized and respected by the public, with knowledge and experience in the administration of state affairs, enterprises or activities of common interest of the public and with apparent integrity. Ombudsmen have the power to investigate failure to perform public duty or abuse of power by government agencies and their officials. The Constitutional Court or Administrative Court, as the case may be, decides the case submitted by the ombudsman without delay.

The Thai judicial system has close links to the civil service system and government administration.[9] The Ministry for Justice is responsible for the budget and general administration of the country's court system. Notwithstanding this 'link' with the government, the Thai judiciary has maintained its independence through the Thai Judicial Council, which is comprised of four government officials, four presiding judges elected by the total judiciary and four highly respected retired judges who are also elected.[10]

In terms of its international links, Thailand is a member of the World Trade Organization, the Association of South-East Asian Nations, the Asia-Pacific Economic Cooperation group, and the East Asian Economic Caucus. As a developing country, Thailand receives preferential treatment on tariffs as a member of the Generalized System of Preferences established under the General Agreement on Tariffs and Trade (now replaced by the World Trade Organization).[11]

2 The Source of Thai Company Law

2.1 *The Constitutional Basis*

The highest form of law in Thailand is the constitution. As a civil law system, Thai laws are derived from and found in codes or statutes. There are four major codes – the Criminal, Civil and Commercial, Civil Procedure and Criminal Procedure codes – completed in 1934.[12] The final arbiter of the constitution is the Constitutional Court established in Chapter VIII of the new constitution which provides:

> Section 255. The Constitutional Court consists of the President and fourteen judges of the Constitutional Court to be appointed by the King upon advice of the Senate from the following persons:
>
> (1) five judges of the Supreme Court holding a position of not lower than Supreme Court judge and elected at a general meeting of the Supreme Court by secret ballot;
>
> (2) two judges of the Supreme Administrative Court elected at a general meeting of the Supreme Administrative Court by secret ballot;
>
> (3) five qualified persons in law elected under section 257;
>
> (4) three qualified persons in political science elected under section 257.
>
> The elected persons under paragraph one shall hold a meeting and elect one among themselves to be the President of the Constitutional Court and notify the result to the President of the Senate accordingly.
>
> Section 266. In the case where a dispute arises as to the powers and duties of organisations under the Constitution, such organisations or the President of the National Assembly shall submit a matter together with the opinion to the Constitutional Court for decision.
>
> Section 268. The decision of the Constitutional Court shall be deemed final and binding on the National Assembly.

2.2 *The Civil and Commercial Code; Public Limited Companies Act*

Commercial transactions in Thailand are governed principally by the Civil and Commercial Code 1928 ('CCC'). Book I of the CCC ('General Principles') provides the basic definitions and principles underlying commercial law transactions in Thailand. Book II ('Obligation') covers the general provisions of contract law. The Thai laws governing companies are found in Book III, Title XXII of the CCC and the Public Limited Companies Act of 1992 ('PLCA'). The CCC contains the provisions dealing with private limited companies and the PLCA regulates public limited companies. These laws cover all matters essential to companies. Book III of the CCC also includes the provisions governing 'Specific Contracts', including carriage of goods, mortgages, hire of services and so on. Other statutes or codes which relate to companies include the Revenue Act 1983, the Bankruptcy Act 1940, the Anti-Monopoly Act 1979 and the Securities Exchange of Thailand Act 1974 and the Commercial Banking Act 1962.[13]

2.3   *The Role of Case Law*

As noted above, the primary source of law is found in the legislation or codes governing companies. Reported court decisions do not constitute the law, but provide useful examples of the provisions of law.

3   The Nature and Powers of Company Regulatory Bodies

3.1   *The Relevant Ministries*

The ministry exercising the general charge of company activities is the Ministry of Finance, which also supervises Thailand's central bank, the Bank of Thailand. Also under the jurisdiction of the Ministry of Finance is the Securities Exchange of Thailand (SET), which was established in 1975.[14]

Other ministries of great importance commercially are the Ministry of Commerce (regulating internal and external trade and responsible for registration requirements of public companies and the enforcement of the public companies legislation) and the Ministry of Industry (in charge of national manufacturing and mining).[15]

3.2   *A Legal Labyrinth*

Depending on the type of business, there are likely to be dozens of different laws and regulations and several government agencies involved. Therefore, it is important for companies doing business in Thailand to do their homework and comply with all the relevant laws, including those governing companies.

4   A Description of the Types of Companies and their Powers

4.1   *Private Limited Companies*

The first type of company in Thailand is the private limited company. These companies tend to be small scale enterprises, owned and operated by a small number of individuals actively involved in the management of the enterprise. Private limited companies are precluded from offering their shares to the public; they cannot sell their shares in any securities market. In addition, the transfer of shares may be restricted or prohibited. Moreover, private limited companies cannot issue debentures.

4.2   Public Limited Companies

The second type of company is the public limited company. These companies tend to be larger than private limited companies. They can offer their shares to the public and sell their shares on the stock market. In addition, the shares of public limited companies are freely transferable. Furthermore, the companies can issue debentures.

5   Company Formation

5.1   Registration

Thai companies can be established by registration under the provisions of the CCC in the case of a private company or the PLCA in the case of a public company. Every kind of company in Thailand is incorporated by one of these methods.

5.2   Memorandum

The formation of a company in Thailand requires certain formalities to be followed. There must be a group of persons (seven or more for a private limited company; 15 or more for a public limited company) who, by subscribing their names to a memorandum and otherwise complying with the provisions of the law, promote and form a limited company by depositing and registering the memorandum at the companies registration office.[16] The memorandum must contain the following particulars:

- the name of the proposed company;
- the part of the region in which the registered office of the company shall be situated;
- the objects of the company;
- a declaration that the liability of the shareholders shall be limited;
- the amount of share capital which the company proposes to be registered and the division thereof into shares of a fixed amount;
- the names, addresses, occupations, nationalities and signatures of the promoters; and
- the number of shares subscribed by each of the promoters.

If the registrar is of the opinion that the name of any company which has applied for registration (whether in a Thai or foreign language name) is the same or similar to the name of a company or private company which has previously registered, the registrar shall reject such application and notify the applicant of the rejection.[17]

5.3   *Share Subscriptions and the Statutory Meeting*

After the registration of the memorandum, the promoters must subscribe and manage the subscription of the shares of the company. When the shares to be paid in money have been subscribed, the promoters must without delay hold a general meeting of subscribers (the statutory meeting).[18] Certain activities must take place at the statutory meeting, including the adoption of the regulations of the company; the ratification of any contracts entered into and any expenses incurred by the promoters in promoting the company; and the appointment of the first directors and auditors and the fixing of their respective powers.[19] After the statutory meeting has been held, the promoters shall with seven days hand over the business to the directors and the directors shall require that promoters and subscribers pay for their shares.[20] In addition, when the amount of the shares has been paid, the directors must apply to have the company registered. The application and entry in the register must contain, in conformity with the decisions of the statutory meeting, certain matters, including the total number of shares subscribed or allotted, (distinguishing ordinary shares and preference shares); the name, occupations and addresses of the directors; and the addresses of the principal business office and all branch offices. When the registrar receives the application, it is examined to see that it has been completed as required by law concerned. When satisfied, the registrar issues a certificate of registration.[21]

Public companies are entitled to offer shares to the public. This shall be done in accordance with the laws governing securities and exchange.[22]

5.4   *The Legal Effect of Company Registration*

The registration of the company has certain legal effects. Most importantly, the registered company is deemed to have a legal personality, namely the law regards the company as a separate legal entity – a distinct form, independent of the persons who manage it (the directors) or those who own its shares (the shareholders). Once the company is registered, creditors of a promoter of the company, in regard to debts incurred in relation to the activities of the company before its registration, cannot take an action against the promoter, but must sue the company because the company has its legal personality.[23]

A company has the power to engage in any activity within the scope of its objects and, unless the articles of association provide otherwise, such power shall include the power to:

1) be a plaintiff, make a complaint, and take any legal proceedings on behalf of the company;
2) purchase, procure, accept, lease, hire-purchase, own, possess, improve, use and otherwise manage any property as well as the interest thereof;
3) sell, transfer, mortgage, pledge, exchange, and otherwise dispose of property;
4) borrow money, guarantee, issue, transfer and endorse bills and other negotiable instruments;
5) request the temporary release of a director, member of staff or employee who is being charged with a criminal offence relating to the performance of his or her duties for the company;
6) hold shares, manage other companies and private companies, and engage in any specific business in cooperation with other companies and private companies;
7) engage in any other operation which a natural person may be able to do within the scope of the objects of the company; except an act that can only be done by a natural person.[24]

5.5   The Share Capital of a Company and Debentures

5.5.1   The share capital of a company   Every company in Thailand has a share capital raised by issuing its shares and selling them to subscribers at the time of the formation of the company or later to the buyers who will become shareholders. The share capital of a company may consist of different types of shares and the rights of different classes of shareholders will be set out in the company's articles.

In Thailand a company's share capital may consist of ordinary shares and preference shares.[25] In the case of ordinary shares, holders have ordinary rights, including voting rights and the right to receive dividends and repayment of capital in the event of a winding up of the company. In practice, the majority of the shares of every company are ordinary shares.

Preference shares may only be issued if they have been authorized by the memorandum or the articles of the company. Holders of preference shares have certain special rights, including receiving priority over other shareholders of the company, for example by obtaining a dividend ahead of the ordinary shareholders; or, in preference to ordinary shareholders, receiving repayment of capital in the event of a winding up of the company.

5.5.2   Debentures   Apart from raising capital through the issue of shares, a public company may raise capital by the issue of debentures. Such debentures are offered to the public who, by purchasing the debenture, loan money to the corporation in return for interest on the money loaned. The offering for sale and issuance of debentures to the public can be made only by public companies[26] and shall be done in accordance with the law governing securities and exchange.[27]

6   The Internal Administration of Companies

6.1   The Rights and Duties of the Shareholders

Ordinary shareholders who are not directors of companies in Thailand have, by virtue of their shareholder status, certain rights and duties in relation to the companies in which they hold shares.

6.1.1   The rights of the shareholders   The shareholders have:

- rights relating to shares, for example to obtain the share certificate, to change the share certificate and to transfer their shares;
- the right to appoint directors and auditors of their companies;
- a right to obtain dividends if their companies have been profitable;
- rights concerning the meetings of their companies, including the right to be present at the company's meetings and at any general meeting; the right to vote (unless they have a special interest in a resolution, which interest disqualifies them from voting on that matter); and for shareholders holding not less than one-fifth of the shares of the company, the right to convene an extraordinary meeting of their company;
- rights to control the management of the company, including the right to examine reports of the board of directors' meetings or of the general meetings of the company; the right to examine the balance sheet, the statement of profits and losses and the report of the auditor of the company; the right to make a motion to a court having jurisdiction over the case to cancel a void or voidable resolution; the right to take an action against directors of the company when the company fails to take such action; and the right to apply to the registrar to inspect and examine the affairs of the company.

6.1.2   The duties of the shareholders   Shareholders have a duty to pay all moneys due and owing on their shares. Shareholders do not have a duty to pay or are not responsible for the debts incurred in the business of the company as the company is a separate legal entity distinct from the shareholders. There is no principle of piercing the corporate veil in Thailand.[28]

6.2 The Management of Companies

6.2.1 In general As a company is an artificial legal person separate from the shareholders of the company, the company is managed by a natural person or a group of natural persons appointed by the shareholders, directors or board of directors. In Thai company law, there are no other persons designated to be responsible for the management of the company; positions such as 'company secretary' are unknown and unrecognized in Thai law and practice.

6.2.2 The number of directors In a private limited company there must be at least one director[29], whereas there shall be at least five directors in a public limited company.[30]

6.2.3 The qualifications of directors In a private limited company, Thai law does not require any particular qualification for directors, but company directors must have capacity to commit any juristic act and not be bankrupt. An act committed by a person without legal capacity shall be void or voidable. On the other hand, the PLCA[31] provides, in relation to the qualifications of a company's directors, that the directors shall:

- be natural persons;
- be *sui juris*, not be bankrupt, incompetent or quasi-incompetent;
- never have been imprisoned on the final judgment of a court for an offence related to property committed with dishonest intent; and
- never have been dismissed or removed from government service, government organization or a government agency in punishment for dishonesty in performing their duties.

In addition, no fewer than half of the directors must reside within Thailand.[32]

6.2.4 The appointment of directors The directors of a company are elected by the shareholders. However, there is a difference between private and public companies. In a private limited company, the directors are appointed by a general meeting by straight voting[33], whereas the directors in a public company are elected by accumulative voting unless otherwise prescribed by the articles of the company.[34] The board of directors elects one of its directors to be the chairman of the board.[35]

Directors must vacate their office upon the occurrence of the following events:

- the expiration of their term;
- death, resignation, lack of qualifications or the possession of prohibited characteristics;
- removal by a resolution of the shareholders' meeting (by a vote of no fewer than three-quarters of the number of shareholders in attendance and who have the right to vote and totalling not less than half the number of shares held by the shareholders attending the meeting and having the right to vote); and
- removal by a court order.[36]

6.2.5   The position of directors   In the management of the company, the directors have an authority as agents of the company.[37] In other words, they have an authority to bind the company.

6.2.6   The powers and duties of directors   A company is managed by a director (in the case of a private limited company) or directors (in the case of a private limited company or a public limited company).[38] In carrying out their duty to manage the company, the director or the board of directors must manage the company in compliance with the provisions of law concerned and the objects and articles of association of the company and under the control of the general meeting of shareholders.[39] These company objects may be distinct from and in addition to those required by various legal provisions, except those provisions of the law concerning moral and public policy, for example the provisions designed to protect outsiders. Where a board of directors engages in conduct not specified by law nor stipulated in the company's articles of association, the directors shall be responsible for such conduct.

In Thailand conduct which is *ultra vires* does not bind the company.[40] Therefore, if directors act outside the objects of the company (*ultra vires*), they will be personally responsible for their conduct. However, the company may ratify such conduct on behalf of the directors, thus binding the company. Alternatively, where the company receives the benefit from such *ultra vires* acts on the part of its director, the company may be liable in accordance with the principle of Thai agency law.[41] Unless the articles of incorporation provide otherwise in its objects and articles, or such action is contrary to the provisions of law concerning moral and public policy, directors must also act in accordance with a resolution of the shareholders' meeting.

In addition to the above duties, directors must, in their conduct of the company's business, apply the diligence of a careful businessman. Directors are jointly responsible for ensuring that shareholders pay for their shares; that the company sets up and maintains its books and documents; that dividends or interest payments be properly distributed; and that resolutions of the general meetings be properly enforced.[42] In doing their duties, directors normally receive remuneration in accordance with the terms of the articles of incorporation or as determined by the company at its general meetings.

6.2.7 The liability of directors Directors are not liable to outsiders for acts committed within the scope of their power. In other words, they will not incur personal liability for *intra vires* contracts, because they act as agents of the company and such acts bind the company in relation to contracts with outsiders. Directors are responsible to outsiders only when they make contracts which are *ultra vires* (exceed the authority conferred on them by the company's articles and memorandum). However, *ultra vires* contracts made by directors can be ratified by a resolution at a general meeting or by the company taking the benefit of such contracts.

In the performance of their duties, directors will be held liable to the company and its shareholders only if they do not comply with the provisions of law concerning moral and public policy, the objects of the company, the articles of association of the company or the resolution of the shareholders' meeting. Directors will also be liable where the director is guilty of gross or culpable negligence in a business sense, for example where directors do not exercise the diligence of a careful businessman in their conduct of the company's business. However, the directors' liability is to the company, not to the shareholders, as directors owe their duties only to the whole company as a corporate body and not to individual shareholders. Thus, claims against the directors for compensation for injury caused by them to the company may be entered by the company. However, if the company refuses to act, shareholders themselves may take an action against the directors for compensation for company losses.[43] In so acting, the shareholders do not bring action against the directors on their own behalf, but on behalf of the company.[44] However, where a director (wilfully or negligently) unlawfully injures an individual shareholder, the director is bound to make compensation to the shareholder in accordance with the ordinary provisions of tort law.

6.3 Shareholders' Meetings

6.3.1 Types of meeting The shareholders can control the directors' management of the company through the general meeting. There are two types of meeting, namely the annual general meeting and the extraordinary meeting.

Every company is required to hold a general meeting of shareholders each calendar year. A private limited company's general meeting is held within six months of the registration and then at least once every 12 months.[45] A public limited company's general meeting is held within four months of the last day of the fiscal year of the company.[46]

An extraordinary meeting is a meeting other than the general meeting, which is usually held when there are special events which cannot wait until the general annual meeting. An extraordinary meeting is usually called by the directors. However, the shareholders holding shares amounting to not less than one-fifth of the total number of shares of the company (in the case of a private limited company)[47] or not less than one-fifth of shares sold or no fewer than 25 shareholders holding shares amounting to not less than one-tenth of shares sold (in the case of a public limited company)[48] may submit their names in a request directing the board of directors to call an extraordinary general meeting.

6.3.2　A quorum　A quorum of a company meeting is the minimum number of shareholders whose presence is required for the legal transaction of business at a meeting. What constitutes a quorum varies between a private company and a public one. In the case of a private company, a quorum requires the presence of at least two shareholders having shares equal to and not less than one-quarter of the capital of the company.[49] However, the quorum requirement for a public company meeting is slightly different, shareholders and proxies (if any) attending a shareholder's meeting in that there should be at least 25 or no fewer than half of the total number of shareholders; and in either case such shareholders shall hold shares amounting to not less than one-third of the total number of shares sold.[50]

6.3.3　Company resolutions and voting procedures　Shareholders are entitled to attend and vote at the shareholders' meeting, but they may authorize other persons as proxies to attend and vote at any meeting on their behalf.[51]

The method employed to decide on a resolution depends on the type of company involved. In the case of a private company, resolutions are decided upon initially by a show of hands unless a poll is demanded. In a show of hands every shareholder has one vote, but in a poll each share carries a vote.[52] Thus, the outcome of the poll is a reflection of the concentration of interests in the company. With respect to the votes in a public company, resolutions are also decided on by a show of hands, unless a poll is demanded. However, whether by show of hands or poll, the shareholders have votes equal to the number of shares held by the voter.[53]

Some matters are decided by ordinary resolution requiring a simple majority, whereas more important matters must be decided by extraordinary or special resolution. However, an extraordinary or special resolution in the two types of companies are somewhat different. An extraordinary or special resolution in a private company must be passed by two successive general meetings, namely the passing of the resolution in the first meeting by a majority of not less than three-quarters of the votes; and the confirmation of such a resolution in a subsequent meeting (which has been summoned and held not less than fourteen days and not more than six weeks after the former meeting) by a majority of not less than two-thirds of the votes.[54] An extraordinary resolution of a public company is required to be passed by a three-quarters majority of those present and entitled to vote.

Resolutions passed by these means are valid and can be enforced. Company resolutions will be invalid and cancelled where a resolution is passed in contravention of a company's articles of association or where the resolution is in breach of some other law. Any shareholder or director (in a private company) or no fewer than five shareholders or shareholders representing not less than one-fifth of the total number of shares sold (in a public company) may make a motion to the court having jurisdiction over the case for an order to cancel such a resolution and the court shall cancel the resolution provided that the application is entered within one month of the date of the resolution.[55]

6.4   Dividends and Reserves

The shareholders have rights in relation to dividends. The distribution of a dividend is made in proportion to the amount paid upon each share, unless otherwise decided with regard to preference shares.[56]

The important principle is that the dividends shall not be paid other than out of profits. If the company still has an accumulated loss, no dividends shall be distributed.[57] This principle is in accord with the principle on maintenance of capital.[58] Moreover, a dividend shall be declared only if it is passed by a resolution agreed in a general meeting. The shareholders shall be notified in writing of such payment of dividends, and the notice shall also be published in a newspaper. The company shall allocate not less than 5 per cent of its annual net profit less the accumulated losses brought forward (if any) to a reserve fund until this fund attains an amount not less than 10 per cent of the registered capital, unless the company's articles of association or other laws require a larger reserve fund.[59]

If a dividend has been paid contrary to the principle previously mentioned, the creditors of the company are entitled to have the amount so distributed returned to the company, provided that a shareholder cannot be obliged to return dividends which he has received in good faith.[60]

6.5   Company Accounts and the Balance Sheet

6.5.1   *In general*   The shareholders' right to information about the company is essential and is one of the crucial means to control the management of the directors of the company. The shareholders must be informed of various matters, for example the accounts, balance sheet and reports of the company.[61]

The directors must deliver the following documents to the shareholders along with written notices calling for an annual general meeting: copies of the balance sheet and the statement of profit and loss examined by the auditor, together with the audit report of the auditor; the annual report of the directors specifying certain matters (for example the name and location of the head office, the category of business, the particulars provided to the company by the directors, remuneration, shares, debentures, other rights and benefits received by the directors from the company, and other particulars as specified in the ministerial regulation).[62]

6.5.2   *Company accounts*   The company must prepare and maintain accounts, including the auditing of accounts as required by the relevant law.[63]

6.5.3   *The balance sheet*   Apart from the accounts, the company is required to prepare, for submission to the shareholders and for consideration and approval at the annual general meeting, a balance sheet as well as a statement of profit and loss at least once during each 12-month period which is a fiscal year of that company. The company balance sheet must be examined by an auditor prior to submission to the shareholders' meeting.[64]

6.6   The Company Audit

The company must have an auditor appointed by the annual general meeting to examine the financial documents of the company and to present an audit report to the annual general meeting.[65] As to qualifications, the auditor may be any competent person but must not be a director, staff member, employee or person holding any position in or having any duty towards the company.[66] This is because duty to examine the company's financial status requires the auditor to be an independent person.

In doing his or her duty, the auditor has the power to examine, during the office hours of the company, certain financial documents of the company, for example the accounts, documents and any other evidence relating to the revenues and expenditures, excluding the assets and liabilities of the company.

The auditor also has the power to question the directors, staff members, employees, persons holding any position in or having any duty towards the company and agents of the company. This includes the power to direct such persons to clarify for the auditor the operation of the business of the company.[67]

The auditor has the right to present a written explanation of the audit report to the shareholders' meeting and has the duty to attend every shareholders' meeting at which the balance sheet, the statement of profit and loss and the problems relating to the accounts of the company are to be considered.[68] In addition to the audit report, a public limited company must deliver to the registrar an annual report, copies of the balance sheet and the statement of profit and loss which has been duly audited and approved by the shareholders' meeting, together with a copy of the minutes of the shareholders' meeting certified to be true by a person authorized to sign on behalf to the company. A public company must also publish the balance sheet for public information in any local newspaper.[69]

6.7 Inspection

Although the shareholders can use the general meeting of their company and other measures to control the management of the company's directors, the directors can still contravene their duties. Thus, Thai company law provides yet another means for the shareholders to control the directors' acts, namely an inspection.[70]

The shareholders, holding not less than one-fifth of the shares of the company (in a private company) or not less than one-fifth of the total number of shares sold or amounting to no fewer than one-third of the shareholders (in a public company) have the right to have the company inspected. These shareholders may submit their names in a written application to the registrar to appoint an inspector to proceed with the examination of the business operations and the financial condition of the company as well as to inspect the conduct of business by the board of directors. In addition, the Minister of Commerce may, on his or her own motion, appoint inspectors to report to the government on the affairs of a private limited company. In the case of a public company, the registrar (the Director-General of the Commercial Registration Department, Ministry of Commerce) may appoint one or more competent officers to be an inspector or inspectors to proceed with the examination of the business operations of the company when the registrar has reasonable ground to suspect certain problems. It may be suspected for example, that the company is committing an act to defraud the creditors of the company or incurring debts that it knew it could not repay; that the company is contravening or not complying with the law or, when applying for registration, making a false statement in the balance sheet, statement of profit and loss or the report which was submitted to the registrar or which was disclosed to the general public; or that the directors or the staff member are carrying out the business contrary to the objects of the company or against the interests of the company or its shareholders.[71]

There are no legal specifications for an inspector's qualifications. However, the inherent nature of the position would suggest an inspector should have knowledge of accountancy and company law.[72] In addition, because an inspector's duty is similar to that of the auditor, an inspector, like that auditor, should not be a director, agent or employee of the company.[73] In performing their duties, inspectors have the power to examine upon oath the directors, employees and agents of the company in relation to the company's business and other relevant conduct in relation to the company.[74]

Following the inspection, the inspector makes a report based on the result of the inspection together with his or her conclusions and submits it, in the case of an investigation of a private company, to the Minister of Commerce or, in the case of a public company, to the registrar.[75]

All expenses of a company inspection must be repaid by the applicants, unless the company, in the first general meeting after such an inspection is completed, consents to that sum being paid out of the assets of the company. A company shall be liable to compensate the persons who paid in advance for the inspection if the anticipated result of the inspection is confirmed by the inspection report.[76]

6.8   Corporate Financial Transactions

6.8.1   Increases of capital   The company may increase the amount of its registered capital by issuing new shares. In the case of a private company, this can be done by a special resolution,[77] however in a public company, a resolution increasing the amount of registered capital requires a resolution to be passed by not less than three-quarters of the total number of votes of the shareholders attending the meeting and having the right to vote.[78] The new shares are allotted as fully or partly paid up in capital.

All new shares must be offered to the shareholders in proportion to the shares held by them, unless decided otherwise by a general meeting.[79] After a portion of the new shares has already been sold by the company, an application to register a change in the paid-up capital may be submitted to the registrar by the company.[80]

6.8.2 Reductions of capital A company may reduce its capital by lowering the par value of each share or by reducing the number of shares. However, the capital of the company must not be reduced to less than one-quarter of its original total amount.[81]

The reduction of a company's capital may be made, in the case of a private company upon a special resolution[82] or, in the case of a public company, upon a resolution passed at the shareholders' meeting by a vote of not less than three-quarters of the total number of votes of the shareholders attending the meeting who have the right to vote.[83]

In the case of a resolution regarding a reduction in its capital, the company must notify in writing the known creditors of the resolution for the reduction of capital and specify in the notification that any objection thereto must be submitted within three months (in the case of a private company) or within two months (in the case of a public company) of the date on which the creditors receive the notice of such resolution. The company must also have the notice of such resolution published in a local newspaper. If an objection is made, the company cannot reduce its capital unless it has paid its debt or given security for the debt.[84] After having proceeded as previously mentioned, the company applies to the registrar to register the reduction of its capital.[85]

7 The External Administration of Companies

7.1 Dissolution

In general terms, a company can be dissolved on one of two grounds, namely grounds specified by provisions of law and by court order.

7.1.1 Dissolution by law The grounds of dissolution specified by provisions of Thai law vary slightly as between private and public companies. A private limited company is dissolved: in a designated situation, if any, as provided for in the company's regulations; if the company was formed for a period of time, by the expiration of such period; if the company was formed for a single undertaking, by the termination of that undertaking; by a special resolution to dissolve (if there is no special resolution, the company cannot be dissolved even though the directors of the company so agreed);[86] and by the company becoming bankrupt or insolvent.[87]

The public limited company is dissolved: by a resolution of shareholders to dissolve by a vote of not less than three-quarters of the total number of votes of shareholders attending the meeting who have the right to vote; or by the company becoming insolvent.[88]

7.1.2   Dissolution by court order   The company may also be dissolved by an order of the court on the following grounds: default made in filing a statutory report or in holding a statutory required meeting; in cases where the business of the company, if operated further, would bring only losses and recovery is hopeless; and in cases where the number of shareholders has decreased to fewer than seven in a private company or fewer than 15 in a public company.[89] An additional ground applicable to private companies occurs in the case of the company failing to commence its business within a year from the date of registration or suspending its business for a whole year.[90]

In the case of a private company, a motion for company dissolution may be brought by only one shareholder holding one or more shares. However, in the case of a public company, a motion for dissolution must be submitted by shareholders holding shares amounting to not less than one-tenth of the total number of shares sold.[91]

In the case of default in filing a statutorily required report or in holding a statutorily required meeting, the court, as it thinks fit, instead of dissolving the company, may direct that the statutory report be filed or the statutory meeting be held. In addition, in the case of a public company, the court, instead of ordering the dissolution of the company, may order the company to rectify or to comply with the law within a specified period of time which may not be more than six months.[92] The court has the discretion not to dissolve a company even in cases where the company has changed its objects, where the directors have commited activities outside the scope of their duties or beyond the objects of the company, or where the company does not carry on its business for over one year;[93] or when the losses of the company cannot be recovered, but there are other grounds not to dissolve the company. An example of the latter situation may occur where the majority of shareholders do not want to dissolve the company and the company still has enough property to pay its debts.[94]

7.2   Liquidation

Upon dissolution, the life of the company is terminated and the process of liquidation follows. In cases where the company is dissolved on grounds other than bankruptcy, the liquidation proceeds in accordance with the provisions of the company law. However if the company is dissolved on the ground of bankruptcy, it must proceed in compliance with the provisions of bankruptcy law. In regard to the dissolution of a private company, the directors become the liquidator unless otherwise provided by the regulations of the company. If there are no persons to be liquidators, they shall be appointed by the court.[95] In the case of a public company, the liquidator is appointed by a meeting of shareholders or by the court.[96]

The liquidator has the following powers and duties: to settle the affairs of the company;[97] to collect and receive money or property to which the company is entitled from other persons or to sell property of the company; to pay its debts and to distribute its assets; to bring or defend any legal proceeding (civil or criminal) and to make compromises in the name of the company; and to do all other acts necessary for the completion of liquidation.[98]

As soon as the affairs of the company are fully liquidated, the liquidator makes up an account of the liquidation showing the conduct of liquidation and the disposal of the company's property; and thereupon calls a general meeting for the purpose of laying before it the account and giving any explanation thereof. After the account is approved, the proceedings of the meeting must be registered.[99] Such registration is taken as being the end of the liquidation.

8 Takeover Rules: the Amalgamation of Companies and Competition Law

8.1 Amalgamation

Two or more companies may be amalgamated to form a new company. Such an amalgamation may take place between two or more private companies to become a new private company, between two or more public companies to become a new public company, or between any private company and any public company to become a public company. In the case of two private companies or a private company amalgamating with a public company, the amalgamation is accomplished by a special resolution of a meeting of shareholders of each of the companies. In the case of public companies, the resolutions in favour of amalgamation must be passed by a vote of not less than three-quarters of the total number of votes of the shareholders attending the meeting who have the right to vote.[100]

During the amalgamation procedure, the company shall notify its creditors in writing of the resolution of amalgamation. If an objection is made, the company cannot proceed with the amalgamation of the company unless it has paid its debt or given security for the debt.[101] In addition, a private company must publish the resolution of amalgamation a minimum of seven times in a local newspaper. With respect to the amalgamation of public companies, after having notified the creditors, the companies to be amalgamated must call a joint meeting of the shareholders of such companies to consider certain matters, including:

- the allotment of shares of the amalgamated company to the shareholders;
- the name to be adopted for the new company;
- the objects of the amalgamated company;
- the capital of the amalgamated company, of which capital the amount shall not be less than the sum of all the companies to be amalgamated;[102]
- the memorandum of association of the amalgamated company;
- the articles of association of the amalgamated company;
- the appointment of the directors of the amalgamated company;
- the appointment of the auditor of the amalgamated company; and
- other matters necessary for the amalgamation of the companies (if any).[103]

When the amalgamation has been completed, it must be registered within 14 days.[104] The new company is entitled to all the rights and is subject to the liabilities of the amalgamated companies.[105]

8.2   Competition Law

A merger or amalgamation must also take into account Thailand's competition laws. In Thailand, competition law is governed by two principal statutes. The oldest is the Trade Association Act BE 2509 (1969) which prevents restraints of trade. Section 22(2) of the Trade Association Act prohibits conduct which aims to 'upset prices or merchandise or service charges'. Section 22(4) catches uncompetitive conduct which increases, reduces or restricts the quantity of production; and Section 22(5) makes it illegal for a business to 'destroy normal business competition'.[106]

More recently, Thailand has passed the Price Control and Anti-Monopoly Act BE 2522 1979. This legislation establishes a central board to determine whether a monopoly has been created in relation to particular goods. In making this determination, the board may consider all relevant circumstances, including:

- the number of products and producers/sellers in a particular market;
- the existence of substitutable goods;
- whether there has been abrupt and sudden changes in the quantities of particular goods available in a market;
- the barriers to entry into a particular market;
- the prices charged by other sellers for similar or identical goods; and

- whether the market share of the major players has remained stable.

If the board finds an anti-monopoly situation to exist, it may declare the business to be a 'controlled business'. This requires the business to file an extensive report on its activities to the government with a view to prohibiting that business from extracting a monopoly price from the sale of its products.[107]

Most recently, in response to the economic crises and devaluation of the Thai baht, the government has announced an economic rehabilitation programme which promises major micro-economic reform to make the Thai economy more competitive.[108] Among the announced reforms are:

- the privitization of state-owned enterprises, the encouragement of competition in production and provision of services and the use of modern technology and management techniques;
- the enactment of the Corporatization Law in order to be able to convert state enterprises' capital to equity and reforms to the Private Participation in State Affairs Act 1992 BE 2535, allowing the private sector to participate in or operate state enterprises and to be more flexible for privatization; and
- the establishment of a regulatory body to monitor fair competition and consumer protection.

The government will also embark on major civil service reforms which will reduce corruption, streamline administration, eliminate waste and change the role of government from that of operator to monitor and coordinator.[109]

9 Securities Regulation in Thailand

9.1 *The History of the Thai Stock Market*

The Thai stock market commenced in 1962. The first market was established by a limited company, which was later incorporated as the Bangkok Stock Exchange Co. Limited and which lasted until the 1970s.[110] The SET came into operation in 1975.[111] It was a non-profit organization under the control of the Ministry of Finance. The SET is one of the fastest-growing capital markets in the world. During the 22 years of its existence, the SET has played a significant part in Thailand's economic and industrial development, mobilizing funds from both domestic and foreign investors. As financial liberalization has taken place in Thailand, market growth has been dynamic, with foreign investors now accounting for over a quarter of trading turn-over.[112]

9.2   *The Regulation of the Thai Stock Market*

The principal legislation governing securities was the Securities and Exchange Act 1974. This legislation was followed by the Securities and Exchange Act 1992 (SEA) which established the Securities and Exchange Commission (SEC).[113] Companies offering securities are required to have a licence from the Ministry of Finance.[114] In order to qualify for a licence, the company must meet specified capitalization requirements and have the application to offer shares approved.[115] The SEA also has various consumer protection provisions which prohibit a company from making misleading and deceptive state-ments (for example as to price, value or the nature of the securities) to the public.[116] Other provisions cover insider dealing,[117] over the counter securities,[118] the qualifications of brokers,[119] the provision of investment advisory services,[120] the management of mutual funds,[121] the management of private funds,[122] associations related to securities businesses,[123] the settlement of disputes concerning securities mat-ters,[124] and the Securities Clearing House and Depository Centre.[125]

Other laws relevant to the regulation of securities include the Fi-nance Act, Securities Act and Credit Foncier Businesses Act. These main pieces of legislation are supplemented by regulations issued by the Ministry of Finance and by the rules of the SET.[126]

9.3   *Features of the SET*

9.3.1   Only limited public companies   All companies listed on the SET are limited public companies. The exact criteria varies according to the Board of Investment Zone in which the company is based and whether or not it is classified under infrastructure or basic industry special categories (described below). These categories apply to newly established companies.

9.3.2   Capitalization requirements   A listed company in Zone 1 must have registered capital in ordinary shares to a value of at least 100 million baht (US$ 4 million). Board of Industry Zones 2 and 3 cover all 60 provinces outside Zone 1, which is Bangkok Metropolitan and five neighbouring provinces. However, that figure is relaxed to 40 million baht for companies based in Zones 2 and 3. Companies fall-ing into the defined special category for infrastructure and basic industry must have 100 million baht of registered capital in ordinary shares. Total market capitalization figures must reach 750 million baht, 200 million baht and 750 million baht respectively.

9.3.3 Special category companies The SET seeks to assist infrastructure project companies and large basic industry companies to register on the market, provided that the business is adjudged beneficial to the economy and society. The project value must be at least 10 billion baht (US$ 400 million) and half of the entire paid-up capital must be held by the company.

9.3.4 Share distribution The SET encourages small shareholders through its listing rules and this in turn benefits the liquidity of stocks. Small shareholders are those who hold not more than 0.5 per cent of the value of total paid-up capital. Applicant companies must provide for small shareholding between 15 and 30 per cent of their registered capital, depending on the paid-up capital value. There must be at least 600 and 300 small shareholders for any listed stock and listed companies in provincial zones respectively.

9.3.5 Business track record Companies applying for a listing must be able to demonstrate a three-year operational track record under the same management. For special category companies, management must be competent and experienced in key areas of management. Normally, companies which have shown a profit of 50 million baht (US$ 2 million) over the previous three years are eligible for listing. This figure is reduced to 15 million baht over two years for companies located in Zones 2 and 3.

9.3.6 Listing fees There are three types of fees payable for listing: application fees, admission fees and annual fees. In addition, fees are payable when capital increases are made in ordinary or preference share listings. All fees are subject to Value Added Tax at 7 per cent.

9.3.7 Listing procedure Under the SEA, the SET may list or delist any security. The listing procedure is as follows:

- initial public offering submitted to the SEC;
- financial advisor appointed;
- listing application submitted to the SET;
- consideration by listing sub-committee;
- company visit;
- company management interview;
- SET Board of Governors' approval;
- trading allowed in listed stocks.

Note that a company must file its listing application to the SET through an authorized finance and securities company which is designated as the 'financial advisor'.

Companies wishing to list should contact The Stock Exchange of Thailand Listing Department.

9.3.8   Investor protection   The SET regulates and supervises member companies in the following areas: trading systems, clearing and settlement, financial advice, margin loans and members' financial status.

9.3.9   Accounting standards   Listed companies' accounting systems must accord with SET standards. The minimum accounting standards comply with the Institute of Certified Accountants and Auditors of Thailand, who themselves accord with standards under the International Accounting Standards Council, the American Institute of Certified Public Accountants and the Financial Accounting Standards Board.

9.3.10   Surveillance system   Since the early 1980s, the SET has operated a stock watch and surveillance system to detect irregularities in price and volume movements. The system is closely used by trained analysts. Should any deviations from the SEA be detected, they will be referred to the SEC for further action.

9.3.11   Supervision signs   The SET operates five supervision signs for investor guidance. These are: NP (notice pending), NR (notice received), DS (designated securities), SP (suspending) and H (trading halted). These signs will be displayed beside the name of a stock on both the price reporting screens and the SET's electronic display board.

9.3.12   Investor information and information disclosure   A company is required to file all the information required by other leading international stock exchanges when listing on the SET. Thereafter, it must disclose specified information accurately, publicly and in the stipulated time.

9.3.13   Information dissemination   In line with its computerized trading system (ASSET), a price reporting system was introduced in 1991 to provide investors with a quoted price and trading information in real time. SET's information management system (known as SIMS) is a computer database system for the general public, which disseminates historical information concerning listed companies as well as trading statistics.

In the SET building, Sindhorn Tower on Wireless Road in Bangkok, are located the Investors' Information Centre and the SET Public Library. These carry previous and latest information and figures on listed companies and their securities. The SET also disseminates relevant trading information through the mass media.

9.3.14 *Arbitration committees* In November 1995, the SET board of governors approved regulations for arbitration committees. These temporary committees will settle disputes between brokers or between a broker and its customer. Three arbitrators will be appointed under the approval of the SET by each of the parties concerned.

9.4 The SEC[127] and the SEA

Although capital market has long played an important role in Thailand's economic system, in the past the development and supervision of Thai capital markets were regulated under various laws and regulations. The SEA, which came into effect on 16 March 1992, was enacted to serve the needs of Thailand's participation in the global economy by facilitating the unity, consistency and efficiency of supervision and development of the Thai capital market.

9.4.1 *The objectives of the SEA* The first objective was to improve the system and SET framework for the supervision and development of the country's capital market by establishing the SEC as a unified regulatory authority to supervise and develop the capital market. The second objective was to enhance direct financing through issuing various kinds of securities. The third was to provide greater investors' protection, and the fourth was to promote the development of the securities business and the capital market.

9.4.2 *The SEC* The SEC was established to supervise and develop the primary and secondary markets of Thailand's capital market system as well as financial or securities-related participants and institutions. The SEC has the responsibility of formulating policies, rules and regulations regarding the supervision, promotion and development of securities businesses as well as other relevant activities pertaining to the securities business, such as issuance and offer of securities for sale to the public, and securities exchange. It also regulates organizations related to the securities business, the acquisition of securities for business takeovers, and the prevention of unfair securities trading practices.

9.4.3 *Membership in the SEC* The SEC comprises:

- the Minister of Finance as the chairman;
- the Governor of the Bank of Thailand;
- the Permanent-Secretary of the Ministry of Finance;
- the Permanent-Secretary of the Ministry of Commerce;
- four to six well-qualified persons, appointed by the Cabinet on the recommendation of the Minister of Finance, who must in-

clude experts from each of the following fields: legal, accounting and finance; and
- Secretary-General of the Office of the SEC.

9.4.4   The major functions of the SEC   The SEC was established pursuant to the SEA Act. The major tasks of the SEC are to:

- create efficiency in fund raising by liberating development of
  new financing alternatives to mobilize funds from the public;
- develop a system that creates confidence, impartiality and protection for disclosure of accurate and adequate information for
  investors; and
- secure a system to maintain long-term stability of the capital
  market.

In carrying out these tasks, the SEC seeks to:

- establish the basic financial infrastructure for the Thai capital
  market by setting up the rules, regulations and legal framework;
- provide opportunities for the private sector to expand its business;
- supervise and examine the securities business and the capital
  market; and
- cooperate at the international level with other securities regulators.

9.4.5   The organizational structure of the SEC[128]   The SEC is organized
into five major departments and a number of offices. These are described below. The SEC is considered to be an independent
governmental agency whose revenue is derived in part from fees of
the application for public offering and licensing of securities businesses and the annual income subsidy from the SET.

The Corporate Finance Department is responsible for the supervision of the public issuance of securities in the primary market to
ensure their accuracy and sufficiency for investors' decision-making.
The department considers and approves public issuing and offering
of securities, and monitors the appropriate disclosure and updating
of data of issuing companies. The department also approves organizations dealing with the disclosure of securities information, for
example financial advisors, auditors, property valuers and credit
rating agencies. It also supervises the acquisition of securities for
business takeovers. It is also charged with making recommendations
for law reforms and the development of new types of financial instruments.[129]

The Department of Securities Business Supervision is responsible for the supervision of securities companies conducting brokerage, and trading and underwriting businesses. It is also involved in the compilation and processing of data from securities companies' reports for use in the supervision and examination of the operations of securities companies.[130]

The Department of Capital Market and Investment Management Supervision is comprised of two major offices. The Office of Market Supervision supervises the SET, the OTC, the Association of Securities Companies and organizations related to the securities business. It is also involved in derivatives regulation generally, including recent law reform proposals in this area. The Office of Investment Management Supervision supervises securities companies conducting mutual fund management, private fund management and investment advisory services.[131]

The Department of Enforcement is responsible for:

- examining the operations of the SET, the OTC, securities-related organizations, and other securities businesses operators that are not under the power and duty of any specific departments;
- inspecting reports, documents, evidences and investigating provisions regarding unfair securities trading practices;
- handling public complaints, investigating practices and collecting materials or evidence which may be deemed to contravene the SEA;
- collecting any factual statements and performing administrative functions for the Settlement Committee; and
- compiling facts and cooperating with competent officers and public prosecutors in gathering documents and evidence to take legal action against wrongdoers.[132]

The Legal Department's tasks are:

- to give advice, consider, draft and construe various notifications, orders and regulations under the jurisdiction of the SEC Office and other related rules and orders which are implemented in the Office;
- to give advice and assistance in relation to the drafting of contracts;
- to compile statistics and give advice in relation to the SEA and related laws;
- to prepare cases for further legal proceedings; and
- to provide advice and assistance to staff involved in initial litigation or work for the Appellate Committee.[133]

Other important offices within the SEC include:

- the Office of Capital Market Research and Development;
- the Office of the Secretary-General which handles the public relations, international administrative and secretariat work for the SEC and the executives of the Office;
- the Office of Information Technology;
- the Office of Human Resource Development;
- the Office of Internal Audit;
- the Office of General Management which manages the office inventory and general administration work, lays down the accounting system and procedures, manages investment and implements the budget and financial administration; and
- the Security Section.[134]

9.5   *The Major Features of the SEA*

9.5.1   The rationale and purpose of SEA   The enactment of the SEA and the establishment of the SEC with the powers to supervise and develop the Thai capital market aim to improve the efficiency, transparency and impartiality of share dealing in Thailand. Such a development will in turn provide an important part of the necessary infrastructure to enable Thailand to achieve sustainable economic development and growth with stability.

9.5.2   Public offerings and types of securities   The SEA allows business sectors to issue and offer various kinds of securities, namely shares, debentures or hybrid instruments for sale to mobilize funds from the public. The issuance must be of benefit to the country's economic prosperity.

9.5.3   Who may issue shares?   Under the SEA, an eligible shares issuer is restricted to a public limited company, whereas an issuer of debt instruments can be either a public limited company or a limited company.

Any issuers who wish to make a public offering of securities must first obtain approval from the SEC Office. However, any of the following securities issuing and offering to the public with conditions as stated hereinafter are considered to have obtained the approval from the SEC already:

> Firstly, the issue and offer of shares that are not worth exceeding 20 million baht within any past period of 12 months;
> Secondly, the issue and offer of securities to no more than 35 investors within any past period of 12 months; or

Thirdly, the issue and offer of securities to investors within 17 types of financial institutions.[135]

9.5.4 Registration   The SEC undertakes to consider an application for the public issuing and offering of securities within 45 days of the receipt of the application and supporting documentation.

Prospective issuers must file the registration statements and draft prospectuses which must disclose accurate, reliable and sufficient information necessary for investors to make an informed decision. The registration statements and draft prospectuses must contain essential information about the issuers, including the amount of registered capital, the nature of the business; its financial condition, the management team, the shareholders' structure, and other necessary information needed for making an investment decision. The registration statements and draft prospectuses will take effect within 30 days, during which period, the public is able to come into the SEC Office to examine the information about the issuers.

9.5.5 The securities business   The SEA also regulates the securities business, which include securities brokerage, securities dealing, securities underwriting, the investment advisory service, mutual fund management, and private fund management.

The private sector is permitted to take part in the securities business by obtaining licences from the Minister of Finance on the recommendation of the SEC. The SEC also sets out policies allowing financial institutions, notably commercial banks and finance companies, to undertake certain types of securities business, such as securities dealing or securities underwriting for debt instruments. In addition, commercial banks and life insurance companies are allowed to act as core applicants in applying for the establishment of new mutual fund management companies. Moreover, non-life insurance companies are allowed to hold shares in those newly established mutual fund management companies.

Under the SEA, mutual fund management is one of the securities businesses which offer investment units to the public to invest in securities and diversify risks for mutual returns. Prior to the launch of each mutual fund, a mutual fund management company must obtain an approval from the SEC Office. In comparison with the previous laws, major changes have been introduced into the SEA of relevance to the management of mutual fund. These are that:

- a mutual fund must be registered as a juristic person;
- a mutual fund supervisor must be appointed as a third party to protect investors and to ensure that the mutual fund

management company manages each mutual fund in accordance with rules and regulations; and
• disclosure of information must be in the prospectus every time new investment units are being offered in order to provide sufficient and accurate information for investors to use as a guideline for investment planning.

9.5.6   Secondary market in securities trading   The SET is considered to be the important secondary market for trading securities which were already issued and offered for sale to the public in the primary market. The SEA empowers the SEC to supervise securities exchanges which include the SET and over the counter exchanges. In addition, under the SEA, securities which are listed for trading in the SET are not allowed to be traded in any other exchanges. However, to accommodate the trading of those securities offered for sale to the public, but not listed on the SET, the OTC is therefore established to serve this purpose, but prior to that it must be granted approval from the SEC.

9.5.7   The SET and its relation to the SEC   The board of directors of the SET is comprised of ten members, five of whom are appointed by the SEC and five of whom are elected from the member securities companies.

These ten members of the board of directors will then elect the manager of the SET who also sits on the board of directors of the SET.

In terms of the relationship between the SEC and the board of directors of the SET, the SEC plays an important role in setting policies and approving the main regulations for the SET, for example listing and delisting rules and commission fee structures. With its important role of monitoring securities trading information, the SET has the primary responsibility for inspection and gathering all related evidence and facts for further actions and cooperation with the SEC whenever any suspicious practices in securities trading occurs.

9.5.8   Unfair securities trading practices   The SEA prohibits various unfair trading practices in relation to securities. These prohibited practices include: the distribution to the public of misleading information in relating to securities; false news reports in relation to securities; and insider trading. Unfair securities trading practices are criminal offences and attract severe penalties under the SEA. The SET and its offices also have wide powers of investigation which enable them to facilitate criminal prosecutions for breaches of the law in relation to securities trading.

9.5.9   The acquisition of securities for business takeovers   The SEA requires the person acquiring or disposing of securities, including shares or certificates representing the rights to purchase shares or other securities which can be converted into shares of public limited companies or limited companies having their securities listed on the SET or traded in the OTC, must report an acquisition or disposition to the SEC within one working day when such acquisition causes the holding to reach or pass 5 per cent of the total number of the securities of a business sold, and when such disposition causes the holding to decrease or pass 5 per cent of the total number of securities of a business sold.

Where a person acquires the securities of a business by means other than a tender offer, then the holding of such securities up to or above the following trigger points requires the person making the acquisition to make a mandatory offer, by which that person must agree to purchase all of the rest of the securities of the target company. These trigger points are:

- an increase in the number of securities held by a person from less than 25 per cent up to 25 per cent or more;
- an increase in the number of securities held by a person from less than 50 per cent up to 50 per cent or more;
- an increase in the number of securities held by a person from less than 75 per cent to 75 per cent or more; or
- any acquisition of more than 5 per cent within any 12-month period while holding securities between 25 and 50 per cent.

Besides the mentioned mandatory offer, a person may also make a voluntary offer in order to purchase and hold 25 per cent or more of the securities of a business under the provisions of the Takeover Code of the SEC.

Through the provisions of the Takeover Code, all shareholders of an offeree company must be treated impartially by an offeror and they must be given sufficient information to enable them to reach a proper decision and must have sufficient time to reach that decision.

9.6 The Continued Reform of Securities Law

9.6.1 The policy on a consolidation of securities companies Acknowledging the operational pressures in a global economy demanding liberalization, increased competition and the need for financial stability and efficiency, as well as the problems associated with a shortage of skilled personnel, the SEC has recently liberalized its rules in relation to the merger of securities companies.[136] This has involved the issuance of various ministerial regulations and related notifications to facilitate such merger activity.

9.6.2   Derivatives legislation   Although Thailand has no specific legislation governing derivatives, derivatives transactions do in fact take place. However, the lack of a legal framework for derivatives has meant that certain financial institutions which are restricted from undertaking such transactions are deprived of an important financial tool, while non-financial institutions can, without any supervision, freely solicit the public to trade in derivatives contracts. In addition, those who have entered into derivatives transactions in good faith have faced uncertainty regarding the legal enforceability of such agreements.

As of June 1998 the proposed derivatives legislation has not yet been enacted.[137] As this publication goes to press, Thailand is seeking comment on its proposed Derivatives Market Act, which was submitted to the Ministry of Finance on 16 May 1997. The aims are to provide a regulatory scheme which will:

- create a legal certainty for derivative contracts;
- provide for a regulatory framework for derivatives markets and intermediaries;
- allow regulators to oversee the financial integrity of the market and take action to prevent adverse systemic effect.

9.6.3   The economic rehabilitation programme[138]   During 1997 Thailand's economy experienced a severe slowdown caused by such problems as a stagnant export growth, volatile foreign exchange rates and non-performing loans of financial institutions. These problems led to a crisis in confidence among Thai and foreign investors and entrepreneurs. Responding to these problems, the Thai government developed an economic rehabilitation programme which includes the following measures:

- changing the foreign exchange system, which used to be pegged to a basket of major currencies, to a floating system;
- securing loans from international organizations such as the International Monetary Fund, the World Bank, the Asian Development Bank, and neighbouring countries;
- addressing the problems of the 58 suspended financial institutions by establishing the Committee to Supervise the Merger and Acquisition of Financial Institutions.[139]

Other economic measures include:

- immediate measures:
  - monetary policy and instruments, and a stabilization programme for financial institutions,

- securing loans from abroad,
- the management of international reserves and the foreign exchange rate system,
- macro-economic targets and management plan;
● Medium-term measures:
- efficiency improvement and competitiveness enhancement, including the reduction of market distortions, privatization and the reform of the civil service,
- industrial restructuring and a financing plan,
- measures to minimize the social and environment at impact from the crisis and rehabilitation programme.[140]

10 Miscellaneous

10.1 Arbitration Law

Perhaps the most utilized remedy to resolve business disputes is arbitration. Thailand's relevant legislation is the Arbitration Act 1987. Section 10 of that Act provides:

In the case where any party commences any legal proceedings in court against any other party to the arbitration agreement in respect of any dispute agreed to be referred to arbitration, the party against whom the legal proceedings are commenced may file with the court a petition prior to the date of taking of evidence, or prior to the passing of the judgement in case where there is no taking of evidence, for an order to stay the legal proceedings, so that the parties may first proceed with the arbitration proceedings. Upon the court having completed the enquiry and it appears that there is nothing that causes the arbitration agreement to be null and void, inoperative or unenforceable by any other reasons or incapable of being performed, the court shall make an order staying the proceedings.

The Act (Sections 29, 30) also recognizes and provides for the enforcement of foreign arbitral awards. In the case of enforcement of foreign arbitral awards, the Arbitration Act provides:

Section 32. An application for the execution of a foreign arbitral award under the auspices of the Convention for the Execution of Foreign Arbitral Awards, signed at Geneva, 26 September 1927, shall be santioned by the court if the party applying for the execution can prove that the award fulfills all the following conditions:

(1) The award has been made in a territory of one of the High Contracting Parties to which the Convention for the Execution of Foreign

Arbitral Awards, signed at Geneva, 26 September 1927 applies, and between persons who are subject to the jurisdiction of one of the High Contracting Parties;

(2)   The award has been made by virtue of an arbitration agreement sanctioned by the Protocol on Arbitration Clauses, signed at Geneva, 24 September 1923;

(3)   The award has been made in pursuance of an arbitration agreement which is valid under the law applicable thereto;

(4)   The award has been made by the Arbitral Tribunal provided for in the arbitration agreement or constituted in the manner agreed upon by the parties;

(5)   The award has been made in conformity with the law governing the arbitration procedure;

(6)   The subject matter of the award is capable of settlement by arbitration under Thai law;

(7)   The award is binding and final in the country in which it has been made;

(8)   The recognition or enforcement of the award is not contrary to Thai law or public policy or good morals.

Section 33. The court may refuse recognition and enforcement of the award under Section 32 if it appears to the court that:

(1)   The award has been annulled in the country in which it was made;

(2)   The party against whom it is sought to use the award was not given notice of the arbitration proceedings in sufficient time to enable him to present his case; or that, being under a legal incapacity, he was not properly represented; or

(3)   The award does not deal with all the differences submitted to arbitration by the parties or contains decisions on matters beyond the scope of the arbitration agreement.

Section 34. An application for the execution of a foreign arbitral award under the auspices of the Convention on the Recognition and Enforcement of Foreign Arbitral Awards, done at New York, 10 June 1958, may be denied by the court, if the party against whom the execution of the award is sought can prove that:

(1)   Any party to the arbitration agreement was, under the law applicable to him, under some incapacity;

(2)   The arbitration agreement is not valid under the law to which the parties have subjected it or, failing any indication thereon, under the laws of the country where the award was made;

(3)   The party against whom the award is invoked was not given proper notice of the appointment of the arbitrator or of the arbitration proceedings or was otherwise unable to present his case;

(4)   The award contains decisions on matters beyond the scope of the submission to arbitration, provided that, if the decisions on matters submitted to arbitration can be separated from those not so submitted, that part of the award which contains decisions on matters submitted to arbitration may be recognised and enforced;

(5)   The composition of the arbitral authority or the arbitral procedure was not in accordance with the agreement of the parties, or, failing such agreement, was not in accordance with the law of the country where the arbitration took place; or

(6)   The award has not yet become binding on the parties, or has been set aside or suspended by a competent authority of the country in which, or under the law of which, that award was made. If merely an application for the setting aside or suspension of the award has been made to a competent authority, the court where the enforcement of the award is sought may, if it deems appropriate, adjourn the decision on the enforcement of the award and may also, on the application of the party claiming enforcement of the award, order the other party to give suitable security.

Section 35. The court may refuse recognition and enforcement of the award under Section 34 if it appears before the court that the subject matter of the dispute is not capable of settlement by arbitration under Thai law, or that the recognition or enforcement of the award would be contrary to the public policy or good morals or the principle of international reciprocity.

10.2   *Civil Remedies: the Law of Juristic Acts*

A detailed discussion of civil remedies is beyond the scope of this chapter. However, an important concept in relation to Thai commercial law is the notion of juristic acts. Parties to a contract must demonstrate not only formation of the contract, but also that they have satisfied the rules in relation to valid juristic acts. Book I of the CCC establishes basic principles underlying commercial conduct governing all 'juristic acts'.[141] To be valid as a juristic act, the parties must have had the capacity to commit the act; the parties will have declared their intent to freely enter into the act; and the form of the act will have been acceptable, that is the contract is in writing if required.[142] A particular juristic act may be held to be void or voidable. If void, it cannot be ratified.[143] However, if voidable, it can be ratified with the act, upon ratification, deemed to be valid from the date of the act.[144]

10.3   Ordinary and Limited Partnerships

In addition to private limited and public limited companies, the two other forms of doing business in Thailand are ordinary partnerships and limited partnerships.[145]

10.3.1   Ordinary partnerships   Ordinary partnerships are governed by the CCC. There are two types of ordinary partnership: registered[146] and unregistered. In the case of an ordinary registered partnership, the partnership is given a separate legal identity[147] and several statutory protections. This includes the right of a partner to claim against any third person who dealt with another partner to the partnership, even though that partner's name does not appear on the transaction. Also, upon ceasing to be a partner, the partner of a registered partnership will only be liable for two years after the resignation.[148] Partners in a registered partnership cannot, without consent of the partners, participate in a competing business.[149] However, a partner in a registered partnership is permitted to be a limited partner in another partnership.

In the case of unregistered ordinary partnerships, there is no separate legal identity and each partner is liable for all of the obligations of the partnership,[150] including for a period of ten years after the resignation of a partner from the partnership.

10.3.2   Limited partnerships   A limited partnership is characterized by one or more partners who are jointly and unlimitedly liable for all the obligations of the partnership and one or more 'limited' partners whose liability is limited to such an amount as they undertake to contribute to the partnership.[151] Management of the limited partnership must be undertaken only by the partners with unlimited liability, and a limited partner who holds himself out as more than that, will be treated as an unlimited partner.[152]

Limited partnerships must be registered and the following information provided:

- the name of the partnership;
- a statement that it is a limited partnership and the object of the partnership;
- the addresses of the principal business and all branch offices;
- the names, trade names, addresses and occupations of all limited partners and the amount of their contributions; and

- the names of the managing partners and the restrictions, if any, on them.[153]

This statement must be signed by every member of the partnership and sealed with the common seal of the partnership.[154] Until it is actually registered, a limited partnership is treated as an ordinary partnership with all members having unlimited liability.[155]

Upon the death of a limited partner, his or her heirs become limited partners in that partner's place.[156] If a limited partner becomes bankrupt, that share must be sold as an asset of the bankruptcy.[157]

10.4 Joint Ventures

Thailand does not recognize a joint venture as a separate legal entity except for taxation purposes. Foreign individuals may enter into a joint venture contract with Thai individuals involving the carrying on of a business in Thailand. A joint venture is usually for a limited purpose and ends on the completion of the particular project. A joint venture may also take the form of a private limited company, in which case it will be treated as described above in the discussion of private limited companies.[158]

10.5 Agency

The legal rules governing agency are found in Title XV of the CCC. Agency is defined as 'a contract whereby a person, called the agent, has authority for another person, called the principal, and agrees so to act'.[159] Agency may be expressed or implied.[160]

10.5.1 The powers of an agent An agent with general authority may do 'all acts of management on behalf of his principal'.[161] However, an agent ordinarily may not, on behalf of the principal, sell or mortgage immovable property, let immovable property for a period longer than three years, make a gift, make a compromise, file an action in court, or submit a dispute to arbitration.[162] Thailand also recognizes the doctrine of an undisclosed principal. An undisclosed principal may declare him or herself and assume any contract entered into on his or her behalf. However, the principal who allows an agent to act as a principal cannot prejudice the rights of the third person against the agent acquired before notice of the agency.[163]

10.5.2 The duties and liabilities of the agent An agent must act according to the express or implied direction of the principal.[164] The agent must give to the principal all moneys and other properties received in connection with the agency.[165] An agent is liable for any injury resulting from his or her negligence or non-execution of the agency, or from an act done without or in excess of authority.[166]

10.5.3   The duties and liabilities of the principal   A principal must advance to the agent such sums as necessary to execute the matters entrusted to him or her.[167] If the agent, in the execution of his or her duties to the principal, has suffered damage without fault on his or her part, the agent may claim compensation from the principal.[168] However, an agent is not entitled to claim compensation in respect of that part of his or her agency which was misconducted.[169] An agent is entitled to retain any part of the property of the principal in his possession by reason of the agency until the agent has been paid what is due to him or her on account of the agency.[170]

10.5.4   The liability of principal and agent to third persons   A principal is liable to third parties for any acts of an agent or sub-agent done on behalf of the principal and within the scope of the agent's authority.[171] A principal is also liable to third parties for the acts of any person held out by the principal as his or her agent or where the principal knowingly allows another person to do hold him or herself out as the principal's agent.[172] When contracting for a principal who is domiciled in a foreign country, an agent is personally liable on a contract to a third party, even though the name of the principal is disclosed, unless the terms of the contract are inconsistent with such liability.[173] A principal is not liable to a third party on a contract made by the agent in circumstances where the agent received consideration of any property or other advantage given privately to the agent by the third person, unless the principal has given his or her consent to such conduct by the third party.[174]

10.5.5   The extinction of agency   The principal may revoke or the agent may renounce the agency at any time, although the acting party may be liable for any consequential damages.[175] Unless the terms of the agreement or the nature of the business indicates otherwise, agency is also extinguished by the death, bankruptcy or incapacity of either party.[176] When an agency is extinguished by the death, bankruptcy or incapacity of the agent, the heir or the person having lawful charge of the agent's estate must notify the principal and take steps to protect the interests of the principal.[177] The extinction of an agency cannot be set up against a third person acting in good faith, unless the third person through his or her own ignorance is ignorant of the extinction of the agency.[178]

10.6   The Alien Businesses Law: Bi-lateral Treaties and Foreign Workers

Thailand places restrictions on the operation of foreign businesses through its Alien Business Law 1972.[179] The Act applies to:

- partnerships or companies formed abroad;
- partnerships or companies formed locally but with 50 per cent or more of the capital owned by foreigners, or where 50 per cent or more of the shareholders are foreigners; and
- locally registered partnership or limited partnership where the managing partner is a foreigner.

In practice, it is possible to get around these limitations by various loopholes. For example, in the case of a company, even though there is a restriction on foreign shareholders, there is no restriction on the number of foreign directors. In this way, foreigners could hold the majority of directors' positions and thus retain control.[180]

The Alien Business Law divides the economy into three classes or sectors in which foreign persons are prohibited or restricted from operating. Class A and B refers to particular businesses, such as rice farming, and services, such as legal practice. The law also restricts the amount of foreign investment in designated businesses, for example in rice farming, and in services, such as legal practice. Even here, however, investment is still possible so long as a majority of shares are held by Thai nationals.[181] In other designated businesses, foreigners may partake and hold a majority of shares, provided they register for and receive an Alien Business Licence.[182]

In addition, Thailand has made special arrangements via treaty. The most significant is the Treaty of Amity and Economic Relations Between the United States of America and the Kingdom of Thailand, which permits a Thai company with a majority of US shareholders or the branch of a US company to operate in designated sectors of the economy, including real estate, communications, transportation, banking, natural resources and agricultural resources.[183]

Finally, foreigners seeking work in Thailand should also be aware that there are restrictions in relation to the employment of foreign workers which must be checked out and complied with.[184]

Notes

* Professor of Law, Thammasat University, Bangkok.
** Dean of Faculty of Management and Professor of Law, University of Canberra.
1 See Hummel, A.L. and Sethsathira, P. (1991), *Starting and Operating a Business In Thailand*, Singapore: Asia Books Co Ltd, 6; see also Anderson, B.J. (1997),

'Thailand', in A. Gutterman and R. Brown (eds), *Commercial Laws of East Asia*, Hong Kong: Sweet & Maxwell Asia, 559–561; P. Phongpaichit and C. Baker (1998), *Thailand's Boom and Bust*, Chaing Mai: Silkworm Books.

2   As note 1 above, 6.

3   URL: http://www.www.parliament.go.th/GE/Chap-0.htm

4   Halligan, J. and Turner, M. (1995), *Profiles of Government Administration in Asia*, Canberra: AGPS, 164.

5   As note 4 above, 164–165.

6   URL: http://www.www.parliament.go.th/GE/Chap-IX.htm

7   As note 4 above, 221–223, 226–229.

8   As note 4 above, 160.

9   As note 4, above.

10   As note 4, above.

11   Anderson, B.J. (1997), 'Thailand', in A. Gutterman and R. Brown (eds), *Commercial Laws of East Asia*, Hong Kong: Sweet & Maxwell Asia, 559–561.

12   See generally, Charoenpanij, S. (1989), 'The Thai Legal system: The Law as an Agent of Environmental Protection', in *Culture and Environment in Thailand: A Symposium of the Siam Society*, Bangkok: the Siam Society, 463–473.

13   Readers are cautioned that commercial law in Thailand, as in many countries, is in a state of constant reform to bring it into line with requirements of a global economy. Readers should thus be careful to ensure that the law has not been updated since the time this chapter was written (January 1998).

14   See section 9, below.

15   See Anderson, as note 1, above, 560.

16   Section 1079 of the CCC and Section 16 of the PLCA.

17   Section 1098 of the CCC and Section 17 of the PLCA.

18   Section 1107 of the CCC and Section 27 of the PLCA.

19   Section 1108 of the CCC and Section 27 of the PLCA.

20   Section 1110 of the CCC and Section 37 of the PLCA.

21   Section 1111 of the CCC and Section 39 of the PLCA.

22   Section 24 of the PLCA. For a discussion of the Securities and Exchange Act, see section 9, below.

23   Supreme Court Decision, Case No. 734 of 1958.

24   Section 42 of the PLCA.

25   Section 1111(1) of the CCC and Section 35(4), (5) of the PLCA.

26   Section 1229 of the CCC. This is because the issue of debentures involves the collection of money from the public – an activity which private companies are prohibited from engaging in.

27   Section 145 of the PLCA.

28   This is in contrast to the corporations laws of England and the United States where the shareholders may, in certain circumstances, be responsible for the corporation's debts. For details of piercing of the corporate veil doctrine in the United Kingdom and the United States, see Cower, L.C.B. (1992), *Cower's Principles of Modern Company Law*, Fifth Edition, London: Sweet & Maxwell, 108–134; and Hamilton, R.W. (1987), *The Law of Corporation*, St. Paul, Minnesota: West Publishing Co. 81–99.

29   Section 1144 of the CCC.

30   Section 67 of the PLCA.

31   Section 68 of the PLCA.

32   Section 67 of the PLCA.

33   Section 1151 of the CCC.

34   Section 70 of the PLCA.

35   Section 77 of the PLCA.

36   Sections 1153–1156 of the CCC and Sections 71–72 of the PLCA.

37 Section 1167 of the CCC and Section 97 of the PLCA.
38 In practice, there is more than one director in every company.
39 Section 1144 of the CCC and Section 77 of the PLCA.
40 The position in Thai law is somewhat different from that occurring in England and the United States, where, at present, the *ultra vires* doctrine has been restricted so that the companies cannot invoke it as a defence to enable the company to avoid responsibility for the *ultra vires* act of its directors. See Cower, as note 28, above, 166–170; and Hamilton, as note 28, above, 51–59.
41 Supreme Court Decision, case No. 992 of 1954.
42 Section 1168 of the CCC and Section 85 of the PLCA; Supreme Court Decision, Case No. 1141 of 1959 and No. 3747 of 1983.
43 Section 1169 of the CCC and Section 85 of the PLCA.
44 Supreme Court Decision, Case No. 220 of 1941.
45 Section 1171 of the CCC.
46 Section 98 of the PLCA.
47 Section 1173 of the CCC.
48 Section 100 of the PLCA.
49 Section 1178 of the CCC. Nevertheless, one of Thailand's distinguished lawyers is of the opinion that even in a situation where one shareholder attends the company meeting, such meeting can be a general meeting. See Charoenpitak, T. (1961), *Explanation in Details on Partnerships and Companies*, Bangkok: Kamchang Co. Ltd., 454. However, the authors are of view that there must be at least two shareholders at a company meeting to constitute a quorum.
50 Section 103 of the PLCA.
51 Section 1187 of the CCC and Section 102 of the PLCA.
52 Sections 1182 and 1190 of the CCC.
53 Section 1020 of the PLCA.
54 Section 1194 of the CCC.
55 Section 1195 of the CCC and Section 108 of the PLCA; Supreme Court Decision, Case No. 2644 of 1977, No. 111 of 1978, No. 2278 of 1984 and No. 2564 of 1989.
56 Section 1200 of the CCC and Section 115 of the PLCA.
57 Section 1201 of the CCC and Section 115 of the PLCA; Supreme Court Decision, Case No. 461 of 1954.
58 For details of this principle, see Cower, as note 28, above, 212.
59 Section 1202 of the CCC and Section 116 of the PLCA.
60 Section 1203 of the CCC and Section 118 of the PLCA.
61 Chapter VIII, Sections 109ff of the PLCA.
62 Sections 113–114 of the PLCA.
63 Sections 1206–1207 of the CCC and Section 109 of the PLCA.
64 Sections 1196–1198 of the CCC and Sections 112, 125 of the PLCA.
65 Section 1209 of the CCC and Section 120 of the PLCA.
66 Section 1208 of the CCC and Section 121 of the PLCA.
67 Section 1213 of the CCC and Section 122 of the PLCA.
68 Section 1214 of the CCC and Section 1253 of the PLCA.
69 Section 127 of the PLCA.
70 See generally, Chapter IX of the PLCA.
71 Section 1215 of the CCC and Section 128 of the PLCA.
72 Ratanakom, S. (1996), *Explanation on the Civil and Commercial Code Concerning Partnerships and Companies*, Fifth Edition, Bangkok: Nitibunakarn, 454.
73 Thannapatoke, L.S. (1960), *Lecture on the Civil and Commercial Code Concerning Partnerships and Companies*, Bangkok: Nitibunakarn, 237.
74 Section 1216 of the CCC and Section 130 of the PLCA.

75　Section 1217 of the CCC and Section 131 of the PLCA.
76　Section 1218 of the CCC and Sections 134–135 of the PLCA.
77　Section 1220 of the CCC.
78　Section 136 of the PLCA.
79　Section 1222 of the CCC and Section 137 of the PLCA.
80　Section 1228 of the CCC and Section 138 of the PLCA.
81　Sections 1224–1225 of the CCC and Section 139 of the PLCA.
82　Section 1224 of the CCC.
83　Section 139 of the PLCA.
84　Section 1226 of the CCC and Section 142 of the PLCA.
85　Section 1228 of the CCC and Section 142 of the PLCA.
86　Supreme Court Decision, Case No. 223 of 1963 and No. 2301 of 1983.
87　Section 1236 of the CCC. The principal law governing insolvency of companies in Thailand is the *Bankruptcy Act* BE 2483 (1940). See generally, Tomasic, R. and Little, P. (1997), *Insolvency Law & Practice in Asia*, Hong Kong: FT Law & Tax, Chapter 8, 229–256.
88　Section 154 of the PLCA.
89　Section 1237 of the CCC and Section 155 of the PLCA.
90　Section 1237 of the CCC.
91　Section 1237 of the CCC and Section 155 of the PLCA.
92　Section 1237 of the CCC and Section 155 of the PLCA.
93　Supreme Court Decision, Case No. 1774 of 1979.
94　Ratariakom, as note 72, above, 468.
95　Section 1251 of the CCC.
96　Section 163 of the PLCA.
97　This power only exist in relation to pending business, not to transacting new business.
98　Section 1259 of the CCC and Section 160 of the PLCA.
99　Section 1270 of the CCC and Section 176 of the PLCA
100　Section 239 of the CCC and Section 146 of the PLCA.
101　Section 1240 of the CCC and Section 147 of the PLCA.
102　If the companies to be amalgamated have already sold their shares according to the number registered, an increase in capital may be made at the same time.
103　Section 148 of the PLCA.
104　Section 1241 of the CCC and Section 151 of the PLCA.
105　Section 1243 of the CCC and Section 153 of the PLCA.
106　See Anderson, as note 1, above, 565–566.
107　As note 106, above.
108　http://www.mof.go.th/dpm/vpongfin.htm (29 October 1997).
109　As note 108, above. Note also the conclusions and recommendations by the Thailand Development Research Institute's Working Group in Economic Structure, reported in 'TDRI Underscores Flaws in Economy', *Nation*, 5 June 1998, A2. Competition law reform is likely to be on the political agenda for some time to come as Thailand continues to fall in its world ranking of competitiveness among nations. See 'Thailand Losing Competitiveness', *Nation*, 6 June 1998, sec. 8 'Business', b2, According to the World Economic Forum's Global Competitiveness Report 1998, Thailand was ranked 21st in 1998, compared to 18th in 1997 and 14th in 1996.
110　Harrison, M. (1991), *Asia-Pacific Securities Markets*, Hong Kong: Longman, 327ff.
111　Legislation authorizing the exchange was passed in 1974: *Securities Exchange of Thailand Act*.
112　URL: http://www.sec.or.th/about/profil4e.html

113 The general organization of the Commission is covered in Chapter 1, Divisions 1 and 2, Sections 8–31.
114 Chapter 4, Sections 90–93 of the SEA.
115 As note 114, above.
116 Sections 114, 238–244 of the SEA.
117 Sections 238–244 of the SEA.
118 Sections 204–217 of the SEA.
119 Sections 112–113, 116 of the SEA.
120 Section 115 of the SEA.
121 Sections 117–132 of the SEA.
122 Sections 133–140 of the SEA.
123 Sections 230–237 of the SEA.
124 Sections 201–203 of the SEA.
125 Sections 204–217 of the SEA.
126 Sections 334–335 of the SEA.
127 The Office of the Securities and Exchange Commission, Thailand, 14th-16th Fl., Diethelm Towers B, 93/1 Wireless Road, Lumpini, Patumwan, Bangkok 10330, Tel.: (662) 252–3223, Fax: (662) 256–7711. Any enquiry or comment to info@sec.or.th
128 URL: http://www.sec.or.th/about/profil4e.html
129 As note 128, above.
130 As note 128, above.
131 As note 128, above.
132 As note 126, above.
133 As note 126, above.
134 As note 126, above.
135 URL: http://www.or.th/indexe.html
136 SEC Meeting 4/2540 dated 3 April 1997.
137 URL: http://www.sec.or.th/indexe.html
138 http://www.mof.go.th/dpm/vpongfin.htm (29 October 1997).
139 As note 136, above.
140 As note 139, above: See also Vinaphol, Dr. 5. (1998), 'Wooing back the necessary overseas capital to Asia', *The Nation*, 5 June, 175.
141 See Anderson, as note 1, above, 569.
142 Sections 112–113 of the CCC.
143 Section 134 of the CCC.
144 Section 140 of the CCC.
145 The law governing partnerships is found primarily in Title XXII, Sections 1012ff of the CCC.
146 See generally, Part V, Sections 1064ff of the CCC.
147 Section 1065 of the CCC.
148 Section 1068 of the CCC.
149 Section 1066 of the CCC
150 Section 1050 of the CCC.
151 Section 1077 of the CCC.
152 Sections 1085–1088 of the CCC.
153 Section 1078 of the CCC.
154 As note 153, above.
155 Section 1080 of the CCC.
156 Section 1093 of the CCC.
157 Section 1094 of the CCC.
158 Hummel and Sethsathira, as note 1, above, at 27.
159 Section 797 of the CCC.
160 As note 157, above.

161   Section 801 of the CCC.
162   As note 159, above.
163   Section 806 of the CCC.
164   Section 807 of the CCC.
165   Section 810 of the CCC.
166   Section 812 of the CCC.
167   Section 815 of the CCC.
168   Section 816 of the CCC.
169   Section 818 of the CCC.
170   Section 819 of the CCC.
171   Section 820 of the CCC.
172   Section 822 of the CCC.
173   Section 824 of the CCC.
174   Section 825 of the CCC.
175   Sections 826–827 of the CCC.
176   Section 826 of the CCC.
177   Section 829 of the CCC.
178   Section 831 of the CCC.
179   National Executive Council, Announcement 281. The Alien Business Law has been much criticized and the last four Thai governments have all promised to reform it, but none has succeeded. See Theparat, C. (1998), 'Japanese firms lobby for Alien Business Law changes', *Bangkok Post*, 30 May, 8.
180   Hummel and Sethsathira, as note 1, above, at 29.
181   As note 180, above, 30–32.
182   As note 180, above, 32–33.
183   Anderson, as note 1, above, 581–582.
184   Hummel and Sethsathira, as note 1, above, 29. The Alien Business Law has been amended to make it easier for foreign investors to carry on a brokerage business in Thailand (Annex C). See K. Urapecpatangpong and K.K. Khamsirivatchara (1998), 'Securities Law Develops to Attract Foreign Investors', *Asia Pacific Legal Developments Bulletin*, **13**(3), October, 50–52.

Further Reading

Asawaroj, S. (1985), *Explanation on Comparative Business Law*, Bangkok: The Faculty of Law, Thammasat University.

Auychai, P. (1987), *Explanation on the Civil and Commercial Code Concerning Partnerships and Companies*, Bangkok: The Legal Institution of the Thai Bar Association.

Chantawirach, T. (1993), *Summary on Law Concerning Partnerships and Companies*, Bangkok: Winyoochon.

Choonhaural, P. (1988), *Explanation on Law Concerning Partnerships and Companies*, Bangkok: Nitibunakarn.

Cliareonpitak, T. (1961), *Explanation of Details on Partnerships and Companies*, Bangkok: Karnchang Co. Ltd.

Gower, L.C.B. (1992), *Gower's Principles of Modern Company Law*, Fifth Edition, London: Sweet & Maxwell.

Hamilton, R.W. (1987), *The Law of Corporation*, St. Paul, Minnesota: West Publishing Co.

Luang, S.T. (1960), *Lecture on the Civil and Commercial Code Concerning Partnerships and Companies*, Bangkok: Nitibunakarn.

Ratanakorn, S. (1996), *Explanation on the Civil and Commercial Code Concerning Partnerships and Companies*, Fifth Edition, Bangkok: Nitibunakarn.

Seline, C. (1997), *Business Guide to Thailand*, Hong Kong: Butterworths Asia.
Setasathien, P. (1991), *Limited Companies*, Bangkok: Nitithum.
Sumawong, P. (1968), *Explanation on the Civil and Commercial Code Concerning Partnerships and Companies*, Bangkok: Praekarnchang.
Wiwatpatrakul, P. (1992), 'Legal Concept on the Company's Share Capital', *Botbundit Cjune*, **48** (2), 49–65.

Relevant World Wide Web Sites About Thailand

History of Thailand
URL: http://pugetsound.com/tha

Country Information – Thailand (Business)
URL: http://www.ait.ac.th/Asia/business.html
URL: http://infomanage.com/int (US State Dept Background Briefing on Thailand)
URL: http://www.thaicon.th.com/trading/thaifact.htm (fact sheets: Thailand Geography. Government. Population. Thailand's Economic Profile)

Organizations in Thailand
Academic and Research Organizations. Government, State Enterprises and Organizations.
URL: http://www.thaicon.th.com/visitors/thaiweb.htm

Thailand Business Directories (SiamBusiness)
URL: http://www.siamweb.co.th/business/finances.htm

Ministry of Finance
URL: http://www.mof.go.th/

The Stock Exchange of Thailand
URL: http://www.sino.net/stock/stock.htm

Thailand – Market Access and Competition
A US perspective on the degree of market access in Thailand.
URL: http://www.stat-usa.gov/b

Asian Financial Markets
URL: http://www.unomaha.edu/~salaymeh/asia.html
(includes Thailand)

Asian & Mid East News & Information Resources
URL: http://www.ozsoft.com/asia.htm
(includes Thai financial markets)

Foreign Banks in Thailand
URL: http://bkk.w3.net.th/FD-o

Currency – Exchange in Thailand
URL: http://www.wiso.gwdg.de/ifbg./currency.html
Provides daily exchange rates for 48 currencies

The 1996 Thailand's Stock Market Review and the Trend in 1997
URL: http://www.tfb.co.th/tfrc96/dec/atfi328b.htm

Thailand: Business: Bank and Investing
URL: http://pundit.ce.kmitl.ac.th/business/bank/

Thailand: News: Business News
Monthly Economic Statistics from Board of Trade.
URL: http://pundit.ce.kmitl.ac.th/news/business/

Banks in Thailand
URL: http://www.siamweb.co.th/business/bank/

Finance and Investment – NetGuide to Bangkok
URL: http://www.bangkoknet.com

Asia's 'Wall-Street'
Financial Institutions in Singapore, Thailand, Malaysia and Indonesia.
URL: http://www.asiatrade.com/

Exchange Regulations in Thailand
URL: http://ipod2.bot.or.th/exchange.html

Thailand-related links on the Net
URL: http://www.hkdata.se/thailand/thailand.html

International Business Practices In Thailand
URL: http://www.smartbiz.com/sbs/arts/bpr80.htm

Taxation in the Asia-Pacific Region/Thailand
Deloitte & Touche
URL: http://www.dtonline.com/asia/thailand.htm

10 Company Law in Malaysia

DR KRISHNAN ARJUNAN*

1 Introduction

The judicial and legal system in Malaysia is essentially based on the English common law model. The Courts of Judicature Act 1964 governs the structure and jurisdiction of the various courts. The highest court in the land is the Federal Court, appeals to the Privy Council having been abolished. The other important courts are the Magistrate's Court, the Sessions Court, the High Court and the Court of Appeal, with the High Court also having some appellate jurisdiction. There is a fused legal profession, practising lawyers being both advocates and solicitors with a right of audience in all courts.

For the purposes of matters connected with the companies legislation, the High Court (or a judge thereof) has original jurisdiction. In some cases specific provision is made granting jurisdiction to lower courts; an example of this is the Magistrate's and Sessions Court's jurisdiction over prosecutions for offences under the Companies Act.

2 Companies Legislation

The Companies Act 1965 (CA) together with the Companies Regulations 1966 and the Companies (Winding-Up) Rules 1972 made thereunder govern the regulation of companies in Malaysia. The CA was modelled on the English Companies Act 1948 and the Australian Uniform Companies Act 1961. The CA is not a self-contained code on companies. Common law principles continue to be relevant and applicable. In view of the historical origins of the CA, company law in Malaysia is greatly influenced by case-law in England and Australia. Although cases from these jurisdictions are not technically binding, they are highly persuasive and are frequently cited in and accepted as authorities by the Malaysian courts. However, with the passage of time and the development of case-law and amendments to companies' legislation in Malaysia, England and Australia, there is an increasing divergence among these jurisdictions.

It is doubtful whether provisions of the English Companies Act may be applied in Malaysia in cases where there is a *lacuna* in the Act. Under Section 5(1) of the Civil Law Act 1956, English law may be applicable to fill the gap 'unless in any case other provision is or shall be made by any written law'. Judicial opinion on the issue is divided. On the one hand, the Federal Court has held in *Tan Mooi Liang v Lim Soon Eng*,[1] that English partnership law was inapplicable in Malaysia as the provisions relating to partnership in the Contracts (Malay States) Ordinance 1950 constituted 'other provisions' within the meaning of Section 5(1) of the Civil Law Act. On the other hand, there are at least two High Court decisions to the contrary: *Re Low Noi Brothers & Co.*[2] and *Sharikat Import dan Export & Perindusterian Timbering Sdn Bhd v Othman bin Taib*.[3] Although both of these decisions were directly concerned with company law provisions and the Federal Court's decision dealt with partnership provisions, the better view is perhaps that the Companies Act would constitute 'other provision' within the meaning of the Civil Law Act. The contrary view would virtually emasculate the Act.

Apart from the CA, there is the Offshore Companies Act 1990 which is part of a scheme of legislation aimed at setting up the Federal Territory of Labuan as an International Offshore Financial Centre. Companies registered under the Offshore Companies Act generally do not come within the purview of the CA. Further, securities and futures are regulated by the Securities Industry Act 1983 and the Securities Commission Act 1993. Under the Malaysian Constitution, the federal government has responsibility, by virtue of the federal power relating to corporations, to legislate and implement laws relating to companies. The CA has a general interpretation section[4] for the purposes of defining terms used in it. Apart from this, the Interpretation Acts 1948 and 1967 and the general law relating to construction of statutes apply.[5]

3   The Nature and Powers of Corporate Regulatory Bodies

The responsibility for overseeing the regulation of companies and the securities and futures industries is dispersed in a number of agencies. The nature and powers of these bodies may be summarized as follows.

3.1   *The Registrar of Companies*

The prime responsibility for the administration of the CA rests with the registrar of companies, appointed by the minister under Section 7(1) of the Act. He or she is assisted by a number of regional registrars, deputy registrars and assistant registrars and other supporting staff. The registrar's primary duty is to ensure that companies are conducted properly in compliance with the provisions of the CA. To do this the registrar is given wide powers, including the right to enter premises, seize documents and compel the giving of oral testimony.[6]

3.2   *The Kuala Lumpur Stock Exchange*

This is a self-regulatory body incorporated as a company in 1976 with the aim of enforcing a set of rules in regard to securities dealings by members. It has primary responsibility for the maintenance of an efficient market and implementation of the listing rules which set out the criteria for public flotation of companies and other obligations. It also oversees the disclosure requirements and corporate conduct of public listed companies. Its rules are subject to amendment by the Minister of Finance. It has an obligation to render any assistance or cooperation as may be necessary to the registrar of companies and the Securities Commission.

3.3   *The Securities Commission*

This commission was established in 1993, pursuant to the Securities Commission Act of that year. Its primary responsibility is to advise the Minister of Finance on matters relating to the securities and futures industries. In this endeavour, it has the duty to supervise and monitor activities of any exchange, clearing house or central depository. It also has the responsibility to stamp out illegal, improper or dishonourable practices in securities and futures dealings. Since its inception, the commission has assumed the functions of the Panel on Takeovers and Mergers.

3.4   *Foreign Investment Committee*

The regulation of mergers and takeovers is further circumscribed by the requirements of the Foreign Investment Committee. This is a government body entrusted with the responsibility of overseeing proposed acquisitions, mergers and takeovers, with a view to ensuring that the activity in question would result in Malaysian control and participation. The committee has issued guidelines – the

Guidelines on the Regulation of Acquisition of Assets, Mergers and Takeovers (better known as the 'FIC Guidelines'). Any proposal for acquisition, merger or takeover must comply with these guidelines, which ensure that the proposal is in the national interest. The onus of proving that the proposal is in the national interest is on the party proposing. However, the guidelines are not relevant in cases where the Malaysian government has approved special projects.

3.5 The Capital Issues Committee

The Capital Issues Committee was set up in 1968 by the Minister of Finance. However, it was not formally established until the advent of the Securities Industry Act 1983. The primary role of the committee is to oversee the orderly development of the capital market by regulating the issue of securities by public limited companies and/or the listing of such securities on a stock exchange in Malaysia. The committee follows a set of guidelines in considering proposals from public companies, in order to ensure consistency. The guidelines relate, *inter alia*, to public issues or offers for sale of securities, public offerings of interests in time-sharing arrangements and club memberships, and issues of securities arising from, among others, rights issues and bonus issues.

4 A Description of the Types of Companies

The CA recognizes[7] four types of local companies which may be incorporated by two or more persons associated for a lawful purpose. These are:

- companies limited by shares;
- companies limited by guarantee;
- companies limited by both shares and guarantee; and
- unlimited companies.

Companies may be public or private companies; public companies may invite the public to invest money in them, whereas private companies are prohibited from doing so. Private companies must also have further clauses stated in their memorandum or articles restricting the transfer of shares, limiting the number of members to 50 and prohibiting the company from inviting the public to deposit money with the company.[8]

The CA also recognizes foreign companies. A foreign company is defined as a company, corporation, society, association or other body incorporated outside Malaysia, or an unincorporated society, association or other body which under the law of its place of origin may sue or be sued, or hold property in the name of the secretary or other officer of the body or association duly appointed for that purpose, and which does not have its head office or principal place of business in Malaysia.[9]

A foreign company intending to establish a place of business in Malaysia must be registered under the CA. The documents required to enable registration are set out in the CA.[10] The provisions of Part XI of Division 2 apply to foreign companies.

Companies, being artificial legal persons, have the capacity of engaging only in activities specified in the objects clause in the memorandum. Companies may also avail themselves of the Third Schedule powers.[11] Any activity outside of the stated objects would be *ultra vires* the company. However, the common law doctrine of *ultra vires* has been modified in Malaysia.[12] Under the modified version, no act or purported act of a company and no conveyance or transfer of property, real or personal, to or by a company is invalid by reason only that the company was without capacity or power to do the act or to execute the conveyance or transfer.[13] Further, the want of capacity or power may be raised only in the circumstances specified,[14] namely:

- in proceedings against the company by any member thereof, or, where the company has issued debentures secured by a floating charge, by the holder of the debentures or his or her trustee to restrain the doing of any act or acts or the conveyance or transfer to or by the company;
- in any proceedings by the company or by any member of the company against the present or former officers of the company; or
- any petition by the minister to wind up the company.

The court has powers to order compensation for loss sustained as a result of the court restraining the performance of a contract to which the company is a party.[15]

5 The Formation of Companies

Persons desiring the incorporation of a company must lodge with the registrar of companies the memorandum and articles (if any) of the proposed company, together with the other documents required by the CA.[16] On payment of the requisite fees and subject to the CA, the registrar will register the company and issue a certificate of incorporation, whereupon the subscribers to the memorandum and others who may become members from time to time, are a body corporate and have all the attributes of a separate legal entity.[17]

The promoters[18] of the company are in a fiduciary relationship with the company and, hence, have an obligation to act *bona fide* and avoid a conflict of interest with the company promoted.

The memorandum and articles of association of a company together form its constitution. The memorandum is the more important document as it contains provisions concerning the relationship of outsiders dealing with the company. Every company which seeks registration must lodge a memorandum of association.[19] The memorandum must contain the name of the company, an objects clause, a share capital clause, a liability clause, an association clause and a subscriber clause setting out the particulars of the subscribers. The association clause is a statement that the subscribers are desirous of forming a company and agree to take the specified number of shares. The subscriber clause states the number of shares the subscribers agree to take, in the case of a company with a share capital.[20]

Although every company must have a memorandum, not all companies need lodge articles; companies limited by shares need not file their own articles.[21] If such a company does not lodge its own articles, the regulations in Table A of the Fourth Schedule of the Act will apply.[22] The articles of a company are the regulations governing its internal management. The memorandum and articles have the effect of a contract under seal between the company and each member and between members *inter se*.[23]

The memorandum may be altered only to the extent and in the manner provided by the CA.[24] The articles may be altered by special resolution, but any alteration is subject to the CA and the memorandum.[25] However, members are not bound by any alteration of the memorandum or articles in so far as the alteration requires them to take, or subscribe for, more shares than the number held at the date of the alteration or in any way increases their liability to contribute to the share capital of, or otherwise to pay money to, the company, unless they have agreed in writing to be bound by such alterations.[26]

As noted above, the name of the company must be stated in the memorandum. However, there are certain formalities and restrictions with regard to the use of names. A company limited by shares or guarantee is required to have the word 'Berhad' or its abbreviation 'Bhd' as part of its name.[27] Further, a private company must have the word 'Sendirian' or its abbreviation 'Sdn' immediately before the word 'Berhad' or 'Bhd'.[28] A company cannot be registered in a name that is, in the opinion of the registrar of companies, undesirable or is a name of a kind that the minister has directed the registrar not to accept for registration. In view of this, a proposed company or foreign company must first apply to the registrar in the prescribed form for a search regarding the availability of the name. If the registrar is satisfied as to the *bona fides* of the application and that the proposed name is not undesirable or one which the minister has directed not to accept, the name is reserved for three months.[29] During this period no company will be registered with the reserved name or one which closely resembles the reserved name.[30] A foreign company is also subject to similar restrictions and cannot use any name other than the one it is registered under.[31]

Upon incorporation, a company is obliged to establish a number of registers. These are registers in respect of:

- directors, managers and secretaries;[32]
- members;[33]
- debenture holders;[34]
- directors' interests in shares, debentures, participatory interests, rights, options and contracts with the company;[35]
- substantial shareholders;[36]
- information regarding beneficial ownership of shares;[37] and
- charges.[38]

6   Internal Administration of Companies

6.1   *The Registered Office*

A company is obliged to have a registered office within Malaysia as from the day it commences business or from the fourteenth day after its incorporation, whichever is the earlier, and the office must be open and accessible to the public for at least three hours during ordinary business hours each day.[39] Notice of the situation of the registered office and any change must be given to the registrar of companies in the prescribed form.[40]

6.2   *The Duties and Powers of Officers*

The two main organs of the company are the general meeting and the board of directors. The general management of the company is usually in the hands of the directors. Article 73 of Table A (the 'model' articles) states that the business of the company shall be managed by the directors and that they may exercise all such powers of the company as are not, by the CA or the articles, required to be exercised by the company in general meeting. The directors' power to manage also includes the power to pay all expenses incurred in promoting and registering the company,[41] to borrow money and to mortgage or charge the company's undertaking, property and uncalled capital.[42]

Directors are in a fiduciary relationship with the company they serve. They have a duty to act *bona fide* in the interests of the company as a whole. This duty is subjective, in the sense that directors will not be in breach if they honestly believe that their action was in the interests of the company, as courts are reluctant to substitute their opinion for that of the business judgment of the directors. The directors normally have to look after the interests of the shareholders. However, when the company is in financial straits, the directors are obliged to take into consideration the interests of creditors as well.

The CA also imposes a like duty on officers. Officers of a company are required at all times to act honestly in the exercise of their duties of office.[43] Breach of this duty renders the officers guilty of an offence and liable to account to the company for any profit made as well as to make good any loss caused to it.[44]

Directors and officers have a duty to exercise powers for proper purposes. This duty is wider than the duty to act in the interest of the company as a whole. Directors may be in breach of this duty even if they honestly believed that their actions were in the interests of the company. Most cases with regard to this duty have had to do with directors' power to issue shares. The courts have generally held that an allotment of shares would be invalidated if the impermissible purpose is causative, in the sense that no allotment would have been made but for its presence.[45]

There is a duty, too, to avoid conflict of interest. Directors must not place themselves in circumstances where their personal interests may conflict with their duty. Consequently, it is generally not permissible for directors to make personal profits out of their office, accept bribes, misuse company funds, use confidential information or compete with the company.[46]

The duties of care, skill and diligence apply to directors. These duties demand that directors carry out their functions with a reasonable standard of care and skill. The traditional approach was seen in *Re Equitable Fire Insurance Co. Ltd.*[47] Recent cases have moved away from the subjective qualities of particular directors applied in *Re Equitable*. The present standard of care and skill expected of directors is much higher.[48]

6.3   Meetings

Inasmuch as the articles are concerned with internal management of a company, they also contain provisions relating to meetings and the manner in which they are to be conducted. The CA also has some provisions in this regard. They are to be found in Division 3, Sections 142–157.

Under these provisions, at least four types of meeting may be identified. These are as follows.

6.3.1   A statutory meeting   Under Section 142(1) of the CA, a public limited company having a share capital must hold a statutory meeting within a period of not less than one month and not more than three months after the date on which it becomes entitled to commence business. The directors are obliged to send members a statutory report containing information relating to certain matters, including the allotment of shares, the amount of cash received, and the particulars of directors, trustees and debenture holders.

6.3.2   An annual general meeting   Under Section 143(1) of the CA, other than the first annual general meeting, a company is obliged to hold an annual general meeting at least once in every calendar year and not more than 15 months after the holding of the last preceding annual general meeting. Certain accounts must be laid before the annual general meeting, including the profit and loss account, the balance sheet and the directors' and auditor's reports. The usual business transacted at an annual general meeting includes the election of directors, the declaration of dividends and the appointment and remuneration of auditors.

6.3.3   An extraordinary general meeting   All meetings other than the annual general meeting are extraordinary general meetings (Table A, Article 43). Power to convene an extraordinary general meeting is usually vested in the directors (Table A, Article 44). However, such a meeting may also be requisitioned by members if the conditions in Section 144(1) of the CA are satisfied. Business transacted at an extraordinary general meeting is known as 'special business' (Table A, Article 46).

6.3.4   A class meeting   Where a company has issued different classes of shares, class meetings may be necessary for obtaining shareholders' consent for variation of their class rights. The CA and the articles make provision for governing the conduct of these meetings (Section 65 and Table A, Article 5).

6.3.5   Other meetings   Members may also convene meetings other than general meetings if the conditions of Section 145(1) of the CA are satisfied. Articles 47–62 of Table A govern the proceedings at general meetings.

6.4   Audit and Accounting

Disclosure of financial information lies at the heart of corporate governance. The CA contains a traditional set of provisions in Division 5 of Part V ('Annual Return') and Part VI ('Accounts and Audit').

Under Section 165(1) of the CA every company having a share capital must make a return containing the particulars in Part I of the Eighth Schedule to the Act. The return is to be accompanied by copies of the documents prescribed by Part II of the Eighth Schedule, together with any relevant certificates. The return must be in the form set out in that Schedule or as near thereto as possible. The return is required to be made up to the date of the annual general meeting of the company or a date not later than the fourteenth day after the date of the general meeting.

Section 165(5) of the CA makes similar provision in respect of companies without a share capital.

Exempt private companies are excused from including certain financial documents, such as the balance sheet and the profit and loss account, with the annual return if the return includes a certificate required by Part II of the Eighth Schedule.

Every company is obliged to keep accounting and other records as would correctly record and sufficiently explain its transactions and financial position. Under Section 167(1) of the CA, the accounting records must be kept in such a manner as to facilitate the preparation of true and fair accounts which may be conveniently and properly audited.

Where related companies operate in a group, directors of holding companies are required by Section 169 of the CA to prepare consolidated accounts dealing with the profit and loss of the holding company and its subsidiaries for their respective financial years. If any director fails to comply or take reasonable steps to secure compliance with the accounts provisions, he commits an offence (Section 171(1)).

Division 2 of Part VI of the CA contains provisions relating to the appointment, duties and powers of auditors. Section 9 sets out provisions with regard to the disqualifications of persons acting as auditors. Every company must appoint an auditor. Appointment must be made before the first annual general meeting of the company. Primary duty to appoint lies with the directors. If the directors do not appoint, the company may do so in the general meeting. If the company does not do so, the registrar of companies may do so on the application of a member.[49]

The principal function of the auditor is to carry out an audit and report on the accounts and financial position of the company. Section 174(2) of the CA requires that his report contain his opinion as to whether the company's accounts have been properly drawn up in accordance with the provisions of the CA and so as to give a true and fair view of the matters required by Section 169 to be dealt with in the accounts and consolidated accounts. Further, under Section 174(3) of the CA, the auditor has a duty to form an opinion on the matters specified therein and state particulars of any deficiency, failure or shortcoming in respect of any of those matters.

6.5 Shareholder Protection

It has already been noted that the general management of the company lies in the hands of the board of directors. It is a basic principle of company law that the majority rule prevails. The directors owe fiduciary duties to the company as a whole. However, except in special circumstances,[50] they do not owe fiduciary duties to individual shareholders.[51] Nevertheless, they must act *bona fide* and fairly in the interests of the shareholders as a group. Violation of this rule is often referred to as a fraud on the minority. Company law, therefore, has had to make provision for the protection of minority interests. Under common law, the right of a member to commence legal proceedings to remedy wrongs done to the company or to rectify internal irregularities is circumscribed by the rule in *Foss v Harbottle*.[52] This rule is twofold: it first stipulates that courts will not generally interfere with internal irregularities of a company; and second that if a wrong is done to the company, the proper plaintiff is the company itself and not individual members. In certain exceptional cases the rule does not apply and individual shareholders may commence an action against the company. These cases are where:

- there is a fraud on the minority;
- the act in question is illegal or *ultra vires*;
- personal rights are infringed;
- special majorities are prescribed; and
- where the justice of the case demands it.

However, in view of the inadequacy of the common law remedies, the legislature has had to make specific provision in the CA for the protection of minority shareholders. The main provision is Section 181, which is broadly based on Section 210 of the English Companies Act 1948. Under Section 181(1), a member, debenture holder or the minister (in the case of declared company under Part IX of the Act), may apply to the court for an order to remedy conduct where:

- the affairs of the company are being conducted or the powers of the directors are being exercised in a manner oppressive to

one or more of the members or holders of debentures, or in disregard of their interests as members, shareholders or holders of debentures of the company; or
- some act of the company has been done or is threatened, or some resolution of the members, holders of debentures or any class has been passed or is proposed, which unfairly discriminates against or is otherwise prejudicial to one or more of the members or holders of debentures.

As is apparent from the above, Section 181 covers a wide range of conduct, including cases of fraud on the minority and the 'just and equitable' ground for winding up under Section 218(1)(i) of the CA. The matters in Section 181(1) also constitute grounds for winding up under Section 218(1)(f) (directors acting in the affairs of the company in their own interests). However, despite its wide terminology, courts are reluctant to intervene in the affairs of companies unless bad faith is established.[53] Although based on the English Companies Act of 1948, the scope of Section 181 is wider than its English counterpart.[54]

As pointed out above, the responsibility for the general management of a company rests with the board of directors. However, the general meeting may also be given specific powers under the Act or the articles. Thus, the board and the general meeting are complementary organs of a company. In the normal course of events, shareholders, even in general meeting, cannot interfere with decisions of the board of directors.[55] Thus, the passing of a resolution by members in general meeting to override the board's decisions is ineffective.[56]

6.6   Corporate Financial Transactions

By virtue of Section 19 and the Third Schedule of the CA, a company has specific powers to issue debentures, give security for loans by charging its uncalled capital and granting floating charges over its property. 'Debenture' is broadly defined in Section 4(1) of the Act to include debenture stock, bonds, notes and any other securities of a corporation, whether constituting a charge on the assets of the corporation or not. The debenture provisions are contained in Part IV, Division 4 of the CA, being Sections 70–83.

The word 'charge' is defined in Section 4(1) as including a mortgage or any agreement to give or execute a charge or mortgage whether upon demand or otherwise. Consequently, a charge may be legal or equitable and includes any security for repayment of a debt.[57] The definition of 'charge' is broad enough to cover other securities such as liens and pledges. The inclusion of the latter is particularly significant in view of the advent of scripless trading of securities.[58] The CA provides a regime for the registration of charges. The provisions are to be found in Part IV, Division 7 of the CA, being Sections 108–118. As the CA does not have a scheme of priorities for charges, the general law applies.

A company enters receivership when a receiver is appointed. Where there is a debenture, the trust deed usually provides for the appointment of a receiver in the event the company defaults in performing its obligations. Alternatively, a receiver may be appointed by the court under the general law or under Order 30 of the Rules of the High Court. Part VIII of the CA, (Sections 182–192) applies to receivership.

The prohibition on a company purchasing its own shares, expounded by the House of Lords in *Trevor v Whitworth*,[59] has been adopted by the CA. Section 67(1) states that, except as is expressly provided by the CA, no company shall:

- give financial assistance[60] for the acquisition of its own shares or shares in its holding company;
- acquire such shares;
- lend money on the security of such shares; or
- purport to acquire shares in its holding company.

Breach of Section 67(1) is an offence by 'officers in default' and not the company, which is seen as the victim. In addition to imposing a penalty under Section 67(3), the court also has power, under Section 67(4), to order the defaulting officer to pay compensation to the company. At common law a transaction which infringed the prohibition was illegal and, hence, any loan granted as financial assistance could not be recovered in court proceedings.[61] This position has, however, been modified by Section 67(6) of the CA and such a loan is now recoverable.

7 The External Administration of Companies

7.1 *Arrangements and Reconstructions*

It has already been noted above that the memorandum and articles of a company constitute a statutory contract between the company and the members and between the members *inter se*. One of the limitations to altering this contract is found in Section 33 of the CA, whereby members are not bound by any alteration requiring them to take more shares or in any way increasing their liability, unless such alteration is agreed to by them in writing. However, if the provisions of Part VII, Sections 176–180 of the CA are invoked, members will be bound by such alterations. These provisions enable the rights and liabilities of members and creditors of a company to be reorganized by a scheme of arrangement or compromise. Such a scheme, once approved, will bind all parties, the company, its members and creditors.[62]

The CA contemplates several types of schemes of arrangements. A compromise between a company and its creditors is one of them. A compromise may be proposed when a company is in financial difficulties and the members and creditors are of the view that there might be some benefit in continuing the business of the company. A scheme of arrangement is usually a moratorium or a compromise scheme. In a moratorium the payment of debts is postponed for a period of time, whereas in a compromise creditors agree to accept payment of less than the amount they are owed in full satisfaction of their debts.

Other types of arrangement involve the reorganization of the rights and liabilities of members by the conversion of one class of shares to another or the transfer of assets of one company to another controlled by the same shareholders. The latter is referred to as a reconstruction. A scheme of arrangement may also be used in a takeover.[63]

7.2   Winding Up

7.2.1   Grounds for winding up   The CA contemplates two types of winding up: voluntary winding up and compulsory winding up (winding up by the court).[64] Voluntary winding up is further divided into members' voluntary winding up and creditors' voluntary winding up. Part X, Division 2 of the CA (Sections 217–253) apply exclusively to compulsory winding up, whereas Part X, Division 3 (Sections 254–276) applies to voluntary winding up. The provisions in Part X, Division 4 (Sections 277–313) apply to both types of winding up.

There are no provisions in the CA for voluntary administration or for judicial management for the rescue of financially ailing companies which might be perceived as being viable.

The grounds for winding up are to be found in Section 218 of the CA. There are 11 grounds, including the most common one, the inability of a company to pay its debts, and the 'just and equitable' ground. The persons who are entitled to file a petition for winding up are specified in Section 217 of the CA. The list includes the company, creditors and contributories.

In the context of winding up on the grounds of a company being unable to pay its debts, the test of insolvency is not whether the company's liabilities exceed its assets. The court must be satisfied that, after taking into account the company's contingent and prospective liabilities, the company is unable to pay its debts as they fall due.

7.2.2   The protection of creditors and the ranking of claims   Upon winding up, the primary function of the liquidator is the proper administration of the affairs of the company with a view to settlement of debts and finally dissolving the company. To this end, the liquidator has the duty to collect, preserve, realize and distribute the assets of the company to those who are entitled. If the company is solvent, these persons are the creditors and the members. The creditors are paid first, the surplus, if any, being paid to members.

The creditors must prove their debts. Generally, secured creditors are paid ahead of unsecured creditors. Section 292 of the CA deals with the ranking of debts of particular classes of unsecured creditors in order of priority. Creditors with priority, known as preferential creditors, are also, as between themselves, ranked in priority. The priority scheme is only relevant if the company is insolvent. In this case, the preferential creditors are paid first, before others. The debts of preferential creditors are listed in Section 292(1) of the CA. Members are only entitled to share in the distribution of the surplus assets after all creditors have been paid in full.

Other than the above provisions in the CA, winding up proceedings also have to comply with the Companies Regulations 1966 and the Companies (Winding-up) Rules 1972.

8   Takeover Rules

8.1   The Framework

The Malaysian Code on Takeovers and Mergers 1987 ('the Takeovers Code'), is the principal regulatory framework for takeovers and mergers. It is broadly based on the English City Code on Takeovers and Mergers. Takeovers are also regulated by other legislation and government policies, such as the Securities Commission Act 1993, the Guidelines on the Regulation of Acquisition of Assets, Mergers and Takeovers (better known as the 'FIC Guidelines'), and the Listing Requirements of the Kuala Lumpur Stock Exchange where the takeover proposal concerns the takeover of a company listed on it.

The Takeovers Code, initially under the purview of the Malaysian Panel on Takeovers and Mergers, is now administered by the Securities Commission. The purpose of the Takeovers Code is to ensure that takeover bids are conducted fairly. The threshold is set at 33 per cent on the premise that persons who hold less than this percentage would be unable to control the affairs of the target company. The

Securities Commission is empowered to grant exemptions and waivers from the obligatory requirement to make a mandatory offer under the Takeovers Code. The Takeovers Code also contains provisions concerning certain prohibited conduct. The board of a target company may not undertake certain actions without the prior approval of the shareholders at a general meeting when it is in receipt of a takeover offer, where it has reason to believe that one is imminent or during the course of the offer. These actions include the issue of any authorized but unissued shares and the entry into contracts other than in the ordinary course of business.

8.2   Disclosure Requirements

There are also provisions in the Takeovers Code regarding the disclosure of certain information in a proposed takeover. The offer must be in writing and contain the following information specified in Part III of the Takeovers Code:

- details of persons acting in concert in the transaction and a statement as to whether the securities acquired in pursuance of the offer would be transferred to another;
- all relevant facts to enable the shareholders to make an informed decision as to the merits of the offer, including:
    - its intentions regarding the continuation of, and major changes to, the business of the target company,
    - the long-term commercial justification of the offer, and
    - its intentions with respect to the continued employment of employees of the target company and its subsidiaries;
- holdings of, and dealings in, shares over the past 12 months by the offeror in the target company, together with the details of share holdings in the target company held by its directors and persons acting in concert;
- confirmation of cash availability; and
- obligations of the offeror and the target company.

Further, the listing requirements of the Kuala Lumpur Stock Exchange (KLSE) may have to be complied with and additional information thereunder will have to be circulated to shareholders of the target company, whether or not the latter is listed.

The Foreign Investment Committee oversees takeover activity in the country. The FIC Guidelines aim to ensure that all proposed acquisitions result directly or indirectly in a more balanced Malaysian participation in ownership and control and lead to net economic benefits including the extent of Malaysian, and in particular, Bumiputra, participation. The FIC Guidelines also ensure that there are no adverse consequences in terms of national policies in such matters as defence, environmental protection or regional development.

9   Securities Regulation

9.1   The Framework

The Securities Industry Act 1983 (the 'Securities Act') was enacted to make provision with respect to 'stock exchanges, stock brokers and other persons dealing in securities, and for certain offences relating to trading in securities, and for other purposes connected therewith'.[65]

The definition[66] of securities in the Securities Act is broad and encompasses all manner of securities, including shares, debentures, government bonds, options in shares, debentures and bonds, and participatory interests in unit trust schemes. The regulation of companies and the regulation of securities cannot, in reality, be considered as separate and unconnected functions. The Securities Act complements the CA, as the latter already provides for disclosure and regulates various aspects of securities, including, the prospectus provisions and participatory interests, allotment of shares, issue of debentures, the accounts provisions and the audit provisions. Further, as noted above, the Takeovers Code regulates the trading in shares during a takeover.

9.2   Stock Exchanges

The Securities Act has provisions with regard to the formation and conduct of stock exchanges. The 'KLSE' was incorporated in 1976 to take over the functions of its predecessor, the Kuala Lumpur Stock Exchange Berhad, and thereafter to implement the provisions of the Securities Act. Under the Securities Act, only existing stock exchanges may provide a stock market.[67] A new stock market may be established only with the consent of the Minister of Finance.[68] The considerations to be taken into account in granting the consent are set out in Section 8(2) of the Securities Act.

The KLSE administers and reviews the listing requirements of the stock exchange. The listing requirements are additional to and complementary to the listed companies' common law and statutory obligations. The listing requirements are a significant element in the regulation of listed companies in Malaysia. They have received judicial and legislative recognition. Under Section 100 of the Securities Act, the registrar of companies and the stock exchange are empowered to apply to the court for an order that the requirements be complied with.

The Kuala Lumpur Commodities Exchange was established in 1980 and is now regulated by the Commodities Trading Act 1985. The Commodities Trading Commission established under this Act is similar to the Securities Commission, but has its jurisdiction exclusively in the area of commodities futures trading.

The Securities Act also has provisions to license persons engaged in the industry. A person is prohibited from acting or holding him or herself out as an investment adviser unless he or she is the holder of an investment adviser's licence.[69] An investment adviser is a person who:

- carries on a business of advising others concerning securities; or
- in the course of a business, issues, publishes, analyses or reports concerning securities.[70]

9.3   *The Regulation of Market Practices*

The Securities Act also makes provisions concerning certain improper market practices which may lead to the establishment of false markets for securities. The provisions relate to the regulation of 'short-selling', which is the practice of selling securities when they are not owned by the seller at the time of sale. There is a possibility of over-selling to the extent that the sellers may not be able to cover their positions, thereby leading to a chaotic market situation. Short-selling is an offence under Section 41(1) of the Securities Act. However, provision is made for some exceptions:[71]

- brokers may short-sell odd lots;
- a person who has entered into a contract to buy securities but who has not completed the purchase may sell the securities; and
- in certain cases where presale arrangements have been made to deliver within three days of sale and the price of the security is not falling.

The Securities Act makes provisions concerning market manipulation and false information. Market manipulation, whereby a false impression of market activity is created, is prohibited.[72] The prohibited activity is the engagement in two or more transactions which are likely to have the effect of raising, lowering or stabilizing the price of the security with the intent of inducing another person to enter the market. 'Transaction' is widely defined in Section 85(4) to include offers or invitations to buy or sell securities.

As regards insider trading, as already noted above, directors owe fiduciary duties to the company. Consequently, they cannot use information acquired by them while acting in their capacity as directors to make a profit for themselves. The general provisions concerning insider trading are to be found in Sections 89 and 90 of the Securities Act. Persons who are connected with a body corporate are prohibited from dealing with securities where they have acquired information in connection with their positions which is not generally available, but which if it were, would materially affect the price of the securities.

10 Miscellaneous

10.1 The Power of the Courts

Aside from the general jurisdiction of the court at common law and under the CA, the court is given various particular powers in order that the Act may be properly enforced. Some of the more important of these may be summarized as follows.

- Where a company is plaintiff in any action and the court has reason to believe that the company will be unable to pay the costs of the defendant if successful, it may require the plaintiff to furnish sufficient security for costs and stay all proceedings in the meantime.[73]
- If in any proceedings for negligence, default, breach of duty or breach of trust against an officer, employee, expert, receiver, receiver and manager or liquidator of a corporation it appears to the court that he or she has acted honestly and reasonably and that, having regard to all the circumstances of the case, he or she ought fairly to be excused for the negligence, default or breach, the court may relieve such person wholly or partly from liability on such terms as the court may think fit.[74]
- No proceeding under the CA shall be invalidated by any irregularity or deficiency of notice or time, unless the court is of the opinion that substantial injustice has been or may be caused thereby which cannot be remedied by any order of court.[75] The court also has the power to declare that the proceeding is valid despite any such defect, irregularity or deficiency.[76] The court is given wide powers to make various orders where any omission, defect, error or irregularity has occurred in the management or administration of a company whereby a breach of the CA has occurred, these including the power to make such order as may be necessary to rectify, or cause to be rectified or to negative, modify or cause to be modified, the consequences in law of any such omission, defect, error or

irregularity or to validate any matter alleged to be invalid by reason of such omission, defect, error or irregularity.[77] The court is also empowered to grant ancillary or consequential directions as it thinks fit.[78]

- The court has the power to enlarge or abridge any time for doing any act or taking any proceeding allowed or limited by the CA upon such terms as the justice of the case may require.[79]
- If any person, in contravention of the CA, refuses to permit the inspection of any register, minute book or document or to supply a copy of the aforesaid, the court may by order compel an immediate inspection of the relevant document or order that a copy of the document be supplied;[80]
- If any officer or former officer of a company has failed to do any act or matter which he is required to do under the CA, the court may by order require such officer to do that act or matter, on the application of the registrar of companies or any member of the company or the official receiver or liquidator.[81]

There are no particular provisions under the CA dealing with civil remedies. Such civil remedies as are available are to be found under the relevant breaches and are interspersed throughout the Act.[82]

10.2   Offences

Part XII, Division 2, of the CA sets out a series of offences. The more important of these may be summarized as follows.

A person is prohibited from going from place to place offering shares for subscription or purchase to the public or any member of the public or seeking or receiving offers to subscribe for or to purchase shares from the public or any member of the public.[83] Exemption from this prohibition may be granted by the Yang di-Pertuan Agong on application in the case of shares of a corporation, if notice of intention to make such application has been advertised in a newspaper circulating generally throughout the country.[84]

A person is also prohibited from offering to the public or any member of the public any shares for purchase, unless it is the ordinary business of the person to buy or sell shares.[85] This prohibition, however, does not apply:[86]

- where the shares to which the offer relates are shares of a class which are quoted on, or in respect of which permission to deal has been granted by, any prescribed stock exchange and the offer so states and the stock exchange is specified;
- where the offer relates to shares which a corporation has allotted or agreed to allot with a view to their being offered for sale

to the public and the offer is accompanied by a document that complies with all enactments and rules as to prospectuses;

- to an application for shares in or debentures of a corporation or to an invitation to deposit money with or lend money to a corporation which is issued, circulated, distributed or made subject to and in accordance with Division 1 of Part IV (dealing with prospectuses);
- where the offer relates to an interest to which Division 5 of Part IV (interests other than shares and debentures) applies and is accompanied by a statement in writing as required by that division or deposits or loans to a corporation of the kind referred to in Section 38(6) (prescribed corporation); and
- to any advice as to the price at which a management company is prepared to buy or sell any interest to which Division 5 of Part IV applies given or sent by the management company to any person to whom the management company has given or sent a statement in writing relating to that interest which complies with that Division within the period of six months immediately preceding the giving or sending of the advice.

Every person who acts or incites, causes or procures any person to act in contravention of the above prohibitions commits an offence punishable by imprisonment for ten years or a fine of 250 000 ringgit.[87] Further, where the person convicted of an offence of breaching any of the above prohibitions is a corporation, every officer concerned in the management of the corporation is also guilty of a like offence unless he or she proves that the act constituting the offence took place without his or her knowledge.[88] Upon conviction, the court may make an order that any contract made as a result of the offer is void and give consequential directions as it thinks fit.[89]

Every corporation which advertises, circulates or publishes any statement of the amount of its capital which is misleading, in which the amount of nominal or authorized capital is stated without the words 'nominal' or 'authorized' or in which the amount of capital, authorized capital or subscribed capital is stated but the amount of paid-up capital or the amount of any charge on uncalled capital is not stated just as prominently, commits an offence and so does every officer of the corporation who knowingly authorizes, directs or consents to the advertising.[90]

A person who makes or authorizes the making of a statement false or misleading in any material particular in any return, report, certificate, balance sheet or other document required by or for the purposes of the CA, is guilty of an offence which is punishable by ten years imprisonment or 250 000 ringgit.[91]

It is an offence for an officer of a corporation, with intent to deceive, to make or furnish, or knowingly and wilfully authorize or permit the making or furnishing of, any false or misleading statement or report to a director, auditor, member, debenture holder (or a trustee thereof), or a prescribed stock exchange or an officer thereof.[92]

A director or manager of a company who wilfully pays or permits to be paid any dividend out of what he or she knows is not profits, commits an offence.[93]

Any person who, by any statement, promises or forecasts that which he or she knows to be misleading, false or deceptive, or by any dishonest concealment of material facts or by the reckless making of such a statement promises or forecasts, induces or attempts to induce another to enter into an agreement to acquire, dispose of, subscribe to or underwrite marketable securities or to lend to or deposit money with a corporation commits an offence.[94]

Conspiracy to commit the above offence is also made an offence under the CA.[95]

It is also an offence for an officer or an agent of a corporation by any deceitful means or false promise and with intent to defraud, to cause or procure any money to be paid or any chattel or marketable security to be delivered to that corporation.[96]

The improper use of the words 'Berhad' or 'Sendirian' is also made an offence.[97]

Every person who, whilst an officer of a company, fraudulently induces a person to give credit to the company or with intent to defraud creditors makes a gift or causes to be made a gift or transfer of or charge on or connived at levying execution against, the property of the company, commits an offence.[98] Likewise, it is an offence for an officer, with intent to defraud creditors, to conceal or remove any property of the company since or within two months before the date of any unsatisfied judgment or order for payment of money obtained against the company.[99]

Apart from the above specific offences, the CA has general penalty provisions to cover breaches of the Act which are not specifically provided for,[100] and for default penalties.[101]

10.3   *The Initiation of Proceedings*

Except where provision is otherwise made in the CA, proceedings for any offence under the Act may be taken by the Registrar of Companies or with the written consent of the minister, by any person.[102] Offences punishable by imprisonment not exceeding three years may be prosecuted in a Magistrate's Court, whereas those punishable with more than three years may be prosecuted either in the Sessions Court or the High Court.[103] Instead of prosecuting, the registrar of companies may offer to compound any offence under the Act, as he deems fit.[104]

The Rules Committee, constituted under the Courts of Judicature Act 1964, is empowered to make rules with regard to various aspects of the enforcement of the CA, including procedure, court fees and costs and winding up of companies.[105]

The Yang di-Pertuan Agong has the power to make regulations with respect to, among others, the duties and functions of the registrar of companies and other assisting officers, the lodging and registration of documents and the prescribing of forms and fees for the purposes of the CA.[106] The Yang di-Pertuan Agong also has the power to amend the schedules to the Act.[107]

Notes

*   Visiting Scholar, Department of Accounting, The Hong Kong University of Science and Technology.
1   [1974] 2 MLJ 60.
2   [1969] 1 MLJ 171.
3   Unreported, High Court, Muar, Civil Suit No. 32 of 1972, reproduced in P.N. Pillay (1986), *Sourcebook of Singapore and Malaysian Company Law*, 2nd Edition, Butterworths, Singapore, Asia.
4   Section 4.
5   For an example of where the general law of construction was applied, see *Pembinaan KSY Sdn Bhd v Lian Seng Properties Sdn Bhd & Another* (1991) 1 MSCLC 90, 746.
6   See Sections 7B, 7C and 7D of the CA.
7   Section 14 of the CA.
8   Section 15(1) of the CA.
9   Section 4(1) of the CA.
10   Section 332(1) of the CA.
11   Section 19 and Third Schedule to the CA.
12   Section 20 of the CA.
13   Section 20(1) of the CA.
14   Section 20(2) of the CA.
15   Section 20(3) of the CA.
16   Section 16(1) of the CA.
17   Section 16(1) and (5) of the CA.
18   For the meaning of 'promoter' for the purposes of the prospectus provisions, see Section 4(1) of the CA; for the common law meaning, see *inter alia*, *Twycross v Grant* (1877) 2 CPD 469; and *Tracy v Mandalay Pty Ltd* (1953) 88 CLR 215.
19   As note 16, above.
20   Section 18 of the CA for details of the information required.
21   Section 29(1) of the CA.
22   Section 30(1) of the CA.
23   Section 33(1) of the CA.
24   Section 21(1) of the CA.
25   Section 31 of the CA.
26   Section 33(1) of the CA.

27   Section 22(3) of the CA.
28   Section 22(4) of the CA.
29   Section 22(7) of the CA.
30   Section 22(9) of the CA.
31   Sections 22(6) and 341(3) of the CA.
32   Section 141 of the CA.
33   Section 158 of the CA.
34   Section 70 of the CA.
35   Section 134 of the CA.
36   Section 69L of the CA.
37   As note 36, above.
38   Section 115 of the CA.
39   Section 119 of the CA.
40   Section 120 of the CA.
41   Table A, Article 73.
42   Table A, Article 74.
43   Section 132(1) of the CA.
44   Section 132(3) of the CA.
45   See, *inter alia, Whitehouse v Carlton Hotel Pty Ltd* (1987) 5 ACLC 421.
46   See, *inter alia, Regal (Hastings) Ltd v Gulliver* [1942] 1 All ER 378; and *Avel Consultants Sdn Bhd v Mohammed Zain Yusof* (1950–1985) MSCLC 145.
47   [1925] Ch 407.
48   See, *inter alia, Daniels v Anderson* (1995) 13 ACLC 614.
49   See generally, Sections 172–175 of the CA.
50   See, for example, *Coleman v Myers* [1977] 2 NZLR 255.
51   *Percival v Wright* [1902] 2 Ch 421.
52   (1843) 67 ER 189.
53   See, for example, *Re Tong Eng Sdn Bhd* [1994] 1 MLJ 451; and *Zephyr Holdings Pty Ltd v Jack Chia (Aust) Ltd* (1989) 7 ACLC 239.
54   For an exposition of the ambit of Section 181, see *Re Kong Thai Sawmill (Miri) Sdn Bhd* [1978] 2 MLJ 227 (PC).
55   See, *inter alia, Northern Counties Securities v Jackson & Steeple Ltd* [1974] 1 WLR 1133; and *Automatic Self-cleansing Filter Syndicate Co. v Cunninghame* [1906] 2 Ch 34.
56   *John Shaw & Sons (Salford) Ltd v Shaw* [1935] 2 KB 113.
57   See *Bensa Sdn Bhd (in liq) v Malayan Banking Bhd* (1993) 3 MSCLC 91, 022, in which a memorandum of deposit in respect of a fixed deposit was held to be a debenture and registrable as a charge under the CA.
58   See the *Securities Industry (Central Depositories) Act* 1991 generally, and Section 40 thereof in particular.
59   (1887) 12 App Cas 409.
60   As to what constitutes 'financial assistance' within the meaning of Section 67(1), see, *inter alia, Chung Khiaw Bank Ltd v Hotel Rasa Sayang Sdn Bhd* [1990] 1 MLJ 356; and *KL Sdn Bhd v LGH* (1990) 1 MSCLC 90, 402.
61   *Dressy Frocks Pty Ltd v Bock* (1951) 51 SR (NSW) 390.
62   Section 176(3) of the CA.
63   Section 180 of the CA.
64   Section 211 of the CA.
65   See the preamble to the Securities Act.
66   Section 2(1) of the Securities Act.
67   Section 7 of the Securities Act.
68   Section 8 of the Securities Act.
69   Section 14 of the Securities Act.
70   See the definition in Section 2(1) of the Securities Act.

71 Section 41(4) of the Securities Act.
72 Section 85 of the Securities Act.
73 Section 351(1) of the CA.
74 Section 354(1) of the CA.
75 Section 355(1) of the CA.
76 Section 355(2) of the CA.
77 Section 355(3) of the CA.
78 Section 355(3)(c) of the CA.
79 Section 355(4) of the CA.
80 Section 362(1) of the CA.
81 Section 362(2) of the CA.
82 See, for example, Section 39(7), the civil remedy available for breach of Section 39 (prospectus provision); Section 67(6), right of recovery of loans made in contravention of Section 67 (dealing by a company in its own shares).
83 Section 363(1) of the CA.
84 Section 363(2) of the CA.
85 Section 363(3) of the CA.
86 Section 363(4)(a)–(e) of the CA.
87 Section 363(5) of the CA.
88 Section 363(6) of the CA.
89 Section 363(7) of the CA.
90 Section 364(1) of the CA.
91 Section 364(2) of the CA.
92 Section 364A(1) of the CA.
93 Section 365(1) of the CA.
94 Section 366(1) of the CA.
95 Section 366(2) of the CA.
96 Section 366(3) of the CA.
97 Section 367(1) and (2) of the CA.
98 Section 368(a) and (b) of the CA.
99 Section 368(c) of the CA.
100 Section 369 of the CA.
101 Section 370 of the CA.
102 Section 371(1) of the CA.
103 Section 371(3) of the CA.
104 Section 371A(1) of the CA.
105 Section 372 of the CA.
106 Section 373 of the CA.
107 Section 374 of the CA.

Further Reading

Arjunan, K. and Low, C.K. (1995), *Lipton & Herzberg's Understanding Company Law in Malaysia*, The Law Book Co. Ltd, BBC Information Services, Sydney.

Woon, W., *The Annotated Statutes of Malaysia, Companies Act 1965 (Act 125)* Singapore: Butterworths Asia.

Pillay, P.N. (1986), *Sourcebook of Singapore and Malaysian Company Law*, 2nd edition, Singapore: Butterworths Asia.

11 Company Law in Singapore

BRENDAN PENTONY*

1 Introduction

The Singapore legal system, as to be expected in a former British colony, was modelled on the English system. Its legal and administrative institutions have that background and the influence of the English common law system prevails. That is not however its exclusive source. Customary law, reflecting the Malay presence in Singapore, is also an influence, as is some Chinese customary law.

Singapore's is not entirely a derivative system. As it developed as an independent nation and established its place in an economically dynamic region, Singapore fashioned its legal system to reflect the local culture and its own values. In this way, it followed many other former British colonies whose systems had the same provenance and a similar pattern of development.

Judicial power in Singapore is vested in the Supreme Court and in such subordinate courts as may be provided for by any written law for the time being in force (Article 93 of the Constitution of the Republic of Singapore). The Supreme Court consists of the Court of Appeal and the High Court. The subordinate courts are the District Court, the Magistrate's Court, the Coroner's Court, the Juvenile Court and the Small Claims Tribunal.

Company law matters, apart from prosecutions, are not dealt with in the subordinate courts. References in the Companies Act (CA) to 'court' are to the High Court or a judge thereof (Section 4). High Court matters are heard before a single judge. Appeals from decisions of the High Court are to the Court of Appeal, which consists of the Chief Justice, who is also the President of the Court of Appeal, and the Judges of Appeal. Since the Judicial Committee (Repeal) Act 1994, appeals to the Judicial Committee of Her Britannic Majesty's Privy Council are no longer possible. Thus, the Court of Appeal is the ultimate court in the Singapore system. Except in appeals on interlocutory matters, the Court of Appeal is made up of at least three judges.

2   A Description of the Corporation Law Statute and Case-law in Singapore

Corporate affairs in Singapore are governed by the CA (Chapter 50), first enacted in 1967 and since amended on several occasions, the Companies Regulations, the Companies (Central Depository System) Regulations and the Companies (Winding- Up) Rules. The Securities Industry Act (Chapter 289) and the regulations made under it regulate the conduct of the market in company securities.

The existence of the CA overcame the effect of Section 5 of the Civil Law Act which provided that in certain areas of law, one of which was 'corporations', the 'law with respect to those matters shall be the same as would be administered in England in the like case, at the corresponding period, if such question or issue had arisen ... '. The English law would apply 'unless in any case other provision is or shall be made by any law having force in Singapore'. This legislation affected other areas of commercial life in Singapore, but corporations were, as explained, not affected and the regulation of corporations was not subject to English statute law. The Civil Law Act was repealed by the Application of English Law Act 1993.

It is not surprising, given the background of the CA, that decisions of Australian courts were relevant to its interpretation, as were decisions of the Judicial Committee of the Privy Council (the British Commonwealth's final appellate court which was part of the Singapore system until 1994) and the English courts. Of course, as litigation developed, the Singapore courts have impressed their own interpretations on the legislation. The most that can now be said of Australian and English decisions is that they provide assistance in the interpretation of the CA, in the same way as the decisions of any foreign jurisdiction. Under the common law system, they are persuasive only and do not bind the Singapore courts.

2.1   The Constitutional Basis of the Company Law

Article 3 of the Constitution of the Republic of Singapore provides that Singapore shall be a sovereign republic to be known as the Republic of Singapore. There is no federal system of government involved and, thus, it is not necessary to consider the distribution of the powers that arises in a federation. The Parliament has unlimited power to make laws with respect to companies.

2.2 How the Company Law Came into Being

The CA is, indirectly, based on the Australian Uniform Companies Act 1961 which was the basis of the Malaysian Companies Act 1965. This, in turn, was adopted in Singapore as the CA 1967. Subsequent amendments to the Act have seen the legislation take on a progressively local form. The vast changes in company law in Australia since 1961 have weakened the legislative link between Singapore and Australia and, in many respects, the Singapore law has stood still by comparison with the Australian reforms.

2.3 Who is Responsible for Changing the Law?

The law-making authority under the Constitution is Parliament. Article 60 of the Constitution requires that legislation will be enacted by the president 'with the advice and consent of the Parliament of Singapore'.

The regulation-making power is granted to the minister (currently the Minister for Finance) under Section 411 of the CA.

2.4 What Principles, if Any, Underlie the Company Law?

The object of the legislation, as with the English and similar systems, is to allow for the creation of the artificial legal entity, the company, and to regulate its conduct and management for the benefit of investors and creditors. The legislation determines the powers and capacity of the company. It allows for and regulates the way in which the company can raise its capital. It protects those who invest in it, as either shareholders or lenders. It seeks to protect creditors of the company from being victims of fraud. It determines the relationship between the company and its members. In this regard, it importantly imposes duties on those who are elected to manage the company. An important aspect of the law is the way in which it makes the managers accountable by way of annual reporting to the members.

2.5 How the Legislation is Interpreted (Rules of Interpretation)

The CA has its own interpretation provisions. Section 4 is the major one, but other definitions appear throughout the CA and the regulations. Where appropriate, the meaning of terms is subject to the Interpretation Act. As with legislation in English-based systems, the courts can play an important role in clarifying the meaning of terms and concepts within the Act.

3   The Nature and Powers of Corporate Regulatory Bodies in Singapore

Under Article 30 of the Constitution, responsibility for a governmental department or subject is assigned to a minister, a member of the Cabinet which exercises the executive authority of Singapore. The ministerial responsibility for the CA currently lies with the Minister for Finance. Section 8 of the CA provides that the minister may appoint 'a Registrar of Companies or such other officers and employees as he thinks necessary for the proper administration of this Act'.

The Registry of Companies and Businesses has as its mission statement 'to provide a system for the registration of business entities and for their compliance with statutory disclosure requirements'. It describes its corporate objectives as being to:

- provide fast and efficient service in the registration of companies and businesses and the various returns and documents filed by them;
- serve the public by providing information pertaining to registered companies and businesses efficiently and speedily;
- take appropriate action against business operators who fail to comply with the registration and disclosure requirements of the law.

Also relevant in the area of corporate regulation is the Commercial Affairs Department which was established in 1984 to combat complex commercial frauds and white collar crime in Singapore. Its mission is to 'maintain the integrity of our financial markets and to protect investors'. The Commercial Affairs Department, an arm of the Ministry of Finance, is responsible for investigating and prosecuting offences under the CA, as well as the Securities Industry Act, the Drug Trafficking (Confiscation of Benefits) Act, and other offences disclosed in the course of investigations.

3.1   *A Description of the Powers of Company Regulatory Bodies*

The registrar has the general responsibility and appropriate powers for the administration of the CA: Section 8. The specific powers which the CA gives to the registrar are to:

- maintain registers and provide certified copies of and extracts from documents lodged (Section 12);
- seek a court order requiring compliance with statutory obligations to lodge returns (Section 13);

- refuse to register a memorandum of association unless satisfied that it complies with the requirements of the CA (Section 20);
- refuse to register a company name (on specified grounds) (Section 27);
- decide whether to register a prospectus (Section 50);
- approve a deed for the appointment of a corporate trustee for the holders of interests other than shares or debentures (Section 109);
- oversee the process of removal of an auditor and to appoint an auditor on the failure of the company to do so (Section 205);
- strike off defunct companies (Section 344); and
- except where the power is given to another agency, undertake proceedings in respect of offences under the CA (Section 409).

Section 409B of the CA empowers the Commercial Affairs Department to 'exercise all or any of the powers in relation to police investigations conferred by the Criminal Procedure Code'. Its legal section undertakes a prosecutorial role and provides advice on enforcement aspects of the relevant legislation.

3.2 The Role of Regulatory Bodies in Policy Formation and Practice

The registrar of companies is primarily an administrative body with responsibility for enforcement of the CA. It has no statutory role to play in the development of policy or in law reform, but its influence in the day-to-day compliance requirements is important.

3.3 Mechanisms for the Review of Regulatory Action

There is a general right under Section 12(6) of the CA which allows a 'party aggrieved' to appeal to the court against a decision by the registrar:

- not to register a corporation;
- not to register a document or receive a document; or
- any other decision.

The court may confirm the decision of the registrar or 'give such directions in the matter as seem proper or otherwise determine the matter'. A person who is adversely affected by the decision but is not a 'party aggrieved' can seek judicial review of the decision.

Where the registrar refuses to register a memorandum of association on public interest grounds, a person aggrieved by that decision has 30 days in which to appeal to the minister whose decision is final (Section 20(3)).

Where registration of a foreign company has been refused, it can appeal to the minister whose decision is final (Section 369(2)).

4   A Description of Types of Companies and their Powers

The concept of an incorporated company is foreign to the common law, so there was only one way by which such a legal entity could have been created, namely by statute. The facilitation of that process is one of the pillars of the English-inspired companies legislation. Singapore legislation follows the style of the English model and provides for three forms of company, based on their liability classification. A further classification reflects the width of membership and the extent to which the company may seek funds from the public.

4.1   A Description of Types of Local Companies

Under Section 17 of the CA, two or more persons may form an incorporated company. It may be one of the following.

- In a company limited by shares, the liability of members is limited to whatever amount remains unpaid on shares issued to them. If the company were to fail, leaving unpaid debts, the most that a member would lose is the amount per share that had not been called up by the company. If the shares had a face value of $ 1 and had been paid up to 45 cents the uncalled amount would be 55 cents. If the shares were issued as fully paid, the liability of the member would be nil. The price of shares on the stock market is not relevant in this process.
- In a company limited by guarantee, the company has no subscribed capital and its members promise/guarantee that when the company is wound up they will pay a certain sum, specified in the memorandum of association.
- In an unlimited company, the liability of members is not limited. Members of such a company are liable for the debts of the company. This degree of liability is not consistent with the notion of a commercial incorporated company and the use of this form of company is not common.

Incorporated companies were conceived as a method of attracting investment. Such a entity, promising limited liability of members, was seen as an attractive vehicle for investment in risky mercantile ventures. Not all companies are formed with the object of raising funds from the public, and the legislation allows for a further classification of incorporated companies. They can be private or public.

A private company is defined in Section 4 of the CA by reference to Section 18. Under Section 18(1), a private company is a company having a share capital whose memorandum or articles of association:

- restricts the right to transfer shares – this may appear in the articles as a requirement that shareholders wishing to dispose of shares must first offer them to existing shareholders or as a provision that the board has the power to decide whether or not to register transfers; this requirement would make it very difficult for a private company to be listed on a stock exchange;
- limits the number of its members to not more than 50 – shares held jointly are treated as if held by one person and employee (current or former) shareholders are not counted in the figure of 50;
- prohibits any invitation to the public to subscribe for any shares in or debentures of the company – this provision would make it impossible for a private company to use the stock exchange as a vehicle for raising funds; and
- prohibits any invitation to the public to deposit money with the company for fixed periods or payable at call, whether bearing or not bearing interest – this is a further restriction on the capacity of a private company to raise funds from the public.

According to the Registry of Companies and Businesses, 99 per cent of Singapore companies are private. A sub-classification of the private company is the exempt private company which is defined in Section 4. Such a company is, according to Section 4, one in whose shares 'no beneficial interest is held directly or indirectly by any corporation and which has not more than 20 members' or which is a private company wholly owned by the government and which has been declared by the minister to be an exempt private company. The exempt company is one that is essentially private, in which there is no need to account to the public in respect of the application of its funds. An exempt private company is not required to disclose for the public record its financial affairs and, in respect of loans to directors, the restrictions that apply to other companies do not apply. Those concessions are appropriate as money is not raised from the public, but, in all other ways, persons dealing with an exempt private company are protected as with dealings with other forms of company.

Section 4 defines a public company as 'a company other than a private company'. A company limited by guarantee is a public company because, in the absence of share capital, it cannot be a private company. An unlimited company that has share capital could be private.

It is possible for a private company to change to public company status (Section 31(2)) and for a public company to convert to a private company (Section 31(1)). Where a private company fails to comply with the statutory requirements for such companies, the court or the registrar may determine that it has 'ceased to be a private company' (Section 32(1) and (2)) and from that time on it shall be a public company (Section 32(3)).

4.2   *The Recognition of Foreign Companies in Singapore*

A foreign company is one that has been incorporated outside of Singapore (Section 4). The CA deals with foreign companies in Part XI (Sections 365–386).

Before it establishes a place of business or commences business in Singapore, Section 368 requires a foreign company to lodge for registration the following documents:

- a certified copy of its certificate of incorporation or equivalent;
- a certified copy of its constituent documents;
- a list of directors showing the same information as is required of directors of Singapore companies;
- a memorandum showing the powers of local directors (if any);
- a formal document identifying two natural persons in Singapore who are authorized to accept service of process and any notices;
- a notice of the local address of the registered office of the company and details of business hours (if it is not open during ordinary business hours); and
- a statutory declaration by the agents of the company in the form prescribed by the companies regulations (Form 80).

Upon the payment of the appropriate fees and registration of these documents, the foreign company is registered. Registration does not necessarily follow the lodgement of the documents – Section 369 empowers the registrar to refuse to register a foreign company if it is 'being used or is likely to be used for an unlawful purpose or for purposes prejudicial to public peace, welfare or good order in Singapore or is acting or likely to act against the national security or interest'.

The CA specifies in Section 366(1) that 'carrying on business' includes establishing or using a share transfer or share registration office or administering, managing or otherwise dealing with property situated in Singapore as an agent, legal representative or trustee, whether by employees or agents or otherwise. Section 366(2) lists some activities which do not, of themselves, amount to carrying on business. These include becoming involved in litigation, holding company meetings or maintaining a bank account in Singapore. An isolated transaction, that is one completed within a period of 31 days, does not come within the notion of carrying on business.

Once registered, a foreign company may, subject to its own constitution, hold immovable property in Singapore (Section 367). That power does not extend to holding residential property.

A foreign company is required by Section 375 to 'conspicuously exhibit' the name and place where it was formed outside its registered office and places of business and on all documents it uses and produces. It must also make clear if the liability of its members is limited.

4.3 The Legal Capacities and Powers of Companies

A company has the powers it is endowed with on creation under its memorandum of association and those which are incidental to achieving the objects set out in the memorandum. Section 23 of the CA adds the following powers:

- to make donations for patriotic or charitable purposes;
- to transact lawful business in aid of Singapore in the prosecution of any war of hostilities in which Singapore is engaged; and
- unless excluded or modified by the memorandum or articles of association, the powers set out in the Third Schedule of the CA, which are numerous and cover a very wide range of company activities.

Section 24 of the CA grants power to a company to provide benefits for its current or former employees upon the cessation of the whole or any part of the business carried on by the company.

A company is limited to doing only what it is authorized to do by the objects clause in the memorandum of association or by the powers granted under the CA. Any activity beyond that is regarded as *ultra vires*, that is beyond its power. In Section 25(1) the CA provides that the fact that the conduct of a company is *ultra vires* will not be invalid by reason only that it was *ultra vires*. Thus, a third party involved in such a transaction is not affected by the fact that the company had no power to undertake the transaction.

Section 25(2), however, keeps alive the *ultra vires* doctrine but not to the extent applied by the common law. The doctrine can be relied on in three specified circumstances:

- in proceedings by a member or a debenture holder or the trustee for debenture holders to restrain the company from doing any act or acts or transferring property to or from the company (the parties who are launching the proceedings can use the fact that the conduct is *ultra vires* to have the company prevented from going on with it; if the company is restrained from carrying out an *ultra vires* contract, the court may, if it regards it as just and equitable to do so, set aside the contract and allow compensation for the loss or damage sustained as a result; if the conduct complained of has been completed then it is too late – the right of action is only to restrain the company from carrying out the act);

- in proceedings by the company or any member against a present or former officer of the company (if the company has acted beyond its power action can be taken to seek compensation for any loss or damages sustained; if the conduct is threatened, an injunction can be sought); and
- in a petition by the minister seeking to have the company wound up.

5   Company Formation

A company is not a natural entity but it is regarded as a legal person. To achieve this status it is necessary for it to be created by legislation. The CA provides the means by which a company comes into existence. It specifies procedures which must be followed and it empowers the entity which has been created as a result of the legislative process. A company needs a name and the persons dealing with it need to be aware that there is a risk associated with it. The risk is that of dealing with a company where the liability of members is limited which would be an important consideration for creditors seeking to be assured about payment of debts.

5.1   *The Registration of Companies*

Section 19(1) provides that 'persons desiring the incorporation of a company' are to lodge certain documents with the registrar. These documents are the memorandum of association, the articles (if any) and such other documents as are required by the registrar. Upon the payment of the prescribed fee, the registrar 'shall register the company'. Once that is done, the registrar is to certify that 'the company is on and from the date specified in the certificate' incorporated in whatever style of company it sought to be registered as (Section 19(4)). The certificate of incorporation shows that the company was one limited by shares, limited by guarantee or unlimited and specifies whether it was a private company. The registration of the company is effectively the birth of the company and the certificate of incorporation is similar to a birth certificate for a natural person.

The registration of a company does not necessarily follow the lodgement of the documents. Section 20 allows the registrar the power to refuse to register unless he is satisfied that the requirements of the CA have been complied with. He is also required to refuse to register where he is satisfied that the proposed company is likely to be used for an unlawful purpose or for purposes prejudicial to public peace, welfare and good order in Singapore, or if it would be contrary to the national security or interest to register it. A person aggrieved by such a decision can appeal to the minister whose decision is final.

The memorandum of association is signed by those who wish to set up the company. They are known as the subscribers and it is they, and other persons who subsequently become members of the company, who become the body corporate referred to in the memorandum. Section 19(5) of the CA explains the effect of the incorporation process in that the body corporate:

- is capable forthwith of exercising all the functions of an incorporated company;
- can sue and be sued;
- has perpetual succession;
- has a common seal; and
- has the power to hold land.

That is to say the company emerges from this process as a legal entity, separate from its members. A trader who supplied goods to the company would expect to be paid by the company not the members, because the company has the capacity to make the contract and, if it failed to pay, the trader would sue the company. Even if a husband and wife were the only shareholders in a company and it was operated for their benefit, the law would recognize the company as a different person. The separation is so complete that the company could employ the husband and wife and would assume the legal obligations of an employer. The members of the company do not own or have any interest in the property of the company and, consequently, they could not seek to insure it against loss or damage. The same separation applies even in a 'family' of companies, that is where one company (the holding company) has subsidiaries which are owned and controlled by it.

The advantages of the corporate form for carrying out sharp practices are well known and, in some places, well developed. The process of 'lifting the corporate veil' is undertaken in some jurisdictions where the courts ignore the legal significance of incorporation and allow the persons who allege they are the victims of such conduct to seek to fix liability for conduct taken in the name of the company on the individuals who control the company. Thus, the people behind the company are made accountable for their actions, they are not able to shelter behind the screen offered by incorporation.

Courts have mixed feelings about lifting the corporate veil and some will do it only where it is specifically authorized by legislation. In Singapore, the CA authorizes it in the following circumstances.

- Where the company operates with fewer than the statutory number of members after a period of six months a member who was aware of that shall be liable for the debts incurred by the company during that period (Section 42).
- If the company, having implied that permission would be sought to list shares and the shares are not listed, does not refund the money paid by applicants, the directors become liable to pay (Section 53(2)).
- In the case of a prospectus naming a person as a director or prospective director and that person has not consented or no longer consents to being a director, the directors responsible for naming that person are made liable personally to indemnify that person against any consequential liability (Section 55(6)).
- If the minimum subscription for a share issue has not been received, the money that has been subscribed is to be refunded within five months of the prospectus. Failure to do so within the time limit makes the directors personally liable to repay the moneys (Section 57(4)).
- The issue, signing or authorization of the issue or signing of a negotiable instrument, for example cheque that does not exhibit the name of the company, will result in the person responsible becoming personally liable, as well as the company (Section 144(2)).
- If it appears that the business of a company has been carried on with intent to defraud creditors or for any fraudulent purpose, any person who was a knowing party to such conduct can, on application to the court, be made personally liable for all or any of the company debts (Section 340(1)).
- Where it appears during a winding up that a company officer was aware, at the time the debt was incurred, that there was no reasonable ground to expect that the company could pay the debt the officer is guilty of an offence (Section 339(3)). Upon conviction, that officer can, on application to the court, be made personally responsible for the payment of part or all of the debt (Section 340(2)).
- Where dividends have been paid out of what directors know

not to be profits, the directors shall be liable to creditors for the amount of the non-profit dividends (Section 403(2)).

It is a feature of an incorporated company that it has full legal capacity at birth – it goes through no period of legal disability. Having perpetual succession, it is capable of living forever, provided it has the minimum number of members. These members need not be the same as those at incorporation, because the company, as a separate legal person, exists independently of its members. The company's legal capacity begins at incorporation, prior to then it had no existence and, thus, it was impossible for it to make contracts or for others to make contracts on its behalf.

There are circumstances where arrangements need to be made about the affairs of a company that has not yet been set up. This is a matter of practicality rather than law. An example could be in renting property or undertaking obligations in respect of a transaction which is the reason for setting up the company. Under the common law, a company cannot be involved in a contract made before it came into existence. The CA recognizes that these transactions could take place and in Section 41 deals with the ratification by the company of contracts made before incorporation. A company may, after it is established, ratify a contract or transaction entered into prior to its formation. The process of ratification authorizes what was done in its name but what was, in legal terms, a transaction without authority. Once having ratified it, the company is bound from the date on which the contract or transaction was made, as if it had been an original party.

Until the contract or transaction has been ratified by the company on whose behalf the person purported to act, that person – the promoter – is personally bound by it. If the company is never incorporated, then ratification is not possible and the promoter remains bound.

5.2 *The Corporate Constitution*

The memorandum of association is a critical document in the company's life cycle. It provides the basic constitution of the company and, being a document on the public record, it informs outsiders about important characteristics of the company.

Section 22 requires that the memorandum be printed, divided into numbered paragraphs, dated and shall state:

- the name of the company which is subject to the registrar's decision (Section 27) – clearly a name already in use or similar to it could not be used (the name under which a company is registered is, as it were, its birth name, but it is not the same as a business name; it is not impossible for a company to be registered under one name but to carry on business under a business name, one which needs to be registered);

- the objects of the company (it is not uncommon to specify a number of objects and then to include a general, all embracing object such as 'to carry on such other businesses as in the opinion of the directors may from time to time be advantageous to the company'; provided there are some specific objects stated in the memorandum it appears that there is no objection to such a general clause);
- unless the company is unlimited, the amount of share capital with which it is to be registered and the division of that capital into shares of a fixed amount (the share capital is variously described as 'authorized', 'registered' or 'nominal' capital; to satisfy the requirement the clause would be expressed to the effect 'the company shall have registered capital of $ 5 million divided into shares of $ 1');
- if the company is one limited by shares, that the liability of members is limited; that is limited to the amount, if any, unpaid on shares respectively held by them (Section 22(3); for persons dealing with the company this is important information and being included in the memorandum ensures that it is on the public record);
- if the company is one limited by guarantee, that the liability of members is limited and that each undertakes on the winding up of the company to contribute to the assets of the company while he or she is a member or within a year after he or she ceases to be a member an amount no more than is specified;
- if the company is an unlimited company, that the liability of members is unlimited;
- the full names, addresses and occupations of the subscribers to the memorandum; and
- that the subscribers 'are desirous of being formed into a company in pursuance of the memorandum and (where the company is to have a share capital) respectively agree to take the number of shares in the capital of the company set out opposite their respective names'.

This is known as the 'incorporating clause' as it satisfies the language of Section 19(1) which makes it possible for companies to be incorporated. The other important document in the life of a company is the articles of association. Section 19 refers to 'the articles, if any' which suggests that it is optional to have articles. That is not so, as the articles can be specifically drafted for the purposes of the company or the company can decide to 'adopt all or any of the regulations contained in Table A' (Section 36(1)). Table A is part of the Fourth Schedule of the CA. In the case of a company limited by guarantee or an unlimited company, Section 35 requires that there be articles.

The articles prescribe the internal regulations for the company. They deal with matters such as the rights attached to shares; the procedure for the transfer of shares (including, in the case of a private company, the right to restrict transfer of shares); meetings, procedure; the appointment of directors; the powers of directors, including the important matter of giving to the directors the power to manage the company; notices; dividends; and the indemnity out of company assets of company officers against the costs of successfully defending themselves against any civil or criminal proceedings or in seeking relief under the CA in respect of negligence, default, breach of duty or breach of trust. Whereas the memorandum lays down the charter of the company, the articles provide the detail for the operation of the company.

Table A will apply if the company does not provide its own articles or if the company articles do not provide for a particular matter.

A critical feature of the memorandum and articles is their contractual nature. This arises from Section 39(1) which provides that:

> Subject to this Act, the memorandum and articles shall when registered bind the company and the members thereof to the same extent as if they respectively had been signed and sealed by each member and contained covenants on the part of each member to observe all the provisions of the memorandum and of the articles.

In effect, the memorandum and articles provide the conditions upon which a person agrees to become a member. They have a right to have the company affairs conducted in accordance with the two documents and the company for its part has rights from the same source and in the same respect. This statutory contract applies to the members in their capacity as members. A member who was also a creditor could not seek to enforce the articles in respect of the debt and nor could the company sue a person who was a party to a contract who also happened to be a member. The contract allows the members and company to enforce the memorandum and articles.

5.3 The Restrictions on the Use of Certain Names

As mentioned earlier, the company memorandum must indicate the company name (Section 19(1)(a)). If this name is registered, it will be the name by which the company is known. The CA makes provision for names in Section 27. A practical matter is that of reserving a name prior to registration. This is possible under Section 27(10) and avoids the problem of having nominated an unavailable name in the memorandum. The reservation, once successful, reserves the name for a period of two months subject to extension for a further two months. Reservation means that the registrar will not allow another company to use that name or a similar one; it does not mean that the applicant has the name, the registrar must still approve the name applied for.

Certain names are not to be registered. They are those that are:

- undesirable, for example where the name is obscene or likely to give offence to a religion or a friendly state;
- identical to that of another company, corporation or business name (clearly, a name that is identically spelt would fail for this reason as would a name that was phonetically similar; a name that is not registered in Singapore but is famously used elsewhere would probably not be accepted for registration);
- so nearly resembling the name of another company, corporation or business name as to be likely to be mistaken for it; or
- of a kind that the minister has directed the registrar not to accept for registration; such names are required to be published in the Gazette.

An important requirement is that persons dealing with the company should be able to know its status. Section 27(7) requires a limited company to have either 'Limited' or 'Berhad' as part of and at the end of its name. Section 27(9) allows for abbreviations to be used, for example 'Pte' in lieu of 'Private' or 'Sdn' in lieu of 'Sendirian'. The purpose of this requirement is to warn a person dealing with the company of the limited liability of members of the company and, thus, to give some idea of its financial depth and the potential risks in dealing with it.

Section 27(8) requires a private company to have the word 'Private' or 'Sendirian' as part of its name inserted immediately before the word 'Limited' or 'Berhad', or, in the case of an unlimited company, at the end of its name. It is also possible to adopt abbreviations for these words, for example 'Ltd' in lieu of 'Limited' and 'Bhd' in lieu of 'Berhad'.

The minister has the power to, by licence, direct that a company be permitted to omit 'Limited' or 'Berhad' from its name (Section 29(1). This concession is available to companies who can satisfy the Minister that they are engaged in what may be termed as useful community activities, that it has some basis of national or general public interest and that it has the financial resources to carry out the objects for which it was formed and dividends cannot be paid to members and profits are to be used to promote the company objects. In granting a licence under this Section 29(1), the minster may impose conditions which, if he or she so directs, are to be inserted in the memorandum or articles of the company (Section 29(3)).

If a company wishes to change its name, it must first pass a special resolution to that effect and apply for the new name (Section 28). The criteria for granting the new name are the same as for the original name under Section 27. Once a new name is approved, the registrar will, for a fee, issue a new certificate of incorporation (Section 28(2)) and the name change is effective once that is done. The changing of the name of a company does not affect its identity nor any rights or obligations of the company. Legal proceedings in progress may be continued in the new name.

5.4 Membership and Share Capital Requirements

The members of the company are, initially, the subscribers to the memorandum of association (Section 19(6). That number may increase as more persons subscribe to the capital of the company or as existing members sell part of their shareholdings to others (assuming that the articles allow for that).

In the case of a company with share capital, the memorandum must state the amount of capital the company is authorized to raise and the denominations of the shares into which the capital is to be divided. Thus, the company may have authorized capital of $ 500 000 divided into $ 1 shares. The amount of $ 1 represents the face, or nominal, value of the shares. That is the amount the company will receive from a person to whom it issues shares. In a secondary disposal of shares, for example on the stock exchange or in a sale between individuals, the price has no relationship with the face value of the shares. The market determines their value and it could exceed or be lower than the face value.

An important rationale for establishing a company was to provide a vehicle for raising capital through the issue of shares and the invitation to lend money to the company. The process by which invitations to subscribe are made to the public is regulated by the CA. This is an example of the CA's role in protecting the investing public. The opportunity for fraud which the company form offers is such that it is appropriate and necessary for the CA to lay down rules about the way in which the company is promoted and the manner of accounting for the money obtained from the public.

Section 43(1) prohibits the issue of application forms for shares or debentures unless it is accompanied by a prospectus that has been registered by the registrar. This prohibition does not apply where the offer was not made to the public (Section 43(2)). An exception is in relation to shares that have previously been issued and are quoted on a stock exchange (Section 43(2A)). Failure to obey the requirements of Section 43 can lead to prosecution. Section 43 cannot apply to a private company because it is constitutionally prohibited from making an offer to the public. Section 44 makes similar provisions in relation to invitations to the public to lend money to or deposit it with the company.

The making of a public offer is the important feature of Section 43 and it offers no definition of that term. Section 4(6) of the CA explains that 'any reference in the Act to offering shares or debentures to the public or to issuing an invitation to public in respect of shares or debentures' shall be construed as an invitation to any section of the public whether selected as clients of the offeror or invitor or in any other manner. This does little more than make it clear that an 'offer to the public' does not have to be made to the world at large. The less specific the target group, the wider the group that is capable of accepting and the larger the number of invitees, the more likely it is that the offer was one made to the public.

The prospectus is basically a selling document and to ensure that it does not create a misleading impression on potential investors it must meet certain requirements as to form and content (Section 45). It must, among other things, be printed in a specified font size and must include what the Fifth Schedule requires as 'matters to be stated'. These matters include:

- the number of founders or management or deferred shares and the interests of the holders of such shares in the property and profits of the company. This is to provide disclosure where the funds being raised are for the purchase of an existing business owned by the founder/s of the company;
- the details of directors, including the share qualifications, if any, for directors specified in the articles and the directors' remuneration;
- the minimum amount needed to be raised where the prospectus relates to a share issue to cover the cost of purchasing assets, the company's preliminary expenses or underwriting commission payable and working capital; also required are details of the identity of the vendors of the property being purchased with the proceeds of the share issue – especially where the vendors include a director or an expert involved in the prospectus; the amount paid for goodwill is also to be disclosed;
- the amounts paid or to be paid to any promoter;
- the details of the subscription, application and allotment process;

- the details of any options in existence to subscribe for shares;
- the details of any shares or debentures issued in the past two years for non-cash consideration;
- the details of the auditor; and
- the reports from an approved company auditor on the company, any guarantor corporation and any subsidiaries, and, where the share issue is being undertaken to pay for the purchase of a business, on that business.

Where a prospectus contains an expert's statement, it must be supported by the expert's written consent to include the statement in the prospectus and a statement that the consent has not been withdrawn (Section 54(1)).

The importance of the prospectus as a means of disclosure is emphasized by the imposition of civil liability on directors, experts and those who authorized the prospectus, for damage arising from any untrue statement or wilful non-disclosure of which they had knowledge (Section 55). There are statutory defences against such liability (Section 55(3)). The CA also imposes criminal liability in respect of a fraudulently untrue statement or non-disclosure (Section 56).

Once the offer has been made in the appropriate form and no later than six months after the issue of the prospectus, the first step in issuing shares is the application by prospective shareholders. The money that is received at this stage, which must be no less than 5 per cent of the nominal value of the shares being subscribed (Section 57(3)), must be held in a special bank account until allotment is undertaken (Section 58).

The second step is the allotment of shares, the process by which shares are set aside for a particular applicant. This is undertaken by directors and in this process they need to act in good faith, rather than allocating shares in a way which will suit their purposes or sustain voting factions within the company. In this regard, Section 161(1) provides that directors 'shall not, without the prior approval of the company in general meeting, exercise any power of the company to issue shares'. That approval, however, can be given in the widest terms or can be expressed as being a power to issue shares at the board's discretion up to a maximum of 10 per cent of the issued capital of the company.

Allocation cannot proceed unless the minimum subscription has been subscribed and the appropriate money received (Section 57(1)). The minimum subscription is the amount determined by the directors and stated in the prospectus. Where the share issue is the initial float, it represents the amount needed by the company to pay for the purchase of property, to meet its preliminary expenses (if any) and to provide for working capital.

If the minimum amount has not been subscribed within four months of the issue of the prospectus, the money received from applicants must be refunded, and, if not done so within five months of the prospectus date the directors are made personally liable (Section 57(4)).

Within a month of an allotment having been made the company must lodge with the registrar a return, stating details of the allotment and the persons to whom shares were allotted (Section 63).

The company is able to determine the amount per share it wishes to raise through an issue of shares. That is to say it is able to maintain an uncalled component and it has the power to make a call or a series of calls for the outstanding amount. Articles 13–19 in Table A of the Fourth Schedule set out the powers of directors and the conditions that may apply.

Once shares are allocated, the person to whom they are allotted has legal title in them. Within seven days of the allotment the company must enter it into its register of members (Section 190(1)(d)). *Prima facie* evidence of legal ownership is provided by the share certificate (Section 123). The certificate must be available within two months of allotment (Section 130). The reason that it is *prima facie* and not conclusive evidence is the possibility that the shares are being held in trust for another by the person named on the certificate. If the shares are further traded, namely from the current shareholder to a purchaser, the company notes the change of ownership by registering it. Except where the articles allow it, the directors cannot refuse to register a transfer. Section 128 deals with the company's refusal to register a transfer.

A feature of Singapore's listed securities trading system is that it is scripless. This does not apply to unlisted companies or private companies. In order to overcome difficulties arising from the traditional view upheld by the CA that a person whose name appears in the company register is a member, the stock exchange established a company – Central Depository Pte. Ltd – which, after shareholders transferred their shares to it, appears in the register of companies as the owner of those shares. This entry remains unchanged despite any trading in the shares. Central Depository Pte. Ltd maintains accounts for each company member and as they trade the account is adjusted up or down with a reciprocal entry being made in the other side's account.

Section 130C is statutory recognition of the existence of the central depository system. Under Section 130D, the CA notes that the central depository is not a member despite being entered in the company's register of members. Those who are depositors with the Central Depository Ptd. Ltd are properly recognized by the CA as company members. Section 130E requires the Central Depository Pte. Ltd to certify the names of persons on its register. In this way, a company is able to establish the names of its members.

5.5 Amendment of Corporate Constitution

Both the memorandum of association and the articles may be altered. Section 26 allows for alteration 'to the extent and in the manner provided by this Act but not otherwise'. If a matter is included in the memorandum and is one for which the CA makes no provision for alteration, it is effectively incapable of being altered. To carry out an alteration requires a resolution carried by a meeting of the company and registered by the registrar.

Section 33 allows for the alteration of the objects clause in the memorandum. This is done by a special resolution requiring 21 days' notice to members and debenture holders. The latter group may not vote on the resolution, but may by application to the court seek the cancellation of the change. The resolution must be lodged with the registrar before it is effective.

The articles may be altered or added to by special resolution (Section 37). There are, however, qualifications to that right. It is subject to the CA and to any condition in the memorandum which may make an article unalterable. Section 39(3) provides that no alteration to the articles can be effective to require a member to take more shares or assume a greater liability unless the member agrees to be bound in writing.

5.6 Company Registers

The CA requires a company to maintain various registers as a formal record of matters regarded by the CA as important. The registers 'may be kept either by making entries in a bound book or by recording the matters in question in any other permanent manner' (Section 395(1)).

5.6.1 The register and index of members   This is required under Section 190. It is to record the names and addresses of members, their shareholdings (where it is a company with share capital), the number of each share or share certificate and the amount paid on those shares. The significance of the register is that it 'shall be prima facie evidence of any matters inserted therein as required or authorised by [the Companies] Act' (Section 190(4)). Failure to maintain the register in accordance with Section 190 is an offence and, if the register is maintained on behalf of the company, that person is liable (Section 193). Where a name is not properly entered or removed from the register the person aggrieved or any member of the company may seek to have the Court rectify the register (Section 194).

The register is open for inspection free of charge by any member (Section 192(2)). A person who is not a member may charged a maximum of $ 1 to inspect the register. It is possible to request the company to make available copies of the register or parts thereof. Failure to permit inspection or to provide a copy can lead to the Court compelling compliance with the Act in that regard (Section 399).

5.6.2 The branch register of members A company having a share capital may maintain at a place outside Singapore a branch register of members and that will form part of the company's register (Section 196(1)). The existence of the branch register is to be notified to the registrar (Section 196(2)).

5.6.3 The register of substantial shareholders Section 82 of the CA requires persons who have a substantial shareholding in a company, which is explained in Section 81 to mean those who have interests in not more than 5 per cent of the aggregate of the nominal amount of all the voting shares in the company, to notify the company of those interests. Where a person's interests change or the person loses the status of being a substantial shareholder, the company is likewise to be notified (Sections 83 and 84). Section 88 requires a company to maintain a register of substantial shareholders at its registered office or principal place of business in Singapore and to make it open for inspection. Failure to keep the register is an offence.

5.6.4 The register of directors, managers, secretaries and auditors This is a requirement under Section 173. In the case of managers, secretaries and auditors, their full names, identity card or passport number and addresses and other occupations, if any, are to be recorded (Section 173(4)).

In the case of directors – including alternate, substitute or local directors – the register is to contain a signed copy of each director's consent to act as director with a statement that the director is not disqualified from acting. Also required are details of the director's name, former name, usual residential address, nationality, business occupation (if any) and identity card or passport number. The register must also contain details of other directorships held in public companies or subsidiaries of public companies.

The details in the register are to be kept up-to-date in respect of changes in address or changes in the persons holding the offices within the company. The register is to be available free of charge for inspection to any member and for any other person a maximum fee of $ 2 is payable. The register details are to be supplied to the registrar.

5.6.5 The register of director's shareholdings Section 164 requires that a company must keep a register showing for each director the particulars of shares, debentures or participatory interests held in the company or a related corporation. The register must also record details of rights or options over the acquisition or disposal of shares in the company or a related corporation held by the director alone or with others. Also to be recorded are contracts which the director is party to or is entitled to a benefit under which a person has a right to call for or make delivery of shares in the company or in a related corporation. The disclosure is not required in respect of shares in a wholly owned subsidiary.

The company is required to make copies of extracts from the registrar available for a small fee per page. The register is to be open and accessible at its annual general meeting.

6 The Internal Administration of Companies

The existence of a company has both an internal and external dimension. The internal facet of company life largely deals with the relationship between the members/shareholders/owners and the controllers of the company. To a significant degree this aspect of corporate life is self-regulated, through the provisions of the memorandum and especially in the articles of association. The CA however makes important provisions in relation to the role and obligations of directors and the process of accountability.

6.1 The Registered Office and Name

A company is required from the date of its incorporation to maintain a registered office in Singapore to which communications and notices may be addressed. The office is to be open and accessible to the public for not less than three hours each ordinary business day (Section 142). Failure to comply with this requirement is an offence.

Section 144 states that the company name, having been approved by the registrar, must appear 'in legible romanized letters' on:

(a)   its seal; and
(b)   all business letters, statements of account, invoices, official notices, publications, bills of exchange, promissory notes, indorsements, cheques, orders, receipts and letters of credit of or purporting to be issued or signed by or on behalf of the company.

The company must also display its name in an easily legible manner in a prominent position on the outside of every office or place in which its business is carried on and its registered office must be identified by those words.

Failure to comply is an offence on the part of a person who uses, issues or authorizes any of the documents referred to. Furthermore, a person who signs a negotiable instrument which does not carry the company name will become personally liable if the company does not honour it.

6.2   *The Duties, Powers and Responsibilities of Officers*

Division 2 of Part V of the CA makes provision for 'Directors and Officers'. The term 'officer' is defined in Section 4. It includes any director or secretary or person 'employed in an executive capacity'. There is no explanation of what 'executive capacity' means, but it should mean a person who is in a position to make decisions affecting the company. Its use makes it clear that not all employees fall into the category of officers. Also included as an officer are a receiver and manager and a liquidator in a voluntary winding up. The definition specifically excludes from the term a receiver who is not also a manager, a receiver and manager appointed by the court, a liquidator appointed by the court or creditors and a judicial manager appointed by the court. It would be inappropriate for the auditor to be an officer and, in any case, Section 10(1)(c) of the CA disqualifies a company officer from being the auditor.

The requirement for directors is found in Section 145 of the CA. Every company shall have at least two directors, one of whom is ordinarily resident in Singapore (Section 145(1)). A director cannot voluntarily resign or vacate the office unless at least two directors remain and the residential qualification is satisfied (Section 145(5) and (6)). A director must be a natural person – not a body corporate – and be of full age (21 years of age) and capacity (Section 145(2)).

The first directors of the company are those named in the memorandum or articles (Section 145(3)). Thereafter, the tenure of directors will be in accordance with the articles of association (see Clauses 63–71 of Table A of the Fourth Schedule).

The steps in appointing a director involve the following considerations.

- Consent to act – Section 146 requires that a signed consent to act as director has been lodged with the registrar.
- Share qualification – if the articles require a director to hold a shareholding qualification that must be satisfied within the period specified by the articles or within two months (Section 147(1)). Failure to do so requires the director to vacate the office under pain of a fine (Section 147(3) and (4)).

- Age limit – the general rule under Section 153 is that no person of or over the age of 70 years can be appointed or act as a director of a public company. The office of a person who attains that age becomes vacant at the following annual general meeting. Section 153(6) provides a qualification to the general rule by allowing directors of or over the age of 70 years to be appointed or re-appointed by resolution passed by a 75 per cent majority of members. The holding of office in this way is on a year-to-year basis.
- Persistent default in lodging documents with the registrar – a director who has, on three occasions in the past five years, been ordered by the court under Section 13 to lodge material with the registrar or has been ordered under Section 399 to comply with the CA in respect of inspection of documents, cannot act as director without the leave of the court (Section 155(1) and (3)). It is a criminal offence to do so without leave being granted.

The CA imposes disqualification on persons acting as directors in the following circumstances.

- Undischarged bankrupts – Section 148 prohibits an undischarged bankrupt from acting as a director or taking part in the management of the corporation unless the leave of the court has been obtained. Conviction for a breach of Section 148 can lead to a maximum fine of $ 10 000 and/or two years' imprisonment.
- Unfit directors of insolvent companies – Section 149 provides that on the application of the minister or the official receiver, the court may order the disqualification of a person from being a director or participating in the management of a corporation for a maximum period of five years. The grounds upon which the court must be satisfied before such an order can be made are that the person is or was a director of an insolvent company that had gone into liquidation and that the person's conduct as a director, alone or as part of the board, 'makes him unfit to be a director of any other company or ... take part in, the management of a company'.
- Conviction for fraud or dishonesty – Section 154(3) provides that a person convicted, in Singapore or elsewhere, for an offence involving fraud or dishonesty punishable by imprisonment for three months or more shall not act as a director or participate in the management of a company.

The members of the company determine the composition of the board of directors. They can appoint and re-appoint directors and have the power to remove a director before the expiration of the term of appointment. In the case of a private company, the power of members so to act depends on the memorandum or articles of association. Depending on what they provide, it is possible for a director of a private company to be, effectively, immune from dismissal by members.

In the case of a public company, Section 152 provides for the removal from office of a director by an ordinary resolution. The removal will apply notwithstanding anything said in the memorandum or articles or any agreement with the director. Depending on what arrangements have been made, a director so removed may be eligible for compensation for loss of office, subject to Section 168.

The role of director is a powerful one, as, in most companies, the directors have control of the management of the company. As will be discussed below, directors have a fiduciary duty to the company and this is supplemented by a regime of disclosure imposed by the CA. Disclosure is required in the following circumstances.

- Interests in contracts with the company, property ownership and offices held – a company director is required under Section 156(1) to disclose to a meeting of directors any interest in a contract or proposed contract of the company. A director's interest includes that of 'a member of the director's family' (Section 156(8)). It is not clear what 'family' encompasses, but the term is defined in Section 163(5) to cover the immediate family, including step children and adopted children. It would be appropriate to take a wide view so that the interests of persons outside the immediate family are comprehended by this section. Disclosure is not required when the director's interest is only that of being a member or creditor of the other company and that interest is not a 'material interest'. That term is not defined and guidance from court decisions is necessary. No doubt it will depend on the circumstances as to whether an interest falls into that category. The holding of an office or the ownership of property which may lead to conflicts of interest arising are to be disclosed (Section 156(5)). This would embrace holding a directorship in a supplier or a rival company or owning property in which the company has an interest. Clause 81 of Table A of the Fourth Schedule prohibits a director from voting on any contract where there is an interest. The CA makes it an offence to fail to disclose (Section 156(10)).
- Loans to directors – there is a prohibition on the making of loans to directors (Section 162). Exceptions apply in the case of an exempt private company or where the loan is to provide the director with funds to meet the expenses of carrying out the

duties as director or, in the case of full-time directors, to provide a home loan or an employee loan. In the case of these transactions, it is necessary that a general meeting has given approval and, in the case of loans for expenses or a home loan, that the particular details are approved. Section 163 closes off the possibility that a loan may be made in breach of Section 162 – lending money to a company in which the director has an interest.

- Directors' shareholdings – a company is required to maintain a register of its directors' holdings of shares, debentures, participatory interests, rights options and contracts by which the directors may obtain shares (Section 164). The information for the register is to be supplied by the directors (Section 165). The register is open to inspection by company members and others.
- Directors' emoluments – a company is required to provide details of emoluments and other benefits received by directors on service of a notice from 10 per cent of members or holders of 5 per cent of the company's nominal capital (Section 165). The CA requires every company to have 'one or more secretaries', who are natural persons with a principal or only place of residence being in Singapore (Section 171). The directors are responsible for taking 'reasonable steps to secure that' each secretary is competent and experienced and has academic or professional qualifications (Section 172(2)). The secretary is an officer of the company and is generally seen as being an administrator of the company.

The duties and liabilities of officers, current and former, of the company are set out in Section 157, which it is stated in Section 157(4) is in addition to other written law and the common law.

Section 157(1) applies only to directors and provides that 'A director shall at all times act honestly and use reasonable diligence in the discharge of the duties of his office'.

This honesty requirement embraces the fiduciary duty owed by directors to the company. The width of that duty is difficult to state exhaustively and it would be safer to think of it as wider rather than narrower. Put briefly, a person in a fiduciary position must act honestly, for the benefit of the person to whom the duty is owed, in this case the company, and must avoid any conflict between personal interest and the obligation to the company. A fiduciary cannot profit from the position. It is because of this that Clause 70 of the articles exists. The only way directors can be paid fees is if the company in a general meeting agrees.

The duty imposed by Section 156 requires directors to give priority to the interests of the company. Section 159, however, provides some protection to directors to the extent that directors 'are entitled to have regard to' the interests of the company's employees generally as well as those of the company members. Directors are also entitled to have regard to the rulings of the Securities Industry Council on the interpretation of the Takeover and Mergers Code.

The duty to use 'reasonable diligence' reflects the common law position. The critical aspect is that the director be reasonably diligent. Part-time directors would not be expected to devote all of their time to their duties.

As to the level of skill expected of directors, the CA makes no provision, but having not excluded the common law, it requires no more than that directors be as skilful as they are capable of being. An accountant who is a director of an electronic communications company would not be expected to know as much about that topic as would an electronics engineer. The standard of performance of directors will depend on the circumstances.

Section 157(2) prohibits the improper use of any information acquired by a company officer or agent by virtue of their position to gain for themselves or others an advantage or to cause a detriment to the company. The type of information that comes within this section has no limitation save that is any information that was acquired from occupying a position with the company. This section appears to uphold the fiduciary principle that a person cannot profit from a position of trust. The abuse of confidential information such as a pricing formula could also come within Section 157(2) and also what would amount to insider trading under Section 103 would be caught.

A breach of the duties imposed by Section 157 could result in the person in breach being liable to compensate the company for any damage suffered as a result of the breach and, as well being liable to criminal sanctions of a maximum fine of $ 5 000 or term of imprisonment of one year (Section 157(3)).

A director against whom action is being taken for negligence or breach of duty can apply for relief to the court in which the proceedings are being taken (Section 391(1)). If it appears to the court that the person is liable but has acted honestly and reasonably and that having regard to all the circumstances of the case 'he ought fairly to be excused', the court may relieve him either wholly or in part from liability. An application for relief may be made to the court prospectively, that is if the applicant has reason to apprehend that action will be taken against him or her for breach of duty or negligence (Section 391(2)).

6.3   Meeting Procedures

Meetings provide the forum in which the company comes together. The most powerful company organ is the company in general meeting. It is here that company controllers can be brought to account for their stewardship. Proper procedures for the calling and conduct of meetings are critical. In some matters the articles provide the rules, whereas in others it is the CA.

6.3.1 Compulsory meetings There is only one meeting that must be held for all companies and that is the annual general meeting which is proscribed by Section 175. It must be held within 15 months of the last annual general meeting. The business to be transacted at an annual general meeting is to present the company accounts (Section 201) and to appoint the auditor (Section 205). The declaration of dividends is a matter for the annual general meeting.

In the case of a public limited company with share capital, it is required to hold a 'statutory meeting' within three months of the date on which it was entitled to commence business (Section 174). That date is to be found by reference to Section 61.

The 'statutory meeting' is a once only event and provides the opportunity for the directors of a newly established company to report to its members about the number of fully and partly paid up shares allotted; the cash raised in the share issue and the receipts from debentures issued; the preliminary expenses to be met; the amount of cash available; the details of the directors, trustee for debenture holders (if any) and the company auditor; and the particulars of any contract which needs the meeting's approval to modify. This meeting is, in effect, a progress report and members are entitled to ask, without notice, any question about the formation of the company. An adjournment of this meeting can lead to a resolution to have the company wound up (Section 174(9)).

6.3.2 Non-compulsory meetings Any general meeting other than the annual general meeting is an extraordinary general meeting. That term has nothing to do with the business being transacted there. What is important about an extraordinary general meeting is the process by which it is convened. Section 176 provides that the directors must convene such a meeting on the requisition of members who hold not less than 10 per cent of the voting power within the company. The requisition must state the objects of the meeting and be signed by the requisitionists. If the meeting is not convened by the directors with 21 days of the requisition being deposited with them, it may be convened by the requisitionists. The company will, initially, be responsible for meeting the reasonable expenses incurred by them, but it will be able to recover the costs from the fees payable to the directors who defaulted in this matter.

Another way of bringing about a meeting is for it to be called by two or more members who hold not less than 10 per cent of the issued share capital or where there is no share capital by not less than five in number (Section 177).

The CA, in Section 182, empowers the court to order a meeting 'if for any reason it is impracticable to call a meeting in any manner in which meetings may be called or to conduct the meeting in the manner prescribed by the articles'. This is done on the motion of the court or by application of a director or member.

The convening of meetings is not the only step involved. It is necessary where an extraordinary general meeting is involved for notice to be given to members. To hold a meeting otherwise would deny members the rights associated with holding shares. The CA requires that, where the business of the meeting does not require a special resolution, there be not less than 14 days' notice given (Section 177). Where a special resolution is to be considered, not less than 21 days' notice is required (Section 184). There are circumstances where special notice is required by the CA, for example the removal of a director of a public company, and Section 185 provides that not less than 28 days be given. If insufficient notice is given, the resolution shall not be effective (Section 185(1)).

The meeting is the opportunity for members to express their views about the business proposed. This is done by voting on resolutions. The CA specifies whether a special resolution is necessary and, if it does not so specify, the matter can be put to the meeting as an ordinary resolution which requires only a simple majority of the votes cast at the meeting. A special resolution is needed where specified by the CA and requires at least 21 days' written notice. It also requires a majority of 75 per cent of the votes cast at the meeting. Special resolutions are to be lodged with the registrar (Section 186).

The procedure at a meeting is largely dealt with by the articles. Section 179, however, provides that:

> So far as the articles do not make other provision in that behalf and subject to Section 64 –
>
> (a)   two persons personally present shall form a quorum;
> (b)   any member elected by the members present at a meeting may be chairman thereof; and
> (c)   in the case of a company having a share capital –
>   (i)   on a show of hands, each member who is personally present and entitled to vote shall have one vote; and
>   (ii)   on a poll, each member shall have one vote in respect of each share held by him ... ; and
> (d)   in the case of a company not having a share capital every member shall have one vote.

A poll is a method of voting whereby each voter signs a paper headed 'for' or 'against' the motion. A poll can be demanded in accordance with the articles (see Article 51).

The reference in Section 179 to Section 64 is to the voting rights of equity shares defined to mean 'any share which is not a preference share', but for the purposes of Section 64 a preference share with voting rights is an equity share and carries one vote.

Meetings of directors are carried out in accordance with the articles (see Articles 79–90).

Other meetings held in the course of a company's life include meetings of classes of shareholders in accordance with the articles; meetings of debenture holders following a breach of the terms of the debenture or trust deed (Section 101(1)(f)); and meetings of creditors in the course of a winding up (Section 295).

An important provision about meetings procedure and notice is Section 392 which allows the court to overlook any procedural invalidity unless it is 'of the opinion that the irregularity has caused or may cause substantial injustice that cannot be remedied by any order of the Court'.

6.4 Audit and Accounting Rules

A tangible way of reporting and measuring the performance of the company and for the company controllers to give an account of their stewardship is through the medium of published accounts. Section 199(1) of the CA requires that there be kept:

> such accounting and other records as will sufficiently explain the transactions and financial position of the company and enable true and fair profit and loss accounts and balance sheets ... to be prepared from time to time and shall cause those records to be kept in such manner as to enable them to be conveniently and properly audited.

The CA recognizes the need for companies to develop internal systems as a protection against fraud and in this respect requires in Section 199(2A) that every public company:

> devise and maintain a system of accounting controls sufficient to provide a reasonable assurance that –
>
> (a) assets are safeguarded against loss from unauthorized use or disposition; and
> (b) transactions are properly authorized and that they are recorded as necessary to permit the preparation of true and fair profit and loss accounts and balance-sheets and to maintain accountability of assets.

Section 201(1) and (3) requires that the directors of every company lay before the company at its annual general meeting a profit and loss account for the preceding period and a balance sheet up to the same date. In the case of a holding company, the requirement is that a consolidated financial report be made. The financial reports, accompanied by the auditor's report are to be made available to members not less than 14 days before the day of the annual general meeting (Section 203).

The form of accounts is specified in the Ninth Schedule. The standard set by the CA is that the reports give a 'true and fair view' of the profits or the state of affairs of the company. That term is not defined in the CA and is probably as confusing in Singapore as it is in the other jurisdictions that use it.

In the interests of presenting reports that are accurate, directors must take reasonable steps to ascertain whether the company has taken action to write off bad debts, to raise a provision for doubtful debts and to ensure that assets are not over-valued (Section 201(3C)).

A directors' report is necessary under Section 201(4A). It must set out detailed information which, apart from identifying the directors and their financial interests in the company, reports on:

- the principal activities of the company and any changes in them during the period under report;
- the financial performance of the company, movements in reserves and details of any capital raising;
- the recommended dividend;
- the action taken in relation to bad debts and doubtful debts, and the accuracy of the asset values recorded in the financial records;
- any contingent liabilities or unrecorded circumstances which might render the accounts misleading;
- any unusual factors over the past year which may have affected the results; and
- any material and unusual post balance day event likely to 'affect substantially' the company results for the period under report.

The CA requires that there be an auditor or auditors (Section 205). The initial appointment is made by the directors, but at the first annual general meeting and at annual general meetings thereafter the members vote to appoint or remove the auditor. The CA protects auditors by:

- laying down procedures to apply in removing the incumbent (Section 205(4)–(9), (14) and (15));

- specifying that the auditor is to report to members (Section 207(1));
- providing the auditor with a right of access to accounting and other records at all times and a right to obtain from company officers such information and explanations as are necessary for the audit (Section 207(4));
- imposing a penalty on any officer who refuses to allow the auditor access to accounting records or 'hinders, obstructs or delays an auditor in the performance of his duties' (Section 207(10));
- imposing a penalty on directors if the CA is not complied with (Section 205(17)); and
- granting qualified privilege against defamation in respect of the reports made by the auditor (Section 208).

Although the appointment of an auditor is mandated by the CA the relationship between the auditor and the company is contractual. The CA, in Section 207, requires the auditor to report to company members on the accounts presented to the annual general meeting. In particular, the CA requires the auditor to state in that report whether the accounts have been prepared to give a true and fair view of the company's financial situation. The auditor is required under Section 207(3) to 'form an opinion' about:

- whether he or she has obtained all the information and explanations required;
- whether proper accounting and other records have been kept in accordance with the CA;
- the adequacy of returns from branch office; and
- the appropriateness of the procedures for the preparation of consolidated accounts.

All of these matters are part of the contractual duty. Other, implied obligations, especially in relation to the auditor's duty of care, are imposed by common law. It appears that an auditor whose report includes deliberately misleading statements about the state of the financial reports is criminally liable under Section 401(2).

The auditor is required to report to the registrar if, in the course of the audit, it appears that there has been a breach of the CA and that the matter will not be adequately dealt with by commenting on it in the report or by notifying the directors (Section 207(9)). In the case of a public company, the auditor is required to notify the minister of any serious offence involving fraudulent or dishonest conduct being committed against the company by its officers or employees (Section 207(9A)).

6.5   *The Annual Return and Other Returns*

Section 197 requires every company having a share capital to make a return in accordance with the Eighth Schedule. The return, to be signed by an officer of the company, is to be lodged with the registrar within two months of the annual general meeting. In the case of an exempt private company, the Eighth Schedule does not require it to disclose details of its financial performance for the year – it is enough that a director, the company secretary and the auditor certify that a financial report has been laid before the annual general meeting of the company.

6.6   *Shareholder Protection Rules*

The limitations of the notion of shareholder control of companies are recognized in Section 216 which provides a remedy in circumstances where the affairs of the company or powers of directors are being exercised in 'a manner oppressive' to one or more of the members or debenture holders or 'in disregard of [their] interests ... ' . The remedy is also available where:

> some act of the company has been done or is threatened or that some resolution of the members, holders of debentures ... has been passed or is proposed which unfairly discriminates against or is otherwise prejudicial to one or more of the members or holders on debentures (including himself).

An application to the court on those grounds can be brought by any member, debenture holder or the minister in certain circumstances. If the court is satisfied that the grounds have been made out, it may make such order as 'it thinks fit'. The CA then specifies some forms of order that the court could make, including:

- an order directing or prohibiting any act or cancelling or varying any transaction or resolution;
- an order regulating the conduct of the company's affairs in future;
- an order authorizing civil proceedings to be brought in the name of, or on behalf of, the company;
- an order providing for the purchase of shares or debentures by other members or holders or by the company;
- a consequential order for the reduction of capital, if it involves the purchase of shares by the company; and
- an order to wind up the company.

The terms 'oppression', 'in disregard of his or their interests as member, shareholders or holders of debentures of the company' and 'unfairly discriminates against or is otherwise prejudicial' are not defined in the CA. They have been considered in a wide range of decisions in Singapore, Australia and the United Kingdom.

Protection of minority shareholders is also afforded by Section 216A which has established a statutory derivative action. That is to say that a member of the company, the minister in certain circumstances, and any other 'proper' person may seek leave from the court to bring an action in the name and on behalf of a company that is not listed on the Singapore stock exchange or to intervene in litigation to which the company is a party for the purpose of prosecuting, defending or discontinuing on behalf of the company.

Before such an action can be brought, Section 216A(3) requires that the court must be satisfied that:

- the person seeking to take action – the complainant – has given 14 days' notice to the company directors of his or her intention to apply to the court if the directors do not take action;
- the complainant is acting in good faith; and
- it appears, *prima facie* in the interests of the company, that the action should be taken.

In granting leave, the court is empowered to make such orders as it thinks fit 'in the interests of justice' (Section 216A(5)). These orders could include that the company pay the reasonable legal costs associated with the proposed action. The fact that a meeting of shareholders has approved or may approve a breach of duty owed to the company is not grounds to prevent an application under Section 216A from proceeding (Section 216B). If the shareholders have approved such an action that may be taken into account by the court in considering a Section 216A application.

This statutory derivative action overcomes the procedural difficulties faced by company members as a result of the proper plaintiff rule – the rule in *Foss v Harbottle* – which holds that the company is the appropriate body to litigate in instances of breaches of the duties owed to it. Under that rule, which has some exceptions, the directors make the decision as to whether the company would undertake such litigation. If the directors were the potential defendants, the difficulties in launching action against them is obvious. The existence of Section 216A empowers members to challenge company controllers who are not acting in the interests of the company.

The power of shareholders to elect and dismiss directors comes from the articles. Although this illustrates that power resides in the members, a more practical assessment is that in a large company voting arrangements can be made to entrench the company control-lers. This is a reason why provisions such as Sections 216 and 216A are necessary.

Another factor to be considered in examining the rights of minori-ties is that of the power to amend the articles. There is no doubt, as many cases have established, that majority rule prevails in this re-gard. The common law rule about exercising the power *bona fide* and for the benefit of the company as a whole is of doubtful value and, in any event, there are many examples of courts being reluctant to interfere. The remedy under Section 216 is a more reliable mode of seeking redress by minorities against what may be abuse of power by the majority within the company.

6.7   The Relationship between Management and Shareholders

In the case of a large, listed company the practical problem of allow-ing members to manage the enterprise needs no elaboration. It would be impracticable for members to be involved at that level. A closely held family company, where the members are the managers, can be managed by the members.

For a company in the first category the articles would provide that the 'business of the company shall be managed by the directors' (see Article 73 in Table A of the Fourth Schedule. The members being bound by such an article would have no right to interfere in the daily operations of the company. If they did not support a particular op-erational decision, their opportunity to change the decision would be through the articles – to remove the directors and replace them with ones who are more sympathetic.

The capacity of members to exercise their rights under the articles is the basis on which they are able to assert their rights as owners of the shares in the company. In a small company, for example one controlled by a dictatorial founding director, this may not be easy to achieve and it may be that the only avenue for redress is through the court.

6.8   Corporate Financial Transactions

A company is able to raise funds through capital raisings and bor-rowing. Security for borrowing can be provided by charges over company assets. These could be in the form of specific charges, such as mortgages, or by floating charges where all of the assets or a class of assets are used as security for borrowings.

Where a charge is created, Section 131 requires that it be registered, with the registrar, within 30 days. Failure to do so will result in the charge being 'void against the liquidator and any creditor of the company', a secured creditor would not in fact be secured. Conclusive proof of registration is in the form of a certificate issued by the registrar (Section 134(2)).

If a charge was not registered within the time limit, it is possible to seek an extension of time by application to the court (Section 137). An application can also be made where the register of charges requires rectification. The court may grant an extension or rectification if it is satisfied that the omission was accidental or due to inadvertence or to some other sufficient cause or is not of a nature to prejudice other creditors or that on other grounds it is just and equitable to do so.

An important concept in the tradition of English-style company law is that of capital maintenance. Put briefly, this exists for the protection of creditors and means that a company must not take action which dilutes its capital base. The company's capital is the fund to which a creditor looks for assurance that a debt will be met. Of course, capital lost through trading is regarded as one of the risks of trading but a deliberate act, such as the company dealing in its own shares, issuing shares at a discount on their nominal value, reducing capital or paying dividends out of capital, is unacceptable. In some circumstances this conduct is possible, but it requires the approval of the court and creditors.

Section 76 of the CA prohibits a company from providing financial assistance for the acquisition of shares in itself or its holding company and also prohibits it from acquiring shares in itself or lending money on the security of its own shares or shares in its holding company. There are exemptions where the company is in the business of lending money and money borrowed from it in the ordinary course of business is used to purchase shares in the company (Section 76(9)(a)). Another exemption is in respect of financial assistance to allow the purchase of its shares by its employees or those of a related corporation or its holding company (Section 76(9)(b)).

Issuing shares at a discount – lower than their nominal value – amounts to a reduction of capital because the shares will not contribute to the company's capital funds what their nominal value indicates should have been. Thus, if a share with a nominal value of $1 was issued for 90 cents, the discount is 10 cents. The fact that shares are selling on a stock exchange for less than their face value is not the same thing as a company issuing them at a discount. Section 68 allows a company to issue shares of a class already issued at a discount provided that:

- such an issue has been authorized by the company in a general meeting and confirmed by the court;
- the resolution specifies the maximum rate of discount;

- not less than a year has elapsed since the company was entitled to commence business; and
- the shares are issued within one month of the court order.

A capital reduction can be achieved by a company provided it has the power under the articles to do so and it is authorized by a special resolution and the court confirms it. The reduction can include the extinguishment or reduction of liability for uncalled capital; the cancellation of paid-up capital that has been lost or is not represented by available assets; and the paying back of capital that is in excess of the needs of the company (Section 73(1)). Where the proposed reduction involves a diminution in the unpaid capital component of a share or a return of paid up capital, every creditor is entitled to object to the reduction (Section 73(2)). The court is required under the CA to pay attention to the rights of the creditors in such a process.

The payment of dividends from funds other than profits could see the subscribed capital of the company diminished. For this reason, there is a requirement in Section 403 that 'no dividend shall be payable to shareholders of any company except out of profits or pursuant to Section 69'. The Section 69 reference is to the share premium account which is raised when shares are issued by the company at a premium, that is above their nominal value. This reserve may be used to finance a dividend but otherwise dividends can be paid only from the profits available at the time of declaration of the dividend.

6.9   Capital Raising

The process of capital raising has been discussed in Section 5.4, above.

7   The External Administration of Companies

There are circumstances where, because of some crisis in the life of the company, its controllers are supplanted by others who have been appointed from outside the company.

7.1   The Rules Regarding Arrangements and Reconstructions

Section 210 provides that where a compromise or arrangement is proposed between a company and its creditors the court may order that a meeting of creditors, or a class of them, be held. If there is a 75 per cent majority of creditors in value at the meeting and it is agreed to accept the compromise, it will be binding on all creditors or class of creditors (Section 210(3)). The binding of the creditors takes place only if the compromise or arrangement is approved by the court and a copy of the court order is lodged with the registrar.

7.2 *Voluntary Administration and Corporate Rescue Provisions*

The scheme of arrangement under Section 210 is a form of corporate rescue appropriate for a company that is in debt but for which there is some hope of making the business profitable.

Another form of rescue is provided in judicial management. Section 227A of the CA provides that, where a company is unable to pay its debts but there is a 'reasonable probability' of rehabilitating it, the company itself, or its creditors, may apply under Section 227B for an order that the company be placed under judicial management. The court needs to be satisfied that:

- the company is or will be unable to meet its debts; and
- the making of the order would achieve one or more of the following:
  - the survival of the company or the whole or part of it as a going concern,
  - the approval of a Section 210 compromise or arrangement,
  - a more advantageous realization of the company's assets than on a winding up.

If the court makes the order, the affairs, business and property of the company are managed by a judicial manager who is appointed by the court (Section 227B(2)). The effect of applying for a company to be put under judicial management is to:

- prevent a resolution being made or an order being made for winding up of the company;
- prohibit, without the permission of the court, any legal proceedings to enforce charges or securities over company property or to repossess property under hire purchase or being leased; and
- stay other proceedings except with the court's permission (Section 227C).

Once the order is made, Section 227D provides that any receiver or receiver and manager is to vacate office and any petition for winding up the company is dismissed. It is also necessary to give notice on every invoice, order or business letter that the company's affairs are being managed by the judicial manager (Section 227E).

The powers and duties of the judicial manager are set out in Section 227G. They are that the judicial manager:

- is to take into custody or control all the property to which the company appears to be entitled;
- whilst the order is in force, has all of the powers and duties that the directors had under the memorandum and articles of association, except that it is not necessary to call meetings of the company. Meetings of creditors may be called;
- shall do all such things as are necessary for the management of the affairs, business and property of the company and such other things as are sanctioned by the court.

The judicial manager may dispose of property which is subject to a security as if it were not (Section 227H) provided the court has made an appropriate order.

Section 227I provides that the judicial manager is the agent of the company and is personally liable on any contract but is entitled to be indemnified in respect of that liability.

An important requirement of the process of judicial management is that the judicial manager shall, within 60 days of the making of the order, provide the creditors and the registrar with a statement of proposals for achieving the purposes mentioned in Section 227B and lay a copy of that statement before a meeting of creditors (Section 227M). It is then a matter for the creditors to decide whether to approve the proposals. This is done at a meeting where a majority (in number and value) of creditors present and voting approves the proposals with modifications subject to the consent of the judicial manager to each modification. If the meeting has not approved the proposals, the judicial manager having reported the outcome of the meeting to the court, the judicial management order may be discharged. If the proposals are approved, the affairs of the company are to be managed in accordance with those proposals (Section 227P). The judicial manager has the power to revise the proposals, but must seek the approval of a creditors' meeting before putting them into effect (Section 227P(2)).

The CA provides a mechanism for any creditor or member of the company to petition the court on the grounds that the affairs of the company have been managed in a way which is or was unfairly prejudicial to the interests of the company creditors or members generally or a single creditor that represents one-quarter in value of the claims against the company (Section 227R). The court has a discretion in making an order to give relief. It may regulate the future performance of the judicial manager or require that the conduct complained of cease or that a meeting of creditors or members be summoned. It also has the power to discharge the judicial management order.

7.3 Company Winding Up Rules, Tests for Insolvency, Grounds for Winding Up and Mechanisms for Initiating Insolvency Proceedings

As a company is an artificial legal person, it cannot die naturally. When it comes to the end of its useful life, that is where it is unable to continue in business or when the purpose for which it was established has been achieved, the company is brought to an end by the legal process of dissolution. Before the company can be dissolved, its affairs must be put in order – its assets realized, its debts paid and, where appropriate, contributions made by shareholders towards any shortfall. This is the winding up of the company.

Winding up of a company in Singapore can be undertaken by the court, as a members' voluntary winding up or as a creditors' voluntary winding up (Sections 247, 291 and 296).

A company may be wound up under an order of the court on the petition of the company, a creditor, a contributory (a member who may be required to contribute to the winding up of the company), the liquidator, the minister under Sections 241 and 254, or the judicial manager (Section 253(1)). The court has a discretion, under Section 254, to order a winding up on the grounds that:

- the company has resolved by special resolution that it be wound up by the court;
- the company has defaulted in holding its statutory meeting or lodging the statutory report;
- the company does not commence business within one year from its incorporation;
- the number of members of the company is reduced to fewer than two;
- the company is unable to pay its debts as defined in Section 254(2);
- the directors have acted in their own interests rather than in the interests of the members as a whole or in any other manner which appears to be unfair or unjust to other members;
- an inspector appointed to investigate the company has reported the opinion that the company cannot pay its debts and should be wound up or that it is in the interests of the public, the shareholders or the creditors that the company should be wound up;
- the period, if any, fixed for the duration of the company by the articles or memorandum has expired;
- the court is of the opinion that it is just and equitable that the company be wound up;
- a banking company's banking licence has been revoked or not renewed;

- the company has carried on banking in contravention of the written banking law;
- the company has carried on multi-level marketing or pyramid selling in contravention of the written law that prohibits such activity; or
- the company is being used for an unlawful purpose or for purposes prejudicial to public peace, welfare or good order in Singapore or against national security or interest.

The court may also have ordered the winding up of the company in an application for relief under Section 216(2)(f), that is where the affairs of the company are being carried on in a manner that is oppressive to members or debenture holders.

The commencement of the winding up is from the time of presenting the petition (Section 255(2)) and the next step is that a liquidator is appointed. The liquidator takes custody or control of all of the property to which the company appears to be entitled (Section 269). The liquidator's powers, which are specified in Section 272 and which may be exercised with the authority of the court or the committee of inspection, are to:

- carry on the business of the company so far as is necessary for the beneficial winding up thereof;
- pay any creditors in full – subject to the CA rules in Section 328 about priority of payments;
- make any compromise or arrangement with creditors;
- compromise any liabilities on debts owing to the company; and
- appoint a solicitor to assist in carrying out the duties of liquidator.

The liquidator has discretionary powers under Section 272(2), which include being able to bring or defend any legal action for the company; to compromise any debt due to the company up to $ 1 500; to sell the property of the company; to transact negotiable instruments in the name of the company; to raise money on the security of the assets of the company; and to do all that is necessary for the winding up of the company. The liquidator's powers are to be exercised subject to directions given by resolution of creditors or contributories and meetings may be summoned to ascertain their wishes (Section 273).

The liquidator's role comes to an end when all the property of the company, or as much as possible, has been realized 'without needlessly protracting the liquidation' and a final dividend has been distributed to creditors or if the liquidator has resigned or been removed from office. In those circumstances, the liquidator may apply to the court for an order to be released and for the company to be dissolved (Section 275).

A voluntary winding up may occur in the circumstances spelt out in Section 290. They are when:

- the period fixed for the duration of the company has expired or when an event occurs on which the memorandum or articles provide the company is to be dissolved and the company resolves to wind up; or
- the company so resolves by special resolution.

If the company is solvent, the winding up is referred to as a members' voluntary winding up. The alternative is a creditors' voluntary winding up.

In the case of a members' voluntary winding up, a majority of the company directors is required to make a statutory declaration of solvency (Section 293(1)). This is to follow an inquiry by the directors into the affairs of the company and the forming of the opinion that the company will be able to pay its debts in full within a period not exceeding 12 months after the commencement of the winding up. The declaration of solvency is to be accompanied by a statement of affairs for the company, showing estimates of the realizable value of the company's assets, its liabilities and the estimated costs of winding up (Section 293(3)). Once the resolution for a winding up has been passed, a liquidator is appointed (Section 294). At that point the powers of the directors come to an end.

If the company directors are unable to make the declaration of solvency, the process proceeds as a creditors' winding up, and, in this regard, within a day of the resolution for winding up being passed, the company must summon a meeting of creditors (Section 296). Section 297 provides that a liquidator shall be appointed. If the company is insolvent and a delay is to occur in launching a voluntary winding up and appointing the liquidator, the company may appoint a provisional liquidator (Section 291). This person has the same powers as a liquidator (Section 291(2)). The liquidator who is appointed is the one nominated by the creditors. The creditors may also appoint a committee of inspection to supervise the liquidator (Section 298).

The winding up commences from the day on which a provisional liquidator is appointed or from the time of passing the resolution for a voluntary winding up (Section 291(6)).

The liquidator has the powers set out in Section 305. These include the same powers as a court-appointed liquidator: the power to settle a list of contributories, that is members who are required to contribute to make up any deficit (this is the point at which the limited liability of shareholders comes into practical operation); the power to make calls; and the power to call meetings in order to obtain the sanction of the company. The liquidator is also empowered to pay the debts of the company and adjust the rights of contributories. Under Section 306, the liquidator has the power to accept shares in another company as consideration for the sale of the property of the company being wound up. In the case of a creditors' voluntary winding up, the liquidator needs the approval of the court or the committee of inspection before exercising this power (Section 306(6)).

Once the company has been wound up, the liquidator is required to hold a meeting of the company or a meeting of the creditors, depending on the type of winding up, and to present an account showing how the winding up was conducted (Section 308(1)). That account and a return of the holding of the meeting is to be lodged with the registrar within seven days of the meeting and three months after that lodging with the registrar and official receiver the company shall be dissolved (Section 308(5)).

7.4   *The Protection of Creditors and the Ranking of Claims*

In the course of a winding up, the critical interest is that of creditors. As far as possible they must be paid. Secured creditors have their own way of ensuring payment. Whether unsecured creditors are paid will depend ultimately on the state of the company. If it is solvent, then the directors have stated that the debts can be paid. If the company goes into a creditors' voluntary winding up, because it is insolvent, it is unlikely that all the creditors will be able to be satisfied. In this regard, Section 328 of the CA makes provision for the priorities to apply in the payment of unsecured debts.

The debts of the company are to be paid in the following order in priority to all other unsecured debts:

- the costs and expenses of the winding up;
- all wages or salary up to the equivalent of five months' salary or $ 7 500 (whichever is the lesser);
- the amount due to an employee as a retrenchment benefit subject to the same limitations as for wages or salary;
- all amounts due in respect of workmen's compensation;
- amounts due in respect of superannuation or provident fund contributions;
- all remuneration payable in respect of vacation leave; and
- payment of taxes.

As a further means of ensuring the orderly payment of debts, Section 329 of the CA allows for the avoidance of transactions that give undue preference. The CA applies the rules in the Bankruptcy Act 1915.

7.5 Control of Insolvency Practitioners

Persons wishing to practise as liquidators must first apply for approval to act as company auditor and then apply to the minister for approval as a liquidator (Section 10). The process of obtaining approval takes into account character, educational and professional qualifications, competence, experience and capacity. Section 11 provides the grounds on which a liquidator is disqualified from acting as a liquidator. These are:

- if indebted to the company for an amount exceeding $ 2 500;
- if an officer of the company, a partner, employer or employee of an officer of the company;
- if a partner or employee of an employee of the company;
- if the person is responsible for, or is the partner, employer or employee of, a person responsible for keeping the members' and debenture holders' registers for the company (Section 10(1));
- if that person is an undischarged bankrupt;
- if that person has assigned his or her estate for the benefit of creditors; or
- if that person has been convicted of an offence involving fraud or dishonesty punishable by a prison term of three months or more.

8 Takeover Rules

Takeovers, the process by which control of a company changes, are regulated by the CA. The key factors in the takeover process are the capacity of the current shareholders to evaluate the offer being made by the offeror for their shares and that shareholders are treated equally.

8.1 An Introduction to Company Takeover Rules

Section 213(4) prevents a takeover for a public company being made unless the offeror corporation has given notice of the terms of the offer to the offeree company (the target) in a prescribed form and within a prescribed period of the offer being made. The prescribed form is set out in Part B of the Tenth Schedule of the CA and the timing requirement is that the notice be given not earlier than 28 days before and not later than 14 days after the offer being made. The offer must also comply with Part A of the Tenth Schedule.

Once the offer has been made, the target company must either provide to the offeror corporation, within 14 days of receiving the notice, a statement as per Part C of the Tenth Schedule or give the same information to the shareholders whose shares are the subject of the takeover bid (Section 213(5)).

An offer can be varied by way of an increase in the consideration offered or by extending the period for acceptance (Section 214). If a shareholder accepted the original offer, he or she is entitled under Section 214(3) to receive any increased consideration later offered. A bid can also be withdrawn (Section 213(10)) and any shareholder who has accepted the offer has an option to treat the acceptance as voidable.

Under section 213(18), a takeover is also required to satisfy the Singapore Code on Takeovers and Mergers. The Code is issued by the Minister for Finance pursuant to a notice made under Section 213(17) of the CA in order to give guidance on the principles of conduct and procedures to be observed in takeover and merger transactions. The Code is, however, non-statutory – being intended to supplement and, in some ways, expand on the statutory provisions dealing with takeovers. As well as the CA and the Code, takeovers and mergers involving listed companies must comply with provisions in the listing manual of the stock exchange.

The Code is drafted with listed public companies in view, but unlisted public companies are expected to observe the letter and spirit of the 'General Principles and Rules', wherever this is possible and appropriate. As with the legislation, the Code does not apply to takeovers of private companies.

Neither the Code nor the Securities Industry Council which administers it is concerned with the evaluation of the financial or commercial aspects of a takeover proposal which is a matter for the shareholders.

The Code is said to represent the collective opinion of those professionally concerned in the field of takeovers and mergers on the proper standard of conduct to be observed in a takeover or merger transaction. It enshrines self-regulation values and applies not only to securities market participants, but also to directors of public companies or persons or groups of persons who seek to gain control of public companies, and professional advisers who are involved in takeovers.

The Code enunciates general principles of conduct to be observed in bid situations and it lays down certain rules, some of which are precise, others no more than examples of the application of the general principles.

8.2   *Takeover Thresholds*

A takeover scheme under the CA is defined as:

the making of offers for the acquisition by or on behalf of a corporation –

(a)   of all the shares in another company or all the shares of a particular class in another company; or

(b)   of any shares in another company which results in the [offeror] acquiring effective control of that other company.

Section 213(3) provides that 'acquiring effective control' means to acquire shares in a company which, when taken with any shares already held, results in being able to exercise or control the exercise of not less than 25 per cent of the votes attached to the voting shares of that company. Once that number of shares has been acquired, an offer must be made for the remaining shares in the company. The CA states that 'a corporation shall be conclusively presumed to have a firm intention to make a takeover offer from the day it acquires effective control' of a target company (Section 213(9)(c)).

8.3   *Disclosure Requirements and Shareholder Protection*

The various Parts of the Tenth Schedule provide details of the material relevant to the takeover offer that must be disclosed to shareholders. The Part A statement which is provided by the offeror corporation specifies the compliance requirements for a takeover offer. The offer must:

- not be conditional on the offeree approving the payment to a director of the target company of compensation for loss of office;
- state whether the offer is conditional on a minimum percentage acceptance;
- state, to the extent that the shares are being acquired by cash, the period by which the payment will be made;
- state, if consideration will be in a non-cash form, when that will be provided;
- in the case of a conditional offer, specify the date at which the offeror can declare the offer to be free of conditions and the new closing date for acceptance; and
- include the following words prominently displayed: 'If you are in any doubt about this offer, you should consult your stockbroker, bank manager, solicitor or other professional adviser.'

Part B of the Tenth Schedule requires the offeror's statement to include:

- the personal details of all of the directors of the offeror corporation;
- a summary of its principal activities;
- the number of shares in the target held by or on behalf of the offeror;
- if the consideration for the target company shares is to be in the form of shares or debentures of the offeror, the reports that would need to be made in the prospectus for those shares or debentures as at the date of the offer (details are also required of any alterations to the capital structure of the offeror company or a subsidiary during the past previous five years);
- details of any restrictions on the right to transfer any shares that form part of the consideration;
- details of arrangements made or being made for the payment of the cash component of the consideration being offered;
- details of any benefits to be paid to the directors of the target company for loss of office or other benefits that may be conditional on the success of the offer;
- where the consideration is, or includes, marketable securities issued or to be issued by the offeror, details of the latest available market sale price on the stock exchange, the highest and lowest market prices over the previous three months, and the latest market price prior to the announcement of the takeover bid; and
- where the securities are not listed, all the details of the number, amount and price at which securities of the offeror were sold in the three months which preceded the making of the offer.

The shareholders who are being asked to consider a takeover offer are entitled to know what might influence the directors of their company when they react to the offer. For this purpose, Part C requires the target company to make a statement which sets out:

- whether the directors recommend acceptance of the offer;
- the number, description and amount of marketable securities held by or on behalf of each of the directors;
- whether each director intends to accept the offer;
- details of each director's holding of marketable securities in the offeror company;
- whether any payment or other benefit is to be made to any director as consideration for retirement from office;
- whether there are any agreements or arrangements in place that are conditional on a successful outcome of the offer;

- whether any director has any direct or indirect interest in any contract entered into by the offeror corporation, and, if so, details of this;
- where shares are being offered as consideration and they are not listed, all the information the target company had as to the details of shares sold in the six months preceding the making of the offer; and
- whether there has been any material change in the financial position of the target company since the date of the last balance sheet.

8.4 The Role of Lawyers, Experts and the Regulator in Takeovers

The Code on Takeovers and Mergers is administered and enforced by the Securities Industry Council, a creature of the Securities Industry Act, whose members are made up of representatives from the government, the Monetary Authority of Singapore and the private sector. The Council issues practice notes on the interpretation of the principles and the rules and the practice to be followed. The role of the Council is 'the enforcement of good business standards and not the enforcement of law'.

The Code involves a process of self-regulation with the primary responsibility of ensuring observance resting with the parties to a takeover and their advisers. Although the documents issued are not required to be submitted to the Council in advance, the practice is that draft documents are submitted to the Council where the takeover involves something unusual. The stock exchange of Singapore, however, does need to see certain documents in advance of publication and takes into account the requirements of the Code.

Any material that is issued to shareholders must not be misleading. A person such as an expert who wilfully makes, or authorizes the making of, a statement that is false or misleading in any material particular is liable to a criminal penalty under Section 401 of the CA.

8.5 The Mechanisms for the Review of Takeover Activity

Where it appears that a breach of the Code has occurred, parties will be required to appear before the Securities Industry Council. Proceedings are informal and no legal representation is permitted, but an alleged offender will be able to call witnesses and have the opportunity to answer the allegations. The Council may also bring witnesses.

The Council is empowered to investigate any dealing in securities that is connected with a takeover transaction. If it finds that there has been a breach, it may deal with it privately or by way of public censure. In a more serious case, it may take action to deprive the offender temporarily or permanently of its ability to enjoy the facilities of the securities market. Should the Council uncover evidence of a criminal offence, it may recommend that prosecution follow.

If the Council feels that the documents contain material that is misleading or incomplete in the way they deal with information of the type the shareholders could reasonably expect, correction will be required by way of further circulars or announcements. Ultimately, however, responsibility for the contents of documents rests with the parties and their advisers and, in this respect, Section 401 of the CA referred to above is relevant.

9   An Introduction to Securities Regulation in Singapore

The securities industry in Singapore is regulated by the Securities Industry Act (Chapter 289) and the regulations made under it. The regulating body is the Monetary Authority of Singapore (the Authority). Also involved in overseeing the market is the Securities Industry Council, comprising representatives of business, government and the Authority, which was established under Section 14 of the Securities Industry Act. The Council's role is primarily advisory, but it is empowered to undertake enquiries into the securities industry and in this regard it has a range of powers. One area in which the Council is active is that of takeovers and mergers. Where the conduct of a market participant has not been satisfactory, the Council has the power to suspend that participant from access to the market.

The scope of the regulations extends to the market participants and to forms of conduct in the market. The thrust of the regulatory system is that it is to protect investors in two ways. The first is by seeking to ensure that the market intermediaries with whom investors deal meet appropriate ethical and prudential standards. This is achieved by a licensing regime and a requirement that market participants, and ultimately the stock exchange, are sufficiently solvent to make good losses incurred by investors as a result of the shortcomings of the market participants. The other form of protection is to prohibit conduct that could result in an innocent investor being taken advantage of or through the market itself being corrupted by manipulation. This arm of investor protection aims to sustain the integrity of the market.

The licensing regime applies to dealers (Section 24), dealers' representatives (Section 25), investment advisers (Section 26) and to investment representatives (Section 27). Only a body corporate can be licensed to carry on business as a dealer (Section 29).

The licensing body is the Authority which can impose conditions and restrictions and revoke licences (Sections 28, 33 and 38). The licences are renewable annually (Section 35). As a further step in protecting investors, the CA requires dealers, dealers' representatives, investment advisers, investment representatives and financial journalists to maintain a register of their interests in securities (Section 42). The Authority can demand production of the register (Section 45) and can require newspaper proprietors to supply personal details of a financial journalist who has contributed advice or analysis in respect of securities (Section 46).

The existence of a stock exchange depends on ministerial approval under the Securities Industry Act (SIA). Requirements are also imposed by the SIA in respect of account keeping, their audit, and, in the case of the stock exchange, a fidelity fund to provide protection to investors who suffered as a result of the dishonest conduct of a stock exchange firm. The stock exchange itself maintains a fund (the Lifeboat Fund) to compensate investors who have suffered financially as result of the failure of a broker. Prudential requirements for brokers are imposed under the regulations.

9.1 The Relationship between the Stock Exchange and Corporate Regulation

The only way in which a stock market can exist is if it is stock market of a securities exchange or an exempt stock market (Section 15 of the SIA). The SIA provides, in Section 16(2), that the minister may approve a body corporate as a stock exchange on being satisfied that:

- at least ten members of the body corporate will carry on the business of dealing in securities independently of and in competition with each other;
- the rules of the body corporate satisfactorily provide for:
  - exclusion from membership of persons not of good character and high business integrity,
  - expulsion, suspension or disciplining of members for 'conduct inconsistent with just and equitable principles in the transaction of business' or for a contravention of the exchange rules or of the SIA,
  - the conditions under which securities are listed for trading on the proposed market,
  - the conditions governing dealings in securities by members,
  - the class or classes of securities that may be dealt with by members,
  - a 'fair representation' of persons in the selection of its committee members and that its membership includes one or more representatives of listed companies and investors not connected with a stockbroker or dealer,

- due regard being paid to the interests of the public in carrying on the business of the stock exchange;
- the interests of the public will be served by granting the application.

The body corporate seeking to establish, maintain or provide a stock market also needs to be approved by the minister as an 'approved securities organisation' (Section 17). The minister must be satisfied that the market will be efficient, honest, fair, competitive and informed; that it will carry on business with due regard to public interest; and that its rules about sanctioning members and the operation of the market will be satisfactory. The approval may be revoked (Section 17(3)).

Where the rules of the exchange are amended, such an amendment is subject to approval by the Authority (Section 18). The Authority may also, with or without consultation with the Securities Industry Council, amend the rules of the exchange (Section 18(3)).

A stock exchange is required, under Section 19(1) of the SIA, to assist the Authority to perform its functions and duties by, among other things, submitting returns and providing information sought by the Authority. It must provide to the Authority details of any disciplinary action taken against a member of the exchange. The Authority is empowered to review the action taken. Notwithstanding the obligations on the exchange, the Authority is able to initiate action against an exchange member.

9.2   The Types of Securities Regulated

Section 2 of the SIA defines 'securities' to mean debentures, stocks or bonds issued or proposed to be issued by a government or by a body corporate or unincorporate or any right or option in respect of such debentures, stocks, shares, bonds or notes or any interest in a company as defined in section 107 of the CA. Specifically excluded from the definition are futures contracts, bills of exchange, promissory notes or certificates of deposit issued by a bank.

9.3   The Legal Effect of Listing Rules and Business Rules of the Stock Exchange

Failure to 'comply with, observe and give effect to the rules or listing rules' of an exchange can lead to the High Court making 'an order giving directions concerning the compliance with, observance or enforcement of, or the giving effect to those rules or listing rules' (Section 20(1)). Such an order may be sought by the Authority, a securities exchange or person aggrieved by the failure. The person against whom such an order can be made is referred to as 'any person who is under an obligation' to so act. The SIA, in Section 20(2), deems a body corporate or a person associated with a body corporate that has been admitted to the official list of an exchange to be 'under an obligation to comply with, observe and give effect to the listing rules' of the exchange. Presumably, a member of the exchange can be ordered to comply with the rules of the exchange.

9.4   *Market Conduct Rules and sanctions for securities misconduct*

Participants in the securities market who are licensed are subject to particular regulations.

- Contract notes of transactions, the evidence that a client's instructions have been carried out, must be issued (Section 49).
- A person making a written recommendation in respect of particular securities must disclose the extent of his or her own interests in the securities involved (Section 50). The penalty for contravention is a maximum fine of $ 5 000 and/or imprisonment for one year.
- Principal dealing is prohibited, unless the client is informed of that fact (Section 52). The penalty for contravention is a maximum fine of $ 10 000 and/or imprisonment for two years.
- Dealers and investment advisers must not extend unsecured credit to an employee to be used to acquire securities (Section 53). The penalty for contravention is a maximum fine of $ 5 000 and/or imprisonment for one year.
- Dealers are required to give priority to a client's instructions in respect of the same securities. That is the dealer cannot, except in limited circumstances, deal with the same class of securities as a principal or on behalf of an associated person. The penalty for contravention is a maximum fine of $ 10 000 and/or imprisonment for one year.

Certain conduct is prohibited and carries criminal sanctions under the general penal section (Section 104). The prohibited forms of conduct affecting securities are as follows:

- creating a false or misleading appearance of active trading of, or with respect to the market for or price of, any securities or manipulating the price of securities by bogus or fictitious transactions; this is variously known as wash sales or churning (Section 97);
- manipulation of the stock market by participating, directly or indirectly, in two or more transactions that intentionally have

the effect or likely effect of raising the price of the securities and inducing persons to purchase or subscribe for such securities (this conduct is also referred to as pooling, whereby securities are sold between members of the pool until the market price has been increased and they can be disposed of at a profit) (Section 98);

- making statements or disseminating information that is false or misleading and likely to induce the sale of purchase of securities or likely to influence the price of securities (Section 99);
- fraudulently inducing persons to deal in securities by making or publishing any misleading, false or deceptive statement, promise or forecast or by any dishonest concealment of material facts (Section 100);
- disseminating information that the price of any securities of a body corporate will or is likely to be affected by reason of transactions that are illegal under Sections 97–100 where the person who is disseminating the information was involved in such transactions (Section 101);
- employment of manipulative and deceptive devices (this is a general omnibus prohibition of conduct that may not satisfy the criteria in respect of the more specific forms of prohibited conduct (Section 102); and
- insider trading by a person who is, or at any time in the preceding six months has been, connected with a body corporate or by a body corporate at a time when any officer of that body corporate is such a person (there are circumstances where a body corporate is, notwithstanding its access to information, not precluded from dealing in the securities) (Section 103).

In brief, insider trading involves a person being in possession of information that:

- is not generally available but, if it were, would be likely materially to affect the price of the securities in question; and
- relates to any transaction (actual or expected) involving two bodies corporate or involving one of them and securities of the other.

Section 157(2) of the CA prohibits the use of sensitive information by an officer of a company – a director, secretary, executive, receiver and manager or a liquidator – and prosecution under Section 157(2) could be seen as an alternative to a charge of insider trading under the SIA.

The penalties for the prohibited conduct are specified in Section 104 and are, in respect of a natural person, a maximum fine of $ 50 000 and/or imprisonment for seven years. The penalty for a body corporate is a maximum fine of $ 100 000. A person convicted is made liable to pay compensation to another person who suffered a loss as a result of the transaction that was affected by his or her conduct (Section 105). Under Section 111, if a company is found guilty of a breach of the CA, the officers of the company are likewise guilty.

10   Miscellaneous

The regulation of companies and those associated with them involves a wide range of issues. In order to make the system of regulation operate there are several classes of provisions.

10.1   The Powers of the Courts

Under the system of law in Singapore, the courts play an important role in resolving disputes between the players in the corporate world – shareholders, company officers, the company and the regulators. Parties in dispute are able to seek adjudication by a court on a matter such as their rights under the articles of association. They may also challenge a decision of the regulators. These rights are in addition to those specified in the legislation. The courts are empowered by Section 409A to grant injunctions.

10.2   Civil Remedies

The CA usually imposes criminal sanctions for breaches of its provisions. In some areas it gives a right to persons who have suffered from a breach of the CA to take action against those who by their breach have caused them loss or damage.

One such area is in respect of misstatements in a prospectus. Section 55 provides that persons who subscribed for shares or debentures on the faith of a prospectus which contained an untrue statement or a wilful non-disclosure may seek compensation for any loss or damage sustained thereby. Those liable are the directors at the time of the issue of the prospectus, a person identified in the prospectus as a current or future director, a promoter of the corporation or a person who authorized the issue of the prospectus. An expert whose opinion is contained in the prospectus is not by that fact alone liable, nor are persons named in various capacities – trustee for debenture holders, auditor, banker, solicitor or stockbroker. The CA provides several defences (Section 55(3) and (5)). This right of action is in addition to the person's common law rights in tort where fraudulent or negligent misrepresentation is relied on. A contractual right could also be available.

Section 157(3)(a) makes a company officer civilly liable for breach of Section 157(1) or (2). The measure of damages is the profit made by the officer in breach or the loss sustained by the company as a result of the breach.

Under Section 105 of the SIA, a person convicted for conduct prohibited by the Act is made liable to compensate a person who suffered a loss as a result of a transaction that had been induced or affected by the conduct of the convicted person. Thus, where the price of shares had been manipulated upwards, a person who paid the artificially high price for shares could seek to recover the difference between that price and what should have been the real price.

10.3   Offences

Where the CA establishes a duty or imposes some restriction, it will at the same time identify the sanction. It is usually a maximum fine and/or a term of imprisonment not exceeding the specified term. In Division 2 of Part XII the CA specifies other offences as follows:

- Share hawking – this occurs where a person goes from 'place to place' offering shares to the public or seeking or receiving offers to subscribe. The penalty for this conduct is a maximum fine of $ 1 000 and/or imprisonment for six months (Section 400).
- False and misleading statements – where a company fails to include the description 'nominal' or 'authorized', is misleading in references to its capital or fails to give equal prominence to the amount of paid-up capital or to the extent of charges over uncalled capital, the company and every officer involved is guilty of an offence (Section 401(1)). A person making a wilfully false or misleading (in a material way) statement in a report, return, certificate, balance sheet or other document is guilty of an offence punishable by a maximum fine of $ 10 000 and/or two years' imprisonment (Section 401(2)).
- False reports – a person making a false report about the company to a director, auditor, debenture holder, trustee for debenture holders, auditor of its holding company or to the stock exchange or Securities Industry Council is guilty of an offence punishable by a maximum fine of $ 10 000 and/or imprisonment for two years (Section 402).
- Payment of dividends except from profits – this is an offence punishable by a maximum fine of $ 5 000 or imprisonment for 12 months. This conduct also makes the directors or managers of the company liable to the creditors of the company up to the amount of dividends paid from sources other than profits (Section 403).

- Fraudulently inducing persons to invest money – the making of 'any statement, promise or forecast' which is known to be misleading, false or deceptive; the reckless making of such a statement; or the concealment of material facts which induces or attempts to induce a person to acquire or sell company securities or lend it money is an offence (Section 404). The penalty is a maximum fine of $ 30 000 and/or a term of imprisonment of seven years.
- Failing to register a corporation or holding out that a business is incorporated – using a name that suggests a business is incorporated or holding out that it is when it is not is an offence punishable by a fine of $ 10 000 and/or imprisonment for two years (Section 405(1)). Improperly using the words 'Private' or 'Sendirian' is an offence subject to a maximum fine of $ 5 000 and a default penalty of a maximum of $ 200 per day for every day on which the conduct continues (Sections 405(2) and 408).
- Frauds by officers on creditors – where a company officer has:
  - (a) by deceitful, fraudulent or dishonest means induced any person to extend credit to the company,
  - (b) executed a charge over assets of the company with intention to defraud creditors, or
  - (c) with intent to defraud creditors, concealed or removed company property since or within two months before the date of any unsatisfied judgment against the company,

  that is an offence. The penalty is a maximum fine of $ 15 000 and/or imprisonment for three years (Section 406).
- General offences – where a person does what the CA forbids, does not do what the CA directs or otherwise contravenes or fails to comply with the CA that is an offence punishable by a maximum fine of $ 1 000 (Section 407).

10.4 *Who May Initiate Proceedings?*

The proper plaintiff rule holds that, in litigation affecting its rights, the company is the appropriate plaintiff. That rule is subject to a statutory derivative action created by Section 216A of the CA.

Prosecutions for breaches of the CA are conducted by the legal section of the Commercial Affairs Department.

10.5 *Registration and Control of Persons under the Legislation*

Section 9(1) of the CA provides that a person may apply to the minister to be approved as a company auditor. The minister is to be satisfied of the applicant's good character and competence to perform the duties of an auditor under the CA (Section 9(2)). An approved auditor may apply to the minister to be approved as a liquidator and the minster, if satisfied of the applicant's experience and capacity, may approve the person (Section 9(3)). The approval is subject to renewal on 31 March of the third year following the year in which approval was granted (Section 9(5)).

No auditor is permitted to consent to be appointed and to act as auditor if not an approved company auditor or if indebted to the company for an amount exceeding $ 2 500, or if an officer of the company, a partner, employer or employee of an officer of the company or a partner or employee of an employee of the company. It is also grounds for disqualification from acting if the person is responsible for or is the partner, employer or employee of a person responsible for keeping the members' and debenture holders' registers for the company (Section 10(1)).

A liquidator is disqualified from acting on similar grounds as an auditor (Section 11(1)). Liquidators are also disqualified if they are undischarged bankrupts, have assigned their estate for the benefit of creditors or have been convicted of an offence involving fraud or dishonesty punishable by a prison term of three months or more.

Note

*   School of Law, University of Canberra.

Further Reading

Pillai, P.N. (1978), *Legal Framework of Business Organisations*, Singapore, Malaya Law Review Faculty of Law, University of Singapore.

Pillai, P.N. (1987), *Company Law and Securities Regulation in Singapore*, Singapore: Butterworths Asia.

Singh, A. (1976), *Company Law of Singapore and Malaysia*, Singapore: Quins.

Lee, F. (1993), *Hong Company Secretarial Practice Manual*, Singapore: Butterworths Asia.

Tay, C.S.K. (1983), *Company Formation Practice Manual*, Singapore: Malayan Law Journal.

Woon, W.C.M. (1995), *Basic Business Law in Singapore*, New York: Prentice Hall.

Woon, W.C.M. and Hicks, A. (looseleaf), *The Companies Act of Singapore: an Annotation*, Singapore: Butterworths Asia.

12 Company Law in Indonesia

PETER LITTLE* AND BAHRIN (KAM)
KAMARUL*

1 Introduction

The Indonesian legal system is pluralistic, reflecting the legacy of Indonesia's colonization by the Dutch until the Japanese occupation in
1942 and different phases of Indonesia's post-colonial constitutional
and political history. The Dutch, as a colonial power, had introduced a
legal system in which different laws were to apply to separate categories of people classified into (a) Europeans, (b) the indigenous people
and (c) foreign Orientals, such as the Chinese. Many laws applied only
to Europeans, whereas the non-European populations were governed
primarily by their respective customary law. Colonial laws which have
continued into post-independent Indonesia have created the basis of a
pluralistic legal system.[1] Although Dutch-based laws are increasingly
being displaced by the enactments of an independent Republic of
Indonesia, the Civil and Commercial Codes introduced by the Dutch
still apply in many areas of commerce and business.

Indonesia's legal pluralism is also the product of different phases
of its legal history.[2] From 1945 to 1949 the Dutch and the Indonesians
had claimed legitimate authority over the territory, resulting in uncertainty in the then existing law. During an eight-month period of
'transfer of sovereignty' in 1949–1950, Indonesian laws were enacted
under a temporary constitution. This was followed, in 1950–1959, by
a system of laws enacted under a liberal parliamentary form of government. The legal system changed with the proclamation of 'Guided
Democracy' in 1959. From 1959 to 1966, rule by presidential decree
became a significant feature of the system. Finally, the legal system
reflects the policy and influence of the New Order government under President Suharto which came to power in 1966. At present, the
sources of law in Indonesia consist of:

- the *Pancasila,* as contained in the Preamble to the 1945 Constitution of the Republic of Indonesia;
- the 1945 Constitution;
- legislative enactments;
- government decrees and decisions;
- judicial decisions;
- customary law; and
- international conventions which have been ratified by the Indonesian government.[3]

The Indonesian Constitution provides for the establishment of a Supreme Court and other courts of law. There are four systems of courts in Indonesia, consisting of:

- General;
- Religious;
- Administrative; and
- Military.

The Supreme Court is the highest court in Indonesia and its functions include the following:

- the review of the decisions from Indonesia's General Courts as a court of cassation (*kasasi*);
- the exercise of general supervisory jurisdiction over the practices and procedures of all Indonesian courts and over the conduct af all judges;
- the provision of legal advice on request from the government;
- the exercise of general supervision over public notaries, lawyers and advocates; and
- the hearing of appeals regarding awards of arbitration over the value of Rp 25 000 or more.

2   The Corporation Law of Indonesia

2.1   *The Constitutional Basis of Company Law in Indonesia*

The *grundnorm* or *rechtsidee* of Indonesian law is *Pancasila* as contained in the Preamble to Indonesia's 1945 Constitution. The philosophy of *Pancasila* consist of five main principles. They are:

- belief in the one supreme God;
- humanity;
- national unity;

- deliberations (*musyawarah*) towards consensus (*mufakat*) or democracy; and
- social justice.

Any Indonesian law or regulation is expected to conform to this philosophy in its details.[4]

The second source of law is the 1945 Constitution, which is regarded as the supreme law of Indonesia. A major source of law are legislative enactments (*undang-undang*) and their accompanying 'elucidations' which are regarded as inseparable parts of the main articles. Other significant sources of law in Indonesia include government regulations, presidential decrees, and other implementing regulations. These commonly provide the details of the *undang-undang*.

2.2 Commercial Law Reform in Indonesia

In 1958 the Institute for the Development of National Law was established with the task of reforming Indonesia laws. However, very few of the Institute's proposals were enacted into formal law by the legislature between 1958 and 1974. The Indonesian legislators, it is suggested, preferred to encourage the organic development of Indonesian law along the principles of Indonesian *adat* or custom.[5] In 1974 the Institute was integrated into the National Law Reform Agency (*Badan Pembinaan Hukum Nasional*) within the Department of Justice. Recent law reforms, in the commercial and business area have shown a greater openness to Western and other foreign ideas and norms.

Current economic law reform is driven primarily by the perceived need to create greater legal certainty in Indonesia's commercial law to promote greater investor confidence and economic growth. One of the objectives of Indonesia's Sixth Five-Year Plan (*Repelita VI*) is 'to organize and improve the national legal system'.[6] The new company law of Indonesia is an example of this process. It is part of the effort by the Indonesian government:

> toward [the] development of the national legal system and the development of our Economic Laws in particular ... [It] is an attempt to find a meeting ground for the elements upheld by Common lawyers on the one hand and those upheld by Continental lawyers on the other.[7]

In this effort, the reform process is much more open to foreign influences.

2.3   *The Enactment of Indonesia's Law on Limited Liability Companies 1995*[8]

Prior to the enactment of Indonesia's Law on Limited Liability Companies (1995) (the 1995 Company Law), Indonesia's law on companies consisted of 21 articles of the Commercial Code 1847 relating to limited companies (together with occasional written and verbal guidance from the Indonesian Ministry of Justice) and the Ordinance of Indonesia Share Enterprise (1939). Both codes were Dutch colonial enactments. Unlike other ex-colonies (for example Singapore), Indonesia did not update its colonial corporate laws until 1995.[9] According to the Preamble to the 1995 legislation, the Commercial Code provisions were 'no longer in keeping with the rapid economic developments either on a national or international scale'. The Commercial Code applies only to Europeans and foreign Orientals, whereas the majority of autochthonous Indonesians remain governed by their own customary law in commercial matters. Although autocthones may choose to avail themselves voluntarily of the institutions of the Code, and that the Commercial Code implicitly applies to transactions among autochthonous Indonesians whenever they enter into a transaction exclusively governed by the Code, there was a high degree of uncertainty in the law. One aim of the new legislation is to provide greater certainty and clarity in the law by replacing the relevant provisions of the Commercial Code and the Ordinance of Indonesia Share Enterprise. Another aim was to integrate the Indonesian economy into the world economy, and to expose it to 'the influences and demands of globalization'. This aim was to be achieved in conjunction with other commercial law reforms, including new laws relating to foreign exchange, foreign investment, enhanced international cooperation, the banking system and the capital market.

2.4   *The Underlying Purpose and Principles of Indonesia's Company Law*

According to the 1995 Company Law's 'Elucidation',[10] the legislation must be 'founded upon and be faithful to the economic principles traced in the Basic Law of 1945, and the principles of brotherhood'. It is also to be guided by the objectives of Indonesia's Second Long Term Development Effort. The Preamble to the 1995 company legislation provides that it must reflect 'the principles of family and economic democracy based on the principles of *Pancasila* and the Constitution of 1945'. Key principles mentioned by the legislation's Elucidation include that all shares subscribed must be fully paid up; that the law 'must consistently be able to protect interests of shareholders, creditors, and other allied persons, as well as the interest of the Limited Company itself'; and, as far as possible, the law should 'restrain monopoly and monopsony in all its forms'.

2.5 The Interpretation of Legislation

A major issue in the interpretation of legislation is the meaning of Article II of the Transitory Provisions of the 1945 Constitution and its effect on a judge's role in deciding the continuing validity of laws, especially Dutch laws, which existed before Indonesia's independence. The Article provides that 'All existing State Bodies and Regulations which are still in force provided that they have not yet been replaced by new ones which are created according to the Constitution'.[11] It is suggested that the Article should be interpreted as:

> [R]ecognizing the competency of judges to preside over civil proceedings and in implementing civil laws, in exceptional cases, if they considered ... that a certain provision was obsolete or was no longer in conformity with existing changes and progress of the times, they then may eliminate the related provision or develop the provision further if the changes and progress of the times require such provision to be developed.[12]

The above principle, it is argued, gives the Indonesian judge the right and discretion to create 'new law' if the circumstances justify it, to 'adjust' the law to the new circumstances, and to decide that a legal provision from the period before the enforcement of the 1945 Constitution is no longer valid.[13] In addition, Article 26 of the Basic principles of the Judiciary (*Undang-Undang Pokok Kekuasaan Kehakiman*) (Law No. 14 , 1970) also provides for a creative role for Indonesian judges. It has been suggested that the article obliges the judge:

> to dig, follow and understand the legal views held by the people. In a community which still has many unwritten laws that are in the process of transition ... a judge is the formulator and digger of legal codes existing amongst the people.[14]

Although the Supreme Court has a leading role in the unifying process of case-law, particularly with regard to unwritten customary law, the theory of binding precedent has no application in the Indonesian courts. In practice, however, the lower courts consider themselves bound by the decisions of higher courts as, otherwise, they lay themselves open to being overturned on appeal.

Indonesian statutes are characteristically very general in nature and lacking in detail.[15] This feature reflects the Indonesian legislators' view that legislation will be difficult to change or amend once it has been enacted. The general nature of legislation poses several problems. First, the enactment of a law does not, in itself, provide sufficient legal certainty. Such legislation requires some implementing rules or regulations from the executive to be applicable with any degree of certainty. Second, the executive does not always respond by enacting the required implementing regulations. Finally, the lack of detail in legislation gives the executive much latitude to reinterpret such legislation. In Indonesia, the detailed application of most statutory provisions depends to a great degree on their elaboration through government regulations (*peraturan pemerintah*), presidential decrees (*keputusan presiden*) and ministerial decisions (*keputusan menteri*).

The 1995 Company Law came into force on 7 March 1996, displacing Articles 36–56 of the Commercial Code which previously governed the operation of limited liability companies. However, regulations enacted to implement the Commercial Code provisions remain valid and applicable, as long as they do not contradict, or have not been replaced by, regulations enacted to implement the new legislation. Consequently, in interpreting the 1995 legislation, the Commercial Code provisions and its regulations may still have relevance.[16]

3   The Nature and Powers of Corporate Regulatory Bodies in the Jurisdiction

3.1   The Minister of Justice

The Minister of Justice is responsible for approving the incorporation of a limited liability company (*perseroan terbatas*). The deed of establishment and articles of association of the company have to be submitted to, and be approved by, the Minister of Justice.[17] The application may be rejected by the minister on a number of grounds[18] (see Section 5 below). In the case of a company which is subject to the Foreign Investment Law 1967, incorporation may be rejected if the company has not met the requirements of that Law, such as presidential approval and the Bank of Indonesia's confirmation of the payment of foreign capital shares. The approval of the minister is also required for some type of amendments to the articles of association of an incorporated company.[19]

3.2   The General Courts

The District Court has been given supervisory powers over company governance by the 1995 company legislation. The chairman of the court in whose jurisdiction the company is situated is given powers to protect the rights of minority shareholders. They include power with regard to general shareholders' meetings, which can be authorized by minority shareholders with more than one-tenth of the shares;[20] and the power to grant an order at the request of minority shareholders that an inspection of the company be made to ascertain whether there has been a breach of the law by the company, the directors or the commissioners causing loss to the shareholders.[21]

3.3 The Capital Investment Coordinating Board (Badan Koordinasi Penanaman Modal, BKPM)

The BKPM, a government non-departmental body to be directly responsible to the Indonesian President, was established in 1973. It manages and administers foreign investment in Indonesia. Such investment is governed by the Foreign Investment Law 1967. The purpose of the legislation is to encourage foreign investment participation in Indonesia's economy, especially in areas of the industrial sector where domestic advanced technology and management skills are not yet available. The functions of the BKPM include:

- advising the president in policy-making regarding capital investment;
- processing approvals of capital investment;
- evaluating policy implementation; and
- advising and assisting foreign and domestic investors.

As a coordinating agency, it has representatives from departments concerned with taxation, tariffs, land purchase and other related investment matters and provides a 'one-stop service' to foreign entrepreneurs seeking to invest in Indonesia.

3.4 The Capital Market Supervisory Agency (BAPEPAM)

The regulation of the capital market is the responsibility of BAPEPAM, which was established in 1977 to administer the Jakarta stock exchange.[22] The Capital Market Decrees of 1990 changed the name of BAPEPAM from the Capital Market Executive Agency to the Capital Market Supervisory Agency, although the acronym BAPEPAM was retained. The Jakarta Stock Exchange was privatized and in 1991 its operational administration was transferred from BAPEPAM to the exchange.[23] In April 1992 BAPEPAM was given a new function as the supervisory agency to ensure the proper and fair operation of the capital market. In 1996, the number of listed companies on the Jakarta stock exchange grew from 238 to 253, and the cumulative value of issues increased from Rp 36 trillion to Rp 50 trillion.[24]

Decree 1548 of 1990 provides that only securities companies licensed to act as broker-dealers, underwriters and investment managers can become members of the securities exchange. These companies are licensed by the Minister of Finance. However, rules regulating the conduct of exchange members are subject to the BAPEPAM approval and BAPEPAM supervises exchange activities. BAPEPAM also supervises other market institutions including: clearing, settlement and depository institutions; securities administration agencies; and custodian banks. Market professionals such as auditors, appraisers and legal consultants are required to register with the BAPEPAM to practise in the capital market. The 1990 decree empowers the BAPEPAM to make regulations to implement the decree. Since 1991 it has issued more than 100 rules, contained in the BAPEPAM Rule Book.[25]

4   A Description of Types of Companies and their Powers

4.1   Types of limited liability company (perseroan terbatas)

The limited liability company is defined as:

> a corporate body which is established on the basis of an agreement, carries on business activities with authorised capital entirely divided into shares, and meets the requirements stipulated in this [limited liability company] law and its enforcement regulations.[26]

The 1995 Law provides for the incorporation of only one type of limited liability company and does not allow for a company whose liability is limited by guarantee. The limited company is required to have its name preceded by the words '*perseroan terbatas*' or the abbreviation 'PT'. Foreign equity investment in Indonesia is required by the Foreign Investment Law 1967 to incorporate in the form of a limited liability company. Such investment can be made through the ownership of shares either in a joint venture or wholly owned limited liability company, with some exceptions.[27] The companies are classified by the BKPM as a foreign investment enterprise (*penanaman modal asing*) and the BKPM's approval is required before a foreign investment enterprise can be registered.

4.2   The Foreign Investment Enterprise (penanaman modal asing)

A limited liability company which is a foreign investment enterprise (whether jointly or wholly owned) must be licensed to operate in Indonesia. A 30-year business licence may be granted by the chairman of the BKMP or by the State Minister for the Mobilization of Investment Funds. The Foreign Investment Law 1967 also requires a foreign wholly owned company to progressively divest a percentage of its shares to Indonesian citizens or companies.[28] Although no specific percentage of the divestment is specified, an interpretation of the regulations suggests that a minimum of 5 per cent within 15 years of commencing commercial production is required.[29] The Indonesian 1995 Company Law breaks new ground in providing protection for minority shareholder rights. In a joint-venture foreign investment company, protection against oppression is given to Indonesian minority shareholders. Under the 1995 legislation, minority shareholders are given certain rights, including the rights of shareholders owning more than one-tenth of the shares:

- to authorize and organize a general shareholders' meeting;[30] and
- to request the District Court to order an inspection of the company to ascertain whether a breach of the law has been committed by the company's directors or commissioners.[31]

The Foreign Investment Law 1967 provides for the granting of a wide range of concessions to the foreign investment company including:

- taxation concessions;
- the choice of the management of the foreign investment company;
- the employment of foreign nationals where no qualified Indonesians are available;
- exemptions from import duties on basic materials;
- loss-carry forwards; and
- international arbitration in the case of compensation to be paid as a result of nationalization of assets.[32]

However, the Foreign Investment Law 1967 also imposes a range of restrictions on foreign investment, including the prohibition of investment in public utilities in telecommunications, shipping, aviation, drinking water, atomic power plants and the mass media, unless the Indonesian state retains sufficient control in its management.[33] Other restrictions on foreign investment are imposed by presidential decree and international agreements, and they include absolute prohibition on investment in the firearms, ammunition and other war equipment industries, and restrictions on investment in small scale industries reserved for domestic capital investment.

4.3   The 'publicly-held' or 'open' limited company (perseroan terbatas terbuka)

A company is publicly held or has open limited liability if it is 'a company with a capital and number of shareholders that meet certain requirements or a company that has made a public offering in accordance with the rules and regulations that govern the capital market'.[34] A public company is required to use the word *'terbuka'* or the abbreviation 'Tbk' after its name to indicate its public company status.[35] The supervision of such companies is the responsibility of the BAPEPAM under Decree 1548 of 1990 and their activities in the capital market are governed by the BAPEPAM Rule Book. Under limited liability company law, the directors of the company are under a duty to submit the annual accounts of the company to a public accountant for audit.[36]

4.4   The Legal Capacities and Powers of Companies

Under the Commercial Code, the limited liability company is not explicitly characterized as a separate legal entity. However, it has been firmly established in practice that a limited liability company is considered to be an independent legal entity. It has its own property, is able to act independently and is separate from the property and actions of the shareholders. It has its own rights and obligations. However, the Law provides that a 'Company shall acquire the status of a legal entity after the Deed of Establishment ... is authorized by the Minister'.[37]

5   Company Formation

5.1   The Registration of Companies and Promoters

The 1995 Company Law continues the existing rule of requiring a minimum of two promoters for the incorporation of a company.[38] The promoters attest to the articles of association of the new company and submit a notarial deed in the Indonesian language to the Minister of Justice to obtain his or her approval.[39] The Minister of Justice may reject the application on the following grounds:

- if the company to be established is against good morals or public order;[40]
- if the articles of association breach other laws and regulations,[41] including complying with 'the principles of good intentions, the principles of fairness, and the principles of decency in managing the company';[42]

- in the case of a company formed under the Foreign Investment Law 1967, that the relevant presidential and ministerial approvals, and confirmation by the Bank of Indonesia of payment of foreign capital shares, have not been obtained; and
- that there is serious objection to the establishment of the company.

Further, the approval by the Minister of Justice may be made on the condition that the limited liability company agrees to be dissolved if the minister finds that the public order so requires.[43] The legislation, however, sets a maximum of 60 days for the finalization of request of approval by the minister from the date of application.[44]

Once a company is incorporated, the directors are required to register with the company register, the deed of establishment (which includes the articles of association) and the letter of authorization from the minister, within 30 days of the date of authorization.[45] Publication of the registration must be made in the Supplementary State Records.[46] Until registration and the announcement of the incorporation are completed, the board of executives of the company are jointly and severally liable for the acts of the company.[47] The legal acts of the founders of the company will bind the company on its ratification of those acts.[48]

5.2 The Corporate Constitution

Unlike the provisions of the Commercial Code, the 1995 Company Law makes a distinction between the articles of incorporation (*akta pendirian*) (Section 1, Chapter II) and the memorandum of association (*anggaran dasar*) (Section 2, Chapter II). The 1995 Company Law provides for certain mandatory provisions in the company's articles. They include:

- the name and domicile of company;
- the purpose, aim and business activity;
- the period of operation;
- the amount of authorized, subscribed and paid-up capital;
- the number and classes of shares;
- the composition and names of members of boards of executives and directors;
- the place and procedure for holding general shareholders' meetings;
- the procedures for electing, appointing, succeeding and dismissing members of the boards of executives and directors;
- the procedures for utilizing profits and distributing dividends; and
- other provisions required by law.[49]

5.3   *Restrictions on the Use of Certain Names*

The name of the company must be preceded by the words *'perseroan terbatas'* or the abbreviation 'PT', and, in the case of a public company, the name must be followed by the abbreviation 'Tbk'. The company shall not use a name that has legally been used by, or resembles the name of, another company.[50]

5.4   *Membership and Share Capital Requirements*

The 1995 Company Law allows incorporation only of those companies whose liability will be limited by shares,[51] and there is no provision for a company limited by guarantee. Shares may be either registered or bearer shares, with bearer shares being required to be fully paid up.[52] Bearer shares were also allowed by Indonesia's Commercial Code, but, since the mid 1980s, the minister has rejected articles of association that allowed for bearer shares because they provided a popular method of evading restrictions on foreign ownership of shares in non-foreign investment companies.[53] Although bearer shares are allowed under the 1995 Company Law, they may not be pledged.[54] Named shares, on the other hand, may be pledged, but the votes in these shares remain with the shareholders.

The minimum authorized capital of a company must be Rp 20 million (approximately US$ 10 000),[55] to be denominated in Indonesian currency only.[56] Other government regulations, however, may prescribe other minimums in particular fields of business.[57] When establishing a company, the promoters are required to subscribe at least 25 per cent of the authorized capital and at least 50 per cent of the nominal value of the shares must be paid up. Further issues of shares thereafter must be fully paid up.[58] Payment for shares can be made in the form of money or other means. If payment by other means is used (for example technology transfer rights or management services), appraisal of the price shall be determined by an expert who has no association with the company. The payment of shares in immovables must be announced in two daily newspapers. However, the issue of capital of a 'publicly held' company must be paid in cash.[59]

Purchase by the company of its own shares is allowed, subject to certain conditions. First, the repurchase must be financed by net profit, must not reduce the net asset value of the company to below the amount of subscribed capital plus compulsory reserves required by law, and the total nominal holding of the company of its own shares must not exceed 10 per cent of its subscribed capital.[60] Second, the repurchase must be authorized by a shareholders' resolution at a meeting attended by shareholders representing not less than two-thirds of the votes. This authority may be delegated to another organ of the company for a maximum period of 10 years, but may be revoked at any time. Finally, shares repurchased by the company or its subsidiaries cannot be used to determine a quorum or cast a vote at shareholders' meetings.[61]

An increase in the company's capital must be authorized by a resolution of a shareholders' general meeting, although that authority may be delegated to the board of directors for a maximum of five years and is revocable at any time.[62] Where the capital of the company is increased, the existing shareholders have the first right of refusal, and if these options are not exercised, then the company employees are granted the option to subscribe ahead of other subscribers. The amount of employee subscription is to be determined by government regulation.[63]

A reduction in the company's capital is permitted by the 1995 Company Law. The proposed reduction may be in respect of one or all classes of shares. Where the reduction relates to all classes of shares, the reduction must be in proportion to the capital represented by such classes of shares. The majority of shareholders in each class of shares must agree to the reduction in that class of shares.[64] The proposal to reduce capital must be authorized by a shareholders' general meeting. All creditors of the company are to be notified of the proposal which is required to be published in the State Gazette.[65] Creditors may object within 60 days of the notification and the company has 30 days to meet creditors' objections. If no resolution can be found, creditors may file their objections in court.[66] The minister will grant approval for the reduction of capital only if there are no creditor objections to the proposal; the solutions to creditors' objections have been achieved; or the lawsuits of the creditors have been rejected by the court.[67]

5.5 The Amendment of the Corporate Constitution

A general shareholders' meeting has all residual powers not explicitly given to the board of executives or directors.[68] A resolution to amend the company's constitution must be authorized by a general meeting attended by shareholders representing at least two-thirds of the shares and approved by two-thirds of shares represented.[69]

5.6 Company Registers

A company is required to keep a register of shareholders in various classes of shares and particulars of bearer shares. It is also required to keep and maintain a register containing details of shares in the company or other companies which are owned by members of the boards of executives or directors. As registered shares can be pledged, unlike bearer shares, a register detailing persons holding rights and other encumbrances to pledged shares is required to be maintained by the company. Changes in share ownership must also be updated by the company.[70]

6   The Internal Administration of Companies

6.1   The Registered Office and Name

A company's name, which must be set out in the articles of association,[71] must not be the same as any name lawfully used by, or identical to that of, another company.[72] Also a company must not use a name which is contrary to public policy or good morals.[73] The name must be preceded by the words '*perseroan terbatas*' or the abbreviation 'PT'.[74] An open company[75] must add the abbreviation 'Tbk'.[76] An alteration of the articles to change the name requires approval of the minister.[77] The company's domicile must also be registered in the articles together with a place where general meetings of shareholders are to take place.[78] The general meeting of shareholders must be held at the place of domicile unless stipulated otherwise in the articles.[79]

6.2   The Duties, Powers and Responsibilities of Officers

Under the 1995 Company Law, management of a company rests in the board of directors[80] and is subject to the supervision of a board of commissioners and, ultimately, the general meeting of shareholders (see Section 6.7, below). Directors are responsible for managing the company in the interests of and in accordance with its objectives and, unless otherwise restricted by statute or the articles, each director may act on behalf of and represent the company.[81] Directors may not, however, transfer or encumber all or a majority of the company's assets or apply for bankruptcy without the approval of a shareholders' resolution.[82]

Directors are required to act in good faith in the interests of the company and are personally liable for the consequences of failing to do so or for acting negligently.[83] These requirements are potentially very onerous as they expose directors to personal liability for well-intentioned errors in the exercise of their powers.[84]

In order to reduce conflicts of interests, Article 84 prevents a director from representing the company while there is a court case between the company and the director or if the director has an interest which conflicts with that of the company.[85] The conflict rule is aided to some extent by the requirement that the shareholding interests of directors and their relatives be disclosed to the company (see further below, however disclosure does not extend specifically to other forms of interest which actually or potentially conflict with the interests of the company.

Furthermore, shareholders holding 10 per cent of the company's voting shares may sue directors in the company's name for fault or negligence. Directors are also jointly and severally liable for losses caused by fault or negligence if the company is declared bankrupt and its assets are insufficient to cover its losses unless they are able to prove that the losses were not due to their fault or negligence.[86]

Specific duties of the directors include:

- the registration of the deed of establishment in the company register and the publication of the registration in the Official Gazette;[87]
- ensuring that any amendments to the articles of association together with the ministerial certificate of approval are registered;[88]
- the preparation and maintenance of a shareholders' register;[89]
- the establishment and maintenance of a special register containing information relating to shares in the company or any other company owned by directors or commissioners and their relatives, together with the dates of acquisition of such shares;[90]
- the preparation of the annual accounts;[91]
- holding an annual general meeting of shareholders;[92] and
- the maintenance of a register of minutes of shareholders' and directors' resolutions.[93]

Directors are appointed by and may be dismissed by the shareholders in a general meeting who also determine their remuneration.[94] A company is required to have only one director, unless it is an open (public) company in which case a minimum of two is required.[95] A person may not be appointed as a director if he or she:

- has ever been declared bankrupt;
- has been a director or commissioner who has been adjudicated to have caused the bankruptcy of a company; or
- has been sentenced for a criminal offence for causing financial loss to the state within five years of appointment.[96]

Only an individual may be appointed as a director.

The 1995 Company Law also obliges a company to appoint a board of commissioners which shall have the authority and duties set out in the articles of association.[97] A minimum of one is required and two in the case of an open company. Appointment, dismissal and qualification requirements are similar to those which apply to directors.[98] The basic statutory duty of commissioners is to supervise the directors' policies and to give them advice. As with directors, they must disclose to the company any shares which they or their relatives hold. They are required to act in good faith in the interests of the company and may be subject to a derivative action brought in the name of the company by the holders of 10 per cent of the company's voting shares if the company suffers loss as a result of their fault or negligence. It has been said that the requirement of both the board of directors and the board of commissioners in a large modern company is undesirable and burdensome and that the onerous liability provisions of the new Indonesian Company Law 1995 may deter people from accepting such positions of responsibility.[99] It has also been suggested that foreign directors of joint venture foreign investment companies could find themselves the targets of vexatious lawsuits for business mistakes.[100]

6.3   Meeting Procedures

A company must hold an annual general meeting, convened by directors at least once every year no later than six months after the end of the financial year and may hold other shareholders' meetings as determined by the board from time to time.[101] Shareholders representing one-tenth of the issued voting shares (unless the articles specify a lower number) can demand a meeting be convened. They must do so by written request setting out the reasons for the request and the meeting may only consider such matters.[102] A shareholders' meeting must be held at the company's domicile unless the articles allow otherwise.[103] The court may also order an annual general meeting to be held if the directors have failed to convene one, or a requisitioned meeting may be ordered where directors or the commissioners did not respond to a shareholders' requisition within 30 days.[104]

Not less than 14 days' prior notice of a meeting must be given by registered mail and, in the case of an open company, notice of the meeting must be advertised in two daily newspapers. Notice must set out the date, time, place and agenda of the meeting and must state that documents relating to the meeting may be inspected and copied, free of charge, at the company's office. Resolutions may be valid notwithstanding a failure to comply with the notice or requirements if the meeting is attended by all shareholders who unanimously approve the resolutions.[105]

Shareholders have a right to attend and vote at a meeting in person or may be represented by an attorney, appointed in writing. However, directors, commissioners and employees of the company cannot be appointed as a shareholders' attorney.[106] Unless otherwise specified in the articles, each share carries one right to vote.[107]

In the first place, resolutions are to be achieved by consensus, failing which a simple majority is required unless the 1995 Company Law or the articles prescribe otherwise.[108] Article 78(1) recognizes, however, that the articles may stipulate other means of passing a shareholders' resolution. They could authorize, for example, video conferenced meetings or resolutions passed by shareholders unanimously signing a copy of a proposed resolution. Special majorities are required in a number of defined situations. First, an amendment of the articles requires a resolution to be approved at a meeting attended by shareholders representing at least two-thirds of the total voting shares and for at least two-thirds of them to vote in favour. If a quorum is not achieved, a similar quorum applies at a reconvened meeting, but only a simple majority is required to pass the resolution.[109] Second, a resolution to approve a merger, consolidation, takeover, bankruptcy application, dissolution, decision to encumber all or a majority of the company's assets, or extension of the company's period of establishment requires the meeting to have been attended by shareholders representing at least three-quarters of the total voting shares and for at least three-quarters to have voted in favour.[110] Minutes of shareholders' meetings must be signed by the chairman of the meeting and at least one shareholder.[111] These and the minutes of directors' resolutions must be entered in a register which the company is to keep at its domicile and make available for inspection by members.[112]

6.4   Audit and Accounting Rules

Within five months of the end of the financial year, directors must prepare an annual report for submission to the annual meeting of shareholders for their approval (see Section 6.3, above) containing:

- the annual accounts: a balance sheet, profit and loss account and an explanation of such documents;
- a consolidated balance sheet for a group of companies;
- a report on the state of the company, its management and the results achieved;
- a description of the company's main activities and any changes during the financial year;
- details of any problems arising during the financial year and their effects on the company;
- the names of the directors and commissioners; and
- the salary and other forms of remuneration paid to directors and commissioners.[113]

If the company raises money from the public, issues debentures or is an open company, the annual report must be audited. The auditor's report must be submitted to the shareholders' meeting through the directors, and advertised in two newspapers.[114] The accounts must be signed by each director and commissioner, and, if any of them refuse to sign, written reasons must be provided.[115] The annual report and annual financial report must be approved by the shareholders in a general meeting.[116] Directors are jointly and severally liable to any person who suffers loss as a result of any untrue or misleading matter in the annual report unless they can prove that the liability was not their fault.[117]

A company is required to establish a reserve fund and contribute to it each year from its net profit until the fund reaches 20 per cent of the company's issued capital. Until that limit is reached, the fund can only be applied to extinguish losses.[118] Otherwise, net profits and the reserve fund may be applied at the discretion of the shareholders' meeting. If shareholders do not decide, net profits must be distributed as dividends.[119]

6.5   The Annual Return and Other Registers

A company is required to establish and maintain a register of shareholders in which details of share ownership are recorded together with details of any pledge over shares and a description of property contributed as capital of the company other than cash.[120] Further, a special register containing details of shares owned by directors or commissioners or their relatives, must be established and maintained.[121] Any change in the ownership (but not of control) of shares referred to in either register must be recorded. If the company issues bearer shares, details (including serial numbers) must also be recorded.[122] These registers, to be kept at the company's domicile, must be available for inspection by shareholders.[123] Shareholders are entitled to documentary evidence of their ownership of shares.[124]

Directors must also establish and maintain a register of minutes of shareholders' and directors' resolutions. Shareholders, on making a request in writing, are entitled to inspect these registers and obtain copies. Importantly, shareholders are also entitled to inspect and take copies of the books of the company although, as the term 'books' is undefined, it is not clear whether this includes all financial records.

6.6   The Shareholder Protection Rules

The shareholder of a limited liability company is liable only to the extent of the nominal value of shares for which he or she has subscribed unless the company is unable to pay its debts in full and the shareholder directly or indirectly has improperly used the company for personal purposes, is involved in a civil wrong committed by the company or has directly or indirectly and unlawfully used the company's assets and caused the deficiency.[125]

Shareholders are afforded significant protection within the 1995 Company Law. In particular, holders of one-tenth of the total votes may bring derivative proceedings in the company's name against directors or commissioners for losses caused through fault or negligence.[126] Further, a shareholder may petition the court in relation to losses sustained because of unfair or unreasonable acts of the company whether as a result of a shareholders' resolution, or that of the directors or commissioners. This is designed to remedy any damage suffered by a shareholder and to prevent the act from being continued or repeated.[127] Protection of shareholders is also provided for in a number of other ways, including:

- a right of redress against directors for having a share buy-back transaction cancelled for exceeding the statutory limit;[128]
- a requirement that unless otherwise provided in the articles, any new issue of shares must be offered *pari passu* to existing holders;[129]
- a requirement that any reduction of capital be proportional;[130]
- a requirement for directors and commissioners and their relatives to disclose their share investments;[131]
- the right to requisition a general meeting of shareholders;[132]
- the right to inspect registers and books;[133] and
- the right to petition the court for an investigation.[134]

See also Section 6.2, above, as to directors' responsibility for a company's bankruptcy.

Shareholders are also given the important right to require the company to purchase their shares at a reasonable price if they have disapproved of, and would suffer loss as a result of, an amendment to the articles of association, a sale encumbrance or exchange of all or a majority of the company's assets, or a merger, consolidation or takeover of a company.[135]

6.7 The Relationship between Management and Shareholders

The general meeting of shareholders which appoints directors and commissioners and has all the powers of the company not entrusted to those boards is given considerable authority by the 1995 Company Law through the special majorities which are required to approve substantial transactions affecting ownership, control and shareholder interests (see further at Section 6.3, above).

6.8   Corporate Financial Transactions

The 1995 Company Law enables a company to buy back its shares providing the source of payment is net profit so long as the company's net assets do not fall below its issued capital plus the statutory reserve fund (see Section 6.4, above) and the total number of shares bought back[136] does not exceed 10 per cent of its issued capital.[137] A buy-back transaction exceeding that limit is void. There is no general register of corporate charges in Indonesia and the company registry only requires the corporate constitution and amendments thereto to be registered. Thus, it is difficult for lenders to establish whether directors may enter into a particular loan and execute the necessary documents.[138]

7   The External Administration of Companies

7.1   The Rules Regarding Arrangements and Reconstructions

Chapter 7 of the 1995 Company Law provides for the first time for merger, consolidation and takeover rules. Thus, one or more companies may merge into one existing company or consolidate with another company to form a new company.[139] In order to implement a plan of consolidation or merger, directors of the companies involved must prepare a plan containing at least the following:

- the names of the companies;
- the reasons for the plan explained by each director, together with the plan's requirements and terms;
- the procedure to connect the shares of the representative companies;
- the draft constitution of the new or consolidated company;
- the balance sheet and profit and loss accounts for the three preceding years for each company involved; and
- any other material information.

Each participating company must approve of the plan by a shareholders' resolution in accordance with Article 102(3). Article 76 further requires a resolution to be passed at a meeting attended by shareholders representing at least three-quarters of the voting shares of whom three-quarters vote in favour.

Importantly, Article 104 imposes a general requirement that during the adoption of any plan consideration be taken of the following interests:

- the company;
- the minority shareholders;
- the employees;
- the public interest; and
- fair competition in business activities.

The official Elucidation states that a plan which would adversely affect these interests may not be carried out. Significantly, it states that minority shareholders are entitled to sell their shares at reasonable prices and, if this will not be possible under the plan, they may disapprove the plan and exercise their rights under Article 55 to have their shares acquired at a reasonable price by the company. In a merger or consolidation, the company which is merged or consolidated is dissolved.[140] This may be carried out without first liquidating the company, in which case the assets and liabilities of the dissolved company are transferred to the surviving company. Similarly, shareholders of the dissolved company become shareholders of the surviving company.

7.2 Voluntary Administration and Corporate Rescue Provisions

Other than the Bankruptcy Code's provisions relating to moratorium and composition (see below), there are no corporate law rules governing voluntary administration or similar procedures.

7.3 Company Winding Up Rules, Tests for Insolvency and Grounds for Winding Up

Corporate insolvency in Indonesia is governed by the little known Bankruptcy Code of 1906 and the 1995 Company Law. The Bankruptcy Code, which was enacted by the former Netherlands-Indies government, has not been modernized and applies to Europeans and foreign Orientals, including corporations. However, any other person may submit him or herself voluntarily to the regulations on bankruptcy by 'partial voluntary submission to European private law', although this is a time-consuming and cumbersome administrative procedure.[141]

Both the Bankruptcy Code and the relevant Articles of the 1995 Company Law implement the following provisions of the Civil Code:

- Article 1131, which states that all assets of the debtor, both present and future, constitute collateral for his or her debts; and
- Article 1132, which provides that the debtor's assets will be distributed '*pro rata pari passu*' in accordance with each

creditor's claim, unless the creditor enjoys a preference by law or other arrangement.

Under both corporate insolvency procedures, priorities are determined in accordance with the Civil Code (see below). In practice, however, neither of these legal procedures is important in dealing with bankrupt or insolvent companies. At present, most corporate liquidation is carried out informally by negotiated settlements.

Under the 1995 Company Law, dissolution and liquidation of a company may be initiated by either a resolution of a general meeting of shareholders or on the expiration of the period for which a company is established as stated in its articles or by a court order. These procedures, although not explained comprehensively, nevertheless surpass the terms of Article 56 of the Commercial Code, which previously required a dissolved limited liability company to be liquidated by the directors unless otherwise provided by the articles of incorporation. Each of the three specified procedures commences with the dissolution of the company and is followed by the administrative process of liquidation.

Under the first procedure, dissolution is effected by a shareholders' resolution which has been proposed by the board of directors.[142] A general meeting of shareholders' resolution is valid in these circumstances if the meeting is attended by shareholders representing at least three-quarters of the total voting shares and if at least three-quarters of them vote in favour of the resolution.[143] Such a resolution may be passed because of, for example, financial distress, internal divisions or the purpose of the company having expired. Dissolution occurs at the time specified in the resolution and is followed by liquidation.[144] If a liquidator is not appointed, the directors serve as the liquidators of the limited liability company.[145]

A limited liability company is also dissolved at the expiration of the period for which it is established as stated in its articles of association,[146] unless the period is extended by the minister acting on a request of the directors who have been authorized to do so by a special resolution of shareholders.[147] The minister must give a decision within 30 days of a request, which may be submitted no later than 90 days before the end of the specified period.[148]

Another winding up procedure enables the District Court to dissolve a company at the request of:

- the public prosecutor where public order is violated;
- members representing not less than 10 per cent of the voting shares;
- a creditor because the company is unable to pay its debts following a declaration of bankruptcy; or

- a party, on the basis of a legal defect in the company's deed of establishment.[149]

The court, if it orders dissolution, appoints the liquidator who must within 30 days register the appointment, apply to advertise the dissolution in the Official Gazette, advertise the dissolution in two daily newspapers and submit a report to the minister.[150] Failure to comply with these administrative requirements renders the liquidator liable to third parties.[151]

The rules governing the appointment, suspension, duties and dismissal of liquidators are similar to those governing directors. Thus, a person may not be appointed if he or she has been declared bankrupt, been a director or commissioner of a company who has been adjudicated to have caused its bankruptcy, or been convicted of having caused financial loss to the state in the previous five years.[152] No formal qualifications are specified for liquidators.

A new liquidator may be appointed by the District Court if it is satisfied on the application of one or more concerned persons or a public prosecutor that the liquidator has not properly performed his or her duties or if the company's liabilities exceed its assets.[153] A liquidator is liable to the shareholders in a general meeting for carrying out the winding up.[154]

The liquidator is required to notify every creditor of the dissolution and specify the claims procedure to be followed.[155] Claims must be submitted within 120 days of receipt of the notice and if rejected, an application to the court may be made within 90 days.[156] If no such claim is made, a creditor may nevertheless submit a claim to the court within two years of dissolution but only in relation to assets which have not been distributed to shareholders.[157] The liquidator is entitled to distribute any surplus assets among shareholders after creditors have been paid.[158]

A company upon dissolution loses its power to commit any legal act other than for purposes of settling the company's assets in liquidation.[159] Therefore, it retains power, *inter alia*, to record and compile the company's assets, to determine the distribution procedure for the assets, to pay creditors and to distribute the surplus to shareholders.[160] Until the liquidator's appointment has been registered and publicly advertised, third parties are not bound by dissolution.[161] During liquidation, the words 'in liquidation' must appear following the company's name in any dealings.[162] At the conclusion of the winding up process, the liquidator is required to register the final results and publish the details of the process in two daily newspapers.[163]

Under the Bankruptcy Code, two avenues are available for dealing with financially troubled companies, namely bankruptcy and moratorium. Each is initiated by a District Court declaration of bankruptcy. A bankruptcy declaration may be made when a company stops paying its debts, regardless of its insolvency, providing more than one debt is owed and unless a reasonable defence is presented to one of the claims.[164] A bankruptcy application may be made by the company, a creditor or the public prosecutor acting in the public interest, however only the company may apply for composition. An application by the directors on behalf of the company must be authorized by a shareholders' resolution.[165]

Following a declaration, management is removed and control of the company's assets passes to an official appointed by the Balai Harta Peninggalan (BHP), an agency of the Department of Justice. The court also appoints a supervisory judge to oversee the official whose responsibilities are to realize the assets and to pay creditors. Either the BHP or the court may appoint a creditors' committee comprising not more than three persons to advise the BHP in its role of custodian and receiver. A creditors' meeting is held within 14 days of the bankruptcy declaration to compose a list of accepted and contested claims.[166] If no plan for composition is submitted,[167] is submitted but rejected by the creditors' meeting or is approved but not ratified by the court, insolvency automatically follows. The BHP will then liquidate the estate and will prepare a distribution schedule.[168]

The ranking of claims on certain and general assets is prescribed the Civil Code in Articles 1139 and 1149 respectively. Pre-bankruptcy acts undertaken knowingly and under no legal obligation, which prejudice creditors' rights, may be challenged. Thus, for example, the BHP may declare null and void a disposition of property for which no valuable consideration was provided or where payment of a mature debt is intended to prefer one creditor over another.[169]

A composition plan may only be adopted if it is submitted at least eight days before the creditors' meeting and is approved by at least two-thirds of known creditors who between them represent at least two-thirds of the unsecured debts. The rights of secured creditors are not affected by a composition plan. A composition plan must be approved by the court and then it binds all unsecured creditors and terminates the bankruptcy. Alternatively, bankruptcy ends after all assets have been distributed and no legal claims against the estate remain.[170]

A debtor may also petition the District Court for a moratorium with respect to its estate. If an order is made, a receiver is appointed to assist with the administration of the estate. An order, initially for three months (a provisional moratorium) prevents creditors from enforcing their claims while the company establishes its right to a permanent moratorium. A permanent moratorium is initially for 18 months, but may be extended for a similar period.

A court will not approve a moratorium if it is opposed by at least one-quarter in value of the claims represented by more than one-third of creditors present and voting at a creditors' meeting. During a moratorium, plans of composition may be proposed. Unsecured creditors may not enforce their claims, but secured creditors' rights are not affected.

7.4 The Protection of Creditors and the Ranking of Claims

If the company is unable to pay its debts in full, distribution of assets amongst creditors is effected in accordance with the provisions in the Civil Code governing bankruptcy. Ranking depends on the type of assets claimed.[171] The ranking of claims on certain assets is set out in Article 1139 and is basically as follows:

- claims for judicial expenses related to enforcement and other efforts to save the assets;
- taxes;
- claims secured with hypothecation and pledge;
- claims for costs and expenses incurred in preserving the assets; and
- unsecured creditors.

The ranking of claims on the general assets of a debtor is set out in Article 1149 of the Civil Code and is basically as follows:

- claims for judicial expenses relating to enforcement and other efforts to save the assets;
- taxes;
- claims secured with hypothecation and pledge;
- salaries;
- claims arising from the supply of daily necessities to the debtor during the last six months; and
- unsecured creditors.

7.5 The Control of Insolvency Practitioners

Under Article 122 of the 1995 Company Law, liquidators are subjected to the same duties and responsibilities as directors. Thus, they must exercise their powers in good faith in the interests of a beneficial winding up. Liquidators may be personally liable for failing to act honestly or for acting negligently.[172] No qualifications for liquidators are specified by the 1995 Company Law, which merely requires that unless the liquidator is appointed by the court, the directors are to act as liquidators.

In practice, very little corporate liquidation occurs under the formal statutory processes. Most is dealt with informally, usually by negotiation. Accordingly, there is no established insolvency profession, although there are firms of lawyers and accountants well versed in the informal processes. Similarly, few matters are handled by the BHP or the courts. As a result, there are few judicial, administrative or professional constraints on the activities of liquidators or others involved in handling insolvent companies.[173]

8   The Takeover Rules

8.1   An Introduction to Company Takeover Rules

The 1995 Company Law provides, for the first time, rules and procedures for company takeovers (see also merger and consolidation in section 7.1, above). According to Article 103, a takeover (*pengambilalihan*) may be accomplished by a legal entity (*badan tiukum*) or a natural person. A takeover may be effected by the acquisition of all or a majority of the company's shares. As with consolidations and mergers, a plan (the takeover plan) must be developed by the offeror and target company, thus discouraging hostile bids.

The takeover plan must set out the names of the parties, an explanation by each director of each company involved of why the takeover is proposed, and the method of acquisition of the shares.

The plan must be approved by shareholders of each of the companies at meetings attended by shareholders representing at least three-quarters of the voting shares of whom at least three-quarters vote in favour. If the offeror is not a company but some other form of legal entity, its management must devise the takeover plan in conjunction with the target company's directors. Approval on behalf of the entity may be obtained either from its members or the management.[174] Similar rules are provided when the offeror is an individual.[175]

8.2   Takeover thresholds

Importantly, the opportunity for an offeror to acquire control under an approved takeover plan does not prevent a legal entity or individual from acquiring control through direct purchases of individual holdings.[176] The legislation provides no thresholds beyond which an acquirer may not proceed without making a formal takeover bid.

The takeover of a company may be rendered more difficult if the articles of association contain a pre-emption clause or other form of transfer restriction as permitted by Article 50. Such an article may require the shares first to be offered to a particular group of share-holders or require the approval of a proposed transfer to be obtained.

8.3 Disclosure Requirements and Shareholder Protection

There are fewer specific disclosure requirements for a takeover plan than for a merger or consolidation plan (see section 7.1, above), which requires shareholders to be provided with 'any other information which may be necessary.' However, the implementation of a takeover plan is subject to the principles contained in Article 104 which may nevertheless raise the disclosure standard. Thus, the interests of the company, its minority shareholders, its employees, the public interest and fair business competition must be taken into account when a takeover plan is proposed. Further, a takeover must not prejudice the rights of minority shareholders to sell out at a reasonable price.[177] Approved plans must be notified to the minister. Takeover plans which adversely affect these interests are not to be carried out.[178] Moreover, a minority shareholder may vote against the plan if he or she is unable to sell his or her shares in the takeover at a reasonable price, and requires the company to acquire them at a reasonable price under Article 55.

9 An Introduction to Securities Regulation

Companies whose shares or debentures are publicly traded are, unless a contrary intention appears in the capital market laws, subject to the provisions of the 1995 Company Law, however public trading in securities is mainly regulated by separate capital market laws. Thus Decrees 53 and 1548 of 1990 instituted the present regulatory framework for the securities industry. The BAPEPAM[179] was created and given powers, similar to those of the US Securities and Exchange Commission, to supervise stock exchanges, disclosure of information, licensed dealers, underwriters and investment managers.[180]

Decree 1548 extensively provides for all aspects of capital market operations and has been supplemented substantially by subsequent rules.[181] Apart from defining the powers and functions of the BAPEPAM, the decree prescribes, *inter alia*, the role of securities exchanges, the operation of investment funds, capital market agencies and associated professionals, and market practices.[182]

Decree 1548 requires securities exchanges to make rules on membership, discipline, listing, disclosure, clearing and settlement, and associated matters.[183] The regulatory philosophy of the capital market laws is to anticipate rather than respond to market problems and to encourage investor confidence through quality structures and practices and disclosure standards which meet the requirements of the international investment community.[184]

10   Miscellaneous

10.1   *The Powers of the Courts*

The District Court is given wide powers to make orders in relation to the conduct of a company's affairs. In particular, orders may be made:

- at the request of a creditor objecting to a capital reduction proposal;[185]
- to protect minority shareholders' interests against unfair or unreasonable conduct;[186]
- to convene meetings at the request of shareholders and to specify the rules to govern the convening and conduct of such meetings;[187]
- to determine the quorum to apply at reconvened meetings;[188]
- to order an investigation of a company and to appoint up to three experts to carry out the investigation;[189] and
- to order the dissolution of a company and make orders against defaulting officers.

Notes

  *   Professor of Business Law, Queensland University of Technology.
  ** Senior Lecturer in Law, University of Canberra.
  1 Gautama, S. (1995), *Indonesian Business Law*, Bandung, Penerbit PT: Citra Aditya Bakti.
  2 ASEAN Law Association (1995), *ASEAN Legal System*, Singapore: Butterworths Asia, 17–22.
  3 As note 2, above, 23.
  4 As note 2, above, 23.
  5 As note 2, above, 24.
  6 Pakpahan, N.S. (1994), 'Legal reform crucial to economic development', *Economic & Business Review Indonesia*, 126, 26.
  7 Oesman, O., Minister of Justice of Indonesia, reported in 'Indonesia-Netherlands Economic Law Dialogue Launched with ELIPS Support', *Bulletin ELIPS*, 2, July 1994, 1.
  8 The Law on Limited Liability Companies (Law No. 1, 1995).
  9 Pulle, A. (1996), 'Indonesia: The New Company Law of Indonesia', *The Company Lawyer*, 17, (4) 122–126.
 10 Elucidation of the Law of the Republic of Indonesia, No. 1, 1995, on Limited Liability Companies.
 11 As note 2, above, 51.
 12 As note 2, above, 54. This principle was formulated by Subekti, R.S.H. (1981), *Pembinaan Hukum Nasional (Development of National Law)* Jakarta: Alumni, 23.

13 As note 12, above, 55.
14 As note 12, above, 56.
15 Surowidjojo, A.T. and Assegal, A.F. (1995), 'Doing Business in Indonesia', *Asian Business Law Review*, 7, 13.
16 As note 1, above, 279.
17 Articles 9 and 7, paragraph 6 of the 1995 Company Law..
18 Articles 2, 4 and 26 of the 1995 Company Law and the Elucidation of the Law.
19 Article 15 of the 1995 Company Law.
20 Chapter V of the 1995 Company Law.
21 Chapter VIII of the 1995 Company Law.
22 See Ruru, B. (1995), 'Development of Equity and Bond Markets: History and Regulatory Framework in Indonesia', *Australian Journal of Corporate Law* 5, (3), 326–333.
23 As note 15, above, 15.
24 McLeod, R.H. (1997), 'Indonesia: Survey of Recent Developments', *Bulletin of Indonesian Economic Studies*, 33, April, 17.
25 As note 22, above.
26 Article 1 of the 1995 Company Law.
27 Article 2 of the Government Regulation, No. 20, 1994, 19 May 1994.
28 Article 7 of the Government Regulation, No. 20, 1994, 19 May 1994.
29 As note 15, above, 14.
30 Article 66, paragraph 2, of the 1995 Company Law.
31 Article 110, paragraph 2, of the 1995 Company Law.
32 Articles 15a, 11, 15a, paragraph 4, 15b (2) of the Foreign Investment Law 1967.
33 Article 6, paragraph 2 of the Foreign Investment Law 1967.
34 Article 1 of the 1995 Company Law.
35 Article 13, paragraph 3 of the 1995 Company Law.
36 Article 59 of the 1995 Company Law.
37 Article 7, paragraph 6 of the 1995 Company Law.
38 Article 7, paragraph 1 of the 1995 Company Law.
39 Article 9 of the 1995 Company Law.
40 Article 2 of the 1995 Company Law.
41 Article 4 of the 1995 Company Law.
42 Article 4 of the Elucidation of the 1995 Company Law.
43 As note 1, above, 284.
44 Article 9, paragraph 2 of the 1995 Company Law.
45 Article 21 of the 1995 Company Law.
46 Article 22 of the 1995 Company Law.
47 Article 23 of the 1995 Company Law.
48 Article 24 of the 1995 Company Law.
49 Article 12 of the 1995 Company Law.
50 Article 13 of the 1995 Company Law.
51 Article 1 of the 1995 Company Law.
52 Article 42 of the 1995 Company Law.
53 As note 9, above, 123.
54 Article 53 of the 1995 Company Law.
55 Article 25, paragraph 1 of the 1995 Company Law.
56 As note 52, above.
57 Article 25, paragraph 2 of the 1995 Company Law.
58 Article 26 of the 1995 Company Law..
59 Article 27 of the 1995 Company Law.
60 Article 30 of the 1995 Company Law.
61 Article 33 of the 1995 Company Law.
62 Article 34 of the 1995 Company Law.

63   Article 36 of the 1995 Company Law.
64   Article 41 of the 1995 Company Law.
65   Article 37 of the 1995 Company Law.
66   Article 38 of the 1995 Company Law.
67   Article 39 of the 1995 Company Law.
68   Article 63 of the 1995 Company Law.
69   Article 75 of the 1995 Company Law.
70   Article 43 of the 1995 Company Law.
71   Article 12(1) of the 1995 Company Law.
72   Article 13(1) of the 1995 Company Law.
73   As note 72, above.
74   Article 13(2) of the 1995 Company Law.
75   That is one capable of making a public offering in accordance with capital market laws.
76   Article 13(3) of the 1995 Company Law.
77   Article 15(1) of the 1995 Company Law.
78   Article 12(a) and (g) respectively of the 1995 Company Law.
79   Article 64 of the 1995 Company Law.
80   Article 79(1) of the 1995 Company Law.
81   Articles 82 and 83 of the 1995 Company Law.
82   Articles 88(1) and 90(1) of the 1995 Company Law.
83   Article 85 of the 1995 Company Law.
84   See Pulle, A. (1996), 'The New Company Law of Indonesia', *The Company Lawyer*, **17**, (4), 122–126.
85   Article 84(1) of the 1995 Company Law.
86   Article 90 of the 1995 Company Law.
87   Articles 21 and 22 of the 1995 Company Law. Article 23 renders directors personally liable for any act committed on the company's behalf until these tasks have been carried out.
88   Article 21 of the 1995 Company Law.
89   Article 43(1) of the 1995 Company Law.
90   Article 43(2) of the 1995 Company Law.
91   Article 56 of the 1995 Company Law.
92   Article 66 of the 1995 Company Law.
93   Article 86 of the 1995 Company Law.
94   Articles 80 and 81 of the 1995 Company Law.
95   Article 79 of the 1995 Company Law.
96   Article 79(3) of the 1995 Company Law.
97   Article 94 of the 1995 Company Law.
98   Articles 95 and 96 of the 1995 Company Law.
99   As note 84, above 125.
100   As note 99, above.
101   Article 65 of the 1995 Company Law.
102   Article 66 of the 1995 Company Law.
103   Article 64 of the 1995 Company Law.
104   Article 67 of the 1995 Company Law.
105   Article 69 of the 1995 Company Law.
106   Article 71 of the 1995 Company Law.
107   Article 72 of the 1995 Company Law.
108   Article 74 of the 1995 Company Law.
109   Article 75 of the 1995 Company Law.
110   Articles 76, 88(3) and 116(2) of the 1995 Company Law.
111   Article 77 of the 1995 Company Law.
112   Article 86 of the 1995 Company Law. See further in section 6.6, below.

113   Article 56 of the 1995 Company Law.
114   Article 59 of the 1995 Company Law.
115   Article 57 of the 1995 Company Law.
116   Article 60 of the 1995 Company Law.
117   Article 60(2) and (3) of the 1995 Company Law.
118   Articles 61 and 62 of the 1995 Company Law.
119   Article 62 of the 1995 Company Law.
120   Article 43(1) of the 1995 Company Law.
121   Article 43(2) of the 1995 Company Law.
122   Article 43(3) of the 1995 Company Law. Note also, Article 53 allows bearer shares to be pledged and for the pledge to be entered in the special register.
123   Article 43(4) of the 1995 Company Law.
124   Article 44 of the 1995 Company Law.
125   Article 3 of the 1995 Company Law.
126   Articles 85(3) and 98(2) of the 1995 Company Law.
127   Article 54(2) of the 1995 Company Law and the official Elucidation relating thereto.
128   Article 30(3) of the 1995 Company Law.
129   Article 36(1) of the 1995 Company Law.
130   Article 41(1) of the 1995 Company Law.
131   Article 43(2) of the 1995 Company Law.
132   Article 66 of the 1995 Company Law.
133   Article 86 of the 1995 Company Law.
134   Article 110 of the 1995 Company Law.
135   Article 55 of the 1995 Company Law.
136   Including those owned by a subsidiary and those which are pledged.
137   Article 30 of the 1995 Company Law.
138   As note 84, above, 122–123; and Tomasic and Little (1997) *Insolvency Law & Practice in Asia*, FT Law and Tax, Hong Kong, 211–212.
139   Article 102(1) of the 1995 Company Law.
140   Article 107 of the 1995 Company Law.
141   Tomasic and Little, as note 138, above, 205.
142   Articles 114(a) and 115(1) of the 1995 Company Law.
143   Articles 76 and 115(2) of the 1995 Company Law.
144   Article 115(3) and (4) of the 1995 Company Law.
145   Article 122 of the 1995 Company Law.
146   Article 114(b) of the 1995 Company Law.
147   Article 116(2) of the 1995 Company Law.
148   Article 116 of the 1995 Company Law.
149   Article 117 of the 1995 Company Law.
150   Article 118(1) of the 1995 Company Law.
151   Article 118(3) of the 1995 Company Law.
152   Articles 79 and 122 of the 1995 Company Law.
153   Article 123 of the 1995 Company Law.
154   Article 124 of the 1995 Company Law.
155   Article 120(2) of the 1995 Company Law.
156   Article 120(2) and (3) of the 1995 Company Law.
157   Article 121 of the 1995 Company Law.
158   Article 124 of the 1995 Company Law; and Commercial Code, Article 49.
159   Article 119 of the 1995 Company Law.
160   As note 159, above.
161   Article 118(2) of the 1995 Company Law.
162   Article 119(3) of the 1995 Company Law.
163   Article 124(3) of the 1995 Company Law.

164   For a good discussion of these rules, see Himawan, C. (1973), *Business Law: Contracts and Business Association*, Bandung: Universitas Padjadjaram, 100.
165   Article 90(1) of the 1995 Company Law.
166   As note 164, above, 101.
167   In practice, the BHP official, upon appointment, attempts to achieve a compromise between interested parties, failing which, winding up follows: see Tomasic and Little, as note 138, above, Chapter 7, note 20.
168   Singam, R.R. (1985), 'Company Insolvency in Singapore, Thailand and Indonesia', *International Business Lawyer*, November, 451.
169   As note 164, above, 102.
170   As note 169, above.
171   Pierce, D.G., Chan, H.H.M., Lacroix, F.E. and Pillai, P.B. (eds) (1995), *Current Issues of International Finance Law*, Singapore: Butterworths Asia, 352.
172   Article 85(3) of the 1995 Company Law.
173   See generally, Tomasic and Little, as note 138, above, 212–222.
174   Article 103(4) of the 1995 Company Law.
175   Article 103(5) of the 1995 Company Law.
176   Article 103(6) of the 1995 Company Law.
177   Article 104(2) of the 1995 Company Law.
178   See the official Elucidation applicable to Article 104.
179   This replaced the first BAPEPAM, which was established in 1977.
180   For a useful discussion of the history, nature and content of the capital market laws, see note 22, above 326.
181   As note 22, above, 329.
182   As note 22, above, 328.
183   As note 22, above, 329.
184   As note 22, above, 328–329.
185   Article 38(3) of the 1995 Company Law.
186   Article 54(2) of the 1995 Company Law.
187   Article 67 of the 1995 Company Law.
188   Article 73(6) of the 1995 Company Law.
189   Articles 110–112 of the 1995 Company Law.

13 The Corporations Law of the Philippines

GEOFFREY NICOLL*

1 A Brief Introduction (the Nature of the Legal System in each Country, its History and Judicial and Regulatory Structure)

In considering the corporations and securities laws of the Philippines, regard must be had to the influences of a variety of enactments which have emerged from the several distinct political periods in the history of the Philippines. The most important of these periods for the purposes of identifying Philippine legislation have been the pre-Spanish period (pre 1521), the Spanish Regime (1521–1898), the Philippine Republic of 1898, the American Regime (1898–1935), the Commonwealth Era (1935–1946), the Japanese Occupation (1941–1944), the Period of the Republic (1946–1972), the Martial Law Period (1972–1986) and the continuation of the Republic.

Emerging from these various periods is an extensive array of legal enactments relevant to the corporations and securities law of the Philippines. The starting point perhaps is a number of codes, originating from the Spanish period and the original Spanish Code of Commerce 1885. Of the 27 codes in force today, the most relevant for the purposes of this chapter are the Civil Code, the Revised Penal Code, the Code of Commerce 1888, the Corporation Code and the Omnibus Investment Code of 1987.

However, attention must also be paid to enacted statutes and Republic Acts and to presidential decrees and executive orders made at various times since the establishment of the US civil government in 1900. Some idea of the variety of these enactments and of their association with the particular historical periods from which they originate may be gleaned from the following account:

> From the establishment of the American civil government in 1900 to 1935, there were 4,275 laws passed by the Philippine Commission and its bicameral successor, the Philippine Legislature. The Commonwealth

period witnessed the enactment of 733 statutes while 6,635 Republic Acts were legislated from 4 July 1946 to 21 September 1972. During the martial law period, a total of 2,035 Presidential Decrees were promulgated as of 20 February 1986, while 891 *Batas* have been passed by the *Batasang Pambansa* since 1 February 1986. A total of 302 Executive Orders have been issued by President Corazon C. Aquino. Congress convened on 27 July 1987 and has enacted 6,636 Republic Acts to date. Thus, there has been a total of 16,000 statutes since 1900.[1]

In addition to this legislation, reference must also be made to an extensive array of issuances, circulars, rules and guidelines promulgated by the Securities and Exchange Commission (SEC) of the Philippines and by other bodies which play lesser regulatory roles, for example the Board of Investments and stock exchanges. This diverse collection of laws relevant to corporations and securities in the Philippines has been conveniently collected together and edited by the editorial staff of the Central Book Supply Inc. in *The New Corporation Code of the Philippines*.[2]

This chapter, utilizing *The New Corporation Code of the Philippines*, deals particularly with the Revised Securities Act (*Batas Pambansa* Blg 178) and associated laws, the Corporation Code of the Philippines (*Batas Pambansa* Blg 68 (1980)) and the Omnibus Investments Code of 1987 (Executive Order No. 226 (1987)). Among the special laws and issuances of the SEC and of the Board of Investments, particular attention is also paid to Presidential Decree 902-A, by which the SEC has been granted extensive new powers, reorganized and placed under the direct administrative supervision of the Office of the President.

It should be mentioned at the outset that although it has been claimed that the influence of the Anglo-US common law system is more evident in the corporations and securities law than in other areas of Philippine law,[3] the features of a codified civil law often appear to remain quite pronounced. For example, in Presidential Decree 902-A there may be seen both a direct executive control of the SEC by the office of the president and an extremely broad regulatory and adjudicative power delegated to the SEC. Furthermore, although the ultimate importance of the constitution may be emphasized and a strong belief expressed in the importance of the separation of powers,[4] the separation of executive, regulatory function and judicial power may not always be so clear in practice. Once again, Presidential Decree 902-A stands as a good example. In this decree extremely broad regulatory functions and judicial powers have been bestowed on the SEC and the line between them may prove difficult to draw. It may well be that because the laws of the Philippines with respect to corporations and securities derive from such a wide variety of constitutional sources, difficulties will continue to arise regarding the relative ambit of legislative, judicial and executive powers.

2 A Description of the Corporation Law Statute (and Case-Law) in the Jurisdiction

2.1 The Constitutional Basis for the Company Law

The constitutional basis for the Corporation Code (*Batas Pambansa* Blg 68 (1980)) and the allied laws with which this chapter chiefly concerns itself, namely the Omnibus Investments Code (Executive Order No. 226 (1987)) and the Revised Securities Act (*Batas Pambansa* Blg 178), is to be found in the Code of Commerce, which became effective on 1 December 1888. This Code of Commerce itself derived from the Spanish Code of Commerce of 1885, which was adopted in the Philippines with some modifications to suit local commercial conditions. The Code of Commerce has been extensively modified, not only by those laws with respect to corporations and securities referred to above, but also by the Insolvency Law,[5] the Chattel Mortgage Law,[6] the Negotiable Instruments Act,[7] the Warehouse Receipts Act,[8] the Trademark Law,[9] the Central Bank Act[10] and the General Banking Law.[11] As a result, the remaining unrepealed portions of the Code of Commerce are now confined to regulation of the relatively narrow areas of merchant qualifications and acts of commerce in general, letters of credit, joint accounts, mercantile registries and book-keeping matters.[12]

The most important enactments relevant to the corporations and securities law of the Philippines today, and to which reference will be chiefly made in this chapter, are:

- the Corporation Code of the Philippines (*Batas Pambansa* Blg 68);
- the Revised Securities Act (*Batas Pambansa* Blg 178);
- the Omnibus Investments Code of 1987 (Executive Order No. 226);
- the special laws and issuances relevant to the SEC, including a number of presidential decrees, commercial Acts and Republic Acts, as well as the SEC's own rules, circulars and sundry guidelines;
- the special laws and issuances relevant to the Board of Investments, including commercial and Republic Acts, executive orders, presidential decrees and sundry rules and regulations.

The Corporation Code of the Philippines and the Revised Securities Act are not particularly lengthy documents and the primary statutory provisions are not detailed. This seems to reflect the dominant role of the SEC, its substantial discretion in the application of the substantive law and the broad ranging regulatory and adjudicative power which it possesses. The Corporation Code is divided into 16 'titles' and the Revised Securities Act into five 'Chapters'. For the purposes of this chapter, it has been found most convenient to refer to relevant groups of Sections of the Corporation Code and the Revised Securities Act, rather than to Title and Chapter headings. Nevertheless, where reference to these has been found particularly useful, such references may be found in the accompanying footnotes.

3   The Nature and Power of Corporate Regulatory Bodies in the Jurisdiction

3.1   A Description of the Powers of Company Regulatory Bodies

On 11 March 1976 Presidential Decree 902-A was passed.[13] This decree recited the national objectives of encouraging investment, both domestic and foreign; encouraging a more active public participation in the affairs of private corporations and enterprises for the promotion of economic development; and promoting a more equitable distribution of wealth. These objectives were seen to give rise to a 'need for an agency of the government invested with ample powers to protect such investment and the public'. Accordingly, the decree goes on to effect the reorganization and restructuring of the SEC to make it a 'more potent, responsive and effective arm of the government [so that it might] help in the implementation of these programmes and ... play a more active role in nation-building'.

In order to meet these national objectives, the administrative supervision of the SEC has been transferred from the Department of Trade to the direct general supervision of the office of the president.[14] The restructured SEC now comprises a chairman and four associate commissioners who are appointed by the president. The chairman has general executive control as well as responsibility for the direction and supervision of the work and operations of the SEC. In addition, there is to be appointed to the SEC, a secretary, who is to act as the recorder and official reporter of SEC proceedings, and an executive director, who is to be responsible for the effective implementation of policies, rules and standards promulgated by the SEC.[15]

It is clear from the decree that the SEC is to exercise very broad regulatory, administrative and judicial functions.[16] In the exercise of these powers and in the enforcement of its decisions, the jurisdiction of the SEC is absolute.[17] The wide adjudicative power of the SEC is evident in Section 5 of the decree, according to which the SEC has the jurisdiction to hear and decide cases involving:

- devices and schemes for fraudulent purposes, devised by corporate management, which are detrimental to the interests of the public;
- intracorporate (or partnership) problems, which arise between or among stockholders;
- problems related to the election and appointment of directors, trustees, officers or managers of corporations, partnerships or associations; and
- problems associated with the appointment of a rehabilitation receiver or a management committee,[18] appointed in situations where the company is unable to pay its debts but holds sufficient assets to make this a possibility in the future.

The specific powers of the SEC are set out in detail in Section 6 of the decree. It is clear that these powers confer a wide judicial power on the SEC and that they permit a degree of influence in private corporate matters that might be considered matters of corporate constitution or private contract in other jurisdictions. Apart from various powers of a procedural nature (such as the power to issue injunctions, writs, attachments and subpoenae and the power to impose fines),[19] and powers which might be generally expected to fall within the SEC's jurisdiction (such as the power to authorize the establishment of stock exchanges),[20] certain powers of the SEC require particular mention.

In the first place, the SEC is empowered to compel meetings of stockholders[21] and to pass judgment on the validity of the issuance and use of proxies and voting trust agreements,[22] matters normally left to private corporate constitutional law in Australia. As noted above, the SEC has the power to create and appoint boards or management committees to undertake the management of corporations following the appointment of rehabilitation receivers or management committees. In these circumstances, the SEC may even take control of the property of the company.[23] These powers are more fully discussed in section 7, below.

Furthermore, the SEC also enjoys particularly wide judicial powers in the conduct of judicial hearings. The jurisdiction to conduct and decide cases involving the comparatively broad range of activities referred to in Section 5 above have already been noted. Under Section 6, the SEC enjoys a wide discretion in the making of judicial orders. For example, it may punish parties for contempt of the SEC,[24] impose fines[25] and revoke, after due notice and hearing, the franchise or certificate of registration of corporations.[26] The SEC is further empowered to pass judgment and to refuse or deny the registration of a corporation, partnership or organization if it is established that the corporation, partnership or organization has not acted consistently with declared national economic policies. Such an order may only be made after consultation with the Board of Industry, the Department of Industry and/or the National Economic and Development Authority, but the power appears a particularly wide one. There is provision for an aggrieved party to appeal to the Supreme Court following a hearing by the SEC.[27]

So far as the organization of the SEC is concerned, it now comprises nine distinct departments, each department headed by a director. These departments are Corporate and Legal; Examiners and Appraisers, Brokers and Exchanges, Money Market Operations, Securities Investigations and Clearing Houses, Investment Research and Statistics, Administration and Finance, Prosecution and Enforcement and Supervision and Monitoring.

The restructured SEC has been further empowered by a number of Commercial and Republic Acts. The powers of the SEC have also been affected by a number of other enactments and presidential decrees.[28]

4   Types of Companies and their Powers

4.1   A Description of Types of Local Companies

The Corporation Code of the Philippines includes specific provisions with respect to particular types of corporation. A fundamental distinction is drawn between stock corporations and non-stock corporations.[29] Within this fundamental division there are provisions relevant to other distinct types of corporation, such as close corporations,[30] and special corporations, including educational corporations[31] and religious corporations.[32] Corporations which are created by special laws or charters are governed primarily by the provisions of the special law or charter creating them or applicable to them, supplemented by the provisions of the Corporation Code, insofar as those provisions may be applicable.[33] There is also a specific section of the Corporation Code which deals with foreign corporations[34] and these provisions are examined more closely in Section 4.2, below.

4.1.1   Stock corporations and non-stock corporations   Stock corporations are those which have capital stock divided into shares and which are authorized to distribute to the holders of those shares dividends or allotments of the surplus profits on the basis of the shares held. All other corporations are non-stock corporations.[35] For stock corporations, provision is made in Section 6 of the Corporation Code for the division of shares into classes with such attendant rights, privileges or restrictions as may be stated in the articles of incorporation. No shares may be deprived of voting rights except those classified as 'deferred' or 'redeemable' shares, unless otherwise provided in the Corporation Code. There must always be a class or series of shares provided for which have full voting rights. Any or all of the shares or shares in a class of shares may have a par value or a no-par value, in accordance with the articles of incorporation.[36] Various types of shares have been specifically provided for, including founders' shares,[37] redeemable shares[38] and treasury shares.[39]

With respect to non-stock corporations, further definitional assistance is provided in Sections 87 and 88 of the Corporation Code. Subject to its specific provisions with respect to non-stock corporations, non-stock corporations may be formed or organized for charitable, religious, educational, professional, cultural, fraternal, literary, scientific, social, civic or similar purposes, or for the purposes associated with trade, industry, agriculture and like activities.[40] A non-stock corporation is defined to be one in which, subject to the provisions of the Corporation Code which apply on the dissolution of the corporation, no part of the income of the corporation may be distributed as dividends to its members, trustees or officers. There is a specific requirement that the non-stock corporation utilize any profits for the furtherance of the purpose or purposes for which the corporation was formed. With respect to non-stock corporations, the code then provides specifically for matters such as the requirements for membership,[41] trustees and officers[42] and for the distribution of assets during winding up.[43]

4.1.2 *Close corporations* With respect to close corporations, the relevant provisions are found in Sections 96–105. A close corporation is defined as one whose articles of incorporation meet three requirements. First, all the corporation's issued stock of all classes, exclusive of treasury shares, must be held by no more than 20 persons. Second, all the corporation's issued stock of all classes must be subject to one or more of the specified restrictions on transfer permitted under the Corporation Code. Third, the corporation must not list on any stock exchange or make any public offerings of any of its stock of any class.[44]

There are other provisions of particular relevance to close corporations, such as the sanctioning of stockholder agreements in close corporations, even though such stockholder agreements might relate to matters of management,[45] the deeming valid of informal board decisions and board decisions made with the express or implied acquiescence of all stockholders,[46] and the statutory right of the stockholder of a close corporation to compel the corporation to purchase his shares at a fair value.[47]

4.1.3   *Special corporations*   The Corporation Code also provides for certain types of special corporations, particularly educational corporations[48] and religious corporations.[49] Educational corporations are to be governed by special laws and by the general provisions of the Corporation Code. Insofar as such educational corporations are organized as stock corporations, the number of directors and their term of office shall be governed by the general provisions with respect to stock corporations. The distinguishing features of educational corporations relate primarily to the prerequisites for incorporation, namely a favourable recommendation of the Department of Education, Culture and Sports, and the requirement that a board of trustees be established, comprising not less than five and not more than 15 members. Religious corporations are to be governed by the specific provisions of the Corporation Code relating to such corporations, as well as by the general provisions which relate to non-stock corporations insofar as those provisions may be applicable. Religious corporations are further sub-categorized into corporations sole and religious societies.

4.2   *The Recognition of Foreign Companies in the Jurisdiction*

The Corporation Code makes specific provision with respect to foreign corporations in Sections 123–136. A foreign corporation is defined to be one '… formed, organized or existing under any laws other than those of the Philippines', whose laws allow Filipino citizens and corporations to do business in the foreign corporation's home state.[50] In order to conduct business in the Philippines, a foreign company must first obtain a licence from the SEC and a certificate of authority. In applying for a licence, a foreign corporation must provide information as to:

- the date of incorporation and the term of the proposed incorporation;
- the name and address of the foreign corporation's resident agent authorized to accept legal process and to participate in legal proceedings;
- the place in the Philippines at which the foreign corporation intends to operate;
- the specific purpose or purposes of the foreign corporation's operation in the Philippines; and
- the authorized capital stock of the foreign corporation, its issued stock and the classes of shares adopted by the foreign corporation.[51]

Further important provisions provide that the resident agent of the foreign corporation may be either an individual residing within the Philippines or a domestic corporation lawfully transacting business in the Philippines,[52] that the law applicable to foreign corporations doing business in the Philippines shall be the law of the Philippines,[53] and that a foreign corporation might merge or consolidate with any domestic corporation provided that the specific requirements with respect to merger or consolidation are followed.[54]

4.3   The Legal Capacities and Powers of Companies

The Corporation Code provides extensively for the powers of corporations in Sections 36–48. Although Sections 46–48 state specifically that the corporation must adopt standard by-laws within one month of incorporation, and must provide for the addition to and amendment of such by-laws, the standard by-laws recommended for adoption are extremely brief.

For this reason, certain powers that might be found in the articles of association of many Western corporations are to be found in the Philippine Corporation Code itself. Several of these statutory powers granted to corporations prompt interesting comparisons with equivalent provisions in the standard articles of association of Western corporations. The statutory powers provided in the Corporation Code sometimes also incorporate provisions otherwise found in the listing rules of stock exchanges in Western jurisdictions. For these reasons, it may be helpful to list the broad range of corporate powers specifically provided for under the Corporation Code before commenting further on particular corporate powers. A corporation has the power to:

- sue and be sued in its corporate name, and trade continuously under its corporate name for the period of time stated in the articles of incorporation and the certificate of incorporation;
- adopt and use a corporate seal, amend the articles of incorporation and adopt and amend by-laws;
- issue and sell stocks and hold and transfer property;
- merge or consolidate with other corporations in accordance with the provisions of the Corporation Code;
- exercise powers other than those already stated above that may be essential or necessary for the carrying out of the purposes stated in the articles of incorporation;[55]
- extend or shorten the corporate term;[56]
- increase or decrease capital stock, incur, create or increase bonded indebtedness;[57]
- deny pre-emptive rights;[58]

- sell or dispose of assets;[59]
- acquire its own shares;[60]
- invest corporate funds in another corporation or business or for any other purpose;[61]
- declare dividends;[62] and
- enter into management contracts.[63]

There is a specific provision that no corporation incorporated under the Corporation Code shall possess or exercise any corporate powers except those conferred by the code or by the articles of incorporation as well as those necessary or incidental to the exercise of the powers so conferred.

5   Company Formation

5.1   *The Registration of Companies and Promoters*

The incorporation and organization of private corporations is provided for in Sections 10–22 of the Corporation Code. Section 19 provides that a private corporation formed or organized under the code commences to have corporate existence and juridical personality, and is deemed to have been incorporated, on the date when the SEC issues a certificate of incorporation under its official seal. Thereafter, the incorporators, stockholders, members and their successors constitute a body politic and corporate, incorporated under the name stated in the articles of incorporation for the period of time provided in the articles, unless that period is extended or the corporation is dissolved earlier by law. The due incorporation of any corporation claiming in good faith to be a corporation incorporated under the Corporation Code, and the right of such a corporation to exercise corporate powers, is not to be challenged in any private suit to which the corporation may be a party.[64] Furthermore, all persons who assume to act as a corporation knowing that they lack the authority to do so shall be liable as general partners for all debts, liabilities and damages incurred or arising as a result of their actions.[65]

Apart from the important requirements with respect to the maintenance of a minimum subscribed capital (requirements which are considered in more detail below), the other general requirements for incorporation are as follows. Any number of natural persons no fewer than five and no more than 15 in number, who are of legal age and resident in the Philippines, may form a private corporation for any lawful purpose or purposes.[66] Each incorporator of a stock corporation must own or be a subscriber to at least one share of the capital stock of the corporation. A corporation shall exist for a period of not more than 50 years from the date of incorporation, unless that period is extended or the corporation is dissolved by law.[67]

It is important to note that the SEC is entitled to reject the articles of incorporation of a proposed corporation and to disapprove any amendments not made in accordance with the requirements of the Corporation Code. The SEC is, however, required to give the incorporators a reasonable time in which to correct or modify any objectionable portions of the articles or of any amendment.[68] Apart from these matters of form, the SEC is entitled to reject the articles of incorporation or disapprove amendments where the purpose or purposes of the corporation are 'patently unconstitutional, illegal, immoral, or contrary to government rules or regulations', and where the required percentage of ownership of the capital stock to be owned by the citizens of the Philippines has not been complied with, as required by existing laws or by the Constitution.

5.2 The Corporate Constitution

The two prime documents which establish the private constitution of the Philippine corporation are the articles of incorporation and the by-laws.

So far as the articles of incorporation are concerned, Section 14 of the Corporation Code requires that the articles of incorporation be filed with the SEC, be duly signed and acknowledged by all of the incorporators and provide for the following specific matters:

- the name of the corporation;
- the specific purpose or purposes for which the corporation is being incorporated;
- the place where the principal office of the corporation is to be located (which must be within the Philippines);
- the term for which the corporation is to exist;
- the names, nationalities and residences of the incorporators;
- the number of directors or trustees (no fewer than five and no more than 15 in number);
- the names, nationalities and residences of the persons who shall act as directors or trustees until the first regular directors or trustees are duly elected and qualified in accordance with the Corporation Code;
- in the case of stock corporations, the authorized capital stock and the number of shares into which it is divided; in the case of par value shares, the par value of each share must be stated as well as the names, nationalities and residences of the original subscribers, and the amounts subscribed and paid by each of

his or her subscription; if some or all of the shares are without par value, such a fact must be stated;

- for non-stock corporations, the amount of capital, the names, nationalities and residences of the contributors and the amount contributed by each; and
- such other matters that are not inconsistent with the law and which the incorporaters may deem necessary and convenient.

Although not specifically required, it would seem necessary for the subscribers to elect a treasurer who must swear a statement of compliance with the minimum capital requirements of Sections 12 and 13 before the SEC is able to accept the articles of incorporation for registration. A standard form of articles of incorporation which incorporates these requirements is set out in Section 15 of the Corporation Code. The articles of incorporation are in fact quite brief by comparison with the articles of Western corporations. As already noted, this is because various other matters typically found in the articles of association of Western corporations are to be found in the by-laws adopted by corporations in the Philippines.

The specific provisions with respect to the by-laws of corporations incorporated in the Philippines are found in Sections 46–48 of the Corporation Code. Every corporation formed pursuant to the code must, within one month of receipt of the official notice of the issuance of its certificate of incorporation by the SEC, adopt by-laws for its government which are not inconsistent with the by-laws provided under the code. At least a majority of stockholders (in the case of stock corporations) or a majority of members (in the case of non-stock corporations) must vote affirmatively to the adoption of the by-laws. A duly signed copy of the by-laws is to be kept at the principal office of the corporation and a further certified copy is to be filed with the SEC and attached to the original articles of incorporation.[69]

Section 47 of the Corporation Code provides for the specific matters which may be dealt with in the by-laws. These include:

- the time, place and manner for calling and conducting regular or specific meetings of the directors or trustees;
- the time and manner for calling and conducting regular or special meetings of the stockholders or members;
- the required quorum in meetings of stockholders or members and the manner of voting therein;
- the form of proxies of stockholders and the manner of voting them;
- the qualifications, duties and compensation of directors or trustees, officers and employees;

- the time for holding the annual election of directors or trustees and the mode or manner of giving notice thereof;
- the manner of election or appointment and the term of office of all officers other than directors or trustees;
- the penalties for violation of the by-laws;
- in the case of stock corporations, the manner of issuing stock certificates; and
- such other matters as may be felt necessary for the proper or convenient transaction of the business and affairs of the corporation.

A majority vote by the board of directors or trustees, supported by a majority of stockholders or members in a general meeting, is required to adopt new by-laws, amend existing by-laws or to repeal by-laws. These same powers may be delegated to the board of directors or trustees by resolution of a two-thirds majority of stockholders or members.[70] In addition to any provisions which may be adopted in the by-laws with respect to meetings, the Corporation Code also makes specific provision for meetings and meeting procedure.[71] These provisions are considered more fully in Section 6.2, below.

Other constitutional matters generally dealt with in the articles of association of Western corporations receive specific statutory attention in the Corporation Code. For example, Section 23 provides for the exercise of corporate powers by the board of directors or trustees, unless otherwise provided in the code. There are specific provisions with respect to close corporations,[72] the articles of incorporation of such close corporations[73] and agreements by stockholders in such corporations.[74] The latter agreements raise interesting constitutional questions with respect to close corporations, because they permit a degree of participation by stockholders in management not always so readily recognized in Western corporations.

5.3 Restrictions on the Use of Certain Names

No corporate name may be allowed by the SEC if the proposed name is identical to, or deceptively or confusingly similar to, that of any existing corporation or to any other name already protected by law, or if the proposed name is patently deceptive, confusing or contrary to existing laws.[75]

5.4 Membership and Share Capital Requirements

A number of provisions of the Corporation Code are relevant to corporate membership and share capital requirements. First, Sections 6–9 deal with the different types of shares that may be held in stock corporations. Second, Sections 60–73 deal generally with the subscription for shares, payment for subscriptions and the sale of shares for non-payment of subscriptions. Third, Sections 81–86 deal with the right of shareholders to exit in the event of merger or sale of the corporate undertaking or amendment to articles, and the right of appraisal associated with this right of exit. Finally, Sections 100–105 deal with intra-shareholder matters such as stockholder agreements, pre-emptive rights and the amendment of articles, arbitration by the SEC and the buy-out of shareholdings in the event of deadlocks. The provisions with respect to membership of non-stock corporations are found in Sections 87–91 of the Corporation Code.

In addition to these requirements with respect to membership and shareholding of stock and non-stock corporations, important provisions with respect to capital requirements are found in Sections 13 and 14 of the Corporation Code. It is convenient to consider the most important aspects of these groups of provisions under three broad headings, namely shareholding and membership in stock corporations, membership in non-stock corporations and the minimum capital requirements.

5.4.1   Shareholding and membership in stock corporations   As noted already, specific provisions are found in the Corporation Code with respect to preferred shares and shares issued without par value, and with respect to the statutory voting rights which attach to non-voting shares provided for in the articles of incorporation.[76] Specific provisions are also made with respect to founders' shares,[77] redeemable shares[78] and treasury shares.[79]

Sections 60–73 deal with the rights and responsibilities of stockholders. There is provision for subscription contracts[80] and pre-incorporation subscriptions.[81] There is a requirement that stocks shall not be issued for consideration less than the par value or issued price of such stocks[82] and provisions with respect to the issue and transferability of stock certificates.[83] Other provisions are made for the charging of interest on unpaid subscriptions[84] and for proceedings upon the non-payment of subscriptions.[85] There is specific provision for a delinquency sale of shares upon which subscriptions due remain unpaid.[86]

With respect to close corporations, there are some provisions of particular interest. For example, there is specific provision for stockholder agreements by which stockholders might reach agreement as to the conduct of any aspect of corporate affairs or as to the voting rights of stockholders.[87] Insofar as such stockholder agreements may potentially blur the line between management and proprietorship interests, Section 101 of the Corporation Code provides specifically for situations in which the need for a formal meeting of directors is dispensed with and for situations in which directors might act without formal resolution. Section 102 provides specifically for the pre-emptive rights of stockholders in close corporations and Sections 104 and 105 provide for the procedures to apply in the event of deadlocks, the withdrawal of stockholders and the dissolution of the corporation.

5.4.2 Membership of non-stock corporations With respect to non-stock corporations, Section 89 provides that the articles of incorporation may limit, broaden or deny voting rights to various classes of members but that unless so limited broadened or denied, each member, regardless of class, retains the entitlement to vote. Membership in a non-stock corporation, and all rights arising therefrom, are stated to be personal and non-transferable unless the articles of incorporation or the by-laws provide otherwise.[88] Again, the articles of incorporation or the by-laws may provide for the termination of membership and, once terminated, all membership rights in the corporation or its property are extinguished.[89]

5.4.3 The minimum capital requirements The requirements for the maintenance of a minimum capital stock for stock corporations are found in Sections 12–14 of the Corporation Code. Section 12 provides that stock corporations incorporated under the Corporation Code shall not be required to have any minimum authorized capital stock except as otherwise specifically provided for by special law, and except as provided in Sections 13 and 14 of the code. Section 13 provides for the minimum capital stock that is to be subscribed and paid for the purposes of incorporation. At least 25 per cent of the authorized capital stock, as stated in the articles of incorporation, must be subscribed at the time of incorporation. In addition, at least 25 per cent of the total subscription must be paid up upon subscription, the balance to be paid on a date or dates fixed in the contract of subscription without need for call, or in the absence of a fixed date or dates, upon a call, for payment by the board of directors.

There is a proviso that in no case shall the paid up capital be less than P 5 000. The SEC is not to accept for registration the articles of incorporation of any stock corporation unless those articles are accompanied by a sworn statement of the treasurer, elected by the subscribers, which attests to the fact that at least 25 per cent of the authorized capital stock of the corporation has been subscribed and that at least 25 per cent of the total subscription has been fully paid to him or her in actual cash and/or in property, the fair valuation of which is equal to at least 25 per cent of the set subscription, and that such paid up capital is not less than P 5 000.

5.5   *The Amendment of Corporate Constitution*

Unless otherwise prescribed by the Corporation Code or by special law, the articles of incorporation may be amended by a majority vote of the board of directors or trustees supported by the vote or written assent of stockholders representing at least two-thirds of the outstanding capital stock, in the case of a stock corporation, or the vote or written assent of two-thirds of the members, in the case of a non-stock corporation.[90] The by-laws of a corporation, by contrast, may be amended by a majority vote of the board of directors or trustees supported by a majority vote of stockholders (in the case of a stock corporation) or a majority of members (in the case of a non-stock corporation).[91]

6   The Internal Administration of Companies

6.1   *The Duties, Powers and Responsibilities of Officers*

Section 23 of the Corporation Code provides that the corporate powers of all corporations formed under the code shall be exercised by the board of directors (in the case of stock corporations) or the board of trustees (in the case of non-stock corporations), unless otherwise provided in the code. The by-laws of a corporation may also create an executive committee, comprising no fewer than three members of the board, and appointed by the board, to act by majority vote on matters within the power of the board. The powers of such an executive committee would necessarily exclude those matters specifically needing shareholders' approval, such as the filling of vacancies on the board, the amendment or repeal of by-laws, the adoption of new by-laws and so on.[92]

All directors must own at least one share of the capital stock of a stock corporation and all trustees must be members of non-stock corporations. There are general provisions with respect to the election, disqualification and removal of directors and trustees.[93] Immediately following their election, the directors of a corporation must formally elect a president, who must be a director, and nominate a treasurer, who may or may not be a director, a secretary, who must be a resident and citizen of the Philippines, and such other officers as may be provided for in the by-laws. Any two or more positions may be held concurrently by the same person, except that no one person is to act as both president and secretary at the same time, or as president and treasurer at the same time.

Unless otherwise provided in the articles or by-laws, a majority in number of directors or trustees as fixed in the articles shall constitute a quorum for the transaction of corporation business.[94] Within 30 days of the election of directors, trustees and officers of the corporation, the secretary must submit to the SEC the names, nationalities and residences of all directors, trustees and officers so elected.[95] In the absence of any provision of the by-laws fixing compensation for directors, the directors shall not receive any compensation apart from their reasonable *per diems*.[96] Stockholders representing at least a majority of the outstanding stock may vote to grant such compensation to directors, but in no case shall the total yearly compensation for directors exceed 10 per cent of the income, before tax, of the corporation in the preceding year.[97]

6.1.1 Directors' liabilities and responsibilities The key provisions regulating the liabilities and responsibilities of directors, trustees or corporate officers are found in Sections 31, 32 and 34 of the Corporation Code. However, the responsibilities of directors, trustees or company officers in related dealings with the corporation (found in Section 32) should be read in conjunction with the general provisions regarding corporate financial transactions dealt with in section 6.6, below.

The type of liability of directors, trustees and corporate officers embraced within Sections 31, 32 and 34 of the Corporation Code include a range of fiduciary, common law and statutory duties. First, there is joint and several liability on such persons if damage is suffered by the corporation, its stockholders, members and other persons, as a result of actions by such persons who:

> willfully and knowingly vote for or assent to patently unlawful acts of the corporation or who are guilty of gross negligence or bad faith in directing the affairs of the corporation or [who] acquire any personal or pecuniary interest in conflict with their duty as such directors, or trustees.[98]

It is further provided in Section 31 of the code that if a director, trustee or company officer acquires, in violation of his duty, any interest adverse to the corporation in any matter entrusted to him in confidence, and in which equity would impose a disability on him dealing on his own behalf, he shall be liable as a trustee for the corporation and must account for the profits which otherwise would have accrued to the corporation.

Section 32 of the Corporation Code is an interesting provision which is specifically directed to the related dealings of corporate directors, trustees and company officers with the corporation. The scheme of Section 32 is to render such contracts voidable at the option of the corporation unless all of the following conditions obtain:

- that the presence of the director or trustee in the board meeting in which the contract was approved was not necessary to constitute a quorum for such meetings;
- that the vote of such director or trustee was not necessary for the approval of the contract;
- that the contract is fair and reasonable under the circumstances; and
- that, in the case of an officer, the contract with the officer has been previously authorized by the board of directors.

In situations where the first two above mentioned conditions may be absent, a contract between the corporation and a director or trustee may nevertheless be ratified by the vote of stockholders representing at least two-thirds of the outstanding capital stock (in the case of a stock corporation) or two-thirds of the members called for that purpose (in the case of a non-stock corporation), provided that there is a full disclosure of the adverse interests of the directors or trustees involved at such a meeting and that the contract is fair and reasonable under the circumstances.

Section 34 of the Corporation Code provides specifically for the 'disloyalty' of a director who acquires for himself a business opportunity which should rightly belong to the corporation. In this circumstance, the director must account to the corporation for all profits earned by him as a result of such an opportunity unless his or her action is ratified by the vote of the stockholders owning or representing two-thirds of the outstanding capital stock. As might be expected of such a provision directed to a director's fiduciary responsibilities, the provision applies notwithstanding that a director might have risked his or her own funds in the venture.

6.2 Meeting Procedures

As noted already, Section 46 of the Corporation Code provides that every corporation formed under the code must, within one month of the issue of its certificate of incorporation, adopt a code of by-laws for its government. Section 47 then specifies the matters which a private corporation may provide for in its by-laws. These matters include:

- the time, place and manner of conducting regular or special meetings of the directors or trustees;
- the time and manner of calling and conducting regular or special meetings of the stockholders or members;
- the required quorum in meetings of stockholders or members and the manner of voting therein;

- the form of proxies to be utilized by stockholders and members and the manner of voting them;
- the qualifications, duties and compensation of directors, trustees, officers and employees;
- the time for holding the annual election of directors or trustees and the mode or the manner of giving notice thereof;
- the manner of election or appointment and the term of officers other than directors and trustees;
- the penalties for violation of the by-laws;
- the manner of issuing stock certificates in the case of stock corporations; and
- such other matters as may be necessary for the proper or convenient transaction of the company's business and affairs.

In addition to providing that the company may adopt by-laws on these matters, there are specific statutory provisions relating to company meetings which may be found in Sections 49–59 of the Corporation Code. The statutory provisions deal with the same sorts of matters on which the corporation may generally adopt by-laws[99] and provide more specifically for many of the matters commonly found in the standard articles of Western corporations. However, worthy of particular mention is Section 59, which provides for voting trusts of stockholders in a corporation, entered into for the purpose of conferring upon a trustee or trustees the right to vote or other rights pertaining to the shares, for a period not exceeding five years. Such voting trusts may be found relevant to those considering the difficult questions associated with the beneficial ownership of shares managed by institutional investors in many Western corporations. Such trusts invite comparisons with the guidelines issued by the Australian Securities Commission permitting agreements between institutional shareholders wishing to vote collectively on certain matters of corporate management.

6.3 The Annual Return and Other Registers

Section 141 of the Corporation Code provides for an annual report to be provided by a company. There is provision in the code for all corporate books to be kept at the principal office of the corporation and for the corporation to keep all minutes of company and board meetings.[100] With respect to the recorded minutes, all protests must be recorded and made available on demand by directors or shareholders. The corporation is required to keep a book recording the capital stock of the corporation together with all acquisitions, diminutions and transfers thereof.

There is a specific right given to stockholders under the Corporation Code to receive copies of all financial statements of the corporation within ten days of their issue.

6.4   *The Shareholder Protection Rules*

The provision of protection for shareholder minorities relies considerably on the provision of 'appraisal rights' afforded to shareholders seeking to exit the corporation in the event of their dissent to a corporate merger, sale of undertaking or amendment to the articles.[101] The circumstances in which a shareholder might exit the corporation, utilizing the appraisal rights referred to, are more fully considered in section 8.3, below, in the context of mergers and takeovers of corporations.

Section 104 of the Corporation Code also provides for shareholder remedies in the event of deadlocks. Deadlocks are generally to be resolved by way of arbitration by the SEC and the buy-back of dissident shareholders' shares. Section 105 of the Corporation Code provides specifically for the dissolution of the corporation.

6.5   *The Relationship between Management and Shareholders*

As noted above, Section 23 of the Corporation Code provides specifically that the corporate powers of all corporations formed under the code are to be exercised by the board of directors or trustees who are to be elected from stockholders or members. This mirrors the kind of provision found in Regulation 66 of the standard Table A Articles adopted by most Australian corporations.

However, in considering the relationship between management and shareholders, particular attention should be paid to the provisions of the Corporation Code dealing with close corporations. These are found in Sections 96–105. Under these provisions, shareholder and director rights might be classified according to the nature of the shares held by those persons and there is specific provision for the corporation to be managed by stockholders, rather than by the board.

6.6   *Corporate Financial Transactions*

Corporate financial transactions must be considered in the context of the general powers of the corporation which have already been considered in Section 4.3 above, and which are to be found in Sections 36 to 44 of the Corporation Code. Some of the key provisions here include the power of the corporation to sell and dispose of its assets,[102] to acquire its own shares for legitimate corporate purposes[103] and to invest corporate funds in another corporation or business or for any other legitimate propose.[104] These important provisions also need to be read in conjunction with the provisions dealing with directors, trustees and company officers, considered in section 6.2, above; the power of the corporation to enter management contracts with related corporations in corporate groups and with interlocking directors;[105] the provisions dealing with corporate mergers and consolidations;[106] and the important exit and appraisal right given to shareholders wishing to exit in the event of any merger, sale of corporate undertaking or amendment to company articles.[107]

Section 40 of the Corporation Code provides that a corporation may, by a majority vote of its board of directors or trustees, sell, lease, exchange, mortgage, pledge or otherwise dispose of all or substantially all of its assets, including its goodwill, on such terms and conditions and for such consideration as the board of directors or trustee may deem expedient. However, the exercise of this power must be authorized by the vote of stockholders representing two-thirds of the outstanding capital stock (in the case of a stock corporation) or by the vote of at least two-thirds of the members (in the case of a non-stock corporation). Most importantly, any 'sale' or 'disposition' will be deemed to cover substantially all the corporate property if the corporation is thereby rendered 'incapable of continuing the business or accomplishing the purpose for which it was incorporated'. Any sale of disposition made in the ordinary course of business will be permissible.

By virtue of Section 42, the corporation is specifically empowered to invest its funds in another corporation or business or for any other purpose agreed on by the majority vote of the board of directors or trustees, ratified by stockholders representing two-thirds of the outstanding capital stock (in the case of a stock corporation) or two-thirds of the members (in the case of a non-stock corporation). There is a proviso that where the investment by the corporation is reasonably necessary to accomplish its primary purpose (stated in the articles of incorporation), the approval of the stockholders or members shall not be necessary. There is a further important proviso that in the event of such a vote, any dissenting shareholders shall have the exit and appraisal rights provided in Sections 81–86 of the code. Section 44 also provides specifically for the corporation to enter management contracts involving management between corporations in corporate groups and interlocking directorates. This specific provision is important to any consideration of corporate financial transactions undertaken under the Corporation Code.

Sections 36–45 of the Corporation Code deal generally with the powers of corporations. Most importantly, the corporation has the power to purchase or acquire its own shares for a 'legitimate' corporate purpose, including the elimination of fractional shares arising out of stock dividends, the collection or compromise of indebtedness to the corporation arising out of unpaid subscriptions in a delinquency sale and the payment of dissenting or withdrawing stockholders entitled to payment for their shares under the provisions of the code. However, before the corporation may exercise this purchase or acquisition power, there must be unrestricted retained earnings in its books to cover the shares to be purchased or acquired.[108] Section 38 is also important in this context, as it provides generally that the corporation is to have the power to increase or decrease its capital stock and incur, create or increase its bonded indebtedness. The exercise of this power by the corporation is prohibited unless first approved by a majority vote of the board of directors and by a two-thirds majority of stockholders duly called to a meeting for that purpose.

Section 38 provides that written notice of the proposed increase or reduction of capital stock must be addressed to each stockholder at his or her place of residence and that a certificate in duplicate must be signed by a majority of the directors of the corporation and countersigned by the chairman and secretary of the stockholders' meeting. This certificate states that the requirements of the Section have been complied with and sets out the details of the increase or the reduction in capital stock. A copy of the certificate must be filed with the SEC attaching a copy of the original articles of the corporation.

The approval of the SEC is required for such a change and the SEC must not accept any certificate which is not accompanied by the sworn statement of the treasurer of the corporation attesting to the fact that at least 25 per cent of such increased capital stock has been subscribed for and that at least 25 per cent of the subscribed stock has been paid for either by way of cash paid to the corporation or by way of transfer to the corporation of property the value of which is equal to 25 per cent of the subscription. There is a further general proviso that the SEC is not to accept such a certificate if the effect of the capital change would prejudice the rights of the corporate creditors.

7 The External Administration of Companies

7.1 An Introduction

The primary provisions dealing with the dissolution of corporations under the Corporation Code are found in Sections 117–121. In these provisions, a fundamental distinction is drawn between the voluntary dissolution of the corporation[109] and involuntary dissolution of the corporation.[110] The provisions with respect to the former are relatively straightforward. On the other hand, Section 121, which states rather simply that a corporation may be dissolved by the SEC upon the filing of a verified complaint and after proper notice and hearing on the grounds provided under the law, demands a closer examination of the extensive regulatory and adjudicative powers of the SEC, given under Presidential Decree 901-A, particularly the provision of the decree which empowers the SEC to appoint receivers of corporate property, 'rehabilitation receivers', management committees, boards or bodies upon commission to undertake the management of corporations, partnerships and other associations which are not supervised or regulated by other governmental agencies.[111] As has been already noted, the SEC enjoys extensive regulatory and adjudicative power in these areas and recourse must be had to the provisions of Presidential Decree 902-A when considering those powers related to the external administration of companies.

In the case of the voluntary dissolution of corporations, a distinction is made between voluntary dissolutions in which no creditors are affected[112] and those voluntary dissolutions in which creditors are affected.[113] In the former, dissolution of the corporation may be effected by majority vote of the board of directors or trustees, and by the resolution in a general meeting of stockholders owning at least two-thirds of the outstanding capital stock or of at least two-thirds of the members of non-stock corporations. Provision is made for due notice and advertisement of such a meeting to be given; for a copy of the resolution authorizing dissolution to be certified by a majority of the board of directors or the trustees and countersigned by the secretary of the corporation; and for the subsequent issue by the SEC of a certificate of dissolution. Where the dissolution of a corporation may prejudice the rights of any creditor, a petition for dissolution may be filed with the SEC. This petition is to be signed by a majority of the board of directors or trustees and verified by the corporation's president or secretary.

The petition must set forth all claims and demands made against the corporation and state that the dissolution of the corporation was resolved by the vote at general meeting of stockholders representing at least two-thirds of the capital stock of a stock corporation, or by at least two-thirds of the members of a non-stock corporation, convened for that purpose. Provided that the petition is sufficient in form and substance, the SEC shall by order fix a date (not less than 30 days and more than 60 days after the date of such an order) on or before which objections to the petition may be filed by any person.

Upon giving five days' notice after the date on which the right to file objections has expired, the SEC shall proceed to hear the petition and try any issue raised by the objections filed. If no such objection is sufficient and the material allegations of the petition are true, the SEC shall render judgment, dissolving the corporation and directing such disposition of its assets as justice demands. The SEC may also appoint a receiver to collect such assets and to pay such debts of the corporation.[114] There is further provision in the Corporation Code for a voluntary dissolution to be effected by an amendment to the articles of incorporation shortening the corporate term. Upon approval of the amended articles of corporation or the expiration of the shortened term, the corporation shall be deemed to be dissolved without any further proceedings.[115]

7.2　*The Rules Regarding Arrangements and Reconstructions*

The primary provisions regarding the merger and consolidation of corporations are found in Sections 76–80 of the Corporation Code and the associated provisions dealing with the exit and appraisal rights of dissenting stockholders in Sections 81–86. As these provisions are not restricted to arrangements and reconstructions undertaken only to assist companies in financial distress, it is probably most appropriate to consider these provisions in the context of the takeover rules and this is done in Section 8, below. Nevertheless, the provisions with respect to the merger and consolidation of corporations dealt with in Section 8, below, may, of course, be of relevance to arrangements and reconstructions undertaken to subsume the liabilities of a corporation in financial difficulty, or to avoid the dissolution of such a company.

7.3　*Voluntary Administration and Corporate Rescue Provisions*

As has been noted already, the SEC is empowered to dissolve a corporation following the receipt of a verified complaint and hearing undertaken on the grounds provided by existing laws, rules and regulations.[116] The SEC is given extensive regulatory and adjudicative powers in matters concerning corporations, partnerships and other associations under Presidential Decree 902-A. In particular, Section 5 of this Decree gives the SEC original and exclusive jurisdiction to hear and decide cases involving:

- the devices, schemes or acts of the board of directors, corporate officers or partners or their business associates, which amount to fraud and misrepresentation and which may be detrimental to the interests of the public, and/or of the stockholders, partners, members of associations or organizations registered with the SEC;
- controversies arising out of intra-corporate or partnership relations, between and among stockholders, members and/or associates, between any and all of them and the corporation,

partnership or association of which they are stockholders, members or associates respectively, and between such corporation, partnership or association and the state in so far as it concerns their individual franchise or their right to exist as such entities;

- controversies in the election or appointment of directors, trustees, officers or managers of corporations, partnerships or associations; and
- petitions of corporations, partnerships or associations, declared while in a state of suspension of payments, when the corporation, partnership or association possess sufficient property to cover all its debts but foresees the impossibility of meeting them when they fall due, or when the corporation, partnership or association has no sufficient assets to cover its liabilities, but is under the management of a rehabilitation receiver or management committee created pursuant to the Decree 902-A.[117]

Further guidance as to the operation of these provisions in matters of voluntary administration and corporate rescue are to be found in the more general powers of the SEC set out in Section 6 of Presidential Decree 902-A. Among the general powers of the SEC is the power to appoint one or more receivers of corporate property which may be the subject of any action pending before the SEC whenever this is necessary to preserve the rights of parties to the litigation and/or the interest of the investing public and creditors.

Perhaps more indicative of the central role played by the SEC, it may also appoint a rehabilitation receiver who shall enjoy enhanced powers, additional to those enjoyed by a regular receiver. It is specifically provided that upon the appointment of a management committee, rehabilitation receiver or board pursuant to the provisions of Presidential Decree 902-A, all actions for and claims against corporations, partnership or associations under management or receivership pending before any court, tribunal court or body shall be suspended.[118]

Most importantly, Presidential Decree 902-A specifically empowers the SEC to create and appoint management committees, boards or bodies upon petition to undertake the management of corporations, partnerships or other associations, not supervised or regulated by other government agencies, when there is imminent danger of dissipation, loss, wastage or destruction of assets or other property or possible paralysis of business operations which may be prejudicial to the interest of minority stockholders, parties-litigants or the general public. Such management committees, rehabilitation receivers, boards or bodies shall have the power to take custody and control of the existing assets and property of entities under management in order to evaluate the existing assets and liabilities, the earnings and operations of such corporations, partnerships or other associations, and thereafter to determine the best way to salvage and protect investors and creditors. They are further empowered to study, review and evaluate the feasibility of continuing operations and/or restructuring and rehabilitating such entities if this is considered feasible by the SEC.

Such management committees shall report and be responsible to the SEC until they are dissolved by order of the SEC. However, the SEC may on the basis of any findings and recommendations made by such management committees, or on its own findings, determine that the continuance in business of such an entity would not be feasible or profitable, nor work to the best interest of the stockholders, parties-litigants, creditors or the general public. In such event, the SEC may order the dissolution of such entities and order that its remaining assets be liquidated accordingly. The management committee may overrule or revoke the actions of the previous management and board of directors of the entity under management, notwithstanding any provision of law, the articles of incorporation or by-laws to the contrary. The management committee will not be liable for actions undertaken or omitted in good faith and in the exercise of its proper functions or powers conferred by virtue of Presidential Decree 902-A.[119]

7.4   Company Winding Up Rules, Tests for Insolvency, Grounds for Winding Up and Mechanisms for Initiating Insolvency Proceedings

As has been noted above, the dissolution of a Philippine corporation may be effected voluntarily[120] or involuntarily by the SEC upon receiving a verified complaint.[121] The wide powers of the SEC under Presidential Decree 902-A (referred to in section 7.3, above), particularly those powers related to the appointment of receivers, rehabilitation receivers, management committees, boards and other bodies, reflect the SEC's central role both as a regulator and in undertaking corporate rescues in appropriate cases.

However, the same provisions also highlight the full extent of the powers of the SEC and of those persons appointed as receivers, rehabilitation receivers and others in deciding whether the corporation is to be dissolved or not. Ultimately, the SEC will decide whether the corporation is to be dissolved and, in doing so, it may act on the advice and reports of those persons it has appointed and on its own findings. Given the extremely broad regulatory and adjudicative powers assigned to the SEC under Presidential Decree 902-A, it might be anticipated that a good deal of discretion will lie with the SEC and its appointees in deciding matters of corporate insolvency and in deciding the fundamental question as to whether a corporation should be dissolved.

8 Takeover Rules

8.1 An Introduction

As has already been seen, the powers of corporations under the Corporation Code include the power to acquire the securities and property of other corporations in the course of transacting the lawful business of the corporation.[122] In addition, the statutory powers of the corporation also include the power to enter into merger or consolidation with other corporations as provided in the Corporation Code.[123] The central provisions concerning the merger and consolidation of corporations are found in Sections 76–80 of the Corporation Code. These provisions are not restricted in their application to cases of merger and consolidation when one participating corporation is in financial distress. Instead, the provisions have a more general application in situations where one corporation might acquire the securities of another with a view to achieving corporate control.

As will be seen, these provisions envisage a cooperative, non-adversarial approach to the building and reorganization of corporate entities, and to the achieving of corporate control. The logic of these provisions rests heavily on the coincidence of the legitimate objectives of participating corporations and on the cooperation between the management of each of the participating corporations. Most importantly, it also rests substantially on the protective role and approval of the SEC and relies on the exit and appraisal rights given to dissenting stockholders, in the event of a merger or consolidation.[124]

8.2 Takeover Thresholds

The Corporation Code provides that two or more corporations may merge into a single corporation (which shall be one of the constituent corporations) or may, alternatively, consolidate into a new single corporation (which shall be a consolidated corporation).[125] In either case the board of directors or the trustees of participating corporations shall approve a plan of merger or consolidation which must set forth the following details:

- the names of the corporations proposing to merge or consolidate;
- the terms of the merger or consolidation and the mode of carrying such merger or consolidation into effect;
- a statement of the changes, if any, in the articles of incorporation of the surviving corporation, in the case of a merger, or in the case of a consolidated corporation following a consolidation, all the statements required to be set forth in the articles of

incorporation for corporations organized under the Corporation Code; and

- such other provisions with respect to the proposed merger or consolidation as may be deemed necessary or desirable.

Upon approval of the plan of merger or consolidation by the majority vote of each of the board of directors or trustees of the participating corporations, the approval for such plan must also be given by stockholders representing two-thirds of the outstanding capital stock of each corporation (in the case of stock corporations) or at least two-thirds of the members (in the case of non-stock corporations). Due notice must be given to stockholders and members respectively of the meeting and such notice must be accompanied by a copy of the plan of merger or consolidation. Any stockholders dissenting to the approval of the plan are entitled to exit the company and to the appraisal right given in Section 81 of the Corporation Code. This process is considered more closely in Section 8.3, below.

Following approval of the plan by stockholders or members, fresh articles of association (annexing a copy of the plan) must be drawn and certified by each participating corporation.[126] These articles are then submitted to the SEC for its approval.[127] In cases involving the merger or consolidation of banks, banking institutions, insurance companies or public utilities which are governed by special laws, the favourable recommendation of the appropriate government agency must first be obtained. Otherwise, once the SEC is satisfied that the merger or consolidation is not inconsistent with the provision of the Corporation Code and the existing laws, it will issue a certificate of merger or consolidation and the merger or consolidation becomes effective from that date. If, upon investigation, the SEC has reason to believe that the proposed merger or consolidation is contrary to, or inconsistent with, the provisions of the Corporation Code or the existing laws it is empowered to set a date for a hearing, giving the corporations concerned an opportunity to be heard.[128] Section 80 of the Corporation Code provides that upon merger or consolidation, the surviving corporation (in the case of a merger) or the consolidated corporation (in the case of a consolidation) shall enjoy the same powers and be subject to the same duties and liabilities of any corporation organized under the Corporation Code.

Most importantly, there is a specific provision that the surviving or consolidated corporation shall be responsible and liable for all the obligations of each of the constituent corporations in the same manner as if such a surviving or consolidated corporation had itself incurred such liabilities or obligations, and any prior claims against constituent corporations subsist following the merger or consolidation. The rights of creditors and holders of security are specifically stated not to be affected by the merger or consolidation.[129]

8.3 Disclosure Requirements and Shareholder Protection

Apart from the disclosure requirements of Section 77 of the Corporation Code (requiring stockholder or member approval to the plan of merger or consolidation) and the protective role exercised by the SEC in approving the merger or consolidation under Section 79 of the Corporation Code, the most important protective feature of the scheme is the exit and appraisal rights given to dissenting stockholders under Title X of the Corporation Code. Any stockholder of a corporation shall have the right to dissent and demand payment of the fair value of his or her shares:

- in the case of amendments made to the articles of incorporation which have the effect of changing or restricting the rights of any stockholders or class of shares, or of authorizing preferences in any respect superior to those of outstanding shares of any class, or of extending or shortening the term of corporate existence;
- in the case of the sale, lease, exchange, transfer, mortgage, pledge or other disposition of all, or substantially all, of the corporate property and assets as provided for in the Corporation Code; and
- in the case of any merger or consolidation.[130]

There is provision for any dissenting stockholder to make a written demand on the corporation for payment of the fair value of his or her shares within 30 days of the date, on which the vote of the general meeting was taken. If, within 60 days of that date the dissenting stockholder and the corporation cannot agree on the fair value of the shares, such value shall be determined and appraised by three impartial persons, one of whom shall be named by the stockholder, another by the corporation and the third by the two thus chosen.

Payment to the dissenting stockholder must be made within 30 days of the making of any award. The costs and expenses of the appraisal are to be borne by the corporation, unless the fair value ascertained by the appraisers is approximately the same as the price initially affected by the corporation to the stockholder.[131] The dissenting stockholder must submit his or her certificates of stock to the corporation for the formal notation that such shares, are dissenting shares within ten days of the stockholder demanding payment for his or her shares.[132]

9   Securities Regulation in the Philippines

9.1   *An Introduction*

The provisions relevant to the regulation of securities trading in the Philippines are found in the Revised Securities Act.[133] Before considering some of the provisions of the Revised Securities Act in greater detail, it is worthwhile noting three distinguishing features of this regulatory system. The most important feature is that regulation relies heavily on registration by the SEC, not only of stock exchanges and brokers and dealers, as might be expected, but also of securities themselves.[134] The most important definitions are found in Section 2 of the Revised Securities Act. This provides essential definitions of the words 'securities' (considered fully in Section 9.2, below), 'Issuer' and 'Dealer', the latter referring to persons primarily responsible for the registration of securities. Section 2 also includes definitions of words such as 'Exchange' and 'Member'. Section 3 makes it clear that the Revised Securities Act is to be administered by the SEC, which, in this endeavour, shall possess the powers and discharge the functions referred to in Presidential Decrees Nos 902-A, 1653, 1758 and 1799 and in Executive Order No. 708.

The procedure for registration of securities is extensively dealt with in Section 8 of the Revised Securities Act and essentially requires the issuer, dealer or underwriter interested in a sale of securities to lodge a sworn registration statement with the SEC. The information required to be included in this registration statement is extensive and suggests an expectation that the SEC is to exercise a substantial protective role in the registration process. Nevertheless, the SEC is to advise the public that, at the end of this process, the issuance of a permit is not to be deemed a finding by the SEC, that the registration statement is true and accurate on its face, or that it does not contain any untrue statement of fact, or that it omits to state a material fact.[135] The extensive information required for inclusion in the registration statement also suggests that the regulatory regime relies more heavily on proper disclosure to the SEC than it does on affording direct protection to those to whom securities might be offered for sale or subscription.

The securities which are to be subject to this registration process are extensively defined in Section 2 of the Revised Securities Act, although provision is also made for exempt securities and exempt transactions.[136] Notwithstanding the central registration requirements found in Sections 4, 5 and 6, certain contracts (such as futures contracts) may also be registered. As has been noted, a number of important regulatory consequences flow from this registration process. For example, periodic and other corporate reports in the vein of continuing reporting requirements must be lodged by the issuer following the registration of securities. In addition, the general limitations on the acquisition of securities, found in Sections 32–34, in effect, rest on the initial registration of those securities. There is provision for the civil liability of those making false statements in the registration statement and in prospectuses, communications and reports, or in any advertising associated with the issue of securities.[137] There is also power in the SEC to suspend any registration of securities and to revoke such a registration.[138]

The second, closely related feature of securities regulation in the Philippines under the Revised Securities Act is the dominant role played by the SEC. This dominant role might by now be anticipated in view of the very wide powers of the SEC, already considered above, and in view of the central importance of the registration of securities, stock exchanges, brokers and dealers to the regulatory scheme.

The requirements for the registration of a stock exchange are found in Section 22 of the Revised Securities Act and the requirements for registration of an exchange are not dissimilar to those generally required elsewhere for the establishment of such institutions. However, it is important to note that the registration statement filed by any intending exchange must include an undertaking to comply with, and to enforce compliance by its members with, the provision of the Act and any amendments thereto, and to implement all rules or regulations made thereunder.[139] Section 22 also permits exchanges to adopt and enforce rules 'not inconsistent with the Act' nor with any rules and regulations thereunder, or any other law.[140] Once again, this regime suggests the central place of the SEC and the relatively less significant role played by the exchange itself in enforcing either listing rules or business rules associated with the regulation of issuers of securities and members of the exchange respectively. It also points to the relatively less significant importance of the contractual relationship which exists between the exchange and corporations listing on that exchange and the exchange and its members, evident elsewhere.

In similar fashion to the registration processes for exchanges and securities, registration with the SEC is also required for brokers, dealers and salesmen.[141] Apart from the potential liability for general market offences considered specifically below, there is particular statutory regulation of certain aspects of the business of brokers, dealers and salesmen which might elsewhere be the subject of regulation by way of business rules promulgated by individual exchanges. For example, the SEC is empowered to make rules with respect to the credit that might be extended on any security[142] and with respect to the restrictions on borrowing that might be made by members, brokers and dealers, aimed at maintaining prudential levels of liquidity.[143]

There are quite specific limitations on dealings by members, brokers and dealers as principals.[144] Finally, there are specific provisions directed at preventing members, brokers and dealers from operating a market removed from the lawful exchange and the facilities of that lawful exchange.[145]

It must also be noted that the central position of the SEC in this regulatory regime is greatly reinforced by the extensive powers invested in the SEC by virtue of Section 38 of the Act. Section 38 empowers the SEC to withdraw its registration of an exchange, to expel members of an exchange and to suspend trading in registered securities on any exchange. It also gives the SEC full powers to ensure that any exchange actively amends its rules, as might be required by the SEC, in the public interest and for the protection of investors. By virtue of Section 37, the SEC enjoys wide powers to examine the records and reports of exchanges, members and other persons. The SEC is also fully empowered to investigate complaints and, in this respect, fulfils an apparent regulatory role.

9.2   Types of Securities Regulated

As noted above, the definition of securities is found in Section 2 of the Revised Securities Act. The definition is an important one as all securities, thus defined, are required to be registered, primarily by the issuers of, or dealers in, such securities, and are thereafter subject to the requirements of periodic and other corporate reporting,[146] the substantial shareholder provisions,[147] and the provisions directed to the regulation of acquisition of shares.[148]

The definition of securities is an exceedingly broad one and includes not only shares, bonds, debentures and other notes evidencing indebtedness, but also:

> preorganization certificates or subscriptions, certificates of interests or participation in a profit sharing agreement, voting trust certificates, interests or instruments commonly considered to be securities, commercial papers evidencing the indebtedness of any person, financial or non-financial entity, issued, endorsed, sold or transferred in any manner to another including, *inter alia*, commodity futures contracts, transferable stock options, pre-need plans, pension plans, life plans, joint venture contracts, and similar contracts and investments where there is no tangible return on investments plus profits but an appreciation of capital as well as enjoyment of particular privileges and services.

9.3 The Legal Effect of Listing Rules and Business Rules of the Stock Exchange(s)

As noted above, the SEC is the administrative agency primarily responsible for the administration of the Revised Securities Act.[149] It is clear that the SEC enjoys a central position in the process of registration of securities and has some responsibility for investor protection in that registration process.[150] Furthermore, the central importance attaching to the SEC in the registration of exchanges[151] and in the registration of brokers, dealers and salesmen[152] points to the primary responsibility of the SEC in regulating not only the relationship between an exchange and listed corporations, but also the relationship between an exchange and its members or dealers.

This responsibility is emphasized by the requirement that an exchange must undertake to comply with, and enforce compliance by its members with, the provisions of the Revised Securities Act.[153] It is also reinforced by direct statutory obligations on brokers with respect to the extension of credit on any registered security and restrictions on the borrowings of members, brokers and dealers.[154] It must also be noted that the powers vested in the SEC include the power to withdraw the registration of a securities exchange, to expel members of that exchange, to suspend trading in securities on the exchange and the residual power to ensure that an exchange adopts its rules or amends its rules in the public interest and for the purposes of the Revised Securities Act.[155]

The central role of the SEC in regulating dealings by members, brokers and dealers is further emphasized by Section 31 of the Revised Securities Act. The SEC is to prescribe the rules and regulations which it may deem necessary or appropriate to safeguard the public interest and to protect investors.[156] These rules may include rules with respect to floor trading by members of securities exchanges, directly or indirectly, or on their own account, and rules directed at segregating and limiting the functions of brokers and dealers. Section 31 further provides that unless otherwise prohibited by such rules and regulations as the SEC may prescribe as necessary or appropriate in the public interest or for the protection of investors, the rules of a securities exchange *may* permit certain specific activities. Nevertheless, the central role of the SEC in this regime remains clear.

9.4 Market Conduct Rules and Sanctions for Securities Misconduct

The primary provisions with respect to the regulation of market conduct are found in Sections 26–30 of the Revised Securities Act. Section 26 deals with the manipulation of securities prices in specific situations. The section specifically prohibits a person from creating a false or misleading appearance of active trading in any security, or a false or misleading appearance with respect to the market for any such security. It prohibits transactions designed to raise or depress the price of securities or to create active trading in those securities for the purpose of inducing a purchase or sale.

Dealers and brokers are specifically prohibited from advertising or participating in such activities. It is also unlawful for any person, broker or dealer to utilize option trading to achieve those ends. In Section 27 there is also a more general prohibition on the use or employment, in connection with the purchase or sale of any security, of any manipulative or deceptive device or contrivance. Under this same Section, it is also generally unlawful to effect a short sale in contravention of any prevailing laws and regulations prescribed by the SEC. Section 28 makes it unlawful for any exchange to adopt and enforce artificial measures of price control of any nature whatsoever without the prior approval of the SEC, whose approval may only be given if such measures serve the public interest and benefit investors.

The most important remaining provisions are found in Sections 29 and 30 of the Revised Securities Act. Section 29 renders unlawful particular dealings undertaken fraudulently or deceitfully. These include untrue statements and omissions of material facts made with respect to registered securities or, importantly, descriptions of registered securities not being offered for sale, whilst receiving an undisclosed consideration directly or indirectly from the issuer or other interested persons.

Section 30 deals with the insider's duty to disclose when trading, although it might be noted that, unlike a number of Western jurisdictions in which insider trading has become essentially a market offence, the Philippine Revised Securities Act defines the insider as the issuer of securities, a director or officer of the issuer, or a person controlling, controlled by, or under common control with, the issuer, or otherwise a person whose relationship or former relationship to the issuer gives him or her access to a fact of special significance about the issuer or about the security that is not generally available. Therefore, 'tipees' of the insider, although not defined as such, are considered to be insiders for the purposes of Section 30.

10 Miscellaneous

10.1   *The Powers of the Courts*

The powers of the courts with respect to matters concerning the corporations law of the Philippines must be considered in the light of

Presidential Decree 902-A. As has been noted many times already, Presidential Decree 902-A provides the SEC with 'absolute jurisdiction, supervision and control over all corporations, partnerships or associations, who are the grantees of primary franchises and/or a licence or permit issued by the Government to operate in the Philippines'. In the exercise of its authority, the SEC is empowered to 'enlist the aid and support of and to deputise any and all enforcement agencies of the government, civil or military as well as any private institution, corporation, firm, association or person'.[157]

In addition to this extremely broad regulatory power, the SEC enjoys broad adjudicative power as well, holding the original and exclusive jurisdiction to hear a wide range of cases involving intracorporate disputes and certain broader matters involving corporations.[158]

The SEC is thus empowered to grant civil remedies to stockholders in disputes between and among stockholders and to stockholders in situations where the actions of directors involve fraud or misrepresentation detrimental to the interests of stockholders or members of the public. Pursuant to the provisions of Section 6 of Presidential Decree 902-A, the SEC is also empowered to impose criminal fines and/or penalties for the violation of Presidential Decree 902-A or of any other laws implemented by the SEC, its rules, regulations, orders, decisions and rulings. The appeal may be made from the decision of such Commissioner to the SEC sitting *en banc* within 30 days of receipt by any person aggrieved of the notice of the Commissioner's decision, ruling or order. Finally, any aggrieved person may appeal the order, decision or ruling of the SEC sitting *en banc* to the Supreme Court by way of a petition for review in accordance with the pertinent provisions of the rules of Court. Notwithstanding any right of appeal to the Supreme Court, the exceedingly broad regulatory and adjudicative power of the SEC remains apparent. This power is reinforced in the preamble to Presidential Decree 902-A and in Section 1 of the decree itself, by which the administrative supervision of the SEC was transferred from the Department of Trade to the direct general supervision of the President.

Notes

* Senior Lecturer in Law, University of Canberra. The author is grateful to Rico Domingo, Attorney and Counsellor-At-Law, Manila, for his assistance with the preparation of this chapter.

1 ASEAN Law Association (1995), *ASEAN Legal Systems*, Singapore: Butterworths Asia, 184.

2 Eighth Edition (1991), Manila: Central Book Supply Inc.

3 As note 1, above, 141.

4   As note 1, above, 152–153.
5   Act No. 1596 (1909).
6   Act No. 1508 (1906).
7   Act No. 2031 (1911).
8   Act No. 2137 (1912).
9   Com Act No. 83 (1937), as amended.
10   Rep Act No. 265 (1948), as amended.
11   As note 1, above, 186.
12   As note 1, above, 186.
13   Presidential Decree No. 902-A, as amended by Presidential Decree Nos 1653, 1758 and 1799.
14   Presidential Decree 902-A, Section 1.
15   Presidential Decree 902-A, Section 2.
16   Presidential Decree 902-A, Sections 5 and 6.
17   Presidential Decree 902-A, Section 3.
18   Presidential Decree 902-A, Section 6(d).
19   Presidential Decree 902-A, Section 6(a), (b), (h) and (i).
20   Presidential Decree 902-A, Section 6(j).
21   As note 20, above.
22   Presidential Decree 902-A, Section 6(f).
23   Presidential Decree 902-A, Section 6(d).
24   Presidential Decree 902-A, Section 6(e).
25   Presidential Decree 902-A, Section 6(i).
26   Presidential Decree 902-A, Section 6(l).
27   Presidential Decree 902-A, Section 6(m).
28   Commercial Act No. 287, an Act transferring to the SEC the powers, duties and functions of the Bureau of Commerce in connection with the registration of corporations and associations; Republic Act No. 62, an Act requiring the presentation of proof of ownership of securities in order to assist in the reconstruction of corporate records; Republic Act No. 1143, an Act providing for a more effective administration of the securities market and other laws by the SEC for the imposition of fines and summary punishment for breaches; Presidential Decree No. 270, a decree requiring the declaration and distribution of surplus profits as dividends to stockholders; and Presidential Decree No. 167, a decree providing for the automatic listing of securities in all stock exchanges.
29   Corporation Code, Sections 3 and 4.
30   Corporation Code, Sections 96–105.
31   Corporation Code, Sections 106–108.
32   Corporation Code, Sections 109–116.
33   Corporation Code, Section 4.
34   Corporation Code, Sections 123–136.
35   Corporation Code, Section 3.
36   Corporation Code, Section 6.
37   Corporation Code, Section 7.
38   Corporation Code, Section 8.
39   Corporation Code, Section 9.
40   Corporation Code, Section 88.
41   Corporation Code, Sections 89–91.
42   Corporation Code, Sections 92 and 93.
43   Corporation Code, Sections 94 and 95.
44   Corporation Code, Section 96.
45   Corporation Code, Section 100.
46   Corporation Code, Section 101.

47   Corporation Code, Section 105.
48   Corporation Code, Sections 106–108.
49   Corporation Code, Sections 109–115.
50   Corporation Code, Section 123.
51   Corporation Code, Section 125.
52   Corporation Code, Section 127.
53   Corporation Code, Section 129.
54   Corporation Code, Section 132.
55   Corporation Code, Section 36.
56   Corporation Code, Section 37.
57   Corporation Code, Section 38.
58   Corporation Code, Section 39.
59   Corporation Code, Section 40.
60   Corporation Code, Section 41.
61   Corporation Code, Section 42.
62   Corporation Code, Section 43.
63   Corporation Code, Section 44.
64   Corporation Code, Section 20.
65   Corporation Code, Section 43.
66   Corporation Code, Section 10.
67   Corporation Code, Section 11.
68   Corporation Code, Section 17.
69   Corporation Code, Section 46.
70   Corporation Code, Section 48.
71   Corporation Code, Sections 49–59.
72   Corporation Code, Sections 96–105.
73   Corporation Code, Section 97.
74   Corporation Code, Section 100.
75   Corporation Code, Section 18.
76   Corporation Code, Section 6.
77   Corporation Code, Section 7.
78   Corporation Code, Section 8.
79   Corporation Code, Section 9.
80   Corporation Code, Section 60.
81   Corporation Code, Section 61.
82   Corporation Code, Section 62.
83   Corporation Code, Sections 63 and 64.
84   Corporation Code, Section 65.
85   Corporation Code, Section 69–72.
86   Corporation Code, Section 68.
87   Corporation Code, Section 100.
88   Corporation Code, Section 90.
89   Corporation Code, Section 91.
90   Corporation Code, Section 16.
91   Corporation Code, Section 48.
92   Corporation Code, Section 35.
93   Corporation Code, Sections 24, 27 and 28.
94   Corporation Code, Section 25.
95   Corporation Code, Section 26.
96   Corporation Code, Section 30.
97   Corporation Code, Section 30.
98   Corporation Code, Section 31.
99   Corporation Code, Section 47.
100   Corporation Code, Sections 74 and 75.

101   Corporation Code, Sections 81–86.
102   Corporation Code, Section 40.
103   Corporation Code, Section 41.
104   Corporation Code, Section 42.
105   Corporation Code, Section 44.
106   Corporation Code, Sections 76–80.
107   Corporation Code, Sections 81–86.
108   Corporation Code, Section 41.
109   Corporation Code, Sections 118–120.
110   Corporation Code, Section 121.
111   Presidential Decree No. 902-A, Section 6(c) and (d).
112   Corporation Code, Section 118.
113   Corporation Code, Section 119.
114   Rule 104.
115   Corporation Code, Section 120.
116   Corporation Code, Section 121.
117   Section 5(d), as added by Presidential Decree No. 902-A by Presidential Decree No. 1758.
118   Section 6(c) of Presidential Decree No. 902-A, as amended by Presidential Decrees Nos 1653, 1758 and 1799, 16 January 1981.
119   Section 6(c) of Presidential Decree No. 902-A, as amended by Presidential Decrees Nos 1653, 1758 and 1799.
120   Corporation Code, Sections 118–120.
121   Corporation Code, Section 121.
122   Corporation Code, Section 36(7).
123   Corporation Code, Section 36(8).
124   Corporation Code, Sections 81–86.
125   Corporation Code, Section 76.
126   Corporation Code, Section 78.
127   Corporation Code, Section 79.
128   Corporation Code, Section 79.
129   Corporation Code, Section 80(5).
130   Corporation Code, Section 81.
131   Corporation Code, Section 85.
132   Corporation Code, Section 86.
133   The Revised Securities Act (*Batas Pambansa* Blg 178).
134   Revised Securities Act, Sections 2 and 4.
135   Revised Securities Act, Section 8.
136   Revised Securities Act, Sections 5 and 6.
137   Revised Securities Act, Sections 12 and 13.
138   Revised Securities Act, Sections 15 and 16.
139   Revised Securities Act, Section 22(a)(1).
140   Revised Securities Act, Section 22 (c).
141   Revised Securities Act, Sections 19 and 20.
142   Revised Securities Act, Section 23.
143   Revised Securities Act, Section 24.
144   Revised Securities Act, Section 31, note particularly Section 31(b).
145   Revised Securities Act, Section 35.
146   Revised Securities Act, Section 11.
147   Revised Securities Act, Section 36.
148   Revised Securities Act, Sections 32 and 33.
149   Revised Securities Act, Section 3.
150   Revised Securities Act, Section 8.
151   Revised Securities Act, Section 22.

152   Revised Securities Act, Section 19.
153   As note 151, above.
154   Revised Securities Act, Section 38.
155   Revised Securities Act, Section 38.
156   Revised Securities Act, Section 31(a).
157   Presidential Decree 902-A, Section 3.
158   These powers, including the central powers in Section 5 of Presidential Decree 902-A, were considered fully in Section 3.1, above.

14 The Company Law of Brunei Darussalam

BAHRIN (KAM) KAMARUL*

1 Introduction

1.1 The State of Brunei Darussalam and Official Ideology

Brunei gained recognition as a sovereign state in 1984, ending its British protectorate status which had been established in 1888. The Brunei state is an absolute monarchy. Its twin pillars are the Constitution 1959 and the official ideology of *Melayu Islam Beraja* (Malay Islamic Monarchy or MIB).[1] The Constitution of Brunei Darussalam 1959 (hereinafter the 1959 'Constitution') vests on the Sultan of Brunei supreme executive authority,[2] power to make laws with the Legislative Council's advice and consent,[3] and reserve powers to enact laws, without the Legislative Council's advice, in the interests of expediency, public order, good faith or good government.[4] The Sultan is also empowered by Section 83(3) of the Constitution[5] to proclaim a state of emergency in Brunei. Since 1962, when a state of emergency was declared, Brunei has been governed by decree. Decrees of the Sultan made under the emergency power have validity notwithstanding anything inconsistent with the Constitution.[6]

Brunei's government operates according to the state ideology of MIB. MIB is officially described as the doctrine which provides 'for a degree of reciprocity in the relationship between subjects and Monarch'[7] in which the Sultan, through a 'capable, effective, clean, honest and accessible administration [is obliged] ... to hear and overcome whatever complaints and difficulties might be faced by the people of Brunei Darussalam'.[8] The ideology is a composite doctrine which 'seeks to consolidate a single national identity, born of convergence on a dominant Malay culture, and long binding a loyal citizenry to an absolute monarchy of the same race, with the blessing of and divine sanction of Islam'.[9]

1.2   *Brunei's Legal System*

While Brunei's Sultan exercises absolute constitutional powers, the legal system of Brunei Darussalam reflects many aspects of the English judicial model, including the ideal of the 'rule of law' in its legal administration. These features have been inherited from Britain, Brunei having been, until 1984, a British protectorate.[10] Consequently, much of Brunei's pre-1984 enactments were based on either British legislation or on regulations with which the British had governed their colonies. Another source of law is English common law, introduced into Brunei through the establishment of the Court of the Resident under the Courts Enactment of 1906. In addition, customary law of the indigenous people is another important source of law. However, all matters concerning Islamic religion, marriage and divorce in Brunei are governed by *shariah* law (Islamic law) administered by the Court of Kathis.

The Brunei judiciary is presided over and supervised by the Chief Justice. The hierarchy of courts comprises of: the Court of Appeal, the High Court, the Intermediate Court and the Magistrate's Court. Appeals from the Intermediate Court or High Court go to the Court of Appeal, which is presided over by a president and two other judges or judicial commissioners. From there, any further appeal will be forwarded to the Judicial Committee of the Privy Council in London. The Judicial Committee in London would report the result of its determination to the Sultan, who may act or make orders as he deems fit.[11] Judges and commissioners of Brunei superior courts are appointed under the Supreme Court (Cap. 5) 1985, Revised Edition.[12]

2   Corporation Law Statute and Case-Law in Brunei

2.1   *Brunei's Companies Act 1956 and Finance Companies Act 1972*

The Companies Act (Cap. 39) 1956 (CA) governs the regulation of companies in Brunei. The legislation, enacted on the advice of the British Resident, was broadly modelled on the United Kingdom Companies Act 1948. In addition, the Finance Companies Act (Cap. 89) 1972 governs the operation of companies engaged 'to carry on financing business', defined as (a) the borrowing of money from the public by acceptance of deposits and the issuing certificates or other evidence of indebtedness to the public and undertaking to repay on call or after an agreed maturity date, or (b) the lending of money to the public, including the financing of hire-purchase agreements.[13]

2.2   English Common Law and Statutory Interpretation in Brunei

English common law rules and statutory interpretation principles apply in Brunei courts. The Brunei High Court Rules which govern civil procedure are similar to civil procedure under English law. The civil jurisdiction of the Brunei High Court, for example, consists of original jurisdiction and authority similar to that of the Chancery, Family and Queen's Bench Divisions of the High Court of England.[14] The Privy Council in England is Brunei's highest court of appeal and English decisions provide the basis of case-law. Entry into Brunei's legal profession is restricted to persons who are qualified to practice as legal practitioners in England, Northern Ireland, Scotland, Malaysia or Singapore. As the University of Brunei does not have a faculty of law, lawyers in Brunei have been, and are, trained in the above countries, especially England and Malaysia.

3   The Nature and Powers of Corporate Regulatory Bodies in the Jurisdiction

3.1   The Registrar of Companies and the Minister of Finance

The prime responsibility for the administration of the CA rests with the registrar of companies. The registrar is appointed by the Sultan of Brunei under the CA and his or her primary duty is to ensure that companies are established and managed in accordance with the provisions of the CA.

The regulation of finance companies, however, is the responsibility of the Minister for Finance under the Finance Companies Act 1972. The Minister is responsible for the licensing of companies which engage in the business of borrowing money from and lending money to the public. The Finance Companies Act 1972 gives the Minister for Finance wide powers of regulation, including the power to prescribe the maximum rates payable on different types of deposits; the maximum percentage that finance companies may hold in different types of loans; the minimum down-payments and maximum maturity periods of loans; the maximum rates of interest or commissions to be charged on loans; and the maximum amount of loans or advances that can be granted.[15] The minister is also empowered to prescribe the minimum holdings of liquid assets to be held by finance companies.[16] To help with this task, the minister is given the power, to occasionally inspect, or cause to be inspected under conditions of secrecy, the books, accounts and transactions of any finance company.[17] Also, the minister may, without instituting proceedings against any person for any offence under the CA, demand and receive any fine or default penalty prescribed for an offence. If such amounts are paid within 14 days of the offence, no proceedings will be instituted, otherwise the minister may institute proceedings in relation to the offence.[18]

3.2   *The Ministry of Development*

The Ministry of Development is responsible for overseeing foreign investment in Brunei. Such investment, particularly by major multi-national companies, is encouraged. The Investment Incentives Act 1975, provides tax and other benefits to such activities. Two industries which are closed to foreign investment, however, are forestry products and deep sea fishing within Brunei territorial waters. A major policy aim of the Ministry of Development is to ensure that foreign investment is carried out through joint ventures between foreign and local companies and businesses, preferably with the Brunei partner holding a 51 per cent stake.[19] The Ministry of Development provides the guidelines which determine the industries which are off limits and those in which foreign investment would be encouraged. The processing of foreign investment approvals is administered by its Industrial Development Unit.

4   A Description of Types of Companies and their Powers

4.1   *Types of Local Companies*

The CA recognizes three types of companies: companies limited by shares; companies limited by guarantee; and, unlimited companies. Companies may be public or private. Public companies are allowed to invite the public to subscribe for their shares or debentures, whereas private companies are prohibited from doing so. Private companies are required to have further clauses stated in their articles restricting the right to transfer shares, limiting the number of members to 50, and prohibiting the invitation to the public to subscribe for shares or debentures.[20]

4.2   *The Recognition of Foreign Companies in the Jurisdiction*

Foreign companies are recognized by the CA. A foreign company includes all companies incorporated outside Brunei which establish a place of business in Brunei.[21] Foreign companies are required to register the following with the registrar: a certified copy of the charter, statutes or memorandum and articles; the directors of the company; and a list of persons authorized to accept service of process or notices.[22]

4.3   The Legal Capacities and Powers of Companies

Upon incorporation, a company acquires a legal personality, it is capable of exercising all the functions of an incorporated company and it has perpetual succession and a common seal.[23] Registered foreign companies have the same power to acquire, hold and dispose of immovable property in Brunei as Brunei incorporated companies have.[24] The CA, however, contains no provision limiting the operation of the common law *ultra vires* doctrine applicable to the company's legal capacity.

5   Company Formation

5.1   Promoters and the Registration of Companies

Persons wishing to incorporate a company must lodge with the registrar of companies the memorandum of the proposed company.[25] Seven or more persons are required to subscribe to a memorandum of a company, but where the company to be formed is a private company, a minimum of two subscribers is required.[26] Whereas in the case of a company limited by shares the filing of its articles of association is not required, in the case of a company limited by a guarantee or an unlimited company, the articles of association of the company must also be lodged with the registrar.[27] Upon payment of the requisite fees and subject to the CA, the registrar will issue a certificate of incorporation.

5.2   The Company Constitution

The memorandum and articles of association together form the constitution of a company. The memorandum must contain the name of the company, the registered office, an objects clause, a liability clause, a share capital clause, an association clause and a subscriber clause setting out the particulars of the subscribers and number of shares taken by each subscriber.[28] The memorandum contains the provisions concerning the relationship of outsiders dealing with the company and is, therefore, the more important document. The articles, on the other hand, are the regulations governing the internal management of the company. The internal management of a company limited by shares which has not filed articles of association with the registrar will be governed by the regulations of Table A of the First Schedule of the CA.[29] The memorandum and articles have the effect of a contract under seal between the company and each member, and between members *inter se*.[30] The memorandum may be altered in the manner provided and only to the extent allowed by the CA.[31] A company may also alter or add to its articles by special resolution, subject to the conditions contained in its memorandum and the provisions of the CA.[32] However, alterations in a memorandum or articles which increase a member's liability to contribute to share capital beyond that which exists at the date of the alteration, do not bind the member, unless the member has agreed in writing to be bound.[33]

5.3   *Company Names and the Restrictions on the Use of Certain Names*

As noted above, the name of the company must be stated in the memorandum. A company limited by shares or guarantee is required to have the word 'Berhad', or the abbreviation 'Bhd' as part of its name. Further, a private limited company must have the word 'sendirian', or the abbreviation 'Sdn' as part of its name, inserted immediately before the word 'berhad' or 'Bhd'. In the case of an unlimited private company, the word 'sendirian' or 'Sdn' must be stated at the end of its name.[34] Company names which cannot be registered include those which are identical or deceptively similar to the name of a Brunei incorporated company; the name of a foreign incorporated company carrying on business and registered in Brunei; or any registered business name. In addition, the registrar shall not register a company name which, in his or her opinion, is likely to mislead the public as to the nature or the objects of the company.[35]

5.4   *Membership and Share Capital*

Under the CA, membership of a company includes the subscribers of the company's memorandum and those who agree to become members and whose names are entered in the company's register of members.[36] A general meeting of a company limited by shares or guarantee, if so authorized by its articles, may alter the conditions of its memorandum to:

- increase its share capital by new shares;
- consolidate and divide all or any of its shares into shares of larger amount than its existing shares;
- convert all or any of its paid-up shares into stock, and re-convert that stock into paid up shares of any denomination;
- sub-divide all of its shares into shares of smaller amount than is fixed by the memorandum; and
- cancel shares which have not been taken up.[37]

By special resolution and subject to confirmation by the court, a company, if authorised by its articles, may also reduce its share capital in any way.[38] The court should sanction a reduction unless what is proposed to be done is unfair or inequitable in the interests of the creditors, the shareholders and the public who may have dealings with the company or may invest in its securities.[39]

5.5   The Company Registers

Upon incorporation, a company is obliged to establish a number of registers, including registers of members,[40] debenture holders,[41] and directors or managers,[42] and every instrument creating a charge must be registered with the registrar.[43]

6   The Internal Administration of Companies

6.1   The Registered Office and Name Change

The memorandum of a company must state the address of its registered office[44] where communications and notices to the company may be addressed and documents served on it. A company may change its name by special resolution and with the prior approval in writing of the Minister of Law.[45] The change does not, however, affect the rights and obligations of the company or render defective any legal proceedings by or against the company under its old name.

6.2   The Duties, Powers and Responsibilities of Officers

The board of directors and the general meeting are the two main organs of the company. The general management of the company is usually in the hands of the directors. A company (except a private company) must have at least two directors. One of the directors must be a Brunei national, and in cases where there are more than two directors, two or no fewer than half of the directors must be Brunei nationals.[46] Article 67 of Table A (the 'model' articles) provides that the business of the company shall be managed by the directors and that they may exercise all such powers that are not, by the CA or the articles, required to be exercised by the company in a general meeting. They include the power to pay all expenses in starting and registering the company[47] and the power to appoint a managing director or manager and to determine the terms of such an appointment.[48]

The duties of directors include fiduciary duties and duties of care and skill. Directors must exercise their powers honestly and in the interests of the company and the shareholders, and they must not put themselves in a position where their duties and interest are likely to conflict. They must act in good faith for the general advantage of the company, and must not make a secret profit out of their position.[49] It is also the duty of a director who is in any way, directly or indirectly, interested in a contract or proposed contract with the company, to declare the nature of his interest at a meeting of the directors of the company.[50] Traditionally, the directors' duties of care and skill are not unduly burdensome. A director need not exhibit in the performance of his or her duties a greater skill than may be reasonably be expected from his or her knowledge and experience. A director is not bound to give continuous attention to the affairs of the company. In respect of duties that, having regard to the exigencies of the business and the articles of association, may properly be left to some other official, a director is, in the absence of grounds of suspicion, justified in trusting that official to perform such duties honestly.[51] Recent English case-law, however, has raised the standard of care expected of directors. This will influence the degree of skill and care expected of company directors in Brunei.

6.3   Meetings

Provisions regarding meetings are found in Part IV, Sections 11–120 of the CA and the articles of association. There are at least four types of meetings.

- **The statutory meeting** Every company limited by shares or limited by guarantee and having a share capital is obliged to hold a statutory meeting within a period of not less than one month and not more than three months of the date at which the company is entitled to commence business. The directors are required to send members a statutory report containing information relating to certain matters, including the allotment of shares, the amount of cash received, and the particulars of directors, trustees and debenture holders.[52]
- **The annual general meeting** A company is obliged to hold an annual general meeting at least once every year and not more than 15 months after the holding of the last general meeting.[53] Accounts and reports which must be laid before the annual general meeting include the profit and loss account, the balance sheet and the directors' and auditor's reports.[54] The usual business transacted at an annual general meeting includes the election of directors in place of those retiring, the declaration of dividends and the appointment and remuneration of auditors.
- **The extraordinary general meeting** Meetings other than the annual general meetings are extraordinary general meetings and these may be convened to transact any 'special business', that is matters other than those belonging to the annual general

meeting.[55] The power to convene such a meeting is vested on the directors.[56] An extraordinary meeting may also be requisitioned by shareholders holding not less than 10 per cent of paid-up capital or votes.[57]

- **Class meetings** Where different classes of shares have been issued by a company, the variation of class rights of these shares requires the sanction of an extraordinary resolution passed at a separate general meeting of the holders of the shares of that class (or the consent in writing of three-quarters of the shareholders).[58]

Meetings other than general meetings may also be called by members under Section 114 of the CA.

6.4   Audit and Accounting

The CA requires the keeping and disclosure of accounting and other records to provide the necessary financial information on the position of the company first to shareholders and, second, to creditors of the company, its employees and the general public. Every company must keep proper books of accounts in respect to monies received and expended, sales and purchases of goods, and assets and liabilities of the company. These books are required to be kept open to inspection by the directors.[59] The publication at the company's annual general meeting of the financial year's profit and loss account and balance sheet is required of the directors.[60] With regard to holding companies, directors must prepare consolidated accounts dealing with profit and loss and balance sheets of the holding company and its subsidiaries for their respective financial years.[61]

A company must appoint an auditor or auditors at its annual general meeting to hold office until the next general meeting. If not, the court, on the application of any member, may may make such an appointment.[62] The CA requires the auditor to report on his or her examination of the company's accounts and to state that he or she is of the opinion that they have been properly drawn up according to the provisions of the CA so as to exhibit a true and correct view of the state of the company's affairs.[63]

6.5   The Annual Return

Every company having a share capital is required to make an annual return containing the particulars set out in the CA.[64] The return is to be made up to the date of the annual general meeting and must be accompanied by copies of documents and certificates set out in Section 109 of the CA. The CA makes a similar provision in respect of companies without share capital.[65] A private company is exempt from having to include certain financial information with their annual return, but is required to certify that it has not issued an invitation to the public to subscribe to the company and that its membership does not exceed 50 in number.[66]

6.6   *Shareholder Protection*

The general management of a company rests with the board of directors, and it is a basic principle of company law that the majority rule prevails. As noted above, directors owe fiduciary duties to the company as a whole. They do not, however, owe fiduciary duties to individual or minority shareholders.[67] If a wrong is done to a company, or if there is an irregularity in its internal management, which is capable of confirmation by a simple majority of the members, the court will not interfere at the suit of a minority of the members.[68] The exceptions to this rule include the right of the individual or minority shareholders to restrain the company from doing an illegal or *ultra vires* act, to prevent a fraud on the minority, and to protect from the invasion of individual rights of members.[69] Under the CA, a shareholder may petition the court for the winding up of a company on the grounds that it is just and equitable that the company should be wound up[70] as in the case where there has been mismanagement or misapplication of funds by the directors who hold the majority of the shares.[71]

6.7   *The Registration of Charges*

The CA requires every charge created by a company as security on the company's property or undertaking to be registered with the registrar, and failure to do so will render these charges void as against the liquidator or any creditor of the company.[72] The charges include:

- a charge securing any of the debentures;
- a charge on uncalled share capital;
- instruments requiring registration as bills of sale;
- a charge on land;
- a charge on the book debts of the company;
- a floating charge;
- a charge on calls made but not paid;
- a charge on a ship or share in ship; and
- a charge on the goodwill, patent, trade mark and copyright property of the company.

A charge includes a mortgage.

7 The External Administration of Companies

7.1 Rules Regarding Arrangements and Reconstructions

The CA provides for a company to enter into schemes of arrangements and reconstructions. Section 151 of the CA allows the company to enter into a compromise or arrangement with its creditors or any class of them, or its members or any class of them, without going into liquidation. A compromise or arrangement can be entered into and will be binding on the company and the creditors or members if:

- the court, on the application of the company or a member of the company (or if the company is being wound up, the liquidator), orders a meeting of the creditors or class of creditors, or of the members, to be summoned;
- the compromise is agreed to by a majority in number representing three-quarters in value of creditors or class of creditors, or members or class of members; and
- it is sanctioned by the court.[73]

In addition to giving effect to arrangements with creditors and members, Section 151 can also be used to carry out a scheme of reconstruction or amalgamation. Under Section 152, the court may sanction a compromise or arrangement for the purpose of reconstruction or amalgamation which involves the transfer of the property of a company (called a 'transferor company') to another company (called a 'transferee company'). The court may order the transfer of the property and liabilities of the transferor company to the transferee company; the allocation of shares or debentures to appropriate persons by the transferee company; the continuation by or against the transferee company of proceedings by or against the transferor company; and the dissolution, without winding up, of a transferor company.[74]

7.2 The Winding Up Rules

The winding up of a company is governed by Part V of the CA, and the Twelfth Schedule, Companies (Winding Up) Rules. A winding up may be by the court, voluntary or subject to the supervision of the court.[75]

A company may be wound up by the court under the following circumstances:

- the company has by special resolution decided that the company be wound up by the court;

- the company defaults in delivering the statutory report or in holding the statutory meeting;
- the company does not commence business within a year of incorporation or suspend business for a year;
- the number of members falls below the statutory minimum;
- the company is unable to pay its debts; or
- the court is of the opinion that it is just and equitable that the company should be wound up.[76]

A company is deemed to be 'unable to pay its debts' if the company neglects to pay a creditor's written demand of payment of a debt exceeding $ 500 for three weeks or more; if the execution of a court's order in favour of a company is returned unsatisfied; or if it is proved to the court's satisfaction that the company is unable to pay its debts, taking into account the contingent and prospective liabilities of the company.[77] A petition for the winding up may be made by the company, creditor or a contributory.[78] The court appoints the liquidator to conduct the proceedings in the winding up of the company.[79] Separate meetings of contributories may appoint a committee of inspection to act with the liquidator during the winding up proceedings.[80]

A company may be wound up voluntarily by an ordinary resolution (if it is in accordance with the articles), by a special resolution or by an extraordinary resolution that the company cannot by reason of its liabilities continue its business and that is advisable to wind up the company.[81] A members' voluntary winding up only takes place when the company is solvent, and the CA requires that before the winding up resolution be made a statutory declaration by the directors that the company will be able to pay its debts in full within a year of the winding up commencement.[82] Without the statutory declaration of insolvency, the winding up will be deemed to be a creditors' voluntary winding up. A members' voluntary winding up is entirely managed by the members and the liquidator appointed by them,[83] and no meeting of creditors is held and no committee of inspection is appointed. A creditors' voluntary winding up requires a meeting of the creditors,[84] which may appoint a liquidator and a committee of inspection.[85]

When a company has passed a resolution for voluntary winding up, the court may order that the voluntary winding up continue but be subject to the supervision of the court as it thinks fit.[86]

7.3   The Protection of Creditors and the Ranking of Claims

In every winding up, all debts and claims against the company are required to be proved.[87] The primary function of the liquidator is the proper administration of the company's affairs with a view to settlement of debts and final dissolution of the company. The liquidator has the duty to collect, preserve, realize and distribute the assets of the company to those entitled, subject to the supervision of the court.[88] Generally, secured creditors are paid ahead of unsecured creditors. The priority is the payment of costs and expenses of the winding up, followed by rates and taxes; wages and salaries of employees up to $ 1 000; and claims of holders and debentures under a floating charge created by the company.[89]

8 Takeover Rules

Section 153 of the CA provides power to a company (a 'transferee company') to acquire shares of dissenting shareholders of another company (a 'transferor company') in a takeover bid which has been approved by the majority. The conditions to be satisfied include:

- there must be a scheme or contract involving the transfer of shares in the transferor company to the transferee company; and
- within four months after it was made, the offer by the transferee company must have been approved by the holders of nine-tenths in value of shares whose transfer is involved (other than shares already held by the transferee company).

Where, at the date of offer, the transferee company holds more than one-tenth of the shares involved, Section 153 does not apply unless the transferee company offers the same terms to all holders of the shares whose transfer is involved; and the holders who approve the scheme or contract, besides holding nine-tenths in value of the shares whose transfer is involved, are also three-quarters in number of the holders of such shares.

9 Securities Regulation

Brunei has no stock exchange. Brokerage and investment services for local investors are provided by Baiduri Securities. The Brunei Investment Agency of the Ministry of Finance is relatively unimportant in terms of local finance. Its main activities are in international investments, where, in conjunction with a consortium of eight US, British and Japanese financial institutions, it manages a large and growing portfolio of foreign assets.[90]

10   Miscellaneous

10.1   *The Powers of the Courts*

Apart from the court's general jurisdiction exercised under common law, the CA gives specific powers to the court in order to properly enforce the legislation. Parts V and VIII of the CA give a wide range of powers to the court with regard to the winding up of companies, and receivers and managers. Other specific powers given to the court include the following.

- Where a company is a plaintiff in an action and there is reason to believe that the company will be unable to pay the costs of the defendant if successful in his or her defence, the court may require sufficient security to be given for those costs, and may stay all proceedings until the security is given.[91]
- The court may grant relief to directors, managers or officers of a company, and persons employed by a company as auditors, in any proceeding against them for negligence, default, breach of duty or breach of trust, if it appears that they have acted honestly and reasonably and ought fairly to be excused from the offence.[92]
- The court may make an order confirming a company's resolution to reduce its capital, after considering the objections that may be brought by creditors.[93]
- On the application of an aggrieved member, the court is empowered to order the rectification of the register of members.[94]
- On the application of shareholders of not less than one-tenth of the shares (one-third in the case of a banking company, and one-fifth of the number of persons in companies not having a share capital), the court may appoint inspectors to investigate the affairs of a company and to report on whether or not offences have been committed by officers of the company.

10.2   *Civil Remedies*

There are no specific provisions dealing with civil remedies. Such civil remedies as are available are found under the relevant breaches and are interspersed throughout the CA.

10.3   *Offences*

Although the CA contains general provisions as to offences (under Sections 314–322), there are no specific provisions dealing with offences. Such offences that are defined in the CA are found under the relevant breaches and are interspersed throughout the CA.

It is an offence to include in a company's memorandum and articles the names of persons who have not consented as directors of a company.[95] It is an offence for any person, being an undischarged bankrupt, to act as director, or directly or indirectly take part in or be concerned in the management, of a company, except with the leave of the court by which he or she was adjudged bankrupt.[96] Failure by a director of a company who is any way interested in a contract or proposed contract with the company to declare the nature of his or her interest at a meeting of the company's directors, is an offence.[97] In regard to a company's resolution to decrease capital, any director, manager, secretary or officer of a company who wilfully conceals the name of any creditor entitled to object to the reduction, or who wilfully misrepresents the nature or amount of the debt, or aids, abets or is privy to any such concealment or misrepresentation, is guilty of an offence.[98]

Notes

* Senior Lecturer in Law, University of Canberra.

1 Brunei (1992), *Brunei Darussalam Profile*, Bandar Seri Bagawan, Government of Brunei, 23.

2 Section 4 of the Constitution.

3 Section 39 of the Constitution.

4 Section 47 of the Constitution.

5 ASEAN Law Association (1995), *ASEAN Legal Systems*, Singapore: Butterworths Asia, 9.

6 Section 83 of the Constitution.

7 As note 1, above, 25.

8 As note 8, above, quoted from a speech of the Sultan of Brunei made on Brunei's National Day in February 1987.

9 Braighlinn, G. (1992), *Ideological Innovation under Monarchy: Aspects of Legitimation Activity in Contemporary Brunei*, Amsterdam: VU University Press, 19.

10 As note 5, above, 3.

11 As note 5, above, 9.

12 As note 5, above, 10.

13 Section 3 of the Finance Companies Act 1972.

14 As note 5, above, 12.

15 Section 24 of the Finance Companies Act 1972.

16 Section 25 of the Finance Companies Act 1972.

17 Section 26 of the Finance Companies Act 1972.

18 Section 34 of the Finance Companies Act 1972.

19 As note 1, above, 163.

20 Section 29 of the CA.

21 Section 298 of the CA.

22 Section 199 of the CA.

23 Section 17 of the CA.

24   Section 300 of the CA.
25   Section 15 of the CA.
26   Section 4 of the CA.
27   Section 9 of the CA.
28   Sections 5 and 14 of the CA.
29   Section 11 of the CA.
30   Section 23 of the CA.
31   Section 8 of the CA.
32   Section 13 of the CA.
33   Section 25 of the CA.
34   Section 5 of the CA.
35   Section 20 of the CA.
36   Section 28 of the CA.
37   Section 53 of the CA.
38   Section 58 of the CA.
39   *Ex parte Westburn Sugar Refineries Ltd* [1951] AC 625.
40   Section 95 of the CA.
41   Section 88 of the CA.
42   Section 143 of the CA.
43   Sections 80 and 88 of the CA.
44   Sections 14 and 323 of the CA.
45   Section 22 of the CA.
46   Section 138 of the CA.
47   Table A, Article 67.
48   Table A, Article 68.
49   *Regal (Hastings) Ltd v Gulliver* [1942] All ER 378.
50   Section 147 of the CA.
51   *Re City Equitable Fire Insurance Co.* [1925] Ch. 407.
52   Section 112 of the CA.
53   Section 111 of the CA.
54   Sections 109 and 122 of the CA.
55   Table A, Article 44.
56   Table A, Article 41.
57   Section 113 of the CA.
58   Table A, Article 3.
59   Section 121 of the CA.
60   Section 122 of the CA.
61   Section 125 of the CA.
62   Section 131 of the CA.
63   Section 133 of the CA.
64   Section 107 and the Fifth Schedule of the CA.
65   Section 108 of the CA.
66   Section 110 of the CA.
67   See the rule in *Percival v Wright* [1902] 2 Ch 421.
68   *Foss v Harbottle* (1843) 2 Ha 461, and *MacDougall v Gardiner* (1875) 1 Ch D 13.
69   See, for example, *Cook v Deeks* [1916] 1 AC 554, and *Pender v Lushington* (1877) 6 Ch D 70.
70   Sections 162 and 164 of the CA.
71   *Loch v John Blackwood Ltd* [1924] AC 783.
72   Section 80 of the CA.
73   Section 151 of the CA.
74   Section 152 of the CA.
75   Section 154 of the CA.
76   Section 162 of the CA.

77   Section 163 of the CA.
78   Section 164 of the CA.
79   Section 177 of the CA.
80   Section 191 of the CA.
81   Section 213 of the CA.
82   Section 218 of the CA.
83   Section 220 of the CA.
84   Section 226 of the CA.
85   Sections 227 and 228 of the CA.
86   Section 243 of the CA.
87   Section 248 of the CA.
88   See Part V of the CA.
89   Section 250 of the CA.
90   Verma, N. (1996), 'Brunei', in R. Edwards and M. Sculley (eds) *ASEAN Business Trade and Development*, Port Melbourne: Butterworth-Heinemann.
91   Section 320 of the CA.
92   Section 321 of the CA.
93   Section 59 of the CA.
94   Section 100 of the CA.
95   Section 139 of the CA.
96   Section 141 of the CA.
97   Section 147 of the CA.
98   Section 63 of the CA.

Further Reading

Ali, A. (1996), *From Penury to Plenty: Development of Oil Rich Brunei, 1906 to Present*, Perth: Murdoch University.

Leigh, M. (1986), *Brunei Darussalam: The Price of Consent*, Canberra: Parliament of Commonwealth of Australia.

Saunders, G. (1994), *A History of Brunei*, Kuala Lumpur: Oxford University Press.

15 Company Law in Papua New Guinea

ANTHONY DEKLIN*

1   A Brief Introduction to the Papua New Guinea Legal System

Any map showing both Asia and the Pacific will invariably show the Island of New Guinea lying across north of Australia like a bridge linking Asia to the Pacific. The independent state of Papua New Guinea (PNG) which occupies the eastern half of the Island of New Guinea, came into existence on 16 September 1975 under its Independence Constitution (the Constitution) when Australia granted PNG its independence after 91 years of colonial rule. At various times during that long colonial period PNG had passed through the hands of three metropolitan powers, namely Britain, Germany and Australia.

In 1884 the colonial rule of the Island of New Guinea was divided between the Dutch, the British and the Germans. The Dutch took possession of the western half of the Island and called it Dutch New Guinea.[1] The Germans claimed the northern portion of the eastern half as their possession and named it German New Guinea. The British, at the insistence of the Australian Colonies which were becoming increasing uncomfortable with the Germans annexing small islands in the Pacific, claimed as their possession the southern portion of the eastern half of the Island and named it British New Guinea.

In 1906 Britain transferred British New Guinea to the Commonwealth of Australia and Australia renamed its new colony Papua. When Germany was defeated during the First World War, the then League of Nations granted a mandate to Australia in 1919 to govern the former German New Guinea, which thenceforth became known as the Mandated Territory of New Guinea. Australia took formal possession of the Mandated Territory in 1921 and began governing it separately from Papua.

The Second World War forced suspension of the civilian rule. After the War, the civil administration was restored and Australia joined both possessions in an administrative union under its Papua New Guinea Act 1949, which remained the basic colonial constitution until it was repealed by the Australian Federal Parliament on 16 September 1975 when PNG gained independence.

The state is unitary, but largely decentralized, and a great deal of policy power, at least according to the letter of the law, is given to the provincial and local-level governments. The system of government is the Westminster form of parliamentary government. There are three levels of government: the national government, the provincial governments and the local-level governments. At the time of writing, there were 20 provincial governments and 262 local-level governments, which together with one national government, were governing a small population of four million people within a total area of 462 840 square kilometres.

The principal law-making institutions established by the Constitution are the national parliament, the provincial parliaments known as provincial assemblies, and the local-level governments which are essentially local governments introduced by the Australian colonial administration in the 1950s.

These institutions enact primary legislation. The power to make subordinate legislation is then delegated by these primary legislations to the executive governments at the national, provincial and local levels. Delegated legislation forms the bulk of the law for daily purposes of government.

Only the national government has three arms – the legislative, the executive and the judiciary – according to the traditional doctrine of separation of powers. As the structural arrangement of the legislative and the executive arms is based on the Westminster system of parliamentary government, there is a high degree of fusion between these two arms of government as the executive is drawn from the legislature.

Courts are organized hierarchically, thus reflecting the influence of the common law system. The Supreme Court and the National Court are the superior courts of record, with the former as the final appeal court. The lower courts are the District Court, the Local Court and the Village Court.

Apart from its special jurisdiction to hear constitutional matters, the Supreme Court has an unlimited jurisdiction. The National Court has a similar unlimited jurisdiction. The Lower Courts have limited jurisdiction. Although a District Court has jurisdiction in all personal actions in both law and equity, it can award damages in civil cases only up to K 10 000. The jurisdictional limit for a Local Court in civil claims is K 1 000. In the case of a Village Court, the limit is also K 1 000 for any compensation order it makes. Strict rules of procedure and evidence are followed in litigation conducted before these courts, except the Village Courts which are intended to apply the customary law through less formal procedures. It is for this purpose that lawyers are not permitted to appear for clients in Village Courts.

The Supreme Court sits in Port Moresby, the national capital. The judges of the National Court are based in four regional centres and go on regular circuits to conduct cases throughout the provinces. Judges of the two superior courts are appointed by the Judicial and Legal Services Commission, which comprises the Minister for Justice, the Chief Justice, the Deputy-Chief Justice, the Chief Ombudsman and a member of parliament. The rationale for this composition is the belief that a judge must have the confidence of all the main power-brokers in the political game if his or her authority is to be respected. A judicial candidate must have had at least ten years of practice of law and a degree in law from the University of Papua New Guinea or an equivalent university.

The Constitution identifies seven types of legal norms as comprising the law of PNG: the Constitution itself, the organic laws, the Acts of the national parliament, emergency regulations, the provincial laws, laws made under or adopted by the Constitution or any of those laws, and the underlying law. The concept of the underlying law as defined by the Constitution, includes both the common law and the customary law. The common law principles include principles of equity. The Constitution, therefore, recognizes the plurality of the country's legal systems.[2] It is a dual system, comprising both the introduced Anglo-Australian common law (which includes the statutory law) and customary law of the indigenous tribal communities. During the colonial period there was a tacit *de facto* recognition of the customary law system as a separate legal system, but no real attempt was made to develop it as such.

The fundamental law is the National Constitution which came into force at midnight on 16 September 1975, the Independence Day. It consists of 60 000 words spread among 275 Sections and five Schedules. Organic laws are part of the Constitution and must deal with a subject-matter specifically designated by the Constitution to be regulated by an organic law. Provincial laws comprise both the primary and delegated legislation of the provincial parliaments. The Constitution also determines the order of validity of these laws by providing that in all cases of inconsistency the Constitution overrides all other laws. Organic laws follow next with an overriding effect where all other laws are inconsistent with them (Sections 9, 10 and 11).

2   The Structure of Company Law: Statutes and Case-Law

Company law is concerned with a certain form of economic organization. It operates effectively in a society that has either created or has captured certain economic conditions favourable for use of capital. In a developing country such as PNG, where these economic conditions are not present in the bulk of the communities, modern company law is largely irrelevant to these communities. Of course, this is bound to change as the commercial life of the nation intensifies. From this perspective, the PNG society may usefully be seen as comprising two sectors: the urban sector and the rural communities.

Eighty-five per cent of the total population lives in the rural villages where every family lives on and off the land. Over 88 per cent of the total land holding is under customary tenure. Customary law regulates much of daily life in these rural communities where there are very few commercial activities. The traditional barter system still operates in some parts of the country, particularly the isolated village communities further away from the urban centres. Modern company law does not as yet play an important role for the benefit of these rural communities. Much of the law applied by Village Court Magistrates at the village level and by the Local Court and the District Court Magistrates at the local and provincial levels respectively, is personal law, the principal one being the criminal law. Both the Local and District Courts apply the state's criminal law, whereas the Village Courts enforce the customary criminal law of the local community.

It is in the commercial centres of the urban enclaves, such as Port Moresby and Lae, that company law has its relevance and continues to be important for the commercial life of the nation. There is very little case-law in the company law area. Consequently, much of this chapter focuses on the provisions of the Companies Act which is the main legislation in the field.

2.1   History

Anthropological evidence shows that humans have been on the Island of New Guinea for over 25 000 years. There are now 1 000 language groups in PNG. Each of these groups has its own customary law. One common aspect of this customary law is that it recognizes tribes, extended families and lineages as corporate entities separate from their members. Thus, ownership of land is vested in the tribe which then grants licence to individual members to use various portions of land to meet their daily needs through activities such as gardening.

The modern statutory law has recently attempted to recognize this traditional corporate principle of customary law as evidenced by such legislation as the Business Groups Incorporation Act (Chapter 144) and the Land Groups Incorporation Act (Chapter 147). Both legislations aim to facilitate traditional groups in commercial activities. The current legislation on the formation and operation of companies in PNG is the Companies Act (Chapter 146). From 1982 all the Acts of the PNG parliament have been compiled into the Revised Laws of Papua New Guinea and are identified by means of Chapters. Thus, Chapter 146 contains the Companies Act, Companies Regulation and Rules.

Although PNG had passed through both the British and German colonial legal systems, the British influence had had more decisive effect, due very much to the ensuing Australian colonial administration. The Germans were interested purely in the economic exploitation of their colony and at any rate their colonization did not last long enough to leave any legal legacy of lasting effect. The origins of the present Companies Act, therefore, go back to the early days of the British colonial rule in what was then the British New Guinea. When Great Britain declared British New Guinea as its colony in 1888, the British law applied to the new colony by virtue of that act of state. This law included the statutory law. Thus, a number of British companies which were incorporated under the companies legislation in Britain were operating in the new colony. Besides these, there were companies incorporated in the new colony by specific ordinances.

The first general statute which attempted to address the form, incorporation and operation of companies was the Companies Ordinance 1912 (No. 29 of 1912) made by the Lieutenant-Governor of Papua in that year. It was based on the Companies Act 1863 of Queensland. The legal position relating to companies was fragmented and, in order to put an end to this, the Companies Ordinance 1912–1926 was enacted in 1926, consolidating all the laws relating to companies into one piece of legislation for the Australian Colony of Papua. When Australia was granted a trusteeship in 1919 by the then League of Nations to govern the former German New Guinea after the First World War, the new Australian Administration with its headquarters in Rabaul to govern what had then become the Mandated Territory of New Guinea under the League of Nations, adopted the Papuan Companies Ordinance for its purposes in the new Mandated Territory. The two legislations became the Companies (Papua) Ordinance 1912–1926 for Papua and the Companies (New Guinea) Ordinance 1921–1926 for the Territory of New Guinea respectively.

The need for two separate legislations, although identical in content, arose from the two separate juristic position of the two possessions. Foreign territories that came into the possession of the Crown of the United Kingdom included those to which the British law applied. These included protectorates and colonies. Papua was an Australian Colony to which Australian law applied, whereas the Territory of New Guinea was a Trust Territory being administered under a trusteeship from the League of Nations and, after the Second World War, the United Nations. The two ordinances were retitled Companies Act respectively at self-government in 1973 when all the existing ordinances were retitled as Acts. The separate Companies Acts remained until 1982 when they were consolidated into the present Companies Act.

2.2   *The Constitutional Basis of Company Law*

Although the Constitution decentralizes a great deal of policy power to provincial legislatures under a highly decentralized system of government, the legal system is essentially a unitary system which is centrally controlled. Thus, technical aspects of the legal system, such as the question of legal personality, remain the national domain. Provincial parliaments are governments of specific powers. The power to determine incorporation and operation of companies is not one of these powers. The pre-independence Companies Acts have been adopted and consolidated as the Companies Act by the Constitution. The Constitution also urges as one of the national goals, 'the use of Papua New Guinean forms of social, political and economic organization'. As explained above, the PNG customary law does recognize the corporate entity of various social groups, such as the tribe, although it did not develop the structure of that entity in as elaborate a way as the introduced company law does. This provides the justification for the use of the introduced company law rather than the customary law by commercial groups.

2.3   *The Creation of Company Law*

As pointed out above, ordinary legislation, rather than the Constitution, has laid down the legal basis of PNG company law, beginning in 1912 when the first legislation in this field was enacted. The present company law comprises: the Companies Act (Chapter 146), the Business Names Act (Chapter 145), the Business Groups Incorporation Act (Chapter 144), the Bodies Corporate (Joint Tenancy) Act (Chapter 143), the Associations Incorporation Act (Chapter 142), the Savings and Loan Societies Act (Chapter 141), the Land Groups Incorporation Act (Chapter 147), the Partnership Act (Chapter 148), the Investment Corporation Act (Chapter 140), and the Cooperative Societies Act (Chapter 150). The Companies Act, and its Companies Regulations and Rules (as amended) remain the principal legislations in the field. Associated with these are those statutes that govern the general commercial field. These include: the Goods Act (Chapter

251), the Hire Purchase Act (Chapter 252), the Bills of Exchange Act (Chapter 250), the Investments Act (Chapter 254), and the Insolvency Act (Chapter 253).

2.4 The Responsibility for Reforming the Law

There is no particular body or instrument set up to oversee the operation of the company law and to recommend changes when these are needed. The responsibility for the administration of the Companies Act, its Regulations and Rules lies with a number of authorities, including the Registrar General, the Attorney-General's Department and the Department of Trade and Commerce. These can act as sources of reform ideas. The PNG Law Society can also be a source of reform proposals. There is a national Law Reform Commission set up by the Constitution to recommend law reform measures to the government. It is a general law reform body and is not given a specific responsibility in the operation of the company law, for instance to update it. So far, the Commission has not been given any reference on review of either the operation of company law generally or of the Companies Act in particular.

2.5 The Basic Principles Underlying the Company Law

The enactment of the Companies Act was not the result of recommendations of any particular body appointed to suggest legislative measures in that field. It was merely an adoption of the Australian model with some adaptations necessitated by the PNG circumstances. Therefore, the underlying principles can be discerned from the provisions of the Companies Act. These are very similar to the ones in the New Zealand legislation (see Chapter 16).

2.6 An Interpretation of the Companies Act

The Constitution provides a number of general principles for interpreting the constitutional laws (which include the Constitution itself) as well as laws generally. These two most important ones are:

- that in interpreting the law the courts shall give paramount consideration to the dispensation of justice (Section 158(2)); and
- that all words, expressions and propositions in, a constitutional law shall be given their fair and liberal meaning (Schedule 1.5(2)).

Interestingly, the Interpretation Act (Chapter 2), which was enacted before the Constitution and has been adopted by it, does not provide any particular rule for interpreting legislation of the national and the provincial parliaments nor has it incorporated any of the interpretive principles contained in the Constitution, particularly the liberal interpretation rule in Schedule 1.5(2). Nevertheless, the Judges of the Supreme Court have been generally applying this liberal interpretation which the Constitution has directed them to apply. However, the Supreme Court also said that this does not mean that the ordinary rules of statutory construction have been replaced. Obviously, the court has been influenced by its primary constitutional responsibility which is to do justice, and this might not be possible if it were restricted to only one method of interpreting statutes.

3 The Nature and Powers of Corporate Regulatory Agencies

Compared with other jurisdictions with external regulatory bodies, such as Australia with its Australian Securities Commission, PNG does not have an equivalent body under the Companies Act or under any other legislation. There is no stock exchange, although the idea of setting one up has been mooted recently by some government ministers as well as PNG business persons. Regulation of companies under the Companies Act is left largely to the Minister for Trade and Industry who may appoint a registrar of companies and such deputy-registrars as he or she sees fit (Section 5). The registrar is responsible for keeping such registers as he or she thinks necessary and in such form as he or she thinks proper (Section 7(1)). The registrar may refuse to register or receive any document submitted, if in his or her opinion, it contains a matter that is contrary to the law (Section 7(5)(a)); by reason of omission or misdescription it has not been duly completed (Section 7(5)(b)); it does not comply with the requirements of the Companies Act (Section 7(5)(c)) or it contains an error, an alteration or an erasure (Section 7(5)(d)). Consequently, the registrar may require that the document be amended and resubmitted, or that a fresh document be submitted in its place.

The registrar or a person authorized by him or her, may inspect and require the production of books and other material or any record required by the Companies Act to be kept (Section 5(6)). A person who fails to produce such documents after having been ordered to so by the registrar is guilty of an offence punishable by a fine of K 1 000 (Section 5(9)). The Companies Auditors Board is another body set up by the Companies Act and is responsible for all matters relating to Part VII of the Act (which covers accounts and audit (Section 10)). The Companies Act prescribes three separate procedures for any investigation into the affairs of a company.

First, the minister may appoint one or more inspectors to investigate the affairs of a company and to report on them in the manner the minister directs. The Companies Act specifies three types of companies to which this procedure applies. In the case of a company (which is not a banking corporation) having a share capital, this procedure may be initiated by an application by more than 200 members, by members holding more than 10 per cent of shares issued or by those members who hold debentures with more than 20 per cent of the nominated value of the debentures issued. In the case of a company not having a share capital, application may be made by members who constitute more than 20 per cent of the total number of persons on the company's register. Where a banking corporation is involved, an application for investigation under the ministerial order may be made by members holding more than one-third of the shares issued (Section 179). The minister is required to give a copy of the report to the company involved in the investigation (Section 179(4)) and the report may also be published (Section 179(5)). Legal action may also be brought on the basis of the report, including prosecution (Section 179(6)) and recovery action (Section 179(7)).

Second, there is a self-regulating mechanism in the Companies Act which requires the company by a special resolution, to order an investigation by one or more inspectors into its affairs provided it is not a company to which Division 4 applies (Section 180(1)). The investigation may extend to any company that is associated with the company at the time (Section 181(1)). The inspector is required to submit the report to the company (Section 180(2)).

Third, the Companies Act gives the minister a power to order special investigations into a company under Division 4 of the Act. However, before such an investigation is set up, the minister is required to give a notice in the *National Gazette*, declaring that the company is the one to which Division 4 applies (Section 183(2)).

In addition, the Companies Act empowers the minister to order any specific investigation into a company whenever the need arises.

4 A Description of Types of Local Companies

The Companies Act provides for five different classes of companies. A company may be limited by shares, by guarantee or by both shares and guarantee. There can also be an unlimited company and, in the case of mining company, a no liability company. A no liability company is one in which due acceptance of a share does not constitute a contract to pay calls (Section 1(1)).

Companies in PNG may be incorporated in one of two ways. The first way is through a special Act of parliament which incorporates a company for the purposes of carrying out a government policy or services.[3] A special Act can also be used to incorporate a group to enable the group to engage in a particular type of commercial activity. Examples of this are the Business Groups Incorporation Act 1974 and the Land Groups Incorporation Act 1974.

The second, and normal, way of incorporating a company is under the Companies Act. The Act prescribes conditions under which incorporation may be effected, depending on the type of company involved. For instance, a proprietary company, that is a company having a share capital (other than a no liability company), may be incorporated as a proprietary company if its memorandum or articles restricts its right to transfer its shares; limits the number of its members to not more than 50; prohibits any invitation to the public to subscribe for shares in, or debentures of, the company; and prohibits any invitation to the public to deposit money with the company for fixed periods or payable at call whether or not interest is payable on the amount (Section 17(1)).

A proprietary company must not have more than two members (Section 16(1)). Companies limited by shares, companies limited by both shares and guarantee, and unlimited companies with a share capital may be incorporated as proprietary companies. Companies limited by guarantee and no liability companies may not be incorporated as proprietary companies (Section 17(1)). Accounts of a proprietary company in which no share is owned by a public company need not be audited if there is a unanimous agreement to that effect by the members (Section 174(19)(a)). The Companies Act also provides for incorporation of public companies. A public company is 'any company that is not a proprietary company' (Section 1(1)).

A public company must have a minimum of five members. There is no upper limit (Section 16(1)). Exempt proprietary companies are also regulated by the Companies Act. An exempt proprietary company is 'a proprietary company no share in which is, or by virtue of Section 2 deemed to be, owned by a public company' (Section 1(1)). For the purposes of the definition of an exempt proprietary company in Section 1(1), a share in a proprietary company is to be deemed to be owned by a public company if a beneficial interest in the share is held directly or indirectly by a public company (Section 2(1)).

The Companies Act imposes a duty of disclosure on any person who holds shares in a proprietary company and renders such person a trustee for or on behalf of the company (Section 165(5)). There are also companies to which Division 4 status (under Part XII) applies. These include both public and proprietary companies. This status has to be applied for, and broadly speaking is available only to, local companies. Division 4 applies to:

- A company or proposed company the membership of which comprises:
  - local persons,
  - companies to which the Division applies,
  - business groups incorporated under the Business Groups Incorporation Act,
  - local government councils,
  - local government authorities,
  - statutory authorities or instrumentalities of the state; and
- a company declared under Subsection (2) of Section 369 to be a company to which Section 369 applies (Section 369(1)).

A company can also be declared to be one to which the Division applies when the head of state, acting on advice, is of the opinion that the membership of the company is substantially composed of persons referred to in Section 369(1)(a) and (b) or that the management of the company is substantially controlled by local persons (Section 369(2)). Such declaration may be notified through the *National Gazette*. Division 4 was added to the Companies Act by the Companies (Amendment) Act 1974. The amendment confers a special status on a company or a proposed company composed or to be composed of either local or substantially local persons or institutions.

Any type of company that may be incorporated under the Companies Act may apply to the registrar for Division 4 status. Division 4 status relieves companies of the payment of some of the fees payable under the Companies Act, and also from compliance with some of the more complex and onerous provisions of the Act. Division 4 status was introduced in response to the criticisms that the Companies Act, as it then stood, was too complex and expensive to operate under and that it imposed onerous obligations on local businesses. It was, therefore, not conducive to the growth and expansion of indigenous enterprises. Where the registrar is satisfied that a company is a company to which this Division applies, he or she may, by notice in writing to the company, relieve the company, the officers of the company or any other person from compliance with all or any of the requirements in the first column of Schedule 10. The registrar may impose such conditions on the grant of relief as he or she considers appropriate (Section 370). The other corporate entities the Companies Act deals with are cooperative companies (Division 5, Part XII).

It appears from Kimuli[4] and Tashjian,[5] the two authors who have written texts in this area of the PNG law, that cooperative companies are subject to, and administered by, both the Companies Act and the Cooperative Societies Act 1982. A cooperative company means a company limited by both shares and guarantee whose articles comply with Section 377 and that includes as part of its name the word 'cooperative' (Section 373). Investment companies are also covered by the Act (Sections 345–354, Division 2, Part XII). The Companies Act imposes a restriction on such a company by requiring that it may not for the purpose of profit, buy, sell or deal in any raw materials or manufactured goods, but it may invest in companies trading in such goods or materials (Section 351(1)). The minister may, by notice in the *National Gazette*, declare to be an investment company, any company that is engaged primarily in the business of investment in marketable securities for the purpose of revenue and for profit and not for the purpose of exercising control (Section 345(2)).

A foreign company is defined as:

> a company, corporation, society, association or other body incorporated outside PNG; or an unincorporated society, association or other body that, under the laws of its place of origin, may sue or be sued, or hold property in the name of the secretary or other officer of the due body or association duly appointed for that purpose, and does not have its head office or principal place of business in PNG (Section 1(1)).

The Companies Act further provides that a foreign company must within one month of establishing a place of business, or commencing business in PNG lodge with the registrar with the intent that it be registered as a foreign company, certain documents which are specified in Section 358(1)(a)–(g).

A foreign company intending to carry on business in PNG must first apply for registration under the provisions of the Investment Promotion Authority Act 1994. The Investment Promotion Authority then considers the application in light of the Investment Priorities Schedule and makes its decision. The purpose of the Schedule is to inform potential investors, and persons and bodies responsible for planning, promoting and encouraging investment, of the priorities attached by the government to investment in particular areas. It also sets out lists of activities in which business by registered foreign enterprises is allowed and those in which business is reserved for local enterprises (the Investment Promotion Authority Act, Section 44).

It has been claimed that a company is foreign if it is more than 25 per cent owned by non-citizens of PNG.[6] This may be a practical executive policy because the Companies Act is silent on the point. The powers of a company include the power to make donations for a patriotic or charitable purpose, except so far as they are expressly excluded or modified by the memorandum or articles. The powers are set out in Schedule Z to the Act and are very broad (Section 36).

The basic provision on the legal capacity is Section 18(4), which provides that on and from the date of incorporation specified in the certificate of incorporation, but subject to the Companies Act, the subscribers to the memorandum, together with such other persons as may from time to time become members of the company, are a corporation by the name contained in the memorandum and are capable of exercising all the functions of an incorporated company. Under the same provision, they have the power to sue and to be sued and have perpetual succession and a common seal with power to hold land. They also carry a liability to contribute to the assets of the company in the event of its being wound up.

5 Company Formation

A person wanting to incorporate a company is required to lodge the memorandum of association and the articles of association (if any) of the proposed company with the registrar, together with other documents required to be lodged by or under the Act. On payment of the appropriate fees the registrar then, subject to the Act, registers the company's memorandum and articles (if any). The formal process of registering the company is thereby completed.

5.1 The Procedural Requirements

In order to incorporate a business, the following documents must be filed with the registrar: a statutory declaration of compliance, which is optional at the discretion of the registrar (Section 18(2)); a list of persons who have consented to be directors (Section 123); and an actual consent of each director to act as a director. Each director must consent in writing to accept the responsibility of being a director (Section 141(2)). The most important document that must be filed to incorporate any type of company is the memorandum of association, which is a mandatory incorporation document (Sections 16(1)(a) and 18(1)).

The memorandum of association 'contains the fundamental conditions upon which alone the company is allowed to be incorporated', per Bowen LJ. in *Guiness v Land Corporation of Ireland* (1882) 22 Ch D 349 and 381. The articles of association, is another important document that needs to be lodged together with the memorandum when incorporating a company limited by guarantee, or shares and guarantee, or an unlimited company (Section 30(1)(b)). However, it need not be lodged for registration when incorporating a company limited by shares or a no liability company (Section 30(1)(a)). Apart from the express statutory requirements under Sections 17(1) and 30(3) and

(4), the contents of the articles will be determined by the promoter's views as to how the company's affairs should be managed.

5.2   *The Promoters*

The position of a promoter is crucial in incorporating a company. The Companies Act defines a promoter in relation to a prospectus issued by or in connection with a corporation, as a promoter of the corporation who was a party to the preparation of a prospectus or any relevant portion of it, but this does not include a person by reason only of his or her action in a professional capacity (Section 1(1)).

In *Twycross v Grant* (1877) 2 CPD 469 at 541, Cockburn LJ. describes a promoter as 'one who undertakes to form a company with reference to a given project and to set it going, and who takes the necessary steps to accomplish that purpose'. In *Erlanger v New Sombrero Phosphate Company* (1878) 3 App Cas 1218 at 1236, Lord Cairns LC. stated:

> promoters have in their hands the creation and moulding of the company; they have the power of defining how and when, and in what shape and under what supervision it shall start into existence and begin to act as a trading corporation.

Promoters have fiduciary duties to the newly formed company and, as such, must act in utmost good faith: *Erlanger v New Sombrero Phosphate Company* (1878) 3 App Cas 1218; *Lagunas Nitrate Co. v Lagunas Syndicate* (1899) 2 Ch 392; and *Gluckstein v Barnes* (1900) AC 240.

There are remedies for the non-disclosure by promoters, for instance their failure to observe the duty of disclosure, which entitles the company to rescind any contract concluded with them: *Erlanger v New Sombrero* (1878) 3 App Cas 1218. Unless a valid contract exists between the company and the promoter, the promoter cannot recover expenses and a company cannot enter into a valid contract before it is incorporated: *Kelner v Baxter* (1866) LR 2 CP 174. However, the articles will normally authorize the directors of the company, in the exercise of the powers of management, to pay all expenses incurred in promoting and registering the company (Schedule 3, Regulation 73 of Table A and Schedule 3, Regulation 56 of Table B). This authority, together with the fact that in most cases a promoter will be one of the first directors, ensures that the promoter is paid his or her preliminary expenses.

5.3   *The Corporate Constitution*

A company is constituted by its memorandum of association and articles of association. The memorandum states the basic purpose, the financial structure and the related matters of the company. The articles are the by-laws by which the daily management of the company is carried on.

5.4 *The Memorandum of Association*

To some extent the contents of both the memorandum and the articles are controlled by the Companies Act. For instance, Section 27 requires that the memorandum of a company shall be printed, divided into numbered paragraphs, dated, and shall state the company's name and objects, share capital, the nature and extent of members' liability, details of subscribers to the memorandum of association, in addition to other requirements as stated in paragraphs (a)–(i) in that section. The provision also requires the memorandum to cover the name of the company and its objects. The objects must be lawful (Section 16(1)). Besides these, the memorandum must:

- set out the purposes for which the company is founded;
- define and delimit the company's area of operation or activity;
- inform the members of the purposes to which their money is being applied so that people dealing with the company can determine whether or not a proposed transaction is within the company's corporate objects (*Cotman v Brougham* (1918) AC 514);
- contain one capital clause, in the case of a company limited by shares, a company limited by shares and guarantee or a no liability company, stating the amount of share capital with which it proposes to be registered (Section 27(1)(c));
- contain the liability clause indicating the liability of members according to the nature of the company: the memorandum of a company limited by shares must state that the liability is limited (Section 27(1)(d)), which means it will be limited to any unpaid amount on the shares held by them. The memorandum of a company limited by guarantee or by both shares and guarantee must state 'that the liability of members is limited'. In addition to this, it needs to state also that each member undertakes to contribute to the assets of the company in the event of its being wound up while he is a member, or within one year after he ceases to be a member, for purposes of payment of debts, and adjustment of rights (Section 27(1)(f)); the memorandum of an unlimited company must state that the members' liability is unlimited (Section 27(1)(f)); and the memorandum of a no liability company must state that the acceptance of shares in the company does not constitute a contract to pay (Section 27(1)(g)); and

- contain the details of subscribers, including their full names, addresses and their occupations (Section 27(1) (h)); the memorandum must also state that the subscribers are desirous of being formed into a company in accordance with the memorandum (Section 27(1)(e)(i)) and, where the company is to have a share capital, that they retrospectively agree to take the number of shares set out opposite their respective names (Section 27(1)(e)(i) and (ii)).

If the company is to have a share capital, each subscriber to the memorandum must state in his or her own handwriting, in words, the number of shares that he or she agrees to take and whether or not the company is to have a share capital. Each subscriber must sign the memorandum in the presence of at least one witness who is not a subscriber (Section 27(2)).

5.5   The Articles of Association

The Companies Act requires the articles of association to be printed, divided into numbered paragraphs, signed by each subscriber to the memorandum in the presence of at least one witness (not being another subscriber) who shall attest the signature and add his or her address (Section 30(2)). In the case of an unlimited company that has a share capital, the articles must state the amount of share capital with which the company proposes to be registered and the division of it into shares of a fixed amount (Section 30(3)). They must also state the number of members (Section 30(4)) and contain the power to increase the membership (Section 30(5)). The articles may adopt all or any of the Regulations contained in Table A of Schedule 3 or, in the case of a no liability company, those in Table B (Section 31(1)).

5.6   Restrictions on the Use of Certain Names

The Companies Act restricts the use of certain names, for instance by prohibiting registration of undesirable names (Section 22(1)) and by requiring a limited liability company to have the word 'limited' or the abbreviation 'Ltd' as part of and at the end of its name (Section 22(3)); a no liability company to have the words 'no liability' or the abbreviation 'NL' as part of and at the end of its name (Section 22(4)); and a proprietary company to have the word 'proprietary' or the abbreviation 'Pty' before the word 'limited' or the abbreviation 'Ltd', or, in the case of an unlimited company, at the end of its name (Section 22(5)).

A person may apply for the reservation of a name set out in the application as:

- the name of an intended company;
- the name to which a company intends to change its name; or
- the name under which a foreign company proposes to be registered either originally, or upon changing its name (Section 22(7)).

Provided that Section 22(1) is not offended, a company may by special resolution, and with the approval of the registrar, change its name (Section 23(1)). Where the minister is satisfied that a proposed limited company being formed is for the purposes of providing recreation or amusement or promoting them, will apply its profits (if any) to other income it may have in promoting its objects, and will prohibit the payment of any dividends to its members, he or she may allow the company to be registered as a company with limited liability without the addition of 'limited' to its name (Section 24(1)).

5.7 Membership and Share Capital Requirements

The Companies Act requires the subscribers to the memorandum to be deemed to have agreed to become members of the company, and on the incorporation of the company, they are to be entered as members in its register of members, and every other person who agrees to become a member of a company and whose name is entered in its register of members is a member of the company (Section 19).

If at any time the number of members is reduced in the case of a proprietary company to fewer than two, or in the case of any other company fewer than five, and the company carries on business for more than six months while the number is so reduced, all members who are cognizant of such carrying on are severally liable and may be severally sued. Furthermore, the company and each of the members are liable to be charged for committing an offence (Section 21).

The Companies Act requires that unless the company is an unlimited company, the amount of share capital (if any) with which the company proposes to be registered, and the division of it into shares of a fixed amount, must be stated in the memorandum (Section 27(1)(c)). In the case of an unlimited company that has a share capital, the articles must state the amount of share capital with which the company proposes to be registered, and the division of it into shares of a fixed amount (Section 30(3)). Articles are mandatory for unlimited companies (Section 30(1)(b)).

If a foreign company increases its authorized share capital, it must, within one month or such further period as required, lodge with the registrar the notice in the prescribed form of the amount from which, and of the amount to which, it has been so increased (Section 359(2)). If it is so authorized by its articles, a company may increase its share capital to consolidate, divide, convert, subdivide or cancel its shares (Section 65(1)). An unlimited company having a share capital may, by a resolution passed for the purposes of Section 25(1) converting from unlimited to limited, increase its shares (Section 65(3)).

5.8 The Reduction of Share Capital by Special Resolution

Subject to confirmation by the court, a company may, if so authorized, reduce its share capital (Section 66(1)) and creditors may, by a special resolution, object to the reduction (Section 66(2)).

5.9 The Amendment of Corporate Constitution

5.9.1 The memorandum of association   In most cases a special resolution is required for an alteration to the clauses in the memorandum. For instance, the objects of the company may be altered only by a special resolution (Section 29(1)) and only after 21 days' notice has been sent by post to all the members and trustees of debenture holders advising them specifically of the intention to alter the objects of the company (Section 29(2) and (3)).

5.9.2 The articles of association   A company may also, subject to the Companies Act and to any conditions in its memorandum, alter or add to its articles by special resolutions (Section 32).

5.10 Company Registers

The Companies Act makes comprehensive provisions which prescribe not only the keeping of a register but also its content. Section 158(1) requires a company to keep a register of all members and such a register, which Section 1(1) refers to as the principal register, is required to record the names, addresses, date of entry into the register, date of cessation of membership if this has occurred within the last seven years, and, where a company has share capital, the date of every allotment of shares to members and the number of shares allotted.

Further provisions cover the place and keeping of registers (Section 160) and their inspection and closing (Section 161).

6 The Internal Administration of Companies

As from the day on which it begins to carry on business or as from the fourteenth day after incorporation, whichever is the earlier, a company must have a registered office which must be accessible to the public for not less than three hours between 8 am and 4 pm each day except Saturday, Sunday and public holidays (Section 118). Upon lodging an application for incorporation with the registrar, a company is also required to present the prescribed form (Form 38) containing the details of the proposed registered office and the days and hours during which it is open and accessible to the public (Section 119(1)). The Companies Act requires the name of the company to appear in legible characters on its seal and all business letters (Section 120(1)) and to be fixed or painted outside every office at which it does business. The registered offices' sign must include the words 'registered office' (Section 120(3)). A foreign company must have a registered office which is open between 9 am and 5 pm Monday to Friday (Saturday, Sunday and public holidays excepted) (Section 358(4)).

A foreign company must lodge with the registrar, within one month, the notice as prescribed in Form 38, if it changes its registered office or hours during which it is open, or the address of its original place of registered office or its name (Section 358(4)).

Directors and officers get their powers to act for or on behalf of the company from the Companies Act, the company memorandum and the articles of association as well as from the common law. Directors include any person occupying the position of a corporation. Public companies must have at least three directors, whereas proprietary companies must have at least one (Section 121(1)). There are comprehensive provisions on the qualifications, duties, liabilities and indemnities of directors, for instance a person's criminal conviction by a court disqualifiies him or her from holding a directorship (Section 142). The Companies Act also makes provisions for voting in directors (Section 126) and for removing them (Section 127) as well as setting their age (Section 128). The common law defines the fiduciary duties of officers and sets down the requirements for them to act in good faith and loyally for the company. The Companies Act imposes on them the statutory duty to exercise honesty and diligence (Section 139(2)), the duty to use information properly (Section 139(3)) and the duty of disclosure (Section 129). Directors are there, fundamentally, to manage the company's business This is not a statutory duty, but is a general power given to them by most articles (Table A, Article 73).

A breach of Section 139(2) exposes a director to both civil and criminal liabilities (Section 139(4) and (6)). *In Re City Equitable Fire Insurance Co.* (1925) 1 Ch 407 Romer J. expounded further on the requirement for due diligence by stating that the performance of duties must be commensurate with the level of skill and knowledge and experience of the director. However, the director is not bound to render continuous attention; and, in the absence of suspicion, a director is justified in trusting other officials to perform certain tasks. The Companies Act also imposes liability on delinquent officers who take part in the formation, promotion, administration and winding up of a company (Section 401). Where a court considers that accounts are not being kept satisfactorily, it may order a director (or manager) to render an account of all moneys received by him, and that such accounts be properly vouched: *Sandy Creek Gold Sluicing Ltd and Others v McEachern* (1965–1966) PNGLR 161. The Companies Act covers insider trading, but the provisions are not confined to directors (Section 139(3)).

6.1   Disclosure

The provisions on disclosure are confined to directors. They require a register to be kept, showing with respect to each director of the company, the number, description and amount of any shares that the director may have in the company (Section 132(1)). The nature of a director's interests is also to be included in register (Section 132(4)). Directors can be required to disclose emoluments and other benefits they receive from the company, including fees, percentages and payments (Section 135). Directors are not, however, permitted to be paid tax-free payments (Section 133). A director must declare the nature of his or her interest in a contract or proposed contract at a directors' meeting as soon as practicable after the relevant facts come to his or her knowledge (Section 129(1)).

6.2   Company Secretaries

Under the Companies Act, a company must have a secretary or secretaries (Section 137(1)). A sole director of a proprietary company cannot be or act as secretary (Section 137(2)). There is a provision requiring a register of the company's secretaries, directors and managers to be kept (Section 141).

6.3   Meetings and Procedures

The Companies Act prescribes certain types of company. A public company that is a limited liability company and has a share capital, and every no liability company must, within a period of no less than one month and no more than three months after the date on which it is entitled to commence business, hold a general meeting of its members (Section 143(1)). The statutory report must, at least seven days prior to the meeting being held, be forwarded to every member (Section 143(2)). An annual general meeting must be held at least once in every calender year, not more than 15 months after the holding of the last annual general meeting. New companies need not hold one in the first year of incorporation and another in the following year, provided that they hold it within 18 months of incorporation (Section 144(1)).

6.4 Extraordinary General Meetings

Extraordinary general meetings of a company must be held on the requisition of members who, at the date of the requisition, hold 10 per cent of the paid up capital of the company or 10 per cent of the total voting rights in the case of a company with no share capital. Directors must convene such a meeting without delay, and not more than two months after receiving the requisition (Section 146(1)).

6.5 Court-ordered Meetings

If for any reason it is impracticable to call a meeting in any manner in which meetings may be called as prescribed by the Companies Act, the court may, either under its own motion or on request, order a meeting to be called (Section 147(1)).

6.6 The Calling of General Meetings

The Companies Act permits shareholders to call meetings at any time if articles do not make provisions for the purpose. In such a case, two or more members holding 10 per cent of the issued share capital may call a meeting of the company; or, where no share capital exists, 5 per cent of the total number of the members (Section 145(1)).

6.7 Pre-meeting Procedure

At least seven days' notice must be given to all members (Section 145(2)), except for a meeting for the passing of a special resolution, which requires a minimum of 28 days' notice (Section 153(1)). Shareholders must be made aware that they have the right to appoint a proxy and the proxy does not have to be a member (Section 150(1)). A member of a proprietary company is not entitled to appoint a proxy under Section 150(1) except in accordance with the articles of the company or with leave of the court (Section 150(2)).

6.8 The Conduct of Meetings

A meeting may proceed once there is a quorum which in a proprietary company is two members and three in any other case unless the articles of the company state otherwise. A 'quorum' refers to a fixed number of members whose presence is essential. Without a quorum, a meeting is a nullity: *Howbeach Coal Co. Ltd v Teague* (1860) 5 H&N 151, 157 ER 1136. A member includes a proxy (Table A, Regulation 47(1)). Table A, Regulation (2) provides that no business is to be transacted at a general meeting unless a quorum is present at the time the meeting proceeds to business. It appears that a quorum is not required when a vote is being taken, so long as it was present at the beginning of the meeting: *Re Hartley Baird Ltd* (1955) Ch 143. However, the articles may demand that a quorum be present through-out the meeting. If, within 30 minutes of the time appointed for the meeting, a quorum is not present, the meeting, if convened on the requisition of members, is dissolved. In any other case, the meeting stands adjourned to the same time and place, or to such other day and at such other time and place as the directors determine (Table A, Regulation 48). The Companies Act requires that if at the adjoined meeting a quorum is not present within 30 minutes of the time ap-pointed for the meeting, the members present (being not fewer than two) are to constitute a quorum. If two members are not present, the meeting must be dissolved (Table A, Regulation 48).

6.9   The Chairman

The articles usually provide that the chairman of the board of direc-tors shall preside at every general meeting. If there is no chairman or if the chairman is absent or is unwilling, the members are required to elect one of their number to be the chairman of the meeting (Table A, Regulation 49). The chairman usually gets the casting vote (Table A, Regulation 53). In the absence of such a provision, no entitlement exists: *Nell v Longbottom* (1894) 1 QB 767.

6.10   Voting

Subject to the articles, voting is required in the first place by a show of hands (Table A, Regulation 54(2)). Unless the articles provide oth-erwise, a proxy cannot vote on a show of hands (Section 150(1)).

6.11   Resolutions

Ordinary resolutions are required under the Companies Act to be passed by a simple majority, whereas a special resolution has to be passed by 70 per cent of the total number of members. Examples of matters to be resolved by special resolution include: the alteration of the company's objectives (Section 29(1)); the alteration of the com-pany's articles (Section 32(1)); the reduction of share capital (Section 66(1)); voluntary winding up (Section 273(1)); and reserve liability

(Section 58(1)). Section 152(1) and (2) deals with special resolutions. A printed copy of every special resolution must, within one month of its passing, be lodged with the registrar (Section 157(1)).

6.12   The Minutes

A company must record minutes of all proceedings of a general meeting and the minutes are to be entered into a book kept for that purpose (Section 155). Such books are to be kept at the company's registered office or principal place of business, and are to be available and open to the inspection of any member without charge (Section 156(1)). Members are entitled to copies at a nominal charge (Section 156(2)).

6.13   Annual Returns

A company must, within one month of each annual general meeting, lodge a return in the prescribed form with the registrar (Sections 166 and 167). Schedule 7 sets out the content and form of annual returns for a company with a share capital, whereas Section 167(2) sets out the particulars that need to be supplied in the case of a company with no share capital. For instance, a public company is exempt if it has more than 500 members and keeps its principal share register at a place where the registry with which it is registered is situated. In addition, the Schedule requires such a company to provide reasonable accommodation and facilities for the purpose of inspection of its annual returns.

6.14   Audit and Accounting Rules

The Companies Act requires accounts to be kept, and such records (in English) as will sufficiently explain the transactions and financial position of the company and enable true and fair profit and loss accounts and balance sheets (Section 169). With the exception of exempt proprietary companies, every company must present its accounts to be audited prior to presentation to the annual general meeting.

6.15   The Appointment of Auditors

At any time before the first annual general meeting, the directors or the company at a general meeting, may appoint a person or persons to be the auditor or auditors of the company. The auditor holds office, subject to the provisions of Section 174, until the first annual general meeting. That provision covers such matters as conditions of appointment, removal and replacement of the auditor. The Companies Act also covers auditor's fees and expenses (Section 175).

6.16   *The Powers and Duties of Auditors as to Reports on Accounts*

An auditor of a company is required to report to the members as to every balance sheet and profit and loss account laid before the company in the general meeting during his or her tenure in office, and is required to state in the report whether, in his or her opinion:

- the balance sheet and profit and loss account are properly drawn up in accordance with the Companies Act so as to give a true and fair view of the state of the company's affairs; and
- the accounting and other records (including registers) examined by him or her are in accordance with the Companies Act (Section 176(1)).

In particular, the auditor is required by the Companies Act where applicable, to state in the report details of any failure or shortcoming in respect of the matters referred to in Section 176(2). The Companies Act further guarantees the right of access to the company's records (Section 176(3)).

6.17   *Shareholder Protection Rules*

One general rule is that the will of the majority of the members of the company prevails, so that resolutions passed in a general meeting are legally the decisions of the company and are binding even on the minority who voted against those resolutions: *Foss v Harbottle* (1843) 67 ER 189. A member who complains that the affairs of a company are being conducted in a way that is oppressive to one or more members, including him or herself, may apply to the court for relief. Section 197 is the basic provision on this. It provides in Section 197(2) that:

if the court is of the opinion that the company's affairs are being conducted in a manner oppressive to one or more of the members, the court may, with a view to bringing to an end the matters complained of:

(a)   make an order that the company be wound up; or
(b)   except where it is of the opinion that winding up the company would unfairly prejudice that member or those members but otherwise the facts would justify the making of a winding up order on the grounds that it is just and equitable that the company be wound up, to make such an order; or

(c) for any other reason, it is just and equitable to make an order (other than a winding up order) under this section, as it thinks proper.

6.18 The Fraud of the Majority

Fraud in this context does not denote dishonesty; it merely connotes conduct which cannot be justified having regard to the power which the creating instrument intends to confer. It may cover the following situations.

6.18.1 *Expropriation of the company's property* The majority cannot, to the prejudice of the minority, expropriate the company's property. In *Cook v Deeks* (1916) 1 AC 554 the directors of a railway construction company obtained a contract for themselves based on the company's reputation and business connections. They held a majority of shares and passed the resolution that the company disclaimed any interest in the contract. The minority were allowed to bring an action against the directors to recover the contract as a part of the company's property.

6.18.2 *The release of directors' duties of good faith* Some seemingly improper or unlawful acts of directors may be retrospectively or prospectively approved at a general meeting (Section 37) provided that adequate disclosure is given: *Winthrop Investments v Winns Ltd* (1975) 2 NSWLR 666. However, a general meeting cannot ratify an act which is a fraud on the company: *Ngurli v McCann* (1954) 90 CLR 425. In *Hogg v Cramphorn* [1967] Ch 254, it was settled that in some cases the directors may clearly have misused their power, but it is in the best interests of the company to ratify such an act.

Where, however, a general meeting ratification is manifestly unreasonable and unfair, the minority may challenge the ratification in court: *Prudential Assurance Company Limited v Newman Industries Limited (No. 2)* [1982] 1 All ER 354.

6.18.3 *Expropriation of another member's property* In *Brown v British Abrasive Wheel Company* (1919) 1 Ch 154, the court held that the majority cannot deprive the minority of their shares in the company. Although in *Sidebottom v Kershaw, Leese and Company* (1920) 1 Ch 154 doubt was cast on the ratio of the *Brown* case, it held that each case must ultimately depend on the judgment as to what benefit would accrue to the company as a whole.

6.18.4 Mala fide *exercise of majority power* It is incumbent on the majority to exercise its power *bona fide* for the benefit of the company as a whole: *Allen v Gold Reefs of West Africa* [1900] 1 Ch 656.

Although the courts generally tend to discourage individual share-holder action, where a fraud on the minority is being or has been committed by those in control of the company, a simple shareholder may sue if the act complained of could not be ratified by a simple majority of the shareholders at a general meeting: *Bamford v Bamford* (1969) 1 All ER 969.

6.19   *Judicial Relief*

If a wrong has been perpetrated against a shareholder, or group of shareholders, the proper defendant is the company in cases of personal actions. Section 179(1) allows the minister to appoint inspectors to investigate the affairs of the company. Therefore, investigators afford the minority some degree of protection from the excesses of the majority. Section 197 also provides that the minority can bring action on the basis of oppression by the majority. The word 'oppression' connotes conducts which are discriminatory, unjustly prejudicial or contrary to the interests of the member, part of the members or the company itself: *Re Five Minute Car Wash* (1966) 1 All ER 242. An action may be brought by a member or members against the company if the affairs of the company are being conducted oppressively. To qualify as oppressive, the conduct must be burdensome, harsh and wrong (*Re Nonvabron Pty Ltd v Fleurs Avenue Pty Co Ltd* (1986) 11 ACLR 33) and must be continuous conduct, not an isolated act.

6.20   *Corporate Financial Transactions*

The Companies Act makes detailed provisions on charges, share buy-backs and receivers. In the case of a charge, a company must lodge within 60 days a statement in the prescribed form for registration of a charge after the charge is created (Section 110).

7   The External Administration of Companies

7.1   *Rules Regarding Arrangements and Reconstructions*

Part VIII of the Companies Act makes detailed provisions on arrangements and reconstructions. The word 'arrangement' is defined as including a reorganization of the share capital by a company by the consolidation of shares of different classes, by division of shares into different classes or by both those methods (Section 192(1)).

Where a compromise or arrangement is proposed between a company and its creditors, or between the company and its members or any class of them, the court may, on the (summary) application of the company, a creditor or a member of the company (or, in the case of a company being wound up, a liquidator), order a meeting of the creditors, the members of the company or class of members to be summoned (Section 192(2)).

If a majority of 75 per cent in value of members or creditors agrees to any compromise which is then approved by order of the court (Section 192(3)), then the compromise is binding on all creditors or class of creditors, members or class of members, and the company. In the case of a company being wound up, the compromise is binding on the liquidation and contributories of the company.

The court may grant its approval to a compromise in management, subject to such alterations and conditions as it thinks just (Section 192(4)).

The Companies Act (Section 194(3)) provides that where:

(a) an application is made to the court under Part VIII for the approval of a compromise or arrangement; and

(b) it is shown to the Court that:

  (i) the compromise or arrangement has been proposed for the purposes of, or in connection with, a scheme for the reconstruction of any company or companies or the amalgamation of any two or more companies; and

  (ii) under the scheme, the whole or part of the undertaking or property of a company concerned in the scheme is to be transferred to another company the Court may, by one order approving the compromise or arrangement or by a subsequent order, provide for all or any of the following matters.

The provision then goes on to specify those matters.

There are a number of reasons for a company wanting to reconstruct or amalgamate. A company may find it necessary to reorganize itself, for example. It may be a successful company that wants to merge with another company or a company that wants to alter its capital structure in a way not open to it under its memorandum or articles. It may also be that it is in financial difficulties and needs to reach a compromise with its creditors.

Section 192 is designed to meet the situation where a compromise or arrangement is proposed between a company and its creditors (or a class of creditors) or between the company and its members (or class of members). It enables the court to summon a meeting of the creditors or members concerned, and, if at that meeting the compromise or arrangement is agreed to by a 75 per cent majority, to order that the approved compromise or arrangement be binding. This is available even where the company is in liquidation.

Section 193 prescribes the information that must be given to those persons called to attend a meeting under Section 192. The Companies Act gives no definition of either a 'compromise' or 'arrangement', although it does state that an arrangement includes a reorganization of share capital by consolidation, division of shares or both.

The ordinary meaning of compromise is an adjustment of conflicting views by a modification of each, and an arrangement is a putting into order of a settlement of a dispute. Thus, the word 'arrangement' probably has a broader application than 'compromise', but, as Section 192 is a discretionary one so far as the court is concerned, the interpretation of both words is fairly liberal.

Section 192 may not be available if what is sought can be achieved by some other express power in the Companies Act. A court has refused to sanction a scheme under the equivalent of Section 192 when what was sought to be achieved could be done by a resolution altering the memorandum: *Re International Harvester Company of Australia Limited* (1953) VLR 669.

The court has the power to order a meeting and to approve of a compromise or arrangement if the required majority agrees to it. The court may grant its approval to a compromise or arrangement subject to such alterations or conditions as it thinks just. Although the power under Section 192 is discretionary, it has been said that the court should be slow to differ from the wishes of the meeting. In *Re English, Scottish and Australian Chartered Bank* (1893) Ch 385, Lord Lindley stated 'if creditors are acting on sufficient information and with time to consider what they are about, and are acting honestly, they are, I apprehend, much better judges of what is to their commercial advantage than the court may be ... '.

The compromise or arrangement may be for the purpose of a scheme for the reconstruction of a company or companies, or for the amalgamation of two or more companies. A reconstruction essentially concerns only one company, whereas an amalgamation results in the redirection of two or more companies into one. A reconstruction involves substantially the same persons carrying on the same business, but in some altered way. If the scheme involves the transfer of part or the whole of the undertaking or property of Company A to Company B, then the court having approved the scheme may make an order to provide for:

- the transfer to Company B of the whole or any part of the undertaking and of the property and liabilities of Company A;
- the allotting or appropriation of Company B of any shares, debentures, policies or similar interests which under the scheme are to be allotted or appropriated by Company B to anyone;
- the continuation by or against Company B of any legal proceedings pending by or against Company A;

- the dissolution without winding up of Company A;
- provision to be made for dissenters from the compromise or arrangement; and
- the incidental consequences and supplementary matters necessary to secure the full and effective carrying out of the reconstruction or amalgamation.

8 Takeover Rules

The basic provision on takeovers is Section 195. A takeover is defined by that provision as an offer or a proposed offer for the acquisition of shares under a takeover scheme. A takeover scheme is a scheme in which a corporation (or some person on its behalf) makes an offer for all the shares or shares of a particular class in a corporation or sufficient shares in another corporation to exercise or control at least one-third of the voting power in it at an annual general meeting. In counting the one-third of the voting power, the shares held beneficially by the corporation making the offer or a corporation related to it are included.

The Companies Act imposes obligations on both the offeror and offeree corporations. A takeover offer must not be made unless the offeror corporation has given the offeree corporation prior written notice of the takeover scheme. This notice must not be earlier than 28 nor later than 14 days before the offer is made. The notice must contain the particulars of the terms of the takeover offer and a statement that complies with Part B of Schedule 9, and must have attached to it a copy of that statement.

Where an offeree corporation receives a notice and statement, it must give or cause to be given to the offeror corporation within 14 days of the receipt of the notice and statement, a written statement that complies with the requirements of Part C of Schedule 9; or within 14 days of the takeover offer first being made under the takeover scheme, it must give or cause to be given the written statement to each holder of shares to which the scheme relates, in the offeree corporation. The Companies Act makes further provisions on shareholders' protection, including the position of dissenting shareholders.

9 Securities Regulation

There is no stock exchange in PNG and the rules of the Australian Stock Exchange apply to securities transactions regarding PNG securities listed on the Australian exchange. (For details of the Australian rules see Chapter 17.)

10   Miscellaneous

The Companies Act confers fairly extensive powers on the courts. These include making orders compelling inspection (Section 406), winding up (Sections 239–268), convicting persons charged with a range of possible offences under Part XIII and imposing penalties on such persons. Offences include falsification of books (Section 385), frauds by officers of the company (Section 386), false and misleading statements (Section 387) and intention to defraud creditors (Section 383(2)). It also provides some limited defences, for instance a person charged with fraud may put up as his or her defence that he or she had no intention to defraud the company (Section 1341(2)).

The power to commence summary prosecution for any offence committed under the Companies Act lies with the registrar although some other person may also exercise that power but only with the consent of the public prosecutor (Section 392(1)). Such proceedings must be brought within three years of the date of the commission of the offence or at any other time thereafter, but only with the consent of the public prosecutor (Section 392(2)). The public prosecutor may also initiate prosecution if it appears that a person has committed an offence under the Companies Act (Section 179(6)).

The Companies Act imposes a civil liability on officers of the company, including promoters for any misleading information in a prospectus or a failure to disclose full and material particulars relating to the purchase of a share or debenture. A person who suffers a loss as a result is entitled to compensation (Section 48). However, a person can put up as defence that he did not consent to the information or that he was not aware of the incorrect information in the prospectus (Section 48(3)). An expert who has been consulted before the issue of the prospectus is liable, but only to the extent that he or she either knew or ought to have known that the information contained in the prospectus was incorrect (Section 48(2)).

As expected, directors carry a heavy responsibility in managing a company. The Companies Act provides that a director who does not act honestly or use reasonable diligence in the discharge of his or her duties of office is guilty of an offence, and is liable to pay to the company any profit made by him or her and to compensate the company for any loss or damage the company has suffered (Section 139).

11   General Conclusions

The indigenous cultures of PNG did not develop any sophisticated system of commerce and trade that would have acted as a catalyst for the development of the kind of company law regime that had developed in response to the commercial needs of modern societies. Virtually all the transactions of commercial nature that took place in the traditional societies before the advent of the colonial rule were conducted on a simple barter system. The barter system is still practised in some of the village societies, particularly those in remote areas.

The colonial rule introduced the modern regime of company law through legislation beginning in 1912 in what was then Papua and was extended to the United Nations Mandated Territory of New Guinea in 1921. The legislation was essentially the Australian legislation with merely formal changes made to it. Its basic aim was to regulate the mining activities of foreign mining companies as those were the main commercial activities in those days. The colonial legislation was improved and extended in response to the growing commercial needs of the country as it moved gradually from the colonial status to the eventual independence in 1975.

The private sector is still small by comparison with the public sector. Much of the commercial life of the country hinges on the exploitation of natural resources, principally minerals, oil, forestry and fishery. The smallness of the private sector and a lack of commercial culture in the modern sense, probably explain the underdevelopment of the case-law aspect of the country's company law. Lawyers have tended to depend on the Australian and the UK case-law in the few company law cases that have been litigated so far in the superior courts. Therefore, the *corpus* of the country's company law can be found in the content of the legislation in this area of the law and in the Australian case-law. The main legislation – the Companies Act – was consolidated in 1982.

In 1996 the government decided to update the legislative framework of the Companies Act and for that purpose looked to the new New Zealand companies legislation as the model. A Draft Bill for a new legislation based on the New Zealand model was submitted to the national parliament at the beginning of 1997, but the debate on it has been delayed by the intervention of national elections in the middle of that year. It is anticipated that the new parliament will debate the Bill early in 1998. The Bill has not been passed at the time of writing. Therefore, the future trend of the PNG company law will be determined by the new model, subject to the modifications that the national parliament, in its wisdom, may make in order to adapt the model to the needs of PNG.

Notes

*   Senior Lecturer in Law, University of Canberra, Barrister and Solicitor of the
    Supreme Court of Papua New Guinea and member of Law Asia. The author is
    grateful to Paul Kerr, a senior law student in the Law School of the University of
    Canberra for his research assistance in the preparation of this chapter.
1   The Dutch surrendered their possession to Indonesia in 1969 after a plebiscite
    supervised by the United Nations was held among the indigenous people of the
    then Dutch New Guinea to see whether they preferred to stay with the Dutch or
    to join Indonesia and they chose the latter course of action.
2   South Pacific countries which include PNG have plural legal systems: see gen-
    erally, Mtumy, M. (ed.) (1993), *South Pacific Islands Legal*, Honolulu: Hawaii
    Press, xx–xxi.
3   See generally Trebilcock, M.J. (1986), *Public Enterprises in Papua New Guinea*, Port
    Moresby: Institute of National Affairs.
4   Kimuli, M.A., Amankwa, H.A. and Mugambwa, J.T. (1990), *Introduction to the
    Law of Business Associations in Papua New Guinea*, Second Edition, Hobart: Pacific
    Law Press, 168–178.
5   See Tashjian, P.C. (1989), *Business Organisations in Papua New Guinea*, Sydney:
    Law Book Co., 204–211.
6   As note 5, above, 56.

16 New Zealand Company Law

PETER FITZSIMONS*

1 Introduction

New Zealand's legal system was derived from the English common law system. The Treaty of Waitangi, signed by the English Crown and Maori in 1840, led to the imposition of English law into New Zealand.[1] The current central document of the New Zealand Constitution is the Constitution Act 1986. This provides for a sovereign to be the head of state of New Zealand (currently Queen Elizabeth II), a governor general to act as the sovereign's representative in New Zealand and to exercise certain royal powers on the sovereign's behalf. It also establishes that parliament will be a unicameral house. The Constitution Act also sets up an executive, consisting of ministers of the crown and members of the executive council and provides for the independence of the judiciary.[2]

New Zealand, in line with the English legal system, has a hierarchy of courts. In the civil arena, it has District Courts which have jurisdiction up to $ 200 000.[3] The second tier of the hierarchy is the High Court, which has all the judicial jurisdiction necessary to administer the laws of New Zealand.[4] There are two levels of appeal above the High Court. The first is the Court of Appeal,[5] followed by the Judicial Committee of the Privy Council.[6]

2 The Source of Corporate Law in New Zealand

2.1 The Constitutional Basis of New Zealand Company Law

New Zealand company law combines common law principles derived from judicial decisions over the past centuries (English and, more recently, New Zealand and other Commonwealth countries) and statute law.

The main corporate statue governing corporations is the Companies Act 1993. It deals with the core elements of company law, such as registration of a company, the constitution of a company, division of powers, duties and remedies, accounts, and dissolution. Other Acts deal with specific areas of corporate operations: for example, the Companies Amendment Act 1963 which governs corporate takeovers; the Financial Reporting Act 1993; the Receiverships Act 1993; the Securities Act 1978 which deal with the raising of funds from the public, and the Securities Amendment Act 1988 which deals with insider trading, the disclosure of substantial shareholdings in listed companies, and regulation of the futures exchange.

2.2   The Enactment of the Companies Act 1993

The recent reforms to New Zealand company law arose out of a review of company law by the New Zealand Law Commission.[7] The Law Commission rejected both the Australian and the English approaches as inappropriate models for New Zealand company law.[8] The Commission instead proposed a new company law model which was based, at least in part, on US corporate law.[9] The emphasis in the reform, which was underpinned by the deregulatory environment in New Zealand after 1984, was on the efficiency of private contractual arrangements and the sanctions provided from markets and private interests of market players.[10] The Companies Act 1993 was based substantially upon the Law Commission's Report.

2.3   Responsibility for Reforming the Law

After the enactment of the Companies Act 1993, the Minister of Justice established an informal group of professionals, called the Company Law Monitoring Group, to advise on any amendments that should be made to the legislation.[11] The Company Law Monitoring Group receives submissions from persons on possible amendments to the legislation and reports to the Minister of Justice.[12]

The New Zealand Securities Commission (NZSC) was established under Part I of the Securities Act 1978. One of the NZSC's functions is to review the law relating to corporate bodies, securities and issuers of securities.[13] Although it mainly confines its review to the area of securities regulation,[14] it has wide powers of investigation.[15] The NZSC may recommend to the governor general regulations covering certain aspects of the primary and secondary securities markets,[16] provided it has first consulted affected parties.[17]

2.4 The Basic Principles of the Companies Act 1993

The basic principles underlying the Companies Act 1993 flow from the Law Commission's Report and are set out in the preamble or long title to the Act:

- a reaffirmation of the economic and social benefits accruing from the aggregation of capital for productive purposes;
- the spreading of economic risk and the taking of business risks;
- the provision of basic and adaptable requirements for the incorporation, organization and operation of companies;
- a definition of the relationship between companies, directors, shareholders and creditors;
- to encourage efficient and responsible management by the provision of wide discretion in matters of business judgment while providing protection for shareholders and creditors against the abuse of management power;
- to provide straightforward and fair procedures for realizing and distributing the assets of insolvent companies.

In essence, the Companies Act is intended to facilitate the economic development of the New Zealand economy while providing shareholders with protection by the inclusion of significant remedies for shareholders. This means that the shareholder remedies in the legislation are quite important, as is the role of the judiciary in giving effect to these remedies and controlling directors' behaviour.[18]

2.5 The Interpretation of Company Legislation

The Interpretation Act 1904 provides general principles for the interpretation of New Zealand legislation. The main principles are that:

- the preamble to every Act shall be deemed to be part thereof, intended to assist in explaining the purport and object of the Act;[19]
- every Act and provision is deemed remedial and, accordingly, shall receive such fair, large, and liberal construction and interpretation as will best ensure the attainment of the object of the Act and of such provision or enactment according to its true, intent, meaning and spirit.[20]

The New Zealand courts have a tradition of using a purposive approach when construing legislation.[21] There are already indications that the judiciary will take into account the purpose of the legislation set out in the long title to the Companies Act.[22]

The New Zealand Bill of Rights Act 1990 is also relevant to the interpretation of legislation. Section 6 provides that the court, when interpreting legislation, should prefer that interpretation which is consistent with the rights set out in that Act. This has been used by the New Zealand courts on a number of occasions, including in the context of securities regulation.[23]

3   The New Zealand Corporate Regulatory Agencies

3.1   *The Powers of Corporate Regulatory Agencies*

Compared to other jurisdictions, such as Australia and United States, New Zealand has a relatively light-handed regulatory regime.[24] The three main regulators of corporate bodies in New Zealand are the registrar of companies, the NZSC and the New Zealand stock exchange.

The registrar of companies, apart from powers relating to the administration of the register required under the Companies Act 1993, has the power to carry out inspections and to require a person to produce documents for the purpose of ascertaining whether a company or a director is complying with the Companies Act 1993 or the Financial Reporting Act 1993, or detecting offences against either of those Acts.[25] The registrar has similar powers of inspection under the Securities Act 1978, subject to the approval of the NZSC.[26]

The NZSC has wide powers to investigate practices in the market and to examine documents and witnesses.[27] It also has power to spend or cancel the registration of a registered prospectus.[28] Under the Securities Amendment Act 1988, it may apply to the court for orders where a person has failed to comply with the requirement of notifying the acquisition of certain interests in voting securities.[29] The NZSC may also approve the appointment of a barrister or solicitor to examine whether there is a cause for action against any person for insider trading.[30] Under Part III of the Securities Amendment Act 1988, the NZSC has the role of authorizing futures exchanges[31] and dealers in futures contracts.[32]

The third regulatory body in New Zealand is the New Zealand stock exchange. Although it is established under the Sharebrokers Amendment Act 1981, the New Zealand Court of Appeal has held that its relationship with listed companies is based on private contract.[33] Under the listing rules, the stock exchange has the power to amend the listing rules, grant waivers, grant listing to companies, to cancel the listing of shares and to cancel or suspend the quotation of any securities.[34] Under the business rules, the stock exchange controls the activities of its members. The operational and surveillance powers of the stock exchange are administered by the Market Surveillance Panel.[35]

3.2 *Review of Regulatory Action*

Any act or decision by the registrar under the Companies Act 1993 is appealable to the court within 15 days of the date of notification of the act or decision.[36]

The NZSC is subject to the usual administrative law requirements when exercising its powers.[37] However, it is not liable under tort for a negligent exercise of its powers.[38]

Although the Court of Appeal recognized the important public role of the stock exchange, it held that it was not subject to judicial review in the exercise of its powers with respect to listed companies.[39] Any dispute with the stock exchange by a listed company would be an issue of contract law.

4 A Description of the Types of Companies and their Powers

4.1 *The Types of Companies Incorporated under the Companies Act 1993*

The Companies Act 1993 requires a company to have one or more shares and one or more shareholders who can have limited or unlimited liability for the obligations of a company.[40] Three types of companies can be registered under the Companies Act 1993. The first is a company with shares, which has limited liability for its shareholders. The second is a company with unlimited liability for shareholders. The third is a company which has limited liability, with any additional liability explicitly provided for in the constitution of the company for any particular shareholder.[41]

4.2 *The Registration of Foreign Companies in New Zealand*

There are two mechanisms for foreign companies to be recognized in New Zealand. A company not incorporated in New Zealand is required to register as an overseas company within ten days of commencing business in New Zealand.[42]

Alternatively, an overseas company may be registered as a company under the Companies Act 1993 by transferring its place of incorporation to New Zealand.[43]

4.3   *The Legal Capacities and Powers of Companies under the Companies Act 1993*

An incorporated company in New Zealand is a legal entity in its own right, is separate from its shareholders and continues in existence until it is removed from the New Zealand register.[44] Subject to any other legal restrictions set out in any other Act, the general law or the company's constitution, a company has full capacity to carry on or undertake any business or activity, do any act, or to enter into any transaction, and, for the purposes of these actions, it has full rights, powers and privileges.[45] Any restriction on the capacity of a company to act does not affect the invalidity of that act merely because of a lack of that power.[46]

A company or a guarantor of an obligation of the company cannot challenge dealings between a person and the company on the basis that a person did not comply with the Act or the constitution of the company.[47] Neither can a company or guarantor challenge such dealings on the basis that the director or company agent was not duly appointed or did not have the usual powers of such a person, unless the person knew or ought to have known by virtue of his or her position with, or relationship to the company of one of these matters, in which case the company or guarantor may challenge the contract or transfer of property.[48] Similarly, a company cannot challenge forged documents, unless the person who has acquired property rights or interests from the company has actual knowledge of the fraud or forgery.[49]

5   Company Formation

5.1   *The Registration of Companies*

Any person may apply for registration of a company under the Companies Act 1993.[50] The application to the registrar of companies for registration has to be in the prescribed form and signed by each applicant.[51] The consent of each director and shareholder is required for the application.[52] If the proposed company is to have a constitution (which would vary in some way from the constitution provided by the Companies Act 1993), then a copy of the company's constitution certified by at least one applicant has to be lodged.[53] If the application is properly completed, the registrar is required to register the application and issue a certificate of incorporation.[54] From the date of incorporation stated on the certificate, the company is incorporated under the Companies Act 1993.[55]

5.2 The Corporate Constitution

The Companies Act 1993 does away with the mandatory requirement for the lodgement of a memorandum of association and articles of association. Instead, it provides for each company to have a constitution. It is not necessary for a company to lodge a formal constitution.[56] If no constitution is adopted, then the provisions of the Companies Act 1993 apply in full to the company.[57]

A company may lodge its own constitution, and the company, board, directors and shareholders have the rights, powers, duties and obligations set out in that constitution.[58] The contents of a constitution can include such matters contemplated by the Companies Act 1993 for inclusion in the constitution (including varying the application of certain provisions of the Act) and such other matters as the company wishes to include.[59] However, a constitution has no effect to the extent that it contravenes or is inconsistent with the Companies Act.[60] The constitution, subject to provisions of the Act, is binding between the company and each shareholder and between each shareholder in accordance with its terms.[61]

5.3 The Company Registered Office and the Company Name

A company is required to have at all times a registered office in New Zealand.[62] A company must register a change of its registered office,[63] and may be required to do so by the registrar of companies.[64]

In order to register a company, it is necessary to reserve a name for the company.[65] If the liability of the shareholders is limited, the registered name of the company must end with the word 'limited' or the abbreviation 'Ltd'.[66] The name of the company has to be stated on all company documents.[67] If the company fails to have its name appropriately stated, then each person who issued or signed the document is liable to the same extent as the company, if the company fails to discharge its obligations.[68]

The registrar cannot reserve a name if it would contravene an enactment, would be identical or almost identical to the name of another company, if the name has already been reserved, or if, in the opinion of the registrar, it is offensive.[69]

5.4 Membership and Share Capital Requirements

Unlike the Companies Act 1955, which required two or more persons to be shareholders in a company, the Companies Act 1993 allows one person companies.[70] There are no upper limits on the number of shareholders. The Companies Act 1993 has removed the distinction between private and public companies.

There are no minimum capital requirements for the registration of a company in New Zealand. All that is necessary is that there be one or more shares.[71] However, if the company is undercapitalized and the directors enter into transactions and the company is unable to perform its obligations, they may incur personal liability.[72] There is also no requirement for the shares to have a par value. The shares can be issued for whatever value the directors determine.

5.5   Amendment of Corporate Constitution

If a company does not have a constitution, the shareholders may adopt a constitution by special resolution.[73] If a company has a constitution, then the shareholders may, by special resolution, alter or revoke it.[74]

The court also has power under Section 34 to alter the constitution of a company if it is satisfied that it is not practicable to alter the constitution, using the procedures set out in the Act or in the constitution itself.[75] The court may exercise its powers on the application of a director or shareholder of the company.[76]

5.6   Company Registers

A company is required by the Companies Act 1993 to keep certain records at its registered office.[77] These are:

- the constitution of the company;
- the minutes of meetings and the resolution of shareholders for the last seven years;
- a register containing the interests of directors;
- the minutes of the meetings and resolutions of directors and directors' committees for the last seven years;
- the certificates given by directors under the Companies Act 1993 for the last seven years;
- the full names and addresses of the current directors;
- all copies of written communications to all shareholders or holders of the same class of shares for the last seven years, including annual reports;
- copies of all financial statements required by the Companies Act 1993 for the Financial Reporting Act 1993 for the last seven completed accounting periods of the company;
- the accounting records required by Section 194 of the Companies Act 1993 for the current accounting period in the last seven completed accounting periods of the Act; and
- the share register.

The records of the company have to be in a written form, or in a manner such that the records are easily accessible and convertible into a written form.[78]

6 The Internal Administration of Companies

6.1 *The Duties, Powers and Responsibilities of Officers*

The Companies Act 1993 removed the requirement to have a company secretary. A company may be formed with only one director,[79] who must be a natural person.[80] Directors are appointed by ordinary resolution by the members of the company,[81] or, in certain circumstances, by the court.[82] A director can be removed by ordinary resolution, subject to the constitution of the company.[83] A company may indemnify or insure a director/employee of the company for certain acts or omissions, provided such an indemnity or insurance is expressly authorized by its constitution.[84]

The Companies Act 1993 imposes duties on directors and defines the word 'directors' broadly. It includes not only persons who are formally appointed as directors,[85] but also those who act as directors, those who direct or instruct a person who occupies the position of director, those who by virtue of the constitution have a power normally exercised by the directors, and those who are delegated powers by the board.[86] The Companies Act 1993, however, excludes a person from being a director to the extent that a person acts only in a professional capacity.[87] A receiver is also excluded from the definition of director.[88]

The Companies Act 1993 incorporates the directors' duties established at common law. These duties are:[89]

- to act in good faith and in what the director believes to be the best interests of the company;[90]
- to exercise a power for a proper purpose;[91]
- to comply with the Companies Act 1993 and the constitution of the company;[92]
- not to engage in reckless trading or entering an obligation that the company cannot perform on reasonable grounds;[93] and
- to exercise care, diligence and skill.[94]

These duties appear to be in addition to any duties imposed by the common law, such as a fiduciary duty to shareholders in particular circumstances,[95] and any duties that the courts may develop, such as a duty to creditors.[96]

Directors also have an obligation to disclose interests in contracts with the company,[97] to refrain from unauthorized use of company information,[98] and to pay compensation if they trade in the shares of the company when in possession of non-public information.[99]

6.2   Meeting Procedures

The Companies Act 1993 provides rules for meetings, some of which may be varied by the constitution of the company.[100] In general terms, notice of a meeting has to be given no fewer than ten working days before the meeting to every shareholder entitled to receive notice of the meeting and to every director and auditor of the company.[101]

Meetings may be held either at a particular place or, subject to the constitution of the company, by means of audio or audio-visual communication, by which all shareholders participating and constituting a quorum, can simultaneously hear each other throughout the meeting.[102] The rules also allow a shareholder to vote either by being present or by proxy.[103] It is also possible for a shareholder to vote by postal vote.[104]

6.3   Audit and Accounting Rules

A company is required to keep at its registered office copies of all financial statements required by the Financial Reporting Act 1993, for the last seven completed accounting periods of the company.[105] These records must be kept in written form in English or in manner in which they are easily accessible and convertible into written form in English (which includes electronic form).[106]

A company must appoint an auditor at each annual general meeting who is required to audit the financial statements of the company.[107] A company may decide not to appoint an auditor, provided there is a unanimous resolution passed by the company. In addition, if the company is an issuer under the Financial Reporting Act 1993 then an auditor has to be appointed.[108]

An auditor has to be a chartered accountant, an officer of the Audit Department of the New Zealand government, or a member of an association of accountants constituted outside New Zealand which has been approved by the registrar; the person should be eligible to act as an auditor in that country and should be approved by the registrar of companies.[109] An auditor is required to give a report to the shareholders on the financial statements audited by him or her.[110]

6.4   The Annual Return

The annual return has to be filed with the registrar of companies.[111] The annual return must contain the matters indicated in the Fourth Schedule of the Companies Act 1993. In general terms, these are details as to the company (registered office, address and so on), the offices of the company, the current and former shareholders of the company, the place where the share register is kept, the shares which have been issued, the classes of shares, the amounts paid or unpaid on those shares, and the shares forfeited, repurchased or redeemed by the company.

6.5   Shareholder Protection Rules

The Companies Act 1993 contains specific protection for shareholders.

The shareholders of a company can require the company to hold a special meeting,[112] or they can apply to the court for the court to call a meeting of shareholders.[113] A shareholder can also demand that the company provide him or her with a statement detailing the number held by the shareholder, as well as the rights, conditions and restrictions attaching to those shares and the relationship of those shares to other classes of shares.[114]

In order to protect the rights attached to shares, the Companies Act 1993 requires that the company cannot take action that affects such rights unless the action has been approved by a special resolution of an interest group.[115] The Act further provides that an issue of shares ranking equally with existing shares is deemed to be an action affecting the rights attached to the existing shares, except where the constitution of the company expressly permits the issue of such shares or the issue is made in accordance with the pre-emptive rights of shareholders under the Companies Act 1993 or constitution.[116]

The Companies Act 1993 further protects a shareholder who is unhappy with the actions proposed by the company, but is a member of an interest group which has approved by special resolution that action. Such a shareholder, provided he or she has voted all his or her shares against approving the action, is entitled to require the company to repurchase the shares.[117] Similarly, if a company adopts, alters or revokes the company's constitution and a shareholder has voted against such a resolution, then the shareholder can also request the company to repurchase his or her shares.[118]

A further protection provided for shareholders is a requirement that shareholders approve a major transaction by special resolution, before it is put into effect.[119] A major transaction is one where the company would acquire or dispose of, or incur abilities, which would represent more than half of the value of the company's assets for the

transaction.[120] If a shareholder votes against the proposed major transaction, he or she is entitled to require the company to buy out his or
her shares.[121]

The Companies Act 1993 retains the oppression remedy for shareholders. A shareholder or a former shareholder may apply to the
court on the basis that the company's affairs have been conducted in
a manner that is, or that is likely to be, oppressive, unfairly discriminatory or unfairly prejudicial to him or her in his or her capacity as
shareholder or in any other capacity.[122] If the court decides that it is
just and equitable to make an order, it can make a wide range of
orders including requiring the company or another person to purchase the shareholder's shares, the regulation of future conduct of
the company's affairs, alterations to the company's constitution,
putting of the company into liquidation or the setting aside of an
action by the company or the board which is in breach of the Companies Act 1993 or constitution.[123] The Companies Act 1993 assists an
applicant in certain circumstances by deeming that a failure to comply with certain sections of the Act is unfairly prejudicial.[124]

A new right of action provided for shareholders is a derivative
action. A shareholder or director may apply to the court for approval
to commence or takeover an action in the name of and on behalf of a
company.[125] A court can only grant the application if it is satisfied
that the company does not intend to deal with an action appropriately or it is in the company's interests that the proceedings not be
left to the directors or the 'determination of the shareholders as a
whole'.[126] If a shareholder applies for an indemnity for the costs of
the statutory derivative action, the court having granted the application for the statutory derivative action, has to make an order that the
costs of the proceedings must be met by the company 'unless the
court considers that it would be unjust or inequitable for the company to bear those costs'.[127]

6.6   *The Relationship between Management and Shareholders*

The Companies Act 1993 attempts to define clearly the roles of
directors and shareholders. In addition, it also creates certain rights
for shareholders and certain duties to shareholders on the part of
directors.

It provides that the business and affairs of the company, subject to
the company's constitution, must be managed by or under the direction or supervision of the board of the company.[128] The board is
granted all the powers necessary to carry out these functions.[129]

The Companies Act 1993 also provides an explicit mechanism for
management review by shareholders. In addition to the requirement
for the board to provide an annual report to the shareholders,[130] the

chairperson has to allow shareholders a reasonable opportunity at a meeting of shareholders to question, discuss or comment on the management of the company.[131] The shareholders are entitled to pass a resolution relating to the management of the company,[132] but unless the constitution provides that the resolution is binding, the resolution will not affect the management of the company.[133]

Certain powers of the company can only be exercised by shareholders so as to limit the powers of the directors. These include transactions providing for the unanimous assent of shareholders,[134] the issue of shares which cannot be issued by reason of the constitution,[135] alteration to the rights of the shareholders,[136] and the entering into the major transaction by a company.[137]

Shareholders are also given two further mechanisms to control directors. The first is the ability to apply to the court for an order restraining the company or director of the company from engaging in conduct that would contravene the constitution, the Companies Act 1993 or the Financial Reporting Act 1993.[138] The second is the ability of a shareholder to apply to obtain information held by the company.[139] The company is required to provide information requested, except if a disclosure of the information would, or would be likely to, prejudice the commercial position of the company or of any other person, or if the request for information is frivolous or vexatious.[140]

The Companies Act 1993 also provides a number of causes for actions by shareholders against directors and against the company. It provides that there are certain duties which directors owe directly to shareholders.[141] These duties include the duty to supervise the share register, to disclose interest and to disclose share dealings.[142] A shareholder is also entitled to apply to the court for an order requiring a director to comply with the constitution, the Companies Act 1993, or the Financial Reporting Act 1993. The court can make such an order if it is satisfied that it is just and equitable to do so.[143] A shareholder has similar rights of actions against a company.[144] In addition, the Companies Act 1993 allows for representative actions to be taken where all or some of the shareholders have the same or substantially the same interest against the company or a director.[145]

6.7 Corporate Financial Transactions

The Companies Act 1993 provides a more flexible regime for financial transactions by a company. A number of transactions previously prohibited are allowed, provided that the company is solvent after the transaction, the relevant procedure has been complied with and the directors sign a certificate to that effect.[146]

A distribution, which includes a dividend, of the company's assets can be made at any time by a company, provided the company will pass the solvency test after the distribution.[147] There is no requirement that a distribution or dividend only be paid out of profits. A company passes the solvency test when it is able to pay its debts as they become due in the normal course of business and when the value of its assets is greater than the value of its liabilities, including contingent liabilities.[148] In the event that a distribution is made and the company is not able to satisfy the solvency test immediately after distribution, the Companies Act 1993 provides that, in certain circumstances, the company can recover from the shareholder who has received a distribution, the amount of the distribution.[149] In addition, directors may be personally liable to repay the company so much of the distribution as cannot be recovered from shareholders, in the event that they have either not followed the procedure set out in the Companies Act 1993 for distributions, or that reasonable grounds for believing that the company would satisfy the solvency test did not exist at the time the certificate was signed.[150]

A company can buy back its own shares, provided the constitution of the company expressly permits a buy back.[151] A buy back can be by a pro-rata offer to all shareholders,[152] an offer to one or more shareholders (provided that either all the shareholders have consented in writing or the board resolves that the offer to those particular shareholders is of benefit to the remaining shareholders and the terms of the offer and the consideration are fair and reasonable to the remaining shareholders)[153] or an offer on the stock exchange.[154]

The company can also redeem its shares, provided this is permitted in any constitution of the company.[155] The company may also provide financial assistance to a person for the purpose of purchasing the company's shares.[156]

The Companies Registration of Charges Act 1993 continues the regime for the registration of charges under the Companies Act 1955.[157] Although the word 'charge' is not fully defined in that Act, there are certain charges which the Act requires to be registered. These are debentures, uncalled share capital, chattels of the company, floating charges, charges on land and book debts.[158] A person who registers a charge gains priority over a subsequent charge over the same assets. It also protects the charge from any claims by unsecured creditors or the liquidator of the company.[159] If a charge is not registered, it is void against a liquidator and any creditor of the company.[160]

6.8   *Capital Raising*

Raising of capital by companies is dealt with both by the Companies Act 1993 and the Securities Act 1978. The Companies Act 1993 entitles the board of the company to issue shares at any time to any person and to any number it thinks fit, subject to the Act and the constitution.[161]

The Securities Act 1978 controls the raising of funds from the public. It prohibits the offer of securities to the public unless there is a registered prospectus.[162] If an allotment of securities is made without a registered prospectus, the allotment is void[163] and the issuer and the directors are required to repay the subscription monies, together with interest.[164] An issuer is required to prepare and issue an investment statement.[165] The purpose of the investment statement is to provide key information which is likely to assist a prudent but non-expert person to decide whether or not to subscribe to securities and to bring to the attention of such a person other important information about the securities that may be available in other documents.[166]

A security is defined in general terms as any interest or right to participate in any capital assets, earnings, royalties or any other property of any person.[167] The definition of security also includes an equity security, a debt security, unit trusts, superannuation schemes, life insurance, life insurance policies, and any interests or rights to be declared by regulations to be a security.[168]

The Securities Act 1978 defines what is included as an offer of securities to the public, as well as defining what does not constitute an offer of securities to the public.[169] An offer to any section of the public, an offer to individuals selected at random, or an offer to a person who has become known to the offeror as a result of any advertisement will constitute an offer of securities to the public.[170] The Securities Act 1978 excludes certain offers of securities, such as an offer made to relatives or close business associates of the issuer, habitual investors or persons who have been selected otherwise than as members of the public.[171] There are also exceptions for offers made to a person to enter into a *bona fide* underwriting or sub-underwriting agreement, a takeover offer under the Companies Amendment Act 1963 or an offer under the Takeovers Act 1993.[172]

The Securities Act 1978 provides specific exemptions for certain types of interest and certain types of offerings. The two most general exemptions for securities are interests in land,[173] and rights to chattels.[174] Securities which have been previously allotted may also be exempt from the provisions of the Securities Act 1978.[175]

The Securities Act 1978 imposes civil and criminal liability for a failure to comply with it or for misleading statements in the prospectus.[176]

7   The External Administration of Companies

7.1   *The Rules Regarding Arrangements and Reconstructions*

The Companies Act 1993 provides for arrangements, amalgamations of companies, and compromises with creditors.[177] An arrangement is defined as including a reorganization of the share capital of a company by the consolidation of the shares of different classes, by the division of shares into different classes, or by both.[178]

It is possible under Part XIII of the Act for the court to approve an amalgamation of two or more companies which may continue as one company or as a new company.[179] This may be effected either by a standard amalgamation application[180] or by a short form amalgamation.[181] In addition, an amalgamation may be effected in the same way that an arrangement may be put into effect.[182]

7.2   *Voluntary Administration and Corporate Rescue Provisions*

New Zealand does not have a formal voluntary administration scheme as in Australia and the United Kingdom. However, it does provide for the approval of a compromise between a company and its creditors.[183] A compromise can include cancelling all or part of the debt of the company, varying the rights of creditors or the term of the debt, or altering the company's constitution.[184] A compromise may also be approved in the same manner as an arrangement.[185]

The Corporations (Investigation and Management) Act 1989 provides for the imposition of statutory management for companies at the direction of the governor-general. The Act can apply to any corporation that is or may be operating fraudulently or recklessly or that wants to apply the Act to preserve the interests of the Corporation's members or creditors, to protect any beneficiary under any trust administered by the corporation, or to protect the public interest, if those interests cannot be adequately protected in any other way.[186]

7.3   *Company Liquidations*

A company is put into liquidation by the appointment of a liquidator.[187] The liquidator has to be a named person or an official assignee of the companies office. There are three ways in which a liquidator may be appointed. These are by special resolution of the shareholders, by the board of the company on the certain events specified in the company's constitution, or by the court on the application of the company, director, shareholder, a person entitled by the constitution, a creditor of the company or the registrar.[188]

The court is able to appoint a liquidator on the grounds that the company is unable to pay its debts,[189] the company or the board has persistently or seriously failed to comply with the Act, the company does not comply with the essential requirements for a company, or it is just and equitable that the company be put into liquidation.[190]

The effect of the liquidation of the company is that the liquidator has custody and control of the company's assets, and the directors cease to have any powers, functions or duties in relation to the company except those required by the Companies Act 1993.[191] In addition no-one can commence or continue legal proceedings against the company or its property, or enforce a right or remedy over or against the property of the company,[192] except a secured creditor.[193]

7.4   *The Protection of Creditors and the Ranking of Claims*

Once a company has been put into liquidation, a creditor (with the exception of a secured creditor) is not entitled to retain the benefit of any execution process, distress or attachment against the property of the company, unless the execution process was completed before the passing of a special resolution by the shareholders, a resolution by the board, the making of an application to the court or the appointment of a liquidator.[194]

The Companies Act 1993 also allows a liquidator to avoid a transaction by a company if at the time of the transaction the company was unable to pay its debts due and it was within two years before the commencement of the liquidation, and enabled another person to receive more towards satisfaction of a debt than the person would otherwise have received or been likely to have received in the liquidation.[195] A liquidator is also entitled to recover from a party where the party received property at an undervalue from the company and the company was unable to pay its debts, and the party received the property within one year prior to the commencement of the liquidation.[196]

Creditors' claims to the assets of the company are determined by whether they are secured, preferential or unsecured creditors. A secured creditor has the right to realize the property subject to the security and claim in the liquidation as an unsecured creditor for the balance due, or surrender the security to the liquidator for the general benefit of creditors and claim in the liquidation as an unsecured credit or for the whole debt.[197]

Out of the assets held and realized by the liquidator, the liquidator has to first pay out the preferential claims.[198] After paying these claims, the liquidator has to apply the assets of the company to satisfaction of all other claims, with those claims ranking equally amongst themselves and must be paid in full.[199] If the assets are insufficient, the unsecured creditors are paid on a *pro-rata* basis.[200]

7.5   *The Control of Insolvency Practitioners*

New Zealand does not have a licensing regime for insolvency practitioners. Any person can act as a liquidator, subject to a number of conditions which are similar to those required by a receiver, namely the person is a natural person,[201] is at least 18 years of age, is not a creditor of the company in liquidation, is not a shareholder, director, auditor or receiver of the company, an undischarged bankrupt, person of unsound mind, or a person who has been prohibited from being a director or promoter of a company.[202]

The court has power to supervise the liquidation of a company,[203] including the power to give directions in relation to any matter arising in connection with liquidation, to confirm, reverse or modify an act or decision of the liquidator, and to review the remuneration of the liquidator.[204] The court may remove a liquidator from office in certain circumstances.[205]

7.6   *Receiverships*

The law relating to receivers in New Zealand is contained in the Receiverships Act 1993. A receiver may be appointed pursuant to a deed or agreement, or by the court in exercise of its inherent jurisdiction.[206] Notice must be given of the receivership.[207] A receiver is given substantial powers under the Act, including the right to demand and recover income of the property in receivership, to manage, insure, repair and maintain the property in receivership, and to inspect and take possession of documents under the control of the guarantor.[208] These powers are in addition to the powers and authorities expressly or impliedly conferred by the deed or by order of the court.[209]

A number of duties are imposed on a receiver. These include a duty to exercise his or her powers in good faith and for a proper purpose,[210] and to exercise the powers in a manner he or she believes on reasonable grounds to be in the best interests of the person in whose interests he or she was appointed.[211] In exercising these powers, the receiver is required to have regard to the interests of the grantor, any person claiming through the grantor an interest in the property in receivership, unsecured creditors of the grantor, and any sureties who may be called on to fulfil obligations of the grantor.[212] In addition, the receiver has a duty to the grantor, the person claiming an interest in the property through the grantor, unsecured creditors of the grantor or sureties to achieve the best price reasonably obtainable as at the time of sale of the property.[213]

The court has extensive powers to control a receivership, including limiting the liability of a receiver, [214] giving directions to a receiver in

relation to any matter arising out of the receivership,[215] and reviewing or fixing the remuneration of the receiver. The court may also
terminate or limit the receivership.[216]

8 Takeover Rules

8.1 An Introduction

New Zealand has, over the last 15 years, engaged in intense debate
over the need for a takeovers regime that models those of overseas
countries.[217] Currently the rules governing takeovers are a combination of statutory and voluntary rules.

8.2 Takeover Thresholds

The Companies Amendment Act 1963 applies if an offer is made for
the acquisition of shares in a company which, together with shares in
which the offeror is already beneficially entitled, carries the right to
exercise or control the exercise of more than one-fifth of the voting
power at any meeting of the offeree company,[218] which has more
than 25 members or shareholders,[219] and where the offer is made to
more than six members of the company.[220] The Act only applies to
written takeover offers.[221]

Under the New Zealand stock exchange listing rules, all listed
companies are required to adopt one of three possible codes for their
respective companies. A bidder has to comply with the relevant code
when the bidder has acquired 20 per cent of the voting securities of
the target company.[222] The codes do not require a bid to be made to
all shareholders or an equal price to be paid to all shareholders.

8.3 Disclosure Requirements and Shareholder Protection

The Companies Amendment Act 1963 requires a bidder to give between 14 and 28 days' notice of the intention to make an offer, and
must include details of the offer.[223] The target company is required to
provide a statement to its shareholders, and the directors must then
provide a recommendation, indicate they do wish to make a recommendation or state they are not justified in making a recommendation.[224]
Directors must also indicate any interest in the bidder and target companies and any payments they will receive for loss of office in the
event of the takeover being successful.[225]

The three codes under the listing rules are the general notice and
pause provisions, the insider only provisions and the minority veto
provisions.[226] Under the general notice and pause provisions if an

offeror is an insider of the company then at least 15 business days' notice of the offer has to be given to the offerees.[227] If the offeree is not an insider, at least three days' notice has to be given of the offer.[228] However, except where a transferee is an insider, if the transaction is effected through the exchange's order matching market then there is only a requirement of giving one business day's notice.[229] Under the insider only provisions, the requirement for 15 days' notice and the provision of an appraisal report only applies if the offeror is an insider.[230]

The information that has to be provided by an offeror is the price or consideration offered for the shares; any conditions of the transaction which are material to the assessment of the price by the shareholders; the identification of the class and the maximum number of securities and the percentage of the relevant class to which the transfer proposal relates; the identity of the persons reasonably expected to acquire relevant interests in the equity securities; the number of equity securities that will be held after the proposed transaction; the times in which the transfers are intended to occur; and how the transfers are to be effected.[231]

Where the offer is made by an insider, the independent directors are required to provide shareholders with an appraisal report in respect of the offer.[232] This report does not have to be provided if all the offerees consent to waive a requirement or if all the disinterested directors certify that the cost and difficulty of providing the appraisal report outweigh the benefits.[233]

Where an offer is made to acquire more than 20 per cent of the shares in a company having a minority veto provision in its constitution, the same period of notice is required as for a general notice.[234] Unless an offer is made to all holders of the equity securities of a class on the same terms, or made through the market, there is a requirement to have the proposed transfer approved by an ordinary resolution of the votes of each affected group of shareholders.[235] In addition, a report has to be prepared by an independent person, commissioned by the directors and approved by the stock exchange, for the shareholders of the company.[236] The report provides an opinion as to the consideration and other terms of the proposed transactions.

A failure to comply with the takeovers code under the listing rules, means that no votes from those shares can be cast on a poll, and the relevant shares may be sold.[237]

The listing rules also provide for compulsory acquisition where the offeror has acquired 90 per cent or more of the shares that were the subject of the bid.[238] The price is to be determined by an independent person where there is an objection to the proposed price.[239]

8.4 Mechanisms for the Review of Takeover Activity

Takeover activity may be reviewed by the NZSC and the Market Surveillance Panel of the New Zealand stock exchange. The NZSC has the power to review practices relating to securities,[240] and this includes the power to examine persons involved with a takeover that is being effected.[241]

The Market Surveillance Panel has been delegated the powers of the stock exchange.[242] In the context of a takeover, it can make rulings regarding aspects of a transaction.[243] If the rulings are not complied with, then the exchange may cancel or suspend the securities or the quotation of the securities.[244] A ruling made by the exchange or the panel is binding upon the issuer.[245]

9   An Introduction to Securities Regulation in New Zealand

9.1 The Relationship Between the New Zealand Stock Exchange and the NZSC

The stock exchange is incorporated under its own Act: the Sharebrokers' Amendment Act 1981. The Court of Appeal has held that the listing rules are a private contract between the stock exchange and the listed companies.[246] The NZSC does not have any statutory oversight of the stock exchange, although this was suggested at one stage after the stock market crash in 1987.[247]

9.2 The Types of Securities Regulated

The NZSC has responsibilities under the Securities Act 1978 and the Securities Amendment Act 1988 for securities as defined in the Securities Act 1978.[248] This includes equity securities, debt securities and what are described as participatory securities.[249] The Securities Amendment Act 1988 is designed to regulate the disclosure of interest in voting securities of listed companies.[250]

The NZSC also has responsibility for regulation of the futures market in New Zealand. It is given the responsibility to authorize a body corporate to conduct a market for trading in futures contracts,[251] as well as to authorize those persons who may carry on the business of dealing with futures contracts.[252] The NZSC also has the obligation to recommend the regulations for the futures exchanges and dealing in futures contracts.[253]

The stock exchange has power over securities which are listed on the stock market. These include not only equity securities, but also debt securities and options.[254]

9.3   *The Market Conduct Rules and the Sanctions for Securities Misconduct*

Regulation of the secondary market for listed companies is covered or controlled by the Securities Amendment Act 1988 and the New Zealand stock exchange's listing rules of 1994.

The Securities Amendment Act 1988 requires the disclosure of substantial shareholdings in listed companies, prohibits insider trading and regulates the futures markets. Under Part I of the Act, members and former members of a public issuer, together with the public issuer, have the right to commence an action against a person who is an insider of the public issuer, either for trading while in the possession of inside information or for tipping (or encouraging) others to trade.[255] In addition, the public issuer also has a right to apply to the court for the insider to be liable for a pecuniary penalty.[256]

There are three statutory exceptions provided for insider trading and tipping. These are where the director or employee follows an approved procedure for trading,[257] where a takeover offer is made in accordance with Section 4 of the Companies Amendment Act 1963,[258] and where a 'Chinese Wall' is put in place to prevent the flow of information within a body corporate.[259]

Part I also provides for a barrister to be appointed with the prior approval of the NZSC to examine whether or not there are grounds for an insider trading action against an insider, with the public issuer being liable for the cost of the opinion.[260] In addition, Part I provides a form of statutory derivative action, which allows a member or former member to apply to the court for approval to commence an action against an insider in the name of the public issuer and at the expense of the public issuer.[261] The court is required to grant approval for the application unless there is 'no arguable case' or there is 'good reason' not to do so.[262]

Section 257 of the Crimes Act 1961 provides that it is an offence for a person to conspire with:

> any other person by deceit or falsehood or other fraudulent means to defraud the public, or any person ascertained or unascertained, or to affect the public market price of stock, funds, shares, merchandise ... whether the deceit or falsehood or other fraudulent means would or would not amount to a false pretence.

This provision, while it may be used against insider trading, is of limited usefulness as it requires a conspiracy and would not apply to an individual (for example a director) trading on inside information.

Part II of the Securities Amendment Act 1988 aims to ensure that the market is informed as to the identity of persons who are entitled to exercise, or control the exercise of, significant voting parcels in a public company.[263] Part II requires a person who obtains a 'relevant interest' in 5 per cent or more of the voting securities of a public issuer to disclose that interest to the public issuer and to the stock exchange.[264] The relevant interest does not have to arise from an enforceable contract.[265] A change by 1 per cent or more of the holdings of the substantial security holder has to be notified to the public issuer and to the stock exchange,[266] as does a change in the nature of any relevant interest.[267]

Part II also provides certain powers to the public issuer to enable it to obtain disclosure. A public issuer (either at its own motion or at the request of members who hold at least 5 per cent of the public issuer's voting securities) has the power to require disclosure by a substantial security holder as to who holds relevant interests in the voting securities held by the substantial security holder.[268] Section 29 is an even more extensive power as it allows the public issuer to request 'any person who the public issuer believes has, or may have, a relevant interest in voting securities of the public issuer' to supply 'such information as [the public issuer] may specify' for the purpose of assisting the public issuer to ascertain who is, or may be, a substantial security holder.

The penalty provisions for Part II are set out in Sections 30–32. Under Section 30, the court has jurisdiction to grant an order under Section 32 where it has 'reasonable grounds to suspect' that a substantial security holder has not complied with Part II.[269] The orders the court can make under Section 32(1) include directions requiring compliance with Part II, prohibiting the exercise of voting rights, suspending registration of transfers of shares, or ordering the forfeiture of any voting securities of the public issuer.

10   Miscellaneous

10.1   The Powers of the Court

In New Zealand the courts play a central role in the control of directors, the enforcement of shareholders' rights and the regulation of market participants.[270]

The Law Commission saw the function of the court under company law as being the imposition of penalties for transgression of the procedural requirements of the Companies Act 1993, granting remedies to dissentient minorities, in the case of fundamental change or in cases of unfair treatment, and determining civil claims for breaches of the Act or constitution.[271] In general terms, the Law Commission saw the role of the court as being essentially supervisory, rather than interventionary.[272] The court was not called on to interfere in the discretion of directors or the majority of shareholders.[273]

The courts are empowered to impose fines for the transgression of the Companies Act.[274] The powers also include the power to prohibit a person from managing a company or to disqualify directors.[275]

10.2   Offences

Part XXI sets out the offences under the Companies Act 1993. These include false statements in relation to documents required by or for the purposes of the Act,[276] and a person who uses or destroys property,[277] falsifies records[278] or carries on a business fraudulently.[279] The penalties for the offences under Part XXI range from a fine not exceeding $ 5 000,[280] to a fine of up to $ 200 000 or five years' imprisonment.[281]

Criminal liability can be imposed for a breach of the Securities Act 1978.[282] The person who makes a takeover offer which contravenes the Companies Amendment Act 1963 can be fined up to $ 10 000.[283]

Notes

*   BCom LLB (UNSW), MComLaw (Hons) (Auck), Bell, Gully, Buddle, Weir, Barristers and Solicitors, Auckland.
1   Gerbic, P. and Lawrence, M. (1994), *Understanding Commercial Law*, Wellington: Butterworths, paragraph 1.3; Mulholland, R. (1995), *Introduction to the New Zealand*, eighth edition, Wellington: Butterworths, paragraph 1.8.1.
2   Mulholland, as note 1, above, paragraph 2.10.
3   As note 2, above, para 3.10.
4   As note 2, above, paragraph 3.13.
5   Judicature Amendment Act 1957; as note 2, above, paragraph 3.16.
6   Judicial Committee Act 1833, as note 2, above, paragraph 3.17.
7   New Zealand Law Commission (1989), *Company Law Reform and Restatement*, NZLC R9, Wellington (1990); *Company Law Reform: Transition and Revision*, NZLC R16, Wellington, 1990.
8   Fitzsimons, P. (1994), 'Australia and New Zealand on Different Corporate Paths', *Otago Law Review*, 8, 267, 284.
9   As note 8, above, 284.
10   As note 9, above.
11   New Zealand Law Society (1995), *Company Law – Practical Experience One Year On*, Wellington, 77.
12   As note 11, above.
13   Section 10(b) and (c) of the Securities Act 1978.
14   See Fitzsimons, P. (1994), 'The New Zealand Securities Commission: The Rise and Fall of a Law Reform Body', *Waikato Law Review*, 2, 87, 88–91.
15   *City Realties Ltd v Securities Commission* [1982] 1 NZLR 74.
16   Section 70(1) of the Securities Act 1978.
17   Section 70(3) of the Securities Act 1978. As note 14, above, 88–91, 119.
18   As note 8, above, 289–291; Fitzsimons, P. (1997), 'Corporate Governance and

the Courts in New Zealand', Australasian Corporate Law Teachers' Conference, University of Melbourne, February, 18.
19 Section 5(e) of the Interpretation Act 1904.
20 Section 5(j) of the Interpretation Act 1904.
21 See, for example, *City Realties Ltd v Securities Commission* [1982] 1 NZLR 74.
22 See Justice Tompkins (1994), 'Directing the Directors: The Duties of Directors Under the Companies Act 1993', *Waikato Law Review*, 2, 13, 18; and Fitzsimons, as note 18, above, 25.
23 *Colonial Mutual Life Assurance Society Ltd v Wilson Neill Ltd* [1993] 2 NZLR 617; *Colonial Mutual Life Assurance Society Ltd v Wilson Neill Ltd* [1994] 2 NZLR 152 (CA).
24 As note 8, above.
25 Section 365(1) of the Companies Act 1993.
26 Section 67 of the Securities Act 1978.
27 Sections 10(b) and (c), 17 and 18 of the Securities Act 1978; *City Realties Ltd v Securities Commission* [1982] 1 NZLR 74.
28 Section 44 of the Securities Act 1978.
29 Sections 31 and 32 of the Securities Amendment Act 1988. See Fitzsimons, P. (1997), 'Part II of the Securities Amendment Act: The Judicial Approach to Penalties for Failure to Notify Relevant Interests', *Companies and Securities Law Bulletin*, 39.
30 Securities Amendment Act 1988, Section 17. See Fitzsimons, P. (1995), 'Enforcement of Insider Trading Laws by Shareholders in New Zealand: An Analysis and Proposals for Reform', *Waikato Law Review*, 3, 97, 112; Fitzsimons, P. (1997), 'Enforcement of Insider Trading Laws in New Zealand', in Rickett, C. and Grantham, R. (eds), *Essays on Securities Regulation and Insider Trading*, Wellington: Brooker's, 206.
31 Section 37(8) of the Securities Amendment Act 1988.
32 Section 38(1) of the Securities Amendment Act 1988.
33 *New Zealand Stock Exchange v Listed Companies Association Inc.* [1984] 1 NZLR 699, 705; See Fitzsimons, P. (1994), 'The New Zealand Stock Exchange: Rights and Powers', in G. Walker and B. Fisse (eds), *Securities Regulation in Australia and New Zealand*, Melbourne: Oxford University Press, 542–543.
34 As note 33, above, 546; New Zealand Stock Exchange, *Listing Rules*, Rule 5.4.
35 As note 33, above, Rule 2.4.
36 Section 370(1) of the Companies Act.
37 *City Realties Ltd v Securities Commission* [1982] 1 NZLR 74.
38 *Fleming v Securities Commission* (1994) 7 NZCLC 260, 410; [1995] 2 NZLR 514 (CA).
39 *New Zealand Stock Exchange v Listed Companies Association Inc.* [1984] 1 NZLR 699, 705; as note 33, above, 543.
40 Section 10 of the Companies Act 1993. See also Section 97(2).
41 Section 97(2) of the Companies Act 1993.
42 Section 332 of the Companies Act 1993.
43 Section 344 of the Companies Act 1993.
44 Section 15 of the Companies Act 1993.
45 Section 16(1) of the Companies Act 1993.
46 Section 17(1) of the Companies Act 1993.
47 Section 18(1) of the Companies Act 1993.
48 Section 18(2). Lodgement of a document on the register does not constitute constructive notice – Section 19 of the Companies Act 1993.
49 Section 18(2) of the Companies Act 1993.
50 Section 11 of the Companies Act 1993.
51 Section 12(1)(a)–(b) of the Companies Act 1993.

52   Section 12(1)(c) and (d) of the Companies Act 1993.
53   Section 12(1)(f) of the Companies Act 1993.
54   Section 13 of the Companies Act 1993.
55   Section 14 of the Companies Act 1993.
56   Section 26 of the Companies Act 1993.
57   Section 28 of the Companies Act 1993.
58   Section 27 of the Companies Act 1993.
59   Section 30 of the Companies Act 1993.
60   Section 31(1) of the Companies Act 1993.
61   Section 31(2) of the Companies Act 1993.
62   Section 186 of the Companies Act 1993.
63   Section 187 of the Companies Act 1993.
64   Section 188 of the Companies Act 1993.
65   Section 20 of the Companies Act 1993.
66   Section 21 of the Companies Act 1993.
67   Section 25(1) of the Companies Act 1993.
68   Section 25(2) of the Companies Act 1993.
69   Section 22(2) of the Companies Act 1993.
70   Section 10(c) of the Companies Act 1993.
71   Section 10(b) of the Companies Act 1993.
72   Section 135 of the Companies Act 1993.
73   Section 32(1) of the Companies Act 1993.
74   Section 32(2) of the Companies Act 1993.
75   Section 34(1) of the Companies Act 1993.
76   As note 75, above.
77   Section 189(1) of the Companies Act 1993.
78   Section 190(1)(a) of the Companies Act 1993.
79   Sections 10(d) and 150 of the Companies Act 1993.
80   Section 151(3) of the Companies Act 1993. Section 151(2)(a)–(g) sets out the
     criteria by which a person would be ineligible to be a director.
81   Section 153(2) of the Companies Act 1993.
82   Section 154(1) of the Companies Act 1993.
83   Section 156(1) of the Companies Act 1993.
84   Section 162 of the Companies Act 1993.
85   Section 126(1)(a) of the Companies Act 1993.
86   Section 126 of the Companies Act 1993; See Rennie QC, H. and Watts, P.
     (1996), *Directors' Duties and Shareholders' Rights*, Wellington: New Zealand
     Law Society Seminar, 2.
87   Section 126(4) of the Companies Act 1993.
88   Section 126(1A) of the Companies Act 1993.
89   See Rennie and Watts, as note 86, above, 7.
90   Section 131(1) of the Companies Act 1993.
91   Section 133 of the Companies Act 1993.
92   Section 134 of the Companies Act 1993.
93   Sections 135 and 136 of the Companies Act 1993.
94   Section 137 of the Companies Act 1993.
95   For example, *Coleman v Myers* [1977] 2 NZLR 225
96   *Nicholson v Permakraft (NZ) Ltd* [1985] 1 NZLR 242.
97   Section 140 of the Companies Act 1993.
98   Section 145 of the Companies Act 1993.
99   Section 149 of the Companies Act 1993.
100 Section 124 of the Companies Act 1993.
101 First Schedule, Clause 2 of the Companies Act 1993.
102 First Schedule, Clause 3 of the Companies Act 1993.

103   Clause 6 of the Companies Act 1993.
104   Clause 7 of the Companies Act 1993.
105   Section 189 of the Companies Act 1993.
106   Section 194(3) of the Companies Act 1993.
107   Section 196(1) of the Companies Act 1993.
108   Section 196(3)(c) of the Companies Act 1993 and Section 4 of the Financial
      Reporting Act 1993.
109   Section 199(1) of the Companies Act 1993.
110   Section 205(1) of the Companies Act 1993.
111   Section 214(1) of the Companies Act 1993.
112   Section 121 of the Companies Act 1993.
113   Section 123 of the Companies Act 1993.
114   Section 83 of the Companies Act 1993.
115   Section 117 of the Companies Act 1993.
116   Section 117(3) of the Companies Act 1993.
117   Section 118 of the Companies Act 1993.
118   Section 110 of the Companies Act 1993.
119   Section 129(1) of the Companies Act 1993.
120   Section 129(2) of the Companies Act 1993.
121   As note 118, above.
122   Section 174(1) of the Companies Act 1993.
123   Section 174(2)(a)–(h) of the Companies Act 1993.
124   Section 175(1) of the Companies Act 1993.
125   Section 165(1) of the Companies Act 1993.
126   Section 165(3) of the Companies Act 1993.
127   Section 166 of the Companies Act 1993; see Fitzsimons, P. (1996), 'Statutory
      Derivative Actions in New Zealand', *Companies and Securities Law Journal*, **14**,
      184.
128   Section 128(1) and (3) of the Companies Act 1993.
129   Section 128(2) of the Companies Act 1993.
130   Section 208(1) of the Companies Act 1993.
131   Section 109(1) of the Companies Act 1993.
132   Section 109(2) of the Companies Act 1993.
133   Section 109(3) of the Companies Act 1993.
134   Section 107 of the Companies Act 1993.
135   Section 34 of the Companies Act 1993.
136   Section 117 of the Companies Act 1993.
137   Section 129 of the Companies Act 1993.
138   Section 164(1) of the Companies Act 1993. See *Mercury Energy Ltd v Power New
      Zealand (No. 2)* (1995) 7 NZCLC 260, 818.
139   Section 178(1) of the Companies Act 1993.
140   Section 178(3) and (4) of the Companies Act 1993.
141   Section 169(1) and (3) of the Companies Act 1993.
142   Section 169(1)(a)–(c) of the Companies Act 1993.
143   Section 170 of the Companies Act 1993.
144   Section 171 of the Companies Act 1993.
145   Section 173 of the Companies Act 1993.
146   Section 52 of the Companies Act 1993.
147   As note 146, above.
148   Section 4 of the Companies Act 1993. See Ross, M. (1994), *Directors' Liability
      and Company Solvency: The New Companies Act*, Auckland: CCH New Zealand
      Ltd, Chapter 3.
149   Section 56(1) of the Companies Act 1993.
150   Section 56(2) of the Companies Act 1993.

151   Section 59(1) of the Companies Act 1993.
152   Section 60(1)(a) of the Companies Act 1993.
153   Sections 60(1)(b) and 61 of the Companies Act 1993.
154   Sections 63 and 65 of the Companies Act 1993; note 34, above, Rule 7.
155   Section 68 of the Companies Act 1993.
156   Section 76(1) of the Companies Act 1993.
157   Section 3(1) of the Companies (Registration of Charges) Act 1993.
158   Section 102(11) of the Companies Act 1955.
159   Section 102(12) of the Companies Act 1955.
160   Section 103(2)of the Companies Act 1955.
161   Sections 42 and 44(1) of the Companies Act 1993.
162   Section 33(1) of the Securities Act 1978.
163   Section 37(4) of the Securities Act 1978.
164   Section 37(6) of the Securities Act 1978.
165   Section 37A(1) of the Securities Act 1978.
166   Section 38D of the Securities Act 19783.
167   Section 2D (1) of the Securities Act 1978.
168   Section 2D(1)(a)–(f) of the Securities Act 1978; see Fitzsimons, P. (forthcoming), 'Offers of Securities to the Public in New Zealand', in Walker and Ramsay (eds), *Securities Regulation in Australian and New Zealand*, second edition, Oxford: Oxford University Press.
169   Section 3(1) and (2) of the Securities Act 1978; as note 168, above.
170   Section 3(1)(a)–(c) of the Securities Act 1978.
171   Section 3(2)(a)(i)–(iii) of the Securities Act 1978.
172   Section 3(2)(b) and (c) of the Securities Act 1978.
173   Section 5(1)(b) of the Securities Act 1978.
174   Section 5(1)(c) of the Securities Act 1978.
175   Section 6(1) of the Securities Act 1978.
176   Sections 56, 57, 58, 59, and 62 of the Securities Act 1978.
177   Parts XIII, XIV and XV of the Companies Act 1993.
178   Section 235 of the Companies Act 1993.
179   Section 219 of the Companies Act 1993.
180   Section 220 of the Companies Act 1993.
181   Section 221 of the Companies Act 1993.
182   Sections 236(1) and 238(a) of the Companies Act 1993.
183   Section 228(1) of the Companies Act 1993.
184   Section 227 of the Companies Act 1993.
185   Sections 236(1) and 238(b) of the Companies Act 1993.
186   Section 4 of the Corporations (Investigation and Management) Act 1989.
187   Section 241(1) of the Companies Act 1993.
188   Section 241(2) of the Companies Act 1993.
189   Section 278 of the Companies Act 1993.
190   Section 241(4)(a)–(d) of the Companies Act 1993.
191   Section 248(1)(a) and (b) of the Companies Act 1993.
192   Section 248(1)(c) of the Companies Act 1993.
193   Section 248(2) of the Companies Act 1993.
194   Section 251(1) of the Companies Act 1993.
195   Section 292(2) of the Companies Act 1993.
196   Section 297(1) of the Companies Act 1993.
197   Section 305(1) of the Companies Act 1993.
198   Section 312(1) and the Seventh Schedule to the Companies Act 1993.
199   Section 313(1) and (2) of the Companies Act 1993.
200   Section 312(2) of the Companies Act 1993.
201   Section 280(2) of the Companies Act 1993.

202 Section 280(1) of the Companies Act 1993.
203 Section 284(1) of the Companies Act 1993.
204 Section 284(1) of the Companies Act 1993.
205 Section 286(5) of the Companies Act 1993.
206 Sections 2(1) and 6 of the Receiverships Act 1993.
207 Section 10 of the Receiverships Act 1993.
208 Section 14(2) of the Receiverships Act 1993.
209 Section 14(1) of the Receiverships Act 1993.
210 Section 18(1) of the Receiverships Act 1993.
211 Section 18(2) of the Receiverships Act 1993.
212 Section 18(3) of the Receiverships Act 1993.
213 Section 19 of the Receiverships Act 1993.
214 Section 32(2), (4) and (7) of the Receiverships Act 1993.
215 Section 34(1) of the Receiverships Act 1993.
216 Section 35 of the Receiverships Act 1993.
217 See Fitzsimons, P. (1996), 'The Regulation of Takeovers in New Zealand', *Agenda*, **3**, 317.
218 Sections 2(1) and 4(1) of the Companies Amendment Act 1963.
219 Section 3(a) of the Companies Amendment Act 1963.
220 Section 3(b) of the Companies Amendment Act 1963.
221 *Multiplex Industries Ltd v Speer* [1966] NZLR 122.
222 As note 34, above, Rule 4.5.2.
223 Section 4(1) of the Companies Amendment Act 1963.
224 The second schedule, Clause 1 of the Companies Amendment Act 1963.
225 The second schedule of the Companies Amendment Act 1963.
226 As note 34, above, Rule 4.
227 As note 34, above, Rule 4.5.3(a).
228 As note 34, above, Rule 4.5.3(b).
229 As note 34, above, Rule 4.5.5.
230 As note 34, above, Rule 4.4.2.
231 As note 34, above, Rule 4.5.2.
232 As note 34, above, Rule 4.5.8.
233 As note 34, above, Rule 4.5.9.
234 As note 34, above, Rule 4.6.1.
235 As note 34, above, Rule 4.6.2.
236 As note 34, above, Rule 4.6.3.
237 As note 34, above, Rule 4.7.2.
238 As note 34, above, Rule 4.8.1.
239 As note 34, above, Rule 4.8.4.
240 Section 10(c) of the Securities Act 1978.
241 *City Realties Ltd v Securities Commission* [1982] 1 NZLR 74.
242 As note 34, above, Rule 2.4.3.
243 As note 34, above, Rule 4.7.8.
244 As note 34, above, Rule 5.4.1 and 5.4.3(b).
245 As note 34, above, Rule 4.7.2(f).
246 *New Zealand Stock Exchange v Listed Companies Association Inc.* [1984] 1 NZLR 699.
247 See *Report of the Ministerial Committee of Enquiry into the Sharemarket*, Ministerial Committee of Enquiry into the Sharemarket, Wellington, 1989 and see Fitzsimons, as note 14, above, 113.
248 Section 2D of the Securities Act 1978.
249 Section 2 of the Securities Act 1978. See Fitzsimons, as note 168, above.
250 Sections 2, 4 and 5 of the Securities Amendment Act 1988; see Fitzsimons, P.

(1997), '"Relevant Interests" and The Securities Amendment Act 1988', *Companies and Securities Law Bulletin*, 15–21.

251 Section 37(8) of the Securities Amendment Act 1988.
252 Section 38(1) of the Securities Amendment Act 1988.
253 Section 41(1) of the Securities Amendment Act 1988.
254 As note 34, above, Rule 1.
255 Sections 7 and 9 of the Securities Amendment Act; as note 168, above.
256 Section 7(2)(g)(i) of the Securities Amendment Act 1988.
257 Section 8(1) of the Securities Amendment Act 1988.
258 Section 82 of the Securities Amendment Act 1988.
259 Section 8(3) of the Securities Amendment Act 1988.
260 Section 17 of the Securities Amendment Act 1988.
261 Section 18 of the Securities Amendment Act 1988.
262 Section 18(2) of the Securities Amendment Act 1988; and see Fitzsimons, as note 255, above.
263 New Zealand Parliamentary Debates, Vol. 490, 1988, 5283.
264 Section 20 of the Securities Amendment Act 1988.
265 See Fitzsimons, as note 250, above.
266 Section 21(1) of the Securities Amendment Act 1988.
267 Section 22(1) of the Securities Amendment Act 1988.
268 Section 28 of the Securities Amendment Act 1988.
269 The court also has jurisdiction under Section 32 where a person has not complied with a request under Sections 28 or 29 of the Act (see Section 32(b)). For a discussion of how the courts have approached the meaning of 'reasonable grounds to suspect' in cases under Part II, see Fitzsimons, P. (1993), *Securities Commission v RE Jones, Waikato Law Review*, 1, 165.
270 Fitzsimons, as note 18, above, 2.
271 As note 7, above, paragraph 136; and see note 18, above.
272 As note 7, above, paragraphs 138 and 139.
273 Fitzsimons, as note 18, above, 18–19.
274 Part XXI of the Companies Act 1993.
275 As note 274, above.
276 Section 377 of the Companies Act 1993.
277 Section 378 of the Companies Act 1993.
278 Section 379 of the Companies Act 1993.
279 Section 380 of the Companies Act 1993.
280 Section 373(1) of the Companies Act 1993.
281 Section 373(4) of the Companies Act 1993.
282 Sections 58, 59 and 60 of the Securities Act 1978.
283 Section 13 of the Companies Amendment Act 1963.

17 Corporations Law in Australia

KETURAH WHITFORD*

1 Introduction

Australia is a federation comprising six states and two self-governing territories, each with its own government. The Commonwealth government has power under the Commonwealth Constitution to make laws with respect to enumerated heads of power.[1] By contrast, the state governments operate under plenary grants of power. In New South Wales, for instance, the state government is given power to make laws for the peace, order and good government of the state.[2] In relation to most areas, state governments have power concurrent with that of the Commonwealth. In the event of an inconsistency between state and Commonwealth law, the Commonwealth law will prevail. This is provided for by Section 109 of the Commonwealth Constitution. The Australian states were originally English colonies which received so much of English law as was appropriate to the condition of the colony at the relevant time.[3] The Commonwealth of Australia was not established until 1901.[4]

The Commonwealth government comprises two houses of parliament, the House of Representatives or lower house and the Senate or upper house. Both senators and members of the House of Representatives are elected. Electoral boundaries for the House of Representatives are drawn in such a way as to ensure that the number of voters in each electorate is similar. Each electorate is a single member constituency and election is based on a preferential voting system. The Senate operates as a house of review. Each state elects the same number of senators regardless of population. This operates to protect the rights of the less populous states. Each electorate is a multi-member constituency and election is based on a proportional representation system combined with preferential voting. The party which forms a government is the party which holds the most seats in the House of Representatives. As a result of the different electoral system for the Senate, it is possible that the government may not control the Senate. The prime minister is the leader of the government. The head of state is the Queen of Australia represented by the governor-general in Australia.

A similar scheme of government operates in the states and territories. The state of Queensland and the two territories (the Australian Capital Territory and the Northern Territory) operate on a unicameral system. In the remaining states there are two houses of parliament. In South Australia and Tasmania the lower house is called the House of Assembly and in the other states it is called the Legislative Assembly. The upper house is called the Legislative Council in all states that have an upper house. Both houses are elected on a representative franchise. Originally, there were restrictions on who could vote for the upper house. This is no longer the case. The leaders of the governments in the states are called premiers and chief ministers in the territories. The state governor is the Queen's representative in the states.

As a consequence of the federal system of government, there is a system of state and federal courts. The ultimate appeal from both sets of courts is to the High Court of Australia. At the federal level there is the Federal Court of Australia, which has federal appellate jurisdiction and some original jurisdiction. In each state and territory the superior court is the Supreme Court, which has appellate and some original jurisdiction and which deals with both state and federal matters.

2   A Description of the Corporations Law in Australia

2.1   *The Constitutional Basis of the Company Law*

The Commonwealth government has power under Section 51(xx) of the Australian Constitution to make laws:

> with respect to the peace, order and good government of the Commonwealth with respect to: ...

> (xx) foreign corporations, and trading or financial corporations formed within the limits of the Commonwealth.

This is the key head of power, but other heads of power may be relevant, for instance the trade and commerce power contained in Section 51(i). Early judicial pronouncements indicated the extent of the limitations on the Commonwealth's power with respect to corporations. The Commonwealth does not have power with respect to corporations generally, but only with respect to foreign, trading or financial corporations. Isaacs J. (dissenting) in *Huddart Parker and Co. Pty Ltd v Moorehead; Appleton v Moorehead*[5] commented *obiter* that:

> it is clear that the power (in s 51 (xx)) is to operate only on corporations of a certain kind, namely, foreign, trading, and financial corporations. For instance, a purely manufacturing company is not a trading corporation ... this leaves entirely outside the range of federal power, as being in themselves objects of the power, those domestic corporations, for instance, which are constituted for municipal, mining, manufacturing, religious, scholastic, charitable, scientific, and literary purposes, and possibly others more nearly approximating a character of trading ... .

This view of Commonwealth power with respect to corporations prevailed for about 70 years. There were then a number of cases which had the effect of expanding the head of Commonwealth power with respect to corporations. In *The Commonwealth of Australia & Another v State of Tasmania & Others*,[6] the High Court upheld a Commonwealth law which sought to prevent the construction of the Franklin Dam in Tasmania. Both the corporation's power and the external affairs' power were relevant to the decision. The Hydro-Electric Commission was found by a majority of the High Court to be a trading corporation because its activities included trading notwithstanding its governmental character. The Commonwealth was able to regulate the activities of the Hydro-Electric Commission merely because it was a trading corporation and the law did not have to be limited to regulating the trading activities of the corporation.

Until 1989 company law was primarily a state matter although a cooperative scheme between the states and the Commonwealth had been put in place which provided for uniform legislation and recognition of companies in states other than their state of incorporation. In 1989 the Commonwealth passed national corporations legislation relying on Section 51(xx) of the Constitution. Originally it had been thought that the Commonwealth lacked sufficient power to do this. However, following the Tasmanian Dams case and a number of other cases it appeared that the Commonwealth's power was wider than was originally thought. It obtained an opinion from Sir Maurice Byers QC to the effect that the Commonwealth had power to enact corporations legislation. This legislation was successfully challenged by a number of the states as being unconstitutional in *The State of New South Wales v The Commonwealth of Australia; The State of South Australia v The Commonwealth of Australia; The State of Western Australia v The Commonwealth of Australia*.[7] The major defect with the legislation was that it regulated the process of incorporation and the

High Court said that the Commonwealth had no power with respect
to the process of incorporation. The Commonwealth only has power
to regulate companies which are already in existence. The High Court
found that the words 'formed within the limits of the Commonwealth' when used in the phrase, 'trading and financial corporations
formed within the limits of the Commonwealth' were words of limitation. The phrase was not used merely to distinguish foreign
corporations from local corporations, but indicated that the corporations must be in existence already. From a practical point of view,
Australia operates under essentially the same legislation as that which
was struck down by the High Court. The effectively national scheme
of regulation of companies depends also on state legislation for its
effect.

2.2   *How the Company Law Came into Being*

Australian corporations law derives from mid-nineteenth century
English company law. In 1844 in England the Joint Stock Companies
Act was passed which provided for corporate status not as a matter
of privilege, as had previously been the case, but as a matter of right
on presentation of certain papers and upon payment of the relevant
fees. In 1855, with the passing of the Limited Liability Act, persons
incorporating a company had the option of forming it on the principle of having their liability limited to the amount that they agreed to
contribute. Both pieces of legislation were then reshaped into the
Joint Stock Companies Act of 1856 and later the Companies Act of
1862, which remains the basis of much of current Australian corporations law.

Prior to the early 1960s Australian states and territories had their
own companies' legislation and there were significant and inconven-
ient differences between them. As a result, there was a move towards
uniform legislation and, following conferences, a draft uniform Companies Bill was prepared based on the Victorian Act of 1958. During
1961 and 1962 all states and the Commonwealth in respect of the
Australian Capital Territory and the Northern Territory passed a
Companies Act based on the draft bill. In 1967 the Standing Committee of Attorneys-General appointed a committee, the Eggleston
Committee, to inquire into the protection afforded to the investing
public by the uniform Companies Acts. As a result of these recommendations, various additional provisions were incorporated into
the legislation in 1971 and 1972. These changes particularly related to
accounts and audit, disclosure of substantial shareholdings, takeovers and insider trading. There were also some departures from
uniformity. New South Wales, for instance, had different provisions
in relation to insider trading.

As a result of a mining boom in the late 1960s and consequent hectic trading on the stock exchange, the Senate Select Committee on Securities and Exchange was set up to inquire into the securities industry. The resulting Rae report recommended the establishment of a national commission similar to the Securities and Exchange Commission in the United States. Four states (New South Wales, Victoria, Queensland and Western Australia) enacted Securities Industry Acts.

In 1976 a novel cooperative companies law regime was established between the Commonwealth and the states. This was proposed in order to achieve uniform and effectively national legislation. There was a Ministerial Council of State and Commonwealth Attorneys-General which oversaw the scheme. A new body, the National Companies and Securities Commission was established with responsibility for policy and administration of company law and the regulation of the securities industry. Most of its powers were delegated to state and territory bodies called Corporate Affairs Commissions.

The scheme was implemented by the Commonwealth passing legislation in the Australian Capital Territory which was enacted in the states by the states passing application of law legislation. Despite the fact that the scheme achieved uniformity, there were criticisms of it. In 1987 the Senate Standing Committee on Constitutional and Legal Affairs in its report, *The Role of Parliament in Relation to the National Companies Scheme*, criticized the Ministerial Council as not being effectively accountable to government. It also pointed to inefficiencies because of the existence of both the National Companies and Securities Commission and the State and Territory Corporate Affairs Commissions. It recommended the introduction of Commonwealth corporations law. The challenge to the corporations legislation is discussed at para 2.1.

To overcome the constitutional problem, the Commonwealth and the states agreed that the legislation which had been struck down by the High Court should form the basis for corporate regulation but that this should be achieved through an applied laws regime. This was brought about by the Corporations Law Amendment Act 1990. The Corporations Act is applied by the Commonwealth as a law of the Australian Capital Territory (using its territories power) and application legislation in each state and the Northern Territory applies the Corporations law as a law of each jurisdiction. The application legislation contains complementary provisions allowing for cross-vesting of court jurisdictions, applying Commonwealth laws relating to offences as if they were state laws, conferring power on the Australian Securities and Investment Commission (ASIC) (the national regulatory body) and the federal police and applying Commonwealth administrative law. These provisions allow the law to operate as if it were Commonwealth law. Since that time the Commonwealth government has enacted the Corporate Law Reform Act of 1992 and 1994 and has embarked on a programme of simplification of the Corporations Law. This work is proceeding in stages. The first Corporate Law Simplification Act was passed in 1995.

2.3   Who is Responsible for Changing the Law?

Each state and the Northern Territory has application legislation which applies the Commonwealth Act 'as in force for the time being' so amendments to the Commonwealth Act automatically flow through to the states and the Northern Territory. The Commonwealth has sole responsibility for reform proposals relating to national markets, including takeovers, securities, public fundraising and futures. The advice of the Ministerial Council must still be tabled in parliament when the legislative amendments are introduced. In relation to proposals for legislative changes related to other subject-matter, the Commonwealth must use its best endeavours to consult with the Ministerial Council.

2.4   What Principles Underlie the Company Law?

One of the chief principles which underpins much of company law is the principle of the separate legal personality of the company from its members which is inextricably linked to the principle of limited liability. The principle of separate legal personality is reflected in Section 124 of the *Corporations Law*. The celebrated case of *Salomon v Salomon*[8] is generally regarded as the common law basis for the principle of separate legal personality. In that case, a sole trader became incorporated with his wife and children subscribing for one share each in order to meet the requirement for seven subscribers. Lord MacNaghten said:

> The company is at law a different person altogether from subscribers to the memorandum; and though it may be that after incorporation the business is precisely the same as before, and the same persons are managers, and the same hands receive the profits, the company is not in law the agent of the subscribers or trustee for them.[9]

Despite the acceptance of this principle in the legislation and the cases, there are examples in the legislation and in the cases where the corporate veil has been disregarded. The legislation, for instance, places personal liability on directors in certain circumstances where the company has traded while insolvent.[10] Cases where the courts have lifted the corporate veil have usually been confined to their facts and have generally been justified on the basis of public policy. Limited liability has its complementary principle of capital maintenance which is reflected in many provisions of the Corporations Law.[11] As there is a limit on the liability of members, creditors have a right to expect that the company's subscribed capital will not be lost otherwise than in the ordinary course of trading. Another theme of the regulation of corporations is that of disclosure. This underpins the provisions relating to directors' duties, the provisions relating to accounts and audit and the prospectus and takeover provisions.

2.5   *How the Legislation is Interpreted*

The Commonwealth and most Australian states have enacted legislation which directs the courts to adopt a purposive approach to interpretation. Section 15AA of the Acts Interpretation Act 1901 (Cth) provides:

> In the interpretation of a provision of an Act, a construction that would promote the purpose or object underlying the Act (whether that purpose or object is expressly stated in the Act or not) shall be preferred to a construction that would not promote that purpose or object.

3   The Nature and Powers of the ASIC

3.1   *A Description of the ASIC's Powers*

The ASIC is the sole regulatory authority under the Corporations Law. It is accountable to the Commonwealth Minister. It was originally created as the Australian Securities Commission by Section 7 of the Australian Securities Commission Act 1989 (ASIC Act) and was renamed the Australian Securities and Investment Commission in 1998. It has power under Division 1 of Part 3 of the ASC Act to conduct investigations. This may arise pursuant to Section 13(1)(a) where the ASIC 'has reason to suspect' that there may be 'a contravention of a national scheme law', or pursuant to Section 13(1)(b) where it 'has reason to suspect' a contravention of Commonwealth, state or territory law concerning 'the management or affairs of a body corporate' or a contravention of a Commonwealth, state or territory law which 'involves fraud or dishonesty and relates to a body corporate, securities or futures contracts'.

Power to investigate also arises pursuant to Section 13(2) where the ASIC 'has reason to suspect that unacceptable circumstances within the meaning of Part 6.9 of the Corporations Law ... have or may have occurred'.

Part 6.9 covers the powers of the ASIC and other bodies in relation to takeovers. Section 732 of the Corporations Law defines when 'unacceptable circumstances' are taken to have occurred. The minister may direct the ASIC to investigate a suspected contravention of the Corporations Law or any Commonwealth, state or territory law relating to company management or involving corporate fraud or dishonesty and other matters listed in Section 14(2) where the minister is of the opinion that it is in the public interest to do so.

The ASIC may also, pursuant to Section 15 initiate an investigation as to whether it should launch a prosecution in relation to matters raised in statutory reports which may be received from a receiver or liquidator under Sections 422 or 533. In conjunction with a Division 1 investigation, where the ASIC suspects or believes on reasonable grounds that a person can give relevant information, it may, pursuant to Section 19 require that person to appear for examination. Under Section 29, the ASIC has the power to inspect any books required to be kept by a national scheme law.

Division 4 of the ASIC Act empowers the ASIC to require disclosure of information about securities and futures contracts from dealers and brokers in particular. As a result of an investigation or examination, the ASIC may decide to initiate a prosecution[12] or commence civil proceedings for damages or recovery of property.[13] The ASIC also has power to hold hearings, pursuant to Section 51 in relation to the exercise of any of its functions or powers. However, this does not apply in relation to a Division 1 investigation or in relation to a declaration of unacceptable conduct.

3.2   The Role of the ASC in Policy Formation and Practice

The Companies and Security Advisory Committee, which comprises the chairperson of the ASIC and such other part-time members as are appointed by the Minister, may on its own initiative, or when requested by the Minister, advise the Minister, and make such recommendations as it thinks fit of a kind referred to in section 148.

The matters listed in Section 148(1) are:

- a proposal to make a national scheme law or to make amendments of a national scheme law;
- the operation of a national scheme law;
- law reform in relation to a national scheme law;
- companies, securities or the futures industry; or
- a proposal for improving the efficiency of the securities markets or futures markets.

Section 1(2) of the ASIC Act provides that:

In performing its functions and exercising its powers, the Commission must strive:

(a) to maintain, facilitate, and improve, the performance of companies, and or the securities markets and futures markets, in the interests of commercial certainty, reducing business costs, and the efficiency and development of the economy; and

(b) to maintain the confidence of investors in the securities markets and futures markets by ensuring adequate protection for such investors; and

(c) to achieve uniformity throughout Australia in how the Commission and its delegates perform those functions and exercise those powers; and

(d) to administer national scheme laws effectively but with a minimum of procedural requirements; and

(e) to receive, process, and store, efficiently and quickly, the documents lodged with, and the information given to, the Commission under national scheme laws; and

(f) to ensure that those documents, and that information, are available as soon as possible for access by the public; and

(g) to take whatever action it can take, and is necessary, in order to enforce and give effect to national scheme laws.

In pursuing these objectives, the ASIC issues practice notes and policy statements, as well as other releases.

3.3 *The Mechanisms for the Review of Regulatory Action*

The Corporations Law provides for review of the merits of a decision by the Administrative Appeals Tribunal. This is provided for by Part 9.4A of the Corporations Law subject to some exceptions. Similarly, Part 15 of the ASIC Act provides for review by the Administrative Appeals Tribunal subject to some exceptions. As the Corporations Law is effectively Commonwealth law, the Administrative Appeals Tribunal Act 1975 (Cth) will extend to reviews of decisions under the Corporations Law as well as the ASIC Act. Section 44 of the Administrative Appeals Tribunal Act provides for an appeal to the Federal Court on a question of law. In addition, the Federal Court has power to review a decision of the Administrative Appeals Tribunal under Section 39B of the Judiciary Act 1903 (Cth).

If the review is sought as to process rather than on the merits of the decision, an application may be made to the Federal Court under the Administrative Decisions (Judicial Review) Act 1977 (Cth). The ASIC is also subject to other legislation which in certain circumstances may provide for review of its actions, including the Ombudsman Act

1976 (Cth), the Freedom of Information Act 1982 (Cth) and the Privacy Act 1988 (Cth).

4   A Description of the Types of Companies and their Powers

4.1   *A Description of Types of Local Companies*

One way of classifying companies is according to the liability of their members. Companies limited by shares are the most common type of companies in Australia. A company limited by shares is defined in Section 9 as 'a company formed on the principle of having the liability of its members limited by the memorandum to the amount (if any) unpaid on the shares respectively held by them'. Generally, pursuant to Section 515, on winding up, a member is liable to contribute an amount which is sufficient to pay the company's debts and liabilities and the cost of winding up. However, in the case of companies limited by shares, the liability of a member is only to the extent of the amount (if any) unpaid on the shares.

A company limited by guarantee is defined in Section 9 as:

> a company formed on the principle of having the liability of its members limited by the memorandum to the respective amounts that the members undertake to contribute to the property of the company if it is wound up.

Under Section 517, on winding up the members may be required to contribute the amounts which they have undertaken to pay. As companies limited by guarantee do not have share capital, they are not generally used for trading. It is a popular form of operation for non-profit-making bodies such as sporting groups or charitable associations or industry lobby groups. Alternatively, non-profit-making bodies may become incorporated and obtain the benefits of limited liability for their members under state and territory legislation relating to the incorporation of associations.[14] In the case of a company limited by both shares and guarantee, Section 518 provided that:

> a member need not contribute more than the aggregate of ... any sums unpaid on any shares held by the member ... [and] the amount the member has agreed to contribute to the company's property if the company is wound up.

This was not a common form of business operation and the Company Law Review Act 1998 eliminated this type of company. An unlimited company is defined in Section 9 as 'a company formed on the principle of having no limit placed on the liability of its members'.

Therefore, in the event of winding up, the general provision of Section 515 would apply. It is not a common form of business operation for this reason. Nevertheless, it may be more convenient to operate as an unlimited company rather than a large partnership, particularly in cases where professional rules prevent persons from operating with limited liability. An unlimited company is able to reduce its share capital without being subject to the restrictions which would otherwise be imposed by Section 195. A no liability company was defined in Section 9 as 'a company that does not have under its constitution a contractual right to recover calls made on its shares from a shareholder who defaults in payment of those calls'.

This type of company was introduced in Victoria in 1871 to assist mining companies to obtain capital. As a result of their speculative nature, mining companies may experience difficulties in raising funds from the public. Only mining companies were permitted to be no liability companies,[15] but mining companies were not required to be no liability companies and many were incorporated as companies limited by shares. In order for a company to be within the definition of mining company in Section 9, it must have had an objects clause which stated that its sole objects were mining purposes. Pursuant to Section 117(1)(f), the memorandum of a no liability company had to state 'that the acceptance of shares in the company does not constitute a contract to pay calls in respect of the shares or to make any contribution towards the company's debts and liabilities'.

Further, Section 254M says that shareholders are not liable to pay calls made by the company on their shares. If they do not pay a call, the shares will be forfeited.[16] As the creditors of a no liability company have no expectation that uncalled capital will be available to them in the event of a winding up, no liability companies are permitted to issue shares at a discount without restriction.[17] This class of company has been removed although existing no liability companies are permitted to continue.

There is a further distinction between public and proprietary companies. Companies limited by guarantee and no liability companies can only be public companies. Other types of companies can be public or proprietary. A public company is defined in Section 9 as 'a company other than a proprietary company'. Proprietary companies are defined in Section 113. They must have fewer than 50 non-employee shareholders and they must not engage in any activity which would require the lodgment of a prospectus under Part 7.12. Therefore, proprietary companies cannot make public issues of shares or other securities.[18] A proprietary company is permitted to make an offer of shares to existing shareholders and to employees.[19]

Both public and proprietary companies need only have one member.[20] Proprietary companies must have a minimum of one director[21] whereas public companies must have a minimum of three.[22] There are further restrictions which apply to directors in public companies. There is a maximum age of 72 years,[23] they must be individually appointed unless the members agree unanimously to do otherwise[24] and they can only be removed by a resolution of the shareholders.[25] Proprietary companies can be of two types: large or small. A proprietary company is a small proprietary company for a financial year if it meets two of the following three criteria:

- the consolidated gross assets at the end of the financial year of the company and any entities which it controls, is less than $ 10 million;
- the value of the consolidated gross assets at the end of the financial year of the company and any entities which it controls, is less than $ 5 million; or
- the company and any entities which it controls have fewer than 50 employees at the end of the financial year.[26]

The chief advantage of being a small proprietary company is that the audit requirements are less stringent. Small proprietary companies need only prepare audited financial statements if requested by the ASIC or by shareholders holding 5 per cent of the shares.[27]

4.2   The Recognition of Foreign Companies

The Corporations Law, although effectively national, still depends on state law for its operation. Companies are incorporated in a particular state or territory. A company is referred to as a recognized company in a jurisdiction outside its home jurisdiction. It can operate, however, in any state or territory without being subject to any further requirements.[28]

A registrable Australian body is defined in Section 9. It is a body corporate which is not a company incorporated in Australia or a foreign company. Exempt public authorities, corporations sole and financial institutions are also excluded from the definition. Unincorporated bodies which have the essential features of bodies corporate, being able to sue and be sued in their own name or being able to hold property in the name of a secretary or other officer, are within the definition. Pursuant to Section 601CA, a registrable Australian body need not be registered under the Corporations Law if it only carries on business within the state or territory of its formation. If it does operate outside its home jurisdiction, it is required to be registered under the Corporations Law. The application must be accompanied by the documents referred to in Section 601CB.

A foreign company, essentially one incorporated outside Australia, must not carry on business in any state or territory unless it becomes registered as a foreign company under Division 2 of Part 5B2. In order to become registered, a foreign company must produce the documentation required by Section 601CE. This includes a certified copy of its certificate of incorporation and of its constitution, a list of directors, information about registrable charges and the address of its registered office or principal place of business in its place of origin and its registered office in Australia. A foreign company must have at least one local agent in Australia who is answerable for the things which a foreign company is required to do under the Corporations Law and who may be personally liable to a penalty for a contravention of the Corporations Law.[29]

4.3 The Legal Capacities and Powers of Companies

Pursuant to Section 124(1), companies have the legal capacity of natural persons and they also have certain corporate powers, including the power:

- to issue debentures or fully or partly paid shares;
- to distribute property among members;
- to charge uncalled capital or to grant a floating charge of company property;
- to obtain registration outside the jurisdiction; and
- to do anything authorized by law.

Companies are not required to specify the objects for which the company was incorporated, although some companies will be indirectly required to have objects clauses.[30] A mining company which wishes to remain a no liability company will require an objects clause in order to be able to comply with the definition of a mining company. Similarly, a company formed for non-profit or charitable purposes which wants to be able to drop the word 'limited' from its name will require an objects clause which limits the company's purposes to those set out in Section 150. Some companies may have been incorporated at a time when an objects clause was required and not have removed it. Other companies may elect to have an objects clause. Even if a company has an objects clause, Section 125(2) states that an act is not invalid merely because it is contrary to or beyond any objects in the company's constitution.

The Corporations Law used to specifiy, in Section 162(D), situations in which an *ultra vires* act could be relied on. None of these situations affected the position of a third party dealing with the company. The situations in which an *ultra vires* act could be relied on were:

- a prosecution under the Corporations Law;
- an application for an order under Section 230, which gives the court power to order certain persons not to manage a corporation;
- an application for an order under Section 260, which effectively gives a remedy to members where the affairs of the company are being conducted in an oppressive, unfairly prejudicial or unfairly discriminatory manner or contrary to the interests of the members as a whole;
- an application for an injunction under Section 1324 to restrain the company from entering into an agreement;
- proceedings by the company or by a member against present or former company officers; or
- an application by the ASIC or by a member for the winding up of the company.

Persons dealing with companies are entitled to make certain assumptions, set out in Section 128, in relation to those dealings. In general terms, a person is entitled to assume that:

- the constitution has been complied with;
- a person whose name is recorded on records with the ASIC as holding a certain office or is held out by the company as holding that office, has the power customarily exercised by a person of that office;
- an officer who has the power to issue a document or to issue a certified copy also has power to warrant that the document is genuine or is a true copy as the case may be;
- a document has been duly sealed if it bears what appears to be the impression of the company seal and the sealing appears to be witnessed by two people who may be assumed to be two directors or a director and secretary on the basis of the ASIC returns or a holding out by the company; and
- directors, secretaries, employees and agents of the company properly perform their duties.

A person is not entitled to make the assumptions if the person, at the time of the dealings, knew or suspected that the assumption was incorrect.[31] A person is not taken to know the contents of a company's memorandum and articles merely because they are lodged with the ASIC.[32] The doctrine of constructive notice does still apply to registered charges.

5 Company Formation

5.1 *Promoters and the Registration of Companies*

The Corporations Law only defines the word 'promoter' for the purposes of the prospectus provisions. The common law has defined promoter in fairly broad terms so as to include those centrally involved in the promotion of the company and also those who play a passive role standing behind the more active promoters.[33] Promoters owe fiduciary duties to the company.[34]

Problems can exist for the promoter and for persons dealing with the promoter in relation to contracts entered into prior to the formation of the company. Sections 131 and 132 are designed to minimize the difficulties inherent in pre-registration contracts. It enables a company to ratify a contract, provided the company is formed within a reasonable time after the contract is entered into.[35] Promoters remain potentially liable if the company is not registered or if it does not ratify the contract.[36] This is relieved to some extent by the fact that the court is given power to make an order against the company if it is registered. Conversely however, even if the company ratifies the contract, the court may still make an order against the promoter if the company fails to perform all or part of the contract.[37] The only way for the promoter to be sure of avoiding personal liability is to be released from liability by the other party to the contract.[38]

In order to register a company, an application must be lodged with the ASIC which must contain the following information:

- type of company;
- the company's proposed name unless the ACN is to be used as its name;
- the names and addresses of proposed members, directors and secretary;
- addresses of proposed registered office and place of business;
- in the case of a company limited by shares or an unlimited company, details of the numbers and classes of shares to be issued and amounts to be paid;
- in the case of a company that is a public company limited by shares or an unlimited company, particulars of shares issued for a non-cash consideration;
- in the case of a company limited by guarantee, the proposed amount of the guarantee.[39]

5.2   *The Corporate Constitution (Memorandum and Articles)*

New provisions in relation to a company's constitution were introduced by the Company Law Review Act 1998. The Corporations Law provides for replaceable rules which can govern the internal management of a company. Alternatively, the company can be governed by a constitution on a combination of both.[40]

Section 140 states that the company's constitution (if any) and any replaceable rules have the effect of a contract:

- between the company and each member;
- between the company and each director and company secretary; and
- between a member and each other member.

Generally a member will be unable to enforce rights granted to him or her in the articles unless they relate to him or her in his or her capacity as a member.[41]

5.3   *The Restrictions on the Use of Certain Names*

A company may simply use its Australian company number as its name.[42] A limited public company must include the word 'Limited' or the abbreviation 'Ltd' as part of its name.[43] A no liability company must include the words 'no liability' or the abbreviation 'NL' as part of its name.[44] A proprietary company must include the word 'proprietary' or the abbreviation 'Pty' at the end of its name or immediately before 'Limited' or 'Ltd' in the case of a limited company.[45]

In order for a company to become registered by a particular name, the name must be available.[46] Section 147(1) provides that a name is available unless the identical name is:

- already reserved or registered;
- included on the national business names register; or
- a name of a kind that is declared by the regulations to be unacceptable.

Regulation 2B.6.01 classes certain names as being unacceptable because they would be misleading. This includes names that imply a connection with the Crown, Commonwealth, state, local authorities or foreign governments and names such as building society, university or stock exchange. Names that are undesirable or likely to be offensive are also unacceptable.

If a name is available, it will be reserved by the ASIC for a period of two months.[47] As the unique identifying feature is a company's

Australian company number, it does not matter that similar names may be registered. Protection in relation to a company's business reputation exists in the common law of passing off and in actions under the Trade Practices Act 1974 and also from laws protecting trade marks.

5.4   *Membership and Share Capital Requirements*

Companies need only have one member.[48] The Corporations Law itself has no minimum capital requirement. Other legislation may impose minimum capital requirements in relation to particular types of companies. Banks, for instance, are required to meet minimum capital requirements under the Banking Act 1959 (Cth).

5.5   *The Amendment of Corporate Constitution*

A company may by special resolution alter its constitution.[49] The constitution may specify a further requirement which has to be met in addition to the special resolution, in order for the alteration to take effect.[50]

An alteration to the constitution may be invalid even where the formal requirements for alteration are met. In the case of *Gambotto & Another v WCP Limited & Another*,[51] the company's articles were proposed to be changed so as to allow a shareholder who was entitled to 90 per cent or more of the company's shares to acquire compulsorily the shares of the remainder. It was conceded that the price offered for the shares was fair, but it was found that the alteration to the articles was made for an improper purpose. Mason CJ., Brennan, Deane and Dawson JJ. said:[52]

> It seems to us that, in such a case not involving an actual or effective appropriation of shares or of valuable proprietary rights attaching to shares, an alteration of the articles by special resolution regularly passed will be valid unless it is *ultra vires*, beyond any purpose contemplated by the articles or oppressive as that expression is understood in the law relating to corporations. Somewhat different considerations apply, however, in a case such as the present where what is involved is an alteration of the articles to allow an expropriation by the majority of the shares, or of valuable proprietary rights attaching to the shares of a minority. In such a case, the immediate purpose of the resolution is to confer upon the majority shareholder or shareholders power to acquire compulsorily the property of the minority shareholder or shareholders ... .
>
> Such a power could not be taken or exercised simply for the purpose of aggrandising the majority. In our view, such a power can be taken if (i) it is exercisable for a proper purpose and (ii) its exercise will not operate oppressively.

5.6   Company Registers

Pursuant to Section 168, a company is required to maintain a register of members. It will also be required to maintain a register of option holders and register of debenture holders if the company issues options or debentures. Such a register must be kept in Australia at:

- the registered office;
- the company's principal place of business;
- an office (whether of the company or of someone else) where the register is maintained; and
- another office approved by the ASIC.[53]

The company must allow anyone to inspect the registers referred to above. Members, registered option holders and registered debenture holders are entitled to inspect the register without charge. The company may make a charge, up to the prescribed amount for inspection by other persons.[54] The use to which information obtained from an inspection of a register can be put is limited by Section 177. The information cannot be used as a mailing list, unless it is relevant to the holding of shares, options or debentures, as the case may be.

6   The Internal Administration of Companies

6.1   Registered Office and Name

A company is required to have a registered office in Australia which has to be open for a minimum number of hours each day. If the company lodges the appropriate notice, the hours can be a minimum of three hours between 9 am and 5 pm.[55] The name of the company and the words 'registered office' must be affixed in a conspicuous position outside its registered office and outside every place of business.[56]

The company may have a common seal with its name (if it has one) and its Australian company number on it.[57]

6.2   The Duties, Powers and Responsibilities of Officers

Directors are subject to common law duties and officers (a word which includes directors, but has an extended meaning) are also subject to statutory duties. Duties of care, skill and diligence are imposed both at common law and under statute.[58] Traditionally, courts were reluctant to impose onerous duties of care, skill and diligence. The words of Romer J. in *Re City Equitable Fire Insurance Co.*[59] are seen as the classic exposition of the duties of directors in relation to care, skill and diligence. He said that directors must act honestly and exercise the degree of care 'an ordinary man might be expected to take in the circumstances on his own behalf'.[60] He went on to make three other general propositions:

(1) A director need not exhibit in the performance of his duties a greater degree of skill than may be reasonably expected from a person of his knowledge and experience. ... directors are not liable for mere errors of judgment. (2) A director is not bound to give continuous attention to the affairs of his company. His duties are of an intermittent nature to be performed at periodical board meetings, at meetings of any committee of the board upon which he happens to be placed. ... (3) In respect of all duties that, having regard to the exigencies of business, and the articles of association may properly be left to some other official, a director is, in the absence of grounds for suspicion, justified in trusting that official to perform such duties honestly.[61]

The modern application of these principles has recently been considered by the New South Wales Court of Appeal in *Daniels v Anderson*.[62] The issue of directors' duties arose indirectly in this case as the action was an action by the company against its auditors. The auditors, however, claimed that the directors were contributorily negligent in relation to the losses which occurred as a result of foreign exchange trading conducted by an employee. Clarke and Sheller JJA. pointed out that '[n]either the law about the duty of directors nor the law of negligence has stood still since the decision in *Re City Equitable Fire Insurance Co.*'[63]. They said:

There is no doubt reason for establishing a board which enjoys the varied wisdom of persons drawn from different backgrounds. Even so a director, whatever his or her background, has a duty greater than that of simply representing a particular field of experience. That duty involves becoming familiar with the business of the company and how it is run and ensuring that the board has available means to audit the management of the company so that it can satisfy itself that the company is being properly run. The board may be assisted by subcommittees consisting of its members, including non-executive directors ... .
    In our opinion the responsibilities of directors require that they take reasonable steps to place themselves in a position to guide and monitor the management of the company.[64]

At common law, directors are under a duty to act *bona fide* in the interests of the company as a whole and to use powers for a proper purpose.[65] An officer is subject to a statutory duty to 'act honestly in the exercise of his or her powers and the discharge of his or her office'.[66]

There is also a duty to avoid conflicts of interest which applies at common law[67] and under statute. The statutory provisions apply to employees as well as officers. The legislation prohibits the improper use of position or of information acquired by virtue of that position 'to gain, directly or indirectly, an advantage for himself or herself or for any other person or to cause detriment to the corporation'.[68] These provisions are in addition to the generally applicable provisions on insider trading.[69]

Related to these provisions are provisions designed to ensure the disclosure of material interests of directors, particularly in relation to proposed contracts with the company. Separate provisions apply to directors of proprietary companies[70] and to directors of public companies.[71] Directors of proprietary companies are required to disclose at a directors' meeting the nature of their interest in a contract or proposed contract, as soon as the relevant facts have come to the director's knowledge.[72] The same applies in relation to offices held or interests in property.[73] It is permissible for a director to make a general declaration that he or she is an officer or member of another company or firm, and is to be regarded as interested in any contract proposed or made after the date of the declaration.[74] Section 232A prohibits a director of a public company from voting or being present during the consideration of a matter where the director has a material personal interest. Section 232A(8) provides that the company's constitution may further restrict a director's entitlement to vote. Section 232A will not apply if the interest that the director has as a member is one which he or she has in common with other company members.[75] The section will not apply if the board resolves that it is satisfied that the interests of the director should not disqualify him or her from considering or voting on the matter.[76]

Chapter 2E also has an impact on the financial relationship between the company and its directors, although it also has a wider application. The object of Chapter 2E is to protect the company's resources by requiring financial benefits to related parties that could diminish or endanger those resources, or that could adversely affect those interests, to be disclosed and approved by a general meeting before they are given.[77]

The key prohibition is contained in Section 243H, which prohibits a public company, including a listed body corporate, from giving a financial benefit to a related party (directors and their immediate relatives, parent or sibling entity and a child entity), except as permitted by Divisions 4 or 5. These Divisions provide for a number of exceptions, including reasonable remuneration for an officer,[78] financial benefits to related parties which are no more favourable than would be given on arms' length terms,[79] and financial benefits approved by shareholders.[80]

Directors' duties are traditionally cast in terms of a duty owed to the company as distinct from the shareholders. Occasionally, the courts have indicated that a broader view of the company should be taken for the purposes of determining to whom directors owe their duties. This applies particularly in the case where a company is facing imminent insolvency. In such a case, the directors must have regard to the interests of creditors. Street CJ. in *Kinsela v Russell Kinsela Pty Ltd (in Liq.)*[81] said:

> But where a company is insolvent the interests of the creditors intrude. They become prospectively entitled, through the mechanism of liquidation, to displace the power of the shareholders and directors to deal with the company's assets. It is in a practical sense their assets and not the shareholders' assets that, through the medium of the company, are under the management of the directors pending either liquidation, return to solvency, or the imposition of some alternative administration.[82]

Directors are also under a statutory obligation to prevent the company from incurring a debt at a time when the company is insolvent or there are reasonable grounds for suspecting that the company is insolvent or would become so if the debt were incurred.[83] Defences are provided, the main defence being that the director took reasonable steps to prevent the company from incurring the debt.[84] It is no defence for the director to say that he or she failed to take part in the management of the company, unless that failure was due to illness or for some other good reason.[85]

6.3 Meeting Procedures

A public company is required to hold an annual general meeting at least once in every calendar year and within five months of the end of the financial year.[86] The first annual general meeting may be held within 18 months of incorporation, but it must still be held within five months of the end of the first financial year.[87] Directors are required to convene a general meeting at the request of:

- members with at least 5 per cent of the votes that may be cast at a general meeting; or
- at least 100 members who are entitled to vote at the general meeting.

The directors must convene the meeting not later than two months after the request is given to the company.[88] The request must be in writing and state any resolution proposed at the meeting.[89] If the directors fail to convene the meeting, the members may proceed to do so.[90] In addition, under Section 249F, a meeting may be convened at their own expense, by members holding at least 5 per cent of the votes that may be cast at a general meeting.

Twenty-one days' notice is required for a meeting,[91] but the meeting will be duly convened if short notice is given if the following requirements are met:

- in the case of an annual general meeting if all members entitled to attend and vote at the meeting agree beforehand; or
- in the case of other meetings, if members holding 95 per cent of the votes which may be cast agree beforehand.

Shorter notice is not allowed in relation to a resolution to:

- remove a director under Section 227;
- appoint a director in place of one so removed;
- appoint or reappoint a director who is 72 years or more of age; or
- remove an auditor under Section 329.

A company that has only one member may pass a resolution by the member, recording it and signing the record.[92]

The court has power under Section 249G to order a meeting to be convened if for any reason 'it is impracticable to call a meeting in any other way'.[93] Meeting procedure is primarily regulated by a company's constitution. Proprietary companies may prohibit the appointment of a proxy, but in relation to other companies there exists a statutory right to appoint a proxy.[94] Members that are bodies corporate are entitled to appoint a representative pursuant to Section 250D. The right of members to demand a poll is also guaranteed by the legislation.[95] Minutes of meetings are required to be kept[96] and in the case of minutes of members' meetings they must be available for inspection by members or a copy may be requested by a member.[97]

Generally any procedural irregularities will be cured by Section 1322. It provides that a proceeding under the Corporations Law is not invalidated because of any procedural irregularity unless, in the opinion of the court, it causes substantial injustice which is not capable of being remedied by an order.[98] More specifically in relation to meetings it provides that a meeting 'is not invalidated only because of the accidental omission to give notice of the meeting or the non-receipt by any person of notice of the meeting' unless the court declares the proceedings void.[99]

6.4   Audit and Accounting Rules

Pursuant to Section 327, a public company must appoint an auditor within one month of incorporation. Proprietary companies may appoint an auditor.[100]

The auditor holds office until the first annual general meeting when the company in a general meeting appoints an auditor.[101] The auditor's consent is required prior to appointment. The person or firm appointed as auditor at that time holds office until his or her death, removal from office or resignation in accordance with Section 329 or until ceasing to be capable to act under Section 324.

Section 324 sets out the qualifications for auditors as individuals and also for firms. The basic qualification is the person, or at least one member of the firm, is a registered company auditor. In addition, in order to preserve the independence of the auditor, it is required that the auditor, or a company in which he or she is a substantial shareholder, not owe more than $ 5 000 to the company, a related body corporate or an entity controlled by the company. In addition, except in the case of a proprietary company, the auditor cannot be an officer of the company, a partner or employee of an officer of the company, or a partner or employee of an employee of an officer of the company. Similar provisions apply where a firm rather than an individual is appointed as auditor.

An auditor of a company may be removed from office by resolution of the company at a general meeting of which special notice has been given.[102] After receiving a copy of the notice the auditor has seven days to make written representations and request that a copy be sent to every member who was sent a notice of meeting.[103] The auditor may also require that the representations be read at the meeting and is entitled to be heard orally.[104] Subject to the ASIC giving its consent to the auditor's resignation, the auditor may resign by written notice to the company.[105] The consent of the ASIC is not required for the resignation of an auditor of a proprietary company.[106]

An auditor of a company has a right of access at all reasonable times to the books of the company and is entitled to require from an officer of the company such information and explanations as are needed for the purposes of the audit.[107] The auditor has a duty to notify the ASIC as soon as possible, if there are reasonable grounds to suspect a contravention of the Corporations Law which will not be adequately dealt with in the auditor's report.[108]

The auditor's report is a report to members.[109] The report must state whether the financial statements are in accordance with the Corporations Law and the accounting standards.[110] The auditor is in a contractual relationship with the company and can be liable for breach of contract and also negligence to the company where the audit is carried out negligently.[111]

There have also been a number of cases where third parties who have relied on the audit report have sought to sue the auditor in negligence. The extent of this duty has not been clear. However, in *Esanda Finance Corporation Ltd v Peat Marwick Hungerfords*,[112] the High Court was called on to consider the extent of an auditor's duty to a third party in relation to the audit of a company's accounts. Esanda was a financier which entered into a number of transactions with a company called Excel, relying on the company's audited accounts. It sued the auditor claiming damages for pure economic loss resulting from the auditor's negligence in connection with the audit of Excel's accounts. The Supreme Court of South Australia struck out certain paragraphs of the statement of claim on the basis that they did not disclose a cause of action. These paragraphs included references to the Australian Accounting Standards, particularly AAS5 which takes into consideration who are likely to be the prime users of financial statements. It was also pleaded that the auditor ought reasonably to have foreseen that Esanda might rely on those accounts. The High Court held that in an action for negligence occasioning economic loss, suffered as a result of a statement made or advice given, it was not sufficient that it be shown that the loss was foreseeable. Something more was required and this could arise in a number of ways. Brennan CJ. quoted[113] from the judgment of Gibbs CJ., Mason, Wilson and Dawson JJ. in *San Sebastian Pty Ltd v The Minister*,[114] where they said in relation to the maker of the statement coming under a duty of care:

> He may warrant the correctness of what he says or assume responsibility for its correctness. He may invite the recipient to act on the basis of the information or advice, or intend to induce the recipient to act in a particular way. He may actually have an interest in the recipient so acting.[115]

Brennan CJ.[116] also referred to the following statement of Lord Bridge of Harwich in the leading English case of *Caparo Industries Plc v Dickman*:[117]

> The salient feature of all these cases is that the defendant giving advice or information was fully aware of the nature of the transaction which the plaintiff had in contemplation, knew that the advice or information would be communicated to him directly or indirectly and knew that it was very likely that the plaintiff would rely on that advice or information in deciding whether or not to engage in the transaction in contemplation.

McHugh J. referred to a number of policy justifications for the decision. He said:

> It is by no means certain that the demands of corrective justice require auditors rather than these sophisticated creditors and investors to absorb the losses that flow from lending or investing in the auditor's client. Auditors can have only a vague idea as to the potential loss that may flow from the failure to detect fraud or error in the affairs of the client being audited. The audited client can reproduce and disseminate the information from an audit at little cost to many persons including groups of potential creditors and investors. If these persons were owed a duty of care, the auditors' liability would effectively be indeterminate.[118]

He also made reference to the fact that in many cases it is 'the client's conduct [which] is the primary cause of the plaintiff's loss; the auditor's role is secondary'.[119]

Part 2M.3 of the Corporations Law deals with accounts. It applies to the following types of companies:

- disclosing entities[120] (disclosing entities are defined in Section 111AC which includes listed companies in the definition). Listed disclosing entities will generally be required by the securities exchange on which they are listed to advise the security exchange of information which is not generally available but which would have a material effect on the price of the shares if it were available. If this is the case, Section 1001A makes it an offence under the Corporations Law for the company to fail to notify the securities exchange of that information and Section 1001B applies in the case of unlisted companies and imposes upon them a requirement to notify the ASIC of material matters as they arise.
- public companies;[121]
- large proprietary companies;[122]
- small proprietary companies if foreign controlled and the companies' profits which are not included by financial reports lodged with the ASIC by the foreign company[123] or if directed by shareholders under Section 293 or the ASIC under Section 294; and
- registered schemes which are managed investment schemes.[124]

A company has an obligation to keep correct financial records so as to enable true and fair financial statements of the company to be prepared and audited.[125] There is an obligation to retain financial records for a seven-year period.[126] The directors can decide where financial records are to be kept, but if they are kept outside of Australia, they must also keep within Australia statements and records which would enable the preparation of true and fair financial statements.[127]

The financial statements must give a true and fair view of the financial position and performance of the company and, where relevant, the consolidated entity.[128] Financial statements must comply with the requirements of Schedule 5 to the regulations.[129] In addition, they must comply with the accounting standards.[130]

In relation to the end of financial year financial statements, the company directors are required to make a declaration under Section 295(4):

- that the financial statements comply with the accounting standards;
- that they give a true and fair view;
- whether there are reasonable grounds to believe that the company will be able to pay its debts as they become due; and;
- whether the financial statements comply with the Corporations Law.

The directors' report must contain the matters set out in Sections 299 and 300. The following information is required:

- a review of operations and results of operations;
- significant changes in the entity's state of affairs;
- principal activities;
- matters which have arisen since the end of the financial year, which would would affect operations, results or the entity's state of affairs in future years;
- likely developments of the entity's operations in future years;
- details of performance in relation to significant environmental regulations, where applicable;
- details of dividends and distributions;
- names of directors;
- details of options issued to directors as part of their remuneration;
- details of shares or interests issued as a result of the exercise of such an option; and
- indemnities given or insurance premiums paid for an officer or auditor.

Further information is required to be given by public companies under Section 300A. Section 317 requires the financial report, the directors' report, and the auditor's report to be laid before the annual general meeting.

6.5   *The Annual Return and Other Registers*

A company must lodge an annual return with the ASIC by 31 January each year unless the ASIC agrees to a different lodgement date.[131]

6.6   *Shareholder Protection Rules*

A member may apply to the court for an order where he or she believes that:

(i) that the affairs of the company are being conducted in a manner that is oppressive or unfairly prejudicial to, or unfairly discriminatory against a member or members, or in a manner that is contrary to the interests of the members as a whole; or

(ii) that an act or omission, or a proposed act or omission, by or on behalf of the company, or a proposed resolution of a class of members, was or would be oppressive or unfairly prejudicial to, or unfairly discriminatory against, a member or members or was or would be contrary to the interests of the members as a whole.[132]

The ASIC may also bring an application where it has undertaken an investigation.[133]

The phrase 'affairs of the company' is given a wide meaning by Section 53. Oppression has been defined at common law.[134] The phrase 'unfairly prejudicial to, or unfairly discriminatory against' encompasses conduct that might not be regarded as oppression. The meaning of these terms was considered in *Wayde v New South Wales Rugby League Ltd.*[135] In that case, the Rugby League decided to exclude the Western Suburbs football team from the competition. Brennan J. said:

It is not necessarily unfair for directors in good faith to advance one of the objects of the company to the prejudice of a member where the advancement of the object necessarily entails prejudice to that member or discrimination against him. *Prima facie* it is for the directors and not for the court to decide whether the furthering of a corporate object which is inimical to a member's interests should prevail over those interests or whether some balance should be struck between them .... . The test of unfairness is objective .... . The court must determine whether reasonable directors, possessing any special skill, knowledge or acumen possessed by the directors and having in mind the importance of furthering the corporate objective on the one hand and the disadvantage, disability or burden which their decision will impose on a member on the other, would have decided that it was unfair to make that decision.[136]

If the application is successful, the court may, subject to Section 246AA(4) make such an order as it thinks fit, including, but not limited to, a range of orders specified in Section 246AA(4).

6.7   *The Relationship Between Management and Shareholders*

The power of management is generally vested in the board of directors who in carrying out this function cannot be effectively controlled or interfered with by the shareholders in a general meeting. The ultimate sanction is to vote the directors out or to amend the constitution. Section 226A provides that the business of the company is to be managed by the directors who:

> may exercise all the powers of the company except any powers that this Law or the company's constitution (if any) requires the company to exercise in general meeting.

It flows from this that it is the company which is the proper plaintiff to take action in relation to any wrongs done to the company. This is the rule in *Foss v Harbottle*.[137] The principle was described by Lord Davey in *Burland v Earle*[138] where he said:

> It is an elementary principle of the law relating to joint stock companies that the court will not interfere with the internal management of companies acting within their powers, and in fact has no jurisdiction to do so. Again, it is clear law that in order to redress a wrong done to the company, or to recover moneys or damages alleged to be due to the company, the action should *prima facie* be brought by the company itself.

There are recognized exceptions to this rule, the most important applies where there is fraud on the minority. Where the interests of the majority are being improperly advanced at the expense of the minority, a minority shareholder may take a derivative action. In *Australasian Agricultural Co. v Oatmont Pty Ltd*,[139] Mildren J. said:

> [W]here the directors are acting in abuse of their powers by knowingly or recklessly acting contrary to the general law, as a result of which the company sustains a loss, this breach of the directors' fiduciary duty could well give rise to a derivative action. In such an action the individual shareholder would seek to bring the action the company has vested in it against the directors for the damages suffered to the company for breach of the fiduciary duty ... . In such a case, the company is a proper party, and if the action is successful, judgment is given in favour of the company.

Other exceptions to the rule in *Foss v Harbottle* include where:

- there is an infringement of a shareholder's personal rights;[140]
- the company is acting *ultra vires*, although this is now dealt with by Section 125(2);
- a special resolution was required, but only an ordinary resolution was obtained;[141] and
- the interests of justice require it, in relation to this exception Ipp J. said in *Biala v Mallina Holdings Ltd*:[142]

> I consider it to be desirable to allow a minority shareholder to bring a derivative claim where the justice of the case clearly demands that such a claim be brought, irrespective of whether the claim falls within the confines of the established exceptions.

The introduction of a statutory derivative action has been recommended by the Companies and Securities Law Review Committee in its report, *Enforcement of the Duties of Directors and Officers of a Company by Means of a Statutory Derivative Action* (November 1990), and by the Companies and Securities Advisory Committee in its report, *Report on a Statutory Derivative Action* (July 1993). The Commonwealth Attorney-General's Department also issued a paper in 1995, *Proceedings On Behalf of A Company (Statutory Derivative Action) Draft Provisions and Commentary.*

6.8 *Corporate Financial Transactions: Charges, Prospectuses, Share Buy Backs and Receivers*

The Australian Register of Company Charges was established under Section 265 of the Corporations Law. Details of registrable charges, which include floating charges, are required to be lodged with the ASIC within 45 days of the creation of the charge.[143] The court does have the power to extend the time for lodgment, but only where the failure was accidental or due to inadvertence and is not of such a nature as to prejudice the position of creditors or shareholders.[144] Section 280 sets out the order of priorities which applies as between registrable charges. Essentially the time of registration determines the order of priorities, but this will be altered if the holder of the first registered charge had notice of an unregistered charge or a subsequently registered charge at the time when the first registered charge was created. If both charges are registrable but unregistered, the time of creation determines the order of priority. A floating charge is at risk of losing priority to a later registered fixed charge if the fixed charge is registered before the floating charge crystallizes. This result can be avoided if it is made a term of the floating charge that creation of a subsequent fixed charge is prohibited and a notice to that effect has been lodged with the ASIC prior to the registration of the fixed charge.[145]

All offers, invitations and issues of securities are required to be made pursuant to a prospectus which complies with the Corporations Law.[146] This does not apply to offers, invitations and issues which are excluded.[147] Generally prospectuses are required to be registered, although there are exceptions to this (the most significant exception relates to listed securities).[148]

The requirements in relation to the contents of prospectuses are set out in Sections 1021 and 1022. A prospectus shall:

> contain all such information as investors and their professional advisers would reasonably require, and reasonably expect to find in the prospectus, for the purposes of making an informed assessment of:
>
> (a)   the assets and liabilities, financial position, profits and losses, and prospects of the corporation; and
> (b)   the rights attaching to the securities.[149]

A company may only reduce its share capital or give financial assistance for the purchase of its shares where there is no material prejudice to the company's ability to pay its creditors.[150] This is consistent with the principle of capital maintenance. Share buy backs are permitted in certain circumstances and are subject to certain safeguards. Companies are only permitted to buy back a maximum of 10 per cent of their shares in a 12-month period.[151] The particular provisions which apply to a share scheme buy back depend upon the type of buy back.

An equal access scheme is defined in Section 257B(2) as one which relates only to ordinary shares, where the offer is for the same percentage of each shareholder's shares and the offer is on the same terms. If the 10 per cent limit in a 12-month period is exceeded, an ordinary resolution of the general meeting is required to approve it.[152]

An on-market buy back is defined in Section 9 as a buy back by a listed company in the ordinary course of trading on the stock exchange. No resolution is necessary unless the 10 per cent limit in a 12-month period is exceeded.[153]

An employee share scheme buy backs is defined in Section 9 as a scheme where the purpose is the acquisition of shares by employees. Such schemes must be approved by the general meeting.

A selective buy back is defined in Section 9 as one which does not meet the requirement to be an equal access scheme, an on-market buy back or an employee share scheme buy back. A selective scheme buy back must be approved by either a special resolution passed at a general meeting with no votes cast by persons whose shares are proposed to be bought back, or by a unanimous resolution of ordinary shareholders at a general meeting.[154] Certain other procedural requirements must be met.

Receivers may be appointed by the court[155] or, more commonly, by private appointment usually pursuant to the terms of a charge. In order to qualify for appointment as a receiver, the person must be a registered liquidator and not be a mortgagee, auditor or officer of the company or an officer of a mortgagee or a related body corporate.[156]

A receiver appointed by the court is an officer of the court. The privately appointed receiver is an officer of the company and is subject to the duties in Section 232. A receiver who is privately appointed will usually be appointed on terms making him or her an agent of the company rather than an agent of the appointor. Section 420 sets out the powers of both court appointed and privately appointed receivers, but these powers are subject to any limitations imposed by the court or the instrument of appointment. Section 420A places receivers under a duty to take all reasonable care when exercising a power of sale to obtain the market value or 'the best price that is reasonably obtainable, having regard to the circumstances existing when the property is sold'.

7   The External Administration of Companies

7.1   *The Rules Regarding Arrangements and Reconstructions*

Since the introduction of the voluntary administration procedure, schemes of arrangement have become less significant at least in relation to insolvent companies. The voluntary administration procedure is less complicated and less costly. Schemes involving reconstructions and amalgamations are more likely to continue to occur than those involving a moratorium or compromise which could be achieved under the voluntary administration procedure.[157]

Generally, reconstructions and amalgamations will not breach the takeover provisions of the Corporations Law because of Section 625, but the court is directed not to approve a scheme of arrangement where it is entered into for the purposes of avoiding the takeover provisions.[158]

There are several stages involved in a scheme of arrangement. A report on the company's affairs needs to be prepared together with an explanatory statement on the proposed scheme. The approval of the court to call a meeting of creditors to consider the scheme must be obtained. If approval is obtained, the meetings of members and creditors are held. If those meetings approve the scheme, it must go back to court again for approval of the draft scheme document. The scheme will be binding only if approved by the required majority of creditors and members and also by the court. It becomes effective when a copy of the court order approving it is lodged with the ASIC.[159]

7.2   *Voluntary Administration and Corporate Rescue Provisions*

The voluntary administration procedure is a relatively new form of insolvency administration and was introduced by the Corporate Law Reform Act 1992. The procedure is founded on the recommendations of the Harmer Report and has similarities to the Chapter 11 procedure in the United States and the administration order procedure in the United Kingdom. The objectives are set out in Section 435A which provides:

> The object of this part is to provide for the business, property and affairs of an insolvent company to be administered in a way that:
>
> (a)   maximises the chances of the company, or as much as possible of its business, continuing in existence; or
> (b)   if it is not possible for the company or its business to continue in existence – results in a better return for the company's creditors and members than would result from an immediate winding up of the company.

The administrator can be appointed by the company under Section 436A if in the opinion of the directors voting for the resolution the company is insolvent or is likely to become insolvent at some future time. The directors need to be satisfied that at the time of the resolution the company is, or is likely to become at some time in the future, unable to pay its debts as they fall due.

One reason that directors may take action to place the company in voluntary administration is to avoid any potential liability for insolvent trading under Section 588G. Section 588G places a positive obligation on directors to prevent insolvent trading. It is a defence to an action for insolvent trading if the director establishes that he or she took all reasonable steps to prevent the company from incurring the debt. One of the things the court is directed to have regard to is any action the director took with a view to appointing an administrator.[160] Similarly directors can be made personally liable for unremitted group tax but again personal liability can be avoided if an administrator is appointed.[161]

The directors' right to appoint an administrator is lost if the company is already being wound up.[162] Again this encourages the directors to take prompt action. The administrator can be appointed by a liquidator or provisional liquidator under Section 436B. Again the person must form the opinion that the company is insolvent or is likely to become insolvent at some time in the future. The liquidator or provisional liquidator will require the court's leave to appoint himself or herself as administrator. The advantage of the liquidator becoming administrator is in the cost saving, but this has to be weighed against a potential conflict of interest.[163]

The administrator can be appointed by a person who is entitled to enforce a charge over the whole or a substantial part of a company's property under Section 436C. This right is lost if the company is already being wound up. The right of a chargee to appoint an administrator only arises where the charge has become enforceable and usually this will mean where the right to appoint a receiver has arisen. No appointment of an administrator can be made if the company is already under administration.[164]

The administrator must consent to act,[165] must be a registered liquidator[166] and cannot be appointed if there is too close a connection with the company.[167] The appointment of an administrator cannot be revoked,[168] although he or she can be removed at the first meeting of creditors and the ASIC or a creditor may apply for an order to remove the administrator.

The administrator's first task is to convene a meeting of creditors within five business days of the commencement of the administration.[169] The purpose of the meeting is to determine whether to appoint a committee of creditors. The function of a committee of creditors is to consult with the administrator.[170] The administrator must give two business days' written notice to as many of the company's creditors as reasonably practicable as well as giving notice through a national newspaper or newspapers in states where the company carries on business. There is no discretion for the court to extend the time for the holding of this first meeting, but an administrator may apply for relief under Section 1322 if he or she has failed to comply strictly with the procedures.[171]

The creditors have the right at that first meeting to remove the administrator and to appoint someone else. Where a creditor believes that the outcome of voting on a resolution was determined by the votes of 'related creditors', that creditor may make an application to the court for an appropriate order[172] In addition, any creditor has the right to apply to the court for the cancellation of any resolution passed by the casting vote of the chairperson.[173] Pursuant to Section 437A(1), while a company is under administration, the administrator:

- has control of the company's business, property and affairs;
- may carry on that business and manage that property and those affairs;

- may terminate or dispose of all or part of that business, and may dispose of any of that property; and
- may perform any function and exercise any power that the company or any of its officers could perform or exercise if the company were not under administration.

The administrator may also seek directions from the court under Section 447D. In carrying out the functions of administrator, the administrator acts as agent of the company pursuant to Section 437B. The administrator incurs a personal liability for debts incurred in the performance of his or her functions under Section 443A, but has a right of indemnity out of the company's assets under Section 443D. While the company is under administration, company officers cannot exercise any power except with the written approval of the administrator.[174] Section 437D provides that any transaction affecting the property of the company entered into during the administration is void, unless:

- the administrator entered into it on the company's behalf;
- the administrator consented to it in writing before it was entered into; or
- it was entered into under an order of the court.[175]

There is an exception for payments made by an Australian bank out of an account of the company in good faith and in the ordinary course of business, provided that the bank has not received notice of the administration. The court also has power to make a validating order under Sub-section (4). Section 438A provides that as soon as practicable after the administration of a company begins the administrator must:

- investigate the company's business, property, affairs and financial circumstances; and
- form an opinion about whether it would be in the interests of the company's creditors:
  - to execute a deed of company arrangement,
  - for the administration to end, or
  - for the company to be wound up.

Directors must deliver up the company books to the administrator as soon as practicable, and within seven days of commencement of the administration must give the administrator a statement about the company's business, property, affairs and financial circumstances. They are also required to assist the administrator as may be reasonably required.[176] Under Sub-section (4), a director is entitled not to comply if he or she has a reasonable excuse, for example legal professional privilege.

If during the administrator's investigation of the company's affairs it appears that a company officer or member may have been guilty of an offence in relation to the company or the other matters listed in Section 438D, the administrator must lodge a report about the matter and assist the ASIC. The essential feature of a voluntary administration is the moratorium provisions.

Under Section 440D, no court proceedings against the company or its property may be begun or proceeded with except with the administrator's consent or the court's leave. This does not apply to criminal proceedings. Likewise, no enforcement process can be begun or proceeded with in the case where judgment has already been obtained.[177]

Section 440B provides that during the administration of a company a person cannot enforce a charge on property of the company except with the administrator's written consent or with leave of the court. Section 440C makes a similar provision preventing an owner or lessor of property that is used or occupied by, or is otherwise in the possession of, the company, from taking possession of the property or otherwise recovering it.[178] Sections 440B and 440C need to be read subject to Division 7, which provides protection from the general moratorium provisions to certain creditors.

The following persons are protected from the moratorium provisions:

- secured creditors who have a charge on the whole or a substantial part of the property of the company who enforce that charge prior to the appointment of the administrator or within ten business days of receiving notice of appointment (the decision period);[179]
- secured creditors who have commenced enforcement of their security prior to the appointment of an administrator[180] (this protects a creditor who has taken action from being thwarted by a company subsequently appointing an administrator; nevertheless a company may still appoint an administrator when it is in default but the secured creditor has not yet taken steps to enforce the charge);
- a creditor who has a charge over perishable property (such a chargee may enforce the charge at any time during the administration);[181]
- lessors and owners of property in the possession of the company under administration, provided that steps have been taken to repossess the property before the administration began;[182] and
- lessors and owners of perishable property (such property may be repossessed at any time during the administration).[183]

On application by the administrator, the court may order a chargee under Sections 441B or 441C who has taken a step or exercised a power in relation to property for the purpose of enforcing a charge on that property, not to perform specified powers except to the extent that the court permits. The court may only make such an order if it is satisfied that what the administrator proposes to do during the administration will adequately protect the interests of the chargee.[184] The administrator can also apply to the court to restrict the rights of an owner or lessor, subject to the same proviso about the protection of their rights.[185]

Where the company in administration has entered into an agreement prior to the administration, pursuant to which the company has the right to use, occupy or be in possession of property of which someone else is the owner or lessor, the administrator has seven days within which to decide whether or not to continue the use of the property. Unless the administrator gives a notice in accordance with Section 443B(3) within seven days of the beginning of the administration, the administrator will be personally liable for the amounts due under the agreement which are attributable to a period arising thereafter and throughout which the company continues to use, occupy or be in possession of the property, and the administration continues, unless the court excuses the administrator from liability.[186]

Within five business days of the end of the convening period, 21 or 28 days from the beginning of the administration (depending on the date the administration commences), a meeting of creditors must be held to decide whether the company will execute a deed of company arrangement or end the administration or wind the company up.[187] Unlike the first meeting of creditors, the court has power to extend the time for the holding of this meeting.[188]

If a deed of arrangement is to be entered into, the administrator shall prepare the deed.[189] It is required to be executed within 21 days of the end of the meeting of creditors.[190] A deed of company arrangement binds all creditors of the company as regards claims arising on or before the day specified in the deed (usually the date the company went into administration).[191] The deed also binds the company, its officers, members and the deed's administrator.[192]

Section 444E is similar to the moratorium provisions and protects the company's property while the deed is in force. The court has the power to limit the rights of a secured creditor or lessor. If such an application is not made, they remain free to enforce their security or repossess their property. Termination of the deed occurs when the court makes an order under Section 445D terminating the deed, when the company's creditors pass a resolution at a meeting convened under Section 445F or if the deed specifies the circumstances in which it is to terminate and those circumstances exist.[193]

7.3 *The Company Winding Up Rules, Tests for Insolvency, Grounds for Winding Up and Mechanisms for Initiating Insolvency Proceedings*

Where it is proposed that a company be wound up voluntarily, the directors may make a declaration of solvency if they are of the opinion that the company will be able to pay its debts in full within 12 months of the commencement of the winding up.[194] It is an offence for a director to make a declaration of solvency without having reasonable grounds for his or her opinion. If the company is unable to pay its debts in full within a year, there is a presumption that the director did not have reasonable grounds for making the declaration.[195] The declaration needs to have a statement of affairs attached to it and it needs to be lodged with the ASIC.[196] A company may be wound up voluntarily if the company so resolves by special resolution.[197] The company in a general meeting appoints a liquidator. If the liquidator at any time forms the opinion that the company will be unable to pay its debts, he or she has three options:

- to apply for the company to be wound up in insolvency;
- to appoint an administrator; or
- to convene a meeting of the company's creditors.[198]

If an application for winding up in insolvency has already been filed, or the court has ordered that the company be wound up in insolvency, a company can only resolve to be wound up voluntarily with the leave of the court.[199] There can be a transition from voluntary administration to voluntary winding up in certain circumstances.[200] There can also be a transition from a members' voluntary winding up to a creditors' voluntary winding up.[201] If there is no declaration of solvency, the winding up proceeds as a creditors' voluntary winding up from the outset. A meeting of creditors is called pursuant to Section 497. The creditors may nominate a different liquidator, subject to a right of application to the court by a member or director for confirmation of the appointment which was made by the company.[202]

The general grounds on which a company can be compulsorily wound up by the court are set out in Section 461. These include where:

- the company has by special resolution resolved that it be wound up by the court;
- the company does not commence business within one year from its incorporation or suspends its business for a whole year; and

- unless the company is a wholly owned subsidiary of another company or of a recognized company or is a proprietary company, the number of members falls below five.

These grounds are technical. Paragraphs (e), (f) and (g) essentially mirror the provisions of Section 246AA which protect minority shareholders. There is a wider range of potential applicants for winding up under Section 461 than under Section 246AA.[203] Paragraph (h) makes it a ground for winding the company up if the ASIC has prepared a report that the company cannot pay its debts and should be wound up or it is in the interests of the public, members or creditors that the company should be wound up. Paragraph (j) makes a similar provision in the case of an application by the Australian Prudential Regulation Authority: it is a ground for winding up where the court is of the opinion that it is in the interests of the public, members or creditors that the company should be wound up. There is a further ground in paragraph (k) where the court is of the opinion that it is just and equitable that the company be wound up. This ground has generally been used in two categories of cases. One is where there has been a failure of the objects or substratum[204] and the other is where the company is similar to a partnership, in which case winding up will be ordered in circumstances where, under partnership law, the partnership would be dissolved.[205]

The most common ground for winding up is that the company is insolvent.[206] Solvency is defined in Section 95A: '(1) A person is solvent if, and only if, the person is able to pay all the person's debts, as and when they become due and payable'. This provides a cash flow definition of insolvency. However, regard should also be had to Section 459D, which states that the court may also take into account a contingent or prospective liability of the company when determining whether or not the company is solvent. In most cases an applicant will be able to rely on a presumption of insolvency without having to prove independently that the company is insolvent in terms of Section 95A. Presumptions of insolvency are set out in Section 459C(2), which provides that:

The court must presume that the company is insolvent if, during or after the 3 months ending on the day when the application was made:

(a)   the company failed (as defined by s 459F) to comply with a statutory demand; or
(b)   the execution or other process issued on a judgment, decree or order of an Australian court in favour of a creditor of the company was returned wholly or partially unsatisfied; or

(c)   a receiver, or receiver and manager, of property of the company
      was appointed under a power contained in an instrument relat-
      ing to a floating charge on such property; or
(d)   an order was made for the appointment of such a receiver, or
      receiver and manager, for the purposes of enforcing such a charge;
      or
(e)   a person entered into possession, or assumed control, of such
      property for such a purpose; or
(f)   a person was appointed so to enter into possession or assume
      control (whether as agent for the chargee or for the company).

The statutory demand procedure is commonly relied on as creating the presumption of insolvency. Pursuant to Section 459E, a person
may serve a statutory demand on a company where there is a debt or
debts which are due and payable, amounting to at least the statutory
minimum of $ 2 000. The demand must require the company to ei-
ther pay the debt or to secure or compound it to the creditor's
reasonable satisfaction within 21 days of the service of the demand.
The demand must also be in writing, in the prescribed form and
signed by or on behalf of the creditor.[207]
Technical defects in the demand are to be ignored unless they
cause substantial injustice.[208] If the defect relates to an overstatement
of the debt, Section 459H provides a formula for determining whether
the demand should be set aside. It should not be set aside if the
amount admitted as owing is above the statutory minimum. Pursuant to Section 459G, the company is given the opportunity to apply
to set aside a statutory demand. This application may only be made
within 21 days of service of the demand. The court has no power to
extend this time limit, although the company may still defend the
application for winding up.[209]

7.4   The Protection of Creditors and the Ranking of Claims

Pursuant to Section 568(1) a liquidator may disclaim property which
consists of:

- land burdened with onerous covenants;
- shares;
- property that is unprofitable or is not readily saleable;
- property that may give rise to a liability to pay money or some
  other onerous obligation;
- property where it is reasonable to expect that the costs, charges
  and expenses that would be incurred in realizing the property
  would exceed the proceeds of realizing the property;
- a contract, whether or not:

- except in the case of a contract – the liquidator has tried to sell the property, has taken possession of it or exercised an act of ownership in relation to it, or
- in the case of a contract – the company or the liquidator has tried to assign, or has exercised rights in relation to, the contract or any property to which it relates.

Except in the case of an unprofitable contract or a lease of land, the liquidator requires the court's leave to disclaim.[210] Pursuant to Section 569, where in the six months prior to the commencement of winding up a creditor has taken action to institute proceedings to attach a debt due to a company or to enforce a charge or a charging order against property of the company, the creditor is required to pay to the liquidator that amount received as a result of the execution, attachment or other action. Floating charges are void against the liquidator if they are created within six months of the relation back day (the commencement of winding up) except in so far as it secures an advance paid in consideration for the charge or associated amounts, such as interest.[211]

Division 2 of Part 5.7B creates a number of categories of transactions which are voidable.[212] The first category is a transaction which meets the definition of an insolvent transaction in Section 588FC and an unfair preference in Section 588FA. The relation back period for such a transaction is six months.[213] A transaction is insolvent if the company was insolvent at the time the transaction was entered into or at the time an act was done to give effect to the transaction, or if the company becomes insolvent as a result of entering into the transaction.[214] Whether or not a transaction is an unfair preference is a question of fact. The question to be asked is whether the transaction results in the creditor receiving more from the company than would be the case if the transaction were set aside and the creditor were to prove for the debt in a winding up.

The second category is a transaction which meets the definition of an insolvent transaction and of an uncommercial transaction. The relation back period is two years.[215] An uncommercial transaction is one which 'a reasonable person in the company's circumstances would not have entered into' having regard to the relative benefits and detriments.[216] The third category is one which is an insolvent transaction and a related entity is party to it. The relation back period is four years.[217] The fourth category is a transaction which is insolvent and is entered into for the purposes of 'defeating, delaying or interfering with, the rights of any or all of its creditors on a winding up of the company'. The relation back period is ten years.[218]

The fifth category is that of an unfair loan. The relation back period is unlimited.[219] An unfair loan is defined in Section 588FD as a loan where the interest rates or the charges were extortionate when the loan was made or have become extortionate since, because of a variation. Regard must be had to the risk and other factors listed in Section 588FD(2) in determining whether the interest or charges are extortionate.

Section 553 provides that:

> all debts or claims against the company (present or future, certain or contingent, ascertained or sounding only in damages), being debts or claims the circumstances giving rise to which occurred before the relevant date, are admissible to proof against the company.

Debts owed to members, in their capacity as members, are not admissible to proof unless all amounts that the member is liable to pay as a member have been paid.[220] Payment of debts owed to members in their capacity as members, is postponed until all other debts are paid.[221] Penalties and fines are not generally admissible to proof.[222] Where there have been mutual dealings between the company and the other party, Section 553C provides that there shall be a set-off of the amounts. The balance is then admissible to proof against the company or payable as the case may be. The benefit of Section 553C is lost if the person dealing with the company had notice of the fact that the company was insolvent at the time of giving credit.[223] Section 554A lays down a procedure to be followed to calculate the debt, where the debt does not bear a certain value. A secured creditor may prove for the debt if the security is surrendered. Alternatively, the balance can be proved for in the event that the security realizes insufficient funds to repay the debt. Procedures also exist for valuing the security if it has not yet been realized.[224]

Pursuant to Section 555, 'all debts and claims proved in a winding up rank equally and, if the property of the company is insufficient to meet them in full, they shall be paid proportionately'. This is subject to other provisions. In particular, Section 556 provides that certain categories of debt must be paid in priority to other unsecured debts. These debts fall broadly into two categories. The first is the expense of winding up or administration and the second is the amount due to employees.[225] Employee claims also enjoy a priority over a floating charge.[226] Third parties with claims against the company for which the company held liability insurance are in a special category. The amounts received from the insurance company, less any expenses are to be paid to the third party in priority to all payments, including those in Section 556. Interest on admitted debts or claims is payable, but payment is postponed until all other debts are paid.[227]

8   Takeover Rules

8.1   *Introduction to Company Takeover Rules*

Once the takeover threshold is reached, the Corporations Law regulates the way in which takeovers may operate for the purpose of protecting the target company's shareholders.

8.2   *Takeover Thresholds*

The key provision in relation to takeovers is Section 615, which provides that where a person would become entitled to more than 20 per cent of the voting shares, the acquisition must occur in accordance with Chapter 6. The same applies where a person is entitled to more than 20 per cent but less than 90 per cent, any increase will be subject to Chapter 6. The concept of 'entitlement to shares' is a broad one in order to minimize the possibility of avoidance. The definitions of 'relevant interest' and 'associate' are also appropriate in this context.

Creeping takeovers of not more than 3 per cent of voting shares in a six-month period are permitted as an exception.[228] Certain other specific exceptions apply.[229] Apart from these exceptions, there are generally two ways in which a takeover is permitted to proceed. One is by way of a takeover scheme[230] and the other is by takeover announcement.[231]

8.3   *Disclosure Requirements and Shareholder Protection*

Under a takeover scheme, an offer is made which must comply with Section 638 and it must be accompanied by a Part A statement and, if available, the Part B statement. The Part A statement must have been served on the target company between 14 and 28 days before the offer was made.[232] The offer and Part A statement are required to be registered.[233] The requirements of the Part A statement are set out in Section 750. The purpose of the Part A statement is to provide disclosure of all information relevant to the offer, including information about the offeror, its interest in the target company, details of how the bid is funded and its intentions in relation to the target company. The Part B statement is provided by the target company to the offeror and must comply with Section 647 and Section 750. It is to be given within 14 days of receipt of the Part A statement. Copies must be lodged with the ASIC and also served on the securities exchange if the target company is listed.[234] The main purpose of the Part B statement is for the directors to make a recommendation in relation to the offer and to disclose details of the directors' interests in both the target company and the offeror. The directors need not make a recommendation in relation to the offer, but should state the reasons for not wishing to make a recommendation.[235]

A takeover announcement occurs where a person or persons causes a dealer to make an announcement at an official meeting that:

> during the period of one month beginning on the first trading day of the company's home exchange after the end of 24 days after the day of the announcement, the dealer offers, on behalf of that person or those persons, to acquire, at a cash price per share specified in the announcement, all shares in that class in respect of which offers made by the announcement are accepted in accordance with section 675.[236]

Similar requirements in relation to disclosure, apply in relation to a takeover announcement. The Part A and B statement being replaced by Part C and D statements.[237]

8.4   The Role of Lawyers, Experts and the Regulator in Takeovers

Part B and Part D statements may refer to an expert's report only if that person has consented to its inclusion in the statement.[238] An independent expert's report will be required in relation to a takeover offer in certain circumstances specified in Section 648. They are where:

- the offeror is already entitled to at least 30 per cent of the voting shares in the target corporation;
- the offeror is or includes a director who is a director of the target corporation; or
- where the offeror includes a corporation, and a director of the target corporation is a director of the offeror.

The expert's report must contain the matters set out in Section 648(2). Particulars must be supplied of the nature of the relationship of the expert with the offeror, with the target company or with an associate of the offeror or the target.

8.5   The Mechanisms for the Review of Takeover Activity

Even though an acquisition of shares contravenes Section 615, the acquisition is not invalid.[239] Where it appears to the ASIC that unacceptable circumstances have, or may have, occurred in relation to an acquisition of shares, or as a result of conduct engaged in by a person in relation to shares, in; or the affairs of a company, the ASIC may apply to the Corporations and Securities Panel for a declaration in relation to the acquisition or conduct. Unacceptable circumstances, are defined in Section 732(1) as occurring if:

(a) the shareholders and directors of a company did not know the identity of a person who proposed to acquire a substantial interest in the company; or

(b) the shareholders and directors of a company did not have a reasonable time in which to consider a proposal under which a person would acquire a substantial interest in the company; or

(c) the shareholders and directors of a company were not supplied with enough information for them to assess the merits of a proposal under which a person would acquire a substantial interest in the company; or

(d) the shareholders of a company did not all have reasonable grounds and equal opportunities to participate in any benefits, or to become entitled to participate in any benefits, accruing whether directly or indirectly and whether immediately or in the future, to any shareholder or to any associate of a shareholder, in connection with the acquisition or proposed acquisition, by any person of a substantial interest in the company; or

(e) a company carries out, or proposes to carry out, a buy-back that is unreasonable having regard to:

  (i) the effect of the buy-back on the control of that company or of another company; and

  (ii) the fact that the disclosure and other procedural safeguards of this Chapter do not apply to the buy-back because of section 632A.

Where the Panel makes a declaration that the acquisition is unacceptable or that conduct is unacceptable, the Panel, on the application of the ASIC, may make one or more of the orders specified in Section 734(2), including:

> any order that it thinks necessary or desirable to protect the rights or interests of any person affected by the acquisition or conduct or to ensure, as far as possible, that a takeover scheme or takeover announcement, or a proposed takeover scheme or proposed takeover announcement, in relation to shares in the company proceeds in the manner in which it would have proceeded if that acquisition had not taken place or that conduct had not been engaged in.[240]

Contravention of a Panel order may result in the ASIC making an application to the court and the court may, under Section 736, make such order or orders as it considers necessary for the purpose of securing compliance with the Panel's order. The court itself is given powers under Part 6.10. The court has power to make such orders as it thinks just where there has been a contravention of Section 615. Specific powers are given to the court in the event that the offeror does not send the offer within 28 days of the service of the Part A statement.[241] The court also has power to protect the interests of person affected by a takeover scheme or announcement where there is a contravention of Chapter 6. The court may make orders where there are agreements providing benefits for directors of the target company which are unfair or unconscionable.[242] The court is also given power to excuse contraventions where it is due to inadvertence, mistake or factors beyond the person's control.[243]

9   An Introduction to Securities Regulation in Australia

9.1   *The Relationship between Securities Exchanges and Corporate Regulation*

Pursuant to Section 776, a securities exchange is required to provide such assistance as the ASIC reasonably requires. In particular, a securities exchange is required to lodge written particulars of any action taken to reprimand, fine, suspend, expel or otherwise discipline a member of the securities exchange.[244] It is also required to lodge a statement where it believes that a person has committed, or is about to commit, a serious contravention of the securities exchange business rules, the listing rules or the Corporations Law.[245] Persons authorized by the ASIC are entitled to full and free access to the trading floor of a securities exchange.

Tomasic, Jackson and Woellner say that:

> To a large degree, regulatory strategies in regard to the securities industry depend more upon self-regulation rather than official governmental regulation. This is despite the number of legislative provisions dealing with the securities industry and the powers of the Commission and the court in regard to the regulation of the industry. This is especially so once persons have become licensed to be dealers. Thereafter, regulation is largely in the hands of the Australian Stock Exchange … , although the Commission may from time to time make inquiries of brokers regarding particular market transactions.[246]

9.2   *The Types of Securities Regulated*

For the purposes of the insider trading provisions, 'securities' are defined in Section 1002A as:

- shares;
- debentures (including convertible notes);
- interests in a managed investment scheme;
- units of shares; and
- an option contract in relation to the above securities, but excluding a futures contract.

In relation to the other provisions, 'securities' bears the meaning given in Section 92, which is similar to the definition in Section 1002A but has a slightly wider meaning.

9.3   *The Legal Effect of the Listing Rules and Business Rules of the Stock Exchange(s)*

Section 777(1) provides that:

> Where a person who is under an obligation to comply with or enforce the business rules or listing rules of a securities exchange fails to comply with or enforce any of those business rules or listing rules, as the case may be, the Court may, on the application of the Commission, the securities exchange or a person aggrieved by the failure and after giving to the person aggrieved by the failure and the person against whom the order is sought an opportunity of being heard, make an order giving directions concerning compliance with, or enforcement of, those business rules or listing rules ... .

Tomasic, Jackson and Woellner say that:

> The enforcement of the [Australian Stock Exchange] Listing Rules takes place in a number of different ways. In its 1990 discussion paper on *The Role of the Australian Stock Exchange and its Listing Rules* (at p 7), the [Australian Stock Exchange] points out that present methods of enforcement include moral suasion, public and private inquiries of listed entities, the issue of press releases, suspensions and delisting. However, the [Australian Stock Exchange] has been reluctant to exercise its powers under the equivalent of Section 777. One reason for this is the reluctance of the [Australian Stock Exchange] to assume liability for the payment of damages in the event that its action to enforce the Listing Rules is unsuccessful. The [Australian Stock Exchange] has been pressing for the amendment of the Corporations Law to exempt it from this possible liability.[247]

9.4   *Market Conduct Rules and Sanctions for Securities Misconduct*

Section 995 is a general provision. It prohibits misleading and deceptive conduct in relation to securities. In addition, there are specific provisions. Section 846 prohibits short selling. It is an offence under Section 846 to sell securities, where the seller does not have a presently exercisable and unconditional right to vest the securities in the purchaser. There are some exceptions provided for, including where a person has entered into a contract to purchase the securities but it has not been completed.[248] Criminal liability is imposed in relation to a breach of Section 846. No civil remedies are available to the buyer, although damages may be awarded under Section 1324(8).

Section 997 prohibits stock market manipulation, whereby a false impression of stock market activity is created. Similar practices are prohibited under Section 998. The making of false or misleading statements which are likely to induce persons to enter the market or to have an effect on the price of securities are prohibited under Section 999. Similar provision is made under Section 1000 which prohibits the making of false or reckless statements to induce another person to deal in securities. Section 1001 prohibits the dissemination of information to the effect that the price of securities may be affected by a transaction which is prohibited by Sections 997–1000. Breaches of Sections 997–1001 constitute criminal offences.[249] In addition, a person who has breached any of these provisions is liable to compensate a person who has entered into a transaction with the person in breach, and who has suffered a loss as a result of the market price being affected by the contravention.[250]

Insider trading is prohibited by Section 232(5).[251] The main difficulty with this provision is that the company is the proper plaintiff to redress a wrong done to the company. It does not readily provide a remedy for the other party to the transaction. Insider trading is also prohibited by Section 1002G, under which an insider is defined as:

- a person who possesses information that is not generally available, and if that information were generally available, a reasonable person would expect it to have a material effect on the price or value of securities of a body corporate; and
- a person who knows, or ought reasonably to know, that:
  - the information is not generally available, and
  - if it were generally available, it might have a material effect on the price or value of those securities.

This definition does not require that the insider have a connection with the company. An insider is prohibited:

- from subscribing for, buying or selling securities, and also from entering into an agreement to do the same;
- from procuring another person to subscribe for, buy or sell any securities, and also from entering into an agreement to do the same; and
- in the case of listed securities, from communicating inside information to another person if the insider knows or ought reasonably to know, that the other person would or would be likely to do any of those things which the insider himself or herself is prohibited from doing.

Section 1002M provides an exception for corporate bodies in certain circumstances. To take advantage of the exception, corporate bodies must have in place an administrative arrangement known as a 'Chinese wall', to prevent the flow of information from the part of the company that has inside information to another part. If a Chinese wall is in place and the decision to enter into the transaction was taken by someone other than a person in possession of the inside information, and the inside information was not communicated, then trading in the securities is permitted. A similar defence exists for the holders of dealers' licences.[252] There are criminal consequences for a breach of Section 1002G.[253] The civil consequences are set out in Sections 1005 and 1013.

10　Miscellaneous

10.1　The Powers of the Courts

The powers of courts are dealt with in Part 9.5. Section 1324 gives the court power to grant an injunction where a person has engaged in or is presently engaging in conduct that contravenes the Corporations Law. This also applies in cases of attempted contravention, aiding, abetting or conspiring in relation to conduct which would contravene the Corporations Law.[254] The court also has power to grant an injunction requiring a person to do an act or thing, which the Corporations Law requires to be done, but which the person either has refused or failed to do, or is proposing to refuse or fail to do.[255]

The court's powers in relation to irregularities are set out in Section 1322. There are two substantive provisions. The first is that a proceeding is not invalidated because of a procedural irregularity, unless the court is of the opinion that the irregularity has caused substantial injustice that cannot be remedied by any court order.[256] The second is that a meeting held for the purposes of the Corporations Law or meeting notice is not invalidated only because of the accidental omission to give notice or the non-receipt by any person of the notice of meeting, unless the court declares the proceedings at the meeting to be void. The court may make the orders specified in Section 1322(4).

Where the ASIC is conducting an investigation or a prosecution, or where a civil proceeding has been commenced under the Corporations Law, the court has the power to make various orders for the purpose of protecting the interests of aggrieved persons.[257] Certain additional powers are given to the court pursuant to Section 1325 in relation to contraventions of Parts 7.11 and 7.12 which relate to securities. The court's power to punish for contempt is preserved[258] and it is also given power to resolve any transitional difficulties.[259]

10.2   Civil Remedies

Certain sections of the Corporations Law are specified as civil penalty provisions.[260] The following provisions are civil penalty provisions:

- Section 232(2), (4), (5) and (6), relating to the directors' and officers' duties of honesty, care, skill and diligence, and the duty not to make improper use of information or position;
- Section 243ZE(2) and (3), relating to receipt by a related party of a financial benefit from a public company;
- Section 588G, relating to the directors' duties to prevent insolvent trading; and
- a number of other provisions.

If the court is satisfied that a civil penalty provision has been contravened, it is to make a declaration to that effect[261] and may make either or both of the following orders:

- an order prohibiting the person, for such period as is specified in the order, from managing a corporation; and
- an order that the person pay to the Commonwealth a pecuniary penalty of an amount so specified that does not exceed 2 000 penalty units.[262]

The court is not to make an order under Paragraph (3)(a) if the person is, nevertheless, a fit and proper person[263] and it is not to make an order under Paragraph (3)(b) unless the contravention is serious.

An application for a civil penalty order may be made on the application of the ASIC or its delegate or a person authorized by the minister.[264]

In addition to civil penalty orders, civil liability is imposed by several provisions of the Corporations Law.[265]

10.3   Offences

Although certain provisions of the Corporations Law are specified as civil penalty provisions, there can still be criminal consequences for a breach of those provisions. Section 1317FA provides that a contravention of a civil penalty provision is an offence if it is done:

- knowingly, intentionally or recklessly;
- dishonestly and intending to gain, whether directly or indirectly, an advantage for that or any other person; or
- with intent to deceive or defraud someone.

Criminal proceedings cannot be commenced if an application for a civil penalty order has already been made.[266] In most circumstances criminal proceedings will preclude the making of an application for a civil penalty order.[267]

Section 1311(1) provides that it is an offence where a person:

- does an act or thing that the person is forbidden to do by or under a provision of the Corporations Law;
- does not do an act or thing that the person is required or directed to do by or under a provision of the Corporations Law; or
- otherwise contravenes a provision of the Corporations Law.

This provision is subject to the specific section making a contrary provision.[268]

Penalties are generally set out in Schedule 3 to the Corporations Law or in the provision itself.[269] Section 1311(5) imposes a fine of five penalty units if there is no penalty otherwise specified.

10.4   Who May Initiate Proceedings?

Subject to the Corporations Law itself, which may specify who may take proceedings, it is the ASIC, its delegate or a person authorized in writing by the Minister, who has power to take proceedings.[270] This does not affect the operation of the Director of Public Prosecutions Act 1983.[271]

10.5   The Registration and Control of Persons Under the Legislation: Auditors and Liquidators

The qualifications for registration as an auditor or liquidator are the same other than that the practical experience must be in auditing or in winding up depending on which registration is sought. In both instances, the applicant must be a member of either the Institute of Chartered Accountants in Australia or the Australian Society of Certified Practising Accountants. The applicant must also meet stipulated educational requirements. Alternatively, the applicant may have qualifications and experience which the ASIC accepts as equivalent to that specified.[272] In both cases, the ASIC shall not refuse registration without first giving the applicant a right to be heard.[273] If the application is refused, the ASIC must supply the applicant with the reasons for the decision.[274]

The scheme for the registration of an official liquidator does not have specific safeguards for applicants. The ASIC may register a registered liquidator as an official liquidator.[275] The Companies Auditors and Liquidators Disciplinary Board was established by Section 202 of the Australian Securities and Investment Commission Act 1989. The Board has power, in specified circumstances, on the application of the ASIC, to cancel or suspend registration as an auditor or liquidator.[276] The Board can only take this action if it has given the person the opportunity to appear at a hearing of the Board and to make submissions to it.[277]

Notes

*   LLB, LLM (Commercial), Dip. Ed. (Adelaide), Head of School, School of Law, University of Canberra, Australia.
1   Section 51 of the Constitution of the Commonwealth.
2   Constitution Act 1902 (NSW).
3   Section 23 of the Australian Courts Act 1828 (UK) (9 Geo IV, c. 83). This applied to New South Wales, which then included what is now Queensland and Victoria, and Van Diemen's Land, now called Tasmania. The date of reception of English law in the other states is the date of foundation.
4   Commonwealth of Australia Constitution Act 1900 (Imp.).
5   (1909) 8 CLR 330 at 393.
6   (1983) 158 CLR 1.
7   (1990) 90 ALR 355.
8   [1897] AC 22.
9   As note 8, above.
10   Section 588G of the Corporations Law.
11   See, for example, Sections 254K, 254T, 256B–256F and 260A–260D of the Corporations Law.
12   Section 49 of the Corporations Law.
13   Section 50 of the Corporations Law.
14   The Associations Incorporation Act 1991 (ACT), the Associations Incorporation Act 1963 (NT), the Associations Incorporation Act 1984 (NSW), the Associations Incorporation Act 1981 (Qld), the Associations Incorporation Act 1985 (SA), the Associations Incorporation Act 1964 (Tas), the Associations Incorporation Act 1981 (Vic) and the Associations Incorporation Act 1987 (WA).
15   Section 115 of the Corporations Law.
16   Section 254Q of the Corporations Law.
17   Section 190(1) of the Corporations Law.
18   Former Section 113(3) of the Corporations Law.
19   As note 18 above.
20   Section 114 of the Corporations Law.
21   Section 221(1) of the Corporations Law.
22   Section 221(2) of the Corporations Law.
23   Section 228 of the Corporations Law.
24   Section 225(1) of the Corporations Law.
25   Section 227 of the Corporations Law.
26   Section 45A(2) of the Corporations Law.
27   Sections 293 and 294 of the Corporations Law.
28   Section 1362A of the Corporations Law.
29   Sections 601CF and 601CJ of the Corporations Law.

30   Section 117(2) of the Corporations Law.
31   Section 128A of the Corporations Law.
32   Section 130 of the Corporations Law.
33   *Tracy & Others v Mandalay Pty Ltd* (1953) 88 CLR 215.
34   *Gluckstein v Barnes* [1900] AC 240.
35   Section 131(1) of the Corporations Law.
36   Section 131(2) of the Corporations Law.
37   Section 131(4) of the Corporations Law.
38   Section 132 of the Corporations Law.
39   Section 117 of the Corporations Law.
40   Section 134 of the Corporations Law.
41   *Eley v Positive Government Security Life Assurance Co.* (1875) 1 Ex D 20, but compare *Quin and Axtens Ltd v Salmon* [1909] 1 Ch 311.
42   Section 148(1) of the Corporations Law.
43   Sections 148(2) and 149 of the Corporations Law.
44   Sections 148(3) and 149 of the Corporations Law.
45   Sections 148(3), 148(5) and 149 of the Corporations Law.
46   Section 148(1) of the Corporations Law.
47   Section 152 of the Corporations Law.
48   Section 114 of the Corporations Law.
49   Section 136(2) of the Corporations Law.
50   Section 136(3) of the Corporations Law.
51   (1995) 13 ACLC 342.
52   As note 51, above, 348.
53   Section 172 of the Corporations Law.
54   Section 173 of the Corporations Law.
55   Sections 142 and 145 of the Corporations Law.
56   Section 144 of the Corporations Law.
57   Section 123 of the Corporations Law.
58   Section 232(4) of the Corporations Law.
59   [1925] 1 Ch 407.
60   As note 59, above, 416.
61   As note 59, above, 416–417.
62   (1995) 16 ACSR 607.
63   As note 62, above, 661.
64   As note 62, above, 664.
65   *Re Smith and Fawcett Ltd* [1942] 1 All ER 542; *Mills v Mills* (1939) 60 CLR 150.
66   Section 232(2) of the Corporations Law.
67   *Regal (Hastings) Ltd v Gulliver* [1942] 1 All ER 378.
68   Section 232(5) and (6) of the Corporations Law.
69   Section 1002G of the Corporations Law.
70   Section 231 of the Corporations Law.
71   Section 232A of the Corporations Law.
72   Section 231(1) of the Corporations Law.
73   Section 232(6) of the Corporations Law.
74   Section 231(5) of the Corporations Law.
75   Section 232A(2) of the Corporations Law.
76   Section 232A(3) of the Corporations Law.
77   Section 243A of the Corporations Law.
78   Section 243K of the Corporations Law.
79   Section 243N of the Corporations Law.
80   Section 243Q of the Corporations Law.
81   (1986) 10 ACLR 395.
82   As note 81, above, 401.

83   Section 588G of the Corporations Law.
84   Section 588H(5) of the Corporations Law.
85   Section 588H(4) of the Corporations Law.
86   Section 250N(2) of the Corporations Law.
87   Section 250N(1) of the Corporations Law.
88   Section 249D of the Corporations Law.
89   As note 88, above.
90   Section 249E of the Corporations Law.
91   Section 249H of the Corporations Law.
92   Section 249B of the Corporations Law.
93   Section 249G(1). See *Re Totex-Adon Pty Ltd & the Companies Act* (1981) ACLC
     40-61.7.
94   Section 249X of the Corporations Law.
95   Section 250K of the Corporations Law.
96   Section 251A of the Corporations Law.
97   Section 251B of the Corporations Law.
98   Section 1322(2) of the Corporations Law.
99   Section 1322(3). See generally *Rivers v Bondi Junction-Waverley RSL Sub-Branch
     Ltd* (1986) 10 ACLR 482.
100 Section 325 of the Corporations Law.
101 Section 327 of the Corporations Law.
102 Section 329(1) of the Corporations Law.
103 Section 329(3) of the Corporations Law.
104 Section 329(4) of the Corporations Law.
105 Section 329(5) of the Corporations Law.
106 Section 329(9) of the Corporations Law.
107 Section 310 of the Corporations Law.
108 Section 311 of the Corporations Law.
109 Section 308 of the Corporations Law.
110 As note 109, above.
111 *Re Kingston Cotton Mill Co. (No. 2)* [1896] 2 Ch 279; *Pacific Acceptance Corpora-
     tion Ltd v Forsyth* (1967) 92 WN (NSW) 29; *Daniels & Others v Anderson &
     Others* (1995) 13 ACLC 614.
112 (1997) 142 ALR 750.
113 As note 112, above, 756.
114 (1986) 162 CLR 341.
115 As note 114, above, 357
116 (1997) 142 ALR 750, 756.
117 [1990] 2 AC 605, 620
118 (1997) 142 ALR 750, 783.
119 As note 118, above, 785.
120 Section 292(1)(a) of the Corporations Law.
121 Section 292(1)(b) of the Corporations Law.
122 Section 292(1)(c) of the Corporations Law.
123 Section 292(2) of the Corporations Law.
124 Section 292(1)(d) of the Corporations Law.
125 Section 286(1) of the Corporations Law.
126 Section 286(2) of the Corporations Law.
127 Section 289 of the Corporations Law.
128 Section 297 of the Corporations Law.
129 Section 296(2) of the Corporations Law.
130 Section 296(1) of the Corporations Law.
131 Section 345 of the Corporations Law.

132   Section 246AA(1)(a) of the Corporations Law.
133   Section 246AA(1)(b) of the Corporations Law.
134   See *Scottish Co-operative Wholesale Society Ltd v Meyer* [1959] AC 324.
135   (1985) 10 ACLR 87.
136   As note 135, above.
137   (1843) 67 ER 189.
138   [1902] AC 83.
139   (1992) 10 ACLC 1220.
140   *Re Caratti Holding Co. Pty Ltd* (1975) 1 ACLR 87.
141   *Edwards v Halliwell* [1950] 2 All ER 1064.
142   (1993) 11 ACSR 785.
143   Section 263 of the Corporations Law.
144   Section 266(4) of the Corporations Law.
145   Section 279(3) of the Corporations Law.
146   Sections 1018 and 1019–20 of the Corporations Law.
147   Sections 66 and 1017 of the Corporations Law.
148   Section 1017A(3) and (4) of the Corporations Law.
149   Section 1022(1) of the Corporations Law.
150   Sections 256B and 260A of the Corporations Law.
151   Section 257B of the Corporations Law.
152   Section 257C of the Corporations Law.
153   Section 257B of the Corporations Law.
154   Section 257D of the Corporations Law.
155   *Bond Brewing Holdings & Others v National Australia Bank Ltd* (1990) 1 ACSR 445.
156   Section 418(1) of the Corporations Law.
157   Section 413 of the Corporations Law.
158   Section 411(17) of the Corporations Law.
159   Section 411 of the Corporations Law.
160   Section 588H of the Corporations Law.
161   Section 222APB of the Income Tax Assessment Act 1936.
162   Section 436A(2) of the Corporations Law.
163   *Re Depsun Pty Ltd* (1994) 12 ACLC 482.
164   Section 436D of the Corporations Law.
165   Section 448A of the Corporations Law.
166   Section 448B of the Corporations Law.
167   Section 448C of the Corporations Law.
168   Section 449A of the Corporations Law.
169   Section 436E of the Corporations Law.
170   Section 436F of the Corporations Law.
171   *Re Vanfox Pty Ltd* (1994) 12 ACLC 357.
172   Section 600A of the Corporations Law.
173   Section 600B of the Corporations Law.
174   Section 437C of the Corporations Law.
175   Section 437D(2) of the Corporations Law.
176   Section 438B of the Corporations Law.
177   Section 440F of the Corporations Law.
178   *Tymray Pty Ltd (Administrator Appointed) v Mercantile Mutual Life Insurance Ltd* (1995) 15 ACSR 203.
179   Section 441A of the Corporations Law.
180   Section 441B of the Corporations Law.
181   Section 441C of the Corporations Law.
182   Section 441F of the Corporations Law.
183   Section 441G of the Corporations Law.

184 Section 441D of the Corporations Law.
185 Section 441H of the Corporations Law.
186 Section 443B of the Corporations Law.
187 Section 439A of the Corporations Law.
188 *Re ATG Developments Pty Ltd* (1994) 12 ACLC 333; 13 ACSR 261.
189 Section 444A of the Corporations Law.
190 Section 444B of the Corporations Law.
191 Section 444D. See *Brash Holdings Ltd v Katile Pty Ltd* (1994) 12 ACLC 472.
192 Section 444G of the Corporations Law.
193 Section 445C of the Corporations Law.
194 Section 494 of the Corporations Law.
195 Section 494(5) of the Corporations Law.
196 Section 494(2) and (3) of the Corporations Law.
197 Section 491 of the Corporations Law.
198 Section 496(1) of the Corporations Law.
199 Section 490 of the Corporations Law.
200 Section 446A of the Corporations Law.
201 Section 446 of the Corporations Law.
202 Section 496(5) of the Corporations Law.
203 Section 462 of the Corporations Law.
204 *Re Tivoli Freeholds Ltd* [1972] VR 445.
205 *Ebrahimi v Westbourne Galleries Ltd* [1972] 2 All ER 492.
206 Section 459A of the Corporations Law.
207 Section 459E(2) of the Corporations Law.
208 Section 459J of the Corporations Law.
209 *David Grant & Co. Pty Ltd v Westpac Banking Corporation* (1995) ACSR 225.
210 Section 568A(1A) of the Corporations Law.
211 Section 588FJ of the Corporations Law.
212 Section 588FE of the Corporations Law.
213 Section 588FE(2) of the Corporations Law.
214 Section 588FC of the Corporations Law.
215 Section 588FE(3) of the Corporations Law.
216 Section 588FB of the Corporations Law.
217 Section 588FE(4) of the Corporations Law.
218 Section 588FE(5) of the Corporations Law.
219 Section 588FE(6) of the Corporations Law.
220 Section 553A of the Corporations Law.
221 Section 563A of the Corporations Law.
222 Section 553B of the Corporations Law.
223 Section 553C(2) of the Corporations Law.
224 Sections 554E, 554F, 554G, 554H and 554J of the Corporations Law.
225 Section 556(1) of the Corporations Law.
226 Section 561 of the Corporations Law.
227 Section 563B of the Corporations Law.
228 Section 618 of the Corporations Law.
229 Sections 619–633 of the Corporations Law.
230 Section 616 of the Corporations Law.
231 Section 617 of the Corporations Law.
232 Section 637 of the Corporations Law.
233 Section 644 of the Corporations Law.
234 Section 647 of the Corporations Law.
235 Section 750 of the Corporations Law.
236 Section 674 of the Corporations Law.
237 Sections 679, 683 and 750 of the Corporations Law.

238   Sections 647 and 683 of the Corporations Law.
239   Section 615(6) of the Corporations Law.
240   Section 734(2)(a) of the Corporations Law.
241   Section 738 of the Corporations Law.
242   Section 740 of the Corporations Law.
243   Section 743 of the Corporations Law.
244   Section 776(2) of the Corporations Law.
245   Section 776(2A) of the Corporations Law.
246   Tomasic, R., Jackson, J. and Woellner, R. (1996), *Corporations Law Principles Policy and Process*, third edition, Sydney: Butterworths, 778.
247   As note 281, above, 789.
248   Section 846(3)(c) of the Corporations Law.
249   Section 1311 of the Corporations Law.
250   Sections 1005 and 1014 of the Corporations Law.
251   See section 6.2 of the Corporations Law, above.
252   Section 1002S of the Corporations Law.
253   Sections 1311 and 1312 of the Corporations Law.
254   Section 1324(1) of the Corporations Law.
255   Section 1324(2) of the Corporations Law.
256   Section 1322(2) of the Corporations Law.
257   Section 1323 of the Corporations Law.
258   Section 1327 of the Corporations Law.
259   Section 1328 of the Corporations Law.
260   Section 1317DA of the Corporations Law.
261   Section 1317EA(1) and (2) of the Corporations Law.
262   Section 1317EA(3) of the Corporations Law.
263   Section 1317EA(4) of the Corporations Law.
264   Section 1317EB of the Corporations Law.
265   See for example Sections 1005, 1006 of the Corporations Law.
266   Section 1317FB of the Corporations Law.
267   Section 1317GC and 1317GD of the Corporations Law.
268   Section 1311(1)(d) and (e) of the Corporations Law.
269   Section 1311(3) and (4) of the Corporations Law.
270   Section 1315(1) of the Corporations Law.
271   Section 1315(3) of the Corporations Law.
272   Sections 1280 and 1282 of the Corporations Law.
273   Sections 1280(8) and1282(10) of the Corporations Law.
274   Sections 1280(9) and 1282(11) of the Corporations Law.
275   Section 1283 of the Corporations Law.
276   Section 1292(1) and (2) of the Corporations Law.
277   Section 1294 of the Corporations Law.

Further Reading

Baxt, R. and Fletcher, K. (1991), *Afterman and Baxt's Cases and Materials on Corporations and Associations*, sixth edition, Sydney: Butterworths.

Bird, H. (1996), 'The Problematic Nature of Civil Penalties in the Corporations Law', *Companies and Securities Law Journal*, **14**, 405.

Blanchard, J. (1997), 'Corporate Accountability and Information', *Australian Journal of Corporate Law*, **7**, 326.

Butterworths, *Australian Corporation Law: Principles and Practice*, Loose Leaf Service, Sydney: Butterworths.

CCH, *Australian Corporations and Securities Law Reporter*, Sydney: CCH.

Crutchfield, P. (1994), *Annotated Corporate Voluntary Administration Law*, Sydney: Law Book Company.

Fisher, S., Wiseman, L. and Anderson, C. (1994), *Corporations Law*, Sydney: Butterworths.

Ford, H.A.J., Austin, R.P. and Ramsay, I.M. (1997), *Ford's Principles of Corporations Law*, eighth edition, Sydney: Butterworths.

Golding, G. (1997), 'Prospectus Liability in the 1990s', *Australian Journal of Corporate Law*, 7, 299.

Greig, J. and Horrigan, B. (1994), *Enforcing Securities*, Sydney: Law Book Company.

Hanks, P. and Newman, S. (1992), 'Standing in the Australian Securities Commission's Shoes: The Administrative Appeals Tribunal and the Corporations Law', *Companies and Securities Law Journal*, 10, 318.

Hanrahan, P. (1997), 'Distinguishing Corporate and Personal Claims in Australian Company Litigation', *Companies and Securities Law Journal*, 15, 21.

Lane, P.H. (1994), *An Introduction to the Australian Constitution*, sixth edition, Sydney: Law Book Company.

Little, P. (1997), *The Law of Company Takeovers*, Sydney: Law Book Company.

Lipton, P. and Herzberg, A. (1995), *Understanding Company Law*, sixth edition, Sydney: Law Book Company.

McDonough, D. (1993), *Annotated Mergers and Acquisitions Law of Australia*, third edition, Sydney: Law Book Company.

O'Brien, D. (1991), 'Administrative Review Under the Corporations Law and the Australian Securities Commission Law', *Companies and Securities Law Journal*, 9, 235.

O'Donovan, J. (1987), *The Law of Company Liquidation*, third edition, Sydney: Law Book Company.

Redmond, P. (1992, 1996 supp), *Companies and Securities Law Commentary and Materials*, second edition, Sydney: Law Book Company.

Sievers, A.S. (1997), 'Directors' Duty of Care: What is the New Standard?', *Companies and Securities Law Journal*, 15, 392.

Tomasic, R. and Bottomley, S. (1995), *Corporations Law in Australia*, Sydney: The Federation Press.

Tomasic, R. and Whitford, K. (1997), *Australian Insolvency and Bankruptcy Law*, second edition, Sydney: Butterworths.

Whincop, M. (1996), 'Developments in Directors' Statutory Duties of Honesty and Propriety', *Companies and Securities Law Journal*, 14, 157.

Index